Get the eBook FREE!

(PDF, ePub, Kindle, and liveBook all included)

We believe that once you buy a book from us, you should be able to read it in any format we have available. To get electronic versions of this book at no additional cost to you, purchase and then register this book at the Manning website.

Go to https://www.manning.com/freebook and follow the instructions to complete your pBook registration.

That's it!
Thanks from Manning!

Haskell in Depth

VITALY BRAGILEVSKY
FOREWORD BY SIMON PEYTON JONES

MANNING
SHELTER ISLAND

Manning Publications Co.
20 Baldwin Road
PO Box 761
Shelter Island, NY 11964

Development editor:	Jenny Stout
Technical development editor:	Marcello Seri
Review editor:	Aleksandar Dragosavljević
Production editor:	Lori Weidert
Copy editor:	Pam Hunt
Proofreader:	Katie Tennant
Technical proofreader:	Alexander Vershilov
Typesetter:	Gordan Salinovic
Cover designer:	Marija Tudor

ISBN 9781617295409
Printed in the United States of America

To my mother

brief contents

contents

foreword

Many introductory books on Haskell are out there, as well as lots of online tutorials, so the first steps in learning Haskell are readily available. But what happens after that? Haskell has a low "floor" (anyone can learn elementary Haskell) but a stratospherically high "ceiling." Haskell is a uniquely malleable medium: its support for abstraction, thorough algebraic data types, higher kinds, type classes, type families, and so on is remarkable. But this power and flexibility can be daunting. What are we to make of the following:

```
traverse :: Applicative f => (a -> f b) -> t a -> f (t b)
```

What are f and t? What on earth does this function do? What is Applicative, anyway? It's all too abstract!

Becoming a power user of Haskell means getting a grip on abstractions like these, not as a piece of theory, but as living, breathing code that does remarkably useful stuff. As we learn these abstractions and see how they work, we realise they are not baked in—they are just libraries—so we can build new abstractions of our own, implemented in libraries.

This book exposes you to many of these techniques. It covers many of the more sophisticated parts of the language: not just type classes, but existentials, GADTs, type families, kinds and kind polymorphism, deriving, metaprogramming, and so on. It describes many of the key abstractions (Functor, Applicative, Traversable, etc.) and a carefully chosen set of libraries (for parsing, database, web frameworks, streaming, and data-type-generic programming). As well as being useful in their own right, each part illustrates in a concrete way how Haskell's features can be combined in powerful and unexpected ways.

Finally, the book covers aspects of software engineering. How do you design a functional program? How do you test it? How do you benchmark it? What error handling is appropriate? These classic issues show up in rather different guises when you are thinking about functional programming.

Functional programming lets you think "big thoughts." It reduces the brain-to-code distance by allowing you to program at a very high level. We are still learning what those high-level abstractions should be. This book will help put you in the vanguard of that journey.

SIMON PEYTON JONES,
SENIOR PRINCIPAL RESEARCHER AT MICROSOFT RESEARCH,
CAMBRIDGE, ENGLAND

preface

The history of Haskell started more than 30 years ago, in 1987 (see "A History of Haskell: Being Lazy with Class" at https://www.microsoft.com/en-us/research/publication/a-history-of-haskell-being-lazy-with-class/ for many exciting details). Nowadays, Haskell is a mature programming language. It is full of features and has a stable implementation, the Glasgow Haskell Compiler, a helpful and friendly community, and a big ecosystem.

Paraphrasing the Haskell 2010 Language Report (https://www.haskell.org/onlinereport/haskell2010/), which is an effective standard description of the Haskell language, we can give it the following definition.

> Haskell is a general-purpose, purely functional programming language featuring higher-order functions, nonstrict semantics, static polymorphic typing, user-defined algebraic data types, pattern matching, a module system, a monadic I/O system, and a rich set of primitive data types (including lists, arrays, arbitrary- and fixed-precision integers, and floating-point numbers).

This definition is feature centric but gives a little information about how to use all these features professionally. Haskell is by far not the most popular programming language in the world, however. Two unfortunate myths contribute a lot to its limited adoption:

- It is hopeless to program in Haskell without a PhD in math.
- Haskell is not ready/suitable for production.

I believe that both of these claims are false. In fact, we can use Haskell in production without learning and doing math by ourselves. The truth is that the deep mathematical concepts behind the language itself give us a tool that can be used to write flexible, expressive, and performant code that is resilient to frequent changes in requirements, well suited to massive refactoring, and less prone to mistakes. If you like these software qualities, then Haskell is definitely for you and your team.

When talking about any programming language in general and its use in industry, we usually discuss the following components:

- Language features, programming style, and how they affect one another
- The set of libraries (packages) available to developers and their distribution
- The tooling that forms a convenient programming environment

Figure 1 presents these components for the Haskell programming language. They form a language ecosystem and make building software for the real world possible.

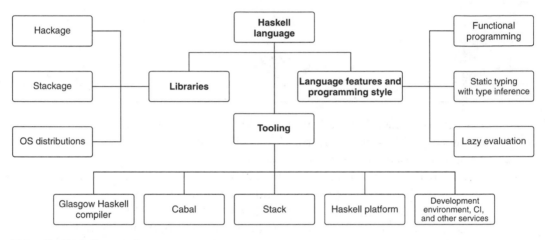

Figure 1   Haskell ecosystem

This is precisely what I talk about in this book: what Haskell is nowadays with respect to the language itself, the tooling around it, the libraries available to get things done, and the programming styles (sometimes known as best practices) supported.

The Haskell definition mentions three of the most valuable Haskell features, namely:

- Support for functional programming
- Static polymorphic typing
- Nonstrict semantics (more often referred to as *lazy evaluation*)

These Haskell features greatly affect the programming style of Haskellers, who write programs by exploiting functional style with higher-order functions and various manipulations over functions. They use Haskell's type system to express their intentions about data and functions. They count on laziness to write clear code without losing performance guarantees. Let's review these three features in general and then talk about the other Haskell ecosystem components.

Functional programming

We often refer to the term *functional programming*, meaning the following programming techniques:

- Composing functions for structuring programs and using recursion instead of loops
- Purity, so that the result of a function is fully determined once its parameters have been fixed
- Absence of side effects (doing literally nothing except evaluating the result)
- Immutability (the inability to change the value of a variable)

Academics would also mention *referential transparency* (the ability to replace a variable with its value without introducing any effects) and *equational reasoning* (the ability to reason about functions and their results). Although all this is true in general, this is not extremely helpful for getting a feel for functional programming.

Functional programming was initially invented, and these ideas crystallized, to fix problems with everyday programming when mutating the state of a global variable in one subroutine caused unwanted effects in another. These problems were pretty common, but now we know how to deal with them without resorting to overly sophisticated tools.

We use functions for structuring programs, and we understand a function in a mathematical sense as a process for transforming arguments into results. That's it. A function is not allowed to do anything else. We call such functions *pure*. They have a useful property: calling the function again with the same parameters must give the same result. This also provides referential transparency: there is no difference between an expression calling a function and its value, so we can replace one with the other without changing anything observable.

In contrast, other programming languages use the term *function* as a synonym for *subroutine* or *procedure*—simply a named part of a program. In object-oriented languages, we have another synonym—*method*—but the idea is the same. In those languages, nothing prevents us from mutating something outside the subroutine (and we are sometimes forced to).

Clearly, it's impossible to write a whole program without any side effects (with I/O being a crucial example). With the functional approach, we are supposed to keep the effectful part of a program as small as possible. In Haskell, even this part can be structured functionally (although not necessarily purely) with such tools as monadic I/O actions. Both pure functions and I/O actions reside in *modules*, which are the main mechanism for structuring code in Haskell.

Functions are so important in functional programming (not surprising, is it?) that we may use them as first-class (as in passengers, not as in OOP classes) values. We can do whatever we like with them: store them in a list, return them as results, or use them as parameters for other functions. This extremely powerful idea of using functions that take other functions as parameters (that is, *higher-order* functions) is built into every functional programming language. Interestingly, we can find higher-order functions in almost every mainstream programming language nowadays. This concept proved itself valuable far beyond traditional functional programming languages.

It is often claimed that functional programming makes it easier to glue functions together, and the truth is as simple as that. Every function gives a result that can be used as a parameter for another function. If it cannot be used directly for some reason, we can always write and call another function to transform it to the needed form—and here we are with three functions glued together.

Embracing purity together with higher-order functions provides us with a convenient way of structuring our programs: we write many small functions for computing this and that from parameters, going all way back to the starting point (the `main` function). Our simplest functions don't use anything except for functions from the standard library, and then we call them on variables inside other functions or use them as parameters to our own or standard higher-order functions.

Type system

Although functional programming, in general, doesn't necessarily require us to use types, they play nicely together: before writing a function, we normally specify what it is going to do using types. The compiler can then check our intentions and warn us if we attempt to do something incorrectly.

The definition of Haskell says that it features static polymorphic typing. "Static" means that types are checked, and any errors are reported at compile time. This static control gives us some degree of confidence that certain kinds of errors can't emerge in our programs. The compiler will prevent us from using price instead of weight, for example, but this will only be the case if we use different types for representing these attributes in a program. As a result, we generally don't want to reuse a type for several things. "Polymorphic" refers to the fact that any typed program entity (function, expression, variable, etc.) can have different types, depending on the context in which it is used. *Type classes* and other type system features are used to express these polymorphic properties of program entities.

The idea of introducing new types all the time contradicts the well-known programming principle of avoiding repetition—often formulated as DRY (don't repeat yourself). Haskell makes it easier to use types without repeating too much via a mechanism of functions over types so that we can use the power of functional programming, even for user-defined types. Although somewhat limited initially, this mechanism has become extremely sophisticated over the years with the introduction of generalized algebraic data types, type families, and kind polymorphism.

There is no need to understand these terms right now. Haskell's philosophy is to gain control via compiler checks and expressiveness with type system advances to write correct and flexible programs. An expressive type system gives us a lot of flexibility to change over time, as always happens in software development.

Interestingly, this flexibility is used in Haskell's development. When something changes significantly in the base library, old code may stop working. The type system ensures that the compiler is able to control this and report it to the user. Nothing goes unnoticed. This is extremely convenient when refactoring code.

In other languages, we may encounter different approaches to type discipline. In *weak* type systems, we can use an integer value instead of Boolean one, and it works like a charm (unless we've done that by mistake—there is no help from the compiler here; it was our choice). With *dynamic* typing, we run a program and then face type errors while trying to multiply a string with an integer (yeah, I know it's fine in some programming languages, but it looks like a disaster to me).

When searching for information about Haskell, we often encounter such mathematical notions as categories, functors and bifunctors, catamorphisms, monads, and so forth. Oddly enough, they are often used to explain Haskell features. That's because Haskell's type system is good for expressing them, too. The truth is, we can apply those mathematical concepts to our code without worrying too much about them. Math is good for applying; it was created and developed over the centuries precisely for that. Nobody bothers about prime numbers and the problem of factorization when buying something with a credit card nowadays.

Another piece of good news is that we can use solid math concepts to make our types more convenient. In Haskell, we can speak in math all the time without even knowing it, thanks to already elaborated concepts built into the language and its libraries.

Control and expressiveness—that's our mantra when using types in Haskell. The language helps us to make fewer mistakes and allows us to use an expressive vocabulary that combines general and domain-specific terms, with math being either one of those domains or a general tool for expressing ideas.

Let me say it again: strong math is not a prerequisite to be a Haskell professional.

Lazy evaluation

Haskell is the only industrial-strength programming language based on lazy evaluation. Although other programming languages may support it in various limited forms, it is supported by default in Haskell.

A traditional misunderstanding exists of the notions of lazy evaluation and nonstrict semantics, which was mentioned in the definition of Haskell. *Semantics* is a term relating to the definition of how things should behave. In Haskell, this means that we can provide a function with an undefined value as one of its parameters and get the result from the function if, for example, it doesn't need that parameter for computation. In other words, an expression could have a value, even if its subexpression couldn't. This is nonstrictness. We may meet it in other programming languages in a limited form of conditional expressions, where a branch is not evaluated if it corresponds to the opposite condition. Haskell brings nonstrictness to every function or operator, giving us tools for controlling it in a way we like.

In contrast, lazy evaluation is a mechanism for implementing nonstrict semantics. Instead of evaluating some value, the compiler gives us a substitute for it: a *thunk*—a recipe for how to compute it in case we need it.

You may wonder why on earth we'd decided to write code for something we don't need. Well, this ability sometimes helps to describe and solve problems more easily.

Here is just one example: Imagine we have to generate a sequence of some objects and then prune it to get those with the required properties. The simplest solution to generate all of the objects and then start pruning is not always efficient, depending on their number and size. In some programming languages, we are forced to interleave the code for generating with the code for pruning, making it strongly coupled and hard to read. In Haskell, we simply compose two functions for generating and pruning, and everything else is done by the compiler and the runtime system.

When we write programs relying on lazy evaluation, we don't have to know how they are *actually* evaluated. We call functional programming *declarative*: we write a program by declaring our intentions, and the compiler decides how to execute it in the most efficient way.

I'm not saying that nonstrictness and lazy evaluation are ideal—they come with their own cost, such as difficulties in predicting performance. If you can't deal with those, you may want to choose another language (and another book)—but we will see many examples of when they simplify code in this book.

Tooling around Haskell

Haskell is often blamed for its lack of tooling. In most cases, this complaint means, "I've googled for the Haskell IDE to write a Hello World program, and there is no such thing." Most Haskellers use text editors: VS Code, vi, or Emacs (see, for example, the survey that Taylor Fausak ran in November 2020: https://taylor.fausak.me/2020/11/22/haskell-survey-results/). Many resources are available online with recommendations on turning your favorite text editor into a real Haskell IDE (see https://wiki.haskell.org/IDEs for a list of options).

So there is no such beast as a dedicated Haskell IDE yet (although there were and there are many attempts). All our tooling is currently based on the following:

- *Glasgow Haskell Compiler (GHC)*—There are other compilers, but this one is the most mature and actively developed.
- *GHCi (an interpreter)*—A program that implements a REPL (read-evaluate-print loop) approach to software development.

Every piece of code in this book was compiled by GHC; I never run other compilers, myself.

We also have the Cabal framework with the `cabal` tool for building software projects containing and using libraries and applications, and the `Stack` tool (based on the Cabal framework) for pretty much the same. I'll get to issues with package management for Haskell software projects in chapter 4.

Apart from Stack or your favorite OS distribution tools, GHC can be distributed by the Haskell Platform (https://www.haskell.org/platform/), a collection of Haskell tools and libraries.

Haskell's ecosystem contains everything we need for the life cycle of our applications. There are tools for configuring, testing, benchmarking, profiling, exploring issues with concurrency, and so forth. We'll meet many of them later in this book. Haskellers often use GitHub or GitLab to develop their software. They may also use Travis CI or AppVeyor services for continuous integration. For example, the code in this book is regularly built with these two CI providers. AppVeyor builds the corresponding package via `stack` for Windows, whereas Travis CI builds it via `cabal` for Ubuntu Linux and via `stack` for macOS. There are plenty of other online services for Haskell development.

What can be done using Haskell: Libraries

Haskell belongs to the family of general-purpose programming languages. In theory, we can write virtually any software in it, from web development to data science. It would be fair to say that in some areas, using Haskell is more challenging than in others. Fortunately, the language is supported by many libraries that make it widely applicable, for example:

- `servant` for building web services
- `pandoc` for transforming text document formats
- `async` for concurrent programming
- `esqueleto` and `persistent` for storing and updating data in databases
- `Frames` for computing with some machine learning methods
- `HaskellR` for bridging with R code
- `accelerate` for GPU programming
- `amazonka` for binding to Amazon cloud-computing services
- `req` for making HTTP requests

These are just some examples (alternatives are also available). Gabriel Gonzalez keeps a record of Haskell's suitability for different programming needs in his extremely useful "State of the Haskell Ecosystem" document (https://github.com/Gabriel439/post-rfc/blob/master/sotu.md). At the time of writing, he considers Haskell support as mature (suitable for most programmers) or even better in such application domains as compiler development, server-side programming, and command-line applications (or scripting). Support for areas such as GUI programming and mobile applications is immature, or even bad, if it exists at all. At the same time, the support for common programming needs such as testing and benchmarking, concurrency, parsing, package management, and more is generally considered very good. Of course, there is always room for improvement, so why not pick one and try to improve it? A reader of *Haskell in Depth* can undoubtedly cope with that, and the Haskell community will be grateful. The language itself is always ready to help.

acknowledgments

I am deeply grateful to the many friends and colleagues who have helped me in learning Haskell and writing this book, and supported me these three years. In particular, I would like to express my gratitude to the following:

- My advisor, recently passed away, Vladimir Stavrovich Pilidi, who let me introduce a course on Haskell into the undergraduate curriculum in 2008 at the Institute of Mathematics, Mechanics and Computer Science of the Southern Federal University (Rostov-on-Don, Russia), and to all my colleagues there.

- Zena Ariola, who hosted me at the University of Oregon (Eugene, OR), where I spent the term of Fall 2018 under the Fulbright Program; Jason Daniels and his beautiful wife Heather Wilson, who made me a part of their family at that time; and all of the people who run the Fulbright Program.

- Alexander Kulikov and Andrey Ivanov, who have created magnificent opportunities for my work since June 2019 at JetBrains and at the Department of Mathematics and Computer Science of Saint Petersburg University (Saint Petersburg, Russia).

- All my students who struggled with learning Haskell in my courses, and were compelled to use it even for non-Haskell courses, simply because it was more convenient for me.

- The great team at Manning Publications, including acquisitions editor Mike Stephens, who believed in me in the first place; development editor Jennifer Stout, who relentlessly pushed me towards this end; technical development editor Marcello Seri, who tried to make me precise and clear in every word (it's entirely my fault if I'm still imprecise and unclear); technical proofreader (and my friend) Alexander Vershilov, who has checked every line of code and commented extensively to make it better (again, anything wrong with my code is still my fault); and all others who dealt with my English, my figures, and me missing almost every deadline.

- The external reviewers, Alexander Myltsev, Andrei de Araújo Formiga, Andres Damian Sacco, Artem Pelenitsyn, Charles C Earl, Christoffer Fink, Dan Sheikh, Daniel Berecz, David Paccoud, Ernesto Bossi Carranza, Federico Kircheis, Giovanni Ornaghi, Jeon-Young Kang, Jose Luis Garcia Baltazar, Justus Sagemüller, Kai Gellien, Kanak Kshetri, Kent R. Spillner, Marcello Seri, Martin Verzilli, Phillip Sorensen, Rohinton Kazak, Tony Mullen, Vincent Theron, and William E. Wheeler, who made this book much better than it would be without their excellent comments and advice, and Aleksandar Dragosavljević, who runs external reviews at Manning Publications (thanks to him, I was introduced to the Manning processes long before starting this book—I knew that I could trust them with my own book).

- The most fabulous Reviewer 4 (well, now I know that was Artem Pelenitsyn, my student and my friend for twenty years), for his valuable comments, suggestions, and all of the time he spent reading the manuscript.

- André van Meulebrouck, who read the MEAP version and sent me an overwhelming number of great suggestions and edits (thanks for teaching me both English and Haskell!).

- Simon Peyton Jones for leading Haskell development for thirty years already (and for writing the Foreword!) and my colleagues at the GHC Steering Committee for engaging discussions about new Haskell features.

- The Russian-speaking Haskell community, I love all of you (even if you don't like each other sometimes!).

- And finally, my family.

about this book

This is a book about the Haskell language as implemented in the Glasgow Haskell Compiler (GHC/Haskell for short). Although I refer to various Haskell libraries from the very beginning, I do that mainly for illustrative purposes to explain Haskell features and to provide a useful toolkit for your own Haskell projects.

Who should read this book

This book is not meant for a Haskell novice. If that's your case, you're better off starting somewhere else. I personally prefer Will Kurt's *Get Programming with Haskell* (Manning Publications; https://www.manning.com/books/get-programming-with-haskell) due to its practical approach and very strong topic development with teaching in mind. Of course, many other alternatives are also available. After grasping the basics, you are certainly welcome to come back to improve your knowledge of Haskell.

Intermediate to advanced Haskell users are very welcome to work through the book or skim the chapters you're interested in. My publisher wants me to mention that you'll double your salary after mastering this book, but as we Haskellers all know, Haskell programming is great fun first off. However, a high salary is not bad, indeed.

How this book is organized: A roadmap

This book contains five parts and 16 chapters in total:

- The first part, "Core Haskell," quickly introduces the reader to main Haskell features and techniques, such as functions, data types and type classes, modules, and developing software with REPL and external libraries. I assume that the reader is already familiar with that, but I try to present those features in pragmatic ways. For example, I embrace Text instead of String for text processing. I also use several recent extensions of GHC/Haskell. In case of severe problems with understanding the first part, I'd suggest working through any introductory Haskell book first.

- In the second part, "Introduction to application design," I talk about language features and tools that support describing software architecture, such as modules, packaging in general, monads, and monad transformers.
- I devote part 3, "Quality assurance," to the ways of achieving several software characteristics generally referred to as *software quality*, namely: fault tolerance (via exception handling and logging), correctness (via extensive testing), and performance (via describing Haskell code behavior at run time, benchmarking, and profiling).
- For part 4, "Advanced Haskell," I chose two topics in Haskell traditionally considered the most difficult: the type system and metaprogramming (using Haskell to generate code in Haskell).
- In part 5, "Haskell toolkit," I present and discuss many idiomatic Haskell libraries used extensively in practice, ranging from concurrent programming to databases. Even in these chapters, however, my main focus stays on the Haskell language itself and its features that make those libraries possible.

As an author, I prefer you to read the book from cover to cover. But, in fact, it's okay to go straight to the topics you are interested in. I give links back when it's helpful to look at the material covered earlier. Besides a couple of projects spanning several chapters, every chapter develops its own topic quite independently and uses its own examples.

About the code

I believe that learning programming is never possible without experimenting with the code. By experimenting, I mean running the source code examples, modifying them, adding tests, implementing new features and reimplementing old ones, profiling, and benchmarking. With that in mind, I provide the full source code for the examples from the book as a Haskell package to make sure that everything stays updated with new releases of GHC, external libraries, and tools. This source code is available on GitHub: https://github.com/bravit/hid-examples. Feel free to do whatever you like with this code. Reporting issues or bugs is welcome. Please ask questions regarding working with the code examples right on GitHub.

All the source code in this book is written in GHC/Haskell, so you will definitely need to get GHC to work with it. Apart from your OS distribution, you can get GHC using one of the following:

- A minimal GHC installation (https://www.haskell.org/downloads)
- The Haskell Platform (https://www.haskell.org/platform/)
- Stack (http://haskellstack.org)

Make sure that you have a relatively recent GHC release. Every example is supposed to be compiled by GHC 8.6 and newer.

In what follows, I give brief instructions on how to work with the source code examples. I support both `stack` and `cabal` tools because they are customary for Haskell projects. Depending on your own preferences, you may choose the packaging and building approach. If you prefer `cabal`, then you should have the latest version installed (3.0 and newer are supported).

Getting the sources

All the source code examples in this book are organized into a Haskell package. The easiest way to get them is to clone the GitHub repository https://github.com/bravit/hid-examples:

```
$ git clone https://github.com/bravit/hid-examples.git
```

This will create the hid-examples folder that readers are free to explore on their own. For example, there is a *Hello world* traditional program in the intro subfolder. Every example that is backed by the source code is accompanied with a block like the following:

EXAMPLE: "HELLO WORLD" IN HASKELL

🗋   intro/hello.hs

⚡ *hello*

☞ We can print "Hello world" in Haskell.

Such blocks inform the reader on the following:

- Where the source code is located (intro/hello.hs): the path is relative to the `hid-examples` package root folder.
- The name of the project component (*hello*): this name can be used to run, explore in GHCi, test, and benchmark the corresponding component (if applicable).
- Key points of the example: this is what the reader is expected to learn while following this example.

Note that smaller examples reside in chXX subfolders, whereas larger projects, some of them spanning several chapters, have their own subfolders in the root folder of the package.

Using cabal

I assume that you have the relatively fresh version (3.0 and up) of the `cabal` tool installed on your system. To build the whole package, issue the following command:

```
$ cabal build
```

This will build and install all the dependencies, so it takes time. When working through a particular example, we can rebuild it by mentioning the corresponding project component name in `cabal build` as follows:

```
$ cabal build hello
```

After building, we can run an executable, as shown next:

```
$ cabal run hello
Up to date
Hello, world
```

The `Up to date` line comes from `cabal`, saying that there is no need to rebuild an executable before running it. We can hide it by setting the *verbosity level* to 0 as follows:

```
$ cabal -v0 run hello
Hello, world
```

If an executable expects command-line arguments, then we supply them using the following syntax:

```
$ cabal run <executable> [ -- <arguments>]
```

For example, to run the *stockquotes* example from chapter 3, we need to specify the CSV file location and (optionally) several flags as follows:

```
$ cabal run stockquotes -- data/quotes.csv -s
```

It is also possible to explore any module in the REPL. For example, let's check the function, defined in the *hello* example, as follows:

```
$ cabal repl hello
<MANY LINES OF OUTPUT>
ghci> hello
"Hello, world"
ghci> :type hello
hello :: String
```

I use the `ghci>` prompt for the code executed in the GHCi REPL. The reader can set the same prompt by issuing the following command:

```
$ ghci
GHCi, version 8.10.1: http://www.haskell.org/ghc/  :? for help
Prelude> :set prompt "ghci> "
ghci>
```

Alternatively, it is possible to tweak the .ghci file to make this change permanent. The GHC User's Guide (https://downloads.haskell.org/~ghc/latest/docs/html/users_guide/)

provides details about the location of the .ghci file: any GHCi command can be written there (e.g., defining values, importing modules, or executing some Haskell code).

If the particular example consists of several modules, then we can access all the functions of the module by loading it. For example, let's look through the `StatReport` module of the `stockquotes` example, shown next:

```
$ cabal repl stockquotes
ghci> :module StatReport
ghci> :type mean
mean :: (Fractional a, Foldable t) => t a -> a
```

First, we run the REPL with all the dependencies compiled. Then, we load the module we are interested in. Finally, we ask the type checker about the type of the `mean` function, which is defined in that module. Instead of the long forms `:module` and `:type`, we could also use `:m` and `:t`.

In addition, we can run tests and benchmarks provided with the package as follows:

```
$ cabal test
$ cabal bench
```

Alternatively, we could ask for testing or benchmarking one particular project component like so:

```
$ cabal test radar-test
...
1 of 1 test suites (1 of 1 test cases) passed.
```

Note that not every example provides tests and benchmarks.

More information about using `cabal` can be found in chapters on packaging, testing, and benchmarking.

Using stack

Most of the operations can also be done with `stack`. To build the whole package, run the following:

```
$ stack build
```

To run one of the executables provided with the package, issue the following command:

```
$ stack exec hello
Hello, world
```

Command-line arguments can be given as follows:

```
$ stack exec stockquotes -- data/quotes.csv -s
```

We can explore modules in GHCi as follows (note the colon before component name):

```
$ stack repl :stockquotes
ghci> :m StatReport
ghci> :t mean
mean :: (Fractional a, Foldable t) => t a -> a
```

It is also possible to run all tests and benchmarks in the package as follows:

```
$ stack test
$ stack bench
```

Running one particular test suite can be done as follows:

```
$ stack test :radar-test
```

liveBook discussion forum

Purchase of *Haskell in Depth* includes free access to a private web forum run by Manning Publications where you can make comments about the book, ask technical questions, and receive help from the author and from other users. To access the forum, go to https://livebook.manning.com/#!/book/haskell-in-depth/discussion. You can also learn more about Manning's forums and the rules of conduct at https://livebook.manning.com/#!/discussion.

Manning's commitment to our readers is to provide a venue where a meaningful dialogue between individual readers and between readers and the author can take place. It is not a commitment to any specific amount of participation on the part of the author, whose contribution to the forum remains voluntary (and unpaid). We suggest you try asking the author some challenging questions lest his interest stray! The forum and the archives of previous discussions will be accessible from the publisher's website as long as the book is in print.

about the author

VITALY BRAGILEVSKY has been teaching Haskell at the university level for more than a decade. He serves as a member of the GHC Steering Committee, a group of people responsible for deciding whether to accept the proposed new features into GHC/Haskell. Vitaly is currently working at JetBrains and at the Department of Mathematics and Computer Science of Saint Petersburg University in Russia. Follow him on Twitter (https://twitter.com/VBragilevsky).

about the cover illustration

The figure on the cover of *Haskell in Depth* portrays the dress of a woman from an ancient Russian nomadic group (Astrakhan Tatars). The illustration is taken from a collection of dress costumes from various countries by Jacques Grasset de Saint-Sauveur (1757–1810), titled *Costumes civils actuels de touse les peoples connus,* published in France in 1788. Each illustration is finely drawn and colored by hand. The rich variety of Grasset de Saint-Sauveur's collection reminds us vividly of how culturally apart the world's towns and regions were just 200 years ago. Isolated from each other, people spoke different dialects and languages. In the streets or in the countryside, it was easy to identify where they lived and what their trade or station in life was just by their dress.

The way we dress has changed since then and the diversity by region, so rich at the time, has faded away. It is now hard to tell apart the inhabitants of different continents, let alone different towns, regions, or countries. Perhaps we have traded cultural diversity for a more varied personal life—certainly for a more varied and fast-paced technological life.

At a time when it is hard to tell one computer book from another, Manning celebrates the inventiveness and initiative of the computer business with book covers based on the rich diversity of regional life of two centuries ago, brought back to life by Grasset de Saint-Sauveur's pictures.

Part 1

Core Haskell

We have many ways to start learning Haskell. You could come to this book from pure mathematics, or from theoretical underpinnings of functional programming, or from practical tutorials. Consequently, Haskell beginners have very different backgrounds. In this part, we'll fly over the main building blocks for Haskell programs—namely, functions, types, type classes, modules, projects, and external packages—to make sure that we are on the same page before diving deeper into Haskell.

Even though there should be nothing new here for a junior Haskell developer, we'll still talk about plenty of good practices ranging from using `Text` instead of `String` and looking for help to the pragmatics of using abstractions in Haskell. In the last chapter of this part, we'll apply all the essential Haskell components to develop a standalone application that reports stock quote data.

Functions and types

This chapter covers

- Using the Glasgow Haskell Compiler (GHC) interpreter to solve problems
- Writing simple functional programs with pure functions and I/O actions
- Using a type-based approach to design programs
- Using GHC extensions for greater code readability
- Efficient processing of text data

Functional programming differs significantly from imperative programming in the ways we design programs. Typing discipline adds some specifics, too. When we code in Haskell, we think in a special way: in terms of the given data and the desired processing results (with both sides expressed by types), instead of focusing on the steps we should execute to get those results.

In this chapter, we'll see several examples of how to solve problems in the most *Haskellish* way:

- By using GHCi REPL (read-evaluate-print-loop) without writing a program
- By writing functions properly

- By keeping pure functions separate from the I/O actions that communicate to users
- By expressing ideas with types

We'll also explore several of Haskell's libraries for *text processing*, which is arguably one of the most common, albeit routine, tasks in software development nowadays.

1.1   *Solving problems in the GHCi REPL with functions*

Suppose we want to analyze the vocabulary of a given text. Many sophisticated methods for such analysis are available, but we will do something quite basic, though still useful:

- Extract all the words from the given text file.
- Count the number of unique words used (size of the vocabulary).
- Find the most frequently used words.

This problem could be a component of a larger social media text analyzer. Such software could mine various pieces of information (ranging from level of education or social position to the risk of financial default) by analyzing texts people post on their social media pages.

   Or, more likely, we've just gotten up in the middle of the night with a desire to explore the size of Shakespeare's vocabulary. How many unique words did Shakespeare use in *Hamlet*? How can Haskell functions help us to answer this question?

EXAMPLE: EXTRACTING A VOCABULARY IN REPL

   ▯   data/texts/hamlet.txt (*The Tragedie of Hamlet*)

   ☞   We can solve problems in the GHCi REPL without writing programs.

We don't have to write a program to use GHCi to compute the number of unique words used in a text file. We just need to fire up GHCi (let's do that in the root folder of the `hid-examples` package), import a couple of modules for processing lists and characters, read the given file into a `String`, and then manipulate its content, as shown in the next code:

```
$ ghci
ghci> :module + Data.List Data.Char
ghci> text <- readFile "data/texts/hamlet.txt"
ghci> ws = map head $ group $ sort $ words $ map toLower text
ghci> take 7 ws
["&","'em?","'gainst","'tane","'tis","'tis,","'twas"]
```

The idea is to make the file's content lowercase and then split it into a list of words, sort them, and remove repetitions by grouping the same words together and taking the first word in each group. Haskellers often check the types of functions they use right in GHCi as follows:

```
ghci> :type toLower
toLower :: Char -> Char
ghci> :type map
map :: (a -> b) -> [a] -> [b]
ghci> :type words
words :: String -> [String]
ghci> :type sort
sort :: Ord a => [a] -> [a]
ghci> :type group
group :: Eq a => [a] -> [[a]]
ghci> :type head
head :: [a] -> a
```

If it's hard to understand what is going on in the `map head $ group $ sort $ words $ map toLower text` expression, I'd advise writing out the specific types in place of the type variables in the type signatures. I'll start here:

```
text :: String = [Char]
toLower :: Char -> Char
map :: (a -> b) -> [a] -> [b]
```

Here, `map` has the following type:

```
map :: (Char -> Char) -> [Char] -> [Char]
```

Consequently,

```
map toLower text :: [Char]
```

and so on.

The results we got in GHCi show that we've forgotten about leading and trailing punctuation, so we need to do some cleanup. The solution is becoming quite long, so I will introduce several temporary variables to make reading easier, as shown here:

```
ghci> text <- readFile "data/texts/hamlet.txt"
ghci> ws = words $ map toLower text
ghci> ws' = map (takeWhile isLetter . dropWhile (not . isLetter)) ws
ghci> cleanedWords = filter (not . null) ws'
ghci> uniqueWords = map head $ group $ sort cleanedWords
ghci> take 7 uniqueWords
["a","abhominably","abhorred","abilitie","aboord","aboue","about"]
ghci> length uniqueWords
4633
```

This is better, although if we look at some other words in the resulting `ws` list, we'll see that we've cleaned words in an incorrect way: for example, the second parts of all the hyphenated words have been removed (due to `takeWhile isLetter`).

1.2   *From GHCi and String to GHC and Text*

The REPL approach to solving problems gets clumsy in time, so let's try to write a complete program to solve the same problem—extracting a vocabulary (a list of used words) from the given text file and computing the size of the vocabulary.

EXAMPLE: WRITING A PROGRAM TO EXTRACT A VOCABULARY

🗋   ch01/vocab1.hs

⚡   *vocab1*

☞   Writing a program as opposed to using REPL

☞   Replacing `String` with much more efficient `Text`

In this attempt, we'll also switch to the `Data.Text` data type, which is much more suitable for handling textual data in terms of both performance and convenience. The whole program can be written as follows:

Imports the modules for working with text

```
import Data.Char
import Data.List (group, sort)
import qualified Data.Text as T
import qualified Data.Text.IO as TIO
import System.Environment

main = do
  [fname] <- getArgs
  text <- TIO.readFile fname
  let ws = map head $ group $ sort $ map T.toCaseFold $ filter (not . T.null)
             $ map (T.dropAround $ not . isLetter) $ T.words text
  TIO.putStrLn $ T.unwords ws
  print $ length ws
```

Imports the module for reading command-line arguments

Reads the command-line arguments into a list of strings

Reads the file content into the Text value

Prints all the words, delimited by spaces

Transforms Text into a list of words

Note that we read the filename from the command line in the first line of the `main` function without worrying too much about incorrect user input. The modules `Data.Text` and `Data.Text.IO` are usually imported with qualifiers to avoid name clashes with `Prelude` (the module that is imported by default). These two modules come with the `text` package, which will be installed when we build the project. The `text` package is listed as a *dependency* in the `vocab1` executable's description in the configuration of the `hid-examples` package. Look at the package.yaml file and search for the `vocab1` entry if you are interested in the details. We'll get back to dependency management in chapter 4.

The `Data.Text` module provides many functions analogous to the list functions from `Prelude` and `Data.List`. It also adds new specific text-processing functions that were used in previous code, such as the following:

```
toCaseFold :: Text -> Text
dropAround :: (Char -> Bool) -> Text -> Text
```

The `toCaseFold` function converts the whole `Text` value to the folded case and does that significantly faster than mapping with `toLower` over every character. In addition, it respects Unicode. The `dropAround` function removes leading and trailing characters that satisfy the given predicate (the function of type `Char -> Bool`).

> **SEARCHING FOR THE FUNCTION**   Haskellers use the website hoogle.haskell.org to find functions by name or, even more usefully, by type annotation. For example, searching for "(Char -> Bool) -> Text -> Text" leads to the `dropAround` function I just described, together with other functions for cleaning text.

Running this program on the text of Shakespeare's *Hamlet* results in something like the next output sample (with the part in the middle stripped away):

```
$ cabal run vocab1 -- data/texts/hamlet.txt
a a'th a-crosse a-downe a-downe-a a-dreames a-foot a-sleepe a-while a-worke
...
4827
```

We won't attempt to make the cleaned-up results even better because the main goal of this chapter is to discuss structuring functional programs. In fact, breaking text on words cannot be done reliably without diving deep into the Unicode rules on text boundary positions. If you are interested, look at the documentation for the `Data.Text.ICU` module from the `text-icu` package; you will find many fascinating details there on what a *word* is. Even then, you will have to add some sort of semantic analysis to come up with a bulletproof solution that works beyond English. Don't forget to check your solution with several text files (I've provided some useful test files in the data/texts folder).

1.3 *Functional programs as sets of IO actions*

The sort of programming presented in the previous sections resembles scripting more than actual programming. In Haskell, we tend to express our ideas in types and functions first and then proceed with implementing them.

> **EXAMPLE: EXTRACTING A VOCABULARY WITH MANY IO ACTIONS**
>
> 🗋   ch01/vocab2.hs
>
> ⚡ *vocab2*
>
> ☞ A Haskell program may be structured as a set of `IO` actions.
>
> ☞ We use types to design our program.

Remember that our task is to explore the vocabulary of a given text file, but let's be more specific here: from now on, we'll regard a *vocabulary* as consisting of entries with words and numbers of occurrences. These entries can be used later for determining the most frequent words, for example. Now that we've agreed on the types of an entry (a word and the number of its occurrences) and a vocabulary (a list of entries), we are ready to write a *type-based* outline for the program, as shown next:

```
type Entry = (T.Text, Int)      ⟵──── One vocabulary entry
type Vocabulary = [Entry]        ⟵
                                      │ List of entries
extractVocab :: T.Text -> Vocabulary
printAllWords :: Vocabulary -> IO ()
processTextFile :: FilePath -> IO ()
main :: IO ()
```

This outline clearly shows that our plan is to read and process the text file (processTextFile) by

1 Extracting a vocabulary from the file's content
2 Using the vocabulary to print all words

But there is more than that in this outline. We plan to read and process command-line arguments (the name of the file, which is a variable of the FilePath type) in the main function. If that is done correctly, proceed with processing the text file (with processTextFile). This function will then read the content of the given file (this is the second component of the user input in this program, after the command-line arguments) into a variable of the Text type, extract the vocabulary (with the extractVocab function), and finally print it (with printAllWords).

Note the extractVocab function here: it is the only *pure* function in this program. We can see that from its type, T.Text -> Vocabulary. There is no IO there.

I've visualized the whole scenario in the flowchart depicted in figure 1.1.

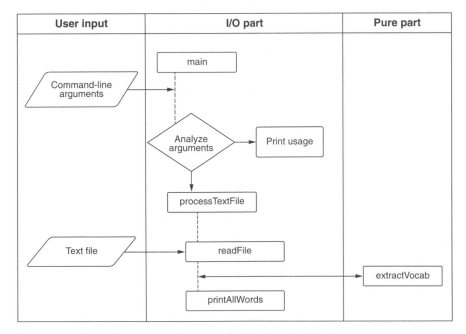

Figure 1.1   Extracting a vocabulary: program structure flowchart

The `extractVocab` function here does what we did before in `vocab1` in the `let` expression inside `main`. It takes a `Text` and returns a `Vocabulary`, as shown in the next piece of code:

```
extractVocab :: T.Text -> Vocabulary
extractVocab t = map buildEntry $ group $ sort ws
  where
    ws = map T.toCaseFold $ filter (not . T.null) $ map cleanWord $ T.words t
    buildEntry xs@(x:_) = (x, length xs)
    cleanWord = T.dropAround (not . isLetter)
```

Once we have a `Vocabulary`, we can print it as follows:

```
printAllWords :: Vocabulary -> IO ()
printAllWords vocab = do
  putStrLn "All words: "
  TIO.putStrLn $ T.unlines $ map fst vocab
```

I prefer to have a separate function for file processing to avoid many lines of code in the `main` function, where I am going to read command-line arguments and check them for correctness, as shown next:

```
processTextFile :: FilePath -> IO ()
processTextFile fname = do
  text <- TIO.readFile fname
  let vocab = extractVocab text
  printAllWords vocab

main = do
  args <- getArgs
  case args of
    [fname] -> processTextFile fname
    _ -> putStrLn "Usage: vocab-builder filename"
```

This program structure is flexible enough to accommodate several task changes. For example, it is easy to print the total number of words in the text file and find the most frequently used words. These new goals can be expressed in types as follows:

```
printWordsCount :: Vocabulary -> IO ()
printFrequentWords :: Vocabulary -> Int -> IO ()
```

Unfortunately, there is a problem with this approach: we tend to stick with IO so that almost every function in the program is an I/O action. In the next section, I'll show how to do the same task in a completely different way.

1.4   *Embracing pure functions*

The problem with functions like `printAllWords`, `printWordsCount`, or `printFrequent-Words` from the previous section is that they are too tightly and unnecessarily coupled with I/O. Even their own names suggest that the same functionality can be achieved by combining the *impure* `print` function with *pure* computations.

There is a consensus within the Haskell community on the role of pure functions. We can get most of the advantages of functional programming when we use pure functions as much as possible. They are easier to combine with other functions. They cannot break anything in other parts of the program, and we can also reason about their correctness.

EXAMPLE: EXTRACTING A VOCABULARY WITH PURE FUNCTIONS AND IO ACTIONS

🗋   ch01/vocab3.hs

⚡   *vocab3*

☞   The only thing IO actions should do is talk to a user.

☞   Main functionality may be implemented by pure functions.

Let's try to follow the path of purity while solving our main problem in this section—extracting a vocabulary—to see how pure functions help us to extend the functionality of the program much more easily.

1.4.1   *Separating I/O from pure functions*

Remember that our initial goal was to write a program that is able to do the following:

- Extract the vocabulary of a text file
- Print all words used in the text
- Count and print the total number of words and the number of unique words (size of a vocabulary)
- Print the given number of the most frequently used words

For example, when running such a program on Shakespeare's *Hamlet*, we'd like to get something like the following:

```
All words:
  a
  a'th
  ...
  zone

Total number of words: 29575
Number of unique words: 4827

Frequent words:
  the: 993
  and: 862
  to: 683
  of: 610
  i: 547
```

The task is more ambitious than what we've programmed so far. Thanks to the clear separation between pure and impure parts of the program, though, we can handle it with pleasure.

The following is the new type-based outline, now with a large choice of pure functions:

```
extractVocab :: Text -> Vocabulary

allWordsReport :: Vocabulary -> Text
wordsCountReport :: Vocabulary -> Text
frequentWordsReport :: Vocabulary -> Int -> Text

processTextFile :: FilePath -> Bool -> Int -> IO ()
main :: IO ()
```

Qualifying imports

Note that I write `Text` instead of the qualified `T.Text` name. The reason is purely aesthetic. We can do the same in the code by using the following simple trick when importing the corresponding `Data.Text` module:

```
import Data.Text (Text)
import qualified Data.Text as T
```

As a result we can use the `Text` identifier without explicit qualification but keep mandatory qualification for all the other identifiers from this module.

Every `*Report` function here is a function that takes a `Vocabulary` with additional arguments, if needed. These functions return the resulting text in the form of `Text` ready for printing. We will use them in `processTextFile`. To prepare these reports, we use the following three pure auxiliary functions:

```
allWords :: Vocabulary -> [Text]
wordsCount :: Vocabulary -> (Int, Int)
wordsByFrequency :: Vocabulary -> Vocabulary
```

The functions in the I/O part of the program (IO actions) now become more trivial: the goal of processTextFile is reading the text file, calling extractVocab to extract the vocabulary, and printing the results of all the *Report functions. To make the program easier to use, I allow skipping the printing of all words: when the Bool argument to processTextFile is False, we don't print the result of allWordsReport. The complete flowchart is depicted in figure 1.2.

We should now deal with the following technical issues:

- How to compute the most frequent words
- How to format reports (We have three of them!)
- How to parse command-line arguments

Let's work on them one by one.

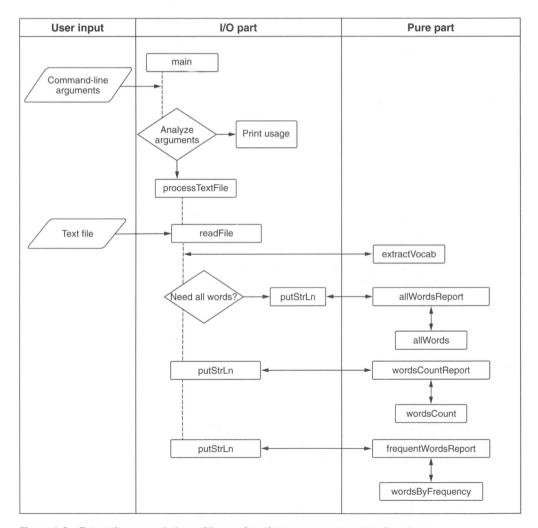

Figure 1.2   Extracting a vocabulary with pure functions: program structure flowchart

1.4.2 *Computing the most frequent words by sorting them*

Note that I've deliberately split the job between two functions, wordsByFrequency and frequentWordsReport, as shown next:

```
wordsByFrequency :: Vocabulary -> Vocabulary
frequentWordsReport :: Vocabulary -> Int -> Text
```

Is this really useful in practice? The wordsByFrequency function can be used later—its goal is to sort the vocabulary by the number of occurrences of each word—but the goal of frequentWordsReport is to prepare the report for printing. It would not be a good idea to add the Int argument to wordsByFrequency because this would greatly limit the function's potential for reuse.

Let's move on to computing the most frequent words. First, we need to sort the vocabulary entries by descending number of occurrences. This can be achieved using the sortBy function from the Data.List module, with the following type:

```
sortBy :: (a -> a -> Ordering) -> [a] -> [a]
```

This function requires using a comparison function, which returns the Ordering data type (whose values can be LT, EQ, or GT, meaning less than, equal, or greater than, respectively). The sortBy function sorts the elements of the list in ascending order by default. To sort in descending order, we can construct a comparison function by using the comparing function from the Data.Ord module over the values, wrapped with the type Down. This implementation reverses the results of comparing two values of the given type, providing us with a sort in descending order instead of the default ascending sortBy behavior, as shown here:

```
wordsByFrequency :: Vocabulary -> Vocabulary
wordsByFrequency = sortBy (comparing $ Down . snd)
```

Note also that calling the snd function over the vocabulary entry enables us to compare numbers of occurrences instead of words themselves.

> **NOTE** I recommend reading Roman Cheplyaka's blog post on the descending sort problem in Haskell (https://ro-che.info/articles/2016-04-02-descending-sort-haskell) to see some of the difficulties behind this seemingly easy task. This post explores the behavior of sortBy and compares it with other sorting functions, such as sortOn and sortWith.

The data for the frequent words report is ready. Let's talk about formatting reports in general.

1.4.3 *Formatting reports*

The formatting boils down to the problem of combining text
and data (see figure 1.3).

This can be done easily by concatenating strings and
data converted to `String` values with `show`, as shown next:

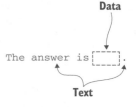

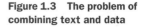

```
ghci> a = 42
ghci> putStrLn $ "The answer is " ++ show a ++ "."
The answer is 42.
```

Because we prefer working with `Text`, we also need the
`T.pack` function, as follows:

Figure 1.3   The problem of combining text and data

```
T.pack :: String -> Text
```

The `Data.Text` module also provides the following function to append `Text` values to
each other:

```
T.append :: Text -> Text -> Text
```

Using these two functions, we could implement the `allWordsReports` function as
follows:

```
wordsCountReport :: Vocabulary -> Text
wordsCountReport vocab = T.unlines [part1, part2]
  where
    (total, unique) = wordsCount vocab
    part1 = T.append (T.pack "Total number of words: ")
                     (T.pack $ show total)
    part2 = T.append (T.pack "Number of unique words: ")
                     (T.pack $ show unique)
```

Unfortunately, this code is not particularly appealing. We don't see any *formatting*; we
just manipulate `Text` values instead. Another problem is that appending `Text` values
may be quite slow, if we have many of them. Just imagine all the memory-copying
operations this would require.

We could avoid explicit calls to the `T.pack` function for `String` literals by teaching
the compiler to regard `String` literals as values of type `Text`. We can do that through
enabling the `OverloadedStrings` GHC extension in the source code by starting the
file with the LANGUAGE pragma, as follows:

```
{-# LANGUAGE OverloadedStrings #-}
```

Using GHC extensions

The use of compiler extensions in other programming languages is somewhat controversial. In C or C++, for example, we have the standard language definition, which is
implemented by many different compilers, and we also have specific compiler extensions. There are no standards for Python or Ruby, which means that there are no extensions: there is only one compiler, and we can legitimately use everything it implements.

In Haskell, the situation is different: there is a standard definition (the Haskell 2010 Language Report is the current version) and only one widely used compiler (the Glasgow Haskell Compiler), which implements many extensions beyond what's defined in the Haskell Report. It is generally considered good practice to use these extensions. Besides providing a programmer with more expressive power, doing so gives the community the experience needed to decide whether to include them in the next standard or, in some cases, to exclude them from the compiler itself.

The `OverloadedStrings` GHC extension saves us a couple of `T.pack` calls, as shown here:

```
wordsCountReport :: Vocabulary -> Text
wordsCountReport vocab = T.unlines [part1, part2]
  where
    (total, unique) = wordsCount vocab
    part1 = T.append "Total number of words: "
                       (T.pack $ show total)
    part2 = T.append "Number of unique words: "
                       (T.pack $ show unique)
```

We'll discuss what is behind this extension in the next chapter. Unfortunately, the situation doesn't become any better.

The key idea here is to employ a *builder*, which is a data type responsible for collecting text components incrementally and then concatenating them into one `Text` value. The builder should be able to absorb data of various types without converting them to `String` or `Text` explicitly. It should also support patterns to specify formats and rules for representing the data in textual form. The task of formatting text is very close to *templating*, where you provide a template of the text with some tokens, which are substituted by values at the final stage of processing.

In Haskell, we have many alternative approaches to text formatting, including the following:

- `Data.Text.Lazy.Builder` from the `text` package provides a very limited builder without any formatting. We can use it when we have many `Text` values that should be combined into one.
- The `printf` function from the `Text.Printf` module provides many format specifiers. It takes a format string and data and produces a `String`.
- The `text-format`, `formatting`, and the more recent `fmt` packages are very close in their goals but different in their interfaces and implementation.
- The `template` package provides a very simple template substitution engine. Other full-blown templating systems are used mainly in web programming.

In this project, we'll use the `fmt` package, but the same work can be easily done with other text-formatting packages as well. After enabling the `OverloadedStrings` GHC extension in GHCi and importing the `Fmt` module, we can construct formatting strings by operators and then use the `fmt` function to create a resulting `Text` value, as shown next:

```
ghci> :set -XOverloadedStrings
ghci> import Fmt
ghci> name = "John"
ghci> age = 30
ghci> fmt $ "Hello, "+|name|+"!\nI know that your age is "+|age|+".\n"
Hello, John!
I know that your age is 30.
ghci> fmt $ "That is "+|hexF age|+" in hex!\n"
That is 1e in hex!
```

The operators `+|` and `|+` are used for including variables and formatters (which are ordinary functions like `hexF` here). Sometimes we need to call `show` for our variable (if the `fmt` package doesn't know how to convert it to textual form). This can be done implicitly via the other pair of operators, `+||` and `||+`. Formatters from the `fmt` package are powerful enough to present tuples, lists, and even associated lists, but we can always provide a formatter for our data by writing a function returning `Builder`, which is the data type used for efficiently constructing `Text` values.

Besides operators for combining string and values, we'll use the following `fmt` features:

- The `nameF` function gives a name to the rest of the output.
- The `unlinesF` function combines elements of the list into one `Builder`.
- The `blockListF'` function formats list elements in the given way and presents them line by line.

All the details about this package and these functions can be found in the documentation for the `fmt` package. Our reports made with `fmt` follow:

```
allWordsReport :: Vocabulary -> Text
allWordsReport vocab =
  fmt $ nameF "All words" $ unlinesF (allWords vocab)

wordsCountReport :: Vocabulary -> Text
wordsCountReport vocab = fmt $
    "Total number of words: " +|total|+
    "\nNumber of unique words: " +|unique|+ "\n"
  where
    (total, unique) = wordsCount vocab

frequentWordsReport :: Vocabulary -> Int -> Text
frequentWordsReport vocab num =
    fmt $ nameF "Frequent words"
        $ blockListF' "" fmtEntry reportData
  where
    reportData = take num $ wordsByFrequency vocab
    fmtEntry (t, n) = ""+|t|+": "+|n|+""
```

1.4.4 *Rule them all with IO actions*

We have the following pure functions by now:

- We can extract a vocabulary from a given text.
- We can prepare data for reports.
- We can format reports.

The only thing we have to do is communicate with the user, so we need some sort of a driver. Our main processing IO action is almost trivial, as expected. It reads the text from a file and then prints all the reports, as shown next:

```
processTextFile :: FilePath -> Bool -> Int -> IO ()
processTextFile fname withAllWords n = do
  text <- TIO.readFile fname
  let vocab = extractVocab text
  when withAllWords $ TIO.putStrLn $ allWordsReport vocab
  TIO.putStrLn $ wordsCountReport vocab
  TIO.putStrLn $ frequentWordsReport vocab n
```

Note the when function from the `Control.Monad` module. It allows printing the corresponding report if the user requests it.

We analyze command-line arguments in the main function as follows:

```
main :: IO ()
main = do
  args <- getArgs
  case args of
    ["-a", fname, num] ->
      processTextFile fname True (read num)
    [fname, num] ->
      processTextFile fname False (read num)
    _ -> putStrLn "Usage: vocab3 [-a] filename freq_words_num"
```

Feel free to analyze any file you want by running the following command:

```
$ cabal -v0 run vocab3 -- -a data/texts/hamlet.txt 10
```

We'll see a much more advanced way to process command-line arguments in chapter 3.

Summary

- Structure programs clearly with types, pure functions, and I/O actions.
- Use the Text type for processing textual information instead of String.
- Enable the OverloadedStrings extension to make it more convenient to use string literals as Text values.
- Choose your own favorite package for representing data in text: formatting and fmt are good candidates.

Type classes

This chapter covers

- Exploiting type classes as tools for writing code that works for values of different types
- Considering type classes as a concept applicable to many types
- Using basic type classes defined in the standard library
- Abstracting computations via type classes

Haskell programmers tend to write code that can be reused in many ways. To achieve that, they avoid using specific types while writing code and use type variables instead. Depending on the types, the actual code may differ. This is possible thanks to *type classes* and their *instances*.

Type classes are usually considered Haskell's most prominent feature. They originated in Haskell and were then taken up by other programming languages. A type class is defined with respect to some type variable. It contains a collection of methods, given by type signatures. We can define as many instances, or implementations, for specific types as we need.

Writing functions with respect to a type class, as opposed to using concrete types, allows you to be more general: a function will work with different types, even if they don't exist at the time of declaring a type class. This makes type classes especially useful for libraries because we don't know in advance which user-defined types will be used with our library in the future.

This chapter is about type classes. We'll start with a simple problem, where we'll use about a dozen type classes. We'll derive (ask GHC to generate) and define (implement manually) instances. We'll even declare our own type classes. Then we'll discuss several issues with numeric and text data regarding type classes. Finally, we'll talk about abstracting computations with type classes and see how this helps us to write generic code.

2.1 Manipulating a radar antenna with type classes

It is useful to think about type classes as abstract concepts. They don't refer to specific types but can be applied to them with the help of instances that materialize those concepts. Whenever we do something in Haskell, chances are we are repeating what is already described by some type class. An experienced Haskeller often looks for a type class first and then starts coding.

In this section, we'll solve the problem of manipulating a radar antenna. This task requires a surprising number of type classes with instances, both derived and implemented manually. We'll also try to invent our own abstract concept and express it using a brand-new type class.

2.1.1 The problem at hand

A radar antenna is a device with the ability to be oriented toward four points of direction (namely, north, east, south, or west).

> **EXAMPLE: MANIPULATING A RADAR ANTENNA**
>
> 🗋 ch02/radar/
>
> ⚡ *radar*
>
> ☞ Type classes define common operations.
>
> ☞ We can declare new type classes.
>
> ☞ We can implement instances manually or derive them.

We can rotate a radar antenna. It supports a limited set of commands to be turned left, right, and all around, as shown in figure 2.1. It can also stay in its current direction.

The task is to write a program that manipulates a radar antenna. The following are the two modes of operation:

- When given a file with a list of turns and a starting direction, the program executes all the turns and reports the final direction with all the intermediate directions.
- When given a file with a list of directions, the program computes and reports the corresponding set of turns to orient the radar antenna as required.

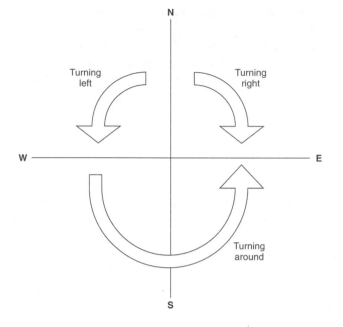

Figure 2.1 **Rotating a radar antenna: directions and turns**

Let's express a radar antenna state and behavior with the following two data types:

```
data Direction = North | East | South | West
data Turn = TNone | TLeft | TRight | TAround
```

Basic operations over a radar includes the following:

- `rotate`: determine a new antenna direction after rotating.
- `orient`: find a rotation to change an orientation from the first given direction to the second one.

As usual, we describe these operations with their type signatures, as shown next:

```
rotate :: Turn -> Direction -> Direction
orient :: Direction -> Direction -> Turn
```

Once we've implemented them, we can define functions over lists as follows:

```
rotateMany :: Direction -> [Turn] -> Direction
rotateManySteps :: Direction -> [Turn] -> [Direction]
orientMany :: [Direction] -> [Turn]
```

We are going to end up processing files and the `main` function, as shown next:

```
rotateFromFile :: Direction -> FilePath -> IO ()
orientFromFile :: FilePath -> IO ()
main :: IO ()
```

It is always a good idea to test our functions. We should do that, too.

No sign of type classes yet? Buckle up!

2.1.2 *Rotating a radar antenna with Eq, Enum, and Bounded*

We could start coding the `rotate` function as follows:

```
rotate :: Turn -> Direction -> Direction
rotate TNone d = d                          <------ Direction is not changed.
rotate TLeft North = West
rotate TLeft East = North
...
```

This is extremely boring, isn't it? This approach requires more than a dozen lines, which could easily go wrong. We definitely don't want to follow this path.

Doing it the Haskell way means that we should abstract a little: going from one direction to another is, in fact, going through the list of the data constructors to the next or previous element (thanks to the order of constructors used in the definition). This is a well-known abstract concept of *enumerating* data constructors expressed in Haskell with the `Enum` type class. The only problem arises when we reach bounds—for those cases, we should restart from the beginning or the end. There is a type class for that, too. `Bounded` is used to specify minimum and maximum bounds among all the data constructors. Note that we should also be able to see whether the two directions are equal. Otherwise, we couldn't tell whether or not we reached one of the bounds. Thankfully, there is the `Eq` type class for that.

EQUALITY, ENUMERATION, AND BOUNDEDNESS

Interestingly, type classes originated in Haskell from the problem of checking the equality of two values. The idea was to do that in a uniform way, whether those values are two `Bool` values, two `Integer` numbers, or whatever.

In Haskell, we have the `Eq` type class with two methods, `(==)` and `(/=)`. The full definition of this class follows:

Two methods with a shared type signature

Head of the class definition, specifying its name and type variable

```
class Eq a where          <-----
    (==), (/=)                   :: a -> a -> Bool      GHC pragma that defines rules
                                                        for inline method definition
    {-# INLINE (/=) #-}   <------
    {-# INLINE (==) #-}
    x /= y                = not (x == y)    <------ Default method implementation
    x == y                = not (x /= y)
    {-# MINIMAL (==) | (/=) #-}   <------| Minimal complete definition: it's enough
                                         | to implement either (==) or (/=)
```

Exploring documentation in GHCi

GHCi provides two commands to get information about type classes: `:info` and `:doc`. The former shows the type class definition with all the instances available at this point. The latter explains goals and expectations on instances. These commands can be used as follows:

(continued)
```
ghci> :info Eq
class Eq a where
  ...
ghci> :doc Eq
  The 'Eq' class defines equality ('==') and inequality ('/=').
  ...
```

It's always a good idea to read this information when using or implementing a new type class.

Other useful concepts are boundedness and enumeration. In Haskell, they are represented by the type classes Bounded (for types with minimum and maximum bounds) and Enum (for types whose values can be enumerated by the Int values). The Bounded type class defines only two methods, shown next:

```
class Bounded a where
  minBound :: a
  maxBound :: a
  {-# MINIMAL minBound, maxBound #-}
```

The Enum type class has the following eight methods:

```
class Enum a where
  succ :: a -> a
  pred :: a -> a
  toEnum :: Int -> a
  fromEnum :: a -> Int
  enumFrom :: a -> [a]
  enumFromThen :: a -> a -> [a]
  enumFromTo :: a -> a -> [a]
  enumFromThenTo :: a -> a -> a -> [a]
  {-# MINIMAL toEnum, fromEnum #-}
```

These methods allow going from the a type to Int and back with the fromEnum and toEnum functions, respectively. This defines an enumeration that can be used to get successors, predecessors, and lists of values of the a type.

We'll apply these type classes shortly, but for now let's build an intuition about them as follows:

- If the values of a type can be checked for equality, we define an instance of the Eq type class.
- If it makes sense to enumerate elements of a type one by one, then it is a good sign that we should implement Enum. The moment we do that, we get a bunch of methods we can use with its values.
- If a data type supports the idea of minimum and maximum values, then we define the Bounded instance—the presence of such an instance serves as a part of this type specification, indicating that it is bounded.

In general, every type class provides cheap added knowledge. If we say which type classes are implemented for a type, everyone gets plenty of information on how this type can be used.

DERIVING INSTANCES

Once we've established useful abstract concepts, it's time to apply them to our types. Haskell gives us two options:

- We can derive instances automatically using some built-in compiler magic (there is a special term for that: *automagically*).
- We can implement those instances manually.

The first option is available for a limited set of type classes including the following, which we need:

```
data Direction = North | East | South | West
  deriving (Eq, Enum, Bounded, Show)

data Turn = TNone | TLeft | TRight | TAround
  deriving (Eq, Enum, Bounded, Show)
```

Besides these three discussed type classes, I've added a Show instance to be able to print values in GHCi. Automatic deriving of these instances follows the natural algorithms:

- For Eq, we get equality for values built from the same data constructors and inequality for all others.
- Enum value constructors are enumerated in order of appearance, so the enumeration starts with North.
- The bounds for Bounded are North (minimum bound) and West (maximum bound), apparently.
- The Show instance allows printing data constructors literally.

The following GHCi session demonstrates that everything works as expected:

```
ghci> succ North
East
ghci> minBound :: Direction
North
ghci> maxBound :: Direction
West
```

> **TIP** Remember, you can follow the GHCi session examples by executing the cabal repl radar command. It loads all the modules and dependencies in GHCi and allows exploring everything available in the example.

We'll get back to deriving instances in chapter 12—there is much more about it to learn.

BUILDING ABSTRACTIONS UPON ABSTRACTIONS: THE CYCLIC ENUMERATIONS

Unfortunately, Enum doesn't allow going from the West to the North because the succ method on West raises an exception, shown next:

```
ghci> succ West
*** Exception: succ{Direction}: tried to take `succ' of last tag
    in enumeration
```

If values of some type can be compared for equality, enumerated, and have bounds (the type has instances of Eq, Enum, and Bounded), then we can enumerate them in a cycle. Let's express this abstract concept in the form of a CyclicEnum type class as follows:

```
class (Eq a, Enum a, Bounded a) => CyclicEnum a where
  cpred :: a -> a
  cpred d
    | d == minBound = maxBound
    | otherwise = pred d

  csucc :: a -> a
  csucc d
    | d == maxBound = minBound
    | otherwise = succ d
```

This class defines two methods with default implementations. We can use them instead of writing our implementation, or we can redefine them in instances. The former is usually done when it's possible to define them more efficiently by exploiting an internal representation of a type.

The default definitions in the CyclicEnum type class (and empty minimal complete definition) allow us to define an instance in one line as follows (note the absence of where):

```
instance CyclicEnum Direction
```

In trivial cases like this one, we could also derive the same instance automatically using the DeriveAnyClass GHC extension. Deriving mechanisms has many gotchas, but for now it suffices to know that we'll get exactly the same instance, shown here:

```
{-# LANGUAGE DeriveAnyClass #-}

data Direction = North | East | South | West
  deriving (Eq, Enum, Bounded, CyclicEnum, Show)
```

Now we are free to go from the West to the North as follows:

```
ghci> csucc West
North
```

It seems we'll never need a corresponding instance for Turn.

IMPLEMENTING RADAR MANIPULATION FUNCTIONS

With all these instances, the definition of rotate becomes rather trivial, as shown next:

```
rotate :: Turn -> Direction -> Direction
rotate TNone = id
rotate TLeft = cpred
rotate TRight = csucc
rotate TAround = cpred . cpred
```

Note the programming pattern here: instead of writing the simplest (but quite cumbersome) definition, we've come up with a straightforward generalization and applied it to the Direction data type.

Remember, we should also define the orient function as follows:

```
orient :: Direction -> Direction -> Turn
```

The simplest idea (maybe not the most efficient one) might be to go over all the possible turns and find which one is the solution, as shown next:

```
orient d1 d2 = head $ filter (\t -> rotate t d1 == d2)
                              [TNone, TLeft, TRight, TAround]
```

It's clear that any two directions can be reached from one another by one turn, so we can safely use head here. There is always exactly one element in the list.

Let's focus on the list [TNone, TLeft, TRight, TAround]. Because we have an instance of Enum for the Turn data type, this list expression can be shortened to [TNone .. TAround]. Also, because we have Bounded, it can be [minBound .. maxBound]—and this can be abstracted again as a list with every value of a bounded enumerable type! We could define yet another type class, but let's write the following generic function instead:

```
every :: (Enum a, Bounded a) => [a]
every = enumFrom minBound
```

The default implementation of enumFrom makes sure that we get the correct finite list for every. Note that we can use it for both Direction and Turn. This is how functions written with respect to type classes work.

Now we can redefine the orient function as follows:

```
orient :: Direction -> Direction -> Turn
orient d1 d2 = head $ filter (\t -> rotate t d1 == d2) every
```

Implementations of functions over lists are almost trivial, as shown next:

```
rotateMany :: Direction -> [Turn] -> Direction
rotateMany = foldl (flip rotate)

rotateManySteps :: Direction -> [Turn] -> [Direction]
```

```
rotateManySteps = scanl (flip rotate)

orientMany :: [Direction] -> [Turn]
orientMany ds@(_:_:_) = zipWith orient ds (tail ds)
orientMany _ = []
```

Make sure you understand what is going on in these functions. I use traditional list-processing functions: `foldl`, `scanl`, and `zipWith`. As usual, the best way to understand them is to explore the types in GHCi with the `:type` command.

2.1.3   *Combining turns with Semigroup and Monoid*

We are not done with abstract concepts yet! Note that rotating a radar antenna twice to the left is the same as rotating it twice to the right—that is, it is the same as rotating it around. Turning an antenna around and then to the left is the same as turning it right in the first place. It looks like we can combine any two turns and get some other turn as a result. Combining turns is an example of a generic binary operation. This concept is captured by the two type classes, `Semigroup` and `Monoid`.

SEMIGROUP AND MONOID

The `Semigroup` type class declares such an operation as follows:

```
(<>) :: Semigroup a => a -> a -> a
```

Many things can be combined with it, as shown next:

```
ghci> import Data.Semigroup
ghci> [1,2,3] <> [4,5,6]
[1,2,3,4,5,6]
ghci> "Hello " <> "world"
"Hello world"
ghci> Sum 2 <> Sum 3
Sum {getSum = 5}
ghci> Product 2 <> Product 3
Product {getProduct = 6}
```

Remember that a `String` is a synonym for a list of `Char`, so the first two examples share an instance for lists (and this operation is just list concatenation). The third and fourth examples apply instances that represent addition and multiplication—two basic operations over numeric types. They feature `newtype` wrappers `Sum` and `Product` for any type a with an instance of `Num a`.

The `Monoid` type class extends `Semigroup` and adds another method

```
mempty :: Monoid a => a
```

which defines a so-called *neutral* element, as follows:

```
ghci> mempty :: [Int]
[]
ghci> mempty :: String
""
```

```
ghci> mempty :: Sum Int
Sum {getSum = 0}
ghci> mempty :: Product Int
Product {getProduct = 1}
```

This element is called neutral because it is expected to satisfy the *monoid laws,* so that for any element a

```
mempty <> a == a
a <> mempty == a
```

The empty list, an empty `String`, and the numbers `Sum` 0 and `Product` 1 satisfy these rules with respect to the corresponding operation.

In general, we use the (`<>`) operation to accumulate information, such as concatenating lists and other containers (`Data.Set` or `Data.Sequence`, to name a few), combining configuration properties, and so forth. When encountering a new data type, it is always a good idea to look for provided instances. If we see instances for `Semigroup` or `Monoid`, then we know that values of this data type can be combined with (`<>`). For example:

```
ghci> import Data.Text
ghci> :info Text
data Text
...
instance Monoid Text -- Defined in 'Data.Text'
...
instance Semigroup Text -- Defined in 'Data.Text'
```

The presence of these instances makes it possible to concatenate `Text` values, as shown next:

```
ghci> :set -XOverloadedStrings
ghci> h = "hello" :: Text
ghci> c = ", " :: Text
ghci> w = "world" :: Text
ghci> h <> c <> w
"hello, world"
```

Demystifying the OverloadedStrings GHC extension

We've met the `OverloadedStrings` GHC extension several times already, so now is a good time to explain it. This extension gives simple but very useful examples of type class usage. When we enable it, types for `String` literals become more generic, as follows:

```
ghci> :type "hello"
"hello" :: [Char]
ghci> :set -XOverloadedStrings
ghci> :type "hello"
"hello" :: Data.String.IsString p => p
```

(continued)
The IsString type class defines only one method, fromString, as shown next:

```
fromString :: IsString a => String -> a
```

The only thing the extension OverloadedStrings is responsible for is replacing every string literal in the source code with a call to the fromString method on that literal. Then it's time for instance resolution algorithms to find the right instance and convert a String to some other type. Note, it should be unambiguous from the context which type is expected at the position of a String literal.

Enabling and disabling GHC extensions in GHCi

The :set GHCi command allows you to manage various GHCi settings and also supports enabling and disabling GHC extensions. In the following session, I enable and then disable the OverloadedStrings GHC extension as an example:

```
ghci> :set -XOverloadedStrings
ghci> :set -XNoOverloadedStrings
```

Besides (<>) and mempty, other methods are available in Semigroup and Monoid. For example, we can apply a binary operation to a list of values, as follows:

```
mconcat :: Monoid a => [a] -> a
```

The mconcat function returns mempty if the given list is empty and applies an operation over all the elements from left to right otherwise.

The Semigroup type class defines the sconcat function, which is similar to mconcat with one exception: there is no neutral element in Semigroup, so we wouldn't be able to return something meaningful in the case of an empty list. This is why the sconcat function takes NonEmpty (provided by the Data.List.NonEmpty module) as an argument, as follows:

```
sconcat :: Semigroup a => NonEmpty a -> a
```

The value of the NonEmpty type is a list, which must have a head and a potentially empty tail. We can construct such a list with the (:|) operation as follows:

```
ghci> import Data.List.NonEmpty
ghci> 0 :| [1,2,3]
0 :| [1,2,3]
ghci> 'x' :| ""
'x' :| ""
```

The sconcat function takes a nonempty list and applies (<>) to all the elements, starting with a head, which accumulates a total value. For example:

```
ghci> sconcat ("x" :| ["y", "z"])
"xyz"
```

NOTE The definitions of the type classes `Semigroup` and `Monoid` are works in progress. A while ago we had only `Monoid`; then `Semigroup` was added, but at that time there were no direct connections between these two classes. In GHC version 8.4, `Semigroup` became a superclass of `Monoid`. If you look at their definitions, chances are you will see traces of their history, such as the `mappend` method, which is the same as `(<>)`. This `mappend` method is expected to be removed from the `Monoid` type class at some time in the future.

We'll meet many examples of using the type classes `Semigroup` and `Monoid` throughout the book. They are truly ubiquitous in Haskell programming.

IMPLEMENTING INSTANCES FOR SEMIGROUP AND MONOID

It should be clear by now that it is possible to implement `Semigroup` and `Monoid` for the `Turn` data type. Let's check all the combinations of the `Turn` values. They are presented in table 2.1. Such tables are called *Cayley tables*. Every value in such a table is a result of applying a `Semigroup` operation to the first elements of the corresponding row and column (in that order). Note that our `Semigroup` of rotations is commutative, meaning that `t1 <> t2` is the same as `t2 <> t1`. This simplifies the definition.

Table 2.1 Cayley table for rotating a radar antenna

	TNone	TLeft	TRight	TAround
TNone	TNone	TLeft	TRight	TAround
TLeft	TLeft	TAround	TNone	TRight
TRight	TRight	TNone	TAround	TLeft
TAround	TAround	TRight	TLeft	TNone

To implement an instance of the `Semigroup` type class, one should express such a table in code as follows:

```
instance Semigroup Turn where
  TNone <> t = t
  TLeft <> TLeft = TAround
  TLeft <> TRight = TNone
  TLeft <> TAround = TRight
  TRight <> TRight = TAround
  TRight <> TAround = TLeft
  TAround <> TAround = TNone
  t1 <> t2 = t2 <> t1
```

The last line in this implementation employs commutativity, whereas all others define half of the table with and over the diagonal.

Clearly, `TNone` is a neutral element, so the `Monoid` instance is trivial, as shown next:

```
instance Monoid Turn where
  mempty = TNone
```

These instances work as expected:

```
ghci> TLeft <> TRight
TNone
ghci> TLeft <> TAround
TRight
ghci> mconcat [TLeft, TRight, TAround, TAround]
TNone
```

So, the `Turn` type is both `Semigroup` and `Monoid`. Do we really need to know that? Well, remember the `rotateMany` function?

```
rotateMany :: Direction -> [Turn] -> Direction
rotateMany = foldl (flip rotate)
```

Instead of rotating the antenna many times to get to the final direction, we could compute the combined turns and rotate it only once, as follows:

```
rotateMany' :: Direction -> [Turn] -> Direction
rotateMany' dir ts = rotate (mconcat ts) dir
```

Imagine how much energy we could save thanks to `Semigroup` and `Monoid`! Of course, if we need to know all the intermediate directions, we have to rotate a radar antenna step by step anyway.

2.1.4 *Printing and reading data with Show and Read*

Suppose we have a couple of files, one with a list of directions and another one with a list of turns, as shown next:

```
$ head -3 data/dirs.txt
East
North
South
$ head -3 data/turns.txt
TLeft
TLeft
TNone
```

Our goal now is to implement the following two functions:

```
rotateFromFile :: Direction -> FilePath -> IO ()
orientFromFile :: FilePath -> IO ()
```

Both functions should read the corresponding files and make them into `[Turn]` and `[Direction]` lists. I assume that lines in the files contain data constructor names. The simplest way to read them is to use the `read` function from the `Read` type class. The following is the type signature of `read`:

```
read :: Read a => String -> a
```

The default implementation of Read can handle this task. Unfortunately, we didn't derive it. We can do that by changing the data type declarations, or, alternatively, we can write a standalone deriving clause as follows:

```
deriving instance Read Direction
deriving instance Read Turn
```

This requires the StandaloneDeriving GHC extension to be enabled. Once we do that, we can use the Read instance as follows:

```
ghci> read "North" :: Direction
North
ghci> read "TRight" :: Turn
TRight
```

We don't have to specify the type explicitly if it can be inferred from the context. For example, in the following GHCi session, types are known to the compiler:

```
ghci> rotate (read "TAround") (read "North")
South
```

With this function it is easy to read the whole file and make it a list of some data type. For example, in some do block we could write

```
do
  f <- readFile fname
  let dirs = map read $ lines f
```

Now reading data is not a problem. What about printing? We have Show instances already. What if we want to print directions or turns differently? For example, we could output something like the following:

```
N W S S N W N W N N
<- || -> <- -> --
```

One option is to leave the existing Show instance for GHCi and apply the fmt package machinery to prepare reports. In the previous chapter, we prepared reports from Text and numbers. To use fmt with user-defined types, we have to implement the Buildable type class. It requires only one method, build, which transforms every value into a Builder. This data type is used to build a final report from its components. An implementation is straightforward, as shown next:

```
instance Buildable Direction where
  build North = "N"
  build East = "E"
  build South = "S"
  build West = "W"

instance Buildable Turn where
```

```
build TNone = "--"
build TLeft = "<-"
build TRight = "->"
build TAround = "||"
```

The `fmt` library uses these instances in its functions. It is also possible to use `Show` instead. The full implementation of the `rotateFromFile` function is given in the following code sample:

Using Read instance

```
rotateFromFile :: Direction -> FilePath -> IO ()
rotateFromFile dir fname = do
  f <- readFile fname
  let turns = map read $ lines f
      finalDir = rotateMany dir turns
      dirs = rotateManySteps dir turns
  fmtLn $ "Final direction: "+||finalDir||+""
  fmt $ nameF "Intermediate directions" (unwordsF dirs)
```

**Using Show instance (note +||
and ||+ operators)**

**Using Buildable
instance**

For example, this is the type of the `unwordsF` function:

```
unwordsF :: (Foldable f, Buildable a) => f a -> Builder
```

In our case, it takes `[Direction]` and applies `build` from `Buildable` to every element.

Note, we don't use `putStr` or a similar function: the `fmt` function is clever enough to print the given value in the context, where `IO ()` is expected. Of course, this is also implemented with type classes and instances. The `fmt` result has the type `FromBuilder b => b`. The `IO ()` instance of `FromBuilder` prints the given value. The `FromBuilder` type class also has an instance for `Text`, so it can be used to return a `Text` value as well.

POLYMORPHIC VALUES The values of the `C a => a` type are called polymorphic, because they can be used in many forms, depending on the required type. For example, we can use numeric values polymorphically without specifying a type, such as `Num a => a`. `String` literals become polymorphic (`IsString s => s`) if we enable the `OverloadedStrings` GHC extension. The `FromBuilder b => b` type follows the same idea.

The `main` function is trivial. Its goal is to analyze command-line arguments and run the corresponding functions, as shown here:

```
main :: IO ()
main = do
  args <- getArgs
  case args of
    ["-r", fname, dir] -> rotateFromFile (read dir) fname
    ["-o", fname] -> orientFromFile fname
    _ -> putStrLn $ "Usage: locator -o filename\n" ++
                    "       locator -r filename direction"
```

We can use this program as follows:

```
$ cabal -v0 run radar -- -r data/turns.txt North
Final direction: North
Intermediate directions: N W S S N W N W N N N
$ cabal -v0 run radar -- -o data/dirs.txt
All turns: <- || -> <- -> --
```

2.1.5 *Testing functions with Ord and Random*

We are not done yet! We have to test our radar manipulation functions. We'll need a couple more type classes for that. Let's discuss corresponding concepts first and then get back to writing tests.

EXAMPLE: TESTING A RADAR ANTENNA

📄 tests/radar/

⚡ *radar-test*

☞ Writing a test suite as a separate package component to test a program

☞ Using randomness for testing

> **Running the test suite in the REPL**
>
> The test suite for the radar-antenna-manipulation program is a separate program. We can run the tests as follows:
>
> ```
> $ cabal test radar-test
> ```
>
> In fact, the same code can be used as an executable (via `cabal run radar-test`) and explored in GHCi (via `cabal repl radar-test`).

ORDER

Many types with values can be ordered. They are not necessarily numeric. For example, `Turn` values can be ordered by the energy required to rotate a radar antenna in the corresponding directions. The concept of being ordered is captured in Haskell by the `Ord` type class. Order depends on equality. It's impossible to introduce order without introducing equality first. That's why `Ord` extends `Eq`. The definition of the `Ord` type class is as follows:

```
class Eq a => Ord a where
  compare :: a -> a -> Ordering
  (<) :: a -> a -> Bool
  (<=) :: a -> a -> Bool
  (>) :: a -> a -> Bool
  (>=) :: a -> a -> Bool
  max :: a -> a -> a
  min :: a -> a -> a
  {-# MINIMAL compare | (<=) #-}
```

Ordering is built upon equality and adds several operators and functions. It is enough to implement only one function, `compare`, or one operator, `(<=)`, to get all the other methods for free. We can also derive an instance; in that case, data constructors are ordered from left to right. Let's do that for `Turn` using the `StandaloneDeriving` GHC extension as follows:

```
deriving instance Ord Turn
```

RANDOMNESS

Introductory Haskell books often avoid discussing randomness, because the corresponding functionality in Haskell is heavily based on type classes and requires `IO` to be used properly.

The main entry point for random numbers in Haskell is the `random` package. This package was heavily revised in 2020, so be aware that most of the educational materials based on the previous versions are outdated. I'll describe here version 1.2, the most current one at the time of writing.

Several parts of the random-numbers interface are available to a Haskell programmer:

- Pure random-number generators
- Stateful random-number generators
- Infrastructure for drawing random values of various types

Random-number generators are basically functions that compute *pseudorandom* numbers by taking them from some sequence of numbers. Depending on the implementation, they can either be the pure functions or use some internal state. The `random` package gives us the `RandomGen` type class for describing pure random-number generators (found in the `System.Random` module) and the `StatefulGen` type class for describing stateful random-number generators (found in the `System.Random.Stateful` module).

We also have the `StdGen` type, a standard random-number generator, which implements the `RandomGen` type class. Every time we need a random number, we have to provide some `StdGen` value first. After generating a random number, we also get a new `StdGen` value that should be used for generating the next one. If we try to use the same `StdGen` twice, we get the same "random" number, because a function that computes a random number from `StdGen` is a pure function. There is also the *global* standard random-number generator available in the `IO` monad. We'll use it in all our next examples.

The `random` package supports generating random values for many different types. This ability is implemented via other type classes, `Uniform` and `UniformRange`, for drawing a value from a whole domain or from a restricted range, respectively. The names of these type classes suggest that they guarantee the uniform distribution of the random numbers we generate. We have instances of these classes for many types in the Haskell standard library.

The simplest way of generating random values of type a is to use one of the following uniform or uniformR functions:

```
uniform  :: (RandomGen g, Uniform a) => g -> (a, g)
uniformR :: (RandomGen g, UniformRange a) => (a, a) -> g -> (a, g)
```

The uniformR function takes a range in the form of (lo, hi) tuple values. We may expect any value x within the specified bounds lo ≤ x ≤ hi as a result.

Note the g generator given and returned in the previous code. These functions are pure, so we need the resulting generator for creating the next random numbers. Where should we get the generator? One option is to access the global one kept in the IO monad. We have the following functions to manipulate it (their types are simplified a little bit):

```
getStdGen    :: IO StdGen
setStdGen    :: StdGen -> IO ()
newStdGen    :: IO StdGen
getStdRandom :: (StdGen -> (a, StdGen)) -> IO a
```

The first two functions get and set the global random number generator. The third one gives us a generator and updates the global one at the same time, so we don't have to set it once we are done generating the numbers we need. The standard generator is *splittable*, meaning that we can produce two generators from the one we have and use them independently. The last function is perfectly suitable to be used with both the uniform and uniformR functions. For example, to generate a random value in the IO monad without thinking too much about managing the global generator, we could write the following IO action:

```
uniformIO :: Uniform a => IO a
uniformIO = getStdRandom uniform
```

The general scenario while working with random numbers is the following:

1 Acquire the random-number generator from the operating system using the newStdGenIO action somewhere close to the main function.
2 Do whatever we like with the generator, generating any number of random values, as long as we keep updating the generator every time we generate a random number.

Later in this book, we'll see how to keep and update random-number generators in a convenient way without going back to the IO part of our program. For now it's okay to generate random values in IO.

GENERATING RANDOM DIRECTIONS AND TURNS

To generate a random Direction or random Turn, we need to provide instances to the Uniform and UniformRange type classes. A minimal complete definition requires the `uniformM` and `uniformRM` methods, respectively. Note the `M` suffix: these methods are defined in the `System.Random.Stateful` module and use the monadic interface more generally. The `uniform` and `uniformR` functions are implemented in the package via `uniformM` and `uniformRM`. The good news is that these methods can be implemented almost trivially, given the `Enum` and `Bounded` instances: the idea is to go to the corresponding `Int` with `fromEnum`, generate a random `Int`, and then return the result with `toEnum`. Instances for `Direction` are presented in the following code:

```
instance UniformRange Direction where
  uniformRM (lo, hi) rng = do
    res <- uniformRM (fromEnum lo :: Int, fromEnum hi) rng
    pure $ toEnum res

instance Uniform Direction where
  uniformM rng = uniformRM (minBound, maxBound) rng
```

Note that we've implemented `Uniform` using the already defined `UniformRange` instance. Instances for `Turn` are identical.

For our testing purposes, we need random lists of directions and turns. Let's implement the next function for random generating lists first:

```
uniformsIO :: Uniform a => Int -> IO [a]
uniformsIO n = replicateM n uniformIO
```

The `replicateM` function comes from the `Control.Monad` module. It executes an `IO` action a given number of times and collects all the results into a list. Now we have to fix a type, and the `uniformsIO` function does the rest, as shown next:

```
randomTurns :: Int -> IO [Turn]
randomTurns = uniformsIO

randomDirections :: Int -> IO [Direction]
randomDirections = uniformsIO
```

These functions can be used to generate a file with random values. We could use such a function to create a file for running the main radar-antenna-manipulating program.

We should be able to generate two sorts of random files: one with directions and another one with turns. The Haskell way is to write a common function for that: it could take a function that generates the given number of any random values (we depend on `Random`) and prints all these values (we depend on `Show`). The function itself, shown next, is shorter than this discussion:

```
writeRandomFile :: (Random a, Show a) =>
                   Int -> (Int -> IO [a]) -> FilePath -> IO ()
writeRandomFile n gen fname = do
  xs <- gen n
  writeFile fname $ unlines $ map show xs
```

We can use this function as follows:

```
$ cabal repl radar-test
ghci> writeRandomFile 10 randomDirections "dirs.txt"
ghci> writeRandomFile 10 randomTurns "turns.txt"
```

WRITING THE TEST SUITE

Finally, we are ready to write tests. I suggest the following three testing scenarios:

- All turns are in use: if we apply the `orient` function to every possible pair of directions, the resulting turns should include all turns.
- Two implementations of `rotateMany` agree with each other for any original `Direction`.
- `orientMany` and `rotateManySteps` agree with each other: starting with any list of directions, then orienting toward them and then rotating again give the same original list of directions.

All these scenarios are implemented in the following functions:

```
test_allTurnsInUse :: Bool
test_allTurnsInUse =
  sort (nub [ orient d1 d2 | d1 <- every, d2 <- every ])
  == every

test_rotationsMonoidAgree :: [Turn] -> Bool
test_rotationsMonoidAgree ts =
  and [ rotateMany d ts == rotateMany' d ts | d <- every ]

test_orientRotateAgree :: [Direction] -> Bool
test_orientRotateAgree [] = True
test_orientRotateAgree ds@(d:_) = ds == rotateManySteps d (orientMany ds)
```

The `nub` function of type `Eq a => [a] -> [a]` from the `Data.List` module removes all duplicates from the given list. Using `sort` in the first function requires `Ord` for `Turn`. Note the three invocations of the `every` function in `test_allTurnsInUse`. It is instantiated for different types: twice for `Direction` and once for `Turn`. Note also the pattern matching in the last function: we want to refer to the whole list as `ds` and to its head element as `d`.

The last question: what does it mean for a program to be a test suite? Very simply, it should exit with a nonzero code if any of the tests fail. The `System.Exit` module provides the `exitFailure` IO action precisely for that. Implementing the `main` function as follows makes this program a test suite:

```
main :: IO ()
main = do
  ds <- randomDirections 1000
  ts <- randomTurns 1000
```

```
when (not $ and [test_allTurnsInUse,
                 test_orientRotateAgree ds,
                 test_rotationsMonoidAgree ts])
    exitFailure
```

NOTE Funnily enough, while preparing this example, I forgot about two equal directions in orient and got an exception in the first test! The fix was to add the TNone data constructor to the Turn data type. See? Even this naive sort of testing can be useful.

We'll get back to much more sophisticated approaches to testing later in this book.

2.2   *Issues with numbers and text*

In this section, we'll discuss several issues with the most used types in every programming language, namely, numbers and text. As we'll see, type classes heavily influence how to work with those types in Haskell.

2.2.1   *Numeric types and type classes*

The Haskell standard library defines many numeric types, including

- Int and Word for fixed-precision integers
- Integer for arbitrary-precision (unbounded) integers
- Float and Double for floating-point numbers, with single and double precision, respectively

Both Int and Word have instances of Bounded, so we can check their bounds as follows:

```
ghci> (minBound, maxBound) :: (Word, Word)
(0,18446744073709551615)
ghci> (minBound, maxBound) :: (Int, Int)
(-9223372036854775808,9223372036854775807)
```

All these types are available by default. They are exported by the Prelude module. After importing the Data.Ratio module, we can use more numeric types, such as Ratio a and Rational (a type synonym for Ratio Integer), and the (%) operator for representing fractions as follows:

```
ghci> 1%4 + 1%4
1 % 2
```

We can also import the Data.Complex module to get the type Complex a and complex numbers with real and imaginary parts represented with the (:+) operator, as shown next:

```
ghci> (0 :+ 1) + (0 :+ (-1))
0.0 :+ 0.0
ghci> (1 :+ (-1))^2
0.0 :+ (-2.0)
```

```
ghci> (1 :+ 1) * (1 :+ (-1))
2.0 :+ 0.0
ghci> (0 :+ 1)^2
(-1.0) :+ 0.0
```

Many useful functions for working with `Ratio a` and `Complex a` are in the corresponding modules.

We expect that numeric types support common operations. At least addition should be implemented for all of them. We don't want to end up with different functions for adding numbers of different types. In Haskell, this problem is solved with numeric type classes.

Numeric type classes, as defined in the Haskell Report, receive a lot of criticism for their mathematical incorrectness, inflexibility, and difficulties with defining instances for user types. The numeric type classes form a hierarchy, which starts with the most abstract numeric type class called `Num`. The `Num` type class defines the most general arithmetic operations, such as addition, subtraction, and multiplication of numbers. Other type classes in this hierarchy include the following:

- `Integral` unifying operations for all integer types, including integer division
- `Real` for operations over real (meaning noncomplex) numbers
- `Floating` for operations with floating-point numbers (`Float` and `Double`)
- `Fractional` for everything that can be used with division

Figure 2.2 presents the whole hierarchy of numeric type classes according to the Haskell Report, with other nonnumeric type classes they extend.

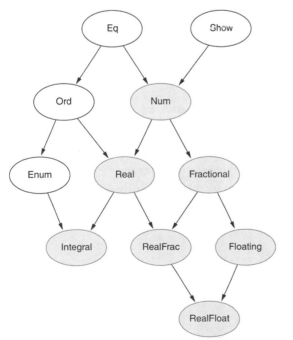

Figure 2.2 Standard Haskell numeric type classes (highlighted with gray)

As usual, the :info GHCi command gives all the information about methods defined in those type classes. The :doc GHCi command also gives additional details regarding usage and rules the instances should follow.

It is often necessary to mix values of different numeric types in a single computation. To do that, we have to convert those values to some common type first.

2.2.2   *Numeric conversions*

Let's start discussing numeric conversions with a small problem of computing the area of a circle with a given radius. Basic high school math teaches us the following:

```
circleArea :: Double -> Double
circleArea r = pi * r * r
```

The pi constant comes from the Floating type class. Consequently, we could make the type of the circleArea function more generic as follows:

```
circleArea :: Floating a => a -> a
circleArea r = pi * r * r
```

One problem with this type is that the argument now can be Complex a, but the radius cannot be a complex number—it must be real. Unfortunately, after changing the type of the argument to Real a, we get the following type error:

```
circleArea :: (Real a, Floating b) => a -> b        Type error: pi and r
circleArea r = pi * r * r                           have different types.
```

Now pi and r have different types, and we cannot use * for them! The solution is to convert the square radius to the appropriate type as follows:

```
circleArea :: (Real a, Floating b) => a -> b
circleArea r = pi * realToFrac (r * r)
```

The realToFrac function has the following type:

```
realToFrac :: (Real a, Fractional b) => a -> b
```

It coerces any real number to a fractional one. Because Floating extends Fractional, we can use it here to get a value of any type b with the Floating instance.

For another example, let's consider the easy problem of computing the mean of a list of Int values as follows:

```
xs :: [Int]
xs = [1,2,3,4,5]
```

Haskell beginners often complain that the straightforward solution shown next doesn't work:

```
ghci> sum xs / length xs

<interactive>:2:1: error:
    • No instance for (Fractional Int) arising from a use of '/'
    • In the expression: sum xs / length xs
      In an equation for 'it': it = sum xs / length xs
```

This example is interesting from the perspective of type inference. The error message clearly says that (/) parameters are required to implement the Fractional type class. Let's explore the following types:

```
ghci> :type (/)
(/) :: Fractional a => a -> a -> a
ghci> :type sum xs
sum xs :: Int
ghci> :type length xs
length xs :: Int
```

So, we are trying to divide two Int values. Int does not have an instance of the Fractional type class. In this case, we can use another coercion function, fromIntegral, as follows:

```
fromIntegral :: (Integral a, Num b) => a -> b
```

The fromIntegral function allows us to treat any integral value as a value of arbitrary numeric type (a type with Num instance). One could use it for computing the mean value of a list as follows:

```
ghci> fromIntegral (sum xs) / fromIntegral (length xs)
3.0
```

The fromIntegral function is able to return the value of any numeric type Num b => b. The type checker limits the resulting type shown here to Fractional b => b for both arguments, and everything runs smoothly:

```
ghci> :type it
it :: Fractional a => a
```

> **WARNING** The fromIntegral function is actually unsafe and should be used with care. The problem is that this function doesn't check for underflows and overflows in data. This could potentially lead to corrupting data when doing incompatible type conversion.

2.2.3 Computing with fixed precision

Sometimes we need to work with fixed precision. This is often the case with financial computations. For example, stock share prices in US dollars traditionally keep two more decimal places after cents to avoid being affected too much by rounding errors.

In Haskell, we can use the `Data.Fixed` module from `base`. It provides types with 0, 1, 2, 3, 6, 9, and 12 decimal places out of the box. These types are `Uni`, `Deci`, `Centi`, `Milli`, and so on. We can use them as follows:

```
ghci> import Data.Fixed
ghci> 3.1415926536 :: Deci
3.1
ghci> 3.1415926536 :: Milli
3.141
ghci> 3.1415926536 :: Pico
3.141592653600
```

Suppose we need a fixed precision of four decimal points. The `Data.Fixed` module suggests the following path to get such a type. First, we need a type that allows the compiler to choose the right resolution for our numeric type (which is 10 to the power of the number of digits after the decimal point we are interested in, so `10000` in this case, as we need four digits).

For specifying such a resolution, the `Data.Fixed` module provides the `HasResolution` type class, which has one method, `resolution`, as shown next:

```
class HasResolution a where
  resolution :: p a -> Integer
```

So, we need a type and an instance of the `HasResolution` type class for it. Because there are no particular requirements for that type apart from having such an instance, we can use an empty data type, as shown here:

```
data E4

instance HasResolution E4 where
    resolution _ = 10000
```

The only role the type `E4` is playing is choosing the right instance, so we don't need any data in there.

The numeric type with a specific number of decimal places is defined as follows with a new type, `Fixed`, parameterized by `E4` (this is why we have the `p a` type signature in the definition of `resolution`: `p` refers to the new type `Fixed` and `a` to its parameter):

```
type Fixed4 = Fixed E4
```

Now we can be sure that the following implementation of the `resolution` method will be applied to the `Fixed4` values in order to limit the number of digits after the decimal point:

```
ghci> pi = 3.14 :: Fixed4
ghci> pi
3.1400
ghci> resolution pi
```

```
10000
ghci> e = 2.7182818 :: Fixed4
ghci> e
2.7182
ghci> resolution e
10000
```

The `Fixed4` type does not round the value but truncates it instead. That's why the `e` constant is shown here as `2.7182` and not `2.7183`.

In the following GHCi session, we can see that this type can be used in computations:

```
ghci> pi * e
8.5351
```

Four decimal places are kept, thanks to the instances of various numeric type classes provided by the `Data.Fixed` module and the `HasResolution` type class itself.

2.2.4 *More about Show and Read*

The type classes `Show` and `Read` are simple and sophisticated at the same time. We use `Show` to turn a value into a `String` and `Read` to recreate a value from a `String`. These type classes can be easily described by two functions: `show` converts a value of any type with an instance of `Show` to a `String`, and `read` converts a `String` to a value of a required type with an instance of `Read`, as follows:

```
ghci> :type show
show :: Show a => a -> String
ghci> :type read
read :: Read a => String -> a
ghci> show [1..5]
"[1,2,3,4,5]"
ghci> read "[1,2,3,4,5]" :: [Int]
[1,2,3,4,5]
```

We don't have to specify the returned type for `read` explicitly if this information can be obtained by type inference. For example:

```
ghci> 2 + read "3"
5
ghci> 1 : read "[2,3]"
[1,2,3]
```

SHOW/READ COMPATIBILITY
Note the following compatibility between the default implementations of the `show` and `read` functions:

```
ghci> v = ([1,2,3,4,5], True) :: ([Int], Bool)
ghci> v == read (show v)
True
```

The String we got from show can be read to the same value. This compatibility is not enforced by the compiler, although it holds for every standard type. Clients may expect the same behavior of user-defined instances for Show and Read. These expectations affect the decision on whether we should derive a Show instance or implement it manually.

SAFE ALTERNATIVES FOR THE READ FUNCTION

The main issue with the read function is that it's almost impossible to use it safely. The problem is that it raises an exception whenever it can't parse the given String. To deal with this problem, we can use the following two functions from the Text.Read module:

```
readMaybe :: Read a => String -> Maybe a
readEither :: Read a => String -> Either String a
```

Unfortunately, dealing with Maybe a or Either a b can also be inconvenient unless we apply monadic tooling to them. We'll discuss this problem in the last section of this chapter and later in chapter 5, devoted to a practical approach to monads.

DERIVING SHOW VS. IMPLEMENTING SHOW

Instances of the Show and Read type classes can be derived automatically for user-defined types via the deriving clause, or they can be implemented manually. Unfortunately, due to limitations of the type classes/instances machinery in Haskell, we can't have both instances, derived and implemented, in one program.

> **NOTE** Some programming languages support named instances. In those languages, we could have one default instance and several named ones. Idris is one example of such a language. In other aspects, type classes in Idris (though called *interfaces* there) are very similar to those in Haskell.

Let's work with the following data type for personal information with a potentially missing age:

```
data Person = Person String (Maybe Int)
```

Our goal is to discuss issues with deriving and implementing Show instances.

> #### EXAMPLE: DERIVING AND IMPLEMENTING SHOW INSTANCES
>
> 🗋   ch02/person/
>
> ⚡ *person-derived, person-implemented*
>
> ☞ Derived Show instances are compatible with Read instances.
>
> ☞ Implemented Show instances break compatibility with Read.

Suppose, we have a couple of persons to look at:

```
homer :: Person
homer = Person "Homer Simpson" (Just 39)

spj :: Person
spj = Person "Simon Peyton Jones" Nothing
```

The OverloadedStrings GHC extension with user-defined types

Types like `Person` can be easily used with the `OverloadedStrings` GHC extension. To do that, we have to implement the `IsString` type class as follows:

```
instance IsString Person where
  fromString name = Person name Nothing
```

With this instance and after enabling the extension, we could write the following definition of the `spj` constant:

```
spj :: Person
spj = "Simon Peyton Jones"
```

Now let's derive the following three instances automatically (we use the `Standalone-Deriving` GHC extension):

```
deriving instance Show Person
deriving instance Read Person
deriving instance Eq Person
```

With these instances, we can compare values defined in the source code with values that come from `read`, as follows:

```
$ cabal repl person-derived
ghci> homer
Person "Homer Simpson" (Just 39)
ghci> show homer
"Person \"Homer Simpson\" (Just 39)"
ghci> homer == read "Person \"Homer Simpson\" (Just 39)"
True
```

Note that the original `homer` value and the value recreated from the `String` coming from `show` are equal.

Printing values in GHCi

In the previous GHCi session, we mentioned the `homer` constant as follows:

```
ghci> homer
Person "Homer Simpson" (Just 39)
```

(continued)
How is this related to `Show`? Well, for every such value, GHCi implicitly adds `print`, which has the following type:

```
print :: Show a => a -> IO ()
```

Consequently, a value is converted to `String` through `show` and then is printed. If the `Show` instance is not implemented or derived, then we get a corresponding complaint from GHC.

If we don't like the derived `show` implementation for `Person`, we could implement it manually as shown next:

```
instance Show Person where
  show (Person name Nothing) = name
  show (Person name (Just age)) = name ++ " (" ++ show age ++ ")"
```

Personal information looks a bit nicer now:

```
ghci> homer
Homer Simpson (39)
ghci> spj
Simon Peyton Jones
```

Unfortunately, reimplementing `Show` manually breaks the compatibility with the `Read` instance. We can't use `read` on a `String` we got from `show` anymore. This `Show`/`Read` incompatibility is not checked by the compiler, but it might surprise the code clients.

  We should address some other issues when implementing `Show`, including the following:

- Constructing a `String` by concatenation is highly inefficient. The `Show` type class gives one fairly limited solution, which we'll discuss shortly.
- Recursive data types introduce the problem of parentheses: when and how should they be inserted into the `String` under construction? This is also addressed in the `Show` type class.
- Implementing `Read` instances to maintain the compatibility with manually implemented `Show` is hard.

Arguably the best advice on `Show` and `Read` is to avoid implementing them manually. In fact, we don't even need to. It's always better to use some formatting (for `Show`) or a parsing library (for `Read`) instead. Derived `Show` and `Read` instances may still be used for simple cases when debugging or exploring code in GHCi.

THE TEXTSHOW TYPE CLASS

I've mentioned many times that `String` is very inefficient and almost never should be used in production code. The `text-show` package provides an alternative for the `Show` type class. The `TextShow` type class implements a similar functionality by building `Text` instead of `String`.

EXAMPLE: IMPLEMENTING A TEXTSHOW INSTANCE

▢ ch02/person/text-show.hs

⚡ *person-text*

☞ We can implement a `TextShow` instance to convert a value to `Text`.

Let's look at the following implementation of `TextShow` for the `Person` data type:

showb returns Builder, not Text.

```
instance TextShow Person where
  showb (Person name Nothing) =          fromString creates
      fromString name                     Builder from String.
  showb (Person name (Just age)) =
      fromString name <> " (" <> showb age <> ")"    Builder supports a
                                                      Semigroup operation.
```

It is enough to implement the `showb` function of the following type:

```
showb :: TextShow a => a -> Builder
```

The resulting `Builder` is the same as in the `fmt` library we've met before. It collects inside itself all the components with the `(<>)` operation without constructing a resulting value because this would be inefficient. Once we are done adding components, we can request a result with `toString`, or `toText`, or print it with `printT`:

```
main = do
  printT homer
  printT spj
```

getting the following as expected:

```
Homer Simpson (39)
Simon Peyton Jones
```

2.2.5 *Converting recursive types to strings*

Computer science often uses arithmetic expressions to illustrate important concepts. Let's use them, too, to look at the difficulties related to the problem of converting values to text form.

EXAMPLE: REPRESENTING ARITHMETIC EXPRESSIONS AND CONVERTING THEM TO TEXT

▢ expr/Expr.hs

⚡ *expr-simple*

☞ `TextShow` supports converting recursive data types to `Text` with parentheses, depending on precedence.

Simple arithmetic expressions can be represented in Haskell programs using the following parametric recursive data type:

```
data Expr a = Lit a
            | Add (Expr a) (Expr a)
            | Mult (Expr a) (Expr a)
```

This definition says that every expression is one of the following:

- A literal (data constructor `Lit`)
- An addition of two expressions (data constructor `Add`)
- A multiplication of two expressions (data constructor `Mult`)

Here is a sample value:

```
expr1 = Mult (Add (Lit 2) (Mult (Lit 3) (Lit 3))) (Lit 5)
```

One good thing about this representation is that it supports the following simple evaluation:

```
myeval :: Num a => Expr a -> a
myeval (Lit e) = e
myeval (Add e1 e2) = myeval e1 + myeval e2
myeval (Mult e1 e2) = myeval e1 * myeval e2
```

For example:

```
ghci> myeval expr1
55
```

We can present the same expression with a treelike view, as shown in figure 2.3.

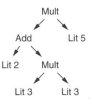

But how can we show this expression? An automatically derived `Show` instance gives us the following:

```
ghci> show expr
"Mult (Add (Lit 2) (Mult (Lit 3) (Lit 3))) (Lit 5)"
```

**Figure 2.3
Arithmetic
expression:
treelike view**

This result is hardly satisfactory. Instead, we'd like something like `(2+3*3)*5`, which is the traditional arithmetic view of this expression. Note the use of parentheses: although the first multiplication is not enclosed with parentheses, the addition is. This is because the addition is an argument to the multiplication. To build such a view, we have to take precedence into account. Addition has lower precedence than multiplication, so addition as an argument to multiplication has to be enclosed with parentheses. Multiplication has higher precedence, so it is not enclosed.

The question is, how should we implement such a conversion? We'll use the `Text-Show` type class in our solution. Although it's possible with `Show`, we'll keep the derived implementation to maintain the `Show`/`Read` compatibility. In fact, it's *simpler* with `Text-Show` because the `TextShow` type class hides the efficient implementation behind the `Builder` type, which supports a `Semigroup` operation to accumulate text representation.

SHOW AND EFFICIENT STRING CONCATENATION At the time the Show type class was designed, many contemporary programming patterns were not in use, if known at all. There was no Monoid type class back then, for example. The inefficiency of String concatenation was already known, however. That's why the Show designers applied another technique, namely, difference lists. The idea was to replace explicit String concatenation by ++ with composition of functions. Every such function appends *something* to its argument, thus producing a new String when required. The base library provides the ShowS type for these functions, together with several utility functions, which enable constructing such functions conveniently.

To deal with precedence, the TextShow type class defines the following method:

```
showbPrec :: TextShow a => Int -> a -> Builder
```

It is enough to implement this method alone in the TextShow instance. The first argument is an integer number from 0 to 11, which corresponds to the precedence of the *outer* context. The same precedence values are used in Haskell itself. For example, the precedence of function application is 10. In the implementation of showbPrec, we use the precedence value to decide whether or not we should enclose the second argument in parentheses.

We have only two operators in our expression data type, addition and multiplication. Consequently, we are free to assign them any precedence, given that multiplication has higher precedence than addition.

Besides showbPrec, the TextShow type class can be implemented via showb of the following type:

```
showb :: TextShow a => a -> Builder
```

This method ignores precedence. Its default implementation calls showbPrec with precedence 0.

There are many utility functions for TextShow. We'll need one to add parentheses, as shown next:

```
showbParen :: Bool -> Builder -> Builder
```

A recursive algorithm for creating a traditional mathematical view of expressions should, therefore, consider two points when given some subexpression:

- Whether we need parentheses to enclose this subexpression
- What precedence should be assigned to the recursive calls for their recursive components

We are going to proceed as follows:

- Literals never need to be enclosed.
- An addition should be enclosed if the precedence of the outer context is higher than that of an addition. Its arguments are processed with the precedence of an addition, because now addition forms the outer context for them.
- A multiplication should be enclosed if the precedence of the outer context is higher than that of a multiplication (which, in fact, is not possible in this particular example). Its arguments are processed with the precedence of a multiplication.

The full implementation of this algorithm is given in the following:

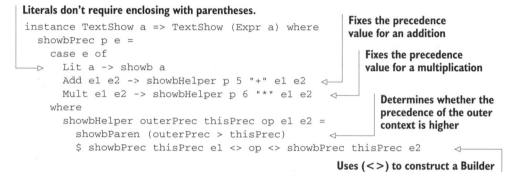

Literals don't require enclosing with parentheses.

Fixes the precedence value for an addition

Fixes the precedence value for a multiplication

Determines whether the precedence of the outer context is higher

Uses (<>) to construct a Builder

```
instance TextShow a => TextShow (Expr a) where
  showbPrec p e =
    case e of
      Lit a -> showb a
      Add e1 e2 -> showbHelper p 5 "+" e1 e2
      Mult e1 e2 -> showbHelper p 6 "*" e1 e2
    where
      showbHelper outerPrec thisPrec op e1 e2 =
        showbParen (outerPrec > thisPrec)
        $ showbPrec thisPrec e1 <> op <> showbPrec thisPrec e2
```

Note that I've chosen precedence values 5 and 6 as something in the middle between the borders of 0 and 11: it is the precedence of addition that is lower than that of multiplication that matters here.

Suppose we have the following expressions:

```
expr1 = Mult (Add (Lit 2) (Mult (Lit 3) (Lit 3))) (Lit 5)

expr2 = Add (Add (Lit 1)
                 (Mult (Add (Lit 1) (Lit 2))
                       (Add (Lit 2)
                            (Mult (Lit 2) (Add (Lit 1) (Lit 2))))))
            (Add (Lit 1) (Mult (Lit 3) (Lit 2)))
```

The next quick tests show that we are good:

```
ghci> printT expr1
(2+3*3)*5
ghci> printT expr2
1+(1+2)*(2+2*(1+2))+1+3*2
```

We can also convert expressions to Text or String as follows:

```
ghci> showt expr1        <——  showt returns Text by using TextShow.
"(2+3*3)*5"
ghci> toString $ showb expr1    <——  toString converts Builder to String.
"(2+3*3)*5"
```

2.3   *Abstracting computations with type classes*

In this section, we'll discuss several type classes that originated in mathematics (mainly category theory). Unfortunately, there is a long tradition of difficulty in grasping them that can be partially attributed to the fact that Haskell's designers kept the mathematical names for these type classes. Consequently, they accidentally created a myth that Haskellers have to know the math behind them in order to work with the corresponding concepts effectively. I strongly believe that the opposite is true. Many programming languages have been adopting once-mathematical ideas for decades. These ideas were then transformed into industrial practices that we exploit without any fear. In Haskell, we have to stick with the somewhat scary names, but a little technical intuition helps us use these type classes for practical needs.

> **NOTE** I recommend reading the Typeclassopedia (https://wiki.haskell.org/ Typeclassopedia) by Brent Yorgey as a brilliant introduction to type classes for abstracting computations for those who are mathematically inclined.

Keep in mind that almost every Haskell type class gives us some abstraction across particular types. In the previous sections, we saw many examples where the same methods were used with values of different types, in the same way, thanks to type classes. We'll continue doing the same in this section. The only new thing is that we'll abstract *computations* over values of various types. The type classes I'm going to discuss here are presented in figure 2.4, where solid arrows represent extending type classes.

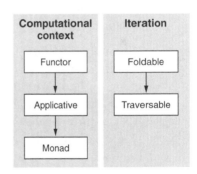

Following are the two most useful groups of type classes:

- *Computational context*—For computing the value of some type in a context, so that computation can be accompanied by some effects
- *Iteration*—For repeated computations over some structure, potentially collecting the results in a context

Figure 2.4   Type classes for abstracting computations

We'll discuss some aspects of these quite abstract descriptions in the remainder of this section and will see many practical examples in this and other chapters.

2.3.1   *An idea of a computational context and a common behavior*

Merriam-Webster gives the following definition of *context*:

> *The interrelated conditions in which something exists or occurs*

So, *computational context* means these *interrelated conditions* occur during the process of computation. Whenever we have a computation, we compute something, so we have a result. In Haskell, we can get this result by using many different computational contexts: some of them allow having side effects, such as input/output (IO), or mutable variables (State, ST), whereas others support the idea of computation with the potential absence of an actual result (Maybe, Either) or with the possibility of storing some additional information along with the computation (Writer). You probably came across some of them when you started learning Haskell.

All these contexts share abstract behavior by allowing us to *map*, *apply*, and *sequence* over them. This behavior is defined in three type classes with fancy names:

- Functor abstracts *mapping* over some value in a computational context.
- Applicative enables *injecting* values into a context and *applying* a function in a context to a value in a context.
- Monad allows *sequencing* of computations in a context so that what is done in the next computation depends on the result of the previous one.

This wording is just a textual representation of the type signatures for the following methods, so look no further:

```
fmap :: Functor f => (a -> b) -> f a -> f b
pure :: Applicative f => a -> f a
(<*>) :: Applicative f => f (a -> b) -> f a -> f b
(>>=) :: Monad m => m a -> (a -> m b) -> m b
```

> **NOTE** Older sources on monads mention the return function. It has the same meaning as injecting a value into a context as the pure function, but it comes from the Monad type class due to historical reasons.

Although these three type classes define other methods as well (we can explore them with the :info GHCi command), these are the most crucial for understanding what is going on here. We often refer to contexts as *functorial*, *applicative*, or *monadic* if there exists a corresponding instance, and we want to specify a particular property.

The phrase *value in a context* relates to the type signatures f a or m a, where a is a type of a value (the result of computation) and f or m restricts the context. In the same way, f (a -> b) is a *function in a context*. Take a look also at the second argument in the type signature of (>>=), (a -> m b)—this is what's meant by "the next computation depends on the result of the previous one" (we call it a *monadic function*). Some call monads "programmable semicolons" for this reason.

When we look at the particular contexts, these methods are concretized and sometimes look quite different, but all of them implement the same ideas of mapping, applying, and sequencing.

Many introductory materials on these three type classes are available—the *Typeclassopedia* includes many links, and unit 5 of *Get Programming with Haskell* by Will Kurt (Manning) describes them in great detail in a very practical way. I will not attempt to repeat those explanations. Instead, I will give examples of three different contexts and operations over values in them, to make sure that we are on the same page.

2.3.2 *Exploring different contexts in parallel*

The type classes we are talking about in this chapter share common ideas about behavior. It is always instructive to go both ways, from common ideas to specific implementations, and vice versa. In this subsection, we'll follow the path of understanding from particular examples toward general notions. We'll focus on the following three contexts:

- IO, which allows us to do input/output
- Writer, which supports logging of additional information along with the process of computations (we can get access to this context after importing the Control.Monad.Writer module)
- [] (a list), which allows extending operations over individual elements to the whole list of values

VALUE IN A CONTEXT

First, let's look at a few examples of what a *value in a context* is:

- getLine :: IO String is a value of type String in a context that is responsible for acquiring it from a side effect of reading user input.
- writer (42, "step 1\n") :: Writer String Int is a value 42 of type Int which is accompanied by the log "step 1\n" in the form of a String.
- [1,2,3] :: [Int] is one of the values 1, 2, or 3 of type Int, but we are not sure which one is the result of the computations (some refer to this uncertainty as a *nondeterminism*).

MAPPING

Now let's check the mapping using the fmap method from the Functor type class as follows:

```
ghci> fmap (++"!") getLine
Hi
"Hi!"
```

The second line, Hi, is the user input, which becomes a value in a context during execution, and the last line is a result of mapping (++"!") over that result.

What about Writer? Take a look:

```
ghci> fmap (+1) (writer (42, "step 1\n")) :: Writer String Int
WriterT (Identity (43,"step 1\n"))
```

Apart from the output mess with WriterT and Identity, which I'll explain later in this book, we can clearly see the new value 43 (the result of mapping (+1) over 42) in an unaltered context—the log does not change.

Now, for the third context:

```
ghci> fmap (+1) [1,2,3]
[2,3,4]
```

We have one of the values 2, 3, or 4, each of them being a potential result of mapping of (+1) over 1, 2, or 3. Clearly, it's an ordinary map for lists.

APPLYING

In the next step, we'd like to look at these contexts in an applicative setting. Let's try to see any similarities, as follows:

```
ghci> pure (++) <*> getLine <*> getLine
hello
world
"helloworld"
ghci> pure (+) <*> writer (42, "step 1\n") <*> writer (10, "step 2\n")
➥ :: Writer String Int
WriterT (Identity (52,"step 1\nstep 2\n"))
ghci> pure (+) <*> [1,2,3] <*> [4,5,6]
[5,6,7,6,7,8,7,8,9]
```

We have a two-argument function that is injected into the context and then applied to two values in a context, and we can clearly see the results of applying ("helloworld", 52, or one of the values in the list [5,6,7,6,7,8,7,8,9]). We can also see that the context does its job by getting two user inputs, combining logs, and exploiting nondeterminism (we had three potential results in the first value in a context and three potential results in the second value in a context, and we got nine (=3*3) of them finally).

SEQUENCING

Let's look at (>>=), pronounced "bind," for our last example, shown here:

```
ghci> getLine >>= putStrLn
hello
hello
ghci> writer (42, "step 1\n") >>= (\a -> writer (a+1, "step 2\n"))
➥ :: Writer String Int
WriterT (Identity (43,"step 1\nstep 2\n"))
ghci> [1,2] >>= (\x -> [x-1, x, x+1])
[0,1,2,1,2,3]
```

Try to work out for yourself what is done here with the result of the first computation and how the contexts reveal themselves. Don't forget to check the type of (>>=) before you start thinking.

2.3.3   *The do notation*

The do notation is a convenient syntactic mechanism for expressing monadic computations, which includes the following:

- Sequencing of operations by writing them one after another (as in imperative programming languages)
- Binding values in a context to names with <-
- Constructing succeeding operations with the names bound previously. (This is the main feature of the Monad type class.)

For example, the following code

```
action t = do
  a <- f t
  b <- g a
  h a
  pure (k a b)
```

is desugared into

```
action t =
  f t >>= \a ->
  g a >>= \b ->
  h a >>
  pure (k a b)
```

which is effectively

```
action t = f t >>= \a -> g a >>= \b -> h a >> pure (k a b)
```

The do notation is desugared into the following monadic operations

```
(>>=) :: Monad m => m a -> (a -> m b) -> m b
(>>)  :: Monad m => m a -> m b -> m b
```

where the last operation, `(>>)`, is a simplified version of `(>>=)` without dependency on the result of the previous computation. You will find details about desugaring do notation in the *Typeclassopedia* (https://wiki.haskell.org/Typeclassopedia#do_notation) and many other sources.

    Linearized definitions like this one are almost impossible to read and very inconvenient to write, so do notation helps a lot.

EXAMPLE: DO NOTATION IN SEVERAL CONTEXTS

   📄   ch02/Contexts.hs

   ⚡   *contexts*

   ☞   We can use do notation with different monads.

Note that we can use do notation in any monadic context. For example, the following three fragments are absolutely legitimate. The first context is `IO`:

```
readNumber :: IO Int
readNumber = do
  s <- getLine
  pure (read s)
```

The second one is `Writer`, where we recursively compute the sum of numbers from 0 to n while logging all intermediate arguments (logging is done via the auxiliary function `tell` from `Control.Monad.Writer`):

```
sumN :: Int -> Writer String Int
sumN 0 = writer (0, "finish")
sumN n = do
  tell (show n ++ ",")
  s <- sumN (n-1)
  pure (n + s)
```

Running this function in the GHCi gives the following:

```
ghci> sumN 5
WriterT (Identity (15,"5,4,3,2,1,finish"))
```

We can see here that the computations resulted in the number 15, and a full log is also provided.

Some monads support so-called *runners*, functions that provide unwrapped results. In the case of `Writer`, we have the `runWriter` function, which returns a pair (`result`, `log`) as follows:

```
ghci> runWriter (sumN 5)
(15,"5,4,3,2,1,finish")
```

The third context is a list, as shown next:

```
cartesianProduct  :: [Int] -> [Int] -> [(Int, Int)]
cartesianProduct xs ys = do
  x <- xs
  y <- ys
  pure (x, y)
```

We can apply the `cartesianProduct` function to some lists and see the results in the following GHCi session:

```
ghci> cartesianProduct [1..2] [1..3]
[(1,1),(1,2),(1,3),(2,1),(2,2),(2,3)]
```

> **NOTE** Every do block corresponds to exactly one monadic context. It's instructive to understand which `Monad` you work in every moment as the observable results crucially depend on that. It is a quite common mistake to expect something that is not handled by the context in use.

2.3.4 *Folding and traversing*

The last two classes in figure 2.4 are `Foldable` and `Traversable`. Both of them capture the idea of processing a container, a collection of values, with different possibilities.

Any `Foldable` instance should implement one of the following methods:

```
class Foldable (t :: * -> *) where
  foldMap :: Monoid m => (a -> m) -> t a -> m
  foldr :: (a -> b -> b) -> b -> t a -> b
  ...
```

Both of them should iterate over `t a`, a container `t` with elements of type `a`; process every element; and combine all the results. `Foldable` contains 16 methods in total. About half of them are various sorts of folding, namely, processing container elements using specific operations; others include `length`, `elem`, `maximum`, and so forth. All of these were once list methods that were later generalized to support other containers, too.

The type class `Traversable` is both simpler (it has only four methods, and two of them repeat the other two in a richer context, existing only for historical reasons) and more complex due to combining the effects of `Functor`, `Applicative`, `Monad`, and `Foldable`. The definition of `Traversable` follows:

```
class (Functor t, Foldable t) => Traversable (t :: * -> *) where
  traverse :: Applicative f => (a -> f b) -> t a -> f (t b)
  sequenceA :: Applicative f => t (f a) -> f (t a)
  mapM :: Monad m => (a -> m b) -> t a -> m (t b)
  sequence :: Monad m => t (m a) -> m (t a)
  {-# MINIMAL traverse | sequenceA #-}
```

The `traverse` method goes over every element in a container (the second argument) and applies its first argument to an element effectfully, as in `Applicative f`. As a result, we receive the same structure as before in a context, but each element is mapped to a new one. Due to constraints to `t` and `f`, the actions performed in `traverse` greatly depend on the particular instances, so it is very hard to talk about it in general.

EXAMPLE: TRAVERSING IN A CONTEXT

   📄   ch02/Contexts.hs

   ⚡   *contexts*

   ☞   We can iterate over containers and collect the results.

Let's look at a simple example. From the type signature of the `traverse` method, we can see that it requires two arguments: a function `a -> f b` returning a value in an applicative context and a container `t a` of elements of type `a`. Let's take a list of `Int` values as a container and `IO` as an applicative context. Then we need some function returning a value in `IO`, as shown next:

```
addNumber :: Int -> IO String
addNumber n = pure (++) <*> pure (show n ++ " ") <*> getLine
```

This function's type is compatible with `traverse`: it takes a number, turns it into a `String`, and concatenates it with the line from the user input. Now we are ready to see `traverse` in action as follows:

```
ghci> traverse addNumber [1..5]
aaa
bbb
ccc
ddd
eee
["1 aaa","2 bbb","3 ccc","4 ddd","5 eee"]
```

Here, I've entered five lines and then numbered them. It is always useful to check the types:

```
ghci> :t traverse addNumber [1..5]
traverse addNumber [1..5] :: IO [String]
```

So, we have a list of `Strings` in the context of `IO`, and this particular call to `traverse` has the following type:

```
(a   -> f  b)       -> t a  -> f  (t b)
(Int -> IO String) -> [Int] -> IO [String]
```

Earlier in this chapter, I suggested using safe alternatives for `read`. For example, we can exploit the `Maybe` context with `traverse` as follows:

```
ghci> :type readMaybe
readMaybe :: Read a => String -> Maybe a
ghci> traverse readMaybe ["1", "2", "3"] :: Maybe [Int]
Just [1,2,3]
ghci> traverse readMaybe ["1", "xxx", "3"] :: Maybe [Int]
Nothing
```

The module `Data.Foldable` provides `traverse_`, a function similar to `traverse`, that does not collect results of the individual computations, shown here:

```
traverse_  :: (Applicative f, Foldable t) => (a -> f b) -> t a -> f ()
```

A simple example of using `traverse_` occurs in the test program for showing arithmetic expressions (*tests/expr/Test1.hs*). I've defined there a function with the following type signature:

```
testexpr :: TextShow a => Expr a -> a -> IO ()
```

This function tests one given expression: it converts it to a `String`, then calls an external interpreter, which evaluates a value of a string representation and then compares expected and actual results. The test fails if values differ. The easiest way to run this function over the exprs list of expressions follows:

```
main = traverse_ (\e -> testexpr e (myeval e)) exprs
```

Always follow the types; they help a lot in understanding abstract functions. Try to use the same approach for sequenceA: choose any container (take a list as the simplest one; Maybe works, too) and any applicative context (try Writer!), and then construct a call to sequenceA. You will definitely see what is going on there.

Writing code with respect to Foldable and Traversable allows changing the container whenever needed, as opposed to relying on a specific container or a data structure. As a result, we can improve the efficiency of our code without rewriting it.

Summary

- Use type classes instead of fixed types to make code more generic.
- Organize abstract common operations in the form of a type class.
- Use instance derivation to make code smaller.
- Do not reinvent operations on values—reuse Semigroup and Monoid.
- Rely on types to get an idea of a computation context and abstract behavior in it.
- Use Foldable and Traversable to change underlying data structures easily and to achieve better performance when needed.

Developing an
application: Stock quotes

3

This chapter covers

- Designing a standalone multimodule Haskell program with dependencies
- Dealing with dates, text, and command-line arguments
- Parsing CSV files and plotting charts
- Employing type classes for practical needs

There is a common pattern for many utility programs: we have some data in a form that is not convenient for analysis and want to present the data, visually or textually. While implementing such a program, we have to address many issues, such as interfacing with a user, designing data types for an application domain, reusing external packages for parts of the program, and more. We should also think about language features that can help us in terms of correctness, performance, and an ability to extend functionality, if needed.

In this chapter, we'll explore the process of developing such a program. I'll start by describing inputs and outputs, then move on to design issues with data types, functions, and modules, followed by a discussion of useful Haskell packages and implementation details. We'll also see how type classes can make our programs much more flexible and resilient to changes.

3.1 *Setting the scene*

The overall task is as follows: we take the historical quotes data for some joint-stock company in CSV format (a text file with comma-separated values), analyze this data, and prepare a statistical report (as a text and an HTML document) with a chart. Figure 3.1 presents the overall data flow of the resulting program: we need to read the CSV file into a collection of some data type values and then process this collection in order to gather statistical information, plot a chart, and prepare a final report.

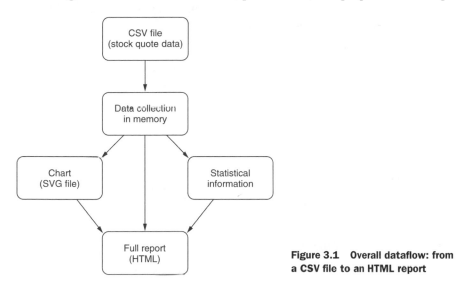

Figure 3.1 Overall dataflow: from a CSV file to an HTML report

Let's discuss expected inputs and outputs for this project. Once we've presented them, we'll talk about project structure that will help us to achieve all our goals.

EXAMPLE: PROCESSING STOCK QUOTE DATA

☐   stockquotes/

☐   data/quotes.csv

⚡   *stockquotes*

☞   We can use Haskell to write a program in any application domain.

☞   It's possible to find a Haskell library for almost any problem.

3.1.1 *Inputs*

Here is a fragment of the input data file, data/quotes.csv:

```
day,close,volume,open,high,low
2019-05-01,210.520004,64827300,209.880005,215.309998,209.229996
2019-05-02,209.149994,31996300,209.839996,212.649994,208.130005
2019-05-03,211.75,20892400,210.889999,211.839996,210.229996
2019-05-06,208.479996,32443100,204.289993,208.839996,203.5
2019-05-07,202.860001,38763700,205.880005,207.419998,200.830002
2019-05-08,202.899994,26339500,201.899994,205.339996,201.75
2019-05-09,200.720001,34908600,200.399994,201.679993,196.660004
...
```

The first line lists the names of the six fields, and every other line of this file contains their corresponding values, as follows:

- day is the date of the stock transaction.
- close is the share price at the close of business.
- volume is the total number of shares of a stock traded during the day.
- open is the price at the opening.
- high is the highest price during the day.
- low is the lowest price during the day.

Besides this file (technically its name), we expect the following to run the application:

- The name of the company, to make information in reports more specific
- The name of the HTML file to generate
- The flag for whether to plot charts
- The flag for whether to print statistical information in text

As usual, we want to give a user some choice so we ask for flags and names.

3.1.2 *Outputs*

This is not a book on financial analysis or trend prediction. I'll limit myself to computing very simple characteristics, such as the mean, minimum, and maximum values of the fields and the number of days between reaching minimum and maximum values. The following is a sample "statistical report" I plan to generate:

```
+-------------+-------------+----------+----------+---------------------+
| Quote Field | Mean        | Min      | Max      | Days between Min/Max |
+-------------+-------------+----------+----------+---------------------+
| Open        | 202.04      | 175.44   | 224.80   | 100                 |
| Close       | 202.16      | 173.30   | 223.59   | 100                 |
| High        | 204.10      | 177.92   | 226.42   | 101                 |
| Low         | 200.32      | 170.27   | 222.86   | 101                 |
| Volume      | 27869192.38 | 11362000 | 69281400 | 28                  |
+-------------+-------------+----------+----------+---------------------+
```

Stock quote information is traditionally presented with charts, so we'll generate them, too. Figure 3.2 demonstrates two sample charts:

- A candlesticks chart with a line for closing prices
- A volumes bar chart

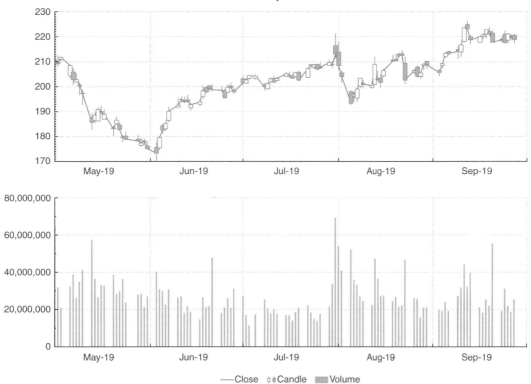

Figure 3.2 Stock quote charts for an imaginary company

Figure 3.3 explains the meaning of a candlestick. It shows all the day prices (open, close, high, and low) and whether the price is rising over the day. If an opening price is lower than a closing one, then a candlestick body is shown as white. Otherwise (a price is lowering over the day), it is filled with a color.

We also want to generate an HTML report that consists of the following:

- Charts
- Statistical information
- Raw data

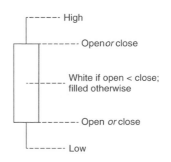

Figure 3.3 Meaning of a candlestick components

The latter two items are best presented with HTML tables. Figure 3.4 illustrates sample tables generated in an HTML document.

Statistics Report

Quote Field	Mean	Min	Max	Days between Min/Max
Open	202.04	175.44	224.80	100
Close	202.16	173.30	223.59	100
High	204.10	177.92	226.42	101
Low	200.32	170.27	222.86	101
Volume	27869192.38	11362000	69281400	28

Stock Quotes Data

Day	Open	Close	High	Low	Volume
2019-05-01	209.88	210.52	215.31	209.23	64827300
2019-05-02	209.84	209.15	212.65	208.13	31996300
2019-05-03	210.89	211.75	211.84	210.23	20892400
2019-05-06	204.29	208.48	208.84	203.50	32443100
2019-05-07	205.88	202.86	207.42	200.83	38763700
2019-05-08	201.90	202.90	205.34	201.75	26339500
2019-05-09	200.40	200.72	201.68	196.66	34908600
2019-05-10	197.42	197.18	198.85	192.77	41208700

Figure 3.4   Tables in HTML report

The next question is how to organize a workflow that will drive us from input data to outputs.

3.1.3   *Project structure*

Let's think what we should do in this project:

- Process command-line arguments.
- Read quote data from a CSV file.
- Compute statistics.
- Plot charts.
- Prepare reports on statistical info in text and HTML.

Depending on the supplied arguments, some of these stages may be skipped.

It is a good practice to split the required functionality over several modules, for example:

- `Params` for describing command-line arguments and processing them
- `QuoteData` for describing data types we are going to use throughout the project
- `StatReport` for computing statistics and preparing a report in a text form
- `HtmlReport` for generating a report in an HTML document
- `Charts` for plotting charts

Surely, we also need the `Main` module to connect the program components all together and drive the whole program. Figure 3.5 demonstrates the module structure for this program, with arrows pointing to the imported modules.

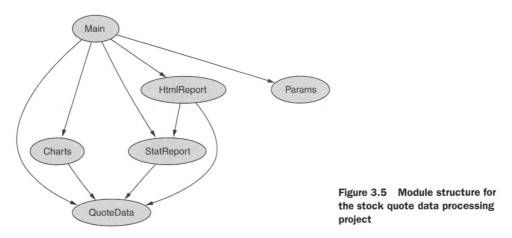

Figure 3.5 Module structure for the stock quote data processing project

TIP This diagram was created with the help of the `graphmod` utility from Hackage, developed by Iavor S. Diatchki. The `graphmod` utility produces a .dot file. These files can be later processed by the `graphviz` set of tools for graph visualization.

While describing this project, I assume that you follow along by reading, exploring in GHCi, and running the code in the `hid-examples` package (the stockquotes folder). Alternatively, you could develop your own solution in an independent manner. For those using the latter way, I'll provide the necessary details to set up a project from scratch.

SETTING UP A CABAL PROJECT

A Haskell package for a project is a directory containing the following:

- Source code, usually organized in subfolders
- A .cabal file, which describes the package content, dependencies, and build instructions, among many other things
- A stack.yaml file, which is a necessary file if we use `stack` as a building tool

Suppose we are in a fresh directory. Let's create an src subfolder with several files for Haskell modules in it, as follows:

- Main.hs
- Params.hs
- QuoteData.hs
- Charts.hs
- StatReport.hs
- HtmlReport.hs

Every module should start with a *module declaration* featuring its name (which should be the same as the filename without an extension), for example:

```
module QuoteData where
```

The Main.hs should also contain the main function. Let's start with the simplest one:

```
main :: IO ()
main = putStrLn "Stock quotes processing project"
```

Once we are done with modules, we create a stockquotes.cabal file in the root folder of the project with the following content:

```
cabal-version:  >= 1.29
name:           stockquotes
version:        0.0.1
synopsis:       Stockquotes processes historical stock quotes data.
build-type:     Simple

executable stockquotes
  hs-source-dirs: stockquotes
  main-is: Main.hs
  other-modules: Params QuoteData StatReport Charts HtmlReport
  build-depends:
      base
  default-language: Haskell2010
```

At this stage we can build and run the project as follows:

```
$ cabal build
$ cabal run stockquotes
```

If we want to use stack, we should also add a one-line stack.yaml file:

```
resolver: lts-14.27
```

This line fixes a set of packages we can use as external libraries. Building and running with stack is done as follows:

```
$ stack build
$ stack exec stockquotes
```

The stack utility reads a .cabal file and builds a project based on information there. In what follows, we'll add some source code and specify additional dependencies in the stockquotes.cabal file (in the build-depends section).

> **NOTE** We'll get back to a Haskell project structure, corresponding files, and cabal/stack commands in chapter 4.

MAIN PROJECT DATA TYPES, FUNCTIONS, AND A FLOWCHART

We are ready to describe the program functionality with types and functions. Figure 3.6 is an informal flowchart that presents the proposed structure of the program. There, you can see user input and both the I/O and pure parts of the program.

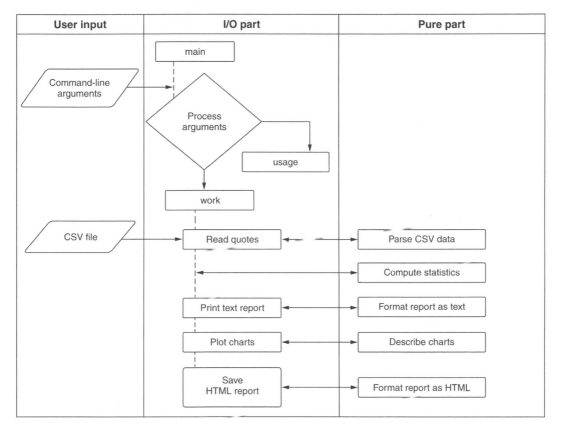

Figure 3.6   Processing stock quote data: program structure flowchart

First, we'll need data types to represent the following:

- Command-line arguments (`Params`)
- Quote data for one day (`QuoteData`)
- Some collection with all the data (let's call it `QuoteDataCollection` for now)
- Computed statistical information (`StatInfo`)
- A report as an HTML document (`Html`)

We'll postpone the definition of these data types until we have enough information on what exactly should be in there.

The program should start by reading user input in the form of command-line arguments (normally a list of `String`s) and then either do its job or inform the user about the correct way to run it. Once we have command-line arguments parsed to `Params`, we can start working with data, as follows:

```
work :: Params -> IO ()
```

In this function, we'll need to read the stock quote data from the CSV file as follows:

```
readQuotes :: FilePath -> IO QuoteDataCollection
```

Compute the statistical information (purely!):

```
statInfo :: QuoteDataCollection -> StatInfo
```

Prepare the text report (again, purely!):

```
textReport :: StatInfo -> String
```

The simplest way to plot a chart is to generate files with them, so we'll have to stick with `IO` for this task, as shown next:

```
plotChart :: QuoteDataCollection -> IO ()
```

Finally, we generate (purely) and save an HTML document to a file:

```
htmlReport :: QuoteDataCollection -> StatInfo -> Html
saveHtml :: FilePath -> Html -> IO ()
```

We'll refine the types and names of these functions later, but even now, they clearly represent the program functionality.

3.2   *Exploring design space*

While implementing this project, we should discuss and solve many common practical problems, including the following:

- *Representing data*—We have to use several data types, including something for dates.
- *Parsing CSV files*—We can either employ an ad hoc solution or use some external library.
- *Formatting reports*—A report is text with data structured in some way. This should be addressed with flexibility and extensibility in mind. Generating HTML is another practical task that should be thought of.
- *Plotting charts*—We do want to use sophisticated packages here.
- *Designing the UI*—We are implementing a terminal application. Consequently, we should deal with command-line arguments. Prepare to see `Semigroup` and `Applicative` in action!
- *Maintaining a clear division between pure and I/O parts of the program*—We'll aim to keep the latter as small as possible.

In this section, I'll present various options and make a choice for this particular project. Remember, this is still a study example. To keep things simple, I'll leave out performance, exception handling, testing, and many other issues for now.

3.2.1 Designing the user interface

I want this application to have a command-line interface because I find that the most efficient. In all the previous examples, we've analyzed the command-line arguments manually. As a result, all our arguments were strictly *positional*: the user had to specify them in positions, expected by the program. Traditionally, mandatory arguments are positional, but program behavior can be tweaked with a set of options or flags beginning with a dash in any position. Consequently, parsing a command line becomes a not-so-easy problem, because we have to analyze all the arguments and build some specific data structure that contains all the parameters.

We've already discussed the set of program parameters. The following is one possible way to include all of them in the command-line arguments:

```
Usage: stockquotes FILE [-n|--name ARG] [-c|--chart] [--html FILE]
                        [-s|--silent]
  Stock quotes data processing

Available options:
  FILE                 CSV file name
  -n,--name ARG        Company name
  -c,--chart           Generate chart
  --html FILE          Generate HTML report
  -s,--silent          Don't print statistics
  -h,--help            Show this help text
```

This is a rather standard way of presenting command-line interfaces. We have one positional argument, namely, the name of the CSV data file, and several short and long flags and options. Remember that flags can be given in any order and any position. Moreover, they can be omitted altogether.

One option could be traversing a list of command-line arguments (retrieved from `getArgs`) and filling some `Map` or associate list with them. Fortunately, we have other options. The two most popular Haskell libraries for parsing command-line arguments are

- `optparse-applicative` by Paolo Capriotti
- `cmdargs` by Neil Mitchell

Both of them force a distinction between command-line arguments and the data type for storing configuration parameters. To use these libraries, we first describe our options by associating them to a configurational data structure. Then, a library based on this description parses a command line and gives us a well-formed configuration if the user specified arguments correctly or generates an error message otherwise. Both libraries can generate an interface description we've seen.

In this book, I've chosen the `optparse-applicative` library because it features a very nice example of `Applicative` in practice. Despite that, both libraries are well suited to be used in industrial applications and are widely adopted by the community.

NOTE In my opinion, these Haskell libraries for dealing with command-line arguments are extremely powerful when compared with other programming languages. As we'll see, unique Haskell features contribute a lot to this power.

3.2.2   *Dealing with input data*

We have a CSV file as the input. Most of its components are simply numbers: `volume` is an integer number, whereas all prices are floating-point numbers. For prices, we could use fixed-point numbers as we discussed in the previous chapter. In fact, share prices deserve their own data type able to deal with rounding errors, different currencies, and localization. One could use the `safe-decimal` or `safe-money` packages to deal with these problems. The simplest solution, though, is to use the `Double` type, so let's stick with it as it perfectly suits our goals.

One of the CSV file fields, `day`, is interesting. Let's discuss representing dates in Haskell.

DATES AND TIMES

You should take into account many factors when using dates and times in software. First, we have to decide which calendar to use. These days, the most straightforward solution is to stick with the Gregorian calendar, but there are other options as well. Processing dates in the first millennium AD would require using the Julian calendar, although writing software for businesses or governments (with fiscal years in mind) might result in employing the ISO week date system (as defined in ISO 8601). Referring to time means dealing with timestamps, moments in time with respect to time zones, or durations. Time zones introduce the issue of Daylight Savings Time. It could get much worse: what about so-called leap seconds, which are irregularly added to some years due to the changes in the Earth's rate of rotation around the Sun?

Fortunately, the `time` package in Haskell is sophisticated enough to deal with all these technicalities. It employs the type system to prevent users from making mistakes in mixing times and dates. The `Day` type represents a date in the Gregorian calendar (which is stored as a count of days, with zero being the day November 17, 1858). We can use it for the `day` field. Many types for times and durations are also available in the `time` package. All of them can be imported from the `Data.Time` module of this package. We'll use some of them later in this book.

Apart from these data types, the `time` package provides many functions, including

- Constructing dates and times from integer values (like years, months, days, hours, minutes, and seconds)
- Parsing dates and times from strings (with an ability to specify an expected format)

- Formatting dates and times into strings (by specified formats and with rather limited localization)
- Getting the current date and time (this clearly requires IO)
- Manipulating dates and times, such as by adding date intervals or computing differences

TIP All the details about the time package are presented in the documentation on Hackage (https://hackage.haskell.org/package/time). I also recommend reading "A Haskell Time Library Tutorial" (https://two-wrongs.com/haskell-time-library-tutorial.html) by Christoffer Stjernlöf.

PARSING CSV FILES

Parsing data files is a well-known programming task. CSV files have very simple structure. To read them we could use basic Text processing facilities, such as lines, splitOn, and read functions. One line of a CSV file could be parsed into the QuoteData type and a complete file into [QuoteData] as follows:

1. Split the file content into a list of lines.
2. Skip the first line with the names of the fields.
3. Transform all other lines into values of the QuoteData type.

Transforming file lines into QuoteData is the most challenging task here: we should split the line into components, parse the date from the first component, and turn the others into Double values. Then we should create the QuoteData value from the extracted components.

Such a naive implementation could use the plain old "garbage in, garbage out" strategy. Any formatting errors in the original file, such as the wrong number of fields, wrong date formats, or NaN (not-a-number) values in other fields would result in an exception, leading to the program halting. We could deal with errors differently, for example:

- Ignore incorrect lines silently, or report them to the user.
- Interpolate missing values somehow using neighboring values.
- Stop reading the file after encountering an error.

All of these strategies make a manual implementation much harder. Alternatively, we could use some powerful parsing libraries, such as parsec. But again, dealing with CSV file irregularities and corner cases can be quite cumbersome.

Fortunately, we have a third path. We could use an external package, cassava, designed specifically for parsing CSV files. The cassava package allows us to avoid hand-rolled CSV parsing and replace it with a carefully crafted, highly efficient implementation. As always, there is a price to pay, as follows:

- We have to describe our data in terms of this package by defining a conversion for file content into stock quote data fields. This can be done by implementing instances of the FromField type class that comes with the cassava package.

- We have to work with `Vector` (found in the `Data.Vector` module from the `vector` package), the data structure that is given to us as a result of parsing. The good news is that doing so can be almost transparent for us, thanks to the `Foldable` type class that has an instance for `Vector`.

It seems that `cassava` is the best approach in this case, so we'll use it here.

Making design decisions

Note the choice we are making here:

- Manual naive implementation—quick and dirty, many issues including dealing with errors and bad performance
- Common powerful instruments (such as full-blown parsers in this case)—may be hard to learn and difficult to use
- Specific tool with its own limitations and choices made for us

This situation is quite common. In general, we have to think carefully before making a choice.

3.2.3 *Formatting reports*

Our expected results include a statistical table in text form, charts, and a full report in HTML. Although the charts seem completely independent from the rest of the results, text and HTML share some formatting. For example, we've decided to use `Double` for prices. Clearly, we should use a fixed number of decimal places when reporting them. For another example, both text and HTML contain tables. Wouldn't it be nice to have some common subsystem for tables? Let's see our options on preparing reports first and then move to charts.

We already know the `fmt` package, which provides a set of functions and type classes for formatting text information. There is no need to look for something similar. This library can be used at the level of formatting individual values as follows:

- If it is a value of some specific type, then we can implement a `Buildable` instance for it.
- If it is a value of some type that is already known to `fmt`, then we can use functions and format expressions to get the desired output.

As an example of the latter, the `fmt` package provides the `fixedF` function, which produces a `Builder` with a fixed number of decimal digits for any `Double`.

Another good thing about the `fmt` library is that it is highly polymorphic. For example, the `pretty` function can take anything of the `Buildable a` type and produce `String`, or `Text`, or even a printed value, depending on what we need in the particular context.

Printing tables can be implemented in several ways. We could prepare a list of rows and format every row as columns via any formatting library. We could also use matrices with a `Text` cell for every value. Unfortunately, with this approach it is quite hard to get a nice output. Dealing with column widths can be quite cumbersome—we need to at least precalculate every value in the column to do that correctly, which would require a lot of manual work. As usual with Haskell, there is also a library for this. In this case, we could use the `colonnade` package. To use this library, we describe our columns first (their names and instructions on how to format individual values) and then provide data for rows (as a list of row data types). The `colonnade` package itself supports printing tables in text form exclusively, but it has adapters for HTML generation also. A good library is a paramount choice for us in this chapter, so let's use the `colonnade` package.

Generating HTML manually is also possible, but it's definitely not a good option. Instead, we could use one of the following libraries:

- The `blaze-html` package by Jasper Van der Jeugt and Simon Meier
- The `lucid` package by Chris Done

Both libraries support HTML generation in a very clear manner. We could use either, but let's take `blaze-html` because it is more popular, judged by the number of downloads on Hackage.

> **TIP** I recommend reading about both the `blaze-html` and `lucid` libraries because they are good examples of designing a library for Haskell that features convenience and performance. The starting point could be a tutorial on `blaze-html` (https://jaspervdj.be/blaze/tutorial.html) and a blog post on `lucid` (https://chrisdone.com/posts/lucid/), both written by the authors of the libraries. The `lucid` library is more novel. Chris Done likes to argue for why his `lucid` library is better. The discussion in the blog post is very instructive.

The `colonnade` package for representing tables can be used together with the `blaze-html` and `lucid` libraries. This is possible thanks to the `lucid-colonnade` and `blaze-colonnade` packages. A generic backend-agnostic library with different backends is an extremely popular approach for designing packages within the Haskell community.

3.2.4 *Plotting charts*

Unfortunately, Haskell is not the best language for presenting data in visual form. Such languages as Python and R provide much better infrastructure and tooling. Nevertheless, we can still draw 2-D charts and plots in Haskell. In this project, we'll use the `Chart` package by Tim Docker for that. It's a good example of a package built on top of other sophisticated Haskell packages, so it's instructive to discuss its ideas and implementation.

The `Chart` package allows describing a chart we want to plot. A chart in terms of this package is a deeply nested data structure. We construct elements we are interested in (such as layouts, axes, legends, data points) one by one, leaving all others with their default values. This package supports line plots, bar plots, pie charts, and even candlestick plots out of the box. One difficulty about this package is that it uses lenses to access elements of the chart structure. This approach is very powerful. In this chapter, we'll see how to use it without a deep understanding of what lenses are. For basic charts with default parameters, it's possible to avoid using lenses altogether because we can use simple wrappers. Unfortunately, this is not our case. We'll cover lenses in greater detail in chapter 14.

The `Chart` package requires a backend for generating image files. We'll use `Chart-diagrams` to generate SVG files because it is the simplest one. It's also possible to generate PNG or JPG images, as well as other graphical formats. Unfortunately, this would require a lot of system dependencies that may be hard to install correctly on Windows. There should be no problems with SVG in any operating system.

The `Chart` package has a wiki page on GitHub (https://github.com/timbod7/haskell-chart/wiki) with several examples on how to use it for plotting various sorts of graphs.

3.2.5 *Project dependencies overview*

I've already mentioned several packages apart from `base` that we'll need for this project. In fact, we'll need two more:

- The `text` package provides `Text` processing facilities that we'll use in almost every example in this book.
- `bytestring` for reading CSV files (`cassava` expects data in the form of a byte string) and saving HTML reports to a file.

All the packages we need are listed in table 3.1.

Table 3.1 Used packages

Package	Used for
text	Efficient text processing and input/output
bytestring	Efficient input/output for binary data
time	Dealing with dates and times
fmt	Formatting text
blaze-html	HTML generation
colonnade, blaze-colonnade	Generating tables in text and HTML form
Chart, Chart-diagrams	Drawing charts
cassava	Parsing CSV files
optparse-applicative	Processing command-line arguments

If you are working with the `hid-examples` package, all these packages are installed automatically on the first build. If you've created your own project for working through this example, then you need to specify all these dependencies in the build-depends section of the stockquotes.cabal file as follows:

```
build-depends:
      base
    , text >=1.2 && <1.3
    , bytestring >=0.10 && <0.11
    , time >=1.8 && <1.11
    , fmt >=0.5 && <0.7
    , colonnade >=1.1 && <1.3
    , blaze-html >=0.9 && <0.10
    , blaze-colonnade >=1.1 && <1.3
    , Chart >=1.8 && <1.10
    , Chart-diagrams >=1.8 && <1.10
    , cassava >=0.5 && <0.6
    , optparse-applicative >=0.14 && <0.16
  default-language: Haskell2010
```

At the first build after editing the .cabal file, all these dependencies will be installed. We'll discuss many issues with version numbers in the next chapter. It may be the case that you need to edit some of the upper bounds to get this package compiled. If you run into problems, the easiest solution could be to find the corresponding section in the hid-examples.cabal file and copy its content.

While installing these packages, many others are also installed as dependencies. In total, there are 108 external packages used to build this project. It is almost impossible to write useful programs without referring to external packages. We'll meet many other packages later in this book that you can use in your own projects.

3.3 *Implementation details*

In this section, I'll go over all the details to implement the stock quote processing project. We already know all the inputs and outputs. We've settled on the external packages we are going to use. My plan is as follows:

1 We'll start with describing data and cooking it in a way suitable for both reading from CSV file and processing (the QuoteData module).

2 Once we have our data ready, we will plot charts. Remember that charts represent only input data, not the statistics (the Charts module).

3 Then we'll move to preparing reports and discuss how to compute all the statistics, format the results, and generate tables both in text and HTML forms (the StatReport and HtmlReport modules).

4 After that, we'll describe program configuration and command-line arguments (the Params module).

5 Finally, we'll connect everything together in the Main module.

Note the style of the descriptions. I don't attempt to present every piece of code. After all, looking over it on GitHub or in a text editor is much more convenient. Instead, I show the most interesting fragments and comment on them in terms of Haskell features used, programming tricks and techniques, and external library facilities.

3.3.1 *Describing data*

Remember that we have input data in the form of the data/quotes.csv file, as shown here:

```
day,close,volume,open,high,low
2019-05-01,210.520004,64827300,209.880005,215.309998,209.229996
2019-05-02,209.149994,31996300,209.839996,212.649994,208.130005
. . .
```

This is a CSV file with named fields. We have six fields in every line: the first one represents the date, the third one is an integer value, and all others are floating-point numbers.

EXAMPLE: REPRESENTING AND PROCESSING DATA

🗋   stockquotes/QuoteData.hs

⚡   *stockquotes*

☞   Type classes and instances help external packages work with our data.

Now it's time to declare a data type corresponding to one line of the CSV file as follows:

```
data QuoteData = QuoteData {
                 day :: Day,
                 volume :: Int,
                 open :: Double,
                 close :: Double,
                 high :: Double,
                 low :: Double
             }
```

This data type should be used in different situations, such as when parsing a CSV file or computing statistics, so we need to make it suitable for that.

COOKING DATA FOR CASSAVA

To describe our data in a form suitable for the cassava package, we'll derive or define instances of several type classes, namely:

- Generic from the GHC.Generics module to give cassava instances for working with our data types using generic programming machinery (more on that in chapter 12).
- FromNamedRecord from the Data.Csv module to allow cassava to read a CSV file with named fields; this will be possible thanks to the same names being used in the CSV file and the QuoteData data type.

- FromField from the Data.Csv module to teach cassava how to parse Day values; cassava can parse values of many types from base, but it doesn't know how to deal with other types.

Note the heavy use of type classes. This is a quite common idiom in Haskell. The library cannot imagine all types it is used with (those types may not even exist yet). Instead, it describes constraints and behavior with type classes. Now it's our responsibility to provide the corresponding instances in order to use the library. Thus, type class instances build a bridge between the library's interface (API in the form of type classes and functions that rely on them) and the client's data types. We'll see the same idea at work many times later in this book.

The code we are going to write requires the following GHC extensions for instance derivation:

```
{-# LANGUAGE DeriveGeneric #-}
{-# LANGUAGE DeriveAnyClass #-}
```

We'll get back to these extensions in chapter 12. For now, it'll suffice to know that they extend the behavior of the deriving clause in data type declarations.

We'll also need to import the following modules:

```
import Data.Time (Day, parseTimeM, defaultTimeLocale)
import Data.ByteString.Char8 (unpack)
import GHC.Generics (Generic)
import Data.Csv (FromNamedRecord, FromField (..))
```

Note how we limit imports: we avoid introducing unnecessary names from the imported modules by specifying what we actually need. The syntax (..) in the import lists refers to everything inside. For example, FromField (..) in the import list for the Data.Csv module refers to the FromField type class and every method of this type class. We can use the same syntax for algebraic data types and their value constructors. Alternatively, we could list names of methods and value constructors explicitly if we want to import only some of them.

The cassava package knows nothing about the Day type, so we need to teach this library how to parse it. We can do this by implementing an instance of the FromField type class, which is defined in Data.Csv as follows:

```
class FromField a where
  parseField :: Field -> Parser a
  {-# MINIMAL parseField #-}
```

This type class defines how to parse a field of type a. The type Field is a synonym for ByteString (that's why we've imported unpack), and Parser is a monadic parser used inside cassava. We already know the monad interface, so we don't even need to think about what this Parser is about—it's a monad, and that's enough. One possible instance for Day follows:

```
instance FromField Day where
  parseField = parseTimeM True defaultTimeLocale "%Y-%m-%d" . unpack
```

We first unpack the given `ByteString` into a `String` and then use the `parseTimeM` function. This function can work in any monad to parse a `Day` value; it will report a failure to the underlying monad in case of errors. For example, we can use it in the `Maybe` context and get `Nothing` if parsing fails. In this case, it will be called in the context of the `Parser` monad.

Reporting failures in monads

Not every `Monad` features an ability to report failures. It comes through the `MonadFail` type class with only one `fail` method. In the past, this method was part of the `Monad` type class. Fortunately, it's not anymore. If some particular monadic context has an ability to report failures, then we expect an instance of the `MonadFail` type class for it.

In addition to a `String` with a value, the `parseTimeM` function takes an expected date or time format, a date/time locale, and a flag for whether to accept leading and trailing spaces in the given `String`.

Exploring functions in GHCi

Remember that you can always explore functions in GHCi yourself as follows:

```
$ cabal repl stockquotes
ghci> import Data.Time
ghci> :type parseTimeM
...
ghci> :doc parseTimeM
...
```

Exploring functions from external packages is easier within a cabal project, because all the dependencies are already available.

Once we have the `FromField` instance for the `Day` type, we can derive a corresponding instance for the `QuoteData` itself as follows:

```
data QuoteData = QuoteData {
                  ...
                }
  deriving (Generic, FromNamedRecord)
```

This is enough for `cassava` to decode a CSV file and create a `QuoteData` value from every line if the given file is parsed correctly. Note that we had to write only nine lines of code for that. Well, technically, it's only one line of code. Everything else is about instances and deriving them.

COOKING DATA FOR COMPUTING STATISTICS

There is not much difference in computing minimums or maximums for opening or closing share prices. If we have an array-like structure for those values, we could process them uniformly. Of course, we have `Int` values for volumes as well, not only `Double`, and we still need to compute minimums and maximums for the `volume` field. We cannot put `Int` and `Double` into one list or any other array-like data structure. This is not a problem for programming languages featuring dynamic typing, such as Python. In Haskell, it is a problem.

My solution is as follows:

- I am going to introduce a data type for referring to those fields of the `Quote-Data` data type that require statistical processing.
- I'll write a function that transforms both `Int` and `DoubleQuoteData` components into `Double`, based on the required field information.

Clearly, transforming everything to `Double` is not the best idea for Haskell, but it's going to work. As an aside, we'll have to ignore the floating-point part later when presenting originally integer data in reports.

The first part of this plan follows:

```
data QField = Open | Close | High | Low | Volume
  deriving (Eq, Ord, Show, Enum, Bounded)

field2fun :: QField -> QuoteData -> Double
field2fun Open = open
field2fun Close = close
field2fun High = high
field2fun Low = low
field2fun Volume = fromIntegral . volume
```

We've defined a value constructor for every numeric field in `QuoteData` and mapped it to the record fields (which are technically accessor functions, `QuoteData -> Double`). As a result, we'll be able to write something like `field2fun qf q` to access any required field qf from a value q of the `QuoteData` type.

That's it for the `QuoteData` module. Note that we never defined the `Quote-DataCollection` data type for storing a collection of the `QuoteData` values. In fact, we don't need it. Any such collection can well be `Foldable t => t QuoteData`. An interface we have from the `Foldable` type class is enough to do whatever we want with the data. Of course, we could do more things and do them with better performance if we knew the exact internal representation of this collection, but that's beyond the scope of this chapter.

Exploring quote data in GHCi

I've implemented a small `readQuotes` wrapper function for loading data from a CSV file to a `[QuoteData]` list to play with them in GHCi as follows:

```
$ cabal repl stockquotes
ghci> quotes <- readQuotes "data/quotes.csv"
ghci> day $ head quotes
2019-05-01
ghci> field2fun High $ last quotes
220.960007
```

All further functions we are going to implement will work with the resulting data, because the list type implements the `Foldable` type class.

3.3.2 *Plotting charts*

Haskell is an old and powerful language. Consequently, over the years, Haskell has acquired many sophisticated ideas and techniques, or styles, which we can use to write our code. Different libraries promote very different programming styles. We'll see one such style in this section on plotting charts. I'd call it a lens-based declarative description.

EXAMPLE: PLOTTING CHARTS

   🗋   stockquotes/Charts.hs

   ⚡   *stockquotes*

   ☞   We can plot charts in Haskell with the Chart package.

   ☞   A chart is a deeply nested data structure with a lens interface.

Let's look at the chart in figure 3.7 and discuss its structure.

First, this chart consists of two charts. In terms of the `Chart` package, this chart has a *stacked layout* with two *layouts* inside it. The layout is one plotting area with a background (grid), axes, a title, a legend, and plotted data. Our first layout contains candles and a line representing closing prices. Our second layout contains volume bars. Stacked layouts share one x-axis; that is a very useful feature in our case.

Layouts in the Chart package

Despite stacked layouts, the `Chart` library also supports individual layouts, two-sided layouts (with different axes on the left- and right-hand sides of the plotting area), and a grid layout when charts are organized in a free-form grid.

Second, let's describe individual layouts. The upper one has a title, two axes, and two plots—one with a line, another with candles. The lower one has two axes and a bar plot, with no title.

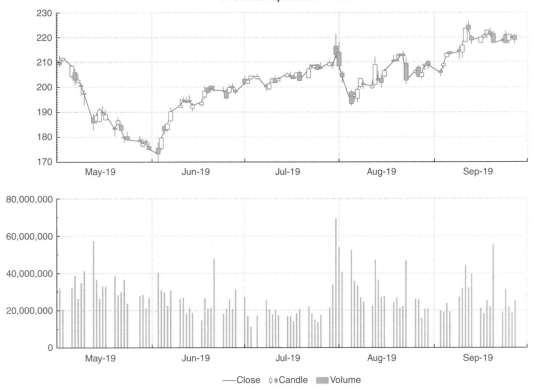

Figure 3.7   Stock quote charts for an imaginary company

Third, we are going deeper. Axes, a legend, and plotting area grids are pretty standard. Thanks to the stacked layout, we have the shared x-axis for dates and the common legend for two charts. It's possible to tweak these components, too, but I prefer the default view.

Fourth, we have data plots, a line, candles, and bars. Besides data, all these plots have many properties like colors, line widths, fill styles, and data row labels. We can either use default values or set them as we like.

Note the pattern. We have some default values on every level of a chart description, and we can set them to something different if we want. We can imagine a big, deeply nested data structure: the chart itself, layouts, layout components, all the way down to individual values. This is the case for the lenses, an approach to work with deeply nested data. We'll use it to set values on the deeper levels of a data structure.

So, we describe our chart level by level and never say how to draw all this stuff. This is an example of a declarative description. The library knows better how to draw. Let's get to the code that follows:

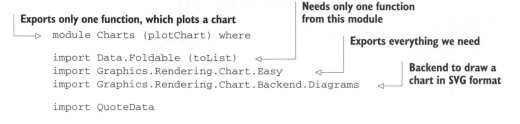

Exports only one function, which plots a chart

Needs only one function from this module

Exports everything we need

```
module Charts (plotChart) where

import Data.Foldable (toList)
import Graphics.Rendering.Chart.Easy
import Graphics.Rendering.Chart.Backend.Diagrams

import QuoteData
```

Backend to draw a chart in SVG format

We have only one function to plot everything:

Interfaces to a data collection

Chart title

```
plotChart :: Foldable t =>
             String
             -> t QuoteData
             -> FilePath
             -> IO ()
```

Quote data collection

Filepath to save a chart image

Saving files requires IO.

The `plotChart` function saves a prepared chart to a file via the `diagrams` backend as follows:

```
plotChart title quotes fname = do
    _ <- renderableToFile fileOptions fname (toRenderable chart)
    pure ()
  where
    fileOptions = FileOptions (800, 600) SVG loadSansSerifFonts
    ...
```

The `chart` variable is the most interesting here. Before defining it, we prepare our data for injecting into a chart description as follows:

```
(candles, closings, volumes) = unzip3 $
  [ (Candle day low open 0 close high,
     (day, close),
     (day, [volume])) | QuoteData {..} <- toList quotes ]
```

Three lists, namely `candles`, `closings` and `volumes`, have a form that is expected by the `Chart` library. To plot candles, we have to provide a list of `Candle` data type values. For lines, it requires a list of pairs `(x, y)`. For bars, we give a list of `(x, [...])` where `[...]` is a list of bars for every data point. We have only one bar here, a `volume`.

Note the `QuoteData {..}` syntax. It requires enabling the `RecordWildCards` GHC extension.

RecordWildCards GHC extension

The `RecordWildCards` GHC extension allows bringing all the record fields into scope without mentioning their names explicitly. We can use it for both accessing these values in pattern matching and constructing records. For example, if we are given the `QuoteData`, we could define a function over it as follows:

```
isRising :: QuoteData -> Bool
isRising QuoteData {..} = close > open
```

Or we can construct a new record, like so:

```
zeroQD :: Day -> QuoteData
zeroQD day = let close = 0
                 open = 0
                 high = 0
                 low = 0
                 volume = 0
             in QuoteData {..}
```

Note that the `day` argument is also captured, so we don't have to introduce a local
binding for it.

Remember, code should have a LANGUAGE pragma mentioning the `RecordWildCards`
extension at the beginning of the file in order to use it.

The chart itself is a data structure with a list of layouts inside it, as shown next:

```
chart = slayouts_layouts .~          ◁─── Sets a field value
    [ StackedLayout candlesLayout,
      StackedLayout volumesLayout
    ]
  $ def          ◁─── Default value for a stacked layout
```

Technically, `chart` is a value of the `StackedLayouts` data type. This is a record with
two fields: one for a list of inner layouts, and another one for a flag for whether to
compress legends from individual layouts into one legend below. We use the lens `(.~)`
operator to set a value for the first field and leave the second one with a default value
(which is `True`).

The `candlesLayout` function describes the first layout with candles and closing
prices, as shown here:

```
candlesLayout =
    layout_title .~ title
  $ layout_plots .~ [ toPlot $ qline "Close" closings green,
                      toPlot $ candle "Candle" candles cyan ]
  $ def
```

This function returns a `Layout`, which is a record with more than a dozen fields. We've
set only two of them here and left all the others with their default values.

The second layout, shown next, is even simpler:

```
volumesLayout =
    layout_plots .~ [ plotBars $ bars "Volume" volumes gray ]
  $ def
```

I set more fields as follows to describe plots themselves, but the idea is the same:

```
candle label values color =
    plot_candle_line_style  .~ lineStyle 1 gray
  $ plot_candle_fill .~ True
  $ plot_candle_rise_fill_style .~ fillStyle white
  $ plot_candle_fall_fill_style .~ fillStyle color
  $ plot_candle_tick_length .~ 0
  $ plot_candle_width .~ 3
  $ plot_candle_values .~ values
  $ plot_candle_title .~ label
  $ def

qline label values color =
    plot_lines_style .~ lineStyle 1 color
  $ plot_lines_values .~ [values]
  $ plot_lines_title  .~ label
  $ def

bars label values color =
    plot_bars_titles .~ [label]
  $ plot_bars_values .~ values
  $ plot_bars_item_styles .~ [(fillStyle color, Nothing)]
  $ def
```

In these descriptions I've used a couple of functions. Let's also mention them as follows:

```
fillStyle color = solidFillStyle (opaque color)

lineStyle n color =
    line_width .~ n
  $ line_color .~ opaque color
  $ def
```

Tweaking charts

I recommend working on this chart description. Change colors and styles, and add plots. Try to use `LayoutLR` to combine all the plots into one plotting area. It's very easy to experiment in GHCi, as shown here:

```
$ cabal repl stockquotes
ghci> quotes <- readQuotes "data/quotes.csv"
ghci> plotChart "Sample quotes" quotes "chart.svg"
```

This will allow you to understand the `Chart` library much better.

TIP   Unfortunately, with a stacked layout, it's impossible to have individual layouts of varying heights. All of them have to be the same height. Why not hack on that? There is an issue on GitHub (https://github.com/timbod7/haskell-chart/issues/152) that discusses this problem. For the chart in this section, I'd like to have a 3:1 relation with three parts for candles and one for volumes. We could do that with a grid layout, but it doesn't support shared axes.

That's it for charts. About 70 lines of code to get a quite informative, professional-looking chart. Not bad, eh?

3.3.3 *Preparing reports*

In this subsection, we'll implement an important piece of functionality: we'll compute statistics about our data and build reports in text form and in HTML.

> **EXAMPLE: PREPARING THE STATISTICAL REPORT**
>
> ☐ stockquotes/StatReport.hs
>
> ⚡ *stockquotes*
>
> ☞ We can use higher-order functions to make code much smaller.
>
> ☞ The `colonnade` package greatly simplifies printing tabular data.

COMPUTING STATISTICS

Remember, we've decided to do all the statistics computations with `Double`, although some of the fields are `Int`, namely, volumes. Even worse, minimum and maximum of volumes are integers, but the mean value should always be a floating-point number.

To deal with these issues, I introduce a default number of floating-point places and a type for representing a statistic value with respect to the number of decimal places expected, as shown next:

```
decimalPlacesFloating = 2

data StatValue = StatValue {
    decimalPlaces :: Int,
    value :: Double
  }
```

When we compute such a value, we know precisely how many decimal places are meaningful for it, either zero or two, or maybe four. Later in this book, we'll see a better way to deliver configuration values than having the `decimalPlacesFloating` constant all over the program.

Once again, this is not the best decision in terms of types and separation of concerns. Why on earth should we combine computations with formatting? Well, it's simple and practical. I'm sorry.

What do we need from the given data? We want to map over it and fold it into a single value, nothing else. Consequently, `(Functor t, Foldable t) => t QuoteData` should suffice. We could require `Traversable t` instead, which conveniently extends both `Functor` and `Foldable`, but there is no need to constrain our data beyond what is actually required.

The analysis has two dimensions: the chosen statistic (minimum, maximum, mean, and number of days between the minimum and the maximum) and the specific record field (`open`, `close`, `high`, `low`, and `volume`). Clearly, computing the minimum is the same for any field, and extracting a field from the quote data does not depend on the computed statistic.

The following data type can be used to represent all the statistics for one field:

```
data StatEntry = StatEntry {
    qfield :: QField,
    meanVal :: StatValue,
    minVal :: StatValue,
    maxVal :: StatValue,
    daysBetweenMinMax :: Int
  }
```

We compute means with almost no information about our actual data. Once we have something Foldable with Fractional values inside, as shown next, we are good to go:

```
mean :: (Fractional a, Foldable t) => t a -> a
mean xs = sum xs / fromIntegral (length xs)
```

Computing a number of days is also quite generic. As we relate prices and volumes to days, we have to supply a Foldable with the whole QuoteData inside, as follows:

```
import Data.Ord (comparing)
import Data.Foldable (minimumBy, maximumBy)
import Data.Time (diffDays)

...

computeMinMaxDays :: (Ord a, Foldable t) =>
                     (QuoteData -> a) -> t QuoteData -> (a, a, Int)
computeMinMaxDays get quotes = (get minQ, get maxQ, days)
  where
    cmp = comparing get
    minQ = minimumBy cmp quotes
    maxQ = maximumBy cmp quotes
    days = fromIntegral $ abs $ diffDays (day minQ) (day maxQ)
```

Note that this function allows us to work with individual fields without changing their type to Double:

```
ghci> :type computeMinMaxDays
  open quotes
computeMinMaxDays open quotes :: (Double, Double, Int)
ghci> :type computeMinMaxDays volume quotes
computeMinMaxDays volume quotes :: (Int, Int, Int)
```

Now we can compute all the statistics into [StatEntry] as follows:

Computes statistics for all the fields in the QField data type

```
statInfo :: (Functor t, Foldable t) => t QuoteData -> [StatEntry]
statInfo quotes = fmap qFieldStatInfo [minBound .. maxBound]
  where
    decimalPlacesByQField Volume = 0
```

Volumes are presented without a fractional part.

```
decimalPlacesByQField _ = decimalPlacesFloating

qfieldStatInfo qfield =
  let
    get = field2fun qfield
    (mn, mx, daysBetweenMinMax) = computeMinMaxDays get quotes
    decPlaces = decimalPlacesByQField qfield
    meanVal = StatValue decimalPlacesFloating
                        (mean $ fmap get quotes)
    minVal = StatValue decPlaces mn
    maxVal = StatValue decPlaces mx
  in StatEntry {..}
```

Decimal places for the particular field → `get = field2fun qfield`, `(mn, mx, daysBetweenMinMax) = computeMinMaxDays get quotes`, `decPlaces = decimalPlacesByQField qfield`

Getter to access the particular field → `get = field2fun qfield`

The mean value always has a fractional part. → `meanVal = StatValue decimalPlacesFloating`

Extracts a Foldable with one field → `minVal = StatValue decPlaces mn`, `maxVal = StatValue decPlaces mx`

Uses RecordWildCards to fill a record → `in StatEntry {..}`

Isn't it interesting to see what we've just computed? Well, we should explain to GHCi how to print all these values before that. That is our next goal.

FORMATTING INDIVIDUAL VALUES

Let's use the `fmt` package to format values. We have at least two types to write `Buildable` instances: `StatValue` and `StatEntry`. In fact, we need the latter to print corresponding values in GHCi. This is still useful.

The `Buildable` instance for `StatValue` is very simple: we just apply formatting for `Double` as follows:

```
instance Buildable StatValue where
  build sv = fixedF (decimalPlaces sv) (value sv)
```

The same formatting should be applied when printing all the prices in the HTML report, so let's define an auxiliary function for that next:

```
showPrice :: Double -> Builder
showPrice = fixedF decimalPlacesFloating
```

The `StatEntry` value has many fields, and we use `Builder` operators to define the final formatting as follows:

```
instance Buildable StatEntry where
  build StatEntry {..} =
          "Stats for "+||qfield||+": "
            +|meanVal|+" (mean), "
            +|minVal|+" (min), "
            +|maxVal|+" (max), "
            +|daysBetweenMinMax|+" (days)"
```

Remember, this code requires two GHC extensions, namely, `RecordWildCards` and `OverloadedStrings`.

With these two instances, we can explore statistics information for our sample quotes data as shown next:

```
ghci> quotes <- readQuotes "data/quotes.csv"
ghci> si = statInfo quotes
ghci> import Fmt
ghci> pretty $ unlinesF si
```

```
Open: 202.04 (mean), 175.44 (min), 224.80 (max), 100 (days)
Close: 202.16 (mean), 173.30 (min), 223.59 (max), 100 (days)
High: 204.10 (mean), 177.92 (min), 226.42 (max), 101 (days)
Low: 200.32 (mean), 170.27 (min), 222.86 (max), 101 (days)
Volume: 27869192.38 (mean), 11362000 (min), 69281400 (max), 28 (days)
```

We definitely need tables, don't we? Stay with me.

PRINTING A TABLE

Let's look at the ideas behind the `colonnade` package. It allows defining the structure of a table that is a collection of columns. Every column is defined by the column header and a function to extract and format a value from the data structure corresponding to one row of the table. Tables in `colonnade` are `Monoid` values. Every column is a one-columned table. If we combine two columns with (`<>`), we get a two-columned table. Once a table structure is ready, we supply a list of row values. The library then prepares data, computes column widths, and formats output in a tabular form. All this functionality is provided by the `Colonnade` module.

To organize tabular printing as a text for [`StatEntry`], we define a list of columns, `mconcat` them, and then call an `ascii` function that produces a `String` formatted as a table, as shown next:

```
textReport :: [StatEntry] -> String
textReport = ascii colStats
  where
    colStats = mconcat
      [ headed "Quote Field" (show . qfield)
      , headed "Mean" (pretty . meanVal)
      , headed "Min" (pretty . minVal)
      , headed "Max" (pretty . maxVal)
      , headed "Days between Min/Max" (pretty . daysBetweenMinMax)
      ]
```

Note how we use the `pretty` function from `fmt`, which formats the given `Buildable` as expected by the context. In this case, the ASCII backend from `colonnade` expects a `String` for every cell value. So the `pretty` function returns a `String`.

Let's print this report immediately as follows:

```
ghci> quotes <- readQuotes "data/quotes.csv"
ghci> putStr $ textReport $ statInfo quotes
+-------------+-------------+----------+----------+----------------------+
| Quote Field | Mean        | Min      | Max      | Days between Min/Max |
+-------------+-------------+----------+----------+----------------------+
| Open        | 202.04      | 175.44   | 224.80   | 100                  |
| Close       | 202.16      | 173.30   | 223.59   | 100                  |
| High        | 204.10      | 177.92   | 226.42   | 101                  |
| Low         | 200.32      | 170.27   | 222.86   | 101                  |
| Volume      | 27869192.38 | 11362000 | 69281400 | 28                   |
+-------------+-------------+----------+----------+----------------------+
```

> ### Writing monadic one-liners with (>>=)
>
> For quick and dirty GHCi exploring, we could have the same table printed as a one-liner as follows:
>
> ```
> ghci> readQuotes "data/quotes.csv" >>= putStr . textReport . statInfo
> ```
>
> I believe that using monadic bind (>>=) explicitly from time to time helps to understand monads better. After all, it's just a function. In this particular case, it is implemented for sequencing IO actions. Nothing special.

That's it. We've combined the following to get a tabular view:

- A data type representing rows
- Formatting of individual values via fmt
- A monoidal table structure (headers, cell data, and their formatting) via colonnade
- ASCII backend from colonnade to produce a resulting String

Let's move to preparing an HTML report and apply the same ideas to get an HTML table.

GENERATING AN HTML DOCUMENT

The structure of the document we want to generate follows:

```
<html>
  <head>
    <title>...</title>
    <style>...</style>
  </head>
  <body>
    <h1>Charts</h1>
    <!-- charts -->
    <h1>Statistics Report</h1>
    <!-- statistics table -->
    <h1>Stock Quotes Data</h1>
    <!-- quote data table -->
  </body>
</html>
```

HTML is quote verbose. Hopefully, it is possible to alleviate this verbosity with a library.

EXAMPLE: PREPARING THE REPORT IN HTML

🗋 stockquotes/HtmlReport.hs

⚡ *stockquotes*

☞ The blaze-html package provides a monadic interface for generating HTML.

☞ The blaze-colonnade generates tables in HTML.

To build an HTML document, we use the following two modules:

```
import Text.Blaze.Html5 as H
import Text.Blaze.Html5.Attributes (src)
```

Note the unqualified aliased import of the `Text.Blaze.Html5` module. We usually do that when some names from the module are ambiguous but others are not. For example, this module provides `head` and `body` functions for the corresponding HTML tags. With such an `import` declaration, we write `H.head` to avoid ambiguity with the `head` function over lists and leave `body` unqualified.

Let's start with tables. We prepare to format individual values first, as shown next:

```
viaFmt :: Buildable a => a -> Html
viaFmt = text . pretty
```

The `text` function expects `Text` for input, and it outputs an `Html` value. Consequently, the `pretty` function from `fmt` will provide `Text` from the given `Buildable`.

Next, we describe table structures:

```
colStats :: Colonnade Headed StatEntry Html
colStats = mconcat
      [ headed "Quote Field" (i . string . show . qfield)
      , headed "Mean" (viaFmt . meanVal)
      , headed "Min" (viaFmt . minVal)
      , headed "Max" (viaFmt . maxVal)
      , headed "Days between Min/Max" (viaFmt . daysBetweenMinMax)
      ]

colData :: Colonnade Headed QuoteData Html
colData = mconcat
      [ headed "Day" (viaFmt . day)
      , headed "Open" (viaFmt . showPrice . open)
      , headed "Close" (viaFmt . showPrice . close)
      , headed "High" (viaFmt . showPrice . high)
      , headed "Low" (viaFmt . showPrice . low)
      , headed "Volume" (viaFmt . volume)
      ]
```

The quote field is formatted as italic, and string converts String to Html.

The showPrice function leaves only two decimal points.

The `Text.Blaze.Colonnade` module provides two useful functions to look at these table structures in action. The `encodeHtmlTable` function takes `Attributes` for the table (it's a `Monoid`, and we can use `mempty` for no attributes), table structure, and a list of raw data. It returns an `Html` value that can be printed via the `printCompactHtml` function. We can look at the HTML code generated with the table structures just defined as follows:

```
ghci> quotes <- readQuotes "data/quotes.csv"
ghci> si = statInfo quotes
ghci> import Text.Blaze.Colonnade
ghci> printCompactHtml (encodeHtmlTable mempty colStats si)
<table>
    <thead>
        <tr>
```

```
          <th>QuoteField</th>
          <th>Mean</th>
          <th>Min</th>
          <th>Max</th>
          <th>DaysbetweenMin/Max</th>
      </tr>
    </thead>
    <tbody>
      ...
    </tbody>
</table>
```

> **NOTE** This representation is so compact that the `printCompactHtml` function has stripped away all spaces inside the `th` tags. Hopefully, the main HTML-rendering function does better. As for this function, the documentation warns: "The implementation is inefficient and incorrect in many corner cases. [...] Use of this function is discouraged." Okay, we just wanted to look at our table in GHCi.

Now we are ready to generate the whole HTML document as shown here:

```
htmlReport :: (Functor t, Foldable t) =>
                String -> t QuoteData -> [StatEntry] -> [FilePath] -> ByteString
htmlReport docTitle quotes statEntries images = renderHtml $ docTypeHtml $ do
    H.head $ do
       title $ string docTitle
       style tableStyle
    body $ do
       unless (null images) $ do
         h1 "Charts"
         traverse_ ((img!).src.toValue) images

       h1 "Statistics Report"
       encodeHtmlTable mempty colStats statEntries

       h1 "Stock Quotes Data"
       encodeHtmlTable mempty colData quotes
  where
    tableStyle = "table {border-collapse: collapse}" <>
                 "td, th {border: 1px solid black; padding: 5px}"
```

Generates the img tags with the src attributes pointing to the image file provided

Only one line of code may be hard to understand; the one where we traverse over the list of images:

```
traverse_ ((img!).src.toValue) images
```

As usual, our main way to understand what is going on is to look at the types. We can use `:type` and `:info` in GHCi after importing all the modules we use, as shown next:

```
images :: [FilePath]
img :: Html
type Html = Markup
type Markup = MarkupM ()
(!) :: Attributable h => h -> Attribute -> h
```

```
src :: AttributeValue -> Attribute
toValue :: ToValue a => a -> AttributeValue
traverse_  :: (Foldable t, Applicative f) => (a -> f b) -> t a -> f ()
```

Now we can use this information to specify types as follows:

```
type Html = MarkupM ()
img! :: Attribute -> Html
(img!).src.toValue :: ToValue a => a -> Html
traverse_ :: (FilePath -> Html) -> [FilePath] -> Html
traverse_ ((img!).src.toValue) images :: Html
```

Finally, we've got `Html` as expected! It turned out, also, that `Html` is a monadic context with the `()` value in it. The resulting HTML for images follows:

```
<h1>Charts</h1><img src="chart.svg"/>
```

We can also note the following style definition for HTML tables with the <> semigroup operation:

```
tableStyle = "table {border-collapse: collapse}" <>
             "td, th {border: 1px solid black; padding: 3px}"
```

Well, HTML and CSS are all about monads and monoids. Checkmate, my cheerful frontend developers.

The `blaze-html` package relies heavily on the `OverloadedStrings` GHC extension to turn every `String` literal into a value of the `Html` type.

I believe everything else in this code is self-explanatory. This is a sign of a good library. A monadic interface with `do` blocks guarantees that we store all the information about a document we provide somewhere inside the `Html` value. Compare this approach with the lens-based interface to the `Chart` library. Both approaches are extensively used in Haskell. It's crucial to get used to both of them.

The `Html` we have is rendered as a `ByteString` that we can export to a file. Note that `htmlReport` is a pure function. We don't have `IO` in its type. Everything in this module works in a pure part of our program.

We are done with reporting. Let's describe a user interface and connect everything together.

3.3.4 *Implementing the user interface*

As usual in Haskell, we struggle to turn the user input into something explicitly typed as quickly as possible. In the case of command-line arguments (a list of `String` values), this means parsing them into some record. The `optparse-applicative` package, which we'll use in this section for parsing command-line arguments, follows exactly this approach. It is an example of a highly regarded, professional, purely declarative (thanks to good abstractions) package with great documentation and many use cases. I don't attempt to describe all of its features but limit myself to a short demonstration.

EXAMPLE: DESCRIBING AND PROCESSING COMMAND-LINE ARGUMENTS

🗋 stockquotes/Params.hs

⚡ *stockquotes*

☞ We can describe command-line arguments declaratively.

The interface we want follows:

```
Usage: stockquotes FILE [-n|--name ARG] [-c|--chart] [--html FILE]
                        [-s|--silent]
  Stock quotes data processing

Available options:
  FILE                  CSV file name
  -n,--name ARG         Company name
  -c,--chart            Generate chart
  --html FILE           Generate HTML report
  -s,--silent           Don't print statistics
  -h,--help             Show this help text
```

And the following is a record with all the information:

```
data Params = Params {
              fname :: FilePath
            , company :: Maybe Text
            , chart :: Bool
            , htmlFile :: Maybe FilePath
            , silent :: Bool
            }
```

The question is this: How do we relate one to another? Well, we describe every field as a command-line argument and provide an injection into a Params value. The optparse-applicative library provides an Applicative interface for that with the <$> and <*> operators. Every field description is combined via <*>, and the final injection is done by the <$>. Field descriptions are constructed with <> from Semigroup. Here is the code:

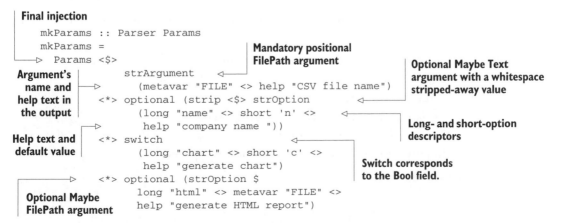

```
Final injection
  mkParams :: Parser Params
  mkParams =
    Params <$>
         strArgument                              Mandatory positional
           (metavar "FILE" <> help "CSV file name")  FilePath argument
    <*> optional (strip <$> strOption                Optional Maybe Text
           (long "name" <> short 'n' <>              argument with a whitespace
            help "company name "))                   stripped-away value
    <*> switch                                       Long- and short-option
           (long "chart" <> short 'c' <>             descriptors
            help "generate chart")
    <*> optional (strOption $                        Switch corresponds
           long "html" <> metavar "FILE" <>          to the Bool field.
           help "generate HTML report")
```

Argument's name and help text in the output

Help text and default value

Optional Maybe FilePath argument

```
<*> switch
    (long "silent" <> short 's' <>
     help "don't print statistics")
```

Remember that `FilePath` is an alias for `String`, so `optparse-applicative` doesn't have to distinguish them.

Note also that `Parser` is an `Applicative`, and the `Params` value is a result of computations in this context. We apply the multiparametric value constructor `Params` via the `<$>` operator from `Applicative`. We know that there should be exactly five arguments (as in the `Params` record). All of them are provided one by one via the `<*>` operator. Every type is checked. It's impossible to describe a `Bool` field as a `String` argument: GHC would complain immediately.

All the `strArgument`, `strOption`, and `switch` functions take `Semigroup`-based combinations of properties, and every such function refers to exactly one `Params` field at the same position.

Now that we've described the correspondence between command-line arguments and `Params` fields, we should supply additional usage information, which will be printed if the user specifies `--help` or `-h` switches and runs the actual parsing. The following code sample demonstrates how to do that:

Parser is an IO action.　　　　　　　　　　　　　**Runs parsing**

```
cmdLineParser :: IO Params
cmdLineParser = execParser opts    <──┘
  where                                       Augments mkParams with
    opts = info (mkParams <**> helper)    <── switches for the help screen
                (fullDesc <> progDesc "Stock quotes data processing")    <──┐
```
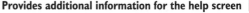

Provides additional information for the help screen

We have an `IO` action here because we need access to command-line arguments. The result of the computation has the `Params` type. In this action, we extend command-line arguments prepared earlier with the standard help screen and execute the parser.

3.3.5   *Connecting parts*

The last thing to do is to connect all the parts of this project together. Namely, we should

- Get `Params` from command-line arguments via `cmdLineParser`.
- Read the CSV file.
- Compute the statistics.
- Prepare and print a text report, if required.
- Generate the charts, if required.
- Prepare and export the HTML report, if required.

Let's do all that now.

EXAMPLE: CONNECTION PARTS IN THE MAIN MODULE

📄 stockquotes/Main.hs

⚡ *stockquotes*

☞ The Main module connects everything in the IO part of the program.

We'll split the job between three functions: main, work, and generateReports. The main function is responsible for running the command-line parser and delegates everything else to work, as shown next:

```
main :: IO ()
main = cmdLineParser >>= work
```

The work function takes the constructed Params as an argument, reads and decodes the CSV file, and runs generateReports, if everything goes well, as follows:

```
work :: Params -> IO ()
work params = do
  csvData <- BL.readFile (fname params)
  case decodeByName csvData of
    Left err -> putStrLn err
    Right (_, quotes) -> generateReports params quotes
```

We read a ByteString (from Data.ByteString.Lazy, imported with the prefix BL) from the file and decode it with the decodeByName function from the cassava package's Data.Csv module. This function has the following type signature:

```
decodeByName :: FromNamedRecord a
             => BL.ByteString
             -> Either String (Header, Vector a)
```

The quotes value is later used as a value of the following type:

```
(Functor t, Foldable t) => t QuoteData
```

The type checker figures out that the a type variable in the type signature for decode-ByName refers to QuoteData. Remember, we've derived an instance of FromNamed-Record for it.

Type Vector comes from the vector package. This package provides an efficient implementation of Int indexed arrays with many optimizations for loop-like operations.

In the case of correct decoding, we get a Vector of QuoteData values. Vector implements both Functor and Foldable type classes. Thus, all our code for computing statistics and preparing reports remains intact (though it performs quite well, thanks to Vector instances of Functor and Foldable).

The generateReports function, shown next, does the rest of the job:

```
generateReports :: (Functor t, Foldable t) => Params -> t QuoteData -> IO ()
generateReports Params {..} quotes = do
  unless silent $ putStr textRpt
  when chart $ plotChart title quotes chartFname
  saveHtml htmlFile htmlRpt
 where
   statInfo' = statInfo quotes
   textRpt = textReport statInfo'
   htmlRpt = htmlReport title quotes statInfo' [chartFname | chart]

   withCompany prefix = maybe mempty (prefix <>) company
   chartFname = unpack $ "chart" <> withCompany "_" <> ".svg"
   title = unpack $ "Historical Quotes" <> withCompany " for "

   saveHtml Nothing _ = pure ()
   saveHtml (Just f) html = BL.writeFile f html
```

Note the use of the maybe function and the Monoid instance for Text in the company name processing (the withCompany function). Once we have Text values of the chart filename and the title, we convert them to Strings expected by other functions with the unpack function.

Unless we were asked to be silent, we print the report to the console. When asked to generate charts, we plot them. Finally, we export the HTML report into the file with the given name if provided. That is all for this project.

Summary

- Use the time package whenever processing dates and times.
- Choose your own favorite package for representing textual data: formatting and fmt are good candidates.
- Drawing charts is easy with the Chart package; give it a try.
- Try the cassava package for parsing CSV files.
- Use the optparse-applicative package for parsing command-line arguments and generating default help screens.
- Learn to build HTML documents with the blaze-html package.
- Monad, Applicative, Functor, Foldable, Semigroup, and Monoid are our friends in practice.
- Use Haskell for everything you need.

Part 2

Introduction to application design

In this part, we'll start talking about developing applications in Haskell. First, we'll discuss topics in package and project management, because we have no applications without external dependencies. Then we'll move to monads and monad transformers as tools for implementing software functionality. I'll use a practical approach—things we'll discuss here are applied in real programs all the time.

Note that these three chapters are no more than a quick intro to the vast application design area in Haskell. For those looking that way, I recommend reading the excellent *Functional Design and Architecture* by Alexander Granin (https://graninas.com/functional-design-and-architecture-book/) after completing this one.

Haskell development with modules, packages, and projects

This chapter covers

- Best practices in structuring programs with modules
- Using custom preludes
- Ideas and approaches behind packaging Haskell projects
- Tools for package and project management

The code in Haskell (data types, function definitions, and so on) is organized into modules. One special module, `Prelude`, is imported into every module by default and exports the most important definitions. Modules form packages, which may contain libraries intended to be used by other packages, standalone applications, or both. One special package, `base`, contains the definitions from the standard library (as defined by the Haskell 2010 Language Report, https://www.haskell.org/onlinereport/ haskell2010/) together with GHC-specific additions. Many professional applications require working on many packages at the same time, so packages are organized into projects to allow application development.

We can't write any useful program in Haskell without importing some modules in addition to `Prelude`. If we stick with the `base` package only, we can do something basic, but that's it. Every Haskell programmer benefits from using libraries that have been created by other programmers and are available in the form of packages on Hackage (https://hackage.haskell.org/), the Haskell community's central package archive. Packages deliver modules ready to be imported into programs. In this chapter, we'll discuss many important issues concerning Haskell modules and a packaging system that every Haskell developer should be aware of.

4.1 *Organizing Haskell code with modules*

Every Haskell application is a collection of modules. The `Main` module, with the `main` function inside it, is an entry point to a program. This and all other modules contain data type definitions, type classes, instances, functions, compiler pragmas, and other components. Every module potentially imports definitions from other modules of a program, the `base` library, and other libraries. A module can also export some of the definitions to make them available to others.

The Haskell Report specifies the only role of a module to be a tool for namespace control and states that any multimodule program can (in theory) be transformed into a single-module program by copying every module entity from all the modules into a single file and then renaming some of those entities to prevent name clashes. Nevertheless, it's generally accepted that splitting any code into modules based on provided functionality (or other principles) makes it easier to maintain it and add new features. We always prefer to import entities from other modules instead of copying them. We've already seen many examples in the previous chapters.

In this section, we'll discuss several lesser-known issues with the Haskell module system. First, we'll talk about module structure, imports and exports, module hierarchy in general, and its correspondence to a particular directory structure in a Haskell project. Then, we'll discuss *custom preludes*, an alternative way to import the most-used definitions. Finally, we'll develop a very basic library implementing a couple of traditional data structures, namely, `Stack` and `Queue`. We'll use this example to discuss issues with imports and exports and also to see how to develop Haskell libraries without using specific package management tools.

4.1.1 *Module structure, imports and exports, and module hierarchy*

Let's start with the anatomy of a single module before diving into multimodule programs. The following is a simplified view of the structure of a Haskell module:

```
module ModuleName (<export list>) where

-- set of imports

-- declarations for
```

```
--  * type classes and instances
--  * type synonyms and data types
--  * functions
--  * etc.
```

A module's name should begin with an uppercase letter (for example, `Fmt`). It is expected to reside in the .hs file with the same name. The only exception is the `Main` module, which is allowed to be placed elsewhere.

IMPORTS AND EXPORTS

We have many options when writing import declarations. For example, we can do the following:

- Import the whole module.
- Import only specific names from the module by listing them in parentheses after the module name.
- Import no names at all with an empty list of names (note that this imports all the instances because they have no names in Haskell).
- Import names with optional or mandatory qualification with an alias (`as`) or a full module name to avoid name clashes.
- Import all names except those listed after the `hiding` keyword.

It is quite common to have a hundred or so import declarations in one module. Note that we can import the same module several times by combining the previously listed options. In that way, we usually bring into scope only the names we need with a qualification when it is unavoidable or if it makes the code easier to read. We should also think about the possibility of adding visual noise through extensive qualification.

> **NOTE** Experienced Haskell developers adore discussions on the right order of import declarations and their formatting style. Many prefer writing them from the most general (`base`, then external libraries) to the most specific (from a package under development) and listing all the names imported in them. They argue that this makes code easier to maintain. Others strongly disagree. The code examples in this book don't follow any specific strategy.

If we develop a module, we should think carefully about what should be exported. We write the export list in parentheses after the module name in the `module` declaration as follows:

```
module ModuleName ( <export list> ) where
```

An export list may contain any of the following:

- Names of the functions.
- Names of the data types (type constructors), with or without data constructors (with the abbreviation (`..`), meaning all of them).
- Names of the type classes, with or without method names.

- A module name or its synonym prefixed with the `module` keyword for exporting all names imported from the corresponding module, or the namespace identified by the synonym. (We call this kind of export reexporting.)

Let's look at the following examples:

```
module ModuleName (          Reexports everything from module X
  module X,        ◁─────────┘
  module Y,
  DataType1,       ◁──────── Only the type constructor is exported.
  DataType2 (..),   ◁─────── Exports the type constructor with all data constructors
  DataType3 (Cons1, Cons2),  ◁
  TypeClass1,                  Exports the type constructor with the
  TypeClass2 (..),             two mentioned data constructors
  TypeClass3 (method1, method2),
  fun1, fun2,   fun3
) where
...
```

After importing `ModuleName` we can use the following:

- Any name exported by the modules (or namespaces) `X` and `Y`.
- The `DataType1` type constructor in the type signatures. (Note that we can't do pattern matching on its data constructors or construct values of this data type with them because they were not exported.)
- The `DataType2` type constructor with all of its data constructors, without any limitations.
- The `DataType3` type constructor and only two of its data constructors. (Others, if they exist, are not exported.)
- The type classes `TypeClass1`, `TypeClass2`, and `TypeClass3`, with similar restrictions on their methods as on the data constructors.
- The functions `fun1`, `fun2`, and `fun3`.

We can't use any other names defined in `ModuleName` because they are not exported.

A `module` declaration without an export list exports everything that is defined inside this module, as shown next:

```
module ModuleName where
```

This is not a good choice except for very small modules. Remember also that instances of type classes are always exported, whereas imported names are never exported by default (unless we do that explicitly with the `module` keyword in the export list).

MODULE HIERARCHY AND DIRECTORY STRUCTURE

The module name can be hierarchical, with components separated by dots (e.g., `Graphics.Rendering.Chart.Backend.Cairo`). The Haskell Report does not set out a meaning for this hierarchy, although existing implementations normally use it as an instruction for finding module source code files in subdirectories.

Figure 4.1 presents the correspondence between the actual position of a module file inside the directory structure, its name as specified in the `module` declaration, and the proper way to import it. We must adhere to this correspondence if we want GHC to compile a program.

Note that a module is always imported by its full name, regardless of whether we import it from the same subdirectory (as in `S.A`) or a neighboring subdirectory (as in `T.B`).

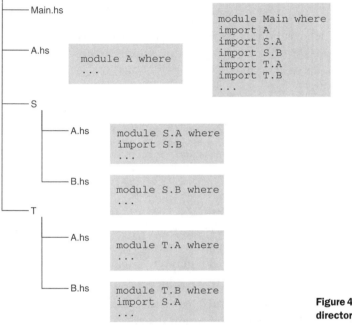

Figure 4.1 Correspondence between directory content and modules

I should stress that whenever we write `import` in a program, we import a particular module but not the whole module subhierarchy. Hierarchical module names are about naming only, and we shouldn't expect anything else. Looking back at figure 4.1, if we provide the S module in the S.hs file in the root directory, then we can do `import` S; otherwise, we can't.

It's easy to observe how GHC searches for modules in subdirectories. Imagine that we run `ghci` from the T subdirectory and try to load the B.hs file providing the `T.B` module in it, as follows:

```
[T]$ ghci B.hs
...
[1 of 1] Compiling T.B                ( B.hs, interpreted )

B.hs:3:1: error:
    Could not find module 'S.A'
    Use -v to see a list of the files searched for.
```

```
  |
3 |  import S.A
  |  ^^^^^^^^^^
Failed, no modules loaded.
```

The suggested flag, -v, gives us a clue:

```
Locations searched:
    S/A.hs
    ...
```

Clearly, there is no such a subdirectory in T. We can help the compiler with the -i..
flag specifying the root directory of this program (note the absence of a space after
the flag name), as shown next:

```
[T]$ ghci B.hs -i..
...
[1 of 3] Compiling S.B         ( ../S/B.hs, interpreted )
[2 of 3] Compiling S.A         ( ../S/A.hs, interpreted )
[3 of 3] Compiling T.B         ( B.hs, interpreted )
Ok, three modules loaded.
ghci>
```

Everything is loaded, and we can work with the T.B module now.

As well as being a key for the compiler to search files containing modules in the
file system, a starting component of a module name says a lot to a programmer. For
example, common names at the top of the hierarchy include the following:

- Data—Modules for working with data (both storing and processing). For example, Data.Map provides an associative container, and Data.Monoid declares the
  Monoid type class with the most important instances.
- Control—Used for control structures. For example, monads with many operations over them reside in Control.Monad, and tools to control concurrency are
  concentrated in Control.Concurrent.
- System—Collects OS-specific interfaces. For example, System.Environment
  allows communicating with the environment where our programs run.
- Text—Pertains to text processing. It contains the various parsing libraries,
  although the Text data type itself resides in Data.Text.
- Network—Contains libraries for network processing. For example, the wreq
  package for writing HTTP requests provides the Network.Wreq module.

There are many other top-level categories. In fact, every library author is free to start a
new category, although it is much more convenient for others to go with an existing
one. This helps you get an idea of what is provided by a library.

There are also conventional names that library authors are encouraged to use
somewhere inside the hierarchy, including the following:

- `Internal` for implementation details normally hidden from users; for example, everything below `Data.Conduit.Internal` from the `conduit` library
- `Tutorial` for examples of how to use the corresponding library, such as `Control.Proxy.Tutorial` from the `pipes` library

4.1.2 Custom Preludes

Haskell is an old language, and it contains many rather awkward features. Using them in production is discouraged. We've already discussed the problem of the highly inefficient `String` data type. There is also consensus on avoiding unsafe functions, such as `head` or `read`, that raise exceptions if given unexpected arguments. Consider the following code fragment:

```
processList xs = otherFunction (head xs)
```

This code contains a hidden source of errors, because it doesn't check whether the `xs` list has any elements. The problem is that there is no help from the compiler; no error or warning. It's possible to exclude such unsafe functions from our code—for example, we can import the `Safe` module from the `safe` package, which provides better alternatives (returning `Maybe` a, a default value, or raising an exception with the specified message), as shown here:

```
headMay :: [a] -> Maybe a
headDef :: a -> [a] -> a
headNote :: String -> [a] -> a
```

If we use `headMay` instead of `head`, we are forced by the type checker to consider both alternatives: the list is either empty (we get `Nothing`) or not (we get `Just something`). Unfortunately, all the unsafe functions and bad types are imported silently from `Prelude`. The beginning programmer has no idea to not use them. Plus, it's easier to use something provided by default than to import some new module.

Another problem with `Prelude` is that it does not export many functions that we use every day—there is no `Text` or `minimumBy` in there, for example—so we have to add many imports, often with qualification, making our code less readable.

Fortunately, Haskell allows us to avoid importing `Prelude` at all. If we enable the `NoImplicitPrelude` GHC extension, as shown next, then there will be no `Prelude` imported in this module:

```
{-# LANGUAGE NoImplicitPrelude #-}

-- no names from Prelude
```

Being alone in the namespace is not the best idea because there is a job to do. We can choose one of the custom preludes. The good news is that there are many of them. A custom prelude may either reinvent everything from scratch, provide brand-new (better, in its author's opinion) abstractions, or be a more conservative extension of the existing `Prelude` that fixes what is broken and unreliable.

Good custom preludes give you what you need to use all the time by default without additional imports and hide things that you are not supposed to use. Certainly you can use those bad parts if you like, but you are forced to import them yourself. You have been warned.

There are several custom preludes that follow that you should definitely know about and consider using in your own projects:

- `Protolude` is a conservative prelude that aims to fix old problems with the standard `Prelude`. It provides a set of names we often need by default (but there is no `String`!). For example, importing `Protolude` in the modules of `stockquotes` from the previous chapter would save us from importing `Data.Ord`, `Data.Foldable`, `Data.Monoid`, `Data.Text`, `Data.Text.IO`, and some others. `Protolude` is often used as a starting point for developing a prelude for a particular project. This can be a good idea for a big project where we want to customize names that are accessible by default. The motivation behind `Protolude` and its main ideas are described by its author Stephen Diehl at http://www.stephendiehl.com/posts/protolude.html.

- `relude` was started by Stephen Diehl also and then developed by the Serokell team. It is now developed by Dmitrii Kovanikov and Veronika Romashkina. This library is an example of a custom prelude developed from strong principles based on productivity, safety, and performance. It can be used for developing Haskell applications from the very beginning because it encourages many good practices.

- `universum` is another custom prelude from the Serokell team based on `Protolude` that aims to speed up productivity.

- `base-prelude` by Nikita Volkov is good for eliminating many lines of import declarations for modules in the `base` package, thanks to reexporting almost all the nonconflicting names.

- `classy-prelude` by Michael Snoyman is different in its approach, reinventing some parts of the standard Haskell type classes. It does a good job of removing noisy qualifications and gives many useful functions by default.

- `foundation` is not just a prelude; it is a project aiming to reimplement the whole standard library with a focus on practicality, performance, and ease of maintenance. One problem with `foundation` is that we may experience communication problems when accessing other libraries outside its ecosystem, although those problems are not insurmountable.

Note that custom preludes are extremely opinionated. That's why it is important to know their authors. All of them are very active within the community. It could be a good idea to follow them on social networks. Information on these and many other custom preludes can be found on Hackage under the "Prelude" category (https://hackage.haskell.org/packages/#cat:Prelude).

4.1.3   *Example: containers-mini*

Suppose we are working on a simple library. We aim to implement traditional data structures, stacks, queues, and deques. We want to use this library while teaching basic computer science (CS) concepts, so the idea is to provide simple interfaces. Data structures in introductory CS courses are traditionally presented as abstract data types. We provide some interface but hide implementation.

The goal of this example is to present the process of library development and turning it into a fully fledged yet simple independent Haskell package. That's why I avoid including it into the `hid-examples` package.

EXAMPLE: LIBRARY WITH SIMPLE DATA STRUCTURES

🗋 https://github.com/bravit/containers-mini/tree/v1.0

☞ We can start development without thinking about packaging.

☞ We use import and export lists to implement abstract data types.

☞ Compiling to an executable is done via `ghc`.

☞ We run source code via `runhaskell`.

While developing a library, we want to make sure that all our functions pass tests. We are also interested in benchmarking them. Let's create a directory with the following structure:

```
$ tree containers-mini
containers-mini
├── Bench.hs
├── Data
│   ├── Deque.hs
│   ├── Queuc.hs
│   └── Stack.hs
├── TestQueue.hs
└── TestStack.hs

1 directory, 6 files
```

The `Data` subdirectory contains our data structure modules: `Data.Stack`, `Data.Queue`, and `Data.Deque`. We have test programs and benchmarks outside it.

The `Data.Stack` module provides the following:

```
module Data.Stack (Stack, empty, isEmpty, push, pop, top) where

newtype Stack a = Stack [a]

empty :: Stack a
push :: a -> Stack a -> Stack a
isEmpty :: Stack a -> Bool
pop :: Stack a -> Stack a
top :: Stack a -> Maybe a
```

The implementation is straightforward, so I've omitted it. Due to the export list, a user of this module has access to the Stack data type (but not the Stack data constructor) and five functions over it. Thus, the only way to manipulate the Stack content is by functions.

Now we can load this file into GHCi as follows:

```
containers-mini $ ghci Data/Stack.hs
ghci> top $ push 10 empty
Just 10
```

Let's write the following simple testing scenario in the TestStack.hs file:

```
import Data.Stack

main = do
  let st = push 15 $ push 10 $ push 5 $ push 0 empty
      -- st == 0, 5, 10, 15 <<-- top
      st' = pop $ pop st -- 0, 5 <<-- top
      st'' = push 100 st' -- 0, 5, 100 <<-- top
      shouldBeTrue = [ top st' == Just 5,
                       top st'' == Just 100,
                       isEmpty $ pop $ pop st']
  print $ and shouldBeTrue
```

To run the test we could compile the program and then run the executable as follows:

```
containers-mini $ ghc TestStack.hs
...
containers-mini $ ./TestStack
True
```

Alternatively, we could use the runhaskell wrapper, as shown next:

```
containers-mini $ runhaskell TestStack.hs
True
```

The deques are implemented by the Sequence data structure that is provided by the Data.Sequence module from the containers package. This package usually comes with GHC, so there is no need to install it.

> **TIP** I recommend reading the Introduction and Tutorial on the containers package (https://haskell-containers.readthedocs.io/en/latest/). It provides many examples and useful advice on how to use such containers as sets, maps, and sequences in Haskell efficiently.

In this module, I've decided to disable implicit Prelude, as shown next, because many Data.Sequence functions have the same names as list functions from Prelude. Alternatively, I could use import Prelude () or name hiding.

```
{-# LANGUAGE NoImplicitPrelude #-}

module Data.Deque (Deque, empty, isEmpty, front, back, push_back,
  push_front, pop_back, pop_front) where

import Data.Sequence hiding (empty)
import qualified Data.Sequence as Seq
import Data.Bool (Bool)
import Data.Maybe (Maybe(..))

newtype Deque a = Deque (Seq a)

empty ::  Deque a
empty = Deque Seq.empty

isEmpty :: Deque a -> Bool
front :: Deque a -> Maybe a
back :: Deque a -> Maybe a
push_front :: a -> Deque a -> Deque a
push_back :: a -> Deque a -> Deque a
pop_front :: Deque a -> Deque a
pop_back :: Deque a -> Deque a
```

Without `Prelude`, we have to import everything, including `Bool` and `Maybe`, with data constructors. Note that I've imported `Data.Sequence` twice to disambiguate `empty`.

Queues are implemented via deques; the implementation is straightforward. The `TestQueue` repeats the `TestStack` scenario as follows:

```
containers-mini $ runhaskell TestQueue.hs
True
```

Finally, let's do simple benchmarking. I suggest checking which is better: using stacks via lists or deques via sequences used as stacks. The scenario is as follows:

   1 I send millions of numbers into a data structure.
   2 I take all the elements back one by one and compute their sum.

This scenario can be implemented for both data structures as follows:

```
fill n insert s = foldl (flip insert) s [1..n]

sumAll s view remove = sum $ unfoldr iter s
  where
    iter s = view s >>= \x -> Just (x, remove s)
```

These functions are designed to be used with both stack and deque as follows:

```
ghci> import Data.Deque as D
ghci> import Data.Stack as S
ghci> sumAll (fill 100 push S.empty) top pop
5050
ghci> sumAll (fill 100 push_front D.empty) front pop_front
5050
```

One problem is how to compute the execution time. I suggest using the `timeit` external package, which can be found on Hackage: http://hackage.haskell.org/package/timeit. With this package, we can implement benchmarking as follows:

```
import System.TimeIt

main = do
  let n = 10^6
  timeItNamed "Stack" $
    print $ sumAll (fill n push S.empty) top pop
  timeItNamed "Deque" $
    print $ sumAll (fill n push_front D.empty) front pop_front
```

Because we've decided to avoid using anything for package management, let's do the installation manually as shown here:

Downloads the package from Hackage as an archive
```
$ curl http://hackage.haskell.org/package/timeit-2.0/timeit-2.0.tar.gz \
    --output timeit-2.0.tar.gz          Unpacks it
$ tar -xf timeit-2.0.tar.gz     ◁
$ cd timeit-2.0                 ◁          Changes the directory
$ runhaskell Setup.hs configure    ◁————  Configures the package
$ runhaskell Setup.hs build      ◁
$ runhaskell Setup.hs install   ◁          Builds it
                                 Installs it
```

It turns out that the Setup.hs file, which comes with every package, does the job. In fact, this file is trivial, as shown next:

```
module Main where
import Distribution.Simple
main = defaultMain
```

It's the Cabal library that does all the work here. Once we are done with installation, we can get back to running our benchmark as follows:

```
containers-mini $ runhaskell Bench.hs
500000500000
Stack:   1.11s
500000500000
Deque:   1.72s
```

The result is as expected. Lists when operated with the head element only are more efficient than sequences used in the same style.

This method for installing dependencies is almost never used in practice. My goal here was to show that it is still possible. We'll get back to this example in the next session and turn it into the real Cabal (Common Architecture for Building Applications and Libraries) package (or *cabalize* it).

4.2 Understanding Haskell packages

Every application or library intended to be used by others should somehow be distributed to its users. In this section, we'll discuss the various issues that arise around package management in Haskell. I'll start with a description of the environment that makes GHC aware of the packages available in the system. This environment by itself is not something that is regularly dealt with by a developer. I believe that understanding it is sometimes crucial for solving problems in dependency management. Then I will move on to Cabal packages, which is a way to distribute Haskell packages.

4.2.1 Packages at the GHC level

Because our applications or libraries use modules provided by other libraries, the compiler needs to know where those libraries reside in the file system. Moreover, there is no information about required external libraries in our Haskell source code. The only information the compiler can get out of it is the set of names of the modules. What is that?

COMPILING PROGRAMS WITH EXTERNAL DEPENDENCIES

Figure 4.2 presents a high-level view of the compilation pipeline, which will give you a clue about what is actually going on at the compiler level.

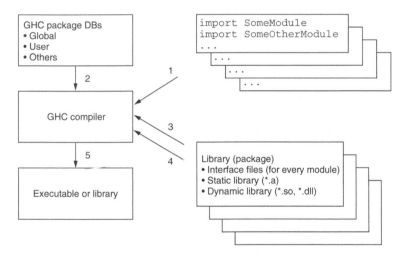

Figure 4.2 High-level view of the GHC compilation pipeline

The compiler performs the following five main steps during compilation:

1 Reads the names of the imported modules from the source files.
2 Consults the package database (associated with the particular distribution of the compiler). This database contains information about all the registered packages. GHC finds out which packages provide required modules and where exactly in the file system all the corresponding artifacts are located.

3 Looks for the interface files of the modules (containing information about what those modules export and import) and uses this information to compile the modules.

4 At the stage of linking, looks for static or dynamic library files provided by the packages.

5 Links all static or dynamic libraries to the program executable or library.

These steps give us the definition of a package from the point of view of the compiler. A package is a collection of the following items:

- Interface files for every exported module
- Compiled library files (either static or dynamic)

The compiler is interested only in library packages. There is no such thing as an application package at this level. Note that the files related to each package and required by the compiler must be located somewhere in the file system. The compiler should be able to get this location from its package database. That means every package must be registered with the compiler in order for it to be able to compile modules that require that package. Technically we can register a package manually by providing all the information the compiler needs to compile modules that require this package via the ghc-pkg utility, which is part of GHC. In fact, we never do that. Instead, we use packaging tools such as cabal-install or stack, which can do all the work of downloading packages, compiling them, placing the packages in the file system, and registering them for us. But remember that all these packaging systems work on top of the compiler and its own low-level packaging system with the registered packages database.

CONSULTING PACKAGE DATABASES

GHC operates two package databases by default: the global one and a user-specific one, arranged in a stack with the user-specific database on top. It starts searching for packages at the top of the stack and continues all the way to the bottom. We can specify additional databases or compile our project against a completely different stack of package databases using the GHC_PACKAGE_PATH environment variable. GHC supports many flags that manipulate package databases and particular packages. Although package database stack tuning is normally done by a higher-level packaging system, the compiler itself is ready to work with any well-formed set of packages—it's the job of the packaging system to provide what is needed for our project.

We can look through all the packages registered with the currently installed GHC with the ghc-pkg list command or get information about the package that provides some module with ghc-pkg find-module. Remember the timeit package we installed manually in the previous section and the System.TimeIt module? Here they are:

```
$ ghc-pkg find-module System.TimeIt
/usr/local/Cellar/ghc/8.8.3/lib/ghc-8.8.3/package.conf.d
    timeit-2.0
```

We can see here that the `System.TimeIt` module is found within the `timeit-2.0` package from the global package database. The compiler needs this information to compile projects using `import System.TimeIt` in some of the source code files.

Once we know the name of the package, we can ask for additional information about it with `ghc-pkg describe` as follows (the output is simplified here for clarity):

```
$ ghc-pkg describe timeit
name:               timeit
version:            2.0
id:                 timeit-2.0-C5F3n19E9zYIMscybjdAzR
copyright:          Copyright © 2009, Lennart Augustsson
maintainer:
    Merijn Verstraaten <merijn@inconsistent.nl>, Lennart Augustsson

author:             Lennart Augustsson
homepage:           https://github.com/merijn/timeit
synopsis:           Time monadic computations with an IO base.
...
```

Information we can get this way includes paths to the library files, external dependencies, exposed modules, and so forth. For example, we can find the interface file as follows:

```
/usr/local/lib/x86_64-osx-ghc-8.8.3/timeit-2.0-
➡ C5F3n19E9zYIMscybjdAzR/System/TimeIt.hi
```

The compiled library file is also there:

```
/usr/local/lib/x86_64-osx-ghc-8.8.3/timeit-2.0-
➡ C5F3n19E9zYIMscybjdAzR/libHStimeit-2.0-C5F3n19E9zYIMscybjdAzR.a
```

The full pathname could be different on other systems, because it is uniquely generated. All this information is available to GHC thanks to package databases. The compiler uses the interface file to compile our program, and the linker then links this library to an executable. As a result, we can run our program.

You can find more on the package databases and the `ghc-pkg` utility in the GHC User's Guide.

PACKAGE ENVIRONMENTS Besides using GHC package databases, we can maintain our own package databases. For example, we can create a package database for a specific project. The packages we have there don't intervene with anything within a system. GHC can be instructed to load a specific package environment, which is a list of package databases and individual package IDs. Thus, we can run GHC in a separate environment created for this particular project. This is usually done using project management tools.

4.2.2   *Cabal packages and Hackage*

GHC bundles the Cabal library, which defines what a Haskell package is and provides tools for manipulating packages, including getting information about them, building them, and registering them. The Cabal library is used by the compiler itself and all the high-level packaging systems. Haskell users usually don't have to work directly with it; its functionality is hidden behind the UI of the packaging systems.

No matter which project management tool is used, Cabal as a library is always used to manipulate Haskell packages. Cooking a package out of the source files is called *cabalizing*.

The Cabal architecture defines a *source package* as a collection of source code files that can be compiled into a GHC package or a standalone application. As such, a Cabal package is both a unit of functionality (set of exposed modules) and a unit of distribution (something that can be distributed over the internet, installed, and used).

Every package has a unique (globally) case-sensitive name that consists of one or more alphanumeric words separated by hyphens. Each package also has a version number with several numeric components separated by dots (e.g., `base-4.11.0.1`, `bytestring-0.10.8.2`, or `timeit-2.0`). We use version numbers to specify precise package implementations we depend on.

Technically a Cabal package is defined in the package description file *package-name.cabal*, usually called the .cabal file. Before discussing its content, let's talk about versioning first.

PACKAGE VERSIONING

Versioning a package should be done with care. Normally one should stick to some versioning policy. This means adding semantic information to version numbers and providing rules on how to change version components, depending on particular changes in the source code. Since 2006, Haskell has adopted the Haskell Package Versioning Policy (PVP, described in full detail at https://pvp.haskell.org/). This policy defines major and minor version components and provides instructions for changing them appropriately.

According to PVP, a version consists of two numbers in a major version component and at least one number in a minor component (more numbers in this part are allowed). For example, the `base-4.11.0.1` package has major version 4.11, where 4 is the generation of the `base` package and 11 is the package version inside this generation; the minor part is 0.1. The latter number signals a patch release without visible changes.

The PVP differentiates between breaking and nonbreaking changes (speaking about the public API), giving attention to extending (say, adding new modules) or deprecating features. Every package author should master the instructions on updating version components and use them in order to guarantee the principle of least astonishment, which helps package users to understand the particular changes made to a package.

ALTERNATIVES TO PVP Clearly, it would be much easier if everybody followed the same policy. Unfortunately, not every Haskeller agrees with PVP, and some prefer to follow another one instead, namely, semantic versioning (https://semver.org/). I personally vote for PVP, which was designed specifically with Haskell in mind, but it's a controversial issue, and there are valid arguments on both sides.

CABAL FILE AS A PACKAGE DESCRIPTION

A Cabal package can contain many components, including the following:

- Library component with modules intended to be used by other packages
- As many executable components as we need
- Test suites
- Benchmarking suites
- Internal libraries to share code between the main library, executables, test suites, and benchmarks

All these components and a package in general are described by a package .cabal file.

A .cabal file is a UTF-8-encoded text file consisting of global package properties such as name, author, license, and so on, plus an optional section for a library (with building information) and any number of sections for describing executables that can be built from the package. Cabal files use a custom format for properties, their values, and sections. They support one-line comments starting with -- and rely on indentation for section properties. Figure 4.3 demonstrates the main parts of a .cabal file.

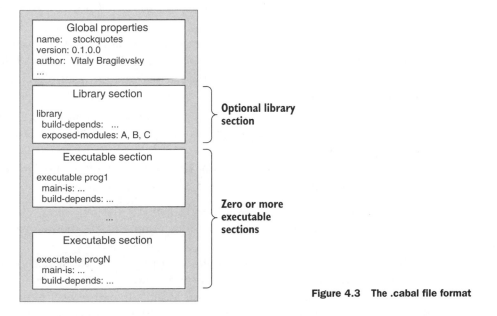

Figure 4.3 The .cabal file format

The Cabal User Guide (https://www.haskell.org/cabal/users-guide/) describes every .cabal file property with possible values. Here I will mention only the most useful and important ones. Global package properties include the following:

- `name` and `version` of the package—the only required properties
- `author`, `copyright`, `license`
- `cabal-version` for specifying requirements on the Cabal specification for reading this .cabal file and processing the source package (with possible value >=1.18)
- `build-type`, which normally has the value `Simple` and specifies how to build this package (more details on this follow)
- `synopsis`, `description`, and `category` for describing this package

The library section starts with the `library` keyword on the first line and contains at least the `exposed-modules` property with the list of names of modules intended to be used by the other libraries and applications as its value. Each executable section starts with the `executable` keyword and requires the `main-is` property for the filename of the `Main` module. There can be other sections, such as `test-suite` and `benchmark`, with information on testing and benchmarking of the package, respectively.

The most important information in the .cabal file is the set of build properties that can be (and normally should be) specified in any section. These include the following:

- `build-depends`, with the list of packages required to build the corresponding package components and constraints on their versions (more on this later in this section)
- `other-modules`, for mentioning all the modules required to build this component (except for those listed in `exposed-modules` and the `main-is` module)
- `hs-source-dirs`, with the list of directories considered as root directories for the module hierarchies
- `default-extensions`, with the list of compiler extensions that will be automatically enabled when compiling every module in this package, regardless of `LANGUAGE` pragmas in the source files
- `default-language`, to specify extensions enabled by default by the corresponding language definition (`Haskell98` or `Haskell2010`, respectively)

The `default-extensions` property can be used to specify the most used extensions only once in the .cabal file, avoiding the need for multiple `LANGUAGE` pragmas in the source files.

Cabal files support setting flags and conditional processing for specifying Cabal properties, depending on the computer architecture and operating system, compiler version, user-defined flags, and so forth. It is also possible to define a set of properties with values in `common` sections and import them into other sections using the `import` property. These features allow us to make packages as general (in terms of environments) as possible and to structure .cabal files in more readable ways. All the details of these and other features can be found in the Cabal User Guide.

The global `build-type` property puts some restrictions on the Setup.hs file. The `Simple` value makes it possible to define this file as follows:

```
import Distribution.Simple
main = defaultMain
```

The Setup.hs file is run by the packaging system with various command-line arguments in order to build this project, test or benchmark it, and perform other kinds of processing. The value `Custom` of the `build-type` property allows you to customize the Setup.hs file, but this is not something that you need to do very often. In most cases, using the value `Simple` for this property and `Distribution.Simple.defaultMain` as the `main` function suffices.

SPECIFYING PACKAGE DEPENDENCIES

All the package components require setting the `build-depends` property. It should list all the dependencies required to build the component with version constraints. We usually specify lower and upper bounds with the operators ==, >=, >, <, and <= followed by a version number and the operators && or || for combining these constraints. Version components use lexicographic ordering.

Consider, for example, the following:

```
build-depends:      base >=4.10 && <4.14, protolude >=0.2.1 && <0.3,
                    ...
```

This specification says that to build the corresponding package component, we have to provide the `base` package with the major component number of at least `4.10` (and any minor component) and the `protolude` package starting with version `0.2.1` and keep `0.2` for the major version component.

More sophisticated versioning operators refer to PVP. For example, `somePackage` `^>= 10.2.3` means that our package is expected to be built with newer versions with the same major `10.2` component of `somePackage`.

The easier part of package versioning is providing lower bounds for dependencies: we can always find out which latest changes you need. The harder part is keeping the upper bounds up to date. New versions of dependencies can be released every day, and PVP expects us to update upper bounds correspondingly to make sure that the client has the freedom to use our package with the latest versions of other packages. One approach is to use tooling for checking upper bounds automatically and updating them as needed. We'll talk about this later in this chapter while discussing specific package management tools.

The `build-depends` property is used by the tools for constructing the build plan—a list of all the packages the project depends on directly or indirectly, with their particular versions. Remember that the compiler is able to build the project against only one version of each package, so technically it is possible that no build plan exists. Consider the following two `build-depends` values from two of the packages some project depends on:

```
build-depends:        somelib >=1.1 && <1.2
```

and

```
build-depends:        somelib >=1.2
```

Clearly there is no way to build this project with one version of the `somelib` library: `somelib-1.2` breaks the first package, and `somelib-1.1` is too old for the second one. It's possible that the author of the first package has simply forgotten to update the upper bound, but if `1.2` really breaks something, that would be unfortunate.

EXAMPLE: CABALIZING CONTAINERS-MINI

Let's get back to the `containers-mini` example from the previous section and cook it as a Cabal package. We already know that we should provide a .cabal file for it.

> **EXAMPLE: containers-mini AS A CABAL PACKAGE**
>
> ☐   https://github.com/bravit/containers-mini/tree/v2.0
>
> ⚡   *stack, queue, bench*
>
> ☞   The Cabal project is described with a .cabal file.

This example contains a library with three modules, a couple of tests, a benchmark, and no executables. To make it a Cabal package with a library, let's add the following containers-mini.cabal file:

```
cabal-version:      2.0
name:               containers-mini
version:            0.1.0.0
build-type:         Simple

library
  exposed-modules:    Data.Stack, Data.Deque, Data.Queue
  other-extensions:   NoImplicitPrelude
  build-depends:      base >=4.10 && <4.15, containers >=0.5 && <0.7
  default-language:   Haskell2010
```

Once we have this .cabal file, we can build this package. All the dependencies are downloaded automatically as follows:

```
containers-mini $ cabal build
```

Our tests should be changed a little bit to become a real test suite. Remember, we were printing either `True` or `False`. The Cabal test suites in their simplest form report failures via a nonzero exit code. This is specified by the `type` field of the corresponding .cabal file section. Changing the `print` instruction to the following should suffice:

```
case and shouldBeTrue of
    True -> pure ()
    False -> exitFailure
```

The `exitFailure` function is imported from the `System.Exit` module, which should also be imported.

Now we add sections for test suites into the package .cabal file as shown next:

```
test-suite stack
  type: exitcode-stdio-1.0
  main-is: TestStack.hs
  other-modules: Data.Stack
  build-depends:
      base >=4.10 && <4.15, containers >=0.5 && <0.7
  default-language: Haskell2010

test-suite queue
  type: exitcode-stdio-1.0
  main-is: TestQueue.hs
  other-modules: Data.Queue, Data.Deque
  build-depends:
      base >=4.10 && <4.15, containers >=0.6 && <0.7
  default-language: Haskell2010
```

Running `cabal test stack` goes smoothly, as shown here:

```
$ cabal test stack
...
Running 1 test suites...
Test suite stack: RUNNING...
Test suite stack: PASS
...
1 of 1 test suites (1 of 1 test cases) passed.
```

Finally, we add our benchmark. Note that only this component depends on the `timeit` package, so we mention it here:

```
benchmark bench
  type: exitcode-stdio-1.0
  main-is: Bench.hs
  other-modules: Data.Stack, Data.Deque
  build-depends:
      base >=4.10 && <4.15,
      containers >=0.5 && <0.7,
      timeit >=2.0 && <2.1
  default-language: Haskell2010
```

Running the benchmark is also successful, as shown next:

```
$ cabal bench
...
Running 1 benchmarks...
Benchmark bench: RUNNING...
500000500000
Stack:   0.10s
500000500000
Deque:   0.09s
Benchmark bench: FINISH
```

To make this package ready for distribution, we also add Setup.hs with the default content.

GENERATING .CABAL FILES WITH HPACK

Writing .cabal files can be rather tedious as it involves specifying too many details that can be defaulted or inferred automatically. One example is the `other-modules` property, where we should list every module of our library that is not exposed to its user or literally every module of our application except for the main module. The `hpack` utility, which comes from the `hpack` Cabal package designed and implemented by Simon Hengel, is an alternative to this boring .cabal file writing. This utility defines its own package description format, which is expected to reside in the package.yaml file and allows generating a .cabal file by running `hpack`. Using the package.yaml file format is based on the following three design principles:

- Obvious things are defaulted or inferred.
- Repetitions can be avoided.
- Everything can be specified with 100% control over the resulting .cabal file.

These principles are quite different from what we have in the case of .cabal files themselves, where we have to specify almost everything. Although newer versions of Cabal support some means for avoiding repetitions (including `common` sections), `hpack` is much more convenient.

Documentation on `hpack` can be found on its GitHub page: https://github.com/sol/hpack#readme. Keep in mind the following to ensure you understand how to read these docs:

- For every package.yaml field, you should know which .cabal file field it corresponds to.
- Note rules for default values.
- You may find value inference rules in the Notes columns.

Once having mastered writing package.yaml descriptions, we can save quite a bit of time because they are much shorter in general. The documentation page contains examples on how to write package.yaml files for several Cabal packages, including `hpack` itself. Both the `hid-examples` package and the final version of `containers-mini` use hpack to generate .cabal files. You can find corresponding package.yaml files in their GitHub repositories.

DISTRIBUTING PACKAGES ON HACKAGE

Developers upload their packages to Hackage and update them with new versions as needed. First-time package authors should decide on a versioning policy and license and follow the directions at https://hackage.haskell.org/upload to upload their packages.

Package users use this archive to look for the packages they need; it is possible to search packages by keywords in their names and descriptions or browse them by particular topics (categories). Downloading the packages is typically left up to the packaging and building tools. They use Hackage as a source of packages and their metadata (roughly understood as .cabal file descriptions). Every package should go through Hackage in order to be distributed within the community.

The cabal utility provides the following commands for distributing packages:

- cabal check to check if the package conforms to some formal rules regarding Hackage packages
- cabal sdist to create a package archive

There is also similar functionality in stack.

Uploaded packages can be curated by the Hackage Trustees (the group of people supervising Hackage). Curation here is the ability to change package metadata (the description in the .cabal file) without altering the package content itself. These changes are called revisions. One goal for revision is to update the build-depends property to account for new versions of the packages in the dependency list that don't break the building of the package. You can read about specific details on the Hackage Upload Package page.

Once the package is uploaded to Hackage, it gets a URL there forever; for example, http://hackage.haskell.org/package/hid-examples corresponds to the package with all the examples accompanying this book. This page is generated using the .cabal file, README file, and the package history.

4.3 Tools for project development

Project development is not only about writing and compiling code; it involves many activities. The most traditional of them are presented in figure 4.4. Some of these activities may not relate to Haskell at all, but belong to general software development practices. Others are deeply affected by Haskell and available tooling. For example, maintaining code under version control is not peculiar to Haskell (though there is the darcs VCS tool that implements an algebra of patches!). Building source code, on the other hand, clearly has its specifics.

In the previous section, we discussed what a package is in Haskell. We can consider it as a unit of project development. In the introduction to this book, I mentioned two

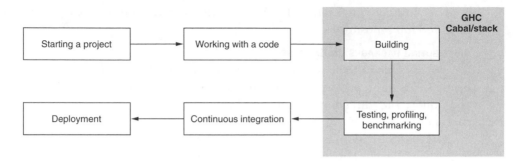

Figure 4.4 Project development overview

main tools to work with Haskell packages, namely, `cabal` and `stack`. Both of them allow us to the following:

- Configure a package under development.
- Find and install its dependencies (make them accessible by the compiler).
- Build a package or its components.
- Prepare a package for distribution (create an archive for uploading to Hackage).
- Install a package (library or application) locally.

Because we have been using these tools from the very first chapter, there is no need to repeat basic operations such as building a package or running tests with them. In this section, we'll look at several project development activities and see how `cabal` and `stack` deal with them and which other tools are also available.

4.3.1 Dependency management

We rely on some packages when we develop our project: we say that our project *depends* on them. Those packages depend on other packages, thus creating a *dependency graph*. When we explored the dependencies of the stock quote project from the previous chapter, we saw that there are more than a hundred Haskell packages that project depends on either directly or indirectly. It's not uncommon to have several hundred if not thousands of packages in dependency graphs for larger projects.

Let's look at the root of the problem first and then discuss several solutions and related tools.

THE BROKEN DEPENDENCY PROBLEM

Imagine the following situation: we've installed packages we want to depend on. All of them are in our local package database available to GHC. We know all the paths. Everything is great.

Problems arise when packages change. These changes are inevitable and, in fact, encouraged: a library's author may fix errors; provide new, better functionality; or extend old functionalities. After making changes in the library, the author releases a new version of the package. Dependencies of the library may change, too. We may be delighted by the new functionality and want to use it as soon as possible in our project. This leads to changes in our dependency graph, and we need to give GHC new versions for some of the packages we depend on. Updating these packages may lead to breaking other packages that were registered previously and depended on the prior versions of the same packages. It is also possible that two packages we need require different versions of a third package, meaning that we cannot use them together. Situations like these are well known within the community as *Cabal hell.*

This situation is illustrated in figure 4.5.

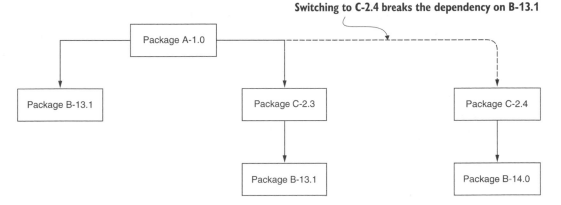

Figure 4.5   Changing versions of a dependency

Fortunately, *Cabal hell* is now history. It doesn't exist anymore with contemporary dependency management systems for Haskell.

APPROACHES TO DEPENDENCY MANAGEMENT

The main goal of the dependency management system is, given the source project and its set of dependencies, to find specific versions of all the packages in the dependency graph that go well together. We call a list of such versions a solution to the dependency problem, or a build plan. Computing a build plan with respect to constraints in the `build-depends` fields of package components and their dependencies is an instance of the well-known constraint satisfaction problem. Besides computing a build plan, we expect a dependency manager to organize packages we need to build our project in the local file system.

We already know how GHC deals with this: it uses the package database and always looks for the latest version available in this database. If the latest versions of several packages are incompatible in terms of their dependencies, or some dependencies are broken, then compilation fails. The compiler will not make an attempt to choose another version. It is the task of the package system to provide the compiler with compatible package versions.

Many years ago, the purpose of the `cabal` tool was simply to populate the GHC package database (either globally or per user). When we asked `cabal` to install some set of packages, it solved a constraint satisfaction problem, thus computing a build plan; downloaded specific versions; and registered them with a compiler. This could potentially lead to breaking packages that had been installed previously and consequently compiled against a different set of dependencies. Remember that all the packages in the dependencies must be built against a single version of every package. Consequently, a small change in one often used package could break almost everything.

The issues with the original `cabal` approach led to the discovery of new approaches, including the following:

- Providing curated sets of packages, with fixed versions of every package in each set and a guarantee to be able to build all of them together
- Sandboxing, or creating a development environment that keeps the set of all required packages on a per-project basis without interfering with the GHC package database
- Persistent storage of uniquely identified package builds, a so-called Nix-style package management system

The first approach makes organizing packages trivial: we are guaranteed that it is okay to download the whole set of packages (or the part we need), register them with the compiler, and build a project under development without there being any broken dependencies. If we want to change one version of a package in the dependencies, then we have to switch to another set of packages that contains the required version. Clearly, a problem may arise when we need a package outside the chosen curated set. This approach is taken by the `stack` tool and the public Stackage package repository, which we'll discuss shortly. Larger Haskell teams often use the same approach internally within the company, keeping their own curated sets of packages and updating them appropriately.

The second approach was originally implemented in `cabal`. Inside sandboxes, `cabal` runs GHC with a specifically crafted package database. We can get breakage in our sandbox, too, but this cannot harm other projects under development. As a negative consequence, if we develop many projects, then we have to keep many copies of packages in our system. Although it is possible to share sandboxes between projects, this can limit our ability to change package versions.

The third approach, first implemented in the `cabal` tool in version 1.24, ensures build reproducibility and alleviates the risk of breaking existing libraries and applications. The inspiration for this approach comes the from `nix` package manager (https://nixos.org/nix), which brings immutability to build artifacts. If some package was built against some dependency once, then this particular dependency (with all its subdependencies) will rest in the system forever. The sole mechanism for deleting a dependency is garbage collection, which can take place only if literally nothing in the system depends on this dependency.

MAINTAINING DEPENDENCIES WITH CABAL 3.0 AND UP

Both older approaches of populating GHC databases and sandboxing are still available with `cabal` 3.0 and newer, but they are considered outdated. The third approach of Nix-style package management is used in `cabal` by default since version 3.0. With this approach, the `cabal` tool keeps every once-required version of every package built against every once-required set of dependencies in a shared environment, at the cost of greater storage requirements. Consequently, when we request an updated package, we get a new build, whereas all older builds are still available. If, while computing a build plan, we have newer versions of some package, `cabal` rebuilds this package and every package depending on it and saves the results in storage.

When we are executing `cabal build`, the `cabal` tool does roughly the following:

- Reads `build-depends` fields of this package and all its dependencies, direct and indirect
- Creates a system of constraints
- Computes a build plan by solving the system of constraints
- Consults the storage if it has any required packages already built against required versions
- Forms a package environment that corresponds to a build plan and runs GHC in this environment
- Saves local package build artifacts in a local directory and all the dependencies in global storage

Changing package properties may lead to a recalculation of a build plan. The `cabal` tool always tries to get the newest versions available, given they satisfy constraints. This passion for novelty is not always desirable. The `cabal freeze` command writes specific versions of the dependencies (that is, the latest build plan) into the cabal.project .freeze file and forces subsequent `cabal build` commands to use them—freezing allows us to recreate the same building conditions in different environments, such as a developer's workstation or testing and production servers.

Such `cabal` commands as `run`, `test`, and `bench` build corresponding components before executing them. The `cabal repl` command executes GHCi in a package environment related to the latest build plan. In fact, all these commands are simple wrappers around the dependency management system itself and are able to prepare an environment where the corresponding programs are executed.

Other useful commands of the `cabal` tool related to dependency management and building follow:

- `cabal clean` cleans all the build artifacts of the local project. It doesn't affect global storage.
- `cabal configure` saves build configuration for subsequent `cabal build` runs.
- `cabal list` and `cabal update` work with the so-called package index, a local representation of Hackage.
- `cabal install` installs Haskell applications and libraries to a local system.

STACKAGE SNAPSHOTS AND RESOLVERS FOR STACK

The curated sets of stack are called snapshots. They are regularly released on Stackage (https://www.stackage.org). Stackage takes packages from Hackage, considering it as upstream. Every snapshot corresponds to a particular compiler release and includes many packages (totaling close to one-fifth of the contents of Hackage at the time of writing) with fixed versions guaranteed to work together. There are two sorts of snapshots, as follows:

- *LTS (Long-Term Support)*—Produced weekly and considered the stable release
- *Nightly*—The bleeding-edge release produced nightly

Every snapshot is in fact a trivial build plan, thanks to fixed versions of packages. The whole stack idea is to develop a project against a specific snapshot. All snapshots are versioned by tags, or resolvers, in the form of lts-<N.M> and nightly-<YEAR-MONTH-DAY>; for example, lts-14.27 (with GHC 8.6.5) or nightly-2020-05-16 (with GHC 8.8.3) resolvers. We are guaranteed that if a project has been built against a specific resolver, it will always work with that resolver. This is called reproducibility.

The stack tool is a local counterpart to Stackage; it is responsible for downloading dependencies (including the compiler itself), building, testing, benchmarking, and installing packages. It also allows developers to prepare and upload packages to Hackage. It uses the Cabal infrastructure (Cabal as a library) under the hood.

The stack tool uses its own configuration file, stack.yaml, which must specify a resolver and is also used for setting other project properties. For example, it is possible to use dependencies outside Stackage snapshots or newer versions of packages found in snapshots. In the following stack.yaml fragment, we ask for quite an old resolver and mention a couple of dependencies missing from the corresponding snapshot:

```
resolver: lts-10.10
extra-deps:
- gtk-0.14.9
- gtk3-0.14.9
```

When building such a package, stack looks for all the packages in the LTS-10.10 snapshot and adds the mentioned extra dependencies to them.

Note that the stack tool relies on a .cabal file or (preferably) a package.yaml file (from hpack) for a package description.

KEEPING UPPER BOUNDS UP TO DATE

Each of the main dependency management approaches looks differently on the problem of setting upper bounds in build-depends. Curation supports the idea of omitting upper bounds, as it is possible to check them automatically while assembling the corresponding set of packages. The constraints satisfaction approach depends on the upper bounds significantly, because omitting them could lead to wrong solutions when we get unbuildable build plans.

The `cabal` tool provides the `cabal outdated` command to check if some of the dependencies were updated according to the local package index. It makes sense to run this command after updating the index first as follows:

```
$ cabal update && cabal outdated
```

There is also a web service that allows hunting for the dependencies of published packages. For example, we can check if there are updated dependencies for the published release of the `hid-examples` package: https://packdeps.haskellers.com/feed?needle=hid-examples.

4.3.2 *Haskell projects as a collection of packages*

Learning Haskell usually starts in the REPL. Then we learn how to write code in a file. At some point, we learn about multimodule programs and start using external dependencies. After that, we usually start to develop and ship applications and libraries as packages. But what about projects? What should we call a project in Haskell?

In industrial environments, a project usually includes many packages. Some of them are published on Hackage; others are internal to an organization. Those packages are usually shared among the developers within a team. Changing code in one of the local packages should affect other local packages depending on it without redistributing.

Both `cabal` and `stack` support working with projects as collections of packages. For example, let's look at the `haskell-chart` collection of packages: https://github.com/timbod7/haskell-chart/. This project contains the following six packages:

- `chart` itself, for plotting charts as we did in the previous chapter
- `chart-diagrams` and `chart-cairo` as backends, for rendering charts in various image formats
- `chart-gtk` and `chart-gtk3` for rendering charts in GTK windows
- `chart-tests` for testing the packages altogether

The root folder of this project has the following structure:

```
haskell-chart
├── Makefile
├── README.md
├── TODO
├── cabal.project
├── cabal.project.local
├── chart/
├── chart-cairo/
├── chart-diagrams/
├── chart-gtk/
├── chart-gtk3/
├── chart-tests/
├── stack.yaml
└── wiki-examples/

7 directories, 6 files
```

There are subfolders for every package and several files describing the project in the root folder, including

- cabal.project and cabal.project.local for `cabal`
- stack.yaml for `stack`

The `cabal` tool looks at the cabal.project file to understand what is in the project, as shown here:

```
packages:
  chart/
  chart-cairo/
  chart-diagrams/
  chart-tests/
  chart-gtk/
  chart-gtk3/
```

The cabal.project.local file describes options referring to particular builds. You will not find this file in the GitHub repository, because it's not checked out. I have it on my machine with the following content:

```
package gtk
  flags: +have-quartz-gtk
```

This says that to build one of the dependencies, the `gtk` package, GHC should be given the `have-quartz-gtk` flag. This flag is required to build this package on macOS exclusively. Placing this flag in cabal.project.local instead of cabal.project doesn't affect any other developers working on this project.

Many options could be specified in cabal.project* files. Most of them correspond to `cabal` or GHC options. For example, to build a version of a package for profiling, one could write the following:

```
profiling: True
```

The `cabal` utility will then run with the `--enable-profiling` option, and the same option will go straight to GHC. We'll talk more about this in the chapter on profiling. In general, many compiler options can be specified in cabal.project* files. We can do that either manually or by running the `cabal configure` command. These files can be also used on a package level with the same idea.

The stack.yaml file plays the same role for the `stack` tool. It can also describe both a standalone package and a project. Let's look at the following file for the `haskell-chart` project:

```
packages:
- chart/
- chart-cairo/
- chart-diagrams/
- chart-tests/
```

```
- chart-gtk/
- chart-gtk3/
flags:
  gtk:
    # This needs to be true on osx
    have-quartz-gtk: false
resolver: lts-10.10
extra-deps:
- gtk-0.14.9
- gtk3-0.14.9
- gio-0.13.5.0
```

This stack.yaml lists all the packages in this project, gives flags to build some of the dependencies, specifies a resolver, and mentions several dependencies outside of Stackage.

4.3.3 *Common project management activities and tools*

When it comes to software development and project management, the number of options becomes so big that it's impossible even to list them. In this short section, I'll try to give an overview of this area with respect to Haskell development and provide links to other resources.

STARTING A PROJECT

Both stack and cabal can help with starting a project. The cabal init command allows you to get an initial .cabal file. The cabal gen-bounds commands allow for setting initial constraints for project dependencies. The stack new command supports project scaffolding using a collection of templates.

Although all these commands come in very handy, I recommend using the Summoner tool (https://kowainik.github.io/projects/summoner). It features generating all the necessary files with sensible initial values. What is more important, it gives us such things as continuous integration for free. Make sure that you read the list of its features. This tool is extremely convenient when it comes to starting a Haskell project.

WORKING ON SOURCE CODE

Most Haskellers, according to the 2020 survey by Taylor Fausak (https://taylor.fausak .me/2020/11/22/haskell-survey-results/#s3q1), tend to use text editors such as vi, Emacs, and Visual Studio Code to work with source code. I recommend consulting the Haskell wiki page on IDEs (https://wiki.haskell.org/IDEs) for a list of options on how to tweak an editor environment.

Besides editing code, we also use code formatters. This area is highly opinionated, so I refrain from commenting on the corresponding tools. I recommend looking at the following projects:

- hindent (http://hackage.haskell.org/package/hindent)
- stylish-haskell (https://hackage.haskell.org/package/stylish-haskell)
- brittany (https://hackage.haskell.org/package/brittany)
- ormolu (https://hackage.haskell.org/package/ormolu)

These tools are very different in their philosophy and usage patterns. It might be a good idea to pick one of them for use in a development process.

The `hlint` tool (https://hackage.haskell.org/package/hlint) is an extremely useful Haskell code linter.

HASKELL AND NIX

One serious problem arises when the development should be done in various system environments. This is often the case because developers tend to prefer their own development environments. One useful approach that is gaining a lot of popularity recently is Nix-based development. It allows getting reproducibility not only for Haskell packages but also for tools and system dependencies. Gabriel Gonzalez created material on this topic: https://github.com/Gabriel439/haskell-nix. He overviews various issues around Haskell development and Nix integration.

CONTINUOUS INTEGRATION AND DEPLOYMENT

Contemporary software engineering practices require building and testing software artifacts as often as possible to make sure that there are no unnoticed long-standing problems. We call it continuous integration (CI), meaning that software components are integrated within bigger software systems continuously, eliminating the need for dedicated integration stages. Because building and testing steps take time, it is quite common to delegate these tasks to continuous integration servers. The Haskell community is not unique in its reliance on https://github.com for storing project source code and using https://travis-ci.com for building them on Linux and macOS. It is also customary to use https://ci.appveyor.com for building Haskell projects for Windows. Some individuals and companies prefer to use GitLab and CircleCI for hosting and building Haskell projects.

The `hid-examples` package uses such services as well, as follows:

- https://github.com/bravit/hid-examples contains source code.
- https://travis-ci.com/github/bravit/hid-examples is used for building on Linux and macOS.
- https://ci.appveyor.com/project/bravit/hid-examples is used for building on Windows.

Note that these services can be used freely for open source projects (although with some limitations).

To get started with CI, an author describes the building and testing environments and stages using a platform-specific file format (e.g., .travis.yml for Travis CI and appveyor.yml for AppVeyor), puts the corresponding files in the project's repository, and then either triggers a build process manually or links it to specific events (such as new commits or pull requests). The rest is done by the CI server. In general, CI servers may be responsible for almost everything from testing to deploying projects and documentation in production.

When it comes to deployment, there are several options also, including the following:

- A collection of static binaries
- A Docker image

The latter option is becoming more and more popular within the community. There is an official Docker image for Haskell development (https://hub.docker.com/_/haskell). At that page are some recommendations on how to use it in production.

Summary

- Know and use the best practices for the import and export sections of your modules.
- Pick a custom prelude, and obey the rules it imposes.
- Understand package system and dependency problems and how to solve them quickly.
- Pick and follow a versioning policy for a package to make it convenient to use by others.
- There is no Cabal hell anymore: we can pick and use either `cabal` or `stack` and get things done in all cases.
- There are many tools available to make Haskell development go smoothly.

Monads as practical
functionality providers

5

This chapter covers

- A pragmatic approach to monads and the
  functionality they provide
- Accessing configuration, writing logs, and
  maintaining state with monads
- Exploiting various approaches to mutability in the
  IO and ST monads

Monads can be seen and taught from many perspectives. The mathematics behind them is just one perspective, and we'll ignore it by focusing on the functionality monads provide. Monads can simplify our code by promoting coherent abstraction and guarantees of the uniformity of the code. In this chapter, we'll talk about using monads in practice. We'll see how they help us to implement difficult algorithms clearly and correctly and to write short and concise code while maintaining readability and ease of support.

This is the approach of this chapter: we'll look at cases and apply monads to them. It makes sense to refresh the idea of abstracting computations from chapter 2 before reading this chapter.

5.1 *Basic monads in use: Maybe, Reader, Writer*

In this section, we'll focus on the following three monads:

- The `Maybe` monad
- The `Reader` monad
- The `Writer` monad

Although the former two monads are often used in practice, the latter one is less used due to memory usage issues (basically, it is too easy to introduce space leaks with it). Nevertheless, all of them are useful to understand the pragmatics behind monads in general.

5.1.1 *Maybe monad as a line saver*

What would we think about a function returning `Maybe a` for some type variable `a`? Well, it represents the result of a computation that may potentially have no result at all. The next question: what if we have several such computations, and our task is to produce an overall result from them? I mean, is there a good way to compose them? In general, there are the following two basic strategies:

- If we need both results to produce a final one, and one of computations gives us `Nothing`, then we answer with `Nothing`.
- If we have only one non-`Nothing` result and that's enough for us, then we answer with it.

The choice of the right strategy depends on our goals. Haskell gives us abstractions for both. The first strategy is implemented by the monadic bind `>>=` for the `Maybe` monad. The second one is captured by the monoid operation over `Maybe` values.

Let's look at several examples.

EXAMPLE: USING MAYBE AS FUNCTOR, APPLICATIVE, AND MONAD

☐ ch05/maybe.hs

⚡ *maybe*

☞ `Maybe` helps deal with missing results of computations.

Suppose we have a `String` representing a number, something like `"21"`. How would we double it? We have to take special care here. What if the given string is incorrect and doesn't represent any number? To deal with such cases, we can use `readMaybe` from the `Text.Read` module as follows:

```
readMaybe :: Read a => String -> Maybe a
```

Now, we definitely don't want to multiply Nothing by 2. Well, we have two options. First, we can pattern match on a readMaybe result as follows:

```
doubleStrNumber1 str =
  case readMaybe str of
    Just x -> Just (2*x)
    Nothing -> Nothing
```

Second, we can apply the Functor functionality, as shown next:

```
doubleStrNumber2 str = (2*) `fmap` readMaybe str
```

It works as expected:

```
ghci> doubleStrNumber2 "21"
Just 42
ghci> doubleStrNumber2 "yy"
Nothing
```

Why is this possible? Because the Functor instance for Maybe already did all the work! Following is its definition from the base library:

```
instance  Functor Maybe  where
    fmap _ Nothing      = Nothing
    fmap f (Just a)     = Just (f a)
```

Functor in general allows applying a function to a result of a computation in a context. Our context here is Maybe, so we double a Just value, leaving Nothing untouched.

If we have two such String represented numbers and need to compute their sum, then that's a job for Applicative, as shown next:

```
plusStrNumbers :: (Num a, Read a) => String -> String -> Maybe a
plusStrNumbers s1 s2 = (+) <$> readMaybe s1 <*> readMaybe s2
```

And it also works as a charm, as follows:

```
ghci> plusStrNumbers "3" "5"
Just 8
ghci> plusStrNumbers "3" "x"
Nothing
```

Imagine all the pattern matches we would have to write here manually if we didn't have the Applicative instance for Maybe!

Let's get to something a little bit more practical. Suppose we have two associated lists: one with pairs of a person name and a phone number, and another one with pairs of a phone number and a corresponding location. For simplicity, let's use String for all values, as follows:

```
type Name = String
type Phone = String
type Location = String
type PhoneNumbers = [(Name, Phone)]
type Locations = [(Phone, Location)]
```

How could we find a location using a person name? We need a function with the following type signature:

```
locateByName :: PhoneNumbers -> Locations -> Name -> Maybe Location
```

This scenario demands the first strategy. We can't proceed without getting the phone number first and are forced to return Nothing if it is missing.

The Prelude module provides the lookup function. It returns a Maybe value, meaning for us that it performs a computation in the Maybe monad, as shown next:

```
lookup :: Eq a => a -> [(a, b)] -> Maybe b
```

Maybe implements the Monad type class, so we can use the (>>=) binding function to search for a location as follows:

```
locateByName :: PhoneNumbers -> Locations -> Name -> Maybe Location
locateByName pnumbers locs name =
  lookup name pnumbers >>= flip lookup locs
```

Although we've had to flip arguments for lookup to get a function suitable for the monadic binding (the flip lookup locs subexpression has the required Phone -> Maybe Location type), the implementation looks quite concise and guarantees that we'll get Just somelocation after two successful lookup calls.

The next implementation without monadic binding looks more tedious:

```
locateByName' :: PhoneNumbers -> Locations -> Name -> Maybe Location
locateByName' pnumbers locs name =
  case lookup name pnumbers of
    Just number -> lookup number locs
    Nothing -> Nothing
```

If we look at the implementation of >>= for Maybe, we'll see the same pattern match over the Maybe a value to the left of >>=, as shown here:

```
instance Monad Maybe where
   (Just x) >>= k = k x
   Nothing  >>= _ = Nothing
   ...
```

So we've just saved a little of typing by reusing >>=. That's all there is to it: we use Functor, Applicative, and Monad instances for the functionality and convenience they provide (not to look smart!). Generally, we try to use the functionality they provide whenever it is sufficient for our goals.

5.1.2 *Carrying configuration all over the program with Reader*

In this section, we'll look at the Reader monad. It proves itself very useful in everyday practical programming in Haskell. We use it to organize read-only access to program configuration. It will be instructive to look at this monad to get an insight into a general approach for defining our own monads or using monads provided by the libraries.

ISSUES WITH ACCESSING CONFIGURATION PARAMETERS

Suppose we've got a configuration from command-line arguments or a config file. We traditionally do that at startup, somewhere close to the main function. The configuration includes several Boolean flags, integer values, and strings. Configuration parameters are required in various parts of our program. How would we transport those parameters to the functions that need them?

One possibility is to pass them as function arguments. Doing this leads to the necessity of adding a configuration to a list of arguments of almost every function in our program. That would be quite cumbersome. In the following example, we read a configuration in main and then pass it to doSomethingSpecial to illustrate this approach:

```
data Config
getConfiguration :: IO Config

main = do
  config <- getConfiguration
  work config ...

work :: Configuration -> ...
work config ... = ... doSomething config ...

doSomething :: Configuration -> ...
doSomething config ... = ... doSomethingSpecial config ...

doSomethingSpecial :: Configuration -> ...
doSomethingSpecial config ... = ... use config ...
```

Although the work and doSomething functions never use the config parameter, they still need to take it as an argument and pass it down further.

Other programming languages solve the same problem with different approaches. For example, it is suggested to use the *Singleton* pattern, which defines a global variable that is guaranteed to uniquely exist and carry a configuration as its value. Global variables are not what we expect in Haskell. Instead, we define a computation with an effect of implicitly passing this information around and an ability to access it whenever we like. This is exactly what the Reader monad is used for.

A COMPUTATION IN THE CONTEXT OF THE READER MONAD

The Reader monad is provided by the Control.Monad.Reader module. Let's see how it helps to deliver configuration parameters where they are required. We start with defining a computation in the corresponding context, and then run this computation in main.

EXAMPLE: USING THE READER MONAD TO CARRY A CONFIGURATION

   📄 ch05/reader.hs

   ⚡ *reader*

   ☞ The Reader monad helps deal with a program configuration.

Suppose we are interested in delivering the verbosity parameter. Our configuration follows:

```
data Config = Config {
    verbose :: Bool
    {- other parameters -}
  }
```

Suppose also we have the following action that reads a configuration in IO:

```
getConfiguration :: IO Config
getConfiguration = pure Config { verbose = True {- ... -} }
```

Any computation with such a configuration should have the following type: Reader Config TypeOfResult. Let's use () as a resulting type for simplicity and introduce a type alias ConfigM for Reader Config to reduce repetition. The main job is done by the following functions:

Starting point of a computation,
calls doSomething

Calls
doSomethingSpecial

```
work :: ConfigM ()
doSomething :: ConfigM ()
doSomethingSpecial :: ConfigM ()
```

Checks for the verbose flag and does
something special verbosely if necessary

The idea of the Reader monad is to pass a configuration *implicitly* (meaning we don't have to do that explicitly) and provide an interface to consult it whenever required. An implicit configuration passing is implemented by the Monad instance for Reader. The interface is described by the following type class:

```
class Monad m => MonadReader r m | m -> r where
    ask    :: m r
    local  :: (r -> r) -> m a -> m a
    reader :: (r -> a) -> m a
```

Note the head of the type class definition: we define multiparametric type class Monad-Reader r m where r refers to the type of configuration (something that can be read inside the computation) and m refers to some monad. The Reader monad implements an instance of the MonadReader type class, but there are other implementations as well.

> **NOTE** To be precise, Reader is not a monad, but Reader r is. So the type of configuration should be uniquely determined by the type of a monad—this is captured by the | m -> r part of the type class head. This syntax comes from the FunctionalDependencies GHC extension, whose goal is to support type inference by prohibiting wrong instances of the same monad m with different r.

The ask method makes a configuration be the result of a computation. Consequently, we can access it by variable binding in do blocks. The reader function adds an ability to ask for some value computed from the configuration, for example, one of its fields. It is often used through the asks alias as follows:

```
asks :: MonadReader r m => (r -> a) -> m a
```

We'll get to the local function shortly. Now let's see how to pass a configuration and consult it when needed. The work and doSomething functions don't need a configuration, as shown next:

```
work :: ConfigM ()
work = do
  -- ...
  doSomething
  -- ...

doSomething :: ConfigM ()
doSomething = do
  -- ...
  doSomethingSpecial
  -- ...
```

These two functions do nothing with a configuration, besides working in the Reader monad. The Monad instance takes care of configuration passing.

The doSomethingSpecial does need access to a configuration as follows:

```
doSomethingSpecial :: ConfigM ()
doSomethingSpecial = do
  -- ...
  vrb <- asks verbose
  when vrb beVerbose
  -- ...
```

We use asks verbose here to access the verbose field in Config. Alternatively, we could ask for a whole configuration and use all the fields somehow, as follows:

```
doSomethingSpecial = do
  -- ...
  Config {verbose} <- ask      ◁──┐  Requires the NamedFieldPuns
  when vrb beVerbose               │  GHC extension
  -- ...
```

Note the use of the `NamedFieldPuns` GHC extension. Unlike the `RecordWildCards` GHC extension, it allows bringing into scope only the fields we are interested in. We list them in {...} and don't mention others.

Sometimes we may want to run a subcomputation in a slightly modified environment (with a different configuration). This is what the `local` function is used for. It takes an argument of the `r -> r` type that is applied to the configuration before running a computation (its second argument). For example, let's do something special silently, ignoring the configuration, as follows:

```
silent :: Config -> Config                        ┌ Uses record
silent config = config {verbose = False}  ◁──┘    │ update syntax

doSomethingSpecialSilently :: ConfigM ()     Runs subcomputation silently ┐
doSomethingSpecialSilently = local silent doSomethingSpecial   ◁──────────┘
```

This is not something that can be easily done with the Singleton pattern approach!

RUNNING A READER COMPUTATION

Note the general idea. We've defined a computation. To get its results, we have to run it. We work at these two stages with every monad, either explicitly or implicitly. Most monads provide explicit runners, which are functions that take a computation as an argument and return its results.

The only way to run the `Reader` computation is via the `runReader` function, as shown next:

```
runReader :: Reader r a -> r -> a
```

It takes a computation itself (of the `Reader r a` type) and a configuration value (of the r type) and returns a result of a computation (of the a type). We can use this function as follows:

```
main :: IO ()
main = do
  config <- getConfiguration                      ┌ Runs the Reader
  let result = runReader work config    ◁──┘      │ computation
  print result
```

The `Control.Monad.Reader` module provides the following two other functions to work with `Reader` computations:

```
mapReader :: (a -> b) -> Reader r a -> Reader r b
withReader :: (r' -> r) -> Reader r a -> Reader r' a
```

The `mapReader` function can be used to transform a result of the given computation purely (with the function of type `a -> b`). The `withReader` function allows modifying the type of configuration. Compare this function with the `local` function: the latter allows changing a configuration but not its type. Both the `mapReader` and `withReader` functions allow us to modify the given computation in different ways: by changing either a result or a configuration, respectively. Modified computations should be run by `runReader` anyway.

5.1.3   *Writing logs via Writer*

Imagine the opposite problem: instead of reading a configuration, as in the previous subsection, we want to write a log of what is going on during the computation. We may want to log either every step or some important moments or errors. The `MonadWriter` type class from `Control.Monad.Writer` defines this functionality as follows:

```
class (Monoid w, Monad m) => MonadWriter w m | m -> w where
    writer :: (a, w) -> m a
    tell :: w -> m ()
    listen :: m a -> m (a, w)
    pass :: m (a, w -> w) -> m a

listens :: MonadWriter w m => (w -> b) -> m a -> m (a, b)
censor :: MonadWriter w m => (w -> w) -> m a -> m a
```

`MonadWriter` is parameterized by the `w` type of the log. Note that this type is constrained by `Monoid w`; thus, appending to a log is a monoid operation. Again note the `| m -> w` part of the type class head: `Writer w` is a monad `m` and as such uniquely determines type `w`. (Once again, this is done with the `FunctionalDependencies` GHC extension.)

The `Writer` monad implements this interface. From the type signatures, we can see that a computation in the `Writer` monad is described by a pair of an actual result and an accumulated log `(a, w)`. By providing such a pair, we can construct a computation using the `writer` function or extract it from a computation with the `listen` function. We can also construct a computation resulting in `()` with the specified log `w` with the `tell` function. It is often followed by the `>>` operator because we are not interested in its result. Other functions such as `pass`, `listens`, and `censor` provide utilities for postprocessing log manipulation.

Binding computations in the `Writer` monad with the `>>=` operator is implemented as appending logs to each other. For example, if we have two computations, `tell [1]` and `tell [2]`, then the resulting log is `[1,2]`.

Just as in the case of the `Reader` monad, we have functions to run a `Writer` computation, as shown here:

```
runWriter :: Writer w a -> (a, w)
execWriter :: Writer w a -> w
```

The first function returns both a result and an accumulated log. The second one returns a log exclusively. We can use it when a result is trivial (say, `()`).

It is also possible to map results of a computation with the `mapWriter` function, as shown next:

```
mapWriter :: ((a, w) -> (b, w')) -> Writer w a -> Writer w' b
```

This function modifies a `Writer` computation by converting both a result and a log to other types.

Note the following points in this short `Writer` monad description:

- We have its functionality (what we can do inside a computation) as the `Monad-Writer`.
- What makes it a monad (appending logs from the consequent computation steps) is an implementation of `>>=`.
- How to run and transform the computation as a whole.

In fact, any particular monad can be described by these three points.

Let's look at two simple examples where the `Writer` monad is quite handy. Suppose we have a text file with the following colon-delimited content:

```
Pen:Bob
Pencil:Alice
Book:Bob
```

Every line contains two elements: an item and its owner. We want to transform this file into a series of SQL queries for inserting all the data into the database, as follows:

```
INSERT INTO items VALUES('Pen','Bob');
INSERT INTO items VALUES('Pencil','Alice');
INSERT INTO items VALUES('Book','Bob');
```

Unfortunately, some file lines may be broken. They may either contain more colon-delimited components or have none at all, as follows:

```
Glass:Mary:10
Bottle
```

Such lines should not be converted to SQL queries and instead should be reported. We can apply the `Writer` monad as follows:

- We convert every correct line to SQL.
- We append an error message to a log for every incorrect line.

We can inspect the reported error messages later. Figure 5.1 demonstrates the overall task.

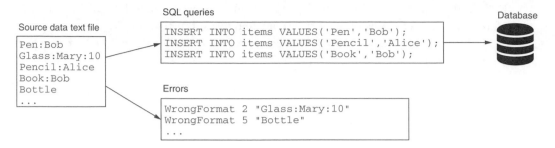

Figure 5.1 **Generating SQL queries from a text data file**

EXAMPLE: TRANSFORMING A DATA FILE INTO SQL

⬜ ch05/genSQL.hs

⚡ *genSQL*

☞ We can log errors during the computation with the `Writer` monad.

Let's declare the following types:

```
type SQL = Text

data ErrorMsg = WrongFormat Int Text
  deriving Show
```

We include a line number and the wrong line itself to an error message.

Our first goal is to implement the following `Writer` computation:

```
genSQL :: Text -> Writer [ErrorMsg] SQL
```

The `genSQL` function takes text and transforms it into SQL, logging into a list of errors as it goes.

Suppose we have the following SQL query generator:

```
genInsert s1 s2 =
  "INSERT INTO items VALUES ('" <> s1 <> "','" <> s2 <> "');\n"
```

> **WARNING** Never construct SQL queries by concatenation as we did in `gen-Insert` because it is highly insecure.

To process one line of the input data accompanied with its number, we check whether it contains exactly two components and construct SQL to report an error otherwise. We can do that as follows:

```
processLine :: (Int, Text) -> Writer [ErrorMsg] SQL
processLine (_, T.splitOn ":" -> [s1, s2]) = pure $ genInsert s1 s2
processLine (i, s) = tell [WrongFormat i s] >> pure ""
```

If the given text line has exactly two components, we return a SQL query. Otherwise, we report an error with `tell` and return an empty result. Note that the `""` literal should be interpreted as a `Text` value. We have to enable the `OverloadedStrings` GHC extension to make that happen.

The ViewPatterns GHC extension

Note the pattern matching expression in the following `processLine` function:

```
(_, T.splitOn ":" -> [s1, s2])
```

It's a pair. We ignore the first component, a line number. The question is what's going on with the second one that should match some `Text` value. The `ViewPatterns` GHC extension allows calling a function on the argument first and then matching a result. Thus, we call `T.splitOn ":"` on the given text, receive a resulting `[Text]` list, and then match on that. If that match fails, the whole pattern match fails, and we continue with the next line of the definition.

Now let's process data as a whole. We take some `Text`, split it into lines, process every line collecting SQL queries and a log of errors, and then combine all the SQL queries into one large SQL query, as shown next:

```
genSQL :: Text -> Writer [ErrorMsg] SQL
genSQL txt = T.concat <$> traverse processLine (zip [1..] $ T.lines txt)
```

One-liners like this one can be very hard to read unless we are used to monadic computations. We have two levels here—first, the following regular computation:

- Splitting text into lines
- Checking every line
- Transforming correct lines into SQL queries
- Concatenating all the SQL queries

Second, we have the following error-reporting infrastructure:

- Reporting an error
- Appending errors from all the computation steps

The second level besides reporting with `tell` is implemented by `traverse` and the `Writer` monad `>>=` machinery. As usual, it is instructive to follow the types to understand what's going on here, as shown next (remember that `SQL = Text`):

```
zip [1..] $ T.lines txt :: [(Int, Text)]          Enumerated input lines
processOneLine :: (Int, Text) -> Writer [ErrorMsg] Text     One-line processor
T.concat :: [Text] -> Text                         Text concatenation
```

We also use the next two generic functions:

```
traverse :: (Traversable t, Applicative f) => (a -> f b) -> t a -> f (t b)
(<$>) :: Functor f => (a -> b) -> f a -> f b
```

We work in the following contexts:

```
Applicative f, Functor f ~ Writer [ErrorMsg]
Traversable t ~ [ ]
```

Remember, `Writer w` is a `Monad`; thus, it is both an `Applicative` and a `Functor`. In these contexts, we can concretize types as follows:

```
traverse :: ((Int, Text) -> Writer [ErrorMsg] Text)
            -> [(Int, Text)]
            -> Writer [ErrorMsg] [Text]
(<$>) :: ([Text] -> Text)
         -> Writer [ErrorMsg] [Text]
         -> Writer [ErrorMsg] Text
```

Now we are ready to compute types of subexpressions, as shown next:

```
traverse processOneLine (zip [1..] $ T.lines txt) :: Writer [ErrorMsg] [Text]

T.concat <$> traverse processOneLine (zip [1..] $ T.lines txt)
        :: Writer [ErrorMsg] Text
```

We finally arrive at a `Text` value with all the SQL queries and a list of all the errors. Once a computation is defined, let's run it. We use the following test data:

```
testData = "Pen:Bob\nGlass:Mary:10\nPencil:Alice\nBook:Bob\nBottle"
```

We are interested in both the resulting SQL and the errors, so we go with `runWriter`, as shown here:

```
testGenSQL = do
  let (sql, errors) = runWriter (genSQL testData)      ◁──┐ Runs the Writer
  TIO.putStrLn "SQL:"                                      │ computation
  TIO.putStr sql
  TIO.putStrLn "Errors:"
  traverse_ print errors      ◁────── Prints all the errors
```

As a result, we get the following output:

```
ghci> testGenSQL
SQL:
INSERT INTO items VALUES ('Pen','Bob');
INSERT INTO items VALUES ('Pencil','Alice');
INSERT INTO items VALUES ('Book','Bob');
Errors:
WrongFormat 2 "Glass:Mary:10"
WrongFormat 5 "Bottle"
```

Not bad. We could now execute the SQL queries to insert the values into a database and provide correct data for lines 2 and 5.

EXAMPLE: LOGGING STEPS IN THE GREATEST-COMMON-DIVISOR COMPUTATION

For another `Writer` example, we'll look at the high school greatest-common-divisor algorithm. The following shows how it can be implemented in Haskell:

```
gcd' :: Integral a => a -> a -> a
gcd' a 0 = a
gcd' a b = gcd b (a `mod` b)
```

EXAMPLE: COMPUTING THE GREATEST COMMON DIVISOR IN A MONADIC CONTEXT

🗋 ch05/gcd.hs

⚡ *gcd*

☞ Turning a regular computation into a monadic one

☞ A computation with steps logged via the `Writer` monad

Suppose we are interested in the following information:

- Which pairs of numbers are we getting along the way?
- How many recursive calls are required in order to compute the greatest common divisor?

Before answering these questions, let's abstract a bit. We want to follow all the steps of the computation and keep some information from every step. We already know that `Writer` implements the latter. What is responsible for the former, then? Well, that is a description of a monadic computation in general: we follow steps of a sequential computation.

With this in mind, let's implement a generic monadic version of the GCD computation as follows:

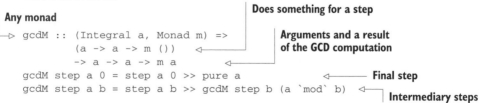

For example, we can use the next generic implementation to print all the steps in the `IO` monad:

```
ghci> gcdM (\a b -> print (a, b)) 27 36
(27,36)
(36,27)
(27,9)
(9,0)
9
```

We could even write `curry print` instead of the lambda here. This answers our first question, though it's better to get these pairs as a list. Why not write pairs to a log as a step? We fix a `Monad` and use `tell` to store values as follows:

```
gcd_logSteps :: Integral a => a -> a -> Writer [(a, a)] a
gcd_logSteps = gcdM (\a b -> tell [(a, b)])
```

Do you remember that we have two runners for `Writer`? Let's look at them in action here:

```
ghci> runWriter (gcd_logSteps 27 36)
(9,[(27,36),(36,27),(27,9),(9,0)])
ghci> execWriter (gcd_logSteps 27 36)
[(27,36),(36,27),(27,9),(9,0)]
```

To answer the second question, we could take the `Sum` type as a log. It's a numeric monoid (we discussed it in chapter 2). If we report `Sum 1` for every step, the whole log accumulates the number of steps using addition as a monoid operation. Let's go for it:

```
gcd_countSteps :: Integral a => a -> a -> Writer (Sum Int) a
gcd_countSteps = gcdM (\_ _ -> tell $ Sum 1)
```

It works as expected, although the answer, shown next, is quite hairy:

```
ghci> runWriter (gcd_countSteps 27 36)
(9,Sum {getSum = 4})
```

If we are interested in the number of steps, we could use `execWriter` and apply the `getSum` field selector to the result as follows:

```
ghci> getSum $ execWriter (gcd_countSteps 27 36)
4
```

Interestingly, `gcd_countSteps` can be implemented using `gcd_logSteps` and the `mapWriter` function. We could keep a result unmodified and change a log, replacing every pair of numbers with (`Sum 1`) or, more generally, every list of pairs with its length wrapped in the `Sum` value constructor as follows:

```
gcd_countSteps' a b = mapWriter mapper (gcd_logSteps a b)
  where
    mapper (v, w) = (v, Sum $ length w)
```

This definition can be shortened (although not simplified) to a one-liner as follows:

```
gcd_countSteps'' = (mapWriter (Sum . length <$>) .) . gcd_logSteps
```

Take my word: I am not a big fan of such cryptic definitions as in the case of gcd_countSteps''. Nevertheless, it's a good exercise to decipher it. Here I suggest several steps—following them helps:

- What is the precedence in the subexpression (Sum . length <$>)? Have you spotted an operator section there?
- Find out how Functor for pairs is implemented. I've used <$>, which is a synonym for fmap from Functor. The first argument of mapWriter is a function over (a, w) pairs.
- The gcd_countSteps'' function is implemented in the so-called pointfree style (https://wiki.haskell.org/Pointfree). The general pattern here is f = (g .) . h. There is the following pointful tool found in the pointful package from Hackage for deciphering such expressions:

```
$ pointful "f = (g.) . h"
f x x0 = g (h x x0)
```

NOTE Now I must confess. I've made gcd_countSteps'' with the help of http://pointfree.io (an online tool built on top of the pointfree tool from the pointfree package on Hackage extracted from the #haskell IRC channel Lambdabot, https://wiki.haskell.org/Lambdabot). Use it to astonish your colleagues, but beware of applying such techniques in production.

5.2 *Maintaining state via the State monad*

Now that we can read data from an external source in Reader and write logs in Writer the question is, can we do both at the same time? Or, alternatively, can we mutate state? Surprisingly, the answer is yes, and this is implemented in the State monad defined in Control.Monad.State.

As usual, let's start with its interface as described by the MonadState type class and several auxiliary functions, as shown next:

```
class Monad m => MonadState s m | m -> s where
    get :: m s
    put :: s -> m ()
    state :: (s -> (a, s)) -> m a

modify :: MonadState s m => (s -> s) -> m ()
gets :: MonadState s m => (s -> a) -> m a
```

The s type variable represents a type of state. It is uniquely determined by the monad m as specified by the | m -> s part. For example State Integer is a concrete monad with a state of type Integer. The get method resembles ask from Reader—it gives access to the current state. The gets function is the counterpart to asks. The put method is analogous to tell—it sets the current state. The state method combines both reader and writer functionalities. Let's compare these three functions as follows:

```
reader :: MonadReader r m => (r -> a) -> m a
writer :: MonadWriter w m => (a, w) -> m a
state :: MonadState s m => (s -> (a, s)) -> m a
```

All of them construct a computation in the corresponding `Monad` from its internal representation (a function, a pair, and a function returning a pair, respectively).

`State` as a `Monad` is responsible for keeping and mutating the state as requested by the user; this is a job for the >>= method implementation. Consequently, the combination of two computations `put 42` and `get` in this particular order (as in `put 42 >> get`; remember that >> is normally implemented via >>=) should reveal 42 as a result of the combined computation.

To work with the computation itself, we can use the following functions (computation runners and modifiers):

```
runState  :: State s a -> s -> (a, s)
execState :: State s a -> s -> s
evalState :: State s a -> s -> a

mapState  :: ((a, s) -> (b, s)) -> State s a -> State s b
withState :: (s -> s) -> State s a -> State s a
```

5.2.1 *Basic examples with the State monad*

Let's do something trivial with the `State` monad to see how some of these functions can be used. In fact, every simple example can be rewritten without `State` at all, so don't take it too seriously.

STATE FOR ACCUMULATING VALUES

For the first example, we'll sum up a list of whole numbers from 1 to 100 using the most basic approach. We'll use `State` for accumulating sum and are not interested in other results except for the sum itself, so our computation will have the `State Integer ()` type.

EXAMPLE: USING THE STATE MONAD AS AN ACCUMULATOR

  ☐   ch05/sumlist.hs

  ⚡   *sumlist*

  ☞ We keep accumulating values in the `State` monad.

There are three parts of the solution: we need to add a number to an accumulator, we need to traverse the list of numbers to sum them up, and we also need to run the computation. The first part follows:

```
addItem :: Integer -> State Integer ()
addItem n = do
  s <- get
  put (s + n)
```

We can think of the addItem function as an assignment operator += found in some other programming languages. For this part, we could also use the modify function, as shown next. It's even better to use its stricter modify' version to prevent creating too many thunks. We'll discuss the problem of excessive laziness later in this book.

```
addItem' :: Integer -> State Integer ()
addItem' n = modify' (+n)
```

We traverse over the list with the familiar traverse_ function as follows:

```
sumList :: [Integer] -> State Integer ()
sumList xs = traverse_ addItem xs
```

At the end of the traversal, the state value keeps the sum we are interested in. Let's run the next computation asking for the state value:

```
ghci> execState (sumList [1..100]) 0
5050
```

> **NOTE** Clearly, we don't need the State monad to sum up numbers in the list. Moreover, for this particular problem, we don't need lists either. Make sure that you know the story of Carl Friedrich Gauss, who solved the same problem efficiently as an elementary school student in the late 1700s.

RANDOM NUMBERS AND THE STATE MONAD

We discussed random numbers in chapter 2. I mentioned there that it's not very convenient to work with StdGen, which should be updated everytime we get a random number. Interestingly, this idea of updating a generator follows the State monad functionality very closely. Note the type of the uniform function again:

```
uniform :: (RandomGen g, Uniform a) => g -> (a, g)
```

That's precisely the type of an argument of the state function, as shown here:

```
state :: MonadState s m => (s -> (a, s)) -> m a
```

The state uniform computation will both return the generated random value as a result and update the generator (provided that the original generator is kept in the state). Let's see how this idea can be used in the following example.

ANALYZING ROCK-PAPER-SCISSORS

Suppose we want to analyze the game of Rock-Paper-Scissors: who wins more often? Let's organize a series of rounds and check all the results.

EXAMPLE: ANALYZING ROCK-PAPER-SCISSORS

⬚ ch05/weapons.hs

⚡ *weapons*

☞ The State monad is compatible with random-number generators.

☞ Applicative and Monad instances simplify using results of computations in a context.

Our types follow:

```
data Weapon = Rock | Paper | Scissors
  deriving (Show, Bounded, Enum, Eq)

data Winner = First | Second | Draw
  deriving (Show, Eq, Ord)
```

One round gives us a pair of weapons, so we have to check who the winner is, shown next:

```
winner :: (Weapon, Weapon) -> Winner
winner (Paper, Rock) = First
winner (Scissors, Paper) = First
winner (Rock, Scissors) = First
winner (w1, w2)
  | w1 == w2 = Draw
  | otherwise = Second
```

The next goal is to generate a random Weapon. We need instances of the Uniform and UniformRange type classes for that. Here we follow the same approach as in chapter 2:

```
instance UniformRange Weapon where
  uniformRM (lo, hi) rng = do
    res <- uniformRM (fromEnum lo :: Int, fromEnum hi) rng
    pure $ toEnum res

instance Uniform Weapon where
  uniformM rng = uniformRM (minBound, maxBound) rng
```

Everything is ready for generating a random Weapon, shown next:

```
randomWeapon :: State StdGen Weapon
randomWeapon = state uniform
```

Thanks to type inference, the randomWeapon function does exactly what we need: it returns a randomly generated Weapon using StdGen as the state and then updates the generator in the state.

Now we can implement one round of the game as follows and get a pair of weapons:

```
gameRound :: State StdGen (Weapon, Weapon)
gameRound = (,) <$> randomWeapon <*> randomWeapon
```

Note that it is not enough to create a pair like (randomWeapon, randomWeapon) because randomWeapon is a computation with a Weapon value as a result. It is not a Weapon itself. Instead, we use an Applicative instance for State that allows us to write this code quite concisely. We execute both randomWeapon computations and collect their results with (,).

Our plan for the whole game follows:

1 Replicate n game rounds with the winner function applied to every one of them.
2 Run all the computations in a monadic sequence, and collect a list of results.
3 Count the number of different outcomes.

Following is an implementation of the plan that is even shorter when expressed by code:

```
game :: Int -> State StdGen [(Winner, Int)]
game n = counts <$> replicateM n (winner <$> gameRound)
  where
    counts xs = map headLength $ group $ sort xs
    headLength xs@(x:_) = (x, length xs)
```

The replicateM function from Control.Monad has the following type:

```
replicateM :: Applicative m => Int -> m a -> m [a]
```

It is useful for replicating monadic (or, technically, applicative) computations and collecting their results in a list.

The only thing that is missing is the random-number generator from IO. With that, we can finally run the game computation in the State monad and print the results as follows:

```
main = do
  g <- newStdGen
  let r = evalState (game 10) g
  print r
```

Note that the State computation is a pure one, so we can do it in a let expression. Now let's run it several times and see what's going on:

```
ghci> :main
[(First,6),(Second,1),(Draw,3)]
ghci> :main
[(Second,4),(Draw,6)]
ghci> :main
[(First,5),(Second,3),(Draw,2)]
ghci> :main
[(First,4),(Second,4),(Draw,2)]
ghci> :main
[(First,6),(Draw,4)]
```

```
ghci> :main
[(First,6),(Second,4)]
ghci> :main
[(First,3),(Second,4),(Draw,3)]
```

If we run it sufficiently many times, there should be a case with only one element in the resulting list. Check whether you are lucky enough to get it quickly. That's not me, unfortunately.

5.2.2 *Parsing arithmetic expressions with State*

Recall converting arithmetic expressions to text form in chapter 2. We've defined the Expr data type as follows:

```
data Expr a = Lit a | Add (Expr a) (Expr a) | Mult (Expr a) (Expr a)
```

We also implemented the TextShow instance for it, resulting in the following pretty printing:

```
ghci> showt $ Mult (Add (Lit 2) (Mult (Lit 3) (Lit 3))) (Lit 5)
"(2+3*3)*5"
```

Now we do the opposite. We implement an algorithm for transforming a regular text representation of arithmetic expressions (in the so-called infix notation) into Expr Integer values. Even if it may sound simple, this is a quite ambitious goal. It's quite difficult to come up with a good solution on our own. Thankfully, it is a well-known and quite popular problem in computer science, so we just borrow a solution and use stateful computations in it extensively!

> **Warning**
>
> Several Manning reviewers were very unhappy about this section. They stated that it's a shame to implement a heavily stateful, extremely boring imperative algorithm to solve this problem. They also suggested using parser combinators, a beautiful, lightweight, purely functional approach. I'm fully content with their indignation. They are absolutely right. Please, skip this section if you agree with them.
>
> My only excuse for retaining this section in the book is that classic CS algorithms are something that we should be able to implement in any programming language. Look, the implementation is still much nicer than in C. Haskell is the best imperative programming language in this part of the galaxy.

DIJKSTRA'S SHUNTING-YARD ALGORITHM

We'll apply the Edsger Dijkstra's shunting-yard algorithm (https://en.wikipedia.org/wiki/Shunting-yard_algorithm). Wikipedia's version of this algorithm solves a slightly different problem, namely, transforming infix notation into reverse Polish notation, or postfix notation. We'll discuss it in the next chapter. Nevertheless, the same algorithm can be easily adapted to build an abstract syntax tree in the form of the Expr a data type.

Let's assume that an expression in infix notation is given as a sequence of tokens in reverse order. Every number, math operator symbol, or parenthesis is a token. Suppose also that we have two mutable data structures, namely, stack and output.

Tokens in reverse order:

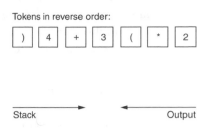

Figure 5.2 **Shunting-yard algorithm: the initial situation**

For example, when given `"2*(3+4)"`String, we split it into tokens and reverse their order, thus arriving at the situation in figure 5.2.

According to the slightly modified shunting-yard algorithm from Wikipedia, we now proceed as follows:

- **while** there are tokens to be read:
  - read a token.
  - **if** the token is `")"`, then:
    - push it onto the stack.
  - **if** the token is `"("`, then:
    - **while** the operator at the top of the stack is not `")"`:
      - ❖ pop the operator from the stack onto the output.
    - pop `")"` from the stack.
    - *if the stack runs out without finding* `")"`, *then there are mismatched parentheses.*
  - **if** the token is an operator, then:
    - **while** (there is an operator at the top of the stack with equal or greater precedence) **and** (the operator at the top of the stack is not `")"`):
      - ❖ pop operator from the stack onto the output.
    - push it onto the stack.
  - **if** the token is a number, then:
    - push it to the output.
- **if** there are no more tokens to read, then:
  - **while** there are still operator tokens on the stack:
    - *if the operator token on the top of the stack is a parenthesis, then there are mismatched parentheses.*
    - pop the operator from the operator stack onto the output.
- exit.

This imperative algorithm is composed of the following two stages:

- Reading and processing tokens (the **while** loop with the huge body)
- Transferring the rest of the operator tokens from the stack to an output (the smaller **while** loop)

Well, neither imperativity nor a mutable state are problems for us. We can run computations in the State monad to have a mutable stack and a mutable output. We can also turn all those awful while loops into perfect recursive functions.

We can build a value of Expr Integer type while we send elements to the output as follows:

- Every number n becomes Lit n.
- Every + operator becomes an Add data constructor with arguments built from the two elements that were sent to the output previously.
- Every * operator becomes a Mult data constructor with arguments built from the two elements that were sent to the output previously.

In case we are given a correct expression, we expect getting one fully constructed value of type Expr Integer as a result.

Before attempting to implement this algorithm, let's follow the steps in an easy example. We start with the situation in figure 5.2. Then we read tokens from left to right and process them as specified by the algorithm as follows:

1. Token ")" is pushed onto the stack.
2. Token "4" as a number is sent to the output.
3. Token "+" is pushed onto the stack (there are no operators at the top of the stack prior to pushing this one).
4. Token "3" as a number is sent to the output.
5. Token "(" causes all the operators from the stack until ")" to be popped onto the output—it's just a "+" in our case; ")" itself is popped from the stack afterward.
6. Token "*" is pushed onto the stack (there are no operators at the top of the stack prior to pushing this one).
7. Token "2" as a number is sent to the output.

The first stage is over: all tokens have been read. For the second stage:

8. "*" from the top of the stack is sent to the output.

Now we are done observing the resulting Mult (Lit 2) (Add (Lit 3) (Lit 4)) in the output. All these steps are illustrated in figure 5.3.

Now we are ready to implement this algorithm in Haskell, exploiting the State monad for maintaining both the stack and the output.

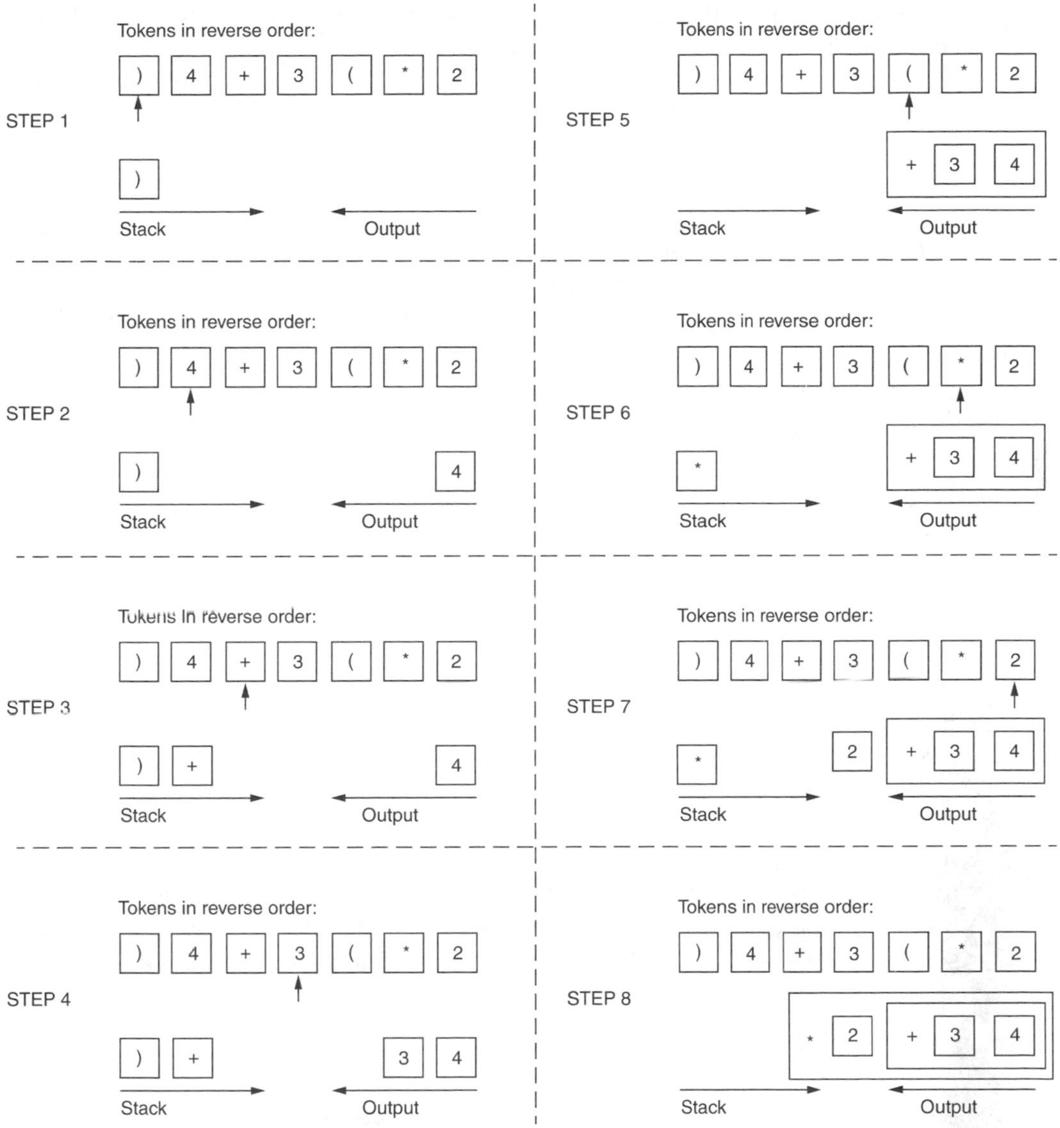

Figure 5.3 Shunting-yard algorithm: all the steps

IMPLEMENTING AN IMPERATIVE ALGORITHM WITH MUTABLE STATE

EXAMPLE: AN IMPLEMENTATION OF THE DIJKSTRA'S SHUNTING-YARD ALGORITHM

◻ expr/ShuntingYard.hs

⚡ *shunting-yard*

☞ The State monad simplifies implementing imperative algorithms with mutable state.

As usual, we start with types. We need them for tokens, stack, output, and state, as shown next:

```
type Token = String
type Stack = [Token]
type Output = [Expr Integer]
type SYState = (Stack, Output)
```

The `Stack` is simply a list of `Token` values, but the `Output` is more sophisticated. We represent it as a list of expressions corresponding to the components of the final expression. Every token sent to the output modifies these components. We'll discuss the details shortly.

We have to implement the following several operations over `Stack`:

- Check whether the stack is empty.
- Look at the top of the stack.
- Pop an element off the stack.
- Push an element onto the stack.

All these operations should be executed in the `State SYState` monad operating over `Stack` without interfering with an `Output`. We start with `isEmpty`, as shown next:

```
isEmpty :: State SYState Bool
isEmpty = null <$> gets fst

notEmpty :: State SYState Bool
notEmpty = not <$> isEmpty
```

In `isEmpty`, we get a `Stack`, which is the first component of `SYState` (we use the `gets` function to extract specific state components) and then turn it into a `Bool` via the functorial operation over the `State` monad. The type of `gets fst` is `State SYState Stack`, where `Stack` is a result of computations within a monad, so it's perfectly fine to apply `null` to it.

Looking at the top of the `Stack` is quite similar, as shown next:

```
top :: State SYState Token
top = gets (head . fst) -- let it crash on empty stack
```

Note that we are not bothering to check for errors; we'll come to that in a later chapter on error handling. For now I assume that everything is gonna be okay!

The following are the two versions of `pop`: one returning the element from the top, and another discarding it (here we follow a tradition of adding the suffix _ to the discarding version):

```
pop :: State SYState Token
pop = do
  (s, es) <- get
  put (tail s, es) -- let it crash on empty stack
```

```
  pure (head s)

pop_ :: State SYState ()   -- let it crash on empty stack
pop_ = modify (\(s, es) -> (tail s, es))
```

I use the do notation in pop and the modify function in pop_. In pop, we have to get a value, change state, and then return a value. The do blocks are more convenient for the computations that have an additional step between acquiring data and returning it to a context. In pop_, we don't return anything, so modify is enough. Note that we left Output as it is.

Finally, we are ready to implement push as follows:

```
push :: Token -> State SYState ()
push t = modify (\(s, es) -> (t : s, es))
```

Let's do one more thing for Stack processing. In the algorithm, we met several times a construction of the following form:

```
while the operator at the top of the stack <satisfies some predicate>:
  <body>
```

Clearly we should check Stack emptiness before every iteration. And what is an iteration (or <body>) here? Well, it's a computation in the State SYState monad. Why not make it an argument? Here we are:

```
whileNotEmptyAnd :: (Token -> Bool) -> State SYState () -> State SYState ()
whileNotEmptyAnd predicate m = go
  where
    go = do
      b1 <- notEmpty
      when b1 $ do
        b2 <- predicate <$> top
        when b2 (m >> go)
```

This is the nastiest function in the whole example. It recursively checks whether some token is on the stack and, if so, checks for a predicate over the top of the stack; executes m if it is satisfied; and goes for another recursive step. If you don't like it, you can reimplement something like this with the convenient functions whileM and andM (or their modifications) from the monad-loops package (but please don't look at how they are implemented themselves!). Argument m can do whatever it wants with the SYState, and thanks to the monadic machinery, everything will be taken into account on the next iteration.

Now let's move to building an expression in Output. The algorithm transfers tokens to the Output in such an order that leaves in the tree Expr a are processed prior to non-leaf nodes. If we process a number, then it becomes a literal Lit a in the Output. If we process an operator token, then we've built its leaves already, so we just take them from the Output and build a new component with Add e1 e2 or Mult e1 e2, depending on the particular operator token. The newly built component is then sent to the Output. This logic is encoded in the output function as follows:

```
output :: Token -> State SYState ()
output t = modify (builder t <$>)
  where
    builder "+" (e1 : e2 : es) = Add e1 e2 : es
    builder "*" (e1 : e2 : es) = Mult e1 e2 : es
    builder n es = Lit (read n) : es -- let it crash on not a number
```

Note the argument of the modify function: here we exploit the Functor instance for pairs, which processes the second component of a pair (an Output in this case). Interested readers may look at the bifunctors package and immediately see how it is possible to simplify an implementation of the functions over Stack (the first component of a SYState pair) in the same spirit.

The algorithm mentions operator tokens and their precedence. We need to do the following:

- Check whether the token is an operator token
- Find out what the precedence is of the given operator
- Compare precedences

Let's implement the following corresponding functions:

```
isOp "+" = True
isOp "*" = True
isOp _ = False

precedence "+" = 1
precedence "*" = 2
precedence _ = 0

t1 `precGTE` t2 = precedence t1 >= precedence t2
```

The precedence of "*" is greater than that of "+". The precedence of all the other tokens except for operators is zero. (This allows stopping conveniently on parentheses—try to find the corresponding condition in the algorithm.)

Now everything is ready for the function that implements the shunting-yard algorithm. Reading this function in parallel with the algorithm reveals that it is an almost exact copy of the algorithm description, as shown next:

```
convertToExpr :: String -> Expr Integer
convertToExpr str = head $ snd $ execState shuntingYard ([], [])
  where
    tokens = reverse $ tokenize str

    shuntingYard = traverse_ processToken tokens >> transferRest

    processToken ")" = push ")"
    processToken "(" = transferWhile (/= ")") >> pop_
```

```
processToken t
  | isOp t = transferWhile (`precGTE` t) >> push t
  | otherwise = output t -- number

transfer = pop >>= output
transferWhile predicate = whileNotEmptyAnd predicate transfer
transferRest = transferWhile (const True)

tokenize = groupBy (\a b -> isDigit a && isDigit b)
         . filter (not . isSpace)
```

We start with an initial state of an empty `Stack` and an empty `Output` and end up by extracting the resulting expression from the `Output`.

The two processing stages in `shuntingYard` are combined with `>>`. In the first stage, we traverse the reverse sequence of tokens from the given `String`. I use `traverse_` here because our computations don't produce results except for `()`; we are interested only in maintaining the state (`traverse_` ignores results of sequential steps).

The `processToken` function is the beautiful heart of our implementation extracted from the ugly body of an awful `while` loop in the original algorithm. No more imperative garbage!

While processing tokens, we have to transfer them into the `Output`. Look how transferring one token is implemented: it's as simple as `pop >>= output`. A token extracted from the `Stack` becomes an argument to the `output` function thanks to monadic bind (`>>=`). With this function, `transfer`, and `Stack` processing machinery implemented in `whileNotEmptyAnd`, it is easy to implement all the `while` loops for transferring tokens.

In the second stage, `transferRest`, we transfer all the tokens left on the `Stack` after processing the string tokens onto the `Output`. (Look at the constant predicate in the implementation of `transferRest`.)

Check out our `tokenize` function, too: it's simple but powerful thanks to the higher-order functions used in its implementation. Two examples of how `convertToExpr` function works follow:

```
ghci> convertToExpr "2+3"
Add (Lit 2) (Lit 3)
ghci> convertToExpr "(2+3) * (3+2)"
Mult (Add (Lit 2) (Lit 3)) (Add (Lit 3) (Lit 2))
```

The /expr/prefix-postfix.hs file implements the conversion of arithmetic expressions to the prefix and postfix notations that is an original goal of the shunting-yard algorithm.

We don't need to stop in fear, facing an imperative algorithm that exploits mutability. We are now equipped with the `State` monad. It helps us to represent any mutable state in our programs. So, we don't have to invent our own purely functional stateless algorithms because this can be quite hard to accomplish sometimes.

5.2.3   *RWS monad to rule them all: The game of dice*

The last monad in this section that I am going to talk about is the `RWS` monad. Its name is short for `ReaderWriterState`. This monad combines all the functionality of the three monads we've discussed previously by allowing the following:

- Accessing the read-only configuration via `ask` and other functions defined by the `MonadReader` type class.
- Writing to a log with `tell` and others from the `MonadWriter`.
- Maintaining state with `get`, `put`, and so on from the `MonadState`.

To use this monad, we need to import `Control.Monad.RWS`. This module provides a monadic type `RWS r w s`, where r refers to the configuration, w to the log, and s to the state, respectively. Remember, we also need to specify another type for the result of the computations. The following three functions run computations inside the `RWS` monad:

```
runRWS  :: RWS r w s a -> r -> s -> (a, s, w)
evalRWS :: RWS r w s a -> r -> s -> (a, w)
execRWS :: RWS r w s a -> r -> s -> (s, w)
```

Let's implement a dice game, quite a strange one, without actual gaming but with a lot of dice rolling.

EXAMPLE: USING READING, WRITING, AND MUTABILITY IN THE RWS MONAD

🗋   ch05/dicegame.hs

⚡   *dicegame*

☞ Some monads combine the effects of other monads.

We represent rolling dice as a computation in the `RWS` monad with the components responsible for the following:

- The `Reader` component keeps dice bounds. Although most die have faces enumerated from 1 to 6, there are other kinds of dice.
- The `Writer` component logs all dice rolled during the whole computation. We can use the resulting log to develop our own dice game strategy for our next vacation in Vegas.
- The `State` component keeps and updates the random-number generator. We already know that it suits this task very well.

We'll use `replicateM` here for rolling a die several times; it will combine all the effects for us.

Our types follow:

```
type Dice = Int
type DiceGame = RWS
                (Int, Int) -- Reader (dice bounds)
                [Dice]     -- Writer (a history of rolls)
                StdGen     -- State (random generator)
```

Note that `DiceGame` is a monadic type. It requires one more result type of computation to become the type of a particular computation.

To roll a die, we need to consult a configuration with `ask` to get the die bounds, then `get` a generator, call the pure `uniformR` function, update the generator with a new value, log the generated random number, and return it as a result of the computation, as shown next:

```
dice :: DiceGame Dice
dice = do
  bs <- ask
  g <- get
  let (r, g') = uniformR bs g
  put g'
  tell [r]
  pure r
```

Surely, we can make it simpler. Note the type of `uniformR` again:

```
uniformR :: (RandomGen g, UniformRange a) => (a, a) -> g -> (a, g)
```

Let's go further and infer the type of `uniformR bs` in our context as follows:

```
uniformR bs :: StdGen -> (Dice, StdGen)
```

This is the exact type of an argument of the `state` function for manipulating state. Whenever our state is `StdGen`, we can construct a stateful computation without doing `get` and `put` explicitly. Now we can write the revised version of the `dice` function as follows:

```
dice = do
  bs <- ask
  r <- state (uniformR bs)
  tell [r]
  pure r
```

Up to this point, the convenience we get (if any) doesn't pay for the troubles. The primitive monadic actions such as `dice` are often quite imperative in their implementations. We could also implement it as a one-liner, as shown next:

```
dice = ask >>= state . uniformR >>= \r -> tell [r] >> pure r
```

However, I'd never recommend writing it this way.

How would you write a function for rolling a die twice and returning a pair? Well, my version follows:

```
doubleDice :: DiceGame (Dice, Dice)
doubleDice = (,) <$> dice <*> dice
```

An `Applicative` at work! Undoubtedly, the bounds are correct and both rolls are logged. What about rolling a die n times? No problem:

```
dices :: Int -> DiceGame [Dice]
dices n = replicateM n dice
```

Again, all dice are rolled with correct bounds and are stored in a log (in addition to everything that was logged previously).

Remember, I warned you this is an awkward game. Well, here it is:

```
diceGame :: DiceGame (Dice, Dice)
diceGame = dice >> dices 5 >> replicateM 2 (dices 3)
              >> dices 10 >> doubleDice
```

Awkward and exciting, isn't it? Let's run it. We should get a random-number generator, initialize the state with it, and provide die bounds (say, traditional 1 to 6). Because we are not interested in the final state, I use `evalRWS`, which omits the state but returns the result (the pair of dice) accompanied with a log (of all 24 dice rolled!), as shown here:

```
main = newStdGen >>= print . evalRWS diceGame (1, 6)
```

Several test runs follow (I use the `:main` GHCi command to run this program):

```
ghci> :main
((2,5),[3,5,6,6,1,3,1,4,2,5,1,6,3,1,5,4,4,3,5,5,3,6,2,5])
ghci> :main
((4,2),[5,5,5,6,2,3,1,3,4,2,4,3,1,1,2,2,4,2,4,4,5,1,4,2])
ghci> :main
((1,4),[6,4,4,6,3,1,3,5,1,5,3,4,2,2,4,2,6,4,5,5,1,1,1,4])
```

Note that the returned pair is always included at the very end of the log along with every other dice ever rolled in the test run.

5.3   *Other approaches to mutability*

The `State` monad is not the only way to achieve mutability in Haskell. In fact, in `State`, there is no mutability; we mimic it by passing arguments inside the internal implementation. As a result we get a *pure* computation that *looks like* mutability. In Haskell, it is also possible to exploit real mutability by changing values in referenced memory cells. We can do it in `IO`, although we are not forced to do that impurely. For example, the `ST` monad is able to convert mutable operations over references to pure computations. Let's see how it works in the rest of this chapter.

5.3.1   *Mutable references in the IO monad*

Imagine we need to count the total number of files in the given directories, including the files in their subdirectories. To accomplish that, we need to arrange a counter and increment it for every file met while traversing the directory hierarchy. Even though this approach is rather imperative, we can still do it in Haskell by exploiting some mutability to implement the counter.

Let's talk about the Data.IORef, which provides mutable references in IO first, and then get back to counting files.

THE DATA.IOREF MODULE

The Data.IORef module from the base package provides a rather simple interface for mutable references in the IO monad. Every reference is a value of the IORef a data type, where a refers to the type of a mutable value itself. First, we need to create a reference with the function newIORef and an initial value as follows:

```
newIORef :: a -> IO (IORef a)
```

Then, we are able to read, write, or modify the referenced value by providing a pure function with the following interface:

```
readIORef :: IORef a -> IO a
writeIORef :: IORef a -> a -> IO ()
modifyIORef :: IORef a -> (a -> a) -> IO ()
modifyIORef' :: IORef a -> (a -> a) -> IO ()
```

Note the final function modifyIORef': traditionally in Haskell, the suffix ' is used to label strict versions of a function, one which evaluates a value up to weak head normal form. We'll talk more about these issues in chapter 9. For now, it's sufficient to know that we'd almost always want to use the strict version modifyIORef' whenever we have simple modifier functions and call this operation often.

These functions are not atomic in the sense that their use in concurrent programs could lead to race conditions. The Data.IORef module provides atomic* versions of them that are more suitable for a concurrent setting.

The following is a simple example of how to use mutable references. A user inputs integer numbers one by one and then gets their sum. I have no doubt that everyone has written such a program while learning an imperative programming language.

EXAMPLE: ACCUMULATING INTEGERS WITH IOREF

☐ ch05/ioref.hs

⚡ *ioref*

☞ We can write imperative programs with mutable variables in Haskell.

The full source code for this example is presented in the following code:

```
import Data.IORef
import Text.Read (readMaybe)

sumNumbers :: IO Int
```

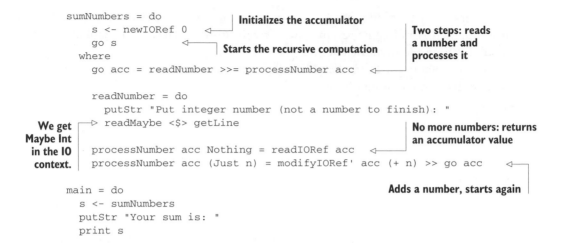

```
sumNumbers = do                    Initializes the accumulator
    s <- newIORef 0                                        Two steps: reads
    go s              Starts the recursive computation      a number and
  where                                                     processes it
    go acc = readNumber >>= processNumber acc

    readNumber = do
      putStr "Put integer number (not a number to finish): "
      readMaybe <$> getLine                         No more numbers: returns
                                                    an accumulator value
    processNumber acc Nothing = readIORef acc
    processNumber acc (Just n) = modifyIORef' acc (+ n) >> go acc

main = do                          Adds a number, starts again
  s <- sumNumbers
  putStr "Your sum is: "
  print s
```

We get Maybe Int in the IO context.

The `sumNumbers` function proceeds as follows:

- We create a reference `s` for the sum of numbers and initialize it with zero.
- We run a recursive process `go`, which reads the number from the user and updates the sum with `modifyIORef'`.
- After finishing a recursive process, we read a value from a reference and return it as a result of a computation in the `IO` monad.

I recommend experimenting with the source code of this example and implementing other basic algorithms that rely on mutability.

IMPLEMENTING DIRECTORY TRAVERSAL WITH COUNTING

Now let's go back to the original task of counting the total number of files in the sub-directories. Apart from the mutable counter, we also need to read lists of files and sub-directories in a given directory. This is definitely a job for the `IO` monad. We could import the `System.Directory` module from the `directory` package that provides various utility functions for working with the file system. Instead, I introduce the `extra` package.

The extra package as a collection of useful utilities

The `extra` package by Neil Mitchell is somewhat exceptional among other packages on Hackage. Instead of providing some new functionality in a specific area, it adds convenient functions to many modules of the most ubiquitous packages, such as `base`, `time`, `directory`, and `filepath`. Whenever we traverse some module documentation, struggling to find the function we need, and find something that is *almost* suitable, chances are we could get precisely what we need in the `extra` package (see it at https://hackage.haskell.org/package/extra).

> For example, it provides the `Data.List.Extra` module, which gracefully reexports all of the `Data.List` functions so that we don't have to import both and extends it with many convenient functions, such as `disjoint` for checking whether two lists are disjoint or `chunksOf` for splitting a list into chunks of the given size.
>
> The `Control.Monad.Extra` module is also very handy: give it and the other `Extra` modules from the `extra` package a chance.

The following are the imported modules and what we actually need from them to implement counting files in subdirectories:

```
import Data.Foldable (traverse_)
import System.Environment (getArgs)
import System.Directory.Extra (listContents, doesDirectoryExist)
import Control.Monad.Extra (whenM, ifM, zipWithM_)
import Data.IORef (newIORef, modifyIORef', readIORef)
```

The implementation follows:

```
fileCount :: FilePath -> IO Int
fileCount fpath = do
   counter <- newIORef 0
   whenM (doesDirectoryExist fpath) $ go counter fpath
   readIORef counter
 where
   go cnt fp = listContents fp >>= traverse_ (processEntry cnt)
   processEntry cnt fp = ifM (doesDirectoryExist fp) (go cnt fp) (inc cnt)
   inc cnt = modifyIORef' cnt (+ 1)
```

We create a new counter. If the given file path is a directory, we start processing it. Finally, we return a counter value. Note that we return 0 for regular files.

The `listContents` function from `System.Directory.Extra` returns a list of absolute paths to files in the given directory `fp` (and differs from `listDirectory` of the `System.Directory` module because the latter returns a list of relative names unsuitable for processing subdirectories without additional manipulations). The returned list is further traversed with `traverse_` by the `processEntry` helper function, which uses `ifM` for differentiating processing of subdirectories and regular files. The function `ifM` has the following type:

```
ifM :: Monad m => m Bool -> m a -> m a -> m a
```

It checks a monadic condition in the first of its arguments and then executes a monadic action in either the second or third arguments, depending on the condition. If we have a subdirectory here, we start traversing it, and increment the counter otherwise.

Note that I'm using the strict `modifyIORef'` for the counter: incrementing is both frequent and simple, so we definitely don't want to use laziness and build thunks here.

In the `main` function, we read command-line arguments, consider all of them as directories, and process as implemented. Then we print all our findings, mentioning both the directory name and the number of files, as shown next:

```
main = do
    args <- getArgs
    xs <- traverse fileCount args
    zipWithM_ printEntry args xs
  where
    printEntry fp n = putStrLn (show n ++ "\t" ++ fp)
```

Running this program in the hid-examples folder gives me the following:

```
hid-examples $ cabal -v0 run filecount -- ch01 ch02 stockquotes ch05
3       ch01
8       ch02
7       stockquotes
11      ch05
```

It works!

As it is often the case with simple examples, we don't have to work so hard. The `System.Directory.Extra` module provides the `listFilesRecursive` function, which traverses subdirectories for us. A solution that uses it follows:

```
fileCount :: FilePath -> IO Int
fileCount fp = length <$> listFilesRecursive fp
```

Easy.

> **WARNING** Both our solutions here will not terminate if any symlinks out there form a loop. Please, consider this a feature, not a bug.

5.3.2 *Mutable references in the ST monad*

A similar interface to mutability is provided by the `ST` monad as defined in `Data.STRef`, shown next:

```
data STRef s a
newSTRef :: a -> ST s (STRef s a)
readSTRef :: STRef s a -> ST s a
writeSTRef :: STRef s a -> a -> ST s ()
modifySTRef :: STRef s a -> (a -> a) -> ST s ()
modifySTRef' :: STRef s a -> (a -> a) -> ST s ()
```

The only difference is that we are allowed to run computations purely with the `runST` function from `Control.Monad.ST` as follows:

```
runST :: (forall s. ST s a) -> a
```

This function has an interesting type, with the `forall` quantifier hiding the `s` type variable inside the parentheses. We'll get back to the `forall` keyword and where it comes from later in this book, but I'll give you the basic idea shortly.

THE FORALL KEYWORD IN THE RUNST TYPE SIGNATURE

EXAMPLE: COMBINING COMPUTATIONS IN THE ST MONAD

⬚   ch05/stref.hs

⚡   *stref*

☞   The Haskell type checker controls the way we combine `ST` computations.

Let's look at the following two computations in the `ST` monad:

```
comp1 :: ST s (STRef s Int)
comp1 = newSTRef 42

comp2 :: STRef s Int -> ST s Int
comp2 ref = readSTRef ref
```

In the first one we create a reference and return it as a result. The second one reads the given reference and returns a referenced value.

The `forall s. ST s a` type in `runST` ensures the following:

- We have no means to specify a particular type for the `s` type variable. If we attempt to write some type, a computation is no longer for all `s`. This `s` type variable is fully managed by the type inference algorithm that GHC runs during the compilation.
- The `s` type stays the same during the whole computation. Any steps should share the same `s`.
- The `s` type variable cannot escape the scope of the `runST` invocation.
- We can't mix results from different `runST` invocations because different `s` type variables are inferred for them.

For example, if we combine these two computations into a sequence and run it with `runST`, everything goes smoothly, as follows:

```
ghci> runST (comp1 >>= comp2)
42
```

The type checker is happy to infer the same `s` type and allows running the combined computation.

If we try to run the first computation independently, then the type checker complains, as shown here:

```
ghci> runST comp1

<interactive>:4:7: error:
    • Couldn't match type 'a' with 'STRef s Int'
```

```
        because type variable 's' would escape its scope
   This (rigid, skolem) type variable is bound by
     a type expected by the context:
       forall s. ST s a
     at <interactive>:4:7-11
   Expected type: ST s a
     Actual type: ST s (STRef s Int)
```

This message reveals some internal type checker mechanics. The words `rigid` and `skolem` basically mean that the type checker can't match the corresponding type variable with any other type due to the `forall` part of the type signature.

Consequently, using a reference returned from `comp1` in `comp2` is also impossible, as shown next:

```
ghci> runST (comp2 (runST comp1))

    Couldn't match type 's1' with 's'
    ...
```

This error message says that the type checker has inferred the two different s1 and s types, and it can't match them with each other. This is how the type checker controls combining computations in the ST monad.

COUNTING ZEROS IN THE ST MONAD

Suppose we have a list of `Int` values and want to count how many zeros are present.

> **EXAMPLE: COUNTING ZEROS IN A LIST**
>
> 🗋   ch05/countzeros.hs
>
> ⚡   *countzeros*
>
> ☞   The ST monad allows hiding mutability inside pure functions.

Any experienced functional programmer would quickly come up with something like the following:

```
countZeros :: [Int] -> Int
countZeros = length . filter (== 0)
```

When solving simple problems like this one, it is almost impossible to boost performance by mutability. GHC does its job pretty well by optimizing such code. Albeit, it never hurts to have something else in your toolbox.

Here is our novel approach (remember your Fortran lessons, if you know what I mean):

- Start by creating a counter with a value of 0.
- Traverse over the given list (well, almost Fortran), and increment the counter for every zero we meet.
- Return the value of the counter.

The following code implements these steps:

```
countZerosST :: [Int] -> Int
countZerosST xs = runST $ do
   c <- newSTRef 0
   traverse_ (\x -> when (x==0) $ inc c) xs
   readSTRef c
 where
   inc c = modifySTRef' c (+1)
```

Now we use mutability inside a pure function with everything under control.

Summary

- Learn interfaces of particular monads, and apply the most suitable functions.
- Monads are practical. We use them when we need the functionality they provide.
- Apply a `Reader` to get access to some configuration in different parts of the code.
- The `Writer` monad is good for logging events inside a pure computation.
- Don't fear computations that require maintaining state: we have `State`, `ST`, and mutability in `IO`.
- Use the `RWS` monad to get all of the features of `Reader`, `Writer`, and `State` at once.

Structuring programs with monad transformers

6

This chapter covers

- Using monad transformers to extend monad functionality
- Describing an application structure with monad stacks
- Defining monad transformers
- Overview of the most common monad transformers provided by the Haskell libraries

We've seen many monads already. We know that every monad specifies a way to combine two computations in a sequence by implementing the >>= operator. We also know that in a monadic setting we have a result of a computation with some additional effects: computations may fail (as in the Maybe monad) or give an opportunity to communicate with the real world by doing input and output (as in the IO monad), or we may mutate the state or consult an environment in some other effectful computations. There are many other monads, but we already know what all of them share in common.

In this chapter, we'll discuss one simple question: how do we express computations that need to use more than one monadic effect at the same time? We'll start with exploring the problem. We'll solve a problem in one monad, find some flaws in that solution, and try to fix them. In Haskell it is often the case that there is a monad for this. But we have a monad already, so the problem now is how to add another monad to a solution. Let's see.

6.1 The problem of combining monads

For the first example, we'll get back to the `State` monad. It turns out that it lacks error-checking functionality. We'll then try to add `Maybe` functionality and face some serious issues. We need corresponding functionality quite often, and it is useful to have both of them at the same time.

6.1.1 Evaluating expressions in reverse Polish notation

Let's take the evaluation of an arithmetic expression given in reverse Polish notation (RPN for short) as an example. This is another nice computer science problem with a good textbook solution. An expression in RPN contains numbers and arithmetic operators (say, +, -, and *). Operators follow numbers. Here are several examples:

- `"2 3 +"` is equivalent to 2+3 in the traditional infix notation, thus it evaluates to 5.
- `"3 2 -"` is 3-2, which evaluates to 1.
- `"2 4 + 3 4 + *"` is (2 + 4) * (3 + 4) and evaluates to 42.

Reverse Polish notation features at least the following two useful properties:

- We don't need parentheses to write expressions.
- There is a simple algorithm to evaluate expressions given in RPN.

A straightforward algorithm uses a stack of numbers as follows:

- For every token of the given expression:
    - If it is a number, push it onto the stack;
    - If it is an operator:
        - Pop two numbers from the stack;
        - Apply the operator to them;
        - Push the result back onto the stack.
- The answer is found at the top of the stack.

Figure 6.1 illustrates how this algorithm works.

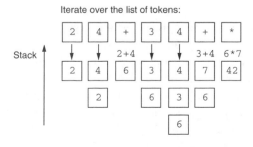

Iterate over the list of tokens:

Stack

Figure 6.1 Evaluating an expression given in reverse Polish notation

EXAMPLE: EVALUATING ARITHMETIC EXPRESSIONS IN REVERSE POLISH NOTATION (VERSION 1)

📄 expr/rpn/EvalRPN.hs

⚡ *evalrpn1*

☞ The State monad can't deal with errors.

A solution using the State monad is pretty straightforward at this point. We need to implement stack-processing functions in the State monad and then use them to implement the evaluation algorithm itself, as shown next:

```haskell
type Stack = [Integer]                    ┐ Defines a type synonym for the State
type EvalM = State Stack        ◁─────┘ monad with a Stack as a state

push :: Integer -> EvalM ()         ┐ Calls modify to add a new
push x = modify (x:)            ◁─────┘ element to the stack

pop :: EvalM Integer                Accesses the current stack content
pop = do
  xs <- get          ◁───────┐ Updates the stack with its tail,
  put (tail xs)    ◁──────┘ thus removing the first element
  pure (head xs)    ◁──┐
                        └ Returns the first element as the result of the computation
```

We could also give a shorter implementation as follows:

```haskell
pop :: EvalM Integer
pop = state $ \(x:xs) -> (x, xs)
```

An algorithmic implementation follows the description closely, as shown here:

```haskell
evalRPN :: String -> Integer              ┐ Runs an EvalM     │ Processes all words, and
evalRPN expr = evalState evalRPN' []  ◁┘ computation      takes the element on top
  where                                                         of the stack
    evalRPN' = traverse step (words expr) >> pop   ◁───┘
    step "+" = processTops (+)
    step "*" = processTops (*)            ┐ The number goes        │ Processes two
    step "-" = processTops (-)            │ to the stack.           elements on top
    step t   = push (read t)       ◁──┘                           of the stack
    processTops op = flip op <$> pop <*> pop >>= push   ◁───┘
```

When having trouble understanding this code, take time to check the types of the modify, state, and evalState functions. Then go in parallel over the algorithmic description and its implementation in the evalRPN' function.

Note the processTops function. The element on top of the stack corresponds to the right-hand-side argument of the operation, whereas the left-hand-side argument is the one below it. For example, for "3 2 -", we'd have 2 on top. Consequently, the first pop gives 2, the second one gives 3. That's why we should write flip op instead of op to get 3-2 instead of the incorrect 2-3.

ANALYZING FLAWS

Everything seems too good to be right at this point. Let's try some other inputs, shown next:

```
$ cabal repl evalrpn1
ghci> evalRPN "2 x"
*** Exception: Prelude.read: no parse
ghci> evalRPN "2 +"
*** Exception: Prelude.head: empty list
ghci> evalRPN "x 2"
2
ghci> evalRPN "1 2 3"
3
ghci> evalRPN ""
*** Exception: Prelude.head: empty list
```

Unfortunately, we've paid no attention to the things that may go wrong. Apparently the problem is in the given expressions. If they are malformed, bad things happen. Let's analyze some of the problems and see how we can identify them while executing the algorithm.

First, every token must be either an operator ("+", "-", or "*") or a number (its textual representation). We check the current token by pattern matching in step and consider it a number unless it's a supported operator. Consequently, the last clause of the step function is the place where we can discover incorrect components. Currently, we call the read function and beg for an exception. This is flaw number one.

Second, an expression may have fewer arguments than required by an operator (as in 2 +). In processTops, we pop twice without checking whether the stack contains those elements. This is flaw number two.

Third, an expression can have more numeric components that are processed by operators (as in 1 2 3). In this case, we end up with extra elements in a stack, although we expect only one (an answer). We are not checking this at all because we are happy to pop the top of the stack after we've finished processing expression components and forget about everything else. Interestingly, right here we can spot one more problem: the stack can be empty here. It's possible if we have an empty String as an expression. This is flaw number three.

The GHC runtime system discovers some of these problems (except for the extra elements on the stack) and raises an exception. Unfortunately, the information we get there is not 100% helpful. Whenever we pop elements from an empty stack, we apply the head and tail list-processing functions to empty lists. This clearly leads to an exception. Accessing empty lists doesn't belong to our RPN domain. We need to figure out such problems earlier. Here the problem is with an empty stack.

AN ATTEMPT TO FIX THE FLAWS: REPORT NOTHING IN CASE OF ERROR

Surely, we can check whether a component is a number. For example, we can do that with the readMaybe function from the Text.Read module. This function returns Nothing given a nonnumeric parameter and Just n otherwise.

We could also check the stack for emptiness with the following functions:

```
isEmpty :: EvalM Bool
isEmpty = null <$> get

notEmpty :: EvalM Bool
notEmpty = not <$> isEmpty
```

We can even check that the stack contains exactly one element, as follows:

```
oneElementOnStack :: EvalM Bool
oneElementOnStack = do
  l <- length <$> get
  pure (l == 1)
```

Anyway, the main question is, what should we do when encountering an error, such as in the `step t` clause shown next?

```
step t = case readMaybe t of
           Just n -> push n
           Nothing -> -- do what?
```

The `State` monad has no means to report a problem. Well, we have the `Maybe` monad designed precisely for that. We know that it is good at handling `case` expressions, as in the previous code. The `Maybe` monad is responsible for stopping the computation in case of any error and reporting `Nothing`. In the next chapter, we'll discuss several more powerful approaches to reporting errors. For now we'll stick with the easiest one. We are going to return `Nothing` in the presence of any error in the given expression.

6.1.2 *Introducing monad transformers and monad stacks*

Now we've come to the idea that we should combine the functionalities of the two monads, `State` and `Maybe`. Which `>>=` operator should work for composing computations, the one of `State` or the one of `Maybe`? Well, in some sense, both. Haskell supports such combinations with the machinery of monad transformers, an apparatus that enables adding the functionality of one monad to another. Let's see how we can do that without diving deep into the implementation details of monad transformers.

EXAMPLE: EVALUATING ARITHMETIC EXPRESSIONS IN RPN (VERSION 2)

☐   expr/rpn/EvalRPNTrans.hs

⚡   *evalrpn2*

☞   We can combine `Maybe` and `State` effects into one monad.

We'll start with types as always. Let's redefine `EvalM`, as follows:

```
type EvalM = StateT Stack Maybe
```

`StateT` is a *monad transformer* (their names traditionally end with `T`). In this code, it adds the functionality of the `State` monad with the `Stack` as a state to the `Maybe` monad (the last type component), or *transforms it*. The `Maybe` monad is called the *base monad* (or *inner monad*). We add the `State Stack` monad on the top of it, arriving at the so-called *monad stack* (don't confuse this term with a particular state data type `Stack` in our example). Figure 6.2 presents the same idea visually.

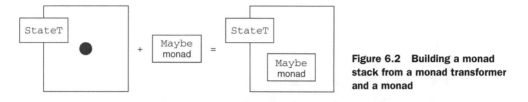

Figure 6.2 Building a monad stack from a monad transformer and a monad

Now let's see how we should modify our code to work in this brand-new monad stack. The `push` function in the next code stays the same because it has nothing to do with the failures:

```
push :: Integer -> EvalM ()
push x = modify (x:)
```

The `pop` function requires some work because this is the place where we can potentially introduce `Nothing`. Remember that we are not interested in an actual reason in this solution, so returning `Nothing` after an attempt of reading from an empty `Stack` is sufficient. We have several options here.

First is the `lift` function with the following type:

```
lift :: (MonadTrans t, Monad m) => m a -> t m a
```

If we use it inside the `EvalM` computation, then the particular type would be as follows:

```
lift :: Maybe a -> (StateT Stack) Maybe a
              t              m    a
```

We can use it to send `Nothing` to the inner `Maybe` monad if the `Stack` is empty, as shown next:

```
pop :: EvalM Integer
pop = do
  xs <- get
  when (null xs) $ lift Nothing
  put (tail xs)
  pure (head xs)
```

Once we send `Nothing`, there will be no subsequent steps due to the monadic bind for `Maybe`, so we can safely use `head` and `tail` after that.

One problem with the `lift` function is that whenever we use it, we fix the monad stack structure. The `lift Nothing` call requires the inner monad to be `Maybe`. This is not always desirable because we could want to change a monad stack somehow later. For example, we could introduce one more layer between `State` and `Maybe`. This breaks explicit `lift` calls.

The second solution is to use the `guard` method from the `Alternative` type class. The `guard False` sends `Nothing` to the `Maybe` monad for us, as shown next:

```
ghci> guard False :: Maybe ()
Nothing
ghci> guard True :: Maybe ()
Just ()
```

The Alternative type class

The `Alternative` type class brings the idea of a monoid operation to computations. It defines the `empty` value for neutral computation and the `(<|>)` for combining them (or choosing between them, depending on the actual implementation). The `(<|>)` operation from the `Alternative` instance for `Maybe` gives back the first non-`Nothing` value.

The `Alternative` type class extends the `Applicative` type class. The `MonadPlus` type class also does the same for `Monad`.

The `StateT` transformer propagates the call to `guard False` to the base monad if the latter implements `Alternative`. We'll see how this propagation is implemented later in this chapter. For now, just note that we can use both `get` and `guard` in our monad stack as if they are implemented for it, as shown next:

```
pop :: EvalM Integer
pop = do
  xs <- get
  guard (not $ null xs)
  put (tail xs)
  pure (head xs)
```

Again, we can safely use `tail` and `head` after `guard`. These functions are called only if the `Stack` is not empty.

Tip

I recommend experimenting with these implementations. To run `EvalM` computations in GHCi, one could do the following:

```
$ cabal repl evalrpn2
ghci> import Control.Monad.State
ghci> evalStateT pop []
Nothing
ghci> evalStateT (push 10 >> pop) []
Just 10
```

The third solution employs the so-called `do` block `MonadFail` desugaring. Here is the basic idea: whenever we use pattern matching in a `do` block, chances are that pattern matching fails. For example, in the following `main` function, the GHC runtime system raises an exception if the number of arguments isn't equal to 1:

```
main = do
  [str] <- getArgs
  putStrLn str
```

When GHC compiles this code, it inserts the call to the `fail` function if pattern matching fails. This method comes from the `MonadFail` type class, as shown next:

```
class Monad m => MonadFail (m :: * -> *) where
  fail :: String -> m a
```

The `Maybe` monad implements an instance of the `MonadFail` type class by returning `Nothing`. The `StateT` monad transformer propagates the call to `fail` to an underlying monad, giving us `Nothing` in case of failed pattern matching, as follows:

```
pop :: EvalM Integer
pop = do
  (x:xs) <- get          If this fails, we
  put xs                 get Nothing.
  pure x
```

Reporting fails in monads

The `fail` method used to be in the `Monad` type class. At that time, incomplete pattern matches were translated to `Monad.fail` in any `do` block. Since GHC 8.6, this is no longer the case. Incomplete pattern matches are now translated to `MonadFail.fail` by default. Thus, it's required for a monad to provide an instance of the `MonadFail` type class to use incomplete pattern matching in `do` blocks.

GHC would object if we write this pattern match in the `do` block of the `State Stack` monad because it doesn't implement the `MonadFail` type class. We can write this here, because the `StateT Stack` monad transformer implements it if the underlying monad implements it.

We can go with either implementation of `pop` because both implement the same behavior. Now let's check whether the `Stack` has exactly one element in the end of processing:

```
oneElementOnStack :: EvalM ()
oneElementOnStack = do
  l <- length <$> get
  guard (l == 1)
```

The only thing that we haven't checked yet is whether we have a number as a component of the given expression. Let's implement the readSafe function, which sends Nothing to our monad stack if not given a number. My goal is to make it as general as possible, as follows:

```
readSafe :: (Read a, Alternative m) => String -> m a
readSafe str =
  case readMaybe str of
    Nothing -> empty
    Just n -> pure n
```

Surprisingly, not many changes occur in the rest of the code. We've done all the low-level jobs already and let monads and monad transformers do their job. Compare the following code with the previous implementation of evalRPN to see the difference:

We return Maybe Integer now.

```
evalRPN :: String -> Maybe Integer
evalRPN str = evalStateT evalRPN' []              ◄── The evalState is replaced
  where                                               with evalStateT.
    evalRPN' = traverse step (words str) >> oneElementOnStack >> pop    ◄──
    step "+" = processTops (+)
    step "*" = processTops (*)                      Adds checking for one-element stack
    step "-" = processTops (-)
    step t   = readSafe t >>= push        ◄──   The readSafe result is pushed
    processTops op = flip op <$> pop <*> pop >>= push   onto the stack unless we've
                                                        got Nothing.
```

The evalStateT is a monadic runner for the StateT monad transformer. We use it to get a computation in the base Maybe monad and return it as a value. We may interpret evalStateT as a tool to execute the State monad functionality and unwrap one level of the computation in the monad stack as shown in figure 6.3. Given an Integer computation in the StateT Stack Maybe monad, we've got an Integer computation in the Maybe monad. Because the Maybe Integer value is an expected result already, we shouldn't go any further in the monad stack processing.

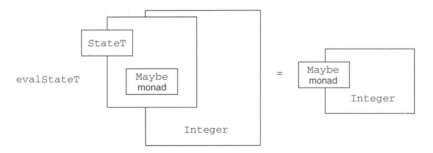

Figure 6.3   Unwrapping one level of the monad stack with evalStateT

Let's see whether it all works:

```
ghci> evalRPN "2 x"
Nothing
ghci> evalRPN "2 +"
Nothing
ghci> evalRPN "x 2"
Nothing
ghci> evalRPN "1 2 3"
Nothing
ghci> evalRPN ""
Nothing
```

Oops, just a second.

```
ghci> evalRPN "2 3 +"
Just 5
```

Phew, it's all right. Let's summarize, what we've achieved in this section:

1 We built a monad stack out of the `StateT` transformer and the `Maybe` monad.
2 We maintain a mutable stack while processing the given RPN expression (`State` effect).
3 We control everything that could go wrong and return `Nothing` in such cases (`Maybe` effect).
4 We can use either explicit `lift` or `Alternative`/`MonadFail` functionality to introduce `Nothing` into a monad stack.

In the rest of this chapter, we use other monads as well, but the idea is the same: build a monad stack and use the effects of the monads it contains.

6.2 *IO-based monad transformer stacks*

Every monad provides some functionality (effect) to our program. If we need the functionality of several monads at once, it's a job for monad transformers. Monad transformers suggest a way of thinking about our application or its independent components: an application is a monad stack built from a base monad with added various monadic functionality via monad transformers. A monad stack is a monad, too, but it is rich in terms of the functionality provided.

For example, the monad stack in figure 6.4 is built from a base monad by the imaginary `Monad1T`, `Monad2T`, and `Monad3T` monad transformers.

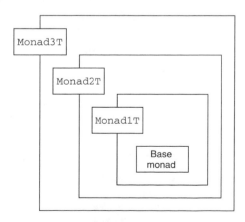

Figure 6.4 Building a complex monad stack from the base monad

One of the most practical monads we usually use as a base monad to build our monad stacks is the IO monad. In fact, IO must be the base monad if we need its functionality. There is no monad transformer to add IO functionality. The good news is that we can transform the IO monad with almost any other monad functionality.

In this section, we'll discuss an application that walks recursively over the given directory and computes various information for every subdirectory down to the given depth. It is also possible to filter files by their extensions. I call this application du, as it resembles the corresponding UNIX command-line utility.

EXAMPLE: COMPUTING INFORMATION FROM A DIRECTORY STRUCTURE

🗋   du/

⚡   *du*

☞   We build a complex monad stack to use many effects at once.

This application provides the following command-line interface:

```
Usage: du [DIRECTORY] [-d|--depth DEPTH] [-e|--extension EXT] [-L]
  Directory usage info

Available options:
  -d,--depth DEPTH         Display an entry for all directories DEPTH
                           directories deep
  -e,--extension EXT       Filter files by extension
  -L                       Follow symlinks (OFF by default)
  -h,--help                Show this help text
```

With no command-line arguments given, we start in the current directory and report information on the whole directory tree. Note that no matter the depth we are given, some tasks may require traversing the whole tree. We use the -d argument to limit reporting directories, not traverse them. Note also that we don't follow symbolic links by default to avoid potential nontermination conditions. Symbolic links can create loops in a directory structure.

For example, let's run this application on the hid-examples/data directory as follows:

```
hid-examples $ cabal -v0 run du -- data -e ".txt" -d1
Directory tree:
data
  tests
  texts
  benchmarks
File counter:
0     data/tests
4     data/texts
0     data/benchmarks
5     data
File space usage:
```

```
0     data/tests
2040941     data/texts
0     data/benchmarks
2326721     data
```

The list of monads we need to build such an application follows:

- IO for traversing over directories and determining file sizes
- Reader for accessing a configuration
- State for maintaining levels of subdirectories and accumulating file sizes
- Writer for logging the resulting information on traversed subdirectories.

An application is built from the following modules:

- AppTypes provides types used throughout the application.
- AppRWST describes our monad stack.
- App reexports definitions used in all other modules.
- Utils provides helpers to traverse a directory and acquire information about files.
- DirTree builds a hierarchical view of a directory structure.
- FileCount counts files in the directories along the way.
- DiskUsage computes file space usage.
- Main provides the main function; it is also responsible for the user interface.

Figure 6.5 presents the dependencies between these modules.

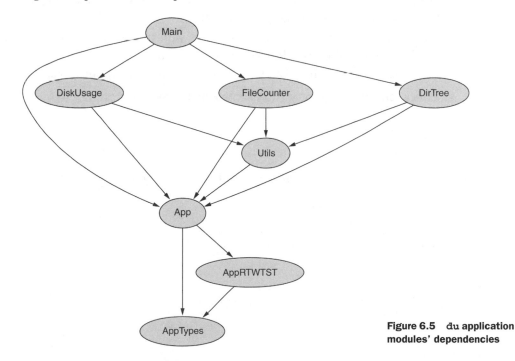

Figure 6.5 du application modules' dependencies

We use the following external packages:

- `mtl` for monad transformer functionality
- `filepath` to work with file paths (concatenating them, taking an extension)
- `directory` to work with directories
- `unix-compat` to access file information in an OS-compatible way
- `extra` to get additional file system utilities
- `optparse-applicative` to read and process command-line arguments
- `text` and `text-show` to work with `Text`

Note, I've enabled the following GHC extensions for all the modules by default:

- `RecordWildCards`
- `NamedFieldPuns`
- `OverloadedStrings`

They are mentioned in the package.yaml and .cabal files for the `hid-examples` project.

In the rest of this section, we'll discuss various issues regarding this application implementation.

6.2.1 *Describing a monad stack*

Let's start with types as usual. This application consists of the following components:

- The configuration from the command-line arguments containing the base path, the maximum depth of reported subdirectories, an optional extension for filtering files, and symlinks following a flag.
- An environment for traversing directories with the current depth and current path; it should also provide access to the configuration.
- The log and state, which can be different for concrete applications.

EXAMPLE: COMPUTING INFORMATION FROM A DIRECTORY STRUCTURE

📄   du/AppTypes.hs

📄   du/AppRWST.hs

The following two data types represent configuration and environment:

```
data AppConfig = AppConfig {
    basePath :: FilePath
  , maxDepth :: Int
  , extension :: Maybe String
  , followSymlinks :: Bool
  }

data AppEnv = AppEnv {
    cfg :: AppConfig
  , path :: FilePath
```

```
, depth :: Int
, fileStatus :: FilePath -> IO FileStatus
}
```

The `fileStatus` field here refers to a function that provides such information about the given path as to whether it corresponds to a directory or a regular file or to its size. Depending on the configuration, we should choose one of the following functions:

- The `getFileStatus` function, when given a symbolic link, gives back information on its destination.
- The `getSymbolicLinkStatus` considers any symbolic link as a regular file and doesn't follow it. Otherwise, it works like the `getFileStatus` function.

The relationship between parameters and environment is best described by the following function, which builds an initial environment from the given configuration:

```
initialEnv :: AppConfig -> AppEnv
initialEnv config @ AppConfig {..} = AppEnv {
    cfg = config
, path = basePath
, depth = 0
, fileStatus = if followSymlinks
              then getFileStatus
              else getSymbolicLinkStatus
}
```

Because we need all of the `Reader`, `Writer`, and `State` functionality, the best choice for us is to build a monad stack with the `RWST` transformer over `IO`, as shown next:

```
type MyApp logEntry state = RWST AppEnv [logEntry] state IO
```

Let's read this type synonym out loud: an application is basically the `Reader`, `Writer`, and `State` functionality with the specified environment, a log entry list, and a state over `IO`. When we see monad stack definitions like this one, we immediately recognize an infrastructure available to an application.

It is also a good idea to define our application runner that incorporates runners of all the monads used here and gives us an `IO` action in the end, as follows:

```
runMyApp :: MyApp logEntry state a -> AppConfig -> state ->
            IO (a, [logEntry])
runMyApp app config st = evalRWST app (initialEnv config) st
```

> **NOTE** The `MyApp logEntry state a` type, together with the `runMyApp` runner function, may resemble application-wrapping classes from GUI frameworks found in other programming languages. The idea is quite the same: we can freely use all the machinery of the framework inside those classes, and we can use the monadic functionality from the handcrafted monad stack here.

6.2.2 *Exploiting monad stack functionality*

Any `MyApp logEntry state a` application is now able to use all the monadic machinery together with the `Reader`, `Writer`, and `State` functionality. Let's start with the simplest problem: how to check the file status for the current path.

EXAMPLE: COMPUTING INFORMATION FROM A DIRECTORY STRUCTURE

📄 du/Utils.hs

The following action consults an environment and then makes a request to a file system:

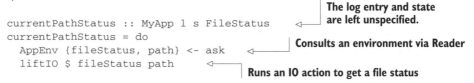

```
currentPathStatus :: MyApp l s FileStatus      ◁── The log entry and state
currentPathStatus = do                              are left unspecified.
  AppEnv {fileStatus, path} <- ask      ◁────── Consults an environment via Reader
  liftIO $ fileStatus path      ◁──
                                    Runs an IO action to get a file status
```

Note the `liftIO` function I've used here. Its goal is to run an `IO` action in any monad stack based on the `IO` monad. This function works no matter the depth of a monad stack. In the next section, we'll discuss how this is possible.

Even though we have an action in the `MyApp` monad stack, we don't have to use all the functionality. For example, in `currentPathStatus` we've used only `Reader` and the base `IO` monad.

TRAVERSING A DIRECTORY

Now we implement the `traverseDirectoryWith` function. It takes some `app` (a computation within our monad stack) as an argument and then traverses over the files in the current directory, as shown next:

```
                              The parameter is a concrete application.
    traverseDirectoryWith :: MyApp le s () -> MyApp le s ()
┌─▷ traverseDirectoryWith app = do
│       curPath <- asks path   ◁──        Accesses the current path
│       content <- liftIO $ listDirectory curPath   ◁──
┌───▷ traverse_ go content                                Lists the directory content
│     where
│       go name = flip local app   ◁──── Runs app in the modified environment
Traverses over every file   $ \env -> env {
in the current directory         path = path env </> name,   ◁──
                        ┌─▷ depth = depth env + 1            Updates an environment
  Increments the        }                                   with a new path
  current depth │
```

Note that this function traverses only one level of subdirectories. It doesn't attempt to go deeper, because that is a task of the concrete application.

The `traverse_` function is responsible for keeping all the effects, such as maintaining state and providing access to the configuration over all the `app` invocations.

The (</>) operator from the System.FilePath module provides a system-agnostic way to include a directory name separator into a file path.

In fact, we don't need the do block in traverseDirectoryWith. Note the pattern here: the name we've bound by <- goes as the last argument in the following step. It's the same as >>=. We could write the following instead:

```
traverseDirectoryWith' app =
    asks path >>= liftIO . listDirectory >>= traverse_ go
  where
  ...
```

This code is much easier to read once you've mastered monads. First, we don't need to introduce any ad hoc names (curPath, content). Second, we have the following very clear pipeline:

1 Access the environment path field.
2 List the corresponding directory lifting to IO.
3 Traverse over the list from the previous step.

The do notation provides more flexibility. The price is that we have to figure out the data flow by looking at the names we've bound.

WALKING OVER THE DIRECTORY TREE

Now we are ready to implement the first concrete application. Let's walk over the directory tree and collect information about subdirectory depths.

EXAMPLE: COMPUTING INFORMATION FROM A DIRECTORY STRUCTURE

🗋 du/DirTree.hs

🗋 du/Main.hs

The implementation is straightforward, as shown next:

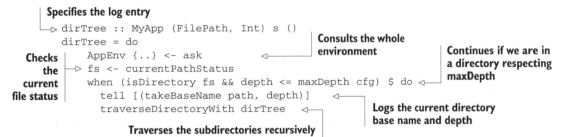

```
Specifies the log entry
  dirTree :: MyApp (FilePath, Int) s ()
  dirTree = do                              Consults the whole
    AppEnv {..} <- ask                      environment
    fs <- currentPathStatus
    when (isDirectory fs && depth <= maxDepth cfg) $ do
      tell [(takeBaseName path, depth)]
      traverseDirectoryWith dirTree
```

We've started using Writer functionality, though we still don't need any state. The information we collect here can be presented as follows:

```
treeEntryBuilder :: (FilePath, Int) -> Builder
treeEntryBuilder (fp, n) = fromString indent <> fromString fp
  where
    indent = replicate (2*n) ' '
```

We define the `Builder` from the `TextShow` module by indenting a given directory name. As a result, we can get the following:

```
Directory tree:
data
  tests
    iplookup
  texts
  benchmarks
    iplookup
```

COUNTING FILES IN DIRECTORIES

Counting files in directories is similar. We traverse a directory tree, respecting `max-Depth`. In every directory, we count the length of the file list. We should also take care of file extensions.

EXAMPLE: COMPUTING INFORMATION FROM A DIRECTORY STRUCTURE

- 🗋   du/Utils.hs

- 🗋   du/FileCounter.hs

The solution is the following:

```
checkExtension :: AppConfig -> FilePath -> Bool
checkExtension cfg fp =
  maybe True (`isExtensionOf` fp) (extension cfg)

fileCount :: MyApp (FilePath, Int) s ()
fileCount = do
    AppEnv {..} <- ask
    fs <- currentPathStatus
    when (isDirectory fs && depth <= maxDepth cfg) $ do
      traverseDirectoryWith fileCount
      files <- liftIO $ listFiles path
      tell [(path, length $ filter (checkExtension cfg) files)]
```

To check whether we need to count files with the specific extension, I use the `maybe` function with the following type:

```
maybe :: b -> (a -> b) -> Maybe a -> b
```

If an extension is not provided, then we return the default `True`. Thus, we accept every file. Otherwise, we use the `isExtensionOf` from the `System.Directory.Extra` module. The function is smart enough to support extensions given both with the dot and without it.

The `fileCount` closely follows the `dirTree` pattern. The only difference is that we access the file system to get the list of files in the current directory. We do that with the `listFiles` function from the `System.Directory.Extra` module. Note that we need to add `liftIO` here because this function knows nothing about our monad stack.

Finally, we are ready to compute disk usage. We need access to files and their names, sizes, and types within the file system. We also need to consult the environment and modify the state.

EXAMPLE: COMPUTING INFORMATION FROM A DIRECTORY STRUCTURE

📄 du/DiskUsage.hs

File size is described by the `FileOffset` type (which normally corresponds to an `Int64`) from the `System.Posix.Types` module. We can use it as a state and a log entry component, as shown here:

```
diskUsage :: MyApp (FilePath, FileOffset) FileOffset ()
```

We use state to compute total space used by files in a directory tree. When encountering a file, we should increase the total space usage by its size. To compute the total space used by some directory, we have to find the difference between the total space used after leaving the directory and before entering it. Note that this task requires tra versing the whole directory tree, no matter the maximum depth given.

Thus, we have two stages. First, we have to decide what to do with the current path. Second, if it's a file, then we record its size. If it's a directory, then we traverse into it. Let's express these stages as a type as follows:

```
data DUEntryAction =
    TraverseDir {dirpath :: FilePath, requireReporting :: Bool}
  | RecordFileSize {fsize :: FileOffset}
  | None
```

We encode this logic in the `diskUsage` function presented in the following:

```
diskUsage = liftM2 decide ask currentPathStatus >>= processEntry      ⟵──┐
  where                                                    The whole pipeline │
    decide AppEnv {..} fs
      | isDirectory fs =
          TraverseDir path (depth <= maxDepth cfg)
      | isRegularFile fs && checkExtension cfg path =
          RecordFileSize (fileSize fs)
      | otherwise = None

    processEntry TraverseDir {..} = do        │ Records the usage when
      usageOnEntry <- get              ⟵──────┘ entering the directory
      traverseDirectoryWith diskUsage
      when requireReporting $ do
        usageOnExit <- get                                Logs the space used by
        tell [(dirpath, usageOnExit - usageOnEntry)]  ⟵── the current directory
    processEntry RecordFileSize {fsize} = modify (+fsize)   ⟵──┐
    processEntry None = pure ()
                                                     Increases the total space
                                                     accumulator in the state
```

Records the usage on exit ⟶

Note the `liftM2` function. Here is its type:

```
liftM2 :: Monad m => (a1 -> a2 -> r) -> m a1 -> m a2 -> m r
```

It runs two actions given by the second and third arguments and then calls its first argument on their results. This is the same as doing the following via an `Applicative`:

```
decide <$> ask <*> currentPathStatus
```

I've decided to use `liftM2` instead, because we are in a monadic setting anyway.

In the `diskUsage` function, we use all the `Reader/Writer/State` functionality, thus fully exploiting our monad stack.

6.2.3 *Running an application*

Our goal in this subsection is to complete the implementation. There is nothing new in processing command-line arguments. The only problem is to run our applications and display the results.

EXAMPLE: COMPUTING INFORMATION FROM A DIRECTORY STRUCTURE

◻ du/Main.hs

We do that in the `work` function as follows:

```
work :: AppConfig -> IO ()
work config = do
  (_, dirs) <- runMyApp dirTree config ()
  (_, counters) <- runMyApp fileCount config ()
  (_, usages) <- runMyApp diskUsage config (0 :: FileOffset)
  let report = toText $
               buildEntries "Directory tree:" treeEntryBuilder dirs
               <> buildEntries "File counter:" tabEntryBuilder counters
               <> buildEntries "File space usage:" tabEntryBuilder usages
  TIO.putStr report
```

When running an application, we have to specify an initial state. Because we don't use it in `dirTree` and `fileCount` anyway, it's OK to use `()`.

The `buildEntries` function combines log entries into a `Builder` as follows:

```
buildEntries :: Builder -> (e -> Builder) -> [e] -> Builder
buildEntries title entryBuilder entries =
  unlinesB $ title : map entryBuilder entries
```

I also use the following helper function to present two columns with a number and a file path, as shown here:

```
tabEntryBuilder :: TextShow s => (FilePath, s) -> Builder
tabEntryBuilder (fp, s) = showb s <> "\t" <> fromString fp
```

Let's review the application structure again. We have the following components:

- Data types for a configuration and an environment
- An application infrastructure in the form of the monad stack built of the RWST monad transformer over the IO monad
- A generic directory traversal based on the infrastructure provided
- Several concrete applications
- The work function as a combined applications runner

6.2.4 Can we do it without RWST?

Before diving into the ideas behind monad transformers, let's see whether we can implement the same application without the RWST helper by using the Reader, Writer, and State monads independently. In fact, we can, but that requires building a bit more complex multilevel monad stack.

EXAMPLE: COMPUTING INFORMATION FROM A DIRECTORY STRUCTURE

🗋 du/AppRTWTST.hs

Recall the following monad stack built from RWST over IO:

```
type MyApp logEntry state = RWST AppEnv [logEntry] state IO
```

Here we apply the RWST monad transformer to the IO monad. The plan now is to take the IO monad, apply the StateT transformer to it, apply the WriterT transformer, and then complete the stack with the ReaderT transformer. We usually do this using new-type definitions, which allows hiding details from a user. The second step is to make sure that this newly built monad stack implements the MonadReader, MonadWriter, and MonadState type classes so that we can use such functions as get, ask, and tell. We should also make sure that we are able to do the liftIO calls (this is a method from the MonadIO type class). Last, but not least, this monad stack should also implement the Functor, Applicative, and Monad type classes—it is a monad after all!

Following is how we will do it:

```
newtype MyApp logEntry state a = MyApp {
    runApp :: ReaderT AppEnv
                (WriterT [logEntry]
                    (StateT state
                            IO)) a
  } deriving (Functor, Applicative, Monad,
            MonadIO,
            MonadReader AppEnv,
            MonadWriter [logEntry],
            MonadState state)
```

The runApp field is the monad stack itself. The deriving clause generates all the functionality required. Deriving is implemented by the GeneralizedNewtypeDeriving

GHC extension—it must be enabled to compile this code. The idea behind it is rather simple. For example, to provide the `tell` method for the `MyApp` s monad, the deriving machinery generates a method body with something like `lift . tell` (one level down along the monad stack to get to the `Writer` monad). The method body for `get` becomes `lift . lift . get` to reach the `State` monad. We'll discuss other details on instance derivation in chapter 12. The overall structure of this `MyApp` s monad stack is presented in figure 6.6.

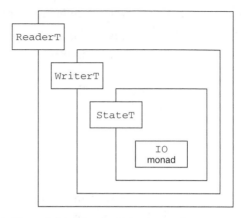

Figure 6.6   A four-level-deep monad stack based on the IO monad

Now we should reimplement a monad runner. The new runner follows the same approach of wrapping other runners inside it, as shown next:

```
runMyApp :: MyApp logEntry state a -> AppConfig -> state -> IO (a, [logEntry])
runMyApp app config st =
  evalStateT
      (runWriterT
          (runReaderT (runApp app) (initialEnv config)))
      st
```

Note the direction of running this monad stack application: we first unwrap `app`, then apply the runner for the `Reader` monad, and then do everything else.

These two monad stacks are identical to each other: we can replace an import declaration in the du/App.hs file without changing the rest of the code.

6.3   *What is a monad transformer?*

We'd expect at least two things of a monad transformer. First, it should define a monad, so that we have the `pure` method and the `>>=` operator. Second, it should give us a way to use the features of both monads: the base monad and the one we intend to lay on top of it.

Remember the following monad stack from the first section of this chapter where we used `StateT` over `Maybe`:

```
type EvalM = StateT Stack Maybe
```

Now we go the other way around. We define a `MaybeT` transformer and build a monad stack with it over the `State` monad. It's instructive to see how the code for that monad stack should be changed (or not). In fact, the `MaybeT` transformer is already available from the `Control.Monad.Trans.Maybe` module (provided by the `transformers` package). Nevertheless, we are interested in the internal details of its implementation. The implementation presented here slightly differs from the one supplied by the package, especially in terms of performance, but we keep the full functionality.

EXAMPLE: IMPLEMENTING A MONAD TRANSFORMER

   🗋   expr/rpn/MyMaybeT.hs

   🗋   expr/rpn/EvalRPNTrans2.hs

   ⚡   *evalrpn3*

   ☞   Writing a monad transformer requires many routine steps.

6.3.1 Step 0: Defining a type for a transformer

The idea behind a monad transformer is to provide a wrapper around any monad m. The question is what we are going to get in the end. We define the MaybeT transformer, so we want to be able to get either Just value or Nothing in the wrapped monad. This dictates a type for the transformer: it's effectively Maybe a in the monad m, where a is the type of the result of the computation, as shown next:

```
newtype MaybeT m a = MaybeT { runMaybeT :: m (Maybe a) }
```

Forget about the newtype wrapping and the traditional naming; the MaybeT transformer is just a Maybe a value in an arbitrary monad. The same works for other transformers, too. For example, ReaderT is a function with access to an environment

```
newtype ReaderT r m a = ReaderT { runReaderT :: r -> m a }
```

so that we can consult r while executing the m a computation for any monad m. If we check other transformer definitions in the transformers package (and I recommend doing that), we'll see the same pattern applied over and over.

Again, there is nothing unusual in the transformer type: it is just a slightly decorated result of the computation a in some monad m. The way we decorate it is determined by the monad we implement.

6.3.2 Step 1: Turning a monad stack into a monad

The transformer builds a monad stack, which is a monad itself. Being a Monad means being a Functor and an Applicative first. Technically, we have to provide instances of these three type classes for the MaybeT m type where m is a Functor, an Applicative, and a Monad, respectively. We'll start with the easiest one, the Functor type class.

MAKE IT A FUNCTOR

The first task is to implement fmap, as in the following snippet:

```
instance Functor m => Functor (MaybeT m) where
  fmap :: (a -> b) -> MaybeT m a -> MaybeT m b
  fmap f v = ...
```

Note the type signature for fmap. Normally, Haskell prohibits type signatures on the class method implementations in the instance declarations. We have to enable the

`InstanceSigs` GHC extension to write them. This extension is extremely helpful in figuring out what should be done in the method: the generic `fmap` type is `(a -> b) -> f a -> f b`, but thanks to `InstanceSigs`, we can see a concrete type here.

We have the following tools at our disposal to implement `fmap`:

- Pattern matching on the `MaybeT` data constructor or the `runMaybeT` accessor function to get access to the internals of the `MaybeT m a` values and to build a final value
- A functional argument `a -> b` to go literally from `a` to `b`
- The `Functor` instance for `m` (`Functor m =>` is a part of the instance head)—we are free to use it whenever we like
- Anything we can do over `Maybe a` values once we've got access to them

This list of available functionality is pretty much everything we need and have. Note that types prevent us doing anything else. For example, we know nothing about `m` except for its functorial ability to do its own `fmap`. Interestingly, this limited list of available tools directs our implementation a lot. In most cases, we have no other choice except for doing the right thing.

Figure 6.7 visualizes our goal: the boxes correspond to the `fmap` arguments and a result.

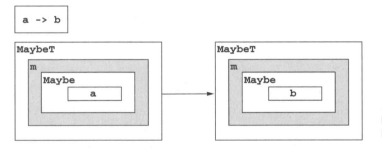

Figure 6.7 The goal: Implementing `fmap`

Note the gray box marked with `m`. This is the most intricate part of the task. The only way to get through it is to use the `fmap` method from `Functor m`. Once we've got a value out of the `MaybeT` data constructor, we are forced to call `fmap` and get the resulting gray box, as shown next:

```
fmap f (MaybeT mma) = MaybeT (fmap f' mma)
```

Now we have to implement `f'`, which should process the result of the computation in the `m` monad (this is what a function in `fmap` always does), so its type should be `Maybe a -> Maybe b`. Technically, we could unwrap `Maybe a`, but it's easier to go with the `Functor` for `Maybe` and implement `f'` by `fmap` with the given `f`, as shown here:

```
f' = fmap f
```

The following snippet shows where we are so far:

```
instance Functor m => Functor (MaybeT m) where
  fmap :: (a -> b) -> MaybeT m a -> MaybeT m b
  fmap f (MaybeT mma) = MaybeT (fmap (fmap f) mma)
```

Note the two `fmap` calls in the right-hand side. They come from the different `Functor` instances: one for `m` and another for `Maybe`.

Using typed holes to fill the gaps

GHC provides a nice tool to find out what is available at a particular point in our program. It is called *typed holes*. If we use an undefined name beginning with an underscore somewhere in our code, GHC prints out everything it can figure out about this point.

For example, we could write the following in `fmap` implementation:

```
fmap f (MaybeT mma) = MaybeT _help
```

As a result, GHC reports a lot of interesting details, including an expected type and everything we have at our disposal to fill the hole, as shown next:

```
• Found hole: _help :: m (Maybe b)
    ...
  • Relevant bindings include
      mma :: m (Maybe a)
      f :: a -> b
      fmap :: (a -> b) -> MaybeT m a -> MaybeT m b
    Constraints include Functor m
   |
23 |    fmap f (MaybeT mma) = MaybeT _help
   |                                 ^^^^^
```

I've cleaned the output a bit to fit the page. In addition to this, GHC reports where all the names (types and values) come from (*are bound*, in terms of GHC itself). Sometimes, GHC reports the `Valid hole fits include` section. Suggestions are not always meaningful, though they are getting better and better with new releases.

Typed holes support an interactive style of development. For example, in this particular case, we could figure out that we need to exploit the `Functor m` constraint and apply `fmap` to `mma`, leaving the hole in the first `fmap` parameter as follows:

```
fmap f (MaybeT mma) = MaybeT (fmap _help mma)
```

Then we run GHC again, analyze its output, and refine the implementation further.

MAKE IT AN APPLICATIVE

Now the instance for `Applicative` follows:

```
instance Applicative m => Applicative (MaybeT m) where
  pure :: a -> MaybeT m a
  pure a = ...
  (<*>) :: MaybeT m (a -> b) -> MaybeT m a -> MaybeT m b
  (MaybeT mf) <*> (MaybeT mx) = ...
```

The list of available tools is mostly the same, apart from the fact that we have an `Applicative m` now. The implementation is also type-directed and straightforward.

For `pure`, we simply wrap the given value with a `Just` to get the `Maybe` computation, then use m's `pure` (there is no other way to get inside the `m` computation), and finally wrap with `MaybeT`.

For `(<*>)`, we should first use pattern matching to unwrap both the `mf` value of type `m (Maybe (a->b))` and the `mx` value of type `m (Maybe a)` out of `MaybeT`. At this stage the only thing we could do is apply the `Applicative m` machinery to those two values to get through `m`, so we need a two-argument function that would take `Maybe (a->b)` and `Maybe a` and return `Maybe b`. This function is precisely `(<*>)` from `Applicative` for `Maybe`, so we apply it applicatively via `(<$>)` and wrap the results back with `MaybeT`. The following code presents the details:

Wraps a value a into the three layers

```
instance Applicative m => Applicative (MaybeT m) where
  pure :: a -> MaybeT m a
  pure a = MaybeT (pure $ Just a)

  (<*>) :: MaybeT m (a -> b) -> MaybeT m a -> MaybeT m b
  (MaybeT mf) <*> (MaybeT mx) = MaybeT ((<*>) <$> mf <*> mx)
```

Applies (<*>) from Maybe to the internals of mf and mx applicatively with (<$>)

Again, note that we've used two different applications of `(<*>)`: one for `Maybe`, and another for `m`. Do you see which `(<$>)` is applied in this implementation?

MAKE IT A MONAD

Finally, we should define an instance of the `Monad` type class as follows:

```
instance Monad m => Monad (MaybeT m) where
  (>>=) :: MaybeT m a -> (a -> MaybeT m b) -> MaybeT m b
  (MaybeT ma) >>= f = ...
```

We are now used to unwrapping `MaybeT` ... first. We know that we'll wrap it back in the end. We have no pattern matching over the functional arguments (`a -> MaybeT m b`), but we can apply them. How can we get access to `a` to do that? Well, we should use `(>>=)` for `m`, which is now a monad. We also know that we'll get `Maybe a` as a result of this monad `m` computation, and our overall result should be either `Nothing` or `Just`, depending on that computation. Pattern matching over that `Maybe a` should do a job. An implementation of these ideas is presented in the following:

Initial unwrapping via pattern matching

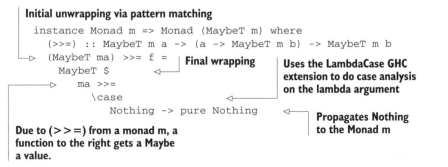

```
instance Monad m => Monad (MaybeT m) where
  (>>=) :: MaybeT m a -> (a -> MaybeT m b) -> MaybeT m b
  (MaybeT ma) >>= f =                      Final wrapping
      MaybeT $
          ma >>=
              \case
                  Nothing -> pure Nothing
```

Final wrapping

Uses the LambdaCase GHC extension to do case analysis on the lambda argument

Propagates Nothing to the Monad m

Due to (>>=) from a monad m, a function to the right gets a Maybe a value.

We have the deeply wrapped value v of type a at last.

```
Just v ->
    runMaybeT (f v)
```

Runs f on v and temporarily unwraps its result to get the types right: we are still inside (>>=) for Monad m.

We are done. I want to stress the inherently mechanical nature of writing these instances. We follow the types and use almost everything we have access to. It's even more mechanical than usual because we've used the preexisting `Functor` and `Applicative` instances for `Maybe`. Note that we didn't use the `Monad` instance for `Maybe`. As we'll see in the next section, in general, when defining these instances for other monad transformers, the corresponding monads are not yet available because those monads are defined using the respective transformers instead.

All right, this is what we've got so far: the `MaybeT` monad transformer defines a monad when given a monad, so a monad stack built with it is a monad.

6.3.3   Step 2: Implementing the full monad stack functionality

Now we have to make sure that our freshly built monad stack is convenient to use. That includes the following two things:

- We should be able to go along the stack with `lift`.
- We should allow automatic lifting to avoid bothering the user with the specific monad stack structure.

GIVE IT A LIFT

First, lifting is defined by the `MonadTrans` type class from the `Control.Monad.Trans.Class` module. We need to define the following instance:

```
instance MonadTrans MaybeT where
  lift :: Monad m => m a -> MaybeT m a
  ...
```

The type signature says that given any monadic computation `m a`, we should produce a new monadic computation in the `MaybeT m a` transformed monad. The lifted computation has nothing to do with the goals of failure management provided by `MaybeT`, so the best solution would be just wrapping its result with the `Just` data constructor and then using `MaybeT` to get the final computation. The following code presents this approach:

Final wrapping
```
instance MonadTrans MaybeT where
  lift :: Monad m => m a -> MaybeT m a
  lift ma = MaybeT $
              fmap Just ma
```

Introduce Just to ma, thus getting the value of m (Maybe a)

In general, lifting means delegating the job further along the stack. That's why its implementation is almost always trivial. For example, let's see how it is implemented for the `WriterT` monad transformer:

```
instance (Monoid w) => MonadTrans (WriterT w) where
    lift :: Monad m => m a -> WriterT w m a
    lift m = WriterT $ do
        a <- m
        return (a, mempty)
```

The same approach is used here: we execute the given action in the underlying monad and then return its result augmented with `WriterT`'s own information (empty log `mempty`). We could rewrite it without a do block as follows:

```
instance (Monoid w) => MonadTrans (WriterT w) where
    lift m = WriterT $ fmap (,mempty) m
```

An empty log with a tuple section (`,mempty`) is analogous to the use of `Just` in the `MaybeT` case. Note that we'd need to enable the `TupleSections` GHC extension for that to work. Otherwise, we'd have to rewrite it with a lambda function.

LIFT-SPECIFIC INTERFACES

Writing `lift m` in our monad stack means that we delegate the job `m` to other monad stack layers. In principle, we could write things like `lift (lift m)` or `lift (lift (lift m))`, thus going deeper and deeper along the stack. There is one problem with this approach: when we write `lift` explicitly, we have to know our stack structure. This is not always practical: changing the stack a little by adding a layer in the middle would break code like this.

The key idea is to provide interfaces for all the monad functionalities. For example, our `MaybeT` transformer has no idea what to do with state-management functions like `put` or `get`. However, if we wrap a monad `m` that knows about them, then why not delegate those tasks by lifting? We can do that for every state-management method. All of them come from the `MonadState` type class, so let's implement it, as shown in the next code sample:

```
instance MonadState s m => MonadState s (MaybeT m)  where
    state = lift . state
```

We are lucky that it's enough to implement `state` because it's the only method in the `MonadState` type class's minimal complete definition. Now, if we use `state` or any other method of the `MonadState` type class inside the monad stack built with `MaybeT`, the method call will be silently replaced by `lift . state`, where `state` comes from the `m` monad `MonadState` instance.

Unfortunately, we have to do the same for every other type class like `MonadState`.

Required GHC extensions

The code in this section requires you to enable several GHC extensions apart from what we've already mentioned, namely:

- `FlexibleInstances` to lift many unnecessary restrictions imposed by the Haskell Report on the instance heads
- `MultiParamTypeClasses` to allow type classes with several type variables like `MonadState s m`
- `UndecidableInstances` to be able to define `MonadState` instances

The last extension may sound the scariest of all: why on earth would we want to introduce *undecidability* into our program? The reason for it is hidden in the way monad transformer libraries are implemented.

6.3.4 *Step 3: Supplying additional functionality*

We are not done yet. The things we already have done are usually done for every monad transformer. Some monads provide additional functionality, so monad transformers should provide it, too. In this section we implement the following:

- The `MaybeT` transformer has natural failing functionality: we can use `Nothing` to express that. This allows writing a `MonadFail` instance.
- We can use monoid operations for `Maybe a`. This is expressed by the `Alternative` and `MonadPlus` type classes.
- We allow using `IO` operations if the base monad is `IO`. This is done via a `MonadIO` instance.

FAIL WITH MONADFAIL

The `MonadFail` type class declares the `fail` method. To implement it, we need to send `Nothing` into the underlying monad. The implementation is trivial, as shown here:

```
instance Monad m => MonadFail (MaybeT m) where
  fail :: String -> MaybeT m a
  fail _ = MaybeT (pure Nothing)
```

With this instance, GHC is able to delegate pattern-matching failures to the `fail` method. Thus, we'll get `Nothing` as expected.

CHOOSE AN ALTERNATIVE

Let's implement the `Alternative` type class. As before, we are going to delegate almost all the work to the `Alternative` instance for `Maybe`. We want to allow users of `MaybeT` to use a `guard` that relies on `Alternative` to stop computations in the monad stacks built with `MaybeT`. The details are presented in the following code sample:

```
instance Applicative m => Alternative (MaybeT m) where
  empty :: MaybeT m a
  empty = MaybeT (pure empty)

  (<|>) :: MaybeT m a -> MaybeT m a -> MaybeT m a
  (MaybeT mx) <|> (MaybeT my) = MaybeT ((<|>) <$> mx <*> my)
```

We want m to be an `Applicative` with no other constraints. In this implementation, we use `empty` for `Maybe a` and `pure` for m. Remember that we have to wrap m (`Maybe a`) with the `MaybeT` constructor.

It is meaningful to implement `Alternative` for `MaybeT`, but what if the transformer under the implementation has no support for `Alternative`? Well, in that case, we can delegate this job along the stack. Here is the beauty of monad stacks: there is always some layer that is aware of how to get the actual job done. Clearly, we have to require that `Alternative` is implemented somewhere along the stack, as shown in the following example:

```
instance (Monoid w, Alternative m) => Alternative (WriterT w m) where
  ...
```

The mentioned requirement comes in the form of an `Alternative m =>` constraint in the instance head. Note that we had no such requirement in the `Alternative` implementation for `MaybeT`.

INPUT AND OUTPUT WITH MONADIO

Finally, we want to allow using `IO` operations in a monad stack built from `MaybeT`, given that the underlying monad allows them. This ability is expressed by the `MonadIO` type class with the (only) `liftIO` method. An implementation is also trivial: we simply `lift` an `IO` action to an underlying monad, as shown next:

```
instance MonadIO m => MonadIO (MaybeT m) where
  liftIO :: IO a -> MaybeT m a
  liftIO = lift . liftIO
```

Once we've lifted it, it's no longer our problem—very convenient.

6.3.5   *Using a transformer*

Remember, we had the following monad stack for evaluating an expression given in RPN:

```
type EvalM = StateT Stack Maybe
```

Now we can switch to our `MaybeT` monad transformer, shown next:

```
type EvalM = MaybeT (State Stack)
```

The changes are minimal. We should import the `MyMaybeT` module and change runners for the `evalRPN` computation. In the previous implementation we had the following:

```
evalRPN :: String -> Maybe Integer
evalRPN str = evalStateT evalRPN' []
  where
    ...
```

Now we need something like this:

```
evalRPN :: String -> Maybe Integer
evalRPN str = evalState (runMaybeT evalRPN') []
  where
    ...
```

We have two runners instead of one, but this comes from the expected result type. In the first implementation, we were interested in `Maybe Integer`, so there was no need to process a value from `evalStateT`. Now we should process our monad stack in full to get the result.

Compare the `EvalRPNTrans` and `EvalRPNTrans2` modules to make sure that everything else stays the same.

6.4 *Monad transformers in the Haskell libraries*

The main monad transformer functionality is split over the two Haskell packages: `transformers` and `mtl` (which is a little bit awkwardly an acronym of *monad transformer library*). This separation is due to historical reasons and is an attempt to distinguish portable and nonportable parts of the library. Although Haskell portability is almost never an issue nowadays, these two libraries still exist and befuddle developers. To make things even more complicated, several implementations exist of the nonportable parts based on different GHC extensions. Apart from `mtl`, which is based on `FunctionalDependencies`, we also have the `monads-tf` package and the now-deprecated `mtl-tf` package, both based on type families.

In what follows, we'll discuss the content of the `transformers` and `mtl` libraries.

6.4.1 *Identity is where it all starts*

Maybe surprisingly, such monads as `Writer` or `State` are actually defined using their corresponding transformers. We already know that transformers add functionality. Now the question is, add to what? The answer is simple. We have the most trivial monad, which is called `Identity`. It's this monad that is transformed in the first place. It's really a `Monad` (and a `Functor`, and an `Applicative`). The `Identity` type and the corresponding (trivial) functionality is defined in the `Data.Functor.Identity` module, which comes with the `base` package.

What is this `Identity`? Well, it's just the following:

```
newtype Identity a = Identity { runIdentity :: a }
```

As usual, every monadic type is accompanied with a type for a result of the computation. `Identity` here is a trivial wrapper over this result. How would we `fmap` with some function `a -> b` over the value a? It's a trivial function application. The `pure` method wraps an `Identity` (remember that due to using `newtype`, all this wrapping is eventually removed anyway). A function in this context is indistinguishable from a function without it. Thus, applying it with `(<*>)` is also trivial. Finally, monadic `(>>=)` becomes a trivial function application also. GHC provides the coerce function, which represents this triviality. Basically, coerce means *leave it without doing anything*. For example, let's see a Functor instance for Identity:

```
instance Functor Identity where
    fmap = coerce
```

The type of fmap in this instance is (a -> b) -> Identity a -> Identity b or, without a wrapper (again, it is removed anyway), (a -> b) -> a -> b. Coercing here can be interpreted as splitting this type signature in two parts—(a -> b) and a -> b—and then saying something like "oh, it's the same thing." The same trick is used for the Applicative and Monad instances.

Interestingly, an IdentityT monad transformer is also defined in the Control .Monad.Trans.Identity module. Can you imagine what functionality it provides?

The reason to use it is highly practical. Suppose we want to call a function parameterized by a monad transformer. If we have a monad instead, we can transform it by the IdentityT monad transformer and pass the result to that function.

6.4.2 An overview of the most common monad transformers

Table 6.1 lists the most common monad transformers. All of them are provided by the transformers package.

Table 6.1   Monad transformers in the **transformers** package

Name	Functionality provided
AccumT	Accumulates data with the ability to read the current value at any time during the computation (something between WriterT and ReaderT, or a limited StateT).
ExceptT	Exits a computation by generating exceptions with the full information about the current context. We'll use this monad transformer in the next chapter extensively.
MaybeT	Exits computations without producing a result.
ReaderT	Implements access to a read-only environment.
StateT	Implements read/write access to a state value.
WriterT	Logs data in the form of appending an element to a monoid.
RWST	Combines the functionalities of the ReaderT, WriterT, and StateT monad transformers.

Other monad transformers are defined in the transformers package. The ContT transformer enables implementing computations with the ability to stop and resume—this is one of the hardest (but rarely used) monad transformers, so feel free to forget about it right now, or read the blog post by Gabriel Gonzalez (http:// www.haskellforall.com/2012/12/the-continuation-monad.html) about it. There is also the SelectT transformer, useful for implementing search algorithms. You can find more information in the documentation on Hackage (make sure that you follow the links to the papers that introduced the corresponding transformers!).

Summary

- Use monad transformers to get the combined functionality of several monads at once.
- Interpret monad stacks as a framework for an application.
- Know the details behind monad transformers—there is no magic there!
- It's okay to use monad transformers without fully understanding the details—remember, we use computers without a PhD in electrical engineering.
- Make sure you have the most common monad transformers at your fingertips.

Part 3

Quality assurance

Software engineering strives to come up with the best practices of developing software at a certain level of quality. We do need correct and performant programs. In this part, we'll talk about errors in our programs and learn ways to handle them. Some of the errors are inevitable at run time, so we have to alleviate their consequences for users. Some of them can be fully avoided by applying smart testing techniques. We'll also cover performance problems, both discovering them and dealing with them. We'll then take a small detour in this part. In chapter 9, we'll talk about internal compiler things, such as Haskell program behavior at run time. I find understanding this topic crucial for developing efficient and performant software in Haskell.

Error handling
and logging

7

This chapter covers

- An idea of exceptions in Haskell and when to use them
- Several exception-handling mechanisms
- Designing exception handling in pure and impure code

Programmers want to control everything within their programs. In Haskell, we can do that via type discipline and reasoning about function behavior. Unfortunately, communication with the outer world sets limits to that control as follows:

- When reading a file, we can never be sure in advance whether it exists.
- Even if it does exist, we have no guarantee its content matches our expectations.
- While we are fetching a web page, a network connection may break.
- Acquiring a resource (even memory allocation) may fail.

How should we react? When can we get information about the problems we have? When do we know how to address them? Are these at the same points in a program or later? Should we halt our application completely? Is it possible to figure out how to proceed instead? These questions have to be answered in every application.

In this chapter, we'll discuss the idea of exceptions and exception-handling mechanisms for getting around these problems. We'll also cover logging as an essential tool for recording information on what is going wrong at run time.

7.1   Overview of error-handling mechanisms in Haskell

Exceptions in Haskell are traditionally complicated. At least two reasons for that follow:

- In Haskell, several distinct exception-handling mechanisms can be used interchangeably in many cases. Thus, we have a problem of choice. Even worse, many interfaces to those mechanisms have a many-to-many relationship.
- Exceptions may indicate a programmer's mistakes or reflect external conditions. We can prepare for some of the latter conditions in advance. Unfortunately, many others are always unpredictable.

In this chapter, I'd like to differentiate between two classes of exception-handling mechanisms as follows:

- Exceptions implemented as a library (I call them programmable exceptions).
- Exceptions supported by the GHC runtime system (known as extensible exceptions).

The first class of exceptions is usually implemented as a monad transformer and uses a monadic approach to computations without any specific language features. The second one has support on both the library level and the GHC runtime system. It can be used via several competing interfaces and is mainly used in IO computations.

Let's talk about the idea of exceptions in general first and then discuss cases when it's better to avoid using them.

7.1.1   The idea of exceptions

An exception is a way to escape regular control flow in a program. If we (or the runtime system) encounter a problematic situation at run time and we don't know how to deal with it, we throw an exception. This stops a regular control flow in our code, and we get back to a point where we can handle (or catch) the exception somewhere along the stack of function calls. At such a point, we can either resume regular control flow or prepare to exit the program. If no such point exists, the program halts with an error message.

Suppose we have a simple function main calling the functions f and g sequentially. If we wrap a call to f with an exception handler, then any exception in f or other function called from it brings us there. Figure 7.1 illustrates this process. In this example, an exception is raised in f12 called from f1 called from f. Note that f13, f2, and f3 are never called. The program execution goes straight to the exception handler at f, and the program then continues with g.

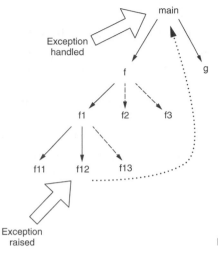

Figure 7.1 Escaping regular control flow with exceptions

Unfortunately, this simple idea becomes a bit more complicated in Haskell due to a combination of purity and laziness. If we call a function and don't get a result from it, this breaks purity. Due to laziness, the computation in f12 may well occur during the execution of g and/or other functions, depending on how the functions are implemented. An exception could become hidden until the result of f12 is actually evaluated. No one knows when this is going to happen.

Things get worse if we acquire some resources before raising an exception. We'd better have them released, or we risk breaking a computing system at some point. Concurrency brings even more complications: our thread could be killed by other threads. Even without concurrency, our thread could be killed by the runtime system while we are doing our nice, safe, pure computations (if, for example, there is not enough memory to accommodate memory allocation requests).

Unfortunately, no one bulletproof, perfectly safe, general solution to these problems exists. The only thing we can do is adhere to some sort of a programming discipline. In short, we should do the right things and shouldn't do the wrong things.

Every exception-handling mechanism provides the following components:

- A representation of an exceptional situation as a value (of some type)
- The means to throw and catch an exception
- Guaranteed finalization (an action that is taken independently whether or not an exception was thrown)

We'd also expect some guidelines on when and how such a mechanism should be used. I'll try to give advice for some of them in the rest of this chapter. Unfortunately, these issues are rather controversial, so feel free not to believe me.

7.1.2   *To use or not to use?*

Exception-handling mechanisms are powerful tools. Nevertheless, it's not a good idea to use them all the time. They introduce significant complexity and potential performance drawbacks. That's why I suggest the following rule: *if we can avoid using exceptions at all, we should avoid using them.*

Moreover, there are cases when using exception handling feels totally wrong to me. By this, I mean programmer faults.

Suppose we write a program that involves division. When we divide by zero, it's our fault that we forget to check whether a divisor equals zero. In the following GHCi session, the runtime system throws an exception when we try to execute such a broken program:

```
ghci> a = 6
ghci> b = 0
ghci> a `div` b
*** Exception: divide by zero
```

This is definitely not the case when we use an exception-handling mechanism to deal with the error. Instead, we prefer to fix the implementation by using, say, the Maybe a type for returning a result as follows:

```
divSafe :: Integer -> Integer -> Maybe Integer
divSafe a 0 = Nothing
divSafe a b = Just (a `div` b)
```

> ### GHC warnings
>
> Although the compiler can deliver us some information about faulty code via exceptions at run time, it's more recommendable to get them as early as possible via compiler warnings, the type system, testing, or other sorts of programming discipline.
>
> For example, we can use the -fwarn-incomplete-patterns GHC flag for compiling our program and get a warning for incomplete pattern matches. In fact, the -W option enables a lot of helpful warnings. There are also -Wall and -Weverything for enabling most of the warnings and all of them, respectively. To write cleaner code, it is generally recommended to use one of the latter flags and disable those particular warnings we don't need. We can set these options for our project via the ghc-option field of the Cabal file.

Exceptions and exception-handling mechanisms are unavoidable when we deal with anything that is not under our control. In Haskell, this is mainly I/O and everything built on top of it. In pure code, it's not always easy to check in advance that everything will go smoothly. Then it's okay to go with exception handling. For example, if we implement a sophisticated algorithm with pure functions, we could be stuck at some point realizing that we have an error in our input. Using exceptions and exception handling here is okay. The good thing about Haskell is that it is possible to do that programmatically without using runtime system exceptions at all.

The point I'd like to stress once again is that it's not always the best idea to go with exceptions. Sometimes we're better off avoiding using them by checking preconditions, exploiting compiler warnings, and so on. That said, we should always be ready to get an exception from the runtime system, no matter the level of purity we have. Memory allocation requests can fail, for example.

7.1.3   *Programmable exceptions vs. GHC runtime exceptions*

A cool thing about Haskell is that we don't need special language support to write code that throws an exception and handles it in separate parts of the code. At the end of the day, it's just some computational effect. We have a tool for that, namely, monads. Everyone could implement such a mechanism by providing a monad with an implementation of >>= that ignores the second argument in the case of getting an exception as a result of evaluating the first argument. Note that the implementation of the `Maybe` monad is very close to this idea. An instance of the `Monad` for `Either` a is even closer. The `Left` value could carry some data describing the exception.

In a scenario like this, handling an exception would mean resuming normal operation. Imagine that we get `Nothing` instead of a result of computation at some stage. If we agree to replace it with some default value or are able to compute it in some other way, then we could continue on, so an exception has been handled.

We call such exception mechanisms *programmable*, meaning that everything is done programmatically by the programmers themselves or the libraries they use. Because we often want to have other effects happen while doing computations, it is usually the case that programmable exceptions are provided by a monad transformer adding one layer to our monad stacks. The `ExceptT` monad transformer helps us to create monadic stacks with this ability. It is best for describing computations that could fail with some known set of exceptional conditions. These conditions are specified by data constructors of an algebraic data type. This is quite often the case with pure computations. It's a good idea to use `ExceptT` for monad stacks based on anything except for the `IO` monad. We'll get back to the `ExceptT` monad transformer later in the next section.

Unfortunately, the real world is full of surprises. It's impossible to predict what will happen at run time. Consequently, the `IO` monad brings a lot of uncertainty. It's impossible to list all the exceptions that could be thrown at run time. Any attempt to apply an `ExceptT`-like approach with a list of exceptional conditions to `IO` computation (including the `main` function) is doomed.

GHC implements another exception-handling mechanism that can be used in any Haskell program. Its main features follow:

- All the exceptions are represented as values of the `SomeException` type.
- We can define our own types for exceptions, provided that they implement the `Exception` type class.

- Exceptions may be thrown everywhere in the code but may only be caught in IO actions.
- Exceptions thrown in pure code are called *imprecise* (meaning an unspecified order of execution in pure code and laziness effects).
- Exceptions may be thrown in some thread by the thread itself (*synchronous* exceptions) or by some other thread (*asynchronous* exceptions). The latter includes exceptions from the runtime system.
- There is no way to specify a list of expected exceptions.

In this chapter, we'll focus on the single-threaded case. Thus, we won't discuss asynchronous exceptions.

GHC runtime exceptions are defined by the Control.Exception module from the base package. It defines many particular types of exceptions, ranging from ArithException to IOException. It provides functions to throw and catch exceptions. This module contains useful documentation as well as a higher-level interface to exceptions defined by the exceptions package (by Edward Kmett).

> **NOTE** GHC runtime exceptions have several competing interfaces. In this chapter, I stick with those defined in the base and exceptions packages. One other solid interface is defined by Michael Snoyman in the safe-exceptions package. This package features good documentation, and it may be useful to learn this approach, too.

To summarize the general picture around exception handling, my personal guidelines follow:

1 We strive to avoid dealing with exceptions by strict programming discipline (types, tests, compiler warnings, etc.).
2 We use approaches with programmable exceptions (Maybe, Either, ExceptT, etc.) to implement pure algorithms if errors in input show themselves at later processing stages and are too hard to discover in advance.
3 We use GHC runtime exceptions for communicating with the real world (IO computations) by throwing and handling them in judicious places.
4 We use GHC runtime exceptions to log any exceptional situations that were not handled by other means (e.g., programmer mistakes that made their way into our program despite our best efforts).

In the rest of this chapter, we'll look at examples of how to use programmable exceptions and GHC exceptions in practice.

7.2 *Programmable exceptions in monad stacks*

In this section, we'll apply one example of programmable exception-handling approaches, namely, the ExceptT monad transformer, to our example of evaluating arithmetic expressions given in reverse Polish notation. In the previous chapter, we dealt with some errors, but the only way to report them was to return Nothing. Meeting something unexpected within an expression is a good reason to throw an exception and let someone work it out later. Before diving into an example, let's look at the `ExceptT` monad transformer closely.

7.2.1 *The ExceptT monad transformer*

The `ExceptT` monad transformer is provided by the `Control.Monad.Except` module from the `mtl` package. It implements an ability to throw errors and suppress execution until errors are handled or a computation is completed.

An interface for this error-handling mechanism is defined by the `MonadError` type class, as shown next:

```
class Monad m => MonadError e m | m -> e where
  throwError :: e -> m a
  catchError :: m a -> (e -> m a) -> m a
```

Using this interface, we can either throw an error at any moment during the computation in the m monad or catch an error thrown earlier. The e type variable refers to the type of an error. Note that there are no restrictions on the e variable, so we can use whatever we like as an error value. When we throw an error with `throwError`, we don't have to think about returning anything meaningful thanks to the m a type of result. The type checker is always happy when we throw an error.

As usual with exceptions, `throwError` creates a new control flow going straight to the `catchError` or to the end of the actions sequence.

The `catchError` method has the following two arguments:

- The first one is an action that potentially may throw an exception or may return a result of type a in a monadic context.
- The second one is an exception handler that is called only if an exception is thrown.

Note that both the action and the handler have the same result type, which becomes the result of the `catchError` itself, though nothing prevents the handler from rethrowing the same or some other error instead of returning something.

To construct a monad stack able to handle these methods, we use the `ExceptT` monad transformer and the `runExceptT` runner as follows:

```
runExceptT :: ExceptT e m a -> m (Either e a)
```

An exception thrown and not caught results in the `Left` component of `Either e a`.

Now let's see how we can use the `ExceptT` monad transformer to evaluate an expression given in reverse Polish notation.

7.2.2 *Example: Evaluating RPN expressions*

To make an example more engaging, let's extend it a little bit. First, we want to evaluate a list of expressions all at once. Second, we want to have variables in our expressions.

Values of these variables may be given by a `Reader`-accessible environment. Third, we want to get a clear indication of what's wrong with an expression. For example, we have the following list of expressions:

```
rpns :: [Text]
rpns = ["answer",
        "12 13 + 1",
        "2 +",
        "x y +",
        "1x +",
        "1 22 1 22 0 2 * * * * *",
        "10 1 2 + 2 2 1 2 * + * * * 1 x 2 + + +"]
```

In an environment with `answer` referring to `42` and `x` to `1`, we could expect the following results:

```
answer = 42
12 13 + 1 Error: There are extra elements in the expression
2 + Error: Not enough elements in the expression
x y + Error: Variable 'y' not found
1x + Error: Expression component '1x' is not a number
1 22 1 22 0 2 * * * * * = 0
10 1 2 + 2 2 1 2 * + * * * 1 x 2 + + + = 244
```

EXAMPLE: EVALUATING RPN EXPRESSIONS WITH EXCEPTT

🗋   expr/rpn/EvalRPNExcept.hs

⚡   *rpnexpr*

☞   The `ExceptT` computation is described by a list of potential errors.

☞   We throw an error when we discover it and catch it later.

CONSTRUCTING A MONAD STACK WITH EXCEPTT

We have a `Stack` as before and a type for the environment where we store values of variables, as shown next:

```
type Stack = [Integer]
type EnvVars = [(Text, Integer)]
```

Let's categorize what could go wrong while evaluating an expression in RPN as follows:

- There are not enough elements in the given expression.
- There are extra elements in the given expression.
- The component that should be a number is not a number.
- The variable mentioned in an expression is not found in the environment.

The `EvalError` type defines these cases as data constructors, as follows:

```
data EvalError = NotEnoughElements
               | ExtraElements
               | NotANumber Text
               | UnknownVar Text
```

Note that we don't have any constraints on the `EvalError` data type. We just list the cases and include any additional information that we've found helpful. To represent these cases in a more friendly way, we can use the following TextShow instance:

```
instance TextShow EvalError where
  showb NotEnoughElements = "Not enough elements in the expression"
  showb ExtraElements = "There are extra elements in the expression"
  showb (NotANumber t) = "Expression component '" <>
                         fromText t <> "' is not a number"
  showb (UnknownVar t) = "Variable '" <>
                         fromText t <> "' not found"
```

Now we can define the monad stack as follows:

```
type EvalM = ReaderT EnvVars (ExceptT EvalError (State Stack))
```

We use `Stack` as our state as before. We also add `ExceptT` to throw errors and `ReaderT` to access the environment.

Just as before, the `push` function doesn't throw any error, so we don't have to change it, as shown next:

```
push :: Integer -> EvalM ()
push x = modify (x:)
```

Once again we see a nice property of monad stacks. We've changed it completely, but don't have to change the implementation of functions that refer to the remaining functionality. All other functions can discover errors. Let's move on to them.

DISCOVERING AND THROWING ERRORS

One problem with the `pop` function is that the stack may be empty. So if the stack is empty, we throw an error as shown in the following example:

```
pop :: EvalM Integer
pop = get >>= pop'
  where
    pop' :: Stack -> EvalM Integer
    pop' [] = throwError NotEnoughElements
    pop' (x:xs) = put xs >> pure x
```

> **The FlexibleContexts GHC extension**
>
> Note the type annotation of the locally defined `pop'` function. If we omit this type anno-
> tation, we'd get a compilation error about a non-type-variable argument in the con-
> straint. The error message may look quite scary, as shown next, but it is instructive:
>
> ```
> expr/rpn/EvalRPNExcept.hs:41:5: error:
>     • Non type-variable argument
>         in the constraint: MonadError EvalError m
>       (Use FlexibleContexts to permit this)
>     • When checking the inferred type
>         pop' :: forall (m :: * -> *) a.
>                 (MonadError EvalError m, MonadState [a] m) =>
>                 [a] -> m a
>       In an equation for 'pop':
>       ...
> ```
>
> The compiler is powerful enough to infer a very general type for `pop'`: the monad we
> are working in must implement the `MonadError EvalError` and `MonadState [a]`
> instances. Unfortunately, constraints with specific types (such as `EvalError`) are
> disallowed in standard Haskell. GHC implements the `FlexibleContexts` extension
> to lift this restriction. It is perfectly safe to enable this extension and get rid of the
> annoying type annotation for the locally defined function.

We know that if an expression is correct, there should be exactly one element on the
stack in the end. Let's check that, as shown in the next example, and throw an exception if it's not the case with the given expression:

```
oneElementOnStack :: EvalM ()
oneElementOnStack = do
  len <- gets length
  when (len /= 1) $ throwError ExtraElements
```

Any other `len` within this monad stack won't be executed after throwing this error
unless we catch it.

In the previous chapter, we had the `readSafe` function, which returned `Nothing` if
the input was not a number. Reading becomes more complicated now. First, we
should check whether we have a number or a variable. I suggest the following simple
check: if a value starts with a letter, it's a variable. Otherwise, it's supposed to be a
number.

If it's a number, we consult an environment and report an error in the case of this
missing variable as follows:

```
readVar :: Text -> EvalM Integer
readVar name = do
  var <- asks (lookup name)
  case var of
    Just n -> pure n
    Nothing -> throwError $ UnknownVar name
```

If it's a number, we try to read it from `Text` as shown here:

```
readNumber :: Text -> EvalM Integer
readNumber txt =
  case decimal txt of
    Right (n, rest) | T.null rest -> pure n
    _ -> throwError $ NotANumber txt9
```

> **NOTE** Facilities to read values from `Text` (such as the `decimal` function) are provided by the `Data.Text.Read` module. These functions try to read the starting part of the given `Text` and return either `Right` with a result and the rest of the `Text` or `Left` with an error message.

An evaluation of one expression is the same as before, though we have to clear the `Stack` before running it as follows:

```
evalRPNOnce ::Text -> EvalM Integer
evalRPNOnce str =
    clearStack >> traverse_ step (T.words str) >> oneElementOnStack >> pop
  where
    clearStack = put []
    step "+" = processTops (+)
    step "*" = processTops (*)
    step "-" = processTops (-)
    step t = readSafe t >>= push
    processTops op = flip op <$> pop <*> pop >>= push
```

Now we are ready to implement the processing of a list of expressions. This requires catching errors and resuming normal operation.

CATCHING EXCEPTIONS WITHIN THE MONAD STACK

The `evalRPNOnce` function makes no attempt to catch an error. Our task now is to run it many times and catch all the errors for every run.

Remember that running a monad stack with the `ExceptT` transformer gives us `Either e a`. Let's prepare to display these results as follows:

```
reportEvalResults :: Either EvalError [Builder] -> Text
reportEvalResults (Left e) = "Error: " <> showt e
reportEvalResults (Right b) = toText $ unlinesB b
```

The `evalRPNMany` function, shown next, takes a list of expressions and transform all of them into one resulting `Text` by running `evalRPNOnce` for every expression and catching errors, if any:

```
evalRPNMany :: [Text] -> EnvVars -> Text
evalRPNMany txts env = reportEvalResults $
    evalState (runExceptT (runReaderT (mapM evalOnce txts) env)) []
  where
    evalOnce txt = (fromText txt <>) <$>
      (buildOk <$> evalRPNOnce txt) `catchError` (pure . buildErr)
    buildOk res = " = " <> showb res
    buildErr err = " Error: " <> showb err
```

Note the `evalOnce` wrapper function. This function catches errors in `evalRPNOnce` and renders the corresponding results, either a value or an error message.

7.3   *GHC runtime exceptions*

The GHC runtime system implements an exception-throwing and -handling mechanism. The main rule is that an exception can be thrown anywhere (including pure code), but it can be caught only in an `IO` computation. The corresponding API is provided by the `Control.Exception` module from `base`. It defines the following:

- A type that encapsulates any exception
- A type class that defines methods for wrapping and unwrapping exceptions
- Types for particular exceptions thrown by the runtime system
- Utilities to throw and catch exceptions

The `Control.Exception` API is heavily based on the `IO` monad. Most of the functions defined there are `IO` actions. To make using this API in monad stacks easier, we use the `Control.Monad.Catch` module from the `exceptions` package. This module reexports the `Control.Exception` API and adds several type classes that can be used in monad stacks that support throwing and catching GHC exceptions. The utility functions are also redefined in terms of monad stacks, as opposed to `IO`.

Now let's see an overview of the components of the GHC exception-handling mechanism using a very simple example of the safe division implementation as follows.

EXAMPLE: SAFE DIVISION WITH GHC EXCEPTIONS

🗋   ch07/div.hs

⚡   *div*

☞ We can define our own types for exceptions.

☞ We can throw exceptions anywhere in code.

☞ We catch exceptions in `IO` computations.

7.3.1   *An idea of extensible exceptions*

Every GHC exception is encapsulated in a value of the `SomeException` type. Its definition from the `Control.Exception` module follows:

```
data SomeException = forall e . Exception e => SomeException e
```

This definition uses the `ExistentialQuantification` GHC extension, which provides the `forall` keyword to be used for data type definitions like this one.

Existential quantification and the forall keyword

You may be surprised that existential quantification is expressed by the `forall` keyword, which is usually used for universal quantification. Shouldn't we use the `exists` keyword instead?

From a logical point of view, these two logical implications are equivalent, as shown next (I leave the proof as an exercise to the reader interested in logic, but please make sure that you use intuitive logic for proving it!):

```
forall x . P x -> Q === (exists x. P x) -> Q
```

Note that we use `Q` here, which doesn't depend on `x`—just as the `SomeException` type doesn't depend on the `e` type of an exception. It's the `SomeException` data constructor that takes a value of `e` as an argument, not the type constructor itself.

The obviously existential type `(exists x. P x) -> Q` allows creating a value of type `Q` from any value of type `x` given that it satisfies the `P` constraint. This means that we could take any exception of the type with an instance of the `Exception` type class and wrap it with the `SomeException` data constructor, getting the value of the `SomeException` type.

Unfortunately, allowing `exists` in arbitrary positions would make type inference undecidable, so the GHC developers decided to go with the limited form of universal quantification where a formula starts with `forall` and contains no other quantifiers. We can be happy that this form happened to be equivalent to what we needed to implement a type for exceptions able to wrap all of them.

Apart from the existential quantification, GHC exceptions make use of type-representation mechanisms provided by the `Data.Typeable` module.

The `Exception` type class provides the following three methods to work with exceptions:

```
class (Typeable e, Show e) => Exception e where
  toException :: e -> SomeException
  fromException :: SomeException -> Maybe e
  displayException :: e -> String
```

These methods have default definitions, given that we implement (or derive) the `Show` instance for our own exception type. They allow us to wrap and unwrap exceptions from the `SomeException` values.

For example, let's define a simple type for arithmetic exceptions as follows:

```
{-# LANGUAGE DeriveAnyClass #-}

data MyArithException = DivByZero | OtherArithException
 deriving (Show, Exception)
```

Now we can throw and catch exceptions of the `MyArithException` type. Thus, we've extended the GHC exceptions hierarchy.

7.3.2   *Throwing exceptions*

The `Control.Exception` module gives us the following four ways to throw an exception:

- The `throw` function to throw an exception in pure code
- The `throwIO` function to throw an exception in the `IO` computation
- The `ioError` function to throw a specific `IOException`
- The `throwTo` function to throw an exception in the target thread (more on this in chapter 16, "Concurrency")

The first function can be used as follows:

```
divPure :: Int -> Int -> Int
divPure _ 0 = throw DivByZero
divPure a b = a `div` b
```

Exceptions thrown from pure code are called imprecise because it may be hard to predict when they reveal themselves. For example, we can't be sure which call leads to the exception in `divPure 1 0 + divPure 2 0` due to the unspecified order of calls. Moreover, due to laziness, we can lose an imprecise exception entirely. Suppose, we have the following multiplication function:

```
mult :: Int -> Int -> Int
mult 0 _ = 0
mult a b = a * b
```

The following code doesn't throw an exception:

```
ghci> mult 0 (divPure 1 0)
0
ghci> p = (divPure 10 2, divPure 5 0)
ghci> fst p
5
```

In addition to the four functions listed earlier, the `MonadThrow` type class from the `exceptions` package defines a class of monads able to throw exceptions, as shown here:

```
class Monad m => MonadThrow m where
  throwM :: Exception e => e -> m a
```

One crucial thing about throwing an exception within a monadic computation is the requirement that no code is executed after an exception is thrown, as shown next:

```
throwM e >> x === throwM e
```

If a monad we use implements an instance of `MonadThrow`, we may raise an exception as a part of our computation.

The following are two examples of division in a monad:

```
divIO :: Int -> Int -> IO Int
divIO _ 0 = throwIO DivByZero
divIO a b = pure (a `div` b)

divM :: MonadThrow m => Int -> Int -> m Int
divM _ 0 = throwM DivByZero
divM a b = pure (a `div` b)
```

The last implementation is easier to use in monad stacks. Otherwise, `divIO` and `divM` share the same semantics.

Now we can use the `divM` function in a monadic sequence as follows:

```
testComputation a b c = divSafe a b >>= divSafe c
```

Let's check this code in the `Maybe` monad as follows (it has a trivial implementation of `MonadThrow`):

```
ghci> testComputation 6 3 10 :: Maybe Int
Just 5
ghci> testComputation 6 0 10 :: Maybe Int
Nothing
```

We see that the exception was thrown in the second expression, and we get `Nothing` in the end (this is what the `MonadThrow` instance for the `Maybe` monad is doing).

> **NOTE** You may get the impression that this example looks more like a programmable exception-handling mechanism than the GHC runtime exception system. This is true. In some sense, the `exceptions` package attempts to unify these approaches with one set of abstractions.

7.3.3 *Catching exceptions*

Before discussing how to catch an exception, let's think about what we are going to do with it. Chances are, we don't have to catch an exception explicitly. We may want to deal with GHC exceptions in the following situations:

- Cleaning up after some operations, especially when working with external resources
- Recovering from errors inside a computation by providing alternative (default) results
- Full-blown exception handling

Both the `Control.Exception` and `Control.Monad.Catch` modules provide utilities for dealing with all these situations. These utilities are defined as `IO` and `MonadCatch m => m` actions, respectively.

Let's discuss these situations separately.

CLEANUP AFTER OPERATIONS

We may want to do something whether or not any exception was raised. This is often the case when we work with external resources. These resources have to be released after use, even if an exception was raised.

In such situations, it's best to use the following functions:

- `finally` for executing some action no matter what
- `onException` for executing some action if an exception was thrown
- `bracket*` for implementing regular resource-aware actions with resource acquisition, use, and guaranteed release in the end

For example, the `bracket` function from the `Control.Exception` module has the following type:

```
bracket  :: IO a -> (a -> IO b) -> (a -> IO c) -> IO c
bracket acquire release use = ...
```

It can be used as follows:

```
bracket
  (openFile "filename" ReadMode)  ⟵─┐  Acquires
  (hClose)                        ⟵──── Releases
  (\fileHandle -> do { ... })     ⟵──┐
                                     │ Uses
```

Note that all these functions hide exception handling behind well-known programming patterns. They provide guaranteed cleanup without diving into particular exception types, thus making programming easier.

The `exceptions` package provides alternatives with the same names to work in monad stacks.

RECOVERY WITH TRY*

Remember, we have the `testComputation` function, which potentially raises a `MyArithException`. Suppose we want to run this computation returning 0 if there was an exception. This is a basic recovery strategy when we return a default value. Let's use the `try` function with the following type:

```
try :: Exception e => IO a -> IO (Either e a)
```

The idea is to run a computation and then recover by case analysis on `Either e a`, as in the following code:

```
divTestWithRecovery ::  Int -> Int -> Int -> IO Int
divTestWithRecovery a b c =
    try (testComputation a b c)  ⟵──── Attempts a computation
    >>= pure . dealWith          ⟵──┐
  where                            │ Analyzes the results
```

```
                 dealWith :: Either MyArithException Int -> Int
Regular  ┌──▷ dealWith (Right r) = r
result   │       dealWith (Left _) = 0      ◁────── Default result
```

Note the type of the `dealWith` function. We have to provide it here. GHC has no way to figure out which exception we plan to recover from. All other exceptions, except `MyArithException`, will be rethrown automatically. Note also that instead of using `>>= pure . dealWith`, we could write `dealWith <$> try (testComputation a b c)`. However, the latter makes the order of execution less obvious.

Apart from `try`, we can also use the following function:

```
tryJust :: Exception e => (e -> Maybe b) -> IO a -> IO (Either b a)
```

The first argument serves here as a predicate. It is executed if an exception of type `e` was raised. Returning `Nothing` from a predicate means that we can't recover at this point, so an exception is rethrown. For example, we could recover from `DivByZero` as follows:

```
divTestWithRecovery2 ::  Int -> Int -> Int -> IO Int
divTestWithRecovery2 a b c =
      tryJust isDivByZero (testComputation a b c) >>= pure . dealWith
   where
    isDivByZero :: MyArithException -> Maybe ()
    isDivByZero DivByZero = Just ()
    isDivByZero _ = Nothing

    dealWith (Right r) = r
    dealWith (Left _) = 0
```

Naturally, there are alternatives to these functions for monad stacks, as shown next:

```
try :: (MonadCatch m, Exception e) => m a -> m (Either e a)
tryJust :: (MonadCatch m, Exception e)
            => (e -> Maybe b) -> m a -> m (Either b a)
```

EXCEPTION HANDLING WITH CATCH* AND HANDLE*

Finally, we have a set of `catch*` and `handle*` functions. In some sense, they are exception-handling primitives. Thus, they allow implementing any exception-handling logic. The `handle*` functions have the same behavior as `catch*` with the arguments swapped.

The two versions of the `catch` function have the following types:

```
Control.Exception.catch :: Exception e => IO a -> (e -> IO a) -> IO a
Control.Monad.Catch.catch ::
  (MonadCatch m, Exception e) => m a -> (e -> m a) -> m a
```

If we have a monadic computation of type `m a` with a result of type `a`, then `catch` requires us to come up with some value of `a`, even if an exception was thrown. The second `catch` argument, an exception handler, is responsible precisely for that.

One more type class is used in the presence of asynchronous exceptions: `Monad-Mask`. It inherits `MonadCatch` and adds methods for dealing with asynchronous exceptions. We'll come to this type class in the chapter on concurrency.

In the following code sample, I use the `catch` function to recover from an error and print an error message at the same time:

```
divTestIO :: Int -> Int -> Int -> IO Int
divTestIO a b c = testComputation a b c `catch` handler
  where
    handler :: MyArithException -> IO Int
    handler e = do
      putStrLn $ "We've got an exception: " ++ show e
                 ++ "\nUsing default value 0"
      pure 0
```

Once again, we have to specify somehow the type of an exception we expect. The previous code works as expected, returning 0 in case of an exception, as shown next:

```
ghci> divTestIO 6 3 10
5
ghci> divTestIO 6 0 10
We've got an exception: DivByZero
Using default value 0
0
```

If we want to have our action written explicitly with the `do` block, then it's more convenient to use a function from the `handle*` family instead (their arguments are flipped).

In addition to `catch`, we have several other convenience functions. For example, it is possible to define a list of handlers for different exceptions and choose among them with the `catches` function. This function dispatches the execution to the suitable handler, depending on the type of exception thrown. We'll see an example later in this chapter.

7.4   *Example: Accessing web APIs and GHC exceptions*

In this section, we'll develop an application that uses several online web APIs to determine sunrise and sunset times based on a given address and the particular date.

EXAMPLE: COMPUTING SUNRISE AND SUNSET TIMES AT THE GIVEN LOCATION

🗋   suntimes/

⚡   *suntimes*

☞ We can use GHC exceptions to inform a user if something goes wrong.

This application works in two modes: an interactive mode for processing exactly one request and batch processing for many requests read from a file. Figure 7.2 presents the basic workflow of this application.

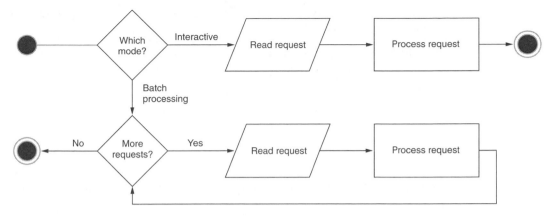

Figure 7.2 Basic workflow of the sunrise/sunset times application

Suppose one request has the following form:

```
[#][<date>@]<address>
```

It includes the following components:

- Line comment symbol # (optional)
- Date (optional)
- Address

A sample file with requests could have the following content:

```
2018-11-05@Deschutes Hall, Eugene, OR
#xx-xx-a@ZZ
Undisclosed Location
2018-12-32@Santa's Village
South Pole
3 Yurkla Way, Eucla, WA, Australia
```

To process one request containing an address and a date, we need to perform the following steps:

1. Determine geographical coordinates (latitude and longitude) for the requested address. We'll use https://nominatim.openstreetmap.org for that.
2. Determine sunset and sunrise times for the given coordinates and the specified date. The web service https://sunrise-sunset.org/ (which we are going to use at this step) returns times in UTC, so we have to process them further to get local times.
3. The https://timezonedb.com/ web service helps us to compute local times of sunset and sunrise for the given address. It uses coordinates to determine a particular time zone. You will need to sign up on this website to get an authentication key required to access their services.

Unfortunately, basic workflows never work as expected due to several potential reasons, including the following:

- A file with a list of requests doesn't exist.
- The user request may be malformed.
- A web API could be down or too busy for a moment.
- The web APIs refuse to serve a request due to an authorization error.
- The results returned from the web APIs are malformed.

This is what happens in the real world, so we need to be ready for that. We don't want our application to crash while encountering these errors. For example, we'd like to get the following results with the sample requests file shown earlier while doing batch processing:

```
05.11.2018 @ Deschutes Hall, Eugene, OR
    06:55:11 PST
    16:56:37 PST
Error in request 'Undisclosed Location': Failed while determining coordinates
Error in request '2018-12-32@Santa's Village': WrongDay "2018-12-32"
Error in request 'South Pole': Failed while determining sunrise/sunset times
12.12.2018 @ 3 Yurkla Way, Eucla, WA, Australia
    04:57:36 +0845
    19:08:45 +0845
```

These results mean that we want to handle all the possible exceptions within one request and go on to the next one within the batch-processing mode. In the opposite direction, we'd like to provide the user with the possibility to fix an incorrect request in interactive mode as follows:

```
Enter your request:
2018-12-32@Santa's Village
There was an error while processing your request: WrongDay "2018-12-32"
Do you want to try again (Y/N)?
Y
Enter your request:
2018-12-31@Santa's Village
31.12.2018 @ Santa's Village
    07:55:40 EST
    16:45:51 EST
```

We'll try to address these and other issues using GHC runtime exceptions.

We have the following modules in this application:

- The `Main` module is responsible for choosing the mode of operation and running the program.
- The `App` module defines a monad stack for the application.
- Interactive and batch requests will be processed as described in the `Process-Request` module.

- We'll need the `GeoCoordsReq` module to determine coordinates for an address in a request.
- The `SunTimes` module is responsible for determining sunrise and sunset times for the given coordinates; it will also deal with time zones and local times.
- We'll define exception types and utilities in the `STExcept` module.
- Types used by all other modules will be defined in the `Types` module.

7.4.1   *Application components*

Before diving into exception handling, which is the main goal of this chapter, let's discuss the application components and the libraries they use. It's often the case that the library dictates how to do exception handling because it defines resources that should be acquired or released and the exceptions that may be thrown.

DATA TYPES WITH JSON ENCODING

We'll start with JSON encoding, one of the most popular text data format nowadays. We'll use it the following two times in this application:

- For fetching data from web APIs
- For storing and reading web authentication information from a configuration file

EXAMPLE: COMPUTING SUNRISE AND SUNSET TIMES AT THE GIVEN LOCATION

   📄   suntimes/Types.hs

We use the `aeson` package in the simplest form by defining a data type and asking `aeson` to generate helpers to deserialize JSON objects into a value of the data type. For example, we need to fetch latitude and longitude for the given address as `Text` values. Suppose the web API returns a JSON value like the following:

```
{
  "lat": "40.355436",
  "lon": "-74.658770"
}
```

We want to transform this value into a value of the following data type:

```
data GeoCoords = GeoCoords { lat :: Text,
                             lon :: Text }
```

The next example contains code that does all the work for the `GeoCoords` data type:

The DeriveGeneric GHC extension enables automatic deriving of the Generic type class instance.

```
{-# LANGUAGE DeriveGeneric #-}
{-# LANGUAGE DeriveAnyClass #-}
```
Allows deriving instances with a default implementation

```
import GHC.Generics
```
The GHC.Generics module contains all the utilities required for building generic data type representations.

```
import Data.Aeson

data GeoCoords = GeoCoords { lat :: Text,
                             lon :: Text }
   deriving (Show,
      Generic,
      FromJSON)
```

The Data.Aeson module provides the main interface to the aeson library.

Deriving the Generic instance allows working with a data type generically, that is, without dependence on its actual definition.

The methods for decoding JSON values into the GeoCoords values are generated by default using the Generic instance.

We'll discuss all the tools to work with data types in a generic way later in this book. For now, it suffices to get the following ideas:

- We derive Generic for any data type we want to convert into JSON and from JSON. This derivation is possible in the presence of the DeriveGeneric GHC extension and the GHC.Generic module we imported.
- We derive default instance implementations of ToJSON and FromJSON, depending on what we need, with the DeriveAnyClass GHC extension.

Let's check the following generated FromJSON instance with the decode function that comes from the Data.Aeson module:

```
ghci> decode "{\"lat\":\"40.355436\", \"lon\":\"-74.658770\"}" ::
   Maybe GeoCoords
Just (GeoCoords {lat = "40.355436", lon = "-74.658770"})
```

Note the return type, Maybe GeoCoords: the aeson library doesn't use exceptions. It returns the Maybe or Either data types instead. This is a clear design decision made by its original author Bryan O'Sullivan. For example, when we have a ByteString with a JSON value (say, read from a file), we could get either a result (in Right) or an explanation of what went wrong (in Left), as shown next:

```
eitherDecode :: FromJSON a => ByteString -> Either String a
```

This function can be used as follows:

```
case eitherDecode bs of
   Right res -> -- do something meaningful with res
   Left err -> -- report an error
```

Thanks to external libraries, we don't need anything else in this project: those libraries are able to run decoding by themselves whenever it is required. It is also possible to define instances of the ToJSON and FromJSON type classes manually. This is usually done when we are not happy with the performance of the methods that were generated for us, when we don't need every component of a data type to be converted into/from JSON, or when dealing with weirdly structured JSON schemas.

There is much more to the `aeson` library. Fortunately, it features quite good documentation, describing the library in greater detail.

ISSUING WEB REQUESTS

Whenever we want to issue a web request and get a response, we have several options beyond the traditional socket API defined by the `network` package, as follows:

- The `http-client` and `http-client-tls` packages for doing low-level HTTP and HTTPS requests. *Low-level* here means that we should construct our request almost completely manually by providing the URL and headers.
- The `Network.HTTP.Simple` module from the `http-conduit` package, providing a somewhat more high-level, although a bit too verbose, interface for the same features.
- The `wreq` package, which defines a powerful API with good support of JSON encoding for requests and responses, and many other features.

Although all these options are widely used, for this example I've chosen another library, namely, `req` by Mark Karpov. The main reason behind this decision is the ease of use for the job at hand: creating and sending HTTP and HTTPS requests to web APIs, fetching responses, and turning them into the data type values we need. The `req` package provides exactly that, and its interface is as simple as possible.

Let's look at one example by using the `req` package to determine the geographical coordinates of a given address. The website https://nominatim.openstreetmap.org/ provides a public API that allows limited noncommercial use with the following requirements (cited here from https://operations.osmfoundation.org/policies/nominatim/):

- No heavy uses (an absolute maximum of one request per second).
- Provide a valid HTTP referer or user agent identifying the application.
- Clearly display attribution as suitable for your medium.
- Data is provided under the ODbL license, which requires sharing alike (although small extractions are likely to be covered by fair usage/fair dealing).

The API itself is described at this web page: https://wiki.openstreetmap.org/wiki/Nominatim. We should access it at the following URL: https://nominatim.openstreetmap.org/search (note the HTTPS scheme) by providing the following URL-encoded fields in the GET request:

- `q` for the given search address.
- `format` to specify that we expect a response in JSON. (HTML and XML are also supported by the API.)
- `limit` for the number of results we expect.
- `email` to identify a requestor.

We will also provide the HTTPS header `"User-Agent"` to specify our application.

The result from the Nominatim API is quite complex—a response body may contain a JSON array of JSON objects. Because we are interested in the latitude and longitude of the first returned object exclusively, we are free to ignore everything else. Our plan is as follows:

1 Prepare request parameters.
2 Issue a request.
3 Receive and interpret a response.

Suppose that we have the following types in addition to `GeoCoords`:

```
type Address = Text
data WebAPIAuth = WebAPIAuth { email :: Text,
                               agent :: Text}
```

The following code sample presents the details. This code differs from the version in the source code. Corresponding changes will be addressed further in this section.

We define a web API endpoint.

```
getCoords :: Address -> WebAPIAuth -> IO GeoCoords
getCoords addr wauth = do
    let
        ep = https "nominatim.openstreetmap.org" /: "search"
        reqParams =
          mconcat [
            "q" =: addr, "format" =: ("json" :: Text), "limit" =: (1 :: Int)
          , "email" =: email wauth
          , header "User-Agent" (encodeUtf8 $ agent wauth)
          ]
        request = req GET ep NoReqBody jsonResponse reqParams
    res <- responseBody <$> runReq def request
    case res of
        [] -> -- ...
        (coords:_) -> pure coords
```

The (=:) operator defines a single named request parameter.

Request parameters are represented by Monoid.

The header function takes two ByteString values and creates a request header.

The req function creates a request as an action but doesn't issue it.

We run a request and return a fetch response body as a list of GeoCoords.

This is a no-answer situation—we'll deal with that later.

We return the first result.

It is crucial to understand the types in this code. First, let's see how the `req` package handles request parameters, including request fields in the query string as well as request headers. All of them are represented via the `Option` type, which has an instance of the `Monoid` type class. This enables accumulation of parameters, which are then routed to the appropriate position (query string or headers) by the library itself.

Explicit types for the =: operator

Note that we had to specify the `Text` and `Int` types explicitly in this code while using the `(=:)` operator. This is necessary because of its highly polymorphic nature. Its type follows:

```
(=:) :: (QueryParam param, ToHttpApiData a) => Text -> a -> param
```

> The second argument is allowed to be of any type with an instance of the `ToHttp-APIData` type class (responsible for turning values into request headers, query string components, etc.). The type inference is not able to choose the suitable type of the right-hand side and the corresponding `ToHttpAPIData` instance.

Second, we return `coords` of type `GeoCoords`, which means that the `res` variable has a type of `[GeoCoords]`. Thanks to the types, the `req` package knows that the HTTP response (array of objects in JSON) should be decoded as `[GeoCoords]`. This decoding is hidden inside the `responseBody` function. The decoding itself is possible via the `FromJSON` instance we defined earlier. Note that `req` was able to figure out that the JSON array should be decoded to the Haskell list.

We don't have to decode JSON manually in this simple example, which is very convenient. We already know that decoding may fail, but we don't see `Maybe` or `Either` here. This is also a design decision: the `req` package raises an exception if the JSON in the response can't be decoded. We'll have to deal with this shortly.

The `req` library is well documented; there are many details on how to use it in the documentation on the `Network.HTTP.Req` module.

DEALING WITH TIMES AND TIME ZONES

I've already mentioned that dealing with time is hard. If we want to determine sunrise and sunset times at a given place, we are interested in local time at that particular place. Unfortunately, the web API at https://api.sunrise-sunset.org gives us UTC times, so we need to convert them. The question is how to determine a local time zone. One way could be to use the `tz` database available to Haskell programs via the `tzdata` and `tz` packages. To use it, we need to know the name of the closest town existing in that database. This is not always feasible.

Instead, we'll use another web API at http://timezonedb.com, which can take geographical coordinates and return some information about the time zone at the specified place, including the GMT offset (in seconds), the time zone abbreviation, and the flag indicating whether daylight savings is in use for this time zone (this requires the exact time of the day to be given in advance!). Once we have this information, we construct a value of the `TimeZone` data type from `Data.Time` and use functions from that module to manipulate the time. This web API requires users to register and get a key to access its services. You may find instructions on the http://timezonedb.com web page.

We'll consider an authentication key as a part of the `WebAPIAuth` record, as shown next:

```
data WebAPIAuth = WebAPIAuth { timeZoneDBkey :: Text,
                               email :: Text,
                               agent :: Text}
```

All of the parameters we can provide and the responses that we can get from both web APIs are presented in the following tables.

Table 7.1   The api.sunrise-sunset.org web API

Name	Description
URL: https://api.sunrise-sunset.org/json	
Parameters	
`lat, lng`	Latitude and longitude.
`formatted`	Whether to format resulting times or not: we'll send `0` to suppress formatting and get results in ISO 8601 (e.g., `2018-12-11T19:52:55+00:00`); the default value is `1`.
`date`	This field is optional. If it is not present, then the current date is used.
Response	
`sunrise, sunset`	Sunrise and sunset times at the specified position and date.

Table 7.2   The timezonedb.com web API parameters and responses

Name	Description
URL: http://api.timezonedb.com/v2.1/get-time-zone	
Parameters	
`key`	Authentication key.
`lat, lng`	Latitude and longitude.
`by`	The method of lookup: we'll use `position` to get a time zone based on geographical coordinates.
`time`	Time in UTC is used to get correct results: time zones may vary during a year due to daylight savings.
`format`	The response format can be either `json` or `xml`.
`fields`	List of fields included in the result; we'll use `gmtOffset, abbreviation, dst`.
Response	
`gmtOffset`	The time offset *in seconds* based on UTC time.
`abbreviation`	Abbreviation of the time zone.
`dst`	Whether daylight saving time (DST) is used; may be either 0 (No) or 1 (Yes).

The code for making these API requests is almost the same as in the case of requesting geographical coordinates by the given address. You may find an implementation in the following functions of the `SunTimes` module in the `suntimes` folder:

- getSunTimesUTC returns sunrise and sunset times in UTC at the specified position.
- lookupTimeZone returns the time zone for the given coordinates.

Note that the api.sunrise-sunset.org API returns a JSON object with the field results, which contains sunset and sunrise times; this requires us to define the SunTimesWrapper type to simplify JSON decoding.

APPLICATION IN GENERAL

The last thing I'd like to discuss before diving into exception handling is organizing this application. We have to implement the following abilities:

- Choosing one of the two modes, interactive or batch processing
- Keeping configuration outside of the application

EXAMPLE: COMPUTING SUNRISE AND SUNSET TIMES AT THE GIVEN LOCATION

📄   suntimes/Main.hs

📄   suntimes/App.hs

As usual, the easiest way to describe the functionality is to present the help output screen as generated by the optparse-applicative package, as shown here:

```
Usage: suntimes ([-f|--file FILENAME] | [-i|--interactive])
                [-c|--conf CONFIGNAME]
  Reports sunrise/sunset times for the specified location

Available options:
  -f,--file FILENAME      Input file
  -i,--interactive        Interactive mode
  -c,--conf CONFIGNAME    Configuration file (default: "config.json")
  -h,--help               Show this help text
```

So, we need to choose between two modes and load the configuration file before running the main functionality.

Parsing command-line parameters is implemented in the following function:

```
data AppMode = FileInput FilePath | Interactive
data Params = Params
                AppMode -- mode
                FilePath -- config file

mkParams :: Opt.Parser Params
mkParams = Params <$> (fileInput <|> interactive) <*> config
  where
    fileInput = FileInput <$> strOption
                (long "file" <> short 'f' <>
                 metavar "FILENAME" <> help "Input file" )
    interactive = flag Interactive Interactive
                (long "interactive" <> short 'i' <>
                 help "Interactive mode")
```

```
config = strOption (long "conf" <> short 'c' <>
                value "config.json" <>
                showDefault <>
                metavar "CONFIGNAME" <> help "Configuration file" )
```

Note how `Alternative` with `Applicative` together allow us to state our intentions clearly in the definition of the `mkParams` function as follows:

```
mkParams = Params <$> (fileInput <|> interactive) <*> config
```

We can read this definition as follows: to create the `Params` value, choose either `file-Input` or `interactive` and then add `config`.

The following is an example of the configuration file (the sample data are given in the data/suntimes.config.sample.json file):

```
{
  "email": "some@email",
  "agent": "SunTimes (Haskell in Depth/sample code from the book)",
  "timeZoneDBkey": "some key"
}
```

We can load this file into the application using `Data.Aeson` functionality. First, we need to teach aeson how to decode records of type `WebAPIAuth` as shown next:

```
data WebAPIAuth = WebAPIAuth { timeZoneDBkey :: Text,
                               email :: Text,
                               agent :: Text}
  deriving (Show, Generic, FromJSON)
```

Second, we should read the file and run decoding as follows (we need to import `Data.Aeson` and `Data.ByteString` as `B` for this code to work):

```
... = do
        wauth <- eitherDecodeStrict `fmap` B.readFile config
        case wauth of
          Right wauth' -> ...
          Left err -> ...
```

Third, we should either report an error (more on this later) or run the main functionality. One issue with the latter is how to deliver config data to the functions that execute web requests. The most traditional approach is to use the `ReaderT` monad transformer in addition to the base `IO` monad, so we arrive at our application monad stack as shown here:

```
newtype MyApp a = MyApp {
    runApp :: ReaderT WebAPIAuth IO a
  } deriving (Functor, Applicative, Monad, MonadIO,
              MonadReader WebAPIAuth)

runMyApp :: MyApp a -> WebAPIAuth -> IO a
runMyApp app config = runReaderT (runApp app) config
```

With this monad stack in use, we could rewrite the geoCoords function as follows:

```
getCoords :: Address -> MyApp GeoCoords
getCoords addr = do
    wauth <- ask
      -- preparing request parameters using wauth
      -- issue request and process response
```

Now we are ready to define the main application functionality as follows:

```
withConfig :: Params -> IO ()
withConfig (Params appMode config) = do
    wauth <- eitherDecodeStrict `fmap` B.readFile config
    case wauth of
      Right wauth' -> runMyApp (run appMode) wauth'
      Left err -> ...
  where
    run :: AppMode -> MyApp ()
    ...
```

This function can be used in main with the traditional execParser function from optparse-applicative as shown next:

```
main = execParser opts >>= withConfig
  where
    opts = ...
```

Let's move to exception handling. We already have many situations within our code where things could go wrong.

7.4.2 Exception-handling strategies

It is convenient to think about exception handling by introducing a set of strategies or particular behaviors in situations when something is wrong. We know that exceptions can be raised either by our code or by some other code that we call (functions from base and external libraries). We can also discover an erroneous situation somewhere in our code (think about discovering a division by zero after checking a divisor). The most common strategies to handle such cases follow:

- IGNORE—We've got an exception, but we are unsure how to deal with it in this particular line of code, so we let it go further along the call stack.
- THROW—We've discovered a bad situation, but we don't know how to deal with it, so we let it go further along the call stack as an exception.
- RETHROW—We've caught an exception, and we can change it somehow (usually to introduce our own type of exceptions) and throw it again.
- DEFAULT—We don't have a requested value due to an exception but are able to return a default value instead; we handle the exception and resume normal operations.

- PRINT, STOP—We don't know how to proceed, so we log an exception and halt.
- PRINT, CONTINUE—We are able to resume normal operations, so we log an exception and continue.
- PRINT, REPEAT—We can try repeating the same operation, so we log an exception and repeat.

PREPARING AN APPLICATION TO RAISE AND HANDLE EXCEPTIONS

Our application is represented by a monad stack. We can make it ready for raising and handling exceptions by deriving instances of the MonadThrow, MonadCatch, and Monad-Mask type classes as follows:

```
newtype MyApp a = MyApp {
    runApp :: ReaderT WebAPIAuth IO a
  } deriving (Functor, Applicative, Monad, MonadIO,
            MonadReader WebAPIAuth,
            MonadThrow, MonadCatch, MonadMask)
```

Thanks to deriving the MonadThrow and MonadCatch type classes instances, we can use throwM, catch, and any other exception-handling functions inside any MyApp a computation. Note that although we are not using concurrency here (at least explicitly), we still need to derive an instance of the MonadMask type class, because it is required by one of the functions we do use, finally.

EXAMPLE: COMPUTING SUNRISE AND SUNSET TIMES AT THE GIVEN LOCATION

📄 suntimes/STExcept.hs

It is also useful to have an exception type for this application, for example:

```
data RequestError = EmptyRequest | WrongDay Text
  deriving Show

data SunInfoException = UnknownLocation Text
                     | UnknownTime GeoCoords
                     | FormatError RequestError
                     | ServiceAPIError String
                     | NetworkError SomeException
                     | ConfigError
    deriving Exception
```

We derive the default implementation of the Exception type class with the DeriveAnyClass GHC extension. We also need the Show instance, shown here:

```
instance Show SunInfoException where
  show (UnknownLocation loc) = "Failed while determining coordinates"
  show (UnknownTime loc) = "Failed while determining sunrise/sunset times"
  show (FormatError er) = show er
  show (ServiceAPIError _) =
```

```
        "Error while communicating with external services"
    show (NetworkError _) = "Network communication error"
    show ConfigError = "Error parsing configuration file"
```

We'll use this code throughout the following subsections.

HANDLING EXCEPTIONS IN COMMUNICATION WITH WEB APIS

The `req` package that we use for issuing web requests is very flexible concerning exception handling. In the simplest form that we are using here, it will raise an exception of the `HttpException` type in the case of errors. A value of this type may be constructed by the following:

- The `VanillaHttpException` data constructor, which wraps `HttpException` from the `Network.HTTP.Client` module used under the hood
- The `JsonHttpException` data constructor with a `String` field describing why JSON decoding failed

The `HttpException` type from the `Network.HTTP.Client` is very complicated; you may find the full documentation on Hackage.

It would be a good idea to turn all the req exceptions into our own `SunInfoException` type once they are raised, so let's follow the RETHROW strategy here. We'll need the following function, which converts exceptions:

```
import qualified Network.HTTP.Client as NC
import Network.HTTP.Req

...

rethrowReqException :: MonadThrow m => HttpException -> m a
rethrowReqException (JsonHttpException s) = throwM (ServiceAPIError s)
rethrowReqException (VanillaHttpException (
                       NC.HttpExceptionRequest _
                         (NC.StatusCodeException resp _ ))) =
    throwM (ServiceAPIError $ show $ NC.responseStatus resp)
rethrowReqException (VanillaHttpException e) =
            throwM $ NetworkError (toException e)
```

You can see that we are converting any `JsonHttpException` into our own `ServiceAPIError`. We also use deep pattern matching to distinguish the case of an unexpected HTTP response status code (e.g., HTTP 404 Not Found) from all other HTTP exceptions and either return a `ServiceAPIError` or `NetworkError`, depending on the case. In real applications, such conversion functions can be quite large, depending on how many exceptions can be thrown by the external libraries.

Note the type of the `rethrowReqException`. We can use it as an exception handler as follows:

```
getCoords ... = handle rethrowReqException $ ...
```

Remember that `getCoords` can get an empty list of results. In this case, we can throw an `UnknownLocation` exception as follows:

```
...
    res <- liftIO $ responseBody <$> runReq def request
    case res of
      [] -> throwM (UnknownLocation addr)
      (coords:_) -> pure coords
```

The same idea of rethrowing a modified exception is used in `getSunTimesUTC`, shown here:

```
getSunTimesUTC ... = handle rethrowReqException $ ...
```

Alternatively, we could ignore an exception for now and defer the problem to the callers: we do that in the `lookupTimeZone` from the `SunTimes` module, so we use the `IGNORE` strategy there. The reason is that any problem in `getCoords` and `getSunTimesUTC` is crucial to our ability to deliver results to the user. On the other hand, if we are unable to look up the time zone, it's fine to go with UTC by default.

The next code shows how we combine results of `getSunTimesUTC` and `lookupTimeZone` to define `getSunTimes`, the only function that is exported from the `SunTimes` module:

```
getSunTimes :: GeoCoords            The When type is defined
                 -> When            as Now | On Day.
Returns ZonedTime                                    Catches SunInfoException,
                 -> MyApp (SunTimes ZonedTime)       which was rethrown earlier
getSunTimes gc d = do
    SunTimes {..} <- getSunTimesUTC gc d `catch` noTimeHandler
    ltz <- lookupTimeZone gc sunrise `catchAll` (const $ pure utc)
    return $ SunTimes (utcToZonedTime ltz sunrise)
                      (utcToZonedTime ltz sunset)    Catches any exception and returns
    where                                            the UTC time zone as a default value
      noTimeHandler :: MonadThrow m => SunInfoException -> m a
      noTimeHandler (ServiceAPIError _) = throwM (UnknownTime gc)
      noTimeHandler e = throwM e                     Rethrows a more specific
Rethrows any other exception without modifications   UnknownTime exception
```

Note that we don't do printing anywhere in these functions—it's the task of the callers to communicate with a user, so we either return results or throw exceptions here.

PARSING USER REQUESTS—NO GHC EXCEPTIONS!

We don't have to use GHC exceptions everywhere. Moreover, if we have pure code, the solution without exceptions would be easier to read. For example, we could use programmable exceptions or return `Either` with some information about the error in the `Left` data constructor.

This is the case with parsing user requests: we have `Text` and want to get `(Text, When)` with address and date information from it. The following computation can be done purely, so we don't need exceptions here:

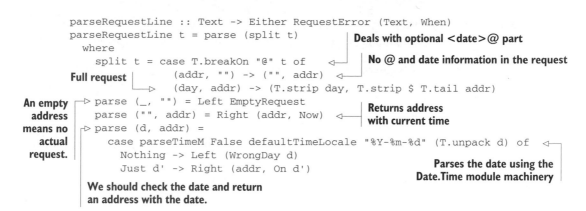

```
parseRequestLine :: Text -> Either RequestError (Text, When)
parseRequestLine t = parse (split t)
  where
    split t = case T.breakOn "@" t of
                (addr, "") -> ("", addr)
                (day, addr) -> (T.strip day, T.strip $ T.tail addr)
    parse (_, "") = Left EmptyRequest
    parse ("", addr) = Right (addr, Now)
    parse (d, addr) =
      case parseTimeM False defaultTimeLocale "%Y-%m-%d" (T.unpack d) of
        Nothing -> Left (WrongDay d)
        Just d' -> Right (addr, On d')
```

Deals with optional <date>@ part

No @ and date information in the request

Full request

An empty address means no actual request.

Returns address with current time

Parses the date using the Date.Time module machinery

We should check the date and return an address with the date.

If the parsing logic was more complex, we could choose to introduce the Except monad here or even employ a parsing library instead.

PROCESSING USER REQUESTS

Now let's move to the most exciting part: we have a request from a user and want to process it using functions that communicate with web APIs. We should deal with processing a single request so that the code could be used in both of the following application modes:

- Processing many requests
- Processing requests interactively

EXAMPLE: COMPUTING SUNRISE AND SUNSET TIMES AT THE GIVEN LOCATION

   🗋   suntimes/ProcessRequest.hs

The best and simplest strategy in such situations is to IGNORE, thus allowing callers to deal with exceptions in their own way. Let's see what is going on in the following processRequest function:

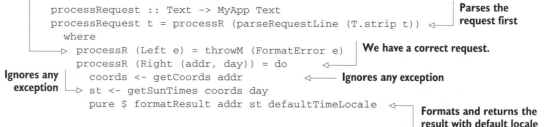

We have no request, so throw an exception.

```
processRequest :: Text -> MyApp Text
processRequest t = processR (parseRequestLine (T.strip t))
  where
    processR (Left e) = throwM (FormatError e)
    processR (Right (addr, day)) = do
      coords <- getCoords addr
      st <- getSunTimes coords day
      pure $ formatResult addr st defaultTimeLocale
```

Parses the request first

We have a correct request.

Ignores any exception

Ignores any exception

Formats and returns the result with default locale

Formatting the result is done as follows:

```
formatResult :: Text -> SunTimes ZonedTime -> TimeLocale -> Text
formatResult req SunTimes {..} loc =
    mconcat [day, " @ ", req, "\n     ", fmt sunrise, "\n     ", fmt sunset]
  where
    day = T.pack $ formatTime loc "%x" sunrise
    fmt t = T.pack $ formatTime loc "%X %Z" t
```

See the documentation on the `Data.Time.Format` module about the `formatTime` function format specifiers. The code here gives us the result in this form:

```
05.11.2018 @ Deschutes Hall, Eugene, OR
    06:55:11 PST
    16:56:37 PST
```

Now that we are able to process a single request, it is time to implement the main functionality. Let's do batch processing first. We need to implement a function of the following type:

```
processMany :: [Text] -> MyApp ()
```

This function takes a list of requests and processes every one of them. In this implementation, if we get an exception from `processRequest`, we print an error message and then continue to process other requests. We're sticking with the PRINT, CONTINUE strategy. In the worst case of a network connection problem, we'll get many similar error messages as a result.

There is one problem we should tackle while doing batch processing. Because we are using public APIs, it would be nice not to overuse their resources. Let's introduce a delay (say, three seconds) between web requests, shown in the next code sample. Note that we should do that no matter whether or not we've got an exception. This is exactly the case for the `finally` method.

Loops over the list with requests
```
processMany :: [Text] -> MyApp ()
processMany = mapM_ processRequestWrapper
  where
    processRequestWrapper r =
      unless ("#" `T.isPrefixOf` r)
           $ (processRequest r >>= liftIO .TIO.putStrLn) `catch` handler r
             `finally` delaySec 3
    delaySec sec = liftIO $ threadDelay (sec * 1000000)
    handler :: Text -> SunInfoException -> MyApp ()
    handler r e = liftIO $ TIO.putStrLn $ "Error in request '" <> r <> "': "
                    <> T.pack (show e)
```

Skips comment lines: we expect # in the beginning of the comment line.

Prints a result or calls a handler

Adds a delay after every call to processRequest

Calls an exception handler for any SunInfoException

As for interactive processing, we don't want to leave the user with an error in the request. Remember that we have the following exceptions:

```
data SunInfoException = UnknownLocation T.Text
                      | UnknownTime GeoCoords
                      | FormatError RequestError
                      | ServiceAPIError String
                      | NetworkError SomeException
                      | ConfigError
```

Clearly, there is not much we can do about `ServiceAPIError` or `NetworkError` here, but we could give the user a chance to edit the request in other cases. This logic is implemented in the `processInteractively` function, as shown next:

An action for regular interactive request processing

```
processInteractively :: MyApp ()
processInteractively = action `catch` handler
  where
    action = do
      liftIO $ TIO.putStrLn "Enter your request:"
      req <- liftIO $ TIO.getLine
      res <- processRequest req
      liftIO $ TIO.putStrLn res
    handler :: SunInfoException -> MyApp ()
    handler e@(ServiceAPIError _) = liftIO $ print e
    handler e@(NetworkError _) = liftIO $ print e
    handler e = do
      liftIO $ TIO.putStr
        $ "There was an error while processing your request: "
        <> T.pack (show e) <> "\nDo you want to try again (Y/N)?"
      yesno <- liftIO $ TIO.getLine
      when (yesno `elem` ["y", "Y", "yes"]) processInteractively
```

A handler for exceptional situations of the SunInfoException type

Prints an error and stops processing

Restarts the processing if the user wants that

Note, in this code, we were able to differentiate exception-handling strategies depending on the error. If it was a user error, then we allow repeating the request; otherwise, we stop processing.

RUNNING THE APPLICATION

Several things could go wrong while firing the application up, such as the following:

- The user may specify incorrect command-line arguments.
- A config file could be missing.
- A config file could be formatted incorrectly.
- A file with requests in batch mode could be missing.

Incorrect command-line arguments will be handled by the `optparse-applicative` package, but to prevent the execution of the code that relies on them, `optparse-applicative` raises an exception of the `ExitCode` type. We can safely hide this exception from the user.

Missing files will result in an exception of the `IOException` type. We can better handle them by reporting the name of the missing file to the user.

We know that the config file is malformed after getting the `Left` data constructor from the `eitherDecodeStrict` call in the `withConfig` function, so there will be no exception in this situation. Let's throw an exception by ourselves to defer handling it to the `main` function.

This is our new implementation of the `withConfig` function, now with exception throwing, as shown next (note that we ignore missing files here; this case will be handled by `main`.):

```
withConfig :: Params -> IO ()
withConfig (Params appMode config) = do
    wauth <- eitherDecodeStrict <$> B.readFile config
    case wauth of
      Right wauth' -> runMyApp (run appMode) wauth'
      Left _ -> throwM ConfigError
  where
    run (FileInput fname) = liftIO (TIO.readFile fname)
                                >>= processMany . T.lines
    run Interactive = processInteractively
```

Finally, we are ready to define `main` in the following example. We have to address many different exceptions here, so this is a good place for the `catches` function, which takes a list of handlers and executes one that is suitable, depending on the exception thrown.

```
main = (execParser opts >>= withConfig)            ┌─ The list of
         `catches` [Handler parserExit,        ◁──┘  exception handlers
                    Handler printIOError,
                    Handler printOtherErrors]
  where
    opts = info (mkParams <**> helper)
       (fullDesc <>
        progDesc "Reports sunrise/sunset times for the specified location")
    parserExit :: ExitCode -> IO ()
    parserExit _ = pure ()                 ◁────── Hides the command-line
    printIOError :: IOException -> IO ()           arguments' exception
    printIOError e
      | isDoesNotExistError e = do
          let mbfn = ioeGetFileName e
          putStrLn $ "File " ++ maybe "" id mbfn  ++ " not found"  ◁──┐
      | otherwise = putStrLn $ "I/O error: " ++ show e                │
    printOtherErrors :: SomeException -> IO ()       Reports the name  │
    printOtherErrors = print                         of the missing file
```

Note the last `printOtherErrors` handler: we are going to print any exception that was not handled before. Hopefully, this will give the user a clue as to what went wrong at run time.

SUMMARIZING EXCEPTION-HANDLING STRATEGIES

The following table summarizes the strategies we've discussed and used in this section.

Table 7.3   Exception handling summary

Component	Module	Function	Strategy
Determining coordinates by address	GeoCoordsReq	getCoords	RETHROW
Determining sunrise/sunset times by coordinates in UTC	SunTimes	getSunTimesUTC	RETHROW
Determining time zone by coordinates	SunTimes	lookupTimeZone	IGNORE

Table 7.3 Exception handling summary

Component	Module	Function	Strategy
Determining local sunrise/ sunset times	`SunTimes`	`getSunTimes`	
1) Unknown time			`RETHROW`
2) Unknown time zone			`DEFAULT`
Processing single request	`ProcessRequest`	`processRequest`	
1) Incorrect format			`THROW`
2) Unknown location			`IGNORE`
3) Unknown times			`IGNORE`
4) Unknown time locale			`DEFAULT`
Processing many requests	`ProcessRequest`	`processMany`	`PRINT, CONTINUE`
Processing request interactively	`ProcessRequest`	`processInteractively`	
1) User error			`PRINT, REPEAT`
2) Network error			`PRINT, STOP`
Reading files with configuration and requests	`Main`	`withConfig`	`IGNORE`
Main function:	`Main`	`main`	
1) Incorrect command-line arguments			`IGNORE`
2) Any other exception			`PRINT, STOP`

In many cases, we use logging instead of printing. In fact, logging is often used as a part of every strategy. This makes it easier to analyze later what went wrong at run time. We'll see how to introduce logging into our application in the next section.

7.5   *Logging*

From the technical point of view, logging is just a process of recording any information during application run time. This information could be as follows:

- Errors, when something is wrong or something unexpected happens
- Events, for recording what is going on in a domain
- History, recording all operations within an application for postauditing

In most programming languages, logging is a rather dull task. Nevertheless, it features some nice properties that make it appealing to implement, for example, clear decomposition into components and stages. When thinking about logging, we usually distinguish the following three components:

- *Source*—Logging instructions in the source code (emitting log records)
- *Object*—Log message that could be a string, data type, JSON object (structured logging), and so on
- *Sink*—Log destination, for example, stdout/stderr, a file, a database, or a cloud stream-processing service

And stages:

- Configuring log formats and sinks
- Acquiring resources (e.g., opening files or establishing connections)
- Writing log records
- Releasing resources

Log records are usually labeled by a log level, such as DEBUG, INFO, WARNING, ERROR, and some others, depending on the implementation. As for the supported sinks, it makes sense to support different backends, able to route logging messages to some particular destinations.

Unfortunately, one inherent property of logging makes it hard to support, namely, that logging instructions are spread over the source code. Figure 7.3 illustrates this idea. Due to this, logging is often used as an example of an aspect (or cross-cutting concern) in aspect-oriented programming.

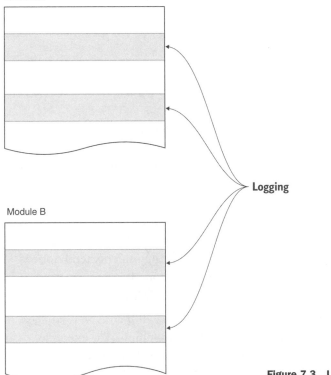

Figure 7.3   Logging as a cross-cutting concern

Logging as a clear and nice problem to solve is extremely popular among Haskellers. At the time of writing, at least 30 packages on Hackage implement logging, with more coming almost every month.

All the logging packages on Hackage fall roughly into one of the following categories:

- Simple, low-level packages (`hslogger`, `fast-logger`, `logging`, `simple-log`, `simple-logger`, `simple-logging`, etc.)
- Industrial-level logging libraries featuring support of monad stacks and various backends (`monad-logger`, `katip`, `log-base`, `logging-effect`, `heavy-logger`, etc.)
- Experimental, proof-of-concept-style libraries (`co-log`, `log-effect`, etc.)

To give you a glimpse of what you should expect from the logging library, we'll extend an application using `monad-logger`, one of the most used logging libraries on Hackage.

7.5.1 *An overview of the monad-logger library*

The `monad-logger` package by Michael Snoyman has been in development since 2012. This library supports `mtl`-style applications. As we'll see in the next subsection, it's super easy to introduce it into any application built with monad stacks. To use this library we have to know the following things:

- It defines the `MonadLogger` type class; we can write logs in every monad that implements it.
- There is the `LoggingT` monad transformer, which introduces `IO` logging into monad stacks based on the `IO` monad.
- There are several runners to run computations with logging into various destinations (`runStdoutLoggingT`, `runFileLoggingT`, etc.).
- We can filter and map computations with logging using the `filterLog` and `mapLoggingT` functions.
- We are not limited to `IO`; the `WriterLoggingT` monad transformer can be used for logging in pure monadic computations.
- The logging itself is done with a convenient set of `logDebug*`, `logError*`, and other functions.
- This library uses the `TemplateHaskell` GHC extension to record line numbers where log messages are emitted. In general, this extension allows us to generate some new code during compilation. We'll get back to this Haskell feature in chapter 12.

EXAMPLE: LOGGING WITH MONAD-LOGGER

🗋 ch07/logging.hs

⚡ *logging*

☞ We can introduce logging into any monad stack.

In the following code is a short example where we are logging in a monad stack built from LoggingT, StateT and IO:

```
popAndLog :: LoggingT (StateT [Int] IO) ()    ◁──── Complex monad stack
popAndLog = do
  _:xs <- lift get    ◁──── Lifts the State monad operation
  lift (put xs)
  $logDebug ("***" <> (pack $ show xs) <> "***")    ◁──── Logs a message

logStateEx :: LoggingT (StateT [Int] IO) Int
logStateEx =  do
  popAndLog
  popAndLog
  pure 5
```

Note the Template Haskell $logDebug splice in the previous code. This splice will be replaced with other code generated when we compile this code as specified by the monad-logger library.

Running this logStateEx action in GHCi, we see the following output:

```
ghci> runStateT (runStdoutLoggingT logStateEx) [1,2,3]
[Debug] ***[2,3]*** @(main:Main example.hs:16:5)
[Debug] ***[3]*** @(main:Main example.hs:19:5)
(5,[3])
```

To compile this code, we need to enable the next two GHC extensions:

```
{-# LANGUAGE TemplateHaskell #-}
{-# LANGUAGE OverloadedStrings #-}
```

We'll inspect Template Haskell and what can be done with it later in this book.

7.5.2 *Introducing logging with monad-logger into the suntimes project*

Now let's see how to add logging to stderr into the suntimes project. We import the Control.Monad.Logger from the monad-logger package for that. First, we should extend our monad stack, as in the following:

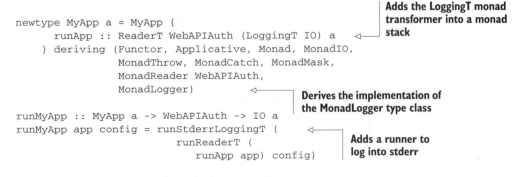

```
newtype MyApp a = MyApp {                                          Adds the LoggingT monad
    runApp :: ReaderT WebAPIAuth (LoggingT IO) a   ◁──┐            transformer into a monad
    } deriving (Functor, Applicative, Monad, MonadIO,                stack
              MonadThrow, MonadCatch, MonadMask,
              MonadReader WebAPIAuth,
              MonadLogger)    ◁────────────┐
                                           │  Derives the implementation of
runMyApp :: MyApp a -> WebAPIAuth -> IO a  │  the MonadLogger type class
runMyApp app config = runStderrLoggingT (   ◁────────┐
                    runReaderT (                      │  Adds a runner to
                      runApp app) config)                log into stderr
```

Once we are done with the monad stack, we can use any logging function from `Control` `.Monad.Logger` anywhere inside computations in the `MyApp` monad (thanks to the derived instance of `MonadLogger`). For example, we could record every request we got to process with the `logInfoN` function, as shown next (this function doesn't use Template Haskell):

```
processRequest :: T.Text -> MyApp T.Text
processRequest t = do
     logInfoN $ "Processing request: " <> t
     processR (parseRequestLine (T.strip t))
  where
    processR ...
```

We could also emit an error instead of plain printing error messages in `processMany`, as shown here:

```
processMany :: [T.Text] -> MyApp ()
processMany = mapM_ processRequestWrapper
  where
    processRequestWrapper ...

    handler :: T.Text -> SunInfoException -> MyApp ()
    handler r e = logErrorN $ "Error in request '" <> r <> "': "
                                <> T.pack (show e)
```

We'd just replace `liftIO $ TIO.putStrLn` with `logErrorN`, and that's it. Now switching to file logging would touch only the `App` module, leaving all the logging instructions unmodified.

Summary

- GHC supports several exception-handling mechanisms, including GHC runtime exceptions and library-defined programmable exceptions.
- The `ExceptT` monad transformer can be used to introduce exception handling into pure (not `IO`-based) monad stacks.
- The GHC exceptions are best used through the interface provided by the `Control.Exception` and `Control.Monad.Catch` modules.
- Exception handling requires careful planning. Think about an appropriate strategy on a case-by-case basis.
- There is a big choice of logging libraries, depending on your needs: `monad-logger` is one of the most used in `mtl`-style applications.

Writing tests

8

This chapter covers

- Writing code and developing with testing in mind
- Unit testing, property testing, and other approaches to testing
- Improving code quality

Every customer is happy to get correct software. It is often claimed that the Haskell type system provides software correctness. Unfortunately, some limitations exist to what the current type system is able to guarantee. That's why we still need to test our code. Haskell supports many approaches to code correctness assurance, ranging from unit testing and property testing to lightweight formal verification. We don't have to apply all of them, but it's a good idea to apply at least some. Once we have tests, it's much easier to refactor the code or make it run faster.

In this chapter, I present testing with an example of IP address processing built from scratch. We'll continue working with this example later in this book to explore code behavior and tune performance.

8.1   Setting a scene: IPv4 filtering application

We will work on a small utility program, namely, an IPv4 filtering application. It should check whether a given IPv4 address falls into some range from a large IP address range database (given as a text file). This utility could be part of a large project implementing an IP firewall in Haskell.

> **EXAMPLE: IPV4 FILTERING APPLICATION**
>
> 🗋   ip/lookup/
>
> ⚡   *iplookup*
>
> ☞   It's too easy to introduce errors into the code without tests.

The task for this utility is not extremely ambitious. Suppose we have the following list of IP addresses ranges:

```
192.168.1.3,192.168.10.14
127.0.0.1,127.0.0.255
220.41.240.89,220.41.241.115
4.159.29.233,5.159.30.77
62.70.22.158,62.70.24.18
```

If we check the IP address `5.12.120.250`, then the answer should be `YES`, because this IP address belongs to the second-to-last range. If we check `127.10.10.1`, then the answer is `NO`, because no range containing the given IP address is in the list.

8.1.1   Development process overview

We start implementing this application in the simplest form as follows:

- Read the IP ranges database from a text file.
- Check a single IP address given as a command-line argument.

Because we aim to cover various approaches to testing, we'll not attempt following any specific methodology (e.g., test-driven development). Instead, we'll be interested in testing the same things in different ways.

> ### Test-driven development and functional programming
>
> The test-driven approach to development (TDD) is based on the following principle: write the tests first and the implementation later. The classical book on TDD, *Test-Driven Development by Example* (Kent Beck, 2003), suggests that writing code is done to pass all the tests, and the tests describe how a user is supposed to use the code.
>
> Functional programming, in general, simplifies this approach due to a clear separation of code (functions) and data. We could write function signatures (with `undefined`) in their bodies, then write tests, run them to see how everything is broken, and then write the functions' bodies.

At this stage, we don't think about performance—that will be done in later chapters.

8.1.2 *Initial implementation*

The first implementation contains the following four modules (see figure 8.1):

- `IPTypes`—Defines types used in other modules
- `ParseIP`—Responsible for parsing single IPv4 addresses, a range of addresses, and a list of ranges
- `LookupIP`—Implements looking up IP ranges database (a list of IP ranges)
- `Main`—Defines the main functionality of reading command-line arguments and processing a user request

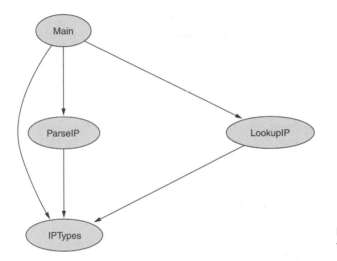

Figure 8.1   Module structure for the IPv4 filtering application

TYPES AND EXCEPTIONS

The types used throughout the application are defined in the `IPTypes` module and presented in the following example:

```
newtype IP = IP {unIP :: Word32}      ◁─── A newtype for IPv4 address
   deriving (Eq, Ord, Show)

data IPRange = IPRange IP IP      ◁─── Data type for IP ranges
   deriving Eq

data IPRangeDB = IPRangeDB [IPRange]      ◁─── Data type for IP ranges database
   deriving Eq
```

We will also define types to deal with parsing errors and exceptions as follows. (This code requires importing the `Control.Monad.Catch` module from the `exceptions` package.)

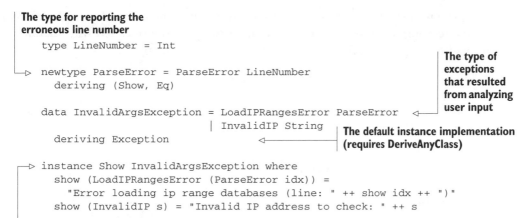

The type for reporting the erroneous line number

```
type LineNumber = Int

newtype ParseError = ParseError LineNumber
    deriving (Show, Eq)

data InvalidArgsException = LoadIPRangesError ParseError
                          | InvalidIP String
    deriving Exception
```

The type of exceptions that resulted from analyzing user input

The default instance implementation (requires DeriveAnyClass)

```
instance Show InvalidArgsException where
    show (LoadIPRangesError (ParseError idx)) =
       "Error loading ip range databases (line: " ++ show idx ++ ")"
    show (InvalidIP s) = "Invalid IP address to check: " ++ s
```

An instance of the Show type class for the exceptions' type

PARSING IPV4 ADDRESSES

We don't use any parsing library to deal with IPv4 addresses to simplify this presentation. Instead, we implement handmade parsing. It'd be fun to compare it with something significantly more sophisticated.

The other parts of the application require the following two functions for parsing a single IP address and a list of IP ranges:

```
parseIP :: String -> Maybe IP
parseIPRanges :: String -> Either ParseError IPRangeDB
```

To parse an IP address given as a `String`, we need to do the following:

1. Split a given `String` on the `.` character.
2. Make sure that we've got exactly four components.
3. Read every component as a number.
4. Make sure that every component fits an octet (eight bits).
5. Build a value of the `IP` type (a `newtype` for `Word32`).

We exploit the functionality provided by the `Monad` and `Alternative` type classes to get a clean implementation. Clearly, we don't want to deal with `Just`/`Nothing` values manually after every processing stage. First, we need the `guarded` function, shown next, which enables checking a condition and returning either a given value or `empty`. (This function was borrowed from the `protolude` custom `Prelude` package.)

```
guarded :: Alternative f => (a -> Bool) -> a -> f a
guarded f a = if f a then pure a else empty
```

For example, we need `guarded` to check the lengths of the lists several times, so let's define the `isLengthOf` predicate function exactly for that as follows:

```
isLengthOf :: Int -> [a] -> Bool
isLengthOf n xs = length xs == n
```

To present processing stages, I prefer using function composition. As we have monadic computations here, it's convenient to apply the so-called fish operator, or monadic composition, from `Control.Monad`, as shown next:

```
(>=>) :: Monad m => (a -> m b) -> (b -> m c) -> a -> m c
```

To build an IP address from the components, we must do some computations. For example, an IP address "192.168.1.1" is built as follows:

```
192.168.1.1
 = 1 + 1 * 256 + 168 * 256^2 + 192 * 256^3
```

So, `foldr` might work, like so:

```
buildIP :: [Word8] -> IP
buildIP = IP . fst . foldr go (0, 1)
  where
    go b (s, k) = (s + fromIntegral b * k, k*256)
```

To parse individual components, we can apply `readMaybe` from the `Text.Read` module. Finally, we are ready to implement the parsing of a single IP address as follows:

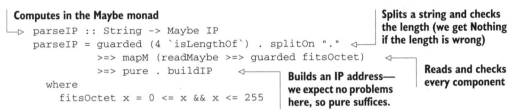

Computes in the Maybe monad

```
parseIP :: String -> Maybe IP
parseIP = guarded (4 `isLengthOf`) . splitOn "."
            >=> mapM (readMaybe >=> guarded fitsOctet)
            >=> pure . buildIP
  where
    fitsOctet x = 0 <= x && x <= 255
```

Splits a string and checks the length (we get Nothing if the length is wrong)

Builds an IP address— we expect no problems here, so pure suffices.

Reads and checks every component

Let's follow the same approach to implement parsing a single range as follows:

```
parseIPRange :: String -> Maybe IPRange
parseIPRange = guarded (2 `isLengthOf`) . splitOn ","
              >=> mapM parseIP
              >=> listToIPRange
  where
    listToIPRange [a,b] = pure (IPRange a b)
    listToIPRange _ = empty
```

Finally, we can parse a whole IP range database, as shown here:

Processes by splitting into lines, adding line numbers, and parsing every line

```
parseIPRanges :: String -> Either ParseError IPRangeDB
parseIPRanges = fmap IPRangeDB . mapM parseLine . zip [1..] . lines
  where
    parseLine (ln, s) = case parseIPRange s of
                          Nothing -> Left (ParseError ln)
                          Just ipr -> Right ipr
```

Computes in an Either ParseError monad

Returns a Right with a parsing result

Returns a Left with a line number to signal an error

Note that an `Either ParseError` monadic instance in `mapM` is responsible for returning either an error message with a line number or a list of IP ranges.

LOOKING UP IP RANGES IN A DATABASE

For now, looking up IP ranges in a database is trivial: we walk through a list of ranges with `find` and see if we've got the range we need, as shown next:

```
lookupIP ::  IPRangeDB -> IP -> Bool
lookupIP (IPRangeDB ips) ip = case find (inRange ip) ips of
                    Nothing -> False
                    Just _ -> True
  where
    inRange ip (IPRange beg end) = beg <= ip && ip <= end
```

Note that we are not interested in an actual range. It's enough to return a `Bool` value. Clearly, this is the slowest implementation possible. Even then, it has an advantage: it's straightforward, easy to test, and hard to implement wrong.

To simplify reporting results, let's also implement a function that takes a database and a list of IP addresses and returns a `String` with a result, as shown next:

```
reportIPs :: IPRangeDB -> [IP] -> String
reportIPs iprdb = unlines . map go
  where
    go ip = show ip ++ ": " ++ yesno (lookupIP iprdb ip)
    yesno True = "YES"
    yesno False = "NO"
```

We'll call this function from the main program.

MAIN FUNCTIONALITY

As usual, the implemented functionality is best described with a help screen, generated by the `optparse-applicative` library as follows:

```
Usage: iplookup FILE IP
  Answers YES/NO depending on whether an IP address belongs to the IP range
  database

Available options:
  FILE                  IP range database
  IP                    IP address to check
  -h,--help             Show this help text
```

Command-line arguments are easily described, as shown here:

```
data Params = Params FilePath String

mkParams :: Opt.Parser Params
mkParams = Params
              <$> argument str (metavar "FILE" <> help "IP range database")
              <*> argument str (metavar "IP" <> help "IP address to check")
```

The main functionality is implemented as follows:

```
run :: Params -> IO ()
run (Params fp ipstr) = do
  iprs <- parseIPRanges <$> readFile fp
  case (iprs, parseIP ipstr) of
    (_, Nothing) -> throwM $ InvalidIP ipstr
    (Left pe, _) -> throwM $ LoadIPRangesError pe
    (Right iprdb, Just ip) -> putStrLn $ reportIPs iprdb [ip]
```

Short question: will this program attempt to load an IP range database if the given IP address to check is invalid? This would be time consuming and useless. We'll see the answer later in this book.

Finally, the `main` function executes the command-line parser followed by the `run` function and deals with exception handling as follows:

```
main = (execParser opts >>= run)
       `catches` [Handler parserExit]
  where
    opts =
      info (mkParams <**> helper)
           (fullDesc <>
            progDesc ("Answers YES/NO depending on whether " ++
                      "an IP address belongs to the IP range database"))
    parserExit :: ExitCode -> IO ()
    parserExit _ = pure ()
```

If we run this program against the IP range database given at the beginning of this section, we'll get the following output:

```
$ cabal -v0 run iplookup -- data/ipranges.txt 5.12.120.250
5.12.120.250: YES
$ cabal -v0 run iplookup -- data/ipranges.txt 127.10.10.1
127.10.10.1: NO
```

All right, we've got a simple working implementation, although it is completely untested. Indeed, what could go wrong here?

8.2   *Testing the IPv4 filtering application*

Testing provides the developer with some confidence that the code behaves correctly. Haskell's type system is able to rule out some errors—it's impossible, or at least quite difficult, to get a null pointer exception in Haskell—but not all of them. This confidence serves not only statically (the code at this point is correct at compile time) but also dynamically, helping to further develop a software project. It's easier to build something new using ingredients we have and trust. Many professionals argue that, when done properly, extensively tested code can be refactored more easily because most of the bugs introduced during refactoring can be caught by failed tests.

8.2.1 Overview of approaches to testing

We have a variety of approaches to test software in general. In this chapter, we are going to discuss testing code components, that is, functions. Code correctness means that the given function behaves as it should. How would we check that? Well, we can do the following:

- Specify an example (test case): at this particular input, this function should give this output.
- Formulate a property: for all inputs satisfying some condition, the function should give an output satisfying another condition.

Usually, we can specify many examples and formulate many properties at once by describing function behavior. We can check those test cases and properties manually (e.g., in GHCi), but it's more effective to use some automation for that. Both case testing and property testing are implemented in many packages—more than 300 packages on Hackage do some sort of testing. In this section, we'll discuss several examples, including the following:

- hspec—The package inspired by the RSpec specifications writing tool from the Ruby community
- hedgehog—The novel property-testing package (with ideas borrowed from the QuickCheck package, the original property-testing package for Haskell)
- doctest—The package for checking test cases given in Haddock comments

No approach to testing is the best one: it's always a good idea to combine them because each one has advantages and disadvantages. Even within one sort of testing packages, we have a lot of choices.

In this section, we also use the tasty package (by Roman Cheplyaka), which allows us to combine test cases and properties from many libraries into a single common test collection and check them all together. With tasty, it's effortless to introduce automated testing in Cabal projects. Let's start with this and then see how the testing packages mentioned earlier can be used to test an IPv4 filtering application.

8.2.2 Testing Cabal projects with tasty

Cabal files used to describe projects in Haskell support the concept of a test suite. In most cases, a test suite is a separate executable that imports the same modules as our application or library. To prevent double compilation of those modules, it's customary to put modules that require testing into a named internal library. Then, both the application and the test suite depend on that library.

EXAMPLE: TESTING IPV4 FILTERING APPLICATION WITH TASTY

- ☐ ip/lookup/
- ☐ tests/iplookup/

⚡ *iplookup-test*

☞ Testing reveals plenty of errors in the original implementation.

In the `iplookup` example, we could define a library containing the `IPTypes`, `ParseIP`, and `LookupIP` modules. The following .cabal file entry does exactly that:

```
library iplookup-lib
  exposed-modules:
      IPTypes
      LookupIP
      ParseIP
  hs-source-dirs:
      ip/lookup
  build-depends:
      base >=4.12 && <4.15
    , <other dependencies>
  default-language: Haskell2010
```

We need to expose all the modules, because both the application and the test suite should depend on them.

Then, we can define the `iplookup` executable as follows:

```
executable iplookup
  main-is: ip/lookup/Main.hs
  build-depends:
      iplookup-lib
    , <other dependencies>
  default-language: Haskell2010
```

Note the dependency on the `iplookup-lib` in the `build-depends` section.

The test suite itself should contain a driver, an executable responsible for running tests and reporting their results. Suppose we call this driver Test.hs. The test suite entry in the .cabal file is defined as follows:

```
test-suite iplookup-test
  type: exitcode-stdio-1.0
  main-is: Test.hs
  other-modules:
  hs-source-dirs:
      tests/iplookup
  build-depends:
      iplookup-lib
    , tasty >=0.11 && <1.4
    , <other dependencies>
  default-language: Haskell2010
```

Note the `type` field. The `exitcode-stdio-1.0` value means that a failing or passing test suite is reported by test driver's exit code. We don't have to bother about it, because `tasty` can do everything for us.

Typically, a test suite consists of many modules. They should be added to the other-modules section of this test-suite entry. Once we have one or more test suites in our project, we can run them with the cabal test or stack test commands, depending on our workflow. It is also possible to run a specific test suite (e.g., with cabal test iplookup-test).

We have no tests yet, but we could create a test driver without tests as follows:

```
import Test.Tasty

main = defaultMain $ testGroup "(no tests)" []
```

Both the defaultMain and testGroup functions come from the tasty package. They simplify defining test suites greatly. If we put the previous code in the tests/iplookup/ Test.hs file, then we can run the empty test suite (successfully!) and see something like this:

```
$ cabal test iplookup-test
Preprocessing test suite 'iplookup-test' for hid-examples...
Building test suite 'iplookup-test' for hid-examples...
Running 1 test suites...
Test suite iplookup-test: RUNNING...
Test suite iplookup-test: PASS
Test suite logged to: hid-examples-iplookup-test.log
1 of 1 test suites (1 of 1 test cases) passed.
```

Now we are all set. Let's see if we find some mistakes in our implementation of the IPv4 filtering application.

8.2.3 *Specifications writing and checking with Hspec*

A specification is almost a sentence in English and describes what should be the result of a function when it is called with specific arguments. The hspec package does a great job of reusing Haskell do notation to write a specification. We use not hspec itself but its provider for tasty, called tasty-hspec, which provides the Test.Tasty .Hspec module.

WRITING SPECIFICATIONS

Remember the following buildIP function:

```
buildIP :: [Word8] -> IP
buildIP = IP . fst . foldr go (0, 1)
  where
    go b (s, k) = (s + fromIntegral b * k, k*256)
```

The specification for it found in the tests/iplookup/ParseIPSpec.hs file follows:

```
spec_buildIP :: Spec          ◁──┐ The Spec type encapsulates a specification
spec_buildIP =                    │ or a collection of specifications.
  describe "buildIP" $ do     ◁──┐ The describe function adds
                                  │ a tag to a specification.
```

```
      it "builds from zero" $                    ◁──────  The single test case is introduced
  ▷    buildIP [0,0,0,0] `shouldBe` (IP 0)                with the it function.
      it "builds from one" $
        buildIP [0,0,0,1] `shouldBe` (IP 1)
      it "builds from localhost" $
        buildIP [127,0,0,1] `shouldBe` (IP $ 1 + 127 * 256^3)
      it "builds from arbitrary address" $
        buildIP [192,168,3,15] `shouldBe`
          (IP $ 15 + 3 * 256 + 168 * 256^2 + 192 * 256^3)
```

The shouldBe function relates a function
application to an expected result.

In principle, it is very easy to write this specification before implementing the function. Once we are done with the implementation and the specification is checked successfully, we can move forward with implementing other functions relying on `buildIP`.

Before running this test, let's add specifications for the following functions:

```
parseIP :: String -> Maybe IP
parseIPRange :: String -> Maybe IPRange
parseIPRanges :: String -> Either ParseError IPRangeDB
```

Again, think of these as functions that are not yet implemented. Our goal is to write specifications that reflect what we expect of the functions, not how they are implemented.

Most of the job is done in the `parseIP` function, so it deserves a precise specification. Read the following example, and enjoy the clarity of the specification:

```
spec_parseIP :: Spec
spec_parseIP =
  describe "parseIP" $ do
    it "parses zero" $
      parseIP "0.0.0.0" `shouldBe` Just (IP 0)              The maxBound value for
    it "parses one" $                                        the Word32 type (this is
      parseIP "0.0.0.1" `shouldBe` Just (IP 1)               inferred automatically)
    it "parses the largest IP address" $
      parseIP "255.255.255.255" `shouldBe` Just (IP maxBound)   ◁──────
    it "parses some random IP address" $
      parseIP "192.168.3.15" `shouldBe`
        Just (buildIP [192,168,3,15])     ◁──────    It's okay to use other
    it "fails to parse 3 components" $                functions here. (buildIP
      parseIP "192.168.1" `shouldBe` Nothing         is already tested.)
    it "fails to parse 4 components with suffix" $
      parseIP "192.168.1.1x" `shouldBe` Nothing
    it "fails to parse empty component" $
      parseIP "192.168..1" `shouldBe` Nothing
    it "fails to parse 5 components" $
      parseIP "192.168.1.0.1" `shouldBe` Nothing
    it "fails to parse large components" $
      parseIP "256.168.1.0" `shouldBe` Nothing
    it "fails to parse extremely large components" $
      parseIP "0.0.0.4294967338" `shouldBe` Nothing
    it "fails to parse negative components" $
```

```
    parseIP "256.168.-1.0" `shouldBe` Nothing
  it "fails to parse non-numeric components" $
    parseIP "192.x.1.0" `shouldBe` Nothing
```

One disadvantage of this approach becomes clear when we get to the larger test cases. It's still manageable for parseIPRange, as shown next:

```
spec_parseIPRange :: Spec
spec_parseIPRange =
  describe "parseIPRange" $ do
    it "parses pair" $
      parseIPRange "192.168.0.1,192.168.3.100" `shouldBe`
        IPRange <$> parseIP "192.168.0.1" <*> parseIP "192.168.3.100"
    it "fails to parse single ip" $
      parseIPRange "192.168.0.1" `shouldBe` Nothing
    it "fails to parse single ip with comma" $
      parseIPRange "192.168.0.1," `shouldBe` Nothing
    it "fails to parse triple" $
      parseIPRange "192.168.0.1,192.168.0.2,192.168.0.4" `shouldBe` Nothing
```

As for the parseIPRanges function, we are limited to rather short examples only, as follows:

```
spec_parseIPRanges :: Spec
spec_parseIPRanges =
  describe "parseIPRanges" $ do
    let sample_range = "192.168.0.1,192.168.3.100"
        sample_range2 = "0.0.0.0,0.0.0.1"
    it "parses empty list" $
      parseIPRanges ""  `shouldBe` Right (IPRangeDB [])
    it "parses single range" $
      parseIPRanges sample_range  `shouldBe`
        Right (IPRangeDB $ catMaybes [parseIPRange sample_range])
    it "parses two ranges" $
      parseIPRanges (sample_range ++ "\n" ++ sample_range2) `shouldBe`
        Right (IPRangeDB $ catMaybes [parseIPRange sample_range,
              parseIPRange sample_range2])
```

Preparing a test case with, say, 10 IP address ranges is extremely inconvenient. Well, lucky for us, there are better ways to do that. I'll present them shortly.

We've defined four specifications, but they can be easily combined into one as follows:

```
parseIPSpecs :: Spec
parseIPSpecs = describe "ParseIP" $ do
  spec_buildIP
  spec_parseIP
  spec_parseIPRange
  spec_parseIPRanges
```

This combined specification can be viewed as a specification for the whole `ParseIP` module. We also need a specification for the `LookupIP` module. It should look very familiar now, as shown here:

```
spec_lookupIP :: Spec
spec_lookupIP =
  describe "lookupIP" $ do
    let empty_iprdb = IPRangeDB []
        sample_iprdb = IPRangeDB [IPRange (IP 0) (IP 1),
                        IPRange (IP 100) (IP 120)]
        ip1 = IP 110
        ip2 = IP 50
    it "no IP in empty list" $
      ip1 `shouldNotSatisfy` lookupIP empty_iprdb
    it "IP in sample list" $
      ip1 `shouldSatisfy` lookupIP sample_iprdb
    it "no IP in sample list" $
      ip2 `shouldNotSatisfy` lookupIP sample_iprdb

lookupIPSpecs :: Spec
lookupIPSpecs = describe "LookupIP" $ do
  spec_lookupIP
```

Note, that I've switched to the `shouldSatisfy` and `shouldNotSatisfy` functions instead of using `shouldBe`. The line

```
ip1 `shouldSatisfy` lookupIP sample_iprdb
```

means the same as

```
lookupIP sample_iprdb ip1 `shouldBe` True
```

You might prefer using `shouldSatisfy` and `shouldNotSatisfy` to give specifications for functions returning `Bool` values.

CHECKING SPECIFICATIONS AND FIXING PROBLEMS

To check all these specifications, we need to do the following:

1. Add the modules with specifications to the test suite (the `other-modules` field).
2. Mention the dependency on the `tasty-hspec` package (the `build-depends` field).
3. Add a test group with the specifications to the `tasty` test suite.
4. Run the tests.

The test group with specifications should be passed to the `defaultMain` function of the Test.hs driver as follows:

```
main = do
  specs <- concat <$> mapM testSpecs
           [ parseIPSpecs
           , lookupIPSpecs
           ]
```

```
defaultMain (testGroup "All Tests" [
                testGroup "Specs" specs
            ])
```

Running tests with `cabal` test gives us the following output:

```
Running 1 test suites...
Test suite iplookup-test: RUNNING...
All Tests
  Specs
    ParseIP
      buildIP
        builds from zero:                            OK
        builds from one:                             OK
        builds from localhost:                       OK
        builds from arbitrary address:               OK
      parseIP
        parses zero:                                 OK
        parses one:                                  OK
        parses the largest IP address:               OK
        parses some random IP address:               OK
        fails to parse 3 components:                 OK
        fails to parse 4 components with suffix:     OK
        fails to parse empty component:              OK
        fails to parse 5 components:                 OK
          fails to parse large components:              FAIL
            expected: Nothing
             but got: Just (IP {unIP = 11010304})
          fails to parse extremely large components: FAIL
            expected: Nothing
             but got: Just (IP {unIP = 42})
          fails to parse negative components:           FAIL
            expected: Nothing
             but got: Just (IP {unIP = 11075328})
        fails to parse non-numeric components:       OK
      parseIPRange
        parses pair:                                 OK
        fails to parse single ip:                    OK
        fails to parse single ip with comma:         OK
        fails to parse triple:                       OK
      parseIPRanges
        parses empty list:                           OK
        parses single range:                         OK
        parses two ranges:                           OK
  LookupIP
    lookupIP
      no IP in empty list:                           OK
      IP in sample list:                             OK
      no IP in sample list:                          OK

3 out of 26 tests failed (0.00s)
Test suite iplookup-test: FAIL
Test suite logged to: hid-examples-iplookup-test.log
0 of 1 test suites (0 of 1 test cases) passed.
cabal: Tests failed for test:iplookup-test from hid-examples.
```

But wait! What's going on? We have failed tests! For example, according to our specification:

```
it "fails to parse extremely large components" $
    parseIP "0.0.0.4294967338" `shouldBe` Nothing
```

Unfortunately, the output says that we've got `Just (IP {unIP = 42})` instead of `Nothing`. We don't trust heartless test automation, so let's fire up GHCi, as shown next:

```
$ cabal repl iplookup-lib
...
ghci> import ParseIP
ghci> parseIP "0.0.0.4294967338"
Just (IP {unIP = 42})
```

Okay, we've got the answer. Now we need a reason. Let's revisit the `buildIP` function type signature, as shown next:

```
buildIP :: [Word8] -> IP
```

Consequently, the `Word8` type is inferred for a result of `readMaybe` in `parseIP`, leading to the following behavior:

```
ghci> import Text.Read
ghci> import Data.Word
ghci> readMaybe "4294967338" :: Maybe Word8
Just 42
```

This behavior is totally correct: the `Word8` type cannot fit such a big value, so we've got a silent overflow. Fortunately, the fix is easy: we control the size of the value anyway, so why not read an unbounded `Integer` value instead? We could read a value with a version of `readMaybe` specialized for `Integer` and then use `fromInteger` to get a `Word8` value as follows:

```
parseIP :: String -> Maybe IP
parseIP = guarded (4 `isLengthOf`) . splitOn "."
        >=> mapM (readMaybe >=> guarded fitsOctet >=> pure . fromInteger)
        >=> pure . buildIP
  where
    fitsOctet x = 0 <= x && x <= 255
```

Running tests again affirms correctness, as follows:

```
$ cabal test
Running 1 test suites...
Test suite iplookup-test: RUNNING...
Test suite iplookup-test: PASS
Test suite logged to: hid-examples-iplookup-test.log
1 of 1 test suites (1 of 1 test cases) passed.
```

In fact, we can do even better with the `toIntegralSized` function from the `Data.Bits` module, as shown here:

```
toIntegralSized :: (Integral a, Integral b, Bits a, Bits b) => a -> Maybe b
```

This function safely converts a value of an integral type to a value of another integral type. So, it's not necessary to use `fitsOctet`. If a value doesn't fit eight bits, then we'll get `Nothing`. One problem is that it's impossible to infer types in the following expression:

```
readMaybe >=> toIntegralSized
```

From the outer context, we can infer that the resulting type is `Maybe Word8`, but what about a type of `readMaybe`, in the next line?

```
readMaybe :: Read a => String -> Maybe a
```

We want the `a` type variable to be an `Integer` here! Then we could safely read any integer number and safely convert it to `Maybe Word8`! One solution could be to write the trivial `readMaybeInteger` function with the type signature `String -> Maybe Integer`. An alternative solution is to use the `TypeApplications` GHC extension. With it, we can specify a particular type for the `a` type variable directly as follows:

```
readMaybe @Integer >=> toIntegralSized
```

Type parameters and the TypeApplications GHC extension

The type signature `Read a => String -> Maybe a` for the `readMaybe` function hides one crucial detail. In fact, this function has a type parameter in addition to the `Read a` type class constraint and a `String` value. We can see this parameter if we enable printing explicit `forall`s as follows:

```
$ cabal repl iplookup-lib --repl-options=-fprint-explicit-foralls
...
ghci> import Text.Read
ghci> :type readMaybe
readMaybe :: forall {a}. Read a => String -> Maybe a
```

By writing `readMaybe @Integer` with the enabled `TypeApplications`, we fix `a` to be an `Integer`, and the `Read a` constraint is automatically satisfied, thanks to the instance of the `Read` type class for `Integer`, as shown next:

```
ghci> :set -XTypeApplications
ghci> :type readMaybe @Integer
readMaybe @Integer :: String -> Maybe Integer
```

As a result, we have the precise version of `readMaybe` we need. We'll talk more about this extension and other type tricks later in this book.

Thus, we arrive at the final implementation of the parseIP function, shown here:

```
parseIP :: String -> Maybe IP
parseIP = guarded (4 `isLengthOf`) . splitOn "."
        >=> mapM (readMaybe @Integer >=> toIntegralSized)
        >=> pure . buildIP
```

All the tests are still passing! No more problems in our implementation! Let's move to the other approaches to testing, though it's unlikely that they will be useful in our project. After all, we've tested everything!

THE HUNIT PACKAGE The HUnit package provides a unit-testing framework for Haskell, inspired by the JUnit tool for Java. It can be used for testing the same things as hspec. In my view, its syntax for test cases is overcomplicated, but it is very popular, so give it a try. Testing with HUnit is described in many sources.

8.2.4 *Property-based testing with Hedgehog*

Sometimes we can describe the behavior of our function, or several functions in general, as a property that has to be true for every input or for some set of inputs. For example, the result of the maximum function called over a list is always greater than or equal to its first element. Clearly, it's not always possible to check a property for all possible inputs. Even if a set of inputs is finite, it could take too much time to check all of them. The solution comes in the form of randomizing inputs: we generate some inputs (many of them) and check a property for them. Surely, we cannot prove that a property holds in this way, but if we are lucky, we could find a counterexample proving that a property is wrong. If a property holds for every random input, then there is a good chance that it holds for all of them. Thus, we gain some confidence that our code is correct.

Property testing consists of the following stages:

1 We define generators for our inputs, describing how to generate them randomly.
2 We formulate properties as equalities or assertions that relate inputs to outputs.
3 We check properties for the generated inputs and analyze the results.

Property testing in Haskell originated in the QuickCheck package in 2002, and it has been actively developed since then. Many tutorials on QuickCheck are available. In this chapter, we use a relatively new property-testing package, Hedgehog, together with tasty and the tasty-hedgehog provider.

EXAMPLE: USING THE HEDGEHOG PROPERTY-TESTING PACKAGE

🗋   ip/gen/

⚡   *ipgen, ipgen-lib*

☞   We can generate data suitable for testing.

To start using Hedgehog, it's enough to import the following three modules:

```
import Hedgehog
import qualified Hedgehog.Gen as Gen
import qualified Hedgehog.Range as Range
```

To use Hedgehog with `tasty`, we would also need the following:

```
import Test.Tasty
import Test.Tasty.Hedgehog
```

Generating inputs can be useful, independent of testing. For example, we could generate a large input to benchmark our application against it. Remember that we split `iplookup` into components: we have the `iplookup-lib` internal library, the `iplookup` executable, and the `iplookup-test` test suite. Let's do the same thing with input generation: we'll define the `ipgen-lib` internal library and the `ipgen` executable. Surely, we need to add the dependency on `ipgen-lib` to `iplookup-test`. Figure 8.2 presents all the internal dependencies for the IPv4 filtering application (an arrow should be read as "depends on").

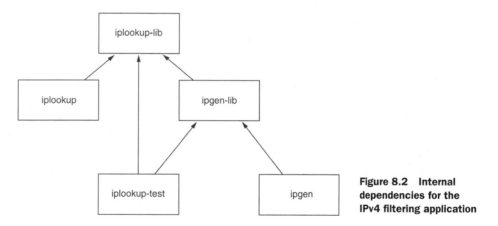

Figure 8.2 Internal dependencies for the IPv4 filtering application

GENERATING INPUTS

Inputs suitable for property-based testing should be distinguished from random data. Although we do want to generate inputs randomly, this randomness should be put bounded; completely random data is not convenient to work with because of its irrelevance to the functions we want to check. Because one of the goals of property checking is providing counterexamples, we'd like to have them as small as possible: we want to see the essence of an error. In programming, it is often the edge cases that are a source of errors, so we want to discover them. Unfortunately, this is not always an easy thing to do. Thus, property-testing inputs are random data plus the following:

- An ability to generate data of various types
- An ability to control sizes and bounds of inputs (depending on their types)

Plus something else, namely:

- A *scaling* strategy to make inputs smaller or larger as needed
- A *shrinking* strategy to make inputs closer to the simplest value (in some sense)

Although scaling allows exploring a space of inputs in an attempt to find a counterexample to a property that is being checked, shrinking is aimed at finding the simplest counterexample that is crucial to revealing the source of the error.

In Hedgehog, these features are implemented by the following components:

- *The* `Size` *type*—An integer value ranging from 0 to 99 and characterizing the size of the randomly generated data (with 0 meaning the smallest)
- *The* `Range` *type*—The lower and upper bounds for generated inputs as a function of `Size` (this is where a scaling strategy lives!) and an origin as the simplest value (the base case for a shrinking strategy!)
- *A collection of generators*—Monadic functions (or values) responsible for providing random data of various types from a specified range

The `Hedgehog.Range` module defines the next four sorts of ranges:

- A singleton range containing exactly one value
- A constant range whose bounds are unaffected by the size parameter
- A linear range with an upper bound depending on the size parameter linearly
- An exponential range with an upper bound depending on the size parameter exponentially

Although creating a range, we may set only bounds, or bounds with an origin, or use `Enum/Bounded` instances to derive both arguments. Figure 8.3 illustrates the idea of a range with bounds, origin, and directions of scaling and shrinking: scaling is responsible for moving bounds, whereas shrinking works by generating values closer to an origin.

Explore the documentation for the `Hedgehog.Range` module to find a variety of `Range`-defining functions.

Generators provided by the `Hedgehog.Gen` module are able to generate inputs of primitive types, enumerations, characters, elements of collections, and collections themselves. We'll see many of them shortly.

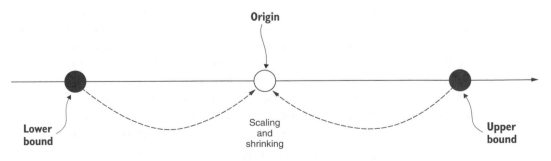

Figure 8.3   A basic Hedgehog range and its components

Let's define a generator for IP addresses. In our example, shown next, an IP address is just an arbitrary `Word32` value, so this should be easy. Indeed, it is:

The Gen monad is a monad for generating random data provided by Hedgehog.

Generates a Word32 value from the given range

```
genIP :: Gen IP
genIP = IP <$> Gen.word32 Range.linearBounded
```

To generate a random IP address, we use a linear range with bounds depending on the `Bounded` instance of the `Word32` type. That means that the lower bound of the range will be `minBound` (which is 0) whereas the upper bound will be `maxBound` with an origin equal to the lower bound. Besides generating a value, the `genIP` generator defines appropriate scaling and shrinking strategies: decreasing the `Size` parameter will tighten the bounds toward zero (the lowest bound) linearly, and shrinking will produce values closer to zero. Thus, we'll see values close to zero in counterexamples often.

Instead of generating an IP address as a whole, we could generate its components instead, as shown here:

```
genIPComponents :: Gen [Word8]
```

We need to generate a list of length 4 containing values from 0 to 255. To generate a list, we can use the following generator:

```
Gen.list :: MonadGen m => Range Int -> m a -> m [a]
```

It has the following two arguments:

- A `Range Int` specifying the expected length of lists
- A single component generator `m a`

Because the only expected length should be 4, we need to define a range containing the value 4 only. There is a `singleton` range for that, shown here:

```
Range.singleton :: a -> Range a
```

We already know about the `word32` generator, but there exists a `word8` generator also.

Using these ingredients, we could arrive at the following generator:

Generates a list with four components

```
genIPComponents :: Gen [Word8]
genIPComponents = Gen.list (Range.singleton 4) genOctet
  where genOctet = Gen.word8 Range.linearBounded
```

Generates a Word8 value for every component

The `linearBounded` range for `Word8` guarantees that we are getting values from 0 to 255.

Now let's generate an IP range. Although we can easily use `genIP` for generating the first IP address in a range, the second one should be greater than or equal to the first one for the IP range to be correct. So, we need to use the first IP address to generate the second one. Let's take one of the following ranges for that:

```
linear :: Integral a => a -> a -> Range a
linearFrom :: Integral a => a -> a -> a -> Range a
```

The `linear` range expects lower and upper bounds (and uses the lower bound as an origin), whereas the `linearFrom` range requires an origin (as a first argument) in addition. The lower bound should be equal to the first IP address. If we use `linear`, then an origin is set to that. Alternatively, we could use the next IP address for an origin, as follows:

```
genIPRange :: Gen IPRange
genIPRange = do
  (IP ip1) <- genIP
  ip2 <- Gen.word32 (Range.linearFrom (ip1 + 1) ip1 maxBound)
  pure $ IPRange (IP ip1) (IP ip2)
```

Uses the generator defined earlier

Generates the second range component, which tends to be next to the first one after shrinking

Returns a range as a pair of generated IPs

Why not generate an invalid IP range with the second component smaller that the first one, as shown next?

```
genInvalidIPRange :: Gen IPRange
genInvalidIPRange = do
  (IP ip1) <- Gen.filter (> (IP minBound)) genIP
  ip2 <- Gen.word32 (Range.linear minBound (ip1 - 1))
  pure $ IPRange (IP ip1) (IP ip2)
```

Note the use of the `Gen.filter` function: we want to avoid getting a zero IP address in the first component, because every such range is valid. This function runs a given generator a sufficient number of times to get an input that satisfies the given predicate.

Following the same course of action, let's next define a couple of generators for a whole IP range database:

```
genIPRangeDBSized :: Int -> Int -> Gen IPRangeDB
genIPRangeDBSized minLen maxLen =
    IPRangeDB <$> Gen.list (Range.constant minLen maxLen) genIPRange
```

The length of a list is expected to be within the specified minLen and maxLen limits.

```
genIPRangeDB :: Gen IPRangeDB
genIPRangeDB = do
  n1 <- Gen.integral (Range.constant 1 100)
  n2 <- Gen.integral (Range.constant n1 100)
  genIPRangeDBSized n1 n2
```

The integral generator is able to generate a value of any Integral type.

n2 is expected to be greater or equal to n1.

We can use the `genIPComponents` generator to generate a `String` representation of a correct IP address as follows:

```
genIPString :: Gen String
genIPString = concat . intersperse "." . map show <$> genIPComponents
```

While defining generators, it's always tempting to see what they actually generate. We can use a convenience function for that: Gen.sample. It takes a generator and returns a single generated value. For example, let's generate and see several IP addresses in their String representation, as shown next:

```
ghci> Gen.sample genIPString
"75.4.60.18"
ghci> replicateM_ 5 $ Gen.sample genIPString >>= putStrLn
32.70.53.42
53.15.14.77
55.8.75.51
27.37.13.77
51.17.6.48
```

It could also be useful to be able to build a String representation of an IP address directly. Let's define the following instances for the corresponding data types (they could go into the IPTypes module):

```
instance Show IP where
  show (IP ip) = concat $ intersperse "." $ map show [b4,b3,b2,b1]
    where
      (ip1, b1) = ip `divMod` 256
      (ip2, b2) = ip1 `divMod` 256
      (b4, b3) = ip2 `divMod` 256

instance Show IPRange where
  show (IPRange ip1 ip2) = show ip1 ++ "," ++ show ip2

instance Show IPRangeDB where
  show (IPRangeDB iprs) = unlines $ map show iprs
```

These instances can be seen at work in GHCi, as shown here:

```
ghci> Gen.sample genIP
55.91.78.115
ghci> Gen.sample $ genIPRange
66.78.147.165,75.47.51.100
ghci> Gen.sample $ genIPRangeDBSized 1 3
49.191.149.19,105.86.77.174
```

Now if we need to get a result of any generator in the form of a String, we can write show <$> genIP or show <$> genIPRange.

The sample function can also be used to generate test data and save it to some file for later uses (e.g., to benchmark the program). The following fragment defines an IO action that creates a file with an IP range list:

```
data Params = Params
                Int         -- number of ranges
                FilePath    -- file name
```

```
writeFileWithRanges :: Params -> IO ()
writeFileWithRanges (Params n fp) = do
  str <- show <$> Gen.sample (genIPRangeDBSized n n)
  writeFile fp str
```

WRITING PROPERTIES

All the functionality to write properties is provided by the `Hedgehog` module. It defines the `Property` type, which encapsulates testing configuration (e.g., number of inputs to check), input generation, and expectation assertions. It is even allowable to do `IO` within a `Property`.

EXAMPLE: TESTING PROPERTIES WITH HEDGEHOG

📄   tests/iplookup/Props.hs

⚡ *iplookup-test*

☞ Property testing is a powerful tool to reveal errors.

Let's start with the `buildIP` function. It is hard to come up with a general property holding for every input. But suppose that we have several implementations, as shown here, less or more performant (we'll see that later):

```
buildIP :: [Word8] -> IP
buildIP = buildIP_foldr

buildIP_foldr :: [Word8] -> IP
buildIP_foldr = IP . fst . foldr go (0, 1)
  where
    go b (s, k) = (s + fromIntegral b * k, k*256)

buildIP_foldl :: [Word8] -> IP
buildIP_foldl = IP . foldl (\s b -> s*256 + fromIntegral b) 0

buildIP_foldl_shl :: [Word8] -> IP
buildIP_foldl_shl = IP . foldl (\s b -> shiftL s 8 + fromIntegral b) 0
```

The first one is the original one and is used by default. The second one, `buildIP_foldl`, uses a smart trick to avoid excessive computations, as follows:

```
192.168.1.1
 = 1 + 1 * 256 + 168 * 256^2 + 192 * 256^3
 = 1 + (1 + (168 + 192 * 256) * 256) * 256
 = (((0 * 256 + 192) * 256 + 168) * 256 + 1) * 256 + 1
 = foldl (\s b -> s * 256 + b) 0 [192, 168, 1, 1]
```

The third one uses smart bitwise computations—it must be super efficient!

Now we can easily formulate a property for their equivalence as follows:

```
prop_buildIPs :: Property
prop_buildIPs = property $ do
```
⟵ **The property function creates a Property from a monadic computation.**

```
ipcs <- forAll genIPComponents
let ip = buildIP ipcs
buildIP_foldr ipcs === ip
buildIP_foldl ipcs === ip
buildIP_foldl_shl ipcs === ip
```

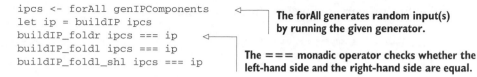

The forAll generates random input(s) by running the given generator.

The === monadic operator checks whether the left-hand side and the right-hand side are equal.

The `do` block in the `prop_buildIPs` property runs in the `PropertyT IO ()` monad. The `PropertyT` monad transformer adds all the testing facilities, such as the generation of test inputs and the assertion of expectations, to the `IO` monad.

For `parseIP`, we could check that it parses results of `show` for all IP addresses correctly, as shown next:

```
prop_parseIP :: Property
prop_parseIP = property $ do
    ip <- forAll genIP
    parseIP (show ip) === Just ip
```

Technically, `show` for IP addresses and `parseIP` form a pair of encoding and decoding functions. Hedgehog provides the following convenience function, `tripping`, exactly for such cases:

```
prop_parseIP_show :: Property
prop_parseIP_show = property $ do
    ip <- forAll genIP
    tripping ip show parseIP
```

It is also the case that `show` for an IP range and IP range database should agree with `parseIPRange` and `parseIPRangeDB`, respectively, as follows:

```
prop_parseIPRange_show :: Property
prop_parseIPRange_show = property $ do
    ipr <- forAll genIPRange
    tripping ipr show parseIPRange

prop_parseIPRanges_show :: Property
prop_parseIPRanges_show = property $ do
    iprdb <- forAll genIPRangeDB
    tripping iprdb show parseIPRanges
```

Remember that we can generate invalid ranges. Let's check `parseIPRange` on them as follows:

```
prop_no_parseInvalidIPRange :: Property
prop_no_parseInvalidIPRange = property $ do
  inv_ip <- forAll genInvalidIPRange
  parseIPRange (show inv_ip) === Nothing
```

Let's also formulate the following two properties for the `lookupIP` predicate (a function returning `Bool`):

1 No IP belongs to the empty IP range database.
2 Borders of every range in the database belong to the database.

The first property can be implemented as follows:

```
prop_lookupIP_empty :: Property
prop_lookupIP_empty = property $ do
  ip <- forAll genIP
  assert (not $ lookupIP (IPRangeDB []) ip)
```

Note the assert function. It checks that the given argument is True (so lookupIP returns False).

The second property is implemented in the following code—we generate an IP range database, choose an arbitrary range from it, and check both its borders:

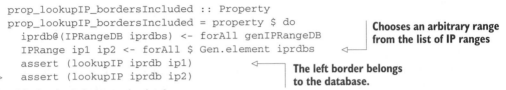

```
prop_lookupIP_bordersIncluded :: Property
prop_lookupIP_bordersIncluded = property $ do
  iprdb@(IPRangeDB iprdbs) <- forAll genIPRangeDB         Chooses an arbitrary range
  IPRange ip1 ip2 <- forAll $ Gen.element iprdbs          from the list of IP ranges
  assert (lookupIP iprdb ip1)
  assert (lookupIP iprdb ip2)             The left border belongs
                                          to the database.
The right border belongs to the database.
```

The last thing we should do with all these properties is connect them to the tasty test suite. Let's define a list of properties using the testProperty function provided by the Test.Tasty.Hedgehog module, as follows:

```
props = [
    testProperty "buildIP implementations agrees with each other" prop_buildIP
      s
  , testProperty "parseIP works as expected" prop_parseIP
  , testProperty "parseIP agrees with show" prop_parseIP_show
  , testProperty "parseIPRange agrees with show" prop_parseIPRange_show
  , testProperty "parseIPRanges agrees with show" prop_parseIPRanges_show
  , testProperty "no parse of invalid IP ranges" prop_no_parseInvalidIPRange
  , testProperty "no ip in empty list" prop_lookupIP_empty
  , testProperty "lookupIP includes borders" prop_lookupIP_bordersIncluded
  ]
```

With this list of properties, we are ready to check all of them.

CHECKING PROPERTIES

To check Hedgehog properties, we should connect them with tasty by passing their lists to the testGroup function along with the hspec specifications in the Test.hs driver as follows:

```
main = do
  specs <- ...
  defaultMain (testGroup "All Tests" [
                  testGroup "Specs" specs         hspec specifications
  Hedgehog    , testGroup "Properties" props
  properties    ])
```

Finally, we can run all the tests, as shown next, and see something interesting:

```
Properties
    buildIP implementations agrees with each other:    OK
        OK
    parseIP works as expected:                     OK
        OK
    parseIP agrees with show:                      OK
        OK
    parseIPRange agrees with show:                 OK
        OK
    parseIPRanges agrees with show:                OK (0.36s)
        OK
    no parse of invalid IP ranges:                 FAIL (0.02s)
        X no parse of invalid IP ranges failed after 1 test and 131 shrinks.

              --- tests/iplookup/Props.hs ---
        44 | prop_no_parseInvalidIPRange :: Property
        45 | prop_no_parseInvalidIPRange = property $ do
        46 |     inv_ip <- forAll genInvalidIPRange
           |     ? 0.0.0.1,0.0.0.0
        47 |     parseIPRange (show inv ip) === Nothing
           |     ^^^^^^^^^^^^^^^^^^^^^^^^^^^^^^^^^^^^^^^^^
           |     ? --- Not Equal ---
           |     ? Just 0.0.0.1,0.0.0.0
           |     ? Nothing
        ...
    no ip in empty list:                           OK
        OK
    lookupIP includes borders:                     FAIL
        X lookupIP includes borders failed after 1 test and 2 shrinks.

              --- tests/iplookup/Props.hs ---
        54 | prop_lookupIP_bordersIncluded :: Property
        55 | prop_lookupIP_bordersIncluded = property $ do
        56 |     iprdb@(IPRangeDB iprdbs) <- forAll genIPRangeDB
           |     ? 0.0.0.0,0.0.0.1
        57 |     IPRange ip1 ip2 <- forAll $ Gen.element iprdbs
           |     ? 0.0.0.0,0.0.0.1
        58 |     assert (lookupIP iprdb ip1)
        59 |     assert (lookupIP iprdb ip2)
           |     ^^^^^^^^^^^^^^^^^^^^^^^^^^^^^^
        ...
2 out of 34 tests failed (0.40s)
```

Well, we've got two failed properties. Note the information we have about those failures. Hedgehog managed to find the following simple counterexamples:

- `0.0.0.1,0.0.0.0` is a clearly invalid range, but it is parsed by `parseIPRange` without complaint.
- `0.0.0.1` should belong to the `0.0.0.0,0.0.0.1` range, but it doesn't, according to our implementation.

Now that we see these problems so clearly, it's easy to fix them. In fact, we never checked that the right border of the range should be greater than or equal to the left one. Let's do that now as follows:

```
parseIPRange :: String -> Maybe IPRange
parseIPRange = guarded (2 `isLengthOf`) . splitOn ","
               >=> mapM parseIP
               >=> listToIPRange
  where
    listToIPRange [a,b]
      | a <= b = pure (IPRange a b)
    listToIPRange _ = empty
```

> **If the guarded condition is not satisfied, then the second clause of the definition is used.**

As for the second failure: I mistakenly wrote < instead of <= in the inRange function (in the LookupIP module). The fix, shown next, is trivial:

```
lookupIP ::  IPRangeDB -> IP -> Bool
lookupIP (IPRangeDB ips) ip = case find (inRange ip) ips of
                    Nothing -> False
                    Just _ -> True
  where
    inRange ip (IPRange beg end) = beg <= ip && ip <= end
```

Running the test suite again reveals no more problems, as shown here:

```
Running 1 test suites...
Test suite iplookup-test: RUNNING...
Test suite iplookup-test: PASS
Test suite logged to: hid-examples-iplookup-test.log
1 of 1 test suites (1 of 1 test cases) passed.
```

Coming up with the correct general properties of your functions is hard, but if you can do that, all the bugs are eaten by Hedgehog automatically!

8.2.5   *Golden tests with tasty-golden*

Including test cases in the code can be problematic for large datasets. To deal with test cases larger than a couple of lines, we can use files. For example, we could read inputs from a file, write output to a file, and then check the output against some reference result. The files used as a reference are called golden files.

We should consider the following issues when applying the technique of checking results against the golden files content:

- Someone should come up with golden files used as a reference first: manual preparation could be infeasible due to their potentially large size.
- Checking many test files at once should be easy.
- Checking file equality should be correct despite platform idiosyncrasies (e.g., newline symbols).
- It should be easy to deal with failures, so we need a way to see what's wrong if a file is too big for manual auditing.

As always, our solution is to use a good library. The `tasty-golden` package provides such a library, clearly integrated with the `tasty` infrastructure.

GOLDEN-TESTING PREPARATIONS

Our main goal is to check the `lookupIP` function (and guarantee its stability as the project evolves), so let's introduce some new, simplified file-based infrastructure around it. Note that we are doing that with golden testing in mind.

First, let's implement two functions for parsing input file content: one for IP ranges and another one for IP addresses themselves. These functions, shown next, use the most basic strategy: they ignore incorrect lines. That's fine because we are not planning to test reading input right now.

```
parseValidIPs :: String -> [IP]
parseValidIPs = catMaybes . map parseIP . lines

parseValidIPRanges :: String -> IPRangeDB
parseValidIPRanges = IPRangeDB . catMaybes . map parseIPRange . lines
```

The `catMaybes` function (provided by the `Data.Maybe` module) strips off all the `Nothing` values we could get while parsing a given `String` as follows:

```
catMaybes :: [Maybe a] -> [a]
```

Second, we need test files with some inputs. Let's put them into the data/tests/ iplookup folder and give them names with meaningful extensions. For example, the following is the potential content of the 1.iprs file with a set of IP ranges:

```
9.166.251.217,20.39.180.175
50.33.43.83,69.2.226.61
27.191.215.182,39.236.185.129
68.66.248.16,95.176.114.135
34.247.148.113,93.161.226.166
23.173.2.219,55.224.252.1
11.188.211.24,40.18.226.141
4.137.106.119,22.197.224.247
```

And here is the 1.ips file with some IP addresses to check:

```
68.66.248.20
127.0.0.1
40.18.226.141
```

In fact, we could generate plenty of files like these using the `ipgen` utility program, and they could be large enough! Suppose all of them have names following the same pattern: N.ip(r)s.

It's easy to write a golden file for the first test case, shown next. Let's call it 1.out.golden.

```
68.66.248.20: YES
127.0.0.1: NO
40.18.226.141: YES
```

Note that we don't attempt writing a golden file for other tests. After all, what if there are thousands of lines there?

WRITING GOLDEN TESTS

EXAMPLE: GOLDEN TESTING FOR THE IPV4 FILTERING APPLICATION

🗋   tests/iplookup/GoldenTests.hs

⚡   *iplookup-test*

☞ Golden tests simplify implementing large test cases.

Let's add the `GoldenTests` module to the `iplookup-test` test suite. The corresponding file starts by importing `tasty` and `tasty-golden` modules together with utilities for file path processing and our own `iplookup-lib` modules, as follows:

```
module GoldenTests where

import Test.Tasty
import Test.Tasty.Golden
import System.FilePath (normalise, takeBaseName, replaceExtension)

import ParseIP
import LookupIP
```

Then, we need to find available test cases. Let's find the .iprs files and create tests for all of them, as follows:

```
testsDir = normalise "data/tests/iplookup/"       ⟵┐ Creates a normalized file path
                                                    for the folder with tests

golden_lookupIP :: IO TestTree
golden_lookupIP = testGroup "lookupIP" . map createTest   ⟵┐ Creates a test group
                <$> findByExtension [".iprs"] testsDir      from a list of tests
      ⟶
Searches for .iprs files in the testsDir folder
```

Now we can define a single test as follows:

```
createTest :: String -> TestTree                Creates a test for
createTest iprsf = goldenVsFile        ⟵        checking file content
                    (takeBaseName iprsf)   ⟵──── Test name
Golden file name  ┌⟶ goldenf
(to check against) │    outf        ⟵──── File for output
                   │    testAction  ⟵
  where                                   An action that creates
    ipsf = replaceExtension iprsf ".ips"   an output file
    goldenf = replaceExtension iprsf ".out.golden"
    outf = replaceExtension iprsf ".out"
```

```
                  testAction = do
                    iprs <- parseValidIPRanges <$> readFile iprsf  ⟵── Reads the IP address ranges
                 ┌─▷ ips <- parseValidIPs <$> readFile ipsf
                    writeBinaryFile outf $ reportIPs iprs ips  ⟵┤ Prepares a report and
                                                                  creates an output file
```

Reads the IP addresses to check (margin annotation, left of code)

Reads the IP address ranges (margin annotation, right of code)

Prepares a report and creates an output file (margin annotation, right of code)

The `goldenVsFile` function is only one of the several available golden tests provided by `tasty-golden`. You may find others in the documentation on the `Test.Tasty.Golden` module.

Finally, we should combine all the golden test groups into a `TestTree` (though, currently, we have only one group), as shown next:

```
goldenTests :: IO [TestTree]
goldenTests = sequence [golden_lookupIP]
```

And add them to the test suite in the Test.hs test suite driver as follows:

```
main = do
  ...
  goldens <- goldenTests
  defaultMain (testGroup "All Tests" [
               ...
               , testGroup "Golden Tests" goldens
               ])
```

We are ready to run these tests and see what's going on.

USING GOLDEN TESTS

Remember that we didn't prepare golden files for test cases beyond the first one. Suppose we trust our current implementation. The `tasty-golden` library creates golden files on the first run if they are missing. When we run the test suite for the first time, we could see the following output:

```
Golden Tests
    lookupIP
      1:                                              OK
      2:                                              OK
        Golden file did not exist; created
```

On all the subsequent runs, `tasty-golden` will check against existing golden files, and you may see something like this as an output:

```
Golden Tests
    lookupIP
      1:                                              OK
      2:                                              OK
```

If some tests fail, the easiest way to see the difference is to analyze the output file and the golden file using any `diff`-like utility. In fact, you may wish to introduce difference analyses right into the test suite via a `goldenVsFileDiff` test. Some useful scenarios concerning the use of golden testing may be found in the article "Introduction to Golden Testing" (https://ro-che.info/articles/2017-12-04-golden-tests), written by Roman Cheplyaka, the `tasty` and `tasty-golden` author.

8.3   *Other approaches to testing*

We've done a lot of work to make sure no errors are in our project. Apart from unit testing, property testing, and golden testing, we have other approaches to guarantee software correctness. In this section, I'll overview some of them briefly and give you links where you can learn more.

8.3.1   *Testing functions à la the REPL with doctest*

If we are writing a Haskell library, we would definitely want to supply documentation for it. We can do that using Haddock, a documentation-generation tool for Haskell libraries (http://hackage.haskell.org/package/haddock). Undoubtedly, you've met documentation looking like that shown in figure 8.4.

```
isLengthOf :: Int -> [a] -> Bool
```

Checks if the list has the given length

```
>>> 4 `isLengthOf` [1,2,3,4]
True
>>> 0 `isLengthOf` []
True
>>> 0 `isLengthOf` [1,2,3,4]
False
```

```
parseIP :: String -> Maybe IP
```

Parses the IP address given as a `String`

```
>>> parseIP "0.0.0.0"
Just 0.0.0.0
```

```
>>> parseIP "192.168.3.15"
Just 192.168.3.15
```

```
>>> parseIP "not an IP address"
Nothing
```

Figure 8.4   A fragment of Haddock-generated module documentation

This documentation can be generated for any cabalized project with the following simple command:

```
$ cabal haddock
```

The good news is that >>> fragments are not just documentation fragments; they can actually be transformed into tests using the doctest library and utility program, written by Simon Hengel.

Suppose we've added the following documentation comments into the ParseIP module:

```
-- | Checks if the list has the given length
--
-- >>> 4 `isLengthOf` [1,2,3,4]
-- True
-- >>> 0 `isLengthOf` []
-- True
-- >>> 0 `isLengthOf` [1,2,3,4]
-- False

isLengthOf :: Int -> [a] -> Bool
...


-- | Parses the IP address given as a 'String'
--
-- >>> parseIP "0.0.0.0"
-- Just 0.0.0.0
--
-- >>> parseIP "192.168.3.15"
-- Just 192.168.3.15
--
-- >>> parseIP "not an IP address"
-- Nothing

parseIP :: String -> Maybe IP
...
```

We've seen the result of processing these lines with cabal haddock in figure 8.4. It may not be the best approach to include tests in code because they create clutter, but these tests still do a good job documenting code. In addition, they could serve as a guarantee that the documentation is fresh.

It is possible to use documentation tests as one of the test suites for a project. To do that, we need to create a test suite driver, say, Doctests.hs (you may find it in the *tests/iplookup-doctest* folder), as shown next:

```
import Test.DocTest

main = doctest ["-iip/lookup", "ip/lookup/ParseIP.hs"]
```

We should also define this test suite in the .cabal file as follows:

```
test-suite iplookup-doctest
  type: exitcode-stdio-1.0
  main-is: tests/iplookup-doctest/Doctests.hs
  ghc-options: -threaded
  build-depends:
      base >=4.12 && <4.15
    , doctest >=0.12 && <0.17
```

Now that we have two test suites, they both run with `cabal test` and report success.

8.3.2   *Lightweight verification with LiquidHaskell*

The LiquidHaskell project brings refinement types to Haskell. Refinement here means extending Haskell types with some information in the form of logically quantified predicates. For example, the `Nat` type is the `Int` type with a predicate, stating that every number is either equal to or greater than zero, as shown here:

```
type Nat = {n : Int | n >= 0}
```

LiquidHaskell is implemented as a standalone application that can be installed via the `liquidhaskell` package from Hackage. This application analyzes comments in the form of `{-@ ... @-}` with refined information on types of functions and checks the code against those refinements.

Suppose we have the following program:

Nat is a refined type.

```
  {-@ v :: Nat @-}      Int is a Haskell type.
  v :: Int
  v = 42                 42 is a value belonging to both Int and Nat.
```

Checking this program with LiquidHaskell (in quiet mode) gives us the following safety guarantee:

```
$ liquid -q v42.hs

**** RESULT: SAFE **************************
```

If we implement a function that adds `v` to any given `Nat` value, we'll retain this guarantee, as shown next:

```
{-@ addV :: Nat -> Nat @-}
addV :: Int -> Int
addV a = a + v
```

Clearly, adding some natural value to another natural value gives us a natural value.

On the contrary, an attempt to subtract a value `v` from the given natural value fails, because such an operation could potentially lead us outside the set of natural numbers, as shown here:

```
{-@ subV :: Nat -> Nat @-}
subV :: Int -> Int
subV a = a - v
```

```
**** RESULT: UNSAFE **************************
```

LiquidHaskell collects types and refined type information and then checks all the operations over corresponding values using another piece of software, namely, SMT solvers. SMT stands for *satisfiability modulo theories*. SMT solvers work with logical formulas over background theories (natural numbers with arithmetic and comparisons, floating-point arithmetic, lists, vectors, etc.). They are able to prove correctness or give up proving and present some unsatisfiable formulas. We call this approach *verification* as opposed to testing, because if LiquidHaskell is able to prove something, then the code is provably correct. The verification is lightweight because we are talking about correctness with respect to our refined types. It's on us to express refined types as strictly as we can, but we are limited here by LiquidHaskell itself.

At the time of writing, LiquidHaskell works with a limited number of GHC versions and supports a relatively small number of background theories. Nevertheless, it belongs to an active area of research and has good prospects. The best way to start learning LiquidHaskell is by following the tutorial at https://liquid.kosmikus.org/, written by Andres Löh. The main web page for this project is https://ucsd-progsys .github.io/liquidhaskell-blog/; you may find an extended tutorial there and plenty of additional information.

8.3.3   Code quality with hlint

Code quality may be considered part of quality assurance. Although no single rule or set of rules defines the right style for Haskell code, it may be helpful to follow some guidelines. One particular set of guidelines is incorporated into the hlint utility. This utility reads Haskell code and provides recommendations on how to improve it.

For example, let's check the ParseIP module using hlint as follows:

```
$ hlint ParseIP.hs
ParseIP.hs:74:17: Warning: Use mapMaybe
Found:
  catMaybes . map parseIP . lines
Perhaps:
  mapMaybe parseIP . lines

ParseIP.hs:77:34: Warning: Use mapMaybe
Found:
  catMaybes . map parseIPRange . lines
Perhaps:
  mapMaybe parseIPRange . lines

2 hints
```

Well, these hints are quite useful; we should definitely apply them to the code!

The hints on `IPTypes` are also promising, as shown next:

```
$ hlint IPTypes.hs

IPTypes.hs:11:18: Suggestion: Use intercalate
Found:
  concat $ intersperse "." $ map show [b4, b3, b2, b1]
Perhaps:
  intercalate "." (map show [b4, b3, b2, b1])

IPTypes.hs:23:1: Suggestion: Use newtype instead of data
Found:
  data IPRangeDB = IPRangeDB [IPRange]
                    deriving Eq
Perhaps:
  newtype IPRangeDB = IPRangeDB [IPRange]
                       deriving Eq
Note: decreases laziness

2 hints
```

Surely, we don't have to follow all the `hlint` hints, but it's always a good idea to look at them. You may find some information on customizing `hlint` in the Hackage page of this package.

Summary

- Testing is a crucial part of quality assurance in the process of software development.
- Unit testing works by specifying test input data for functions and checking the results against given correct output.
- Property testing works by checking functions and their combinations against a large set of randomly generated data.
- Golden testing is checking program output against presumably correct "golden" output.
- Testing is able to discover errors, though it can't guarantee correctness.
- It's a good idea to check code with the `hlint` utility to ensure that it follows community-supported guidelines and better coding practices.

Haskell data and code at run time

9

This chapter covers

- Representing data and code in memory at run time
- Haskell features that affect performance
- Code optimizations done by the compiler

Haskell performance is a tricky story. It may be difficult to predict and explain, and it's not the easiest thing to achieve in our programs. With functional and other declarative programming languages, code running on actual hardware tends to be much further from code written by a programmer than in the case of imperative languages. One of the consequences of this fact is that a programmer sometimes has a somewhat limited ability to affect performance directly. Although it is considered a task for a compiler to produce the best executable code possible, this goal is crucial for a developer also. Haskell laziness adds much to this intricacy. A programmer should be able to predict what is executed and what is not. Thanks to laziness, significant parts of the code may well not be evaluated at all.

In this chapter, we'll discuss various Haskell features that affect performance and learn ways to use them wisely. We'll start with Haskell memory usage and find out how Haskell data and code are represented in memory. Then we'll look at the memory representation used to implement lazy evaluation and learn how to control it. Finally, we'll discuss several examples of optimizations that affect executable code and see what's going on with the code during compilation and execution. Note that this chapter is very specific to GHC implementation. Whenever I say *Haskell*, I mean GHC/Haskell, the Haskell language as implemented in the Glasgow Haskell Compiler.

The knowledge of all these implementation details will help us in the next chapter to analyze and boost the performance of our IP filtering application from the previous chapter. It is also helpful to explore drawbacks in other programs and fix them.

9.1 A mental model for Haskell memory usage at run time

In this section, we'll look at GHC/Haskell memory usage: what's going on in memory at run time. We'll focus on the simple model and discuss the storage of data and code in memory. These details will help us understand how Haskell code is executed at run time. I call it a simple model because the compiler may affect memory usage profoundly due to various optimizations.

9.1.1 General memory structure and closures

The memory of every running Haskell program comprises the following three main components:

- Static memory (containing static objects known at compile time)
- Stack (used to store immediate values, addresses of where to go next, etc.)
- Heap (containing dynamic objects, i.e., everything created at run time including values, partial function applications, and many other run-time program entities)

Figure 9.1 presents these components with their content.

The heap is the most used part of the address space of the process. Haskell immutability affects heap usage a lot, because it is necessary to create a new object whenever something is changed. Imagine that we have a list of numbers and want to increment every element, as shown next:

```
ys = map (+1) xs
```

Now we have two lists in the heap, so we've doubled heap usage. That's why we shouldn't be surprised by a program's amount of memory usage. Even for simple programs, the GHC runtime system allocates a lot of memory.

At the same time, Haskell compilers try hard to minimize heap usage and use sharing as much as possible, as shown in the following example:

```
p = (xs, xs)
```

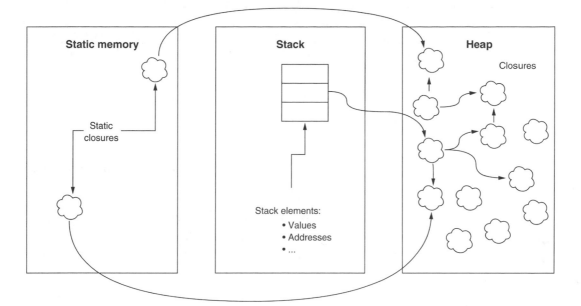

Figure 9.1   Run-time memory structure for a Haskell program

Here we've built a pair of values, but we don't have to keep xs in the heap twice, so it's shared.

Sharing is used by the compiler almost everywhere to save heap space. For another example, let's look at the replicate 1000 'a' expression. Only one dynamic object is responsible for keeping the 'a' character. It is referenced by every (:) data constructor in the resulting list.

GHC/Haskell uses garbage collection to free up the heap so that there is space to create new dynamic objects in place of those that are not needed anymore. Haskell uses pointers to implement sharing, and yes, we are back to plain old C pointers while discussing memory usage.

The heap itself is a collection of closures, entities used for representing everything in the heap. Every character and every Integer value in our program is represented by some closure. Every closure is a pair: it has a description and a payload, whose content depends on the description. We don't have to know the exact content of a description, but it is used by the runtime system to deal with a closure as follows:

- First, there is an info table describing the exact content of a closure's payload.
- Second, the closure's description contains an entry code, which is evaluated whenever we enter the closure. Closures are used for representing both data and code; that's why we need code out there.

Figure 9.2 presents the high-level closure model.

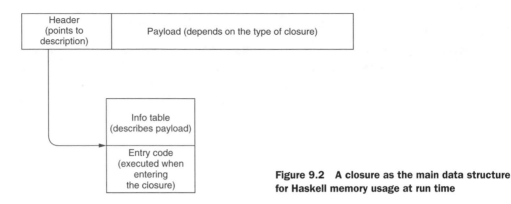

Figure 9.2   A closure as the main data structure for Haskell memory usage at run time

The closures' structure may be affected in some compilation modes. For example, when we compile a program for profiling, we have an additional pointer to a data structure with various counters. This is one reason why we need to compile all the external libraries in a profiling mode from scratch to profile our programs.

Descriptions are heavily shared. For example, every data constructor of an algebraic data type definition refers to one such description in the heap. Many values can be built with that data constructor, but all of them share the same description.

Closures may well reference each other so that we have a graph of dependencies in the heap that is analyzed and processed by the garbage collector. Values on the stack may reference heap closures also. Static objects in static memory may be represented by closures themselves (we call them static closures) or reference dynamic ones.

Further, we'll see how closures are used to represent Haskell data, and after that, we'll move to representing code with closures. Interestingly, the latter allows implementing lazy evaluation of Haskell programs.

9.1.2   *Primitive unboxed data types*

Storing absolutely everything with closures is not extremely efficient. Sometimes we'd like to use the CPU's registers or plain memory cells. Haskell, being a high-level programming language, struggles to hide these implementation details, but we have ways to access them anyway.

Values that support storing in memory directly are called unboxed because they don't require a closure (a box). We call the types of those values unboxed also. The opposite, boxed types, require a closure to store every individual value. Most of the Haskell types are boxed. In this subsection, we discuss primitive unboxed types, which are built into the language and compiler. We'll get to defining our own unboxed types in the next section.

The GHC.Prim module exports several primitive types that can be used for storing primitive unboxed values, including the following:

- `Int#` and `Word#` for native-sized (32- or 64-bit, depending on the machine architecture) signed and unsigned integers, respectively
- `Int8#`, `Int16#`, `Word8#`, and `Word16#` for storing smaller-size integers
- `Char#` for storing 31-bit characters
- `Float#` and `Double#` for storing 32- and 64-bit floating-point numbers, respectively
- `Addr#` for storing machine addresses

In order to refer to these types, we should enable the `MagicHash` GHC extension, which allows referring to identifiers with # in them.

The literals of these types require the # suffix as seen in the following GHCi session:

```
ghci> :set -XMagicHash
ghci> :t 3#
3# :: GHC.Prim.Int#
ghci> :t 3.14#
3.14# :: GHC.Prim.Float#
ghci> :t 'x'#
'x'# :: GHC.Prim.Char#
```

Using # in names for unboxed values and types is conventional, though not mandatory. In addition to types, the `GHC.Prim` module exports many primitive operations over primitive values. The programmer rarely needs to use all this stuff directly, but it is useful to know that it is possible. It is also useful to understand that traditional Haskell types are defined through them, for example:

```
data Int = I# Int#
```

```
data Char = C# Char#
```

These definitions are located in the `GHC.Base` module, which is accessible from every Haskell module when compiled with GHC. Note that `I#` and `C#` are regular data constructors and are stored in memory with closures, as described in the next subsection, but their fields are special because they are primitive and stored directly in memory.

9.1.3 *Representing data and code in memory with closures*

There is not much difference between code and data in Haskell, and in functional programming in general. On the one hand, we can store code (a function) as a field of a data constructor. On the other hand, data may be unevaluated due to laziness and thus be represented as a thunk—code that is able to evaluate a value whenever needed—so the distinction is rather superficial.

FULLY EVALUATED DATA IN MEMORY

Let's suppose for now that every data value is fully evaluated and discuss its representation in memory. We'll see how laziness affects this representation shortly.

Here is the basic principle: a payload of closures corresponding to data constructors contains pointers to closures of the constructor's fields. Say we have the following data type representing geometric shape sizes:

```
data Shape = Rectangle Int Int | Circle Int
```

We already know that the type Int is defined as

```
data Int = I# Int#
```

where Int# is a primitive type whose values are stored in memory as one machine word. We denote them with a hashtag such as 1#. Thus, we have three constructors playing this game with three info tables generated to describe them as follows:

- Rectangle
- Circle
- I#

Suppose that the following two values were created at run time:

- Circle 3 to be stored as Circle (I# 3#)
- Rectangle 5 3 to be stored as Rectangle (I# 5#) (I# 3#)

Our simple memory model suggests generating the following five closures to store these values in memory:

- Three distinct closures to store the I# values 3#, 5#, and one more 3#
- One closure to store the Rectangle value
- One closure to store the Circle value

Figure 9.3 presents the corresponding memory layout.

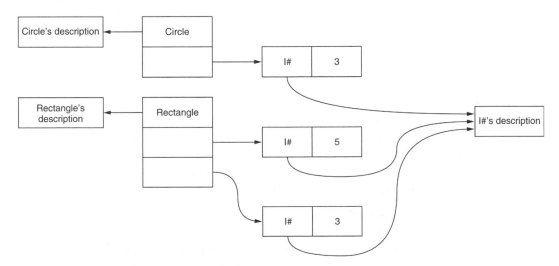

Figure 9.3   Closures and their descriptions in memory

The GHC compiler may optimize some of these closures away, especially closures for small, strict Int values, but the general idea is that we do need closures for most fields of the data constructor. If the constructor has no fields (e.g., True, False, or Nothing), then there will be precisely one closure for it at run time with its own description. Whenever this constructor is used somewhere, this closure is referenced.

EXAMPLE: COMPUTING MEMORY USAGE

Remember that data constructor descriptions are shared, so they don't increase dynamic memory usage. Thus, storing Rectangle 5 10 and Circle 3 in memory would require 11 words in total because we have the following:

- Eight pointers referencing descriptions and other closures (every box with an outgoing arrow in figure 9.3 represents a pointer).
- Three primitive I# values.

Now let's try to compute memory usage for replicate 1000 'x' as a list of 1,000 characters. Suppose that the list built with replicate is defined as follows. (Note that I use pseudocode here.)

```
data [a] = (:) a [a]
       | []
```

We can predict the existence of the following closures in memory, assuming that the list is fully evaluated:

- There will be one closure storing the 'x' value (C# 'x'#, two words).
- We'll have 1,000 closures for every list element, with every such closure containing one pointer to the (:) data constructor description; one pointer to the closure storing the 'x' value; and one pointer to the closure with the next list element, thus taking three words per closure and 3,000 words in total (not counting the constructor's description).
- There will be a closure storing the [] data constructor (empty list) referenced by the last element (one word-size as it is the constructor with no fields).

Summing everything up, we get 2 + 3000 + 1 = 3003 words that equals to 3003 * 8 = 24024 bytes, or about 23.5Kb on 64-bit machines.

CODE IN MEMORY AND LAZY EVALUATION

We've already discussed that there is no significant difference between code and data in Haskell and in other functional programming languages. To store code in memory, we use the same concept of a closure with a slightly different payload and description. The following two essential types of closures are used to represent code:

- Functions—the payload, in this case—contain references to values that occur freely in the code. GHC generates static closures for top-level functions and dynamic ones for those that are created at run time. The entry code for these closures is the function code itself.

- Thunks are very close to functions. They are used to represent code that should be executed to evaluate an expression. As such, they represent unevaluated expressions. Their payload contains references to free variables of the expression, and their entry code in the closure's description is the code to evaluate the corresponding expression.

One of the main features of thunks as closures is their ability to be updated when their value is evaluated. In that case, a thunk's closure changes its type and becomes an indirection—a closure that references another closure containing the result of an evaluation.

Haskell laziness effectively boils down to creating thunks instead of evaluating expressions in the first place. The evaluation itself is then followed in the form of an updating thunk with an indirection to the results of the evaluation when they are needed.

EXAMPLE: EVALUATING A THUNK

Suppose that we have the following expression somewhere in a program:

```
let x = a + 2 in ...
```

Figure 9.4 shows the three stages of evaluating the value of x as represented in memory:

- Before the value of x is required
- After the value of x is required
- After garbage collection (we assume that the value of x is still needed within a program).

First, note that the a variable occurs freely in the a+2 expression. Second, GHC will not attempt to evaluate this expression immediately. Instead, it will generate a thunk for it with the code to evaluate it when needed (stage 1). Once this moment comes at run time, the program accesses the value of a (and forces its evaluation if it is also

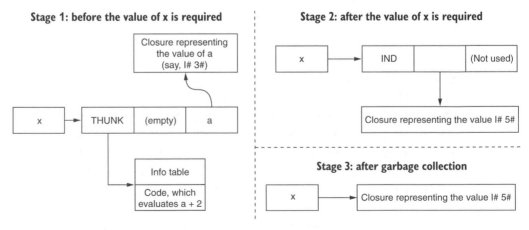

Figure 9.4   Expression evaluation time line: thunks and indirections

represented as a thunk—we assume that it evaluates to I# 3#), evaluates a + 2, creates a closure to store the result in memory, and updates the thunk with an indirection pointing to the closure with the result (stage 2).

The indirection will be removed during garbage collection, and if the x variable survives (say, it is still used somewhere), it will reference the closure with its value directly (stage 3).

The thunk's payload is specifically designed to be easily updated with an indirection: it has an empty field that becomes a pointer to a closure with the result of a computation.

FORMS OF A VALUE: NORMAL FORM AND WEAK HEAD NORMAL FORM

As we have seen, almost all the values in our programs are represented in memory with closures. These closures are thunks at first (and their value is unevaluated) and are then updated with the results of an evaluation (the value becomes evaluated). The next question is, how deeply is this value evaluated? The answer is trivial for the value x from our previous example as presented in figure 9.5.

Unevaluated

Fully evaluated

Figure 9.5   An unevaluated and fully evaluated variable: the trivial case

If we have a value of a more complex type, things get more interesting. Consider, for example:

```
let z = (length [1..5], "hello" ++ " world") in ...
```

We start with an unevaluated expression with z represented by a thunk, and we end up in a situation where z equals the pair (5, "hello world"), which is fully evaluated. But between these two forms of the z variable is a whole bunch of other forms in which z is partially evaluated, for example:

- (thunk, thunk)—z is a pair.
- (5, thunk)—z is a pair with the first component equal to 5.
- (5, 'h':thunk)—z is a pair with the first component equal to 5 and a partially evaluated second component.

Figure 9.6 presents the first and the last of these partially evaluated forms in memory.

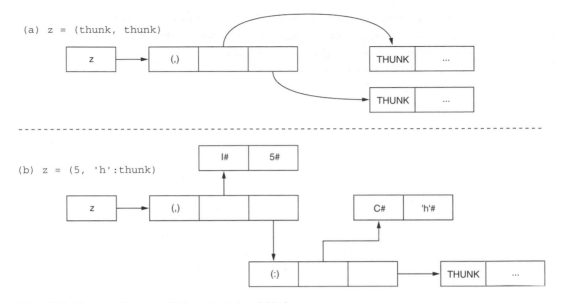

Figure 9.6   Representing a partially evaluated variable in memory

Let's give several formal definitions of the forms we are discussing in this subsection. We say that a value is *unevaluated* if it is represented by a thunk. We say that a value is in *normal form* if it is fully evaluated. We say that a value is in a *weak head normal form* (WHNF) if it is represented by a closure corresponding to a data constructor.

9.1.4   *A detour: Lifted types and the concept of strictness*

Let's get away from memory representation details and take a detour to the theoretical ideas that are implemented with this approach to memory usage.

LIFTED AND UNLIFTED TYPES

A type is said to be lifted if its values may take the special value undefined (called *bottom* and often denoted as ⊥). Most Haskell types are necessarily lifted due to thunks: we don't know in advance whether the evaluation will be successful, so we include the possibility of failure. Thus, we assume that the bottom value is automatically added to every type we define in Haskell.

The type is called unlifted if its values cannot be bottom. For example, unboxed types are always unlifted, because there is no way to represent bottom for them because there are no thunks—their values are precisely what is stored in the corresponding memory cells.

Boxed types can be both lifted and unlifted. A traditional example of an unlifted boxed type is a low-level Array#, which is typically represented by a pointer to a contiguous block of memory. It is boxed because it is not stored directly in a memory cell or a CPU's register; it is unlifted because it doesn't include bottom (we cannot construct a thunk for it).

Figure 9.7 presents possible relations between lifted/unlifted and boxed/unboxed types.

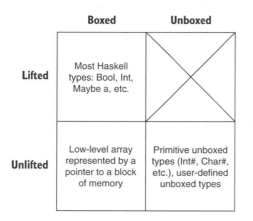

	Boxed	Unboxed
Lifted	Most Haskell types: Bool, Int, Maybe a, etc.	
Unlifted	Low-level array represented by a pointer to a block of memory	Primitive unboxed types (Int#, Char#, etc.), user-defined unboxed types

Figure 9.7 Relations between lifted/unlifted and boxed/unboxed types

Note the strong connection between evaluating a value and the liftedness of its type: if a type is unlifted, then there is no way to delay evaluating the value because we can't construct a thunk for it. Interestingly, function types in Haskell are always lifted because they are represented in memory by closures, which can be thunks.

Kinds for unboxed unlifted types and levity polymorphism

Should we attempt to dive deeper into the run-time representation of Haskell values, we soon realize that most of the Haskell machinery available to programmers is provided for lifted boxed types only. For example, we can't use values of primitive unboxed types as elements of a list or send them to a polymorphic function. The reason is that all these features of Haskell extensively use memory closures in their implementations. They count on a heap structure and a value size.

Haskell uses its kind system to differentiate lifted types from unlifted ones. The kind * (or its synonym, the `Type` kind) refers to lifted boxed types only. In fact, it is defined via more general machinery briefly presented as follows:

```
TYPE :: RuntimeRep -> Type

data RuntimeRep = LiftedRep      -- for things like `Int`
                | UnliftedRep    -- for things like `Array#`
                | IntRep         -- for `Int#`
                | ...

type Type = TYPE LiftedRep    -- Type is just a type synonym
```

An ability to work with different run-time representations is called levity polymorphism. See the corresponding section in the GHC User's Guide for more details.

STRICTNESS

Another theoretic concept that significantly depends on the run-time memory representation in Haskell is strictness. It is supposed to be used in connection with lifted types. Let's give a formal definition of a strict function.

A one-argument function f is called strict if, given the bottom value as an argument, it returns the bottom value as follows:

```
f ⊥ = ⊥
```

If a function has more than one argument, we could say that it is strict in the first (or second, or any other) argument.

In Haskell, to represent bottom, we can use either undefined or a computation running forever. Clearly, not all Haskell functions are strict. Consider the following const function:

```
const a b = a
```

It is definitely strict in the first argument, but it's not strict in the second one, for example:

```
ghci> const 1 undefined
1
```

Functions head and (+1) are strict, as shown here:

```
ghci> undefined + 1
*** Exception: Prelude.undefined
ghci> (length $ repeat 1) + 1
(loops forever)
ghci> head undefined
*** Exception: Prelude.undefined
```

But the next function, (True ||), is not strict:

```
ghci> True || undefined
True
```

In most programming languages, many functions are strict in all the arguments (the notable exception to this rule is short-circuiting Boolean operations that don't require evaluating the right-hand side if the result is already clear). In Haskell, whether a function is strict in some of its arguments depends on how the argument is used. Due to laziness, arguments to functions are initially represented by thunks, which potentially might never be evaluated.

DETERMINING STRICTNESS OF A FUNCTION Sometimes it may be too inefficient to create a thunk for an argument in which the function is clearly strict. GHC implements an optimization technique called demand analysis (also known as strictness analysis) whose goal is to determine whether a value of an argument is used to evaluate a function result. Knowing this in advance could potentially lead to generating more efficient code.

In the next section, we'll see how a programmer can control the strictness of a function and reduce the number of thunks created at run time.

9.2 Control over evaluation and memory usage

The ability to control the process of evaluating Haskell values is quite limited. First, we can add more strictness to the code, reducing the number of thunks created and, if we are lucky enough, achieving better performance. Second, we can exploit unboxed types, eliminating the creation of thunks altogether. In this section, we'll explore both approaches.

In some sense, we are departing from regular Haskell programming here. The corresponding techniques are better thought of as a necessary evil to achieve performance (especially in computation-intensive code) and should be applied very carefully. In most cases, they make the code less readable and less idiomatic.

9.2.1 Controlling strictness and laziness

Let's look at the following Haskell function, which computes the sum of all the numbers from 1 to a given n:

```
sumN :: Int -> Int
sumN n = go 0 n
  where
    go acc 0 = acc
    go acc n = go (acc+n) (n-1)
```

We focus on evaluating the go inner function when we want to get the result of sumN 5, as follows:

```
sumN 5 = go 0 5 = go (0+5) 4 = go ((0+5)+4) 3 =
go (((0+5)+4)+3) 2 = go ((((0+5)+4)+3)+2) 1 =
go (((((0+5)+4)+3)+2)+1) 0 = (((((0+5)+4)+3)+2)+1) = 15
```

Note that nothing forces this function to evaluate the acc value. So with every call to go, the thunk for the first argument is created. As for the second argument, there are no thunks for it because with every recursive call, we have to check whether or not it is zero.

In terms of strictness, the go function is not strict in its first argument unless the second one equals 0. We could avoid creating all these thunks if we specify somehow that go is strict in the first argument also.

THE SEQ FUNCTION

Haskell provides the somewhat magic `seq` function, which is defined in terms of strictness. Its type is `a -> b -> b`, so it looks like it ignores the first argument. In fact, it's not, because its implementation is guaranteed to adhere to the following two rules:

- `seq ⊥ b = ⊥`
- `seq a b = b`

Basically, this function is strict in its first argument by definition.

How does this function check whether or not the first argument is bottom? Well, it evaluates it to a weak head normal form. Remember that values are normally represented by closures, as follows:

- If the first argument is represented by a data constructor's closure, then it's not the bottom for sure.
- If it is represented by a thunk, we need to evaluate it to weak head normal form.

It is enough to evaluate it only one step further from an unevaluated value. The corresponding closure becomes a data constructor closure or a closure of some other type, which may well contain references to thunks or whatever.

Misunderstandings around seq

A common source of misunderstandings around the `seq` function lies in the idea that it evaluates the first argument and then returns the second one. In fact, the only thing that is done by `seq` is to check if its first argument is not `undefined`. Technically, this is done by consulting the corresponding closure and evaluating it (computing a thunk, calling a function, etc.) until it's clear whether it is `undefined`.

For example, it makes no sense writing the following:

```
ghci> (undefined, undefined) `seq` 5
5
```

The first argument here is not `undefined`; it's a pair. There are more interesting cases. Compare the following two expressions and their results:

```
ghci> seq ((\True x -> "") undefined) "OK"
"OK"
ghci> seq ((\True -> \x -> "") undefined) "OK"
*** Exception: Prelude.undefined
```

The `(\True x -> "") undefined` expression is a partial application because there is only one argument to the lambda, so the result is some function and definitely not `undefined`. The `seq` function doesn't attempt to match `undefined` against the `True` pattern here, because this is done only for full-function applications.

The second `seq ((\True -> \x -> "") undefined)` expression is a function call, so `seq` checks the result and attempts to evaluate it, pattern matches `True` against `undefined`, and gets an exception.

The best way to understand the `seq` function is to understand its technical side of evaluating a closure corresponding to its first argument.

Getting back to the `sumN` function, we could avoid creating almost all of the thunks by sending `acc` to `seq`. An `Int` value is either a thunk or an `I#` closure without any references to other closures.

The following implementation of the `sumN` function demonstrates the usage of the `seq` function to avoid creating unnecessary thunks:

```
sumN n = go 0 n
  where
    go acc 0 = acc
    go acc n = acc `seq` go (acc+n) (n-1)
```

Once we do this, the computation goes smoothly as follows:

```
sumN 5 = go 0 5 = go (0+5) 4 = go (5+4) 3 =
go (9+3) 2 = go (12+2) 1 =
go (14+1) 0 = 14+1 = 15
```

The `seq` function is usually introduced to improve performance by avoiding unneeded laziness. It is relatively rarely seen in production code because it is too low-level. Several syntax extensions (implemented via the `seq` function) provide a more convenient experience. Let's have a look at them.

BANG PATTERNS

The `BangPatterns` GHC extension enables adding `!` (bang) to patterns with the following effect, as defined by the GHC User's Guide:

> *Matching the pattern* `!pat` *against a value* v *behaves as follows:*

- If v is bottom, the match diverges.
- Otherwise, `pat` is matched against v.

Bang patterns can be described by translation to `seq` calls as follows:

```
case v of { !pat -> e; _ -> e' }
  = v `seq` case v of { pat -> e; _ -> e' }
```

This translation reveals that whenever we match some value against a bang pattern, the following occurs:

- We check whether it is defined (in the same way as the first argument to `seq`).
- If yes, we match it as usual.

The code of the `sumN` function in the presence of the `BangPatterns` GHC extension could look as follows:

```
{-# LANGUAGE BangPatterns #-}

sumN n = go 0 n
  where
    go acc 0 = acc
    go !acc n = go (acc+n) (n-1)
```

The result is the same as in the implementation with seq.

Bangs have no effect on patterns other than variables or wildcards. For example, there is no sense in writing !(x, y) or ![x] because a value that is matched against this pattern will be checked if it's a pair or a list first anyway (and this clearly subsumes checking that it's not a bottom). Writing !_ as a pattern is okay as you may see in the following GHCi session:

```
ghci> let _ = undefined in "OK"
"OK"
ghci> :set -XBangPatterns
ghci> let !_ = "BAD" in "OK"
"OK"
ghci> let !_ = undefined in "OK"
"*** Exception: Prelude.undefined
```

We can use bang patterns almost everywhere common patterns are allowed, including the following:

- Left-hand sides of the function definitions
- Case expressions
- Let expressions

The ($!) function as a strict application and a case for levity polymorphism

The Haskell Prelude exports the ($!) function, called strict application, defined via bang patterns and levity polymorphism as follows:

```
($!) :: forall r a (b :: TYPE r). (a -> b) -> a -> b
f $! x = let !vx = x in f vx
```

First, note that this function is defined for the resulting b type with any run-time representations (lifted/unlifted or boxed/unboxed). Second, this implementation uses a bang pattern for the x argument before applying the f function, so the argument will be evaluated to weak head normal form before sending it to the function.

STRICT FOLDS

The base GHC library defines strict versions of some well-known functions, such as foldl', foldl1', scanl', scanl1', and iterate'. In all of them, the supplied function argument is applied strictly, meaning that the result of an application is forced with seq (or a bang pattern) to be evaluated to weak head normal form. This works great when the accumulator is WHNF-strict (its weak head normal form is the same as normal form, for example, a number). In the following GHCi session, I compare the strict and nonstrict versions of foldl by looking at the execution time and memory usage (the +s GHCi flag is very helpful):

```
ghci> import Data.List
ghci> :set +s
ghci> foldl' (+) 0 [1..10^7]
```

```
50000005000000
(0.26 secs, 880,075,648 bytes)
ghci> foldl (+) 0 [1..10^7]
50000005000000
(2.43 secs, 1,612,372,904 bytes)
```

The strict version is clearly less demanding in both time and space consumption, thanks to the reduced number of thunks. But remember that strict application means evaluating to weak head normal form, so if the accumulator looks like

```
data MyInteger = MI Integer
```

the strict fold won't help because it won't attempt to compute anything inside the MI data constructor. We have to take other precautions in such cases: for example, we use strictness flags in data constructors, as I'll describe shortly.

STRICTNESS FLAGS IN DATA CONSTRUCTORS

When we create some value with a data constructor (i.e., apply a data constructor), its arguments are normally not evaluated. Instead, a thunk is created for every field. We may force evaluating them to weak head normal form by adding a strictness flag (which is conveniently a bang symbol: !) to their definitions as follows:

```
data MyInteger = MI !Integer
data Point = Point {x :: !Double, y :: !Double}
```

The GHC runtime system will then apply seq to the corresponding arguments of the data constructor (thus evaluating them to a weak head normal form) before applying it. We don't need to enable any GHC extension to use strictness flags, as they are part of the Haskell Report.

STRICT AND STRICTDATA GHC EXTENSIONS

Using strictness flags and bang patterns aggressively within a module may well lead to visual pollution in our code. To alleviate this, we may enable the following two GHC extensions:

- StrictData, which makes all the fields of all the data types defined in the current module strict by default
- Strict, which makes all function arguments and other bindings strict by default (evaluated to weak head normal form!) and implies StrictData

The following code example is identical to the previous one; all the data constructors will have strict fields:

```
{-# LANGUAGE StrictData #-}

data MyInteger = MI Integer
data Point = Point {x :: Double, y :: Double}
```

These extensions may be needed in high-performant computational parts of our code. They can be enabled on a per-module level and allow reverting to laziness occasionally by adding ~ to a pattern or a data constructor field.

Note that `Strict` and `StrictData` affect definitions in the current module only; everything imported from modules defined without them will be lazy, as in regular Haskell code.

Interestingly, switching to programming in "strict Haskell" does not necessarily make our programs run faster. It's always a good idea to do benchmarking first, as described in the next chapter.

STRICT VERSIONS OF CONTAINERS

Strictness, as opposed to laziness, has a great effect on the performance of data structures. That's why it is extremely important to think about which version of the container we actually need. As always, the difference boils down to the evaluation to weak head normal form as opposed to leaving unevaluated thunks whenever possible.

For example, each function in `Data.Map.Strict` forces values to weak head normal form before adding them to a `Map`, and the functions manipulating `Map` in other ways return a `Map` with values in weak head normal form. Though subject to extensive benchmarking, the strictness of values in a container often leads to better performance unless some laziness is required by the algorithms.

THE DEEPSEQ FUNCTION AND EVALUATION TO NORMAL FORM

Sometimes evaluating to weak head normal form is not enough, and we want to have fully evaluated data. In this case, we may use the `deepseq` function from the `Control.DeepSeq` module provided by the `deepseq` package. This function is able to force evaluation to normal form.

It is not always clear how to reach the normal form; the right evaluation order may depend on the data structure. That's why the `deepseq` function works via the `NFData` type class. The `deepseq` package provides several useful instances for many Haskell types. It is relatively easy to write instances for your own types.

The following is a type signature for `deepseq`:

```
deepseq :: NFData a => a -> b -> b
```

Apart from the `NFData a` section, it is the same as the one for `seq`.

There is also the `force` function, as shown next:

```
force :: NFData a => a -> a
```

This function returns a value that is guaranteed to be evaluated to normal form when it's evaluated to WHNF.

Similar to a strict application via (`$!`) is the deeply strict application operator, (`$!!`).

WARNING The deepseq function, as opposed to seq, always evaluates the given value in full, even if it was already evaluated. This is necessary to make sure that we have a normal form. Due to the representation with closures, we have no way to distinguish partially evaluated and fully evaluated values until we go over all the closures. Consequently, it's not a good idea to use deepseq all the time.

IMPORTANT Let me stress it again: all the techniques mentioned in this section should be seen as a departure from regular Haskell, a declarative, lazy programming language. Drawbacks that result from connecting strict and lazy code may appear very quickly.

9.2.2 *Defining data types with unboxed values*

GHC provides several tools to ask for unboxing. Let's overview them in this section.

THE UNPACK PRAGMA AND CORRESPONDING OPTIMIZATIONS

As we discussed in the previous section, storing values like Rectangle 3 5 requires many closures for the value itself and for each of its fields. If our fields are small, it may be helpful to put them directly into the payload of the constructor's closure. This is done with the UNPACK pragma, which can be used as follows:

```
data Shape = Rectangle {-# UNPACK #-} !Int
                       {-# UNPACK #-} !Int
           | Circle {-# UNPACK #-} !Int
```

Note that it is required to have strictness flags on all the unpacked fields. The UNPACK pragma has an effect only when optimizations are turned on (compilation with the -O family of flags). Note also that this pragma has no effect on polymorphic values.

Depending on what we are doing with the fields after matching over the constructor pattern, it may be necessary to rebox them, so this optimization does not always lead to reduced memory usage. Anyway, GHC tries hard to avoid reboxing.

GHC OPTIONS ON UNBOXING In addition to the UNPACK pragma, GHC provides the -funbox-strict-fields flag, which has the effect of adding {-# UNPACK #-} to every strict constructor field. Note that using it could lead to performance drawbacks if we copy a data structure extensively because all the unboxed fields have to be copied. Remember that any change in a data structure leads to copying in Haskell. This is not a problem for small, strict fields if their size is no bigger than a pointer—the pointer has to be copied anyway. That's why GHC enables the -funbox-small-strict-fields flag by default.

UNBOXED TUPLES AND UNBOXED SUMS

We are not allowed to define primitive unboxed types, but we are able to define unboxed tuples and unboxed sums using the UnboxedTuples and UnboxedSums GHC extensions. The idea behind these extensions is to make possible declaring complex types without the need to create closures for storing their values. Both unboxed tuples and unboxed sums don't exist at run time, but their components do exist and are stored in memory, depending on their own types.

EXAMPLE: UNBOXING TUPLES AND SUMS

◻   ch09/unboxed.hs

⚡   *unboxed*

☞ We can reduce memory allocation thanks to unboxing.

Let's define a function that computes the sum and product of two numbers and returns them as an unboxed tuple, as shown next:

```
{-# LANGUAGE UnboxedTuples #-}

sum_prod :: Num a => a -> a -> (# a, a #)
sum_prod a b = (# a + b, a*b #)
```

To use this function, we pattern match on its result right after calling it as follows:

```
test_sum_prod = case sum_prod 5 6 of
                     (# s, p #) -> print (s + p)
```

In this case, we avoid creating closures for tuples in memory. Doing so may be beneficial if we call this function many times and use its results right away.

The function returning an unboxed tuple may be recursive, as shown here:

```
{-# LANGUAGE UnboxedTuples #-}

fib_next :: Int -> (# Integer, Integer #) -> (# Integer, Integer #)
fib_next 0 p = p
fib_next n (# a, b #) = fib_next (n-1) (# b, a+b #)

main = case fib_next 100 (# 0, 1 #) of
         (# a, b #) -> print a
```

In this program, we compute the 100th Fibonacci number in a relatively efficient way without creating tuples at all.

Unboxed sums allow sending and receiving alternative values without storing additional closures in memory. The following function takes one or two Double values and finds the smallest of them:

```
{-# LANGUAGE UnboxedTuples #-}
{-# LANGUAGE UnboxedSums #-}

smallest :: (# Double | (# Double, Double #) #) -> Double
smallest (# d | #) = d --                              ◁─── First alternative
smallest (# | (# x, y #) #) = min x y      ◁─────┐
                                                 │ Second alternative
```

```
test_smallest = do
  print $ smallest (# 5.4 | #)              ◁———| First alternative
  print $ smallest (# | (# 2.3, 1.2 #) #)   ◁——— Second alternative
```

Note how we use | to specify the alternative we want in patterns and constructors. Using primitive Double# instead of Double could save you even more memory and provide additional performance because there is no unnecessary boxing/unboxing.

9.3   *Exploring compiler optimizations by example*

As I've mentioned in the introduction to this chapter, when using a declarative programming language, there is always a distance between what is written by a programmer and what is actually executed. Let's see how we can understand and predict the resulting code by analyzing a small numerical example.

EXAMPLE: CHECKING A NUMBER FOR PRIMALITY

🗋   ch09/isprime/

⚡   *isprime*

☞   Declarative high-level code can be compiled effectively.

Remember that a number is called prime whenever it has no other divisors except for 1 and the number itself. Let's use this definition to check whether a given number is prime.

The function in the following code snippet creates a list of potential divisors using a range from 2 to n-1, and checks if every potential divisor actually divides the given number:

```
isPrime :: Integer -> Bool
isPrime n = all notDividedBy [2 .. n-1]
  where
    notDividedBy m = n `mod` m /= 0
```

The main program takes a command-line argument, converts it to an Integer number, passes it to isPrime, and prints True if all the potential divisors don't divide the given number (so it's prime) and False otherwise. To measure timing, I use the timeIt function from the timeit package, as follows:

```
import System.Environment
import System.TimeIt

import IsPrime

main :: IO ()
main = getArgs >>= timeIt . print . isPrime . read . head
```

Clearly, this is an extremely naive implementation. Nevertheless, it has one crucial advantage: it corresponds directly to the mathematical notion of a prime number. As a result, it is quite simple and trivially correct.

Let's build this program first and then run it twice with different arguments as follows:

```
$ cabal -v0 run isprime -- 78680101
True
CPU time:   2.24s
$ cabal -v0 run isprime -- 78680100
False
CPU time:   0.00s
```

The second run stops almost immediately. This means that almost nothing is done when the number is divisible by the very first potential divisor 2. In that case, the program doesn't check any other divisor, although nothing in the code asks for that. Compare this result with the following imperative pseudocode:

```
for d in [2 .. n-1]:
  if n `mod` d == 0:
    return False
return True
```

Here we have to clearly specify that we should exit the function when a divisor is found. Although we never specified that in the Haskell implementation, it is executed exactly like this. This behavior is made possible by laziness: Haskell doesn't attempt to execute anything that is not necessary to produce a result. Let's see how this is possible.

9.3.1   *Optimizing code manually*

To understand what is actually executed, we'll unfold the syntax and the functions we've used.

This unfolding involves several things that are done by GHC, namely:

- Desugaring, when syntactic sugar is replaced with function calls
- Inlining, when the function call is replaced with the body of the function
- Rewriting, when the code that matches some pattern is rewritten to something else

Let's see how GHC applies these processing stages while compiling our small example.

UNFOLDING [..] SYNTAX

The [n .. m] syntax is desugared to a call of the enumFromTo n m method from the Enum type class, so in this case, we'll get enumFromTo 2 (n-1). The following is an implementation of this method for the Integer type that we are using in this example:

```
enumFromTo x lim = enumDeltaToInteger x 1 lim
```

This implementation belongs to the GHC.Enum module, an internal GHC module that provides several Enum instances for the base package, including one for Integer. This instance contains the INLINE pragma, which advises the compiler to inline the definition of enumFromTo as follows:

```
{-# INLINE enumFromTo #-}
```

Inspecting the code, we find an implementation of enumDeltaToInteger, as shown here:

```
enumDeltaToInteger :: Integer -> Integer -> Integer -> [Integer]
enumDeltaToInteger x delta lim
  | delta >= 0 = up_list x delta lim
  | otherwise  = dn_list x delta lim
```

We know that delta is always 1 in this case, so now we need to look for the up_list function. Here it is:

```
up_list :: Integer -> Integer -> Integer -> [Integer]
up_list x0 delta lim = go (x0 :: Integer)
                    where
                        go x | x > lim   = []
                             | otherwise = x : go (x+delta)
```

Great! No other function is used here, so we can imagine unfolding [2 .. n-1] manually as follows:

```
[2 .. n-1] ===                          Desugaring
enumFromTo 2 (n-1) ===                          Inlining
enumDeltaToInteger 2 1 (n-1) ===           Calculating (1 ≥ 0)
up_list 2 1 (n-1) ===
go 2                                     Calculating
```

We could also continue calculating go 2 as follows:

```
                                2 ≤ n-1
go 2 ===
2 : go (2+1) ===                3 ≤ n-1
2 : 3 : go (3+1) ===            4 ≤ n-1
2 : 3 : 4 : go (4+1) ===
...
2 : 3 : 4 : ... : n-1 : go n ===          n > n-1
2 : 3 : 4 : ... : n-1 : []
```

But this is not what is actually done at run time. In fact, there will be no such a list at all. We'll see the details shortly.

REWRITING ENUMERATION

Haskell code (especially in libraries) often contains rewriting rules, in which case the compiler tries to apply them. Some rules should be applied before other rules. To facilitate this order, the compiler uses phase numbers, which decrease to zero (so zero is the last phase).

Rewriting rules are introduced by the RULES GHC pragma as follows:

```
{-# RULES
  <rewriting rules>
 #-}
```

Every rule has a name, an optional phase number, a code pattern that should be rewritten, and the result of rewriting, for example (the actual rule usually takes one line):

```
"efdtInteger1"
   [~1]
   forall x l.    enumDeltaToInteger x 1 l
   =
   build (\c n -> enumDeltaToInteger1FB c n x l)
```

The [~1] phase number specification means that this rule should be applied *before* phase 1. Note that this particular rule can be applied to enumDeltaToInteger 2 1 (n-1) and rewrites it to build (\c n' -> enumDeltaToInteger1FB c n' 2 (n-1)). Surely, the compiler is smart enough not to interfere with our variable n here.

The build function, which was introduced by this rewrite rule, is defined as follows:

```
build g = g (:) []
```

Apparently, it has something to do with constructing lists. The function enumDelta-ToInteger1FB, shown next, is also new to us:

```
enumDeltaToInteger1FB :: (Integer -> a -> a) -> a
                        -> Integer -> Integer -> a
enumDeltaToInteger1FB c n x0 lim = go (x0 :: Integer)
                  where
                     go x | x > lim   = n
                          | otherwise = x `c` go (x+1)
```

This function combines the functionality of enumDeltaToInteger and up_list, which we saw before, but eliminates checks as to whether delta is greater than 0. (Well, delta is equal to 1 after all.)

Now we've got the following:

```
                                  | Desugaring
[2 .. n-1] ===                  <──────┘
enumFromTo 2 (n-1) ===                 | Inlining
enumDeltaToInteger 2 1 (n-1) ===    <──────┘
build (\c n' -> enumDeltaToInteger1FB c n' 2 (n-1))    <─── Rewriting
```

Attempting to inline the `build` function definition with

```
build (\c n' -> enumDeltaToInteger1FB c n' 2 (n-1)) ===      ⟵———— Inlining
enumDeltaToInteger1FB (:) [] 2 (n-1)
```

would make it possible to apply one more rewriting rules as follows:

```
"enumDeltaToInteger1" [1] enumDeltaToInteger1FB (:) [] = enumDeltaToInteger1
```

where `enumDeltaToInteger1` is defined as

```
enumDeltaToInteger1 :: Integer -> Integer -> [Integer]
enumDeltaToInteger1 x0 lim = go (x0 :: Integer)
                   where
                     go x | x > lim   = []
                          | otherwise = x : go (x+1)
```

At this moment, one may feel that we are going in circles. Well, this is really the case if we inline `build`. So, let's not do that and see what is going on with the call to the `all` function instead.

UNFOLDING ALL

The `all` function is defined in the current base as follows:

```
all :: Foldable t => (a -> Bool) -> t a -> Bool
all p = getAll #. foldMap (All #. p)
```

Although quite short, this definition hides a lot inside it, as shown here:

- `all` uses the `Foldable` instance and the `Monoid` instance for `Bool` in conjunction with newtype `All`.
- `all` deals with newtype wrapping/unwrapping effectively via the `(#.)` function composition.

Let's unfold all this stuff function by function. First, `foldMap` has a default implementation in the `Foldable` type class, as shown next:

```
foldMap :: Monoid m => (a -> m) -> t a -> m
foldMap f = foldr (mappend . f) mempty
```

The `foldr` method in the `Foldable []` instance refers to the following `foldr` for lists:

```
foldr :: (a -> b -> b) -> b -> [a] -> b
foldr k z = go
        where
          go []     = z
          go (y:ys) = y `k` go ys
```

As for the mappend method, it will be defined by the Semigroup and Monoid instances as follows:

```
class Semigroup a => Monoid a where
  ...
  mappend = (<>)
  ...

instance Semigroup All where
  (<>) = coerce (&&)
  ...

instance Monoid All where
  mempty = All True
```

What is coerce? It's a method of a somewhat magic Coercible a b type class. Its goal is to say that the internal memory representations of the a and b type values are the same, so it is safe to use the same function to process them. In this example, any All value All t is represented at run time as just the Bool value t, so we can apply the (&&) function to it directly. Whenever we apply the coerce function, we want to make sure that the types are in fact coercible, and the compiler is able to check that.

Getting back to the implementation of all, (#.) uses the same trick. It is defined as follows:

```
(#.) :: Coercible b c => (b -> c) -> (a -> b) -> (a -> c)
(#.) _f = coerce
```

In this case, it coerces a function of type a -> Bool to a function of type a -> All (making it suitable for foldMap) and back to extract Bool from All. This approach eliminates all wrapping and unwrapping newtype values at run time, so we end up with the following:

```
all notDividedBy ===            <——┐  │ Inlining
foldMap notDividedBy ===          <—— Remember, mappend === (&&)
foldr ((&&) . notDividedBy) True
```

Now it's time to combine this result with the desugared enumeration, as shown next:

```
all notDividedBy === foldr ((&&) . notDividedBy) True
[2 .. n-1] === build (\c n' -> enumDeltaToInteger1FB c n' 2 (n-1))
```

After combining them we get the following:

```
all notDividedBy [2 .. n-1] ===
foldr ((&&) . notDividedBy)
      True
      (build (\c n' -> enumDeltaToInteger1FB c n' 2 (n-1)))
```

So far, so good.

LIST FUSION

List fusion is a well-known optimization technique that eliminates intermediate lists in situations like this one. It is implemented via a set of rewriting rules as follows:

```
"fold/build"    forall k z (g::forall b. (a->b->b) -> b -> b) .
                foldr k z (build g) = g k z
```

As a result, in our example, we can get the following:

```
all notDividedBy [2 .. n-1] ===
enumDeltaToInteger1FB ((&&).notDividedBy) True 2 (n-1)
```

Now it's time to follow this `INLINE` pragma with

```
{-# INLINE [0] enumDeltaToInteger1FB #-}
```

and inline the definition of `enumDeltaToInteger1FB`, arriving at

```
all notDividedBy [2 .. n-1] ===
go 2
 where
   go x | x > n-1 = True
        | otherwise = x `(&&).notDividedBy` go (x+1)
```

Note that there is no list anymore. We've fused two list-processing functions and thrown the intermediate list away.

FINAL OPTIMIZATIONS

Now let's deal with `(&&).notDividedBy`. It's a function over two `Integer` values returning `Bool` as follows:

```
((&&).notDividedBy) :: Integer -> Integer -> Bool
```

We can inline it when given two arguments to something like the following:

```
((&&).notDividedBy) x y ===
(notDividedBy x) && y ===
case notDividedBy x of
  True -> y                   We don't need the right
  False -> False ===          argument in this case.
case n `mod` x /= 0 of
  True -> y
  False -> False
```

Combining all of the above and turning pattern guards in `go` to `case` expressions, we arrive at the following resulting code that is going to be executed at run time:

```
isPrime n ===
all notDividedBy [2 .. n-1] ===
go 2
```

```
  where
    go x = case x > n-1 of
             True -> True
             False -> case n `mod` x /= 0 of
                        True -> go (x+1)
                        False -> False
```

All the optimizations that we've done here manually can be performed by the compiler when we compile code with the -O1 flag. In fact, the compiler produces the same code for the following two isPrime implementations:

```
isPrime :: Integer -> Bool
isPrime n = all notDividedBy [2 .. n-1]
  where
    notDividedBy m = n `mod` m /= 0

isPrime:: Integer -> Bool
isPrime n = go 2
  where
    go x = case x > n-1 of
             True -> True
             False -> case n `mod` x /= 0 of
                        True -> go (x+1)
                        False -> False
```

We'll get more evidence in support of this claim in the next chapter.

> **IMPORTANT**   This was an example of how we do things in Haskell: we write pretty functional, declarative code, and the compiler transforms it into something extremely efficient.

9.3.2   *Looking at GHC Core*

Interestingly, I can easily prove that GHC is able to transform our program in the same way we did manually in the previous subsection by presenting the code in the intermediate programming language GHC Core, which is used inside GHC when compiling Haskell programs. We can dump Core while compiling the code with the following command:

```
$ ghc isPrime -O1 -ddump-simpl -dsuppress-idinfo -dsuppress-coercions \
               -dsuppress-type-applications -dsuppress-uniques \
               -dsuppress-module-prefixes
```

We need numerous flags to suppress printing irrelevant details, but the result is still tough to read, so don't expect to understand everything. I accompany this code with the corresponding code in our isPrime function:

```
let {
    lim :: Integer
    lim = minusInteger x main5 } in    ◁— n–1
 joinrec {
```

```
go :: Integer -> String
go (x1 :: Integer)
  = case gtInteger# x1 lim of {        <———— First case expression in isPrime
      __DEFAULT ->
        case eqInteger# x1 main4 of {     <———— Prevents division by zero
          __DEFAULT ->
            case neqInteger# (modInteger x x1) main4 of {
              __DEFAULT -> $fShowBool4;          <—
              1# -> jump go (plusInteger x1 main5)      Returns False
            };                                          (already as a String)
          1# -> case divZeroError of wild6 { }
        };
      1# -> $fShowBool2     <———— Returns True (already as a String)
    }; } in
jump go main3;            <———— Calculates go 2
```

Second case expression in isPrime (label pointing to the `case neqInteger#` line)

ON READING GHC CORE   In many cases, a programmer has to look at GHC Core to get ideas on what is wrong with the generated code. This is usually a hard job, but reading Core can be insightful: we can learn that some optimizations we were thinking about were not applied and try to understand why this is the case.

Summary

- Haskell programs are very demanding on memory due to inherent immutability and storing almost everything in closures in the dynamic memory (heap).
- Closures are used to implement lazy evaluation.
- We have many ways to control laziness.
- Adding strictness to our code and fine-grained control over memory usage may boost its performance.
- Benchmarking is usually required when switching to low-level laziness and memory control.
- GHC implements many sophisticated optimizations that turn your lazy declarative code into efficient executable code.

Benchmarking
and profiling

This chapter covers
- Benchmarking code in Haskell
- Exploring time and space consumption
- Tips and tricks to optimize code

In this chapter, we'll discuss how to check the performance of our code. As usual, we are interested in time and space usage characteristics. We'll discuss how to compare different implementations of the same function in terms of execution time using benchmarking and choose the most suitable implementation. We'll explore time and space consumption of our programs (we call it profiling) and use this information to find drawbacks in the implementation, such as space leaks. Finally, we'll see how to use benchmarking and profiling to make our programs run faster.

Remember, we've already implemented the first version of the IP filtering application and tested it intensively. We'll continue working on the same project in this chapter. Let's make the following assumptions on how this utility program is intended to be used:

- The list of ranges might be rather large, containing thousands of them.
- The range database is fixed at run time, so we don't have to reload it.
- IP addresses for filtering are processed as they go; hence, there might be millions of them.

These assumptions, together with the benchmarking results, gives us insights on what we should do to make this program run faster. Then, we'll try to optimize this program using different approaches and compare them in terms of performance. Note that all the times we make changes to achieve better performance, our tests accompany us and help to assure us that everything works correctly.

10.1   *Benchmarking functions with criterion*

We've already done a little bit of benchmarking earlier in this book. In this chapter, my goal is to introduce the `criterion` library, which is a de facto standard for benchmarking (measuring execution time) of our functions. The goal of benchmarking is to determine the performance characteristics and compare different implementations.

The basic ideas of benchmarking with `criterion` are covered next. The library does the following:

- Runs the given function with the given argument many times (an *experiment*)
- Counts the execution time of every run (population unit) and creates a *sample* (collection of units)
- Analyzes the sample using statistical methods and presents the results to the user in both textual and visual forms

The `criterion` library tries to alleviate the influence of laziness by preparing arguments, warming up prior to running experiments, evaluating results to normal form, and so on. The process of benchmarking depends on what we actually benchmark, as follows:

- Is it a pure function or an `IO` action?
- Where do we get arguments?
- How complex are the arguments?

In this section, we'll discuss how to organize benchmarking in different situations and how to interpret results.

10.1.1   *Benchmarking implementations of a simple function*

In the previous chapter, we had two implementations of the `isPrime` function. The first one was purely declarative and the second one was rather low-level. I tried to argue that they behave at run time in the same way. Let's find more evidence in support of this fact using benchmarking.

EXAMPLE: BENCHMARKING TWO IMPLEMENTATIONS OF ISPRIME

📄   ch09/isprime/

📄   benchmarks/primcheck.hs

⚡   *primcheck*

☞   We benchmark functions to compare them.

DEFINING AND RUNNING A BENCHMARK

We've already discussed earlier in this book that benchmarking suites are parts of Cabal projects. The package.yaml and hid-examples.cabal files both provide an example of how to introduce them (search for primcheck in those files).

The simplest benchmarking module with criterion is presented in the following example:

```
import Criterion.Main        ⟵──┐  Imports all the
                                 │  criterion functionality

import qualified IsPrime as IP
import qualified IsPrimeUnfolded as IPU
                            ┌─  Argument for functions
primeNumber :: Integer      │   to benchmark
primeNumber = 16183   ⟵─────┘
                            ┌─  Default implementation
main :: IO ()               │   of a benchmarking suite
main = defaultMain [  ⟵─────┘
    bench "isPrime (declarative)" $ whnf IP.isPrime primeNumber
  , bench "isPrime (unfolded)" $ whnf IPU.isPrime primeNumber
  ]
```

Benchmarking
one function

The defaultMain function has the following type signature:

```
defaultMain :: [Benchmark] -> IO ()
```

This function takes a list of individual benchmarks, prepared with the bench function. The types of the bench and whnf functions we use in this example as shown next:

```
bench :: String -> Benchmarkable -> Benchmark
whnf :: (a -> b) -> a -> Benchmarkable
```

The whnf function evaluates the result of the given a -> b function to weak head normal form (WHNF). This is obviously enough because we are computing the Bool value in isPrime. The bench function makes sure that an argument to a function under benchmarking is fully evaluated and then runs it.

Once we have our benchmark suite defined, we can start benchmarking as follows:

```
$ cabal bench primcheck
```

This command builds the benchmark suite executable first and then runs it. We can also use the `cabal bench` (or `stack bench`) command to run all the benchmarking suites in the project.

Passing options to a benchmark suite

We can send command-line options to an executable with `--benchmark-options`. For example, the following code allows seeing the many arguments that we can give to the default `main` function provided by `criterion`:

```
$ cabal bench primcheck --benchmark-options="--help"
Running 1 benchmarks...
Benchmark primcheck: RUNNING...
Microbenchmark suite - built with criterion 1.5.6.2

Usage: ...
```

In this way, it is possible to tweak many parameters of benchmarking, for example, exporting raw data or a summary to file, listing specific benchmarks to run, and setting some statistical parameters.

Running the previous benchmark gives us the following results:

```
$ cabal bench primcheck
Running 1 benchmarks...
Benchmark primcheck: RUNNING...
benchmarking isPrime (declarative)
time                 448.5 µs   (445.5 µs .. 451.6 µs)
                     1.000 R²   (0.999 R² .. 1.000 R²)
mean                 451.9 µs   (448.8 µs .. 456.8 µs)
std dev              12.46 µs   (8.794 µs .. 22.23 µs)
variance introduced by outliers: 20% (moderately inflated)

benchmarking isPrime (unfolded)
time                 448.4 µs   (445.7 µs .. 451.3 µs)
                     1.000 R²   (1.000 R² .. 1.000 R²)
mean                 447.7 µs   (445.9 µs .. 450.0 µs)
std dev              6.952 µs   (5.239 µs .. 8.974 µs)

Benchmark primcheck: FINISH
```

The difference in `time` is negligible. The results may differ from run to run, but the difference is always small. This is evidence that these two quite different implementations are compiled into almost the same code.

READING AND INTERPRETING BENCHMARKING RESULTS

First, let's make sure that we understand the units `criterion` uses to report times, as shown in table 10.1.

Table 10.1   Time units used by `criterion`

Unit	Full name	Comment
s	seconds	
ms	milliseconds	1000 ms = 1 s
μs	microseconds	1000 μs = 1 ms
ns	nanoseconds	1000 ns = 1 μs
ps	picoseconds	1000 ps = 1 ns

Thus 1 s = 1000 ms = 1,000,000 μs = 1,000,000,000 ns = ...

Now let's look at the results provided by the `criterion` library once again:

```
benchmarking isPrime (declarative)
time                  448.5 μs   (445.5 μs .. 451.6 μs)
                      1.000 R²   (0.999 R² .. 1.000 R²)
mean                  451.9 μs   (448.8 μs .. 456.8 μs)
std dev               12.46 μs   (8.794 μs .. 22.23 μs)
variance introduced by outliers: 20% (moderately inflated)
```

Remember, when we run a benchmark, a corresponding function is called a lot of times. The library then measures every run and comes up with several statistical characteristics, namely:

- *Time* is computed by so-called OLS regression, a method for computing good estimates for execution time by eliminating as many constant factors as possible.
- *R-squared goodness-of-fit* characterizes the accuracy of measurements; something is going wrong if it's under 0.99.
- *Mean* is the average execution time; it is usually close to time.
- *Std dev*, or standard deviation, reflects the distance between the mean value and specific results; a larger value here testifies to scattered results.
- *Variance introduced by outliers* reports a share of units that lay far from the mean value (outliers); a large share means that execution times for different runs differ a lot from each other.

Column 2 shows estimates, whereas columns 3 and 4 show lower and upper bounds of the 95% samples; the closer they are to each other, the better. Fortunately, we don't have to learn statistics to interpret these results (as I try to show in this chapter).

Reading console output is not the only way to get benchmarking results. The `criterion` library is able to generate nice-looking reports in HTML with interactive graphs when running with the `--output isprime.html` option as follows:

```
$ cabal bench primcheck --benchmark-options="--output isprime.html"
```

Figure 10.1 presents the results we get on this run. Note that they differ a little bit from what we saw earlier; this is normal.

criterion performance measurements

overview

want to understand this report?

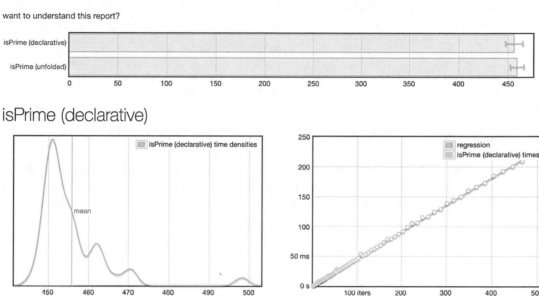

isPrime (declarative)

	lower bound	**estimate**	upper bound
OLS regression	452 µs	455 µs	457 µs
R² goodness-of-fit	0.999	1.000	1.000
Mean execution time	454 µs	456 µs	460 µs
Standard deviation	5.36 µs	8.80 µs	15.0 µs

Outlying measurements have moderate (11.0%) effect on estimated standard deviation.

Figure 10.1 Criterion report in HTML: function performance measurements

> **NOTE** The criterion tutorial (http://www.serpentine.com/criterion/tutorial.html) explains how to understand graphs.

Graphs present data for every benchmarking experiment visually using traditional statistical tools. We will not use this option in this book, because it is much more convenient to look at text output in most cases.

OPTIMIZING A FUNCTION AND RERUNNING A BENCHMARK

Let's introduce one small optimization into the implementation of isPrime as follows:

```
isPrime :: Integer -> Bool
isPrime n = all notDividedBy [2 .. n `div` 2]
  where
    notDividedBy m = n `mod` m /= 0
```

Clearly, there is no need to check all of the 2..n-1 divisors. How is it better in terms of running time? Let's modify the benchmarking list in defaultMain by adding the following:

```
, bench "isPrime (rewritten)" $ whnf isPrime primeNumber
```

Running the benchmark again proves that this change was a great idea, as shown here:

```
benchmarking isPrime (declarative)
time                 446.7 µs    (444.2 µs .. 449.6 µs)
...
benchmarking isPrime (unfolded)
time                 450.9 µs    (447.1 µs .. 454.5 µs)
...
benchmarking isPrime (rewritten)
time                 223.5 µs    (222.2 µs .. 224.9 µs)
...
```

Great—we've made this function twice as fast. Well, we had to check a twice-smaller number of potential divisors, after all—no surprise.

When we run benchmarks many times, it doesn't make sense to run all of them. The `criterion` library allows running only those we are interested in. For example, we can ask for the rewritten implementation with the `-m pattern` option, which allows matching on benchmarks names, as follows:

```
$ cabal bench primcheck --benchmark-options="-m pattern rewritten"
benchmarking isPrime (rewritten)
...
```

The `-m` option takes `prefix`, `pattern`, `ipattern`, or `glob` as an argument so that we can conveniently describe a set of benchmarks to run.

10.1.2 *Benchmarking an IPv4 filtering application*

Now, after dealing with simple technical details, we are ready to benchmark our IPv4 filtering application. We'll discuss how to design particular benchmarks in the following subsections. This depends greatly on the nature of the functions we want to benchmark, whether they are pure, whether they need some data prepared in advance, and so on.

EXAMPLE: BENCHMARKING IPV4 FILTERING APPLICATION

- 🗋 ip/lookup/

- 🗋 benchmarks/iplookup/

- ⚡ *iplookup-bench*

- ☞ We compare different implementations and choose the most performant one.

- ☞ We search for bottlenecks in our code and decide what should be optimized.

We have an `iplookup-bench` benchmark defined in our project. The goal is to benchmark functions from the `iplookup-lib` internal library. Besides `criterion`, we also need the `deepseq` package to deal with the evaluation to normal form.

The easiest task for `criterion` is to benchmark pure functions. We'll start with pure functions from the IPv4 filtering application, `buildIP` and `parseIP`, and then move to `IO` actions. Apart from that, we'll pay attention to structuring the benchmark suite in a way that enables easy filtering.

CHOOSING THE MOST EFFICIENT IMPLEMENTATION OF BUILDIP

We'll start with the `buildIP` function from the `ParseIP` module as follows.

EXAMPLE: BENCHMARKING IPV4 FILTERING APPLICATION

🗋 ip/lookup/ParseIP.hs

🗋 benchmarks/iplookup/BenchBuildIP.hs

🗋 benchmarks/iplookup/Bench.hs

⚡ *iplookup-bench*

Remember that we have three well-tested implementations of the `buildIP` function, which uses various approaches to combine a list of octets into a 4-byte IP address as shown next:

```
buildIP :: [Word8] -> IP
buildIP = buildIP_foldr

buildIP_foldr :: [Word8] -> IP
buildIP_foldr = IP . fst . foldr go (0, 1)
  where
    go b (s, k) = (s + fromIntegral b * k, k*256)

buildIP_foldl :: [Word8] -> IP
buildIP_foldl = IP . foldl (\s b -> s*256 + fromIntegral b) 0

buildIP_foldl_shl :: [Word8] -> IP
buildIP_foldl_shl = IP . foldl (\s b -> shiftL s 8 + fromIntegral b) 0
```

Now it's time to choose the most efficient implementation with the help of benchmarking. Let's see which of the implementations is the best one for processing the [17,0,32,2] list of octets.

The `buildIP` function gives us an `IP`, which is a `newtype` for `Word32`, so it is represented by a `Word32` in memory. This means that it's enough to evaluate it to WHNF. The following list of benchmarks does what we need:

```
bench_buildIP :: [Benchmark]
bench_buildIP = [
    bench "buildIP-foldr" $ whnf buildIP_foldr theip
  , bench "buildIP-foldl" $ whnf buildIP_foldl theip
```

```
    , bench "buildIP-foldl-shl" $ whnf buildIP_foldl_shl theip
    ]
  where
    theip = [17,0,32,2]
```

We also need to send this benchmark to `defaultMain` in the Bench.hs file, as shown next:

```
main :: IO ()
main = defaultMain benchmarks
  where
    benchmarks = bench_buildIP
```

Executing `cabal bench iplookup-bench` gives us the following results:

```
Running 1 benchmarks...
Benchmark iplookup-bench: RUNNING...
benchmarking buildIP-foldr
time                 41.20 ns    (41.10 ns .. 41.31 ns)
...
benchmarking buildIP-foldl
time                 11.82 ns    (11.79 ns .. 11.85 ns)
...
benchmarking buildIP-foldl-shl
time                 11.91 ns    (11.84 ns .. 12.00 ns)
...
Benchmark iplookup-bench: FINISH
```

Looking at these results reveals at least the following two interesting insights:

- The original version of `buildIP` implemented via `foldr` is about four times slower than other implementations.
- Two other implementations are close to each other in terms of running time.

One potential problem with our approach is that we use only one list of octets for benchmarking. This is okay in this case because the running time of `buildIP` shouldn't depend on the actual numbers in the list. In general, it's better to test implementations considering several different inputs. For example, we could prepare a list of inputs as follows:

```
ipcomps = [ [0,0,0,1]
          , [192,168,1,1]
          , [255,255,252,41]
          , [255,255,252,41]
          , [17,0,32,2]
          ]
```

Then we could benchmark `map buildIP_foldr` and other functions on `ipcomps`. The result now becomes a list of `IP` addresses, so evaluating it to WHNF is not enough. Here we need the `deepseq` function to evaluate a result to a normal form.

The criterion library provides the following nf function to evaluate results to a normal form, thus avoiding lazy evaluation influencing the overall timing:

```
nf :: NFData b => (a -> b) -> a -> Benchmarkable
```

The nf function requires that the result of the function we are going to benchmark supports the evaluation to normal form (implements the NFData instance). In this case, we should provide an instance for the IP data type.

EXAMPLE: BENCHMARKING IPV4 FILTERING APPLICATION

🗋 benchmarks/iplookup/NFUtils.hs

☞ We can generate the NFData instance automatically.

The NFData instance can be derived automatically, thanks to the machinery of GHC.Generics, as follows:

```
{-# LANGUAGE StandaloneDeriving #-}
{-# LANGUAGE DeriveGeneric #-}
{-# LANGUAGE DeriveAnyClass #-}

module NFUtils where

import Control.DeepSeq (NFData)
import GHC.Generics (Generic)

import IPTypes

deriving instance Generic IP
deriving instance NFData IP
```

We'll discuss what is going on here later in this book. Now we can rewrite our benchmark using the nf function to benchmark functions over lists of IP as follows:

```
bench_buildIP :: [Benchmark]
bench_buildIP = [
    bench "buildIP-foldr" $ nf (map buildIP_foldr) ipcomps
  , bench "buildIP-foldl" $ nf (map buildIP_foldl) ipcomps
  , bench "buildIP-foldl-shl" $ nf (map buildIP_foldl_shl) ipcomps
  ]
  where
    ipcomps = ...
```

The results follow:

```
Benchmark iplookup-bench: RUNNING...
benchmarking buildIP-foldr
time                 241.3 ns   (240.5 ns .. 242.3 ns)
...
benchmarking buildIP-foldl
time                 94.53 ns   (94.24 ns .. 94.87 ns)
```

```
...
benchmarking buildIP-foldl-shl
time                 94.46 ns   (94.10 ns .. 94.78 ns)
...
```

The `buildIP_foldr` still demonstrates the worst performance, so it could be a good idea to replace `buildIP` with either of the `buildIP_foldl` or `buildIP_foldl_shl` implementations. The choice between the latter implementations is more difficult because the difference is negligible. We have at least one reason to go with `buildIP_foldl`: it is easier to read. Multiplying by 256 is arguably better in terms of readability than shifting eight digits. Finally, we've ended up with the following implementation:

```
buildIP :: [Word8] -> IP
buildIP = buildIP_foldl
```

Remember that we had tests for all of the implementations, so switching them shouldn't introduce any problems. Let's run the tests via `cabal test` and check the results as follows:

```
Test suite iplookup-test: RUNNING...
All Tests
  Specs
    ParseIP
      buildIP
        builds from zero:                            OK
        builds from one:                             OK
        builds from localhost:                       OK
        builds from arbitrary address:               OK
...
  Properties
    buildIP implementations agrees with each other:      OK
...
```

Well, we are on the safe side. The joy of testing, you know.

GROUPING AND FILTERING BENCHMARKS

It could be a good idea to keep all the benchmarks in one place instead of replacing one with another. This allows analyzing degrading performance in case we introduce any changes to the code. It is also convenient to keep inputs to the functions closer to the benchmarks. The `criterion` package provides the `bgroup` function, which is useful for grouping several benchmarks into one, as shown next:

```
bgroup :: String -> [Benchmark] -> Benchmark
```

It is easy to define groups of groups of benchmarks.

EXAMPLE: BENCHMARKING IPV4 FILTERING APPLICATION

☐   benchmarks/iplookup/BenchBuildIPGroups.hs

☞   We can build a hierarchy of benchmarks with groups.

In the following example, we have a group of all the benchmarks related to `buildIP` split into two subgroups: one processing a single IP and the other one processing a list of IPs:

```
bench_buildIP :: [Benchmark]
bench_buildIP = [
    bgroup "buildIP" [
      let theip = [17,0,32,2] in
      bgroup "single" [
        bench "default" $ nf buildIP theip
      , bench "foldr" $ nf buildIP_foldr theip
      , bench "foldl" $ nf buildIP_foldl theip
      , bench "foldl-shl" $ nf buildIP_foldl_shl theip
      ]

    , let ipcomps = [[0,0,0,1], [192,168,1,1], [17,0,32,2],
                     [255,255,252,41], [255,255,252,41]] in
      bgroup "several" [
        bench "default" $ nf (map buildIP) ipcomps
      , bench "foldr" $ nf (map buildIP_foldr) ipcomps
      , bench "foldl" $ nf (map buildIP_foldl) ipcomps
      , bench "foldl-shl" $ nf (map buildIP_foldl_shl) ipcomps
      ]
    ]
  ]
```

Note how we use the `let`/`in` expression to bring inputs closer to benchmarks.

This new structure of benchmarks is also reflected in the `criterion` output, as shown here:

```
...
benchmarking buildIP/single/default
...
benchmarking buildIP/single/foldr
...
benchmarking buildIP/single/foldl
...
benchmarking buildIP/single/foldl-shl
...
benchmarking buildIP/several/default
...
```

Even better, we can now run only those benchmarks that test a single IP as follows:

```
$ cabal bench iplookup-bench --benchmark-options="buildIP/single"
Running 1 benchmarks...
Benchmark iplookup-bench: RUNNING...
benchmarking buildIP/single/default
...
benchmarking buildIP/single/foldr
...
benchmarking buildIP/single/foldl
...
benchmarking buildIP/single/foldl-shl
...
Benchmark iplookup-bench: FINISH
```

Note that running a benchmark suite with `--benchmark-options="buildIP/single"` is equivalent to using `--benchmark-options="-m prefix buildIP/single"`. We can also ask for all the benchmarks matching `"foldr"` as shown next:

```
$ cabal bench iplookup-bench --benchmark-options="-m pattern foldr"
...
benchmarking buildIP/single/foldr
...
benchmarking buildIP/several/foldr
...
```

In what follows, we use the `bgroup` function to structure all the benchmarks for the IPv4 filtering application.

GETTING PARSEIP PERFORMANCE

Now that we have the more efficient implementation of `buildIP`, it's time to look at the `parseIP` function that calls it.

EXAMPLE: BENCHMARKING IPV4 FILTERING APPLICATION

- ip/lookup/ParseIP.hs

- benchmarks/iplookup/BenchParseIP.hs

- benchmarks/iplookup/Data.hs

Our current implementation (explained in full detail in chapter 8) follows:

```
guarded :: Alternative f => (a -> Bool) -> a -> f a
guarded f a = if f a then pure a else empty

isLengthOf :: Int -> [a] -> Bool
isLengthOf n xs = length xs == n

parseIP :: String -> Maybe IP
parseIP = guarded (4 `isLengthOf`) . splitOn "."
        >=> mapM (readMaybe @Integer >=> toIntegralSized)
        >=> pure . buildIP
```

Let's prepare a list of inputs for benchmarking it, implement one more benchmark, and add it to the list of benchmarks in `defaultMain` as follows:

```
iptexts = ["0.0.0.1", "192.168.1.1", "17.0.32.2",
           "255.255.252.41", "255.255.252.42"]

bench_parseIP :: [Benchmark]
bench_parseIP = [
    bench "parseIP/current" $ nf (map parseIP) iptexts
  ]

main = defaultMain benchmarks
  where
    benchmarks = bench_buildIP
                <> bench_parseIP
```

Running this benchmark with `--benchmark-options="parseIP/current"` gives the following results:

```
benchmarking parseIP/current
time                 24.46 µs   (24.40 µs .. 24.52 µs)
...
```

Is 24.46 microseconds of running time good or bad? Well, it depends. We know that this function is used very intensively. For example, it will take about half a minute to parse 1,000,000 IP addresses. That's a significant time to be bothered with. We'll attempt to do something about this function later in this chapter.

Now let's benchmark other parts of our program.

BENCHMARKING IO ACTIONS

Sometimes we need to benchmark functions that do `IO`. Clearly, we should take care of laziness. The `criterion` library provides the `nfIO` function, which gives us all the necessary guarantees.

Let's benchmark our code that reads an IP-range database file. Suppose we have the following files (the `wc -l` command gives us the number of lines in the corresponding files):

```
$ wc -l data/benchmarks/iplookup/*.iprs
       8 data/benchmarks/iplookup/1.iprs
     100 data/benchmarks/iplookup/2.iprs
   10000 data/benchmarks/iplookup/3.iprs
```

How much longer does it take to read file number 3 compared to reading file number 2? 100 times? We'll find out shortly.

Data files in Cabal projects

Including data files in Cabal projects creates a problem. We know where those files are located within the project folder. Moreover, it is required to list all of them in the .cabal file (in the `data-files` section). The problem is that we don't know in advance where those files will be located when the corresponding package is installed—this depends on the system distribution and other factors. For example, a user can change the actual path with flags when installing a package.

The `Cabal` library provides the following solution to this problem: for every executable or library in a project, `Cabal` generates a special module with the `Paths_<PACKAGE_NAME>` name. For example, we have `Paths_hid_examples` here. Note that - in the package name was replaced with _. This module provides the `getDataFileName` function, which takes the path name relative to a project folder and gets the full path within the file system back.

EXAMPLE: BENCHMARKING IPV4 FILTERING APPLICATION

🗋   benchmarks/iplookup/Data.hs

🗋   benchmarks/iplookup/BenchRanges.hs

Suppose we have the following IO action to read the IP range database file:

```
import Paths_hid_examples (getDataFileName)

-- ...

readIPRDBFile fname = getDataFileName (ipBenchDir ++ fname)
                      >>= readFile
  where
    ipBenchDir = "data/benchmarks/iplookup/"
```

Let's benchmark it as follows:

```
bench_ranges :: [Benchmark]
bench_ranges = [
  bgroup "ranges" [
      bgroup "read" $
        map (\(desc, fname) ->
              bench desc $ nfIO (readIPRDBFile fname))
          rangeFiles
  ]
  where
    rangeFiles = [("small", "1.iprs"),
                  ("middle-sized", "2.iprs"),
                  ("large", "3.iprs")]
```

Note that I use the map function to generate the list of benchmarks for all the input files I've prepared. Running the benchmarking suite with `"ranges/read"` as an argument shows that our hypothesis about execution times was wrong, as shown next:

```
$ cabal run iplookup-bench -- "ranges/read"
...
benchmarking ranges/read/small
time                 26.73 µs   (26.61 µs .. 26.85 µs)
...
benchmarking ranges/read/small
time                 44.76 µs   (44.54 µs .. 44.99 µs)
...
benchmarking ranges/read/small
time                 1.841 ms   (1.830 ms .. 1.854 ms)
...
```

Reading the file, which is 100 times larger, is only 70 times slower. In fact, there is nothing amazing here because files are read in blocks, not lines. In addition, many factors could influence reading times.

Let's use the `readIPRDBFile` function to measure parsing the IP range database as a whole.

BENCHMARKING WITH A PREPARED ENVIRONMENT

The crucial question we should always answer when benchmarking is, what exactly do we want to measure? For example, if our goal is to benchmark the `parseIPRanges` function, it is not a good idea to consider the time spent reading the file with the IP range database. This means that the database should be read in advance. Then it can be used to benchmark several functions that use its data.

This leads to the idea of a benchmarking environment, which can be prepared in advance and then used in a benchmarking process. The following `env` function from `criterion` is able to create benchmarks that use an environment evaluated to normal form before passing to the functions we want to measure:

```
env :: NFData env => IO env -> (env -> Benchmark) -> Benchmark
```

The following example shows how to use this function. We'll add it to the `"ranges"` group we already have, as shown next:

```
bench_ranges :: [Benchmark]
bench_ranges = [
  bgroup "ranges" [
      ...
    , bgroup "parse" $
        map (\(desc, fname) ->
            env (readIPRDBFile fname) $        <—    An environment here
              \iprdbf ->                    <—            is a file content.
            bench desc $ nf parseIPRange iprdbf)    Variable to refer to an
              rangeFiles                             environment inside a
    ]                                                measured function
  ]
  where
    rangeFiles = ...
```

Benchmark with access to the environment

We also need an environment to benchmark the `lookupIP` function.

EXAMPLE: BENCHMARKING IPV4 FILTERING APPLICATION

☐ ip/lookup/LookupIP.hs

☐ benchmarks/iplookup/Data.hs

☐ benchmarks/iplookup/BenchLookupIP.hs

This function has the following type signature:

```
lookupIP ::  IPRangeDB -> IP -> Bool
```

Let's reuse the `iptexts` list of IP addresses we've used for benchmarking `parseIP` and prepare an environment for measuring. We take the larger file, as shown here:

```
iptexts :: [String]
iptexts = ["0.0.0.1", "192.168.1.1", "17.0.32.2",
           "255.255.252.41", "255.255.252.42"]

ips :: [(String, IP)]
ips = map (\s -> (s, fromJust $ parseIP s)) iptexts

iprdb :: IO IPRangeDB
iprdb = parseValidIPRanges <$> readIPRDBFile "3.iprs"
```

Now we are ready to implement a benchmark for `LookupIP`. But before doing that, let's revisit the following techniques I introduced earlier in this section:

- Calling a function for a single input and for a list of inputs
- Using `whnf` or `nf`, depending on the type of result
- Grouping related benchmarks
- Generating a list of benchmarks from a list of data

The following code incorporates all the techniques:

```
bench_lookupIP :: [Benchmark]
bench_lookupIP = [
    env iprdb $ \ iprdb' ->
      bgroup "lookupIP" [
        bgroup "single" $
          map (\ (textip, ip) ->
                bench textip $
                  whnf (lookupIP iprdb') ip) ips
        , bench "several" $ nf (map (lookupIP iprdb')) $ map snd ips
        ]
  ]
```

The `"lookupIP/several"` benchmark numbers can be used when deciding whether some other implementation is better or not on average as follows:

```
benchmarking lookupIP/several
time                 85.23 µs   (84.59 µs .. 85.96 µs)
```

By the way, the `"lookupIP/single"` benchmark groups reveal the following interesting fact about the current implementation:

```
benchmarking lookupIP/single/0.0.0.1
time                 32.26 µs   (32.16 µs .. 32.35 µs)
...
benchmarking lookupIP/single/192.168.1.1
time                 12.33 ns   (12.30 ns .. 12.36 ns)
...
benchmarking lookupIP/single/17.0.32.2
time                 39.60 ns   (39.45 ns .. 39.76 ns)
...
benchmarking lookupIP/single/255.255.252.41
time                 15.17 µs   (15.08 µs .. 15.29 µs)
```

```
...
benchmarking lookupIP/single/255.255.252.42
time                   38.31 µs   (38.12 µs .. 38.49 µs)
```

Let's sort these times, check whether the answer is yes or no, and try to interpret the results. Remember that we can use `cabal run` for checking answers as follows:

```
$ cabal run iplookup -- data/benchmarks/iplookup/3.iprs 192.168.1.1
192.168.1.1: YES
```

Table 10.2 summarizes our findings.

Table 10.2   Sample `iplookup` benchmarking results

IP	Time	Answer
192.168.1.1	12.33 ns	YES
17.0.32.2	39.60 ns	YES
255.255.252.41	15.17 µs	YES
0.0.0.1	32.26 µs	NO
255.255.252.42	38.31 µs	NO

Now we can clearly see that we get NO after going over the whole database, and it takes the longest time. The first two IP addresses in the table belong to a range at the beginning of the database. The 255.255.252.41 is somewhere close to the end. There is nothing strange in these results. After all, we use a plain list to store the database. Clearly, we should work harder to achieve better performance. We'll do something about it in the last section of this chapter.

10.2   *Profiling execution time and memory usage*

Profiling allows us to get information about the time and memory usage of our code. Although it's not always necessary to profile software, we may encounter unexpectedly long execution times for some operations or too-high memory usage at run time. In these cases, profiling is able to provide us with many useful insights on the real reasons. GHC profiling tools can give us a lot of details about how our program behaves at run time, including the following:

- How much time the program spends in a particular function.
- How much time is required to evaluate the expression we are interested in.
- How much memory is allocated at run time in total and by a particular function.
- How much memory is allocated on the heap at a particular moment in time. (We call this characteristic memory residence.)

With all this data, we can decide what is going wrong in our program and which parts of it require the most attention. We can also avoid optimizing something that is not a problem, thus not falling into the premature optimization sin.

The goal of this section is to learn how to use the profiling tools that come with GHC. To achieve it, we'll design and implement a simulation for the IPv4 filtering application and then profile it as much as we can. Later, we'll use profiling information to make the corresponding functionality much faster.

10.2.1 *Simulating iplookup usage in the real world*

Suppose we have a database with 10,000 IP address ranges. It can be generated randomly using the ipgen utility as follows:

```
$ cabal run ipgen -- 10000 data/ipdb.txt
$ wc -l data/ipdb.txt
   10000 data/ipdb.txt
$ head -3 data/ipdb.txt
44.162.171.187,44.176.142.166
195.223.149.165,195.238.83.205
157.194.109.142,157.207.92.50
```

We'll run the simulation by generating half a million IP addresses and checking whether they belong to the ranges from the database. Because we don't want everything to be printed to the output, let's print only the total number of YES and NO answers instead. This will force GHC to evaluate the results of every lookupIP call.

EXAMPLE: SIMULATING IPLOOKUP USAGE

🗋   ip/iplookup-simulation.hs

⚡   *iplookup-simulation*

☞   We simulate real-world behavior.

The following example contains the full simulation program:

```
module Main where

import IPTypes
import ParseIP
import LookupIP

ipdb :: String
ipdb = "data/ipdb.txt"

nReqs :: Int
nReqs = 500000

genIPList :: Int -> [IP]
genIPList n = map IP $ take n $ iterate (+step) 0
  where
    step = maxBound `div` fromIntegral n

simulate :: IPRangeDB -> [IP] -> (Int, Int)
simulate iprdb ips = (yes, no)
```

```
  where
    yes = length $ filter id $ map (lookupIP iprdb) ips
    no = length ips - yes

report :: (Int, Int) -> IO ()
report info = putStrLn $ "(yes, no) = " ++ show info

main :: IO ()
main = do
  iprs <- parseIPRanges <$> readFile ipdb
  let ips = genIPList nReqs
  case iprs of
    Right iprs' -> report $ simulate iprs' ips
    _ -> print "Can't read IP ranges database"
```

In this program, we do the following:

- Set initial simulation parameters: the file with the IP range database and the number of requests to check an IP address.
- Generate the list of IP addresses by going from zero almost to the end of the IPv4 address set.
- Run the simulation itself with the given IP range database and the list of IP addresses.
- Report simulation results.

If we run it, we get the following results:

```
$ cabal -v0 run iplookup-simulation
(yes, no) = (346647,153353)
```

Let's analyze the time and memory allocation for this program.

10.2.2 Analyzing execution time and memory allocation

The GHC runtime system can provide useful information about time and memory usage after running a program. We request this information by providing the +RTS <profiling_options> -RTS block in the command line. The -RTS argument is optional if there are no other arguments. For example, we could ask for some statistics with the -s flag as follows:

```
$ cabal run iplookup-simulation -- +RTS -s
(yes, no) = (346647,153353)
    531,147,936 bytes allocated in the heap
     74,534,336 bytes copied during GC
     20,700,048 bytes maximum residency (17 sample(s))
      3,421,296 bytes maximum slop
             19 MB total memory in use (0 MB lost due to fragmentation)

                                    Tot time (elapsed)  Avg pause  Max pause
  Gen  0       493 colls,     0 par    0.021s   0.022s    0.0000s    0.0006s
  Gen  1        17 colls,     0 par    0.023s   0.036s    0.0021s    0.0140s
```

```
INIT     time     0.000s  (  0.003s elapsed)
MUT      time    20.949s  ( 21.046s elapsed)
GC       time     0.044s  (  0.058s elapsed)
EXIT     time     0.000s  (  0.002s elapsed)
Total    time    20.994s  ( 21.109s elapsed)

%GC      time        0.0%  (0.0% elapsed)

Alloc rate    25,354,211 bytes per MUT second

Productivity  99.8% of total user, 99.7% of total elapsed
```

The runtime system reports about 21 seconds of running time. We also have information on memory allocation and garbage collection. Note that about a half a gigabyte was allocated in total. This is quite a lot for such a small program. This amount should not be confused with the maximum memory residence, which is about 20 megabytes. The report says that there were 17 samples, so RTS checks for memory residence about every second.

To get more information, we need to compile a program with profiling support.

Compiling with profiling support

In the previous chapter, I mentioned that profiling requires a different memory layout for closures. Thus, compiling with profiling support is required for base and every external dependency we have. GHC compiles for profiling when given the -prof flag.

The cabal utility has the --enable-profiling flag to compile a package with all the dependencies for profiling. We can pass it to cabal run. Note that passing it to cabal build is not enough, because the subsequent call to cabal run without this flag recompiles everything without profiling support due to a changed configuration.

Another option is to make profiling permanent by setting profiling: true in the cabal.project.local file. Then all the subsequent calls to cabal build and cabal run compile for profiling.

With stack, we can build the whole package for profiling with stack build --profile and then execute a program as follows:

```
$ stack exec --profile -- <executable_name>
```

For example, we can start profiling as follows:

```
$ cabal run iplookup-simulation --enable-profiling -- +RTS -P
```

The -P flag means that we want to get a report on execution time and allocations. This is the basic form of a profiling report we usually start with. The report itself is saved into the iplookup-simulation.prof file. Let's look into it. The profiling report starts with the title and general information about the run, as shown next:

```
Tue Jun 16 07:13 2020 Time and Allocation Profiling Report   (Final)

       iplookup-simulation +RTS -P -RTS

   total time  =       22.75 secs   (22750 ticks @ 1000 us, 1 processor)
   total alloc = 558,968,504 bytes  (excludes profiling overheads)
```

WARNING Note that it takes a little bit longer to run the simulation under profiling. There is always some overhead when profiling programs. Nevertheless, a very slow function is usually slow under profiling, too. If we make it much faster under profiling, we have a good chance that it becomes faster without profiling, too. Unfortunately, this is not always the case, so we still need to have benchmarks.

The next part of the report provides information about the most demanding functions (or cost centers), as shown here:

```
COST CENTRE    MODULE                     SRC       %time %alloc  ticks       bytes

lookupIP       LookupIP                   <...>      99.1   0.0   22503           0
parseIP        ParseIP                    <...>       0.5  56.3     118   314810608
breakDelim     Data.List.Split.Internals  <...>       0.1  14.4      21    80518256
genIPList      Main                       <...>       0.1  10.7      16    59999960
parseIPRanges  ParseIP                    <...>       0.1   6.9      14    38529952
...
```

A cost center is a function, or an expression, or anything else requiring time and memory resources to be evaluated. The report shows the name of the cost center, the module, the exact source location (removed in the example above to fit the page), the percentage of time and memory allocated for this cost center, and the actual time and memory data.

From this part of the report, we can see that our simulation spends most of the time (99.1%) looking up the IP address in the IP range database. The memory allocated by the lookupIP function is 0.0%. (Even if it allocates some memory, it is rounded to zero.)

What about breakDelim? We've never called this function in our program, so where does it come from? And why does it allocate 14% of the memory? To answer these questions, we have to look at the last part of the report, which contains the call graph of the program. To make things visible, I've removed several columns and many rows, as shown next:

```
individual     inherited
COST CENTRE         entries  %time %alloc   %time %alloc

MAIN                     0    0.0   0.0    100.0  100.0
  ...
  main                   0    0.0   2.1     99.9   89.1
   report                1    0.0   0.0      0.0    0.0
   simulate              1    0.0   0.0     99.1    0.0
```

lookupIP	500000	99.1	0.0	99.1	0.0
parseIPRanges	0	0.1	6.8	0.8	87.1
parseIPRange	0	0.0	0.2	0.7	80.3
...					
parseIP	0	0.5	56.3	0.6	70.9
...					
splitOn	0	0.0	0.0	0.1	14.5
...					
breakDelim	285389	0.1	7.0	0.1	8.1
...					
splitOn	0	0.0	0.0	0.1	9.2
...					
breakDelim	285389	0.0	7.4	0.1	7.6
...					

Now we see that the mysterious breakDelim function is used by the splitOn function called from parseIP and parseIPRange. Both times it takes about 7% of total memory allocation. Big numbers for memory allocation are not necessarily a bad thing, but all this data should be garbage collected and may affect performance.

Thus, the report data suggests dealing with lookupIP to optimize execution time and with parseIP (including splitOn) and genIPList to optimize memory allocation.

Controlling cost centers in time and allocation reports

It was relatively easy to find the most demanding cost centers in this small program. GHC allows some degree of flexibility to control what is taken as a cost center. In bigger programs, we would definitely need to use the following GHC options in addition to -prof when compiling programs for profiling:

- -fprof-auto-top makes every top-level definition a cost center.
- -fprof-auto-exported makes every exported definition a cost center.
- -fprof-auto-calls makes every call site a cost center.
- -fprof-auto is the default choice for --enable-profiling; it makes almost every top-level or nested definition a cost center.

These options can be specified by either the --ghc-option flag to cabal or on a per-module basis with the OPTION_GHC pragma.

To introduce a new cost center for an expression, we can use the SCC (set cost center) pragma in our code as follows:

```
simulate iprdb ips = (yes, no)
  where
    yes = {-# SCC "answer yes" #-}
          length $ filter id $ map (lookupIP iprdb) ips
    no = {-# SCC "answer no" #-} length ips - yes
```

These pragmas create additional cost centers when compiled with -prof.

10.2.3 *Analyzing memory usage*

We were able to look at time and memory allocation. The next goal is to look more closely at memory residence: how much memory we use in every moment at run time. This can be achieved using the -h flag, which enables generating a heap usage report. We can visualize it with the hp2pretty utility, shown next, which can be installed via cabal install hp2pretty:

```
$ cabal run iplookup-simulation --enable-profiling -- +RTS -h
$ hp2pretty iplookup-simulation.hp
```

The hp2pretty utility creates the iplookup-simulation.svg file presented in figure 10.2.

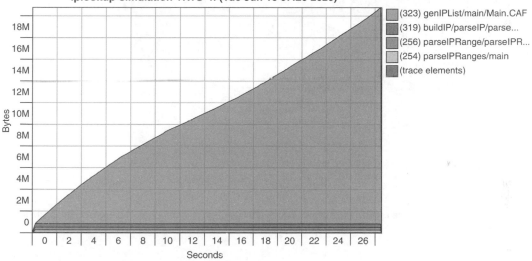

Figure 10.2   Heap usage report in the iplookup-simulation.svg file

Figure 10.2 shows that most of the heap usage is due to the genIPList function, which generates the huge list of IP addresses, and it takes more and more memory as the simulation progresses. The question is, do we really need to keep this list in memory as a whole? Why are the already processed elements not garbage collected?

Let's look at the simulate function again:

```
simulate iprdb ips = (yes, no)
  where
    yes = length $ filter id $ map (lookupIP iprdb) ips
    no = length ips - yes
```

How many times do we refer to the list of IP addresses? Well, twice: first in yes, second in no. Is it a good idea to compute the number of elements by length? Clearly, no!

We've just generated this list, and we know that it contains nReqs elements! Let's eliminate this second usage of the list of IP addresses as follows:

```
simulate iprdb ips = (yes, no)
  where
    yes = length $ filter id $ map (lookupIP iprdb) ips
    no = nReqs - yes
```

Running this simulation once again gives us the new diagram presented in figure 10.3.

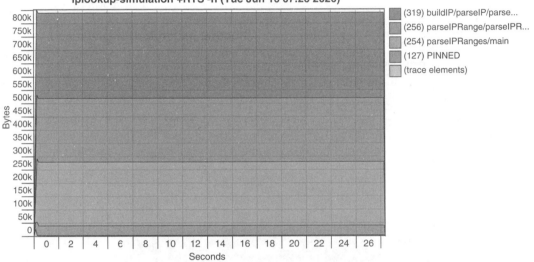

Figure 10.3   Heap usage report in the iplookup-simulation.svg after eliminating the second use of the list of IP addresses

Now it's clear that we've done the right thing: we work in constant memory, and the memory residence has been reduced dramatically.

You can find many additional tweaks of the memory profiler in the corresponding section of the GHC User's Guide. In the next section, we'll apply our findings to making the IPv4 filtering application much faster.

10.3   *Tuning performance of the IPv4 filtering application*

Thanks to profiling reports from the previous section, we know we have at least the following two issues in our program right now:

- Almost all the time is spent in lookupIP, which traverses over the list of ranges again and again.
- The parseIP function is doing too many memory allocations and is not extremely efficient.

Let's attack both these issues in this section.

10.3.1 Choosing the right data structure

How is it possible to make `lookupIP` faster? Well, we could switch from the linear search over the list of IP ranges to a logarithmic search over some tree of ranges. Is it a good idea to implement something from scratch? Certainly not, because implementing data structures correctly is a very sophisticated job. Although there is no collection in `base` that could work for us, we could use one from the external package. The best candidate here is the `fingertree` package. It provides the so-called interval map, which implements what we need. This data structure allows storing intervals of any type and supports linear time construction with logarithmic time search.

EXAMPLE: OPTIMIZING LOOKUPIP

🗇 ip/lookup/FastLookup.hs

⚡ *iplookup-lib*

☞ The right data structure drastically changes performance characteristics.

Let's add the `FastLookup` module to the internal `iplookup-lib` library as follows:

```
module FastLookup (FastIPRangeDB, fromIPRangeDB, lookupIP) where

import IPTypes
import Data.IntervalMap.FingerTree

newtype FastIPRangeDB = IPRDB (IntervalMap IP ())

fromIPRangeDB :: IPRangeDB -> FastIPRangeDB
fromIPRangeDB (IPRangeDB iprdb) = IPRDB $ foldr ins empty iprdb
   where
     ins (IPRange ip1 ip2) = insert (Interval ip1 ip2) ()

lookupIP :: FastIPRangeDB -> IP -> Bool
lookupIP (IPRDB imap) ip = not $ null $ search ip imap
```

This module declares a data type for the IP range database that supports fast lookup operations together with the following two functions:

- `fromIPRangeDB` to create a fast database from the `IPRangeDB` we had earlier
- `lookupIP` to search over it

Their implementation is very small, thanks to the functionality provided by the `fingertree` package. In the first function, we insert IP ranges one by one by folding the given list of ranges. In the second one, we refer to the `search` function for finger trees and interpret their results.

EXAMPLE: SIMULATING IPLOOKUP USAGE

🗇 ip/iplookup-simulation.hs

⚡ *iplookup-simulation*

Now we can easily switch to `FastIPRangeDB` in `iplookup-simulation` by changing `import LookupIP` to `import FastLookup`, `IPRangeDB` to `FastIPRangeDB`, and creating a fast database in `main`.

Profiling with the `-P  -h` flags gives us the following characteristics of this new implementation:

- Total time is now 3.69 secs (almost seven times faster!).
- Total allocation is 13 times larger.
- Maximum heap size is twice as large.

This is a traditional trade-off: we've got a huge speed boost paid for with a significantly larger memory footprint.

EXAMPLE: BENCHMARKING IPV4 FILTERING APPLICATION

◻ benchmarks/iplookup/BenchLookupIP.hs

⚡ *iplookup-bench*

Benchmarking the new implementation shows even better results. Compare the following:

```
benchmarking lookupIP/several
time                 88.43 µs   (88.05 µs .. 88.95 µs)
...
benchmarking lookupIP (fast)/several
time                 6.702 µs   (6.684 µs .. 6.722 µs)
```

We are 13 times faster with our new implementation of `lookupIP` thanks to the new data structure. Clearly, this optimization technique is not Haskell-specific, but this is something we should try first from the onset.

10.3.2 *Squeezing parseIP performance*

Let's turn to the performance of the `parseIP` function. We targeted the following goals while writing and fixing `parseIP` in chapter 8:

- It should be bulletproofed, and we've provided a lot of tests.
- It should be concise, and we've applied monadic machinery to achieve that.
- We didn't want to implement things by ourselves, so we've used standard library functions and functions from external libraries as well (`splitOn`, for example).

Although these goals are quite useful while developing Haskell (and, in fact, any other) programs, none of them guarantee performance. Moreover, both monadic machinery and functions from external libraries may well be a huge source of performance issues. Let's come up with another implementation that targets performance instead in the first place. Once we've got it passing the tests and make sure that it performs better through benchmarking, it's all right to replace the current implementation.

It seems that the fastest (and, unfortunately, rather low-level) way to parse IP addresses should proceed as follows:

- Go over the characters of the given string.
- At every digit, accumulate the current IP address component.
- At dots and in the end, accumulate the IP address itself.
- Control the number of digits in the current component and the number of components.
- Control the component range (0 to 255).

EXAMPLE: OPTIMIZING PARSEIP

📄 ip/lookup/ParseIP.hs

📄 benchmarks/iplookup/BenchParseIP.hs

⚡ *iplookup-bench*

☞ Low-level implementation can be faster.

Let's rewrite the parseIP function, forgetting about readability, as follows:

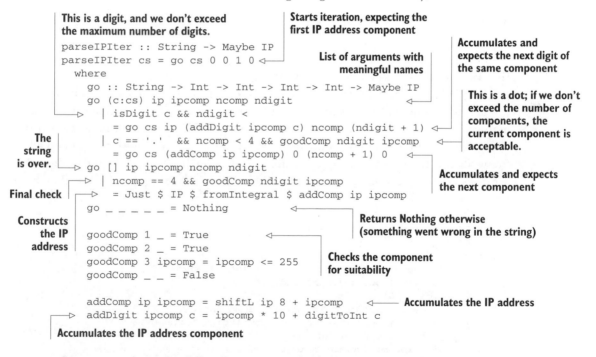

This is a digit, and we don't exceed the maximum number of digits.

Starts iteration, expecting the first IP address component

Accumulates and expects the next digit of the same component

```
parseIPIter :: String -> Maybe IP
parseIPIter cs = go cs 0 0 1 0
  where
    go :: String -> Int -> Int -> Int -> Int -> Maybe IP
    go (c:cs) ip ipcomp ncomp ndigit
      | isDigit c && ndigit <
        = go cs ip (addDigit ipcomp c) ncomp (ndigit + 1)
      | c == '.'  && ncomp < 4 && goodComp ndigit ipcomp
        = go cs (addComp ip ipcomp) 0 (ncomp + 1) 0
    go [] ip ipcomp ncomp ndigit
      | ncomp == 4 && goodComp ndigit ipcomp
        = Just $ IP $ fromIntegral $ addComp ip ipcomp
    go _ _ _ _ _ = Nothing

    goodComp 1 _ = True
    goodComp 2 _ = True
    goodComp 3 ipcomp = ipcomp <= 255
    goodComp _ _ = False

    addComp ip ipcomp = shiftL ip 8 + ipcomp
    addDigit ipcomp c = ipcomp * 10 + digitToInt c
```

List of arguments with meaningful names

This is a dot; if we don't exceed the number of components, the current component is acceptable.

The string is over.

Final check

Constructs the IP address

Accumulates and expects the next component

Returns Nothing otherwise (something went wrong in the string)

Checks the component for suitability

Accumulates the IP address

Accumulates the IP address component

Suppose we have the following structure in the ParseIP module:

```
parseIP :: String -> Maybe IP
parseIP = parseIPMonadic
```

```
parseIPMonadic = -- original implementation via monadic operations

parseIPIter = -- new iterative implementation
```

Now let's compare these two implementations by running the following benchmark:

```
iptexts = ["0.0.0.1", "192.168.1.1", "17.0.32.2",
           "255.255.252.41", "255.255.252.42"]

bench_parseIP :: [Benchmark]
bench_parseIP = [
    bench "parseIP/current" $ nf (map parseIP) iptexts
  , bgroup "parseIP" [
      bench "monadic" $ nf (map parseIPMonadic) iptexts
    , bench "iterative" $ nf (map parseIPIter) iptexts
    ]
  ]
```

The results are as follows:

```
benchmarking parseIP/monadic
time                24.84 µs    (24.78 µs .. 24.90 µs)
...
benchmarking parseIP/iterative
time                564.9 ns    (563.1 ns .. 566.6 ns)
...
```

Fantastic! 564.9 nanoseconds of the running time is 44 times faster than 24.84 microseconds. What a success! It looks like a good compensation for losing readability.

Can we do better? How about making it twice as fast? This implementation uses many accumulating values, and we already know that GHC may use thunks for storing them. Not all of them will be evaluated at every iteration because we don't need all of them all the time. Let's introduce bang patterns on the accumulating values (this requires enabling the BangPatterns GHC extension) as follows and see if they help here:

```
parseIPIterStrict :: String -> Maybe IP
parseIPIterStrict cs = go cs 0 0 1 0
  where
    go :: String -> Int -> Int -> Int -> Int -> Maybe IP
    go (c:cs) !ip !ipcomp !ncomp !ndigit
      | isDigit c && ndigit < 3
        = go cs ip (addDigit ipcomp c) ncomp (ndigit + 1)
      | c == '.'  && ncomp < 4 && goodComp ndigit ipcomp
        = go cs (addComp ip ipcomp) 0 (ncomp + 1) 0
    go [] !ip !ipcomp !ncomp !ndigit
      | ncomp == 4 && goodComp ndigit ipcomp
        = Just $ IP $ fromIntegral $ addComp ip ipcomp
    go _ _ _ _ _ = Nothing

    goodComp 1 _ = True
```

```
goodComp 2 _ = True
goodComp 3 !ipcomp = ipcomp <= 255
goodComp _ _ = False

addComp !ip !ipcomp = shiftL ip 8 + ipcomp
addDigit !ipcomp !c = ipcomp * 10 + digitToInt c
```

The only difference with the previous implementation is that I've added bangs for every argument that is not scrutinized via pattern matching (without thinking too much, I should confess). Let's check the following benchmarking results:

```
benchmarking parseIP/iterative-strict
time                 250.4 ns   (249.8 ns .. 251.1 ns)
...
```

More than twice as fast! This implementation is 100 times faster than the original one. This is an extremely good result, although a little bit upsetting for those who prefer abstractions and high-level programming.

But we are not done yet. Our job is over once we've tested this new implementation. After replacing the original implementation of `parseIP` to `parseIPIterStrict`, we get the following:

```
All 39 tests passed (0.06s)
```

You should have no doubt that I've made a lot of mistakes while implementing this very efficient version of `parseIP`. It seems impossible to write this algorithm at once without errors, but the traditional iterative approach supported by tests was extremely helpful to make it.

Summary

- We use benchmarks to compare different implementations of a particular functionality.
- The `criterion` package is a de facto standard tool for benchmarking in Haskell.
- Profiling gives us information about the most resource-demanding components of our code as well as directions on what should be optimized first.
- Profiling heap usage saves us from wasting memory in memory leaks.
- We should explore both general programming techniques (such as choosing the right data structure) and some specific to Haskell to make our software run faster.
- Tests keep confidence in the correctness of our code while doing various optimizations.

Part 4

Advanced Haskell

Haskell is the first programming language that allows applying type system advances to software development needs. In this part, we'll discuss all the major topics in Haskell types, such as polymorphism, generalized algebraic data types, and type families. We'll also talk about programming techniques based on the concept of dependent typing. Although we don't have dependent types in Haskell at the time of writing, we can still use the corresponding techniques in our programs.

One of the chapters in this part is devoted to metaprogramming, that is, a way to generate code and deal with it in a generic way. Metaprogramming is very popular within the Haskell community, because it allows writing less code while still solving all the problems. Sounds good, doesn't it?

Type system advances

11

This chapter covers

- Classifying program entities such as terms, types, and kinds
- Specifying code behavior with a bunch of type-level features
- Dealing with type errors

This chapter is devoted to programming at the level of types. We'll explore a variety of Haskell features that makes it possible. As we've discussed earlier in this book, types help us to control software behavior and express our ideas on what the code should and shouldn't do. Heavily typed code is highly resistant to some sorts of bugs. It also enables aggressive refactoring. If we do something wrong, the Haskell type checker would report that.

We'll discuss features and techniques available to any Haskell programmer. While presenting them, I limit myself to simple, contrived examples. In particular, we'll discuss the types and kinds system, data kinds, type families, generalized algebraic data types, and polymorphism. I conclude this chapter with ways to deal with errors while programming at the type level.

Almost everything discussed in this chapter is not standard Haskell and is implemented in GHC via extensions. By the end of this chapter, you will understand and be able to use all the following GHC extensions:

```
{-# LANGUAGE DataKinds #-}
{-# LANGUAGE PolyKinds #-}
{-# LANGUAGE TypeFamilies #-}
{-# LANGUAGE ScopedTypeVariables #-}
{-# LANGUAGE KindSignatures #-}
{-# LANGUAGE TypeApplications #-}
{-# LANGUAGE TypeOperators #-}
{-# LANGUAGE AllowAmbiguousTypes #-}
{-# LANGUAGE ExplicitForAll #-}
{-# LANGUAGE GADTs #-}
{-# LANGUAGE GADTSyntax #-}
```

The chapter "GHC Language Features" in the GHC User's Guide (for GHC 8.8) contains 40 sections in total, and about two-thirds of them describe various type-level features. Some of them are old and stable whereas others are novel. Some of them are rather large and deep; others are small additions to the ways we specify types in Haskell.

In this chapter, I attempt to draw a group portrait of Haskell type-level programming features, leaving thorough individual descriptions to the GHC User's Guide and the papers behind them.

11.1 *Haskell types 101*

Let's start with Haskell features that create the basis for type-level programming. We should understand the distinction between terms, types, and kinds first. Then I'll talk about ways to deliver information about types that are not necessarily accompanied with values.

11.1.1 *Terms, types, and kinds*

We all know that Haskell is the world's most powerful calculator. For example, we could define a function for converting Fahrenheit degrees to Celsius and use it as many times as we like right in the interpreter as follows:

```
ghci> f2c f = (f-32)*5/9
ghci> f2c 32
0.0
ghci> f2c 86
30.0
```

Note that we don't need types for doing that, either in the definition or in the applications. Surely, we know that there are always types in Haskell, and GHC infers them, as we can immediately see via the :type GHCi command (often used with the :t shortcut) shown next:

```
ghci> :type f2c
f2c :: Fractional a => a -> a
ghci> :type f2c 32
f2c 32 :: Fractional a => a
```

So, f2c is a function with both the argument and the result belonging to a type with an instance of the Fractional type class. The Fractional type class has instances for Float and Double but also for the less-known Ratio type from the Data.Ratio module, as shown here:

```
ghci> import Data.Ratio
ghci> f2c (100%3)
20 % 27
```

Sometimes we don't need this freedom and want to limit types to something less vague as follows:

```
f2c :: Double -> Double
f2c f = (f-32) * 5/9
```

Or, as before, in the interpreter, as shown here:

```
ghci> f2c f = (f-32) * 5/9 :: Double
ghci> :type f2c
f2c :: Double -> Double
```

Now we are sure that the term f2c 32 is Double, as shown next:

```
ghci> :type f2c 32
f2c 32 :: Double
```

So, we classify terms by types. But what about types? Can we classify them? Many years ago, Haskell got the term *kind* for that, and for a long time it was a rather limited way for doing exactly that, as follows:

```
ghci> :kind Double
Double :: *
ghci> :kind Integer
Integer :: *
```

The Double and Integer types both belong to the * kind as well as many other types that have values. Type constructors, such as Maybe and Either, fit nicely in the kind system as they naturally become functions over types, as shown next:

```
ghci> :kind Maybe
Maybe :: * -> *
ghci> :kind Either
Either :: * -> * -> *
ghci> :kind Maybe Int
```

```
Maybe Int :: *
ghci> :kind Either String Bool
Either String Bool :: *
```

The `Maybe` type constructor has the kind `* -> *`, so we need to give it a type of kind `*` to get another type of kind `*`, for example, `Maybe Int`.

The `*` and `->` symbols allow distinguishing concrete types and type constructors, but it was determined quickly that this is not enough. For example, we'd like to include type classes into the same kind systems. It is also useful to be able to classify concrete types more thoroughly than by just sending all of them to the `*` kind. This is possible in modern Haskell.

First, let's enable the `NoStarIsType` GHC extension and see how the `:kind` command reacts to this as follows:

```
ghci> :kind Integer
Integer :: Type
ghci> :kind Maybe
Maybe :: Type -> Type
ghci> :kind Maybe Integer
Maybe Integer :: Type
```

We don't have `*` anymore. Instead, we have a `Type` and a function over `Type`. So far, so good, but what about type classes, as shown next?

```
ghci> :kind Fractional
Fractional :: Type -> Constraint
```

We have a special kind for constraints, but to build them, we need to specify an exact type to a type class as follows:

```
ghci> :kind Fractional Double
Fractional Double :: Constraint
```

Monads also have their kinds, as shown here:

```
ghci> :kind Monad
Monad :: (Type -> Type) -> Constraint
```

And now we can see, as shown here, why `Maybe` can be a `Monad` and `Int` can't:

```
ghci> :kind Maybe
Maybe :: Type -> Type
ghci> :kind Monad Int

<interactive>:1:7: error:
    • Expected kind 'Type -> Type', but 'Int' has kind 'Type'
    • In the first argument of 'Monad', namely 'Int'
      In the type 'Monad Int'
```

Well, that's because the *kind checker* (by analogy with a type checker) rules this out.

Interestingly, we are not allowed to test kinds for things like `Maybe a` or `Monad m` because a or m are not defined within the interpreter. Thankfully, we have a trick we can use. We can define them explicitly right in the type using the `ExplicitForAll` GHC extension as follows:

```
ghci> :set -XExplicitForAll
ghci> :kind forall a. Maybe a
forall a. Maybe a :: Type
ghci> :kind forall m. Monad m
forall m.Monad m :: Constraint
```

The `forall` keyword is normally implicit in all the Haskell types with type variables. The `ExplicitForAll` extension allows specifying it explicitly. This extension is also implied by several other type-level GHC extensions.

We'll meet other kinds besides `Type` and `Constraint` later in this chapter. But now let's answer the final question for this explorational subsection: can we classify kinds? The answer may be a bit surprising. The names `Type` and `Constraint` are not available by default, but they can be imported from the `Data.Kind` module. Let's find out whether they have type or kind or something else in the next code sample:

```
ghci> import Data.Kind (Type, Constraint)
ghci> :type Type

<interactive>:1:1: error: Data constructor not in scope: Type
ghci> :kind Type
Type :: Type
ghci> :kind Constraint
Constraint :: Type
```

So, the `Type` kind is not defined at the term level (at least for now). As a result, we can't use `:type` for it, but it has a kind `Type`! It's the same with the `Constraint` kind. All this means that kinds are nowadays also types and can be classified by kinds. There is ongoing research on unifying types and terms in Haskell so types could become terms, and we could classify them by types. When this is implemented, we would not need kinds anymore and could safely forget about them. Strangely, there was a period in GHC history when kinds were classified by *sorts* (please don't ask me about classifying sorts at those times, because there was only one sort, called BOX), but that period is over. Chances are, we will not need kinds in Haskell either in some near future. Figure 11.1 illustrates the current division between terms and types in Haskell with mappings over them.

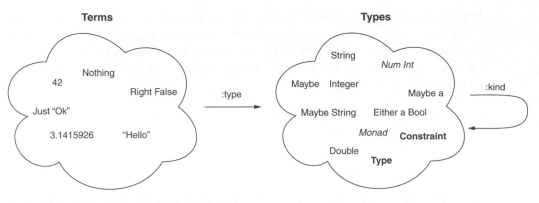

Figure 11.1 Terms, types, and kinds in Haskell

11.1.2 *Delivering information with types*

Now let's look at several basic Haskell features that enable interesting and quite popular techniques. We already know that every term has a type. Moreover, this should be a type of kind Type. There are types of other kinds, and they don't have terms belonging to them. Does it make sense to have a type of kind Type without any terms at all? Well, it does. Those types can be used as *phantom parameters*, and this gives us the first example of type-level programming in this chapter. We use those parameters to deliver information with types, not terms.

PHANTOM PARAMETERS AND EMPTY TYPES

Suppose we want to distinguish Celsius and Fahrenheit degrees but don't want to define separate data types to store and process the corresponding temperatures. Let's try to do that with types.

EXAMPLE: STORING TEMPERATURES IN DIFFERENT SCALES

📄   ch11/temperature/TempPhantom.hs

⚡   *temp-proxies*

☞   Phantom type parameters deliver additional information about types.

We start with defining a type for storing temperatures. This type is parameterized with the unit type variable as follows:

```
newtype Temp unit = Temp Double
  deriving (Num, Fractional)
```

Note that the unit type variable is not used in the right-hand side; it is a phantom parameter. We derive the Num and Fractional instances to be able to use numeric literals as Temp values and have arithmetic operations from scratch. This requires the GeneralizedNewtypeDeriving GHC extension.

We also define a couple of types which serve as units as follows:

```
data F
data C
```

There are no values of these types. They both have an empty declaration.

Now we can define a couple of temperatures using type signatures to specify the desired unit, as shown next:

```
paperBurning :: Temp F
paperBurning = 451

absoluteZero :: Temp C
absoluteZero = -273.15
```

Although we can't create values of the F and C types, we can safely use them as types by using them instead of the unit type variable. This prevents the following sort of error:

```
$ cabal repl temp-proxies
ghci> paperBurning - absoluteZero
<interactive>:1:4: error:
    • Couldn't match type 'C' with 'F'
      Expected type: Temp F
        Actual type: Temp C
  ...
```

Of course, we have no problems when we use values with the same units as follows:

```
ghci> paperBurning - paperBurning
0.0°F
```

Note the output—I'll define the Show instance for the Temp unit shortly. This is where we'll need to get information about the particular type.

It's easy to implement the converting function with the type stating what is going on in there, as shown next:

```
f2c :: Temp F -> Temp C
f2c (Temp f) = Temp ((f-32)*5/9)
```

After converting units, things go smoothly, as shown here:

```
ghci> f2c paperBurning - absoluteZero
505.92777777777775°C
```

Unfortunately, we don't have much control over the type we can use instead of unit, besides which, it should be of kind Type. So, the following awkward definition works, too, without any meaning at all:

```
nonsense :: Temp Bool
nonsense = 0
```

We'll find another way to deal with this inconvenience; but still, we may often see phantom parameters in actual code.

PROXIES

Sometimes we do have a value of a type, but the sole purpose of that value is to refer to a type. The value itself is never used. Such types and values are called *proxies*. The base package contains the `Data.Proxy` module, which declares the following data type:

```
data Proxy t = Proxy
```

The `t` parameter is a phantom, and the only value of this type is `Proxy` (the data constructor itself). We may want to use proxies in situations when something we do depends on the type but not on a value. Let's use this type to define the `Show` instance for `Temp unit` to enable it to show unit names.

EXAMPLE: USING PROXIES TO DELIVER INFORMATION WITH TYPES

🗋 ch11/temperature/UnitNameProxies.hs

⚡ *temp-proxies*

☞ Proxies bring information about types to the level of terms.

For example, let's define a type class with a function, which gives the name of the unit as follows:

```
class UnitName u where
  unitName :: Proxy u -> String
```

To define this function for different types, we have to use type class/instance mechanisms. The reason is straightforward: in Haskell, we don't have pattern matching over types. The only way to distinguish different types in the same function is to define instances. I use the `InstanceSigs` GHC extension to specify the precise type of the function definition inside an instance.

For example, let's define instances for F and C as follows:

```
instance UnitName C where
  unitName :: Proxy C -> String
  unitName _ = "C"

instance UnitName F where
  unitName :: Proxy F -> String
  unitName _ = "F"
```

In both instances, we aren't interested in `Proxy` values so we use `_` instead.

To call the `unitName` function in GHCi, we have to provide not only a parameter—which is `Proxy`, apparently—but also its type, as shown next. The compiler would have no clue which implementation to choose otherwise.

```
ghci> import Data.Proxy
ghci> unitName (Proxy :: Proxy F)
"F"
ghci> unitName (Proxy :: Proxy C)
"C"
```

We can also define an instance of this type class for the `Temp u` type as follows:

```
instance UnitName unit => UnitName (Temp unit) where
  unitName _ = unitName (Proxy :: Proxy unit)
```

Note that we use the `unit` type variable from the instance header inside the method body. This requires enabling the `ScopedTypeVariables` GHC extension. As an implementation, we call the `unitName` for another type.

With these instances at hand, it's easy to define the `Show` instance for `Temp unit` as follows:

```
instance UnitName unit => Show (Temp unit) where
  show (Temp t) = show t ++ "°" ++ unitName (Proxy :: Proxy unit)
```

It's also very easy to introduce a new unit

```
data K
```

```
instance UnitName K where
  unitName _ = "K"
```

which can be used in the same way as before, as shown next:

```
ghci> 0 :: Temp K
0.0°K
```

It could also be convenient to get a unit from a value. Let's define a function for that as follows:

```
unit :: forall u. UnitName u => Temp u -> String
unit _ = unitName (Proxy :: Proxy u)
```

We need to have access to the `u` type variable in the right-hand side of the function body. The `ScopedTypeVariables` GHC extension makes that possible, too. It allows introducing the `u` variable explicitly with the `forall` keyword and referring to it later within the function's body. Now the client of our code may avoid mentioning proxies at all, as shown here:

```
ghci> unit paperBurning
"F"
ghci> unit absoluteZero
"C"
```

Let's look again at the definition of the `UnitName` type class:

```
class UnitName u where
  unitName :: Proxy u -> String
```

One question could be, what is the kind of a type behind the `u` type variable? It turns out that it is `Type` by default. So this declaration has the same meaning as the following:

```
import Data.Kind (Type)

class UnitName (u :: Type) where
  unitName :: Proxy u -> String
```

Consequently, we are not allowed to implement instances for types of other kinds, for example, `Temp`, which is of kind `Type -> Type`. Why does Haskell limit us? Because kinds in type classes are not polymorphic by default. We need kind polymorphism to do that. Fortunately, we have another GHC extension, `PolyKinds`, which enables the desired behavior. Once we enable it, it is possible to define an instance for `Temp` as follows:

```
instance UnitName Temp where
  unitName _ = "_unspecified unit_"
```

And it works. The `Proxy` may be a value of `Proxy Temp` now, as shown next:

```
ghci> unitName (Proxy :: Proxy Temp)
"_unspecified unit_"
```

Figure 11.2 summarizes the role of the `PolyKinds` GHC extension in class definitions.

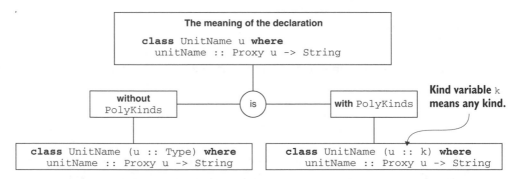

Figure 11.2 Type variables in class definitions with or without `PolyKinds`

In case you're wondering why we need this proxy stuff, I'll show you one practical example. The following is the definition of the `JSONSchema` type class from the `json-schema` package using the same idea of proxies to provide type information exclusively without any meaningful value:

```
class JSONSchema a where
  schema :: Proxy a -> Schema
```

A schema describes the structure of a JSON data file for the specified data type. It doesn't depend on the value of the data type—that's why that package developer decided to use `Proxy`.

Sometimes it makes sense to combine `Proxy` with an additional value or, in other words, to use a phantom type with a value. The `tagged` package provides the `Tagged s b` type of kind `k -> Type -> Type` (with `PolyKinds` enabled), which supports converting to and from a `Proxy`.

We may also occasionally come up with code like the following:

```
someFunc :: proxy a -> String
someFunc _ = "OK"
```

Don't be fooled by its appearance. The `proxy` we see here is a type variable, not the `Proxy` type. It may be instructive to think about its kind and how one could call this function. We can supply any argument with a type that is a type constructor with a type argument, for example:

```
ghci> someFunc (Just 'x')
"OK"
ghci> someFunc (Right 'x')
"OK"
ghci> someFunc []
"OK"
ghci> someFunc (Proxy :: Proxy Bool)
"OK"
```

Although this technique is also used, the specific `Proxy` or `Tagged` type gives much more control over kinds and should be preferred nowadays.

VISIBLE TYPE APPLICATIONS

In the previous subsection, we used proxies to deliver information about types. With the `TypeApplications` extension, GHC supports providing this information explicitly in a use site, that is, at the moment we call the function. One classic example is the `read` function. What is the type of `read "42"`? Well, it depends on where it is used: it may be `Int` or `Double`, or it may cause an exception (if we expect `Bool`, for example).

The type of `read` is as follows:

```
read :: Read a => String -> a
```

So it gives back the value of type `a`, given that this type has an instance of the `Read` type class. When we call this function, Haskell injects two inferred implicit parameters, namely, a specific type itself and a dictionary with an implementation of the `Read` type class methods. The `read` function has those two parameters, but we never think of them because they are always inferred. By the way, we can ask GHCi to print them as follows:

```
ghci> :set -fprint-explicit-foralls
ghci> :type read
read :: forall {a}. Read a => String -> a
```

Notice this implicit {a} parameter? We can give it a value (specify a required type) explicitly as follows:

```
ghci> :set -XTypeApplications
ghci> read @Int "42"
42
ghci> :type it
it :: Int
```

The result is now of type Int, as was required. We may think of @ as a visible type application. The read function has the following three parameters in total:

- *A type variable* a *of the* Type *kind*—We can provide it via type application with an @.
- Read a *of the* Constraint *kind*—It is always injected by GHC.
- *A* String *value*—We provide it as usual.

For another example of type applications, let's revisit the implementation of the UnitName type class.

EXAMPLE: USING TYPE APPLICATION TO DELIVER INFORMATION WITH TYPES

    📄   ch11/temperature/UnitNameTypeApps.hs

    ⚡   *temp-type-apps*

    ☞   Type application allows us to provide a specific type at a use site.

```
class UnitName u where
  unitName :: String        ◁——— No Proxy or other arguments

instance UnitName C where
  unitName = "C"

instance UnitName F where
  unitName = "F"

instance UnitName Temp where       ◁——— We need kind polymorphism here.
  unitName = "_unspecified unit_"

instance UnitName u => UnitName (Temp u) where
  unitName = unitName @u                        ◁——— Type application
```

We have to use the AllowAmbiguousTypes GHC extension here. It is quite subtle. GHC is unable to give a type to the unitName function until we call it. Without this extension, it would be a type error. As we can see in the following GHCi session, the only way to assign a type to the function is to specify the type explicitly using type application:

```
ghci> :type unitName

<interactive>:1:1: error:
    Ambiguous type variable 'a0' arising from a use of 'unitName'
    prevents the constraint '(Describe a0)' from being solved.
```

```
    ...
ghci> :set -XTypeApplications
ghci> :type unitName @F
unitName @F :: String
```

Just as before, we can use the new `UnitName` type class to define the `Show` instance for temperatures, as shown next:

```
instance UnitName u => Show (Temp u) where
  show (Temp t) = show t ++ "°" ++ unitName @u
```

We can also revisit the implementation of the `unit` function, which returns a unit name given a temperature value as follows:

```
unit :: forall u. UnitName u => Temp u -> String
unit _ = unitName @u
```

Visible type applications are not something we should use often. In regular Haskell programming, we provide actual parameters, and all the types are inferred for us by the compiler. Nevertheless, while doing type-level programming, type applications become unavoidable sometimes.

> **CAN WE GET RID OF PROXY ENTIRELY?** When learning a new Haskell feature, it may be tempting to think that this feature can replace something old. Unfortunately, this in not often the case. Visible type applications can't help us to get rid of the `Proxy` type. Richard Eisenberg explains why in the following video: https://www.youtube.com/watch?v=FFZXWoqviBo.

11.1.3 Type operators

In the final subsection on the basic type-level machinery, we'll discuss type operators, a purely syntactic way to give nice names to types.

EXAMPLE: USING TYPE OPERATORS

📄 ch11/type-operators.hs

⚡ *type-operators*

☞ We can use operators in types.

In the following example, we define algebraic data types from scratch as sums and products of any type and use convenient + and * operators to denote them:

This extension allows operators in type names.

```
{-# LANGUAGE TypeOperators #-}
data a + b = Inl a | Inr b
  deriving Show

data a * b = a :*: b
  deriving Show
```

The element of the sum is a value of either left or right type.

The element of the product contains values of both left and right types.

```
infixl 6 +    │  Addition has lower precedence than
infixl 7 *    │  multiplication; both are left associative.
```

Now we have types like `Bool + Int` or `String * Maybe Integer` with values like `Inl False` or `"Hello" :*: Nothing`, respectively. Note that infix data constructor names are required to start with : to distinguish them from regular operators that manipulate expressions.

For products, it is useful to define a couple of getters, as follows:

```
first :: a * b -> a
first (a :*: _) = a

second :: a * b -> b
second (_ :*: b) = b
```

Type operators make type signatures shorter and more evident. Compare the type `Either Char (Bool, Bool)` with the following:

```
val1 :: Int + Bool * Bool
val1 = Inl 0

val2 :: Int + Bool * Bool
val2 = Inr (True :*: False)
```

We can use type operators to define type synonyms or other types, for example:

```
type Point a = a + a * a + a * a * a

zero2D :: Point Int
zero2D = Inl (Inr (0 :*: 0))
```

The value of the `Point` type may be used to store a point in one-dimensional, two-dimensional, or three-dimensional space. Note that we've used `infixl` declarations to give the precise meaning to the declarations, like `Point a` earlier. Left associativity with the specified precedence means that a + a * a + a * a * a is parsed as follows:

```
type Point a = (a + (a * a)) + ((a * a) * a)
```

Thus, to define a 2-D point, we have to use `Inl` followed by `Inr`.

11.2 *Data kinds and type-level literals*

We are ready to discuss the workhorse of type-level programming in Haskell: defining and using new kinds besides `Type` and `Constraint` that we've seen before.

11.2.1 *Promoting types to kinds and values to types*

Let's get back to the example with temperatures and agree on the following:

1. We'd like to have one type to store them.
2. We want the type checker to prevent mixing units without explicit conversion in one expression.
3. We'd like to fix a list of units.

Earlier with phantom types, we had 1 and 2, but not 3. Now we are ready to get 3. The idea is to bring data type values to the type level with the `DataKinds` GHC extension.

EXAMPLE: EXPRESSING TEMPERATURE UNITS WITH DATAKINDS

◻ ch11/temperature/temp-kinds.hs

⚡ *temp-kinds*

☞ We may fix a list of units at the level of types.

We start with defining a type with units as values as follows:

```
data TempUnits = F | C
```

With `DataKinds` enabled, this line defines both the `TempUnits` data type with values `F` and `C` and the `TempUnits` kind with types `F` and `C` belonging to it (with strictly no others). Now we have not only `Type` and `Constraint` kinds but also `TempUnits`. We say that `F` and `C` values are *promoted* to types. Consequently, the `TempUnits` type is promoted to kind.

Now we can define temperature as follows:

```
newtype Temp (u :: TempUnits) = Temp Double
  deriving (Num, Fractional)
```

`Temp` is a new parameterized type with a type variable limited to a specified kind, so the only possible types for it are `F` and `C`, as shown here:

```
paperBurning :: Temp F
paperBurning = 451

absoluteZero :: Temp C
absoluteZero = -273.15

f2c :: Temp F -> Temp C
f2c (Temp f) = Temp ((f-32)*5/9)
```

The `DataKinds` GHC extension *promotes* data type definitions to the level of types as follows:

- Type constructors become kind constructors.
- Data constructors become type constructors.

So, `F` is both a value and a type. `TempUnits` is a type and a kind (which, as we know, is also a type). The following GHCi session illustrates this behavior:

```
ghci> :set -XNoStarIsType -XDataKinds
ghci> :type F
F :: TempUnits
ghci> :kind F
F :: TempUnits
ghci> :kind TempUnits
TempUnits :: Type
```

Now, the following is allowed:

```
ghci> f2c paperBurning - absoluteZero
505.92777777777775°C
```

And this is not:

```
ghci> paperBurning - absoluteZero

<interactive>:6:16: error:
    • Couldn't match type ''C' with ''F'
    ...
ghci> 0 :: Temp Bool

<interactive>:7:11: error:
    • Expected kind 'TempUnits', but 'Bool' has kind 'Type'
    ...
```

Note the names 'F and 'C in the first error message in the previous code sample. Sometimes we or the compiler need to disambiguate equally named values and corresponding promoted types. In these situations, the ' prefix is used to mention a *type* and not a value.

We can also mention our new kind in type class declarations as follows:

```
class UnitName (u :: TempUnits) where
  unitName :: String
```

Now we are not allowed to define instances for anything except F and C.

11.2.2 *Type-level literals*

All the DataKinds machinery works not only for user-defined data types but also for types in the base library, including natural numbers, strings, and lists. Moreover, we can freely use the values of those types at the type level. They are called type-level literals.

The GHC.TypeLits module defines the following types, which are automatically promoted to the kinds:

- Nat *for natural numbers, such as* 0, 1, 2,...—These literals become types under promotion.
- Symbol *for strings, such as* "hello" *and* "bye"—These literals become types, too.

In the following GHCi session, we explore the kinds of those promoted types:

```
ghci> :set -XDataKinds -XNoStarIsType
ghci> :kind 42
42 :: Nat
ghci> :kind Nat
Nat :: Type
ghci> :kind "hello"
"hello" :: Symbol
ghci> :kind Symbol
Symbol :: Type
```

It is also possible to use list literals for lists at the type level, as shown next:

```
ghci> :kind []
[] :: Type -> Type
ghci> :kind [Int, String, Bool]
[Int, String, Bool] :: [Type]
```

As before, if we need to disambiguate types and terms, we use the ' prefix as follows:

```
ghci> :kind '[Int, String, Bool]
'[Int, String, Bool] :: [Type]
```

EXAMPLE: ALIGNED POINTERS

For the first example of using natural numbers at the type level, let's take low-level memory pointers. Hardware sometimes requires pointers to be aligned or divisible by some fixed number.

EXAMPLE: KEEPING POINTERS ALIGNED WITH TYPE LITERALS

🗋 ch11/type-lits/Pointers.hs

⚡ *type-lits*

☞ Type controls the interpretation of a pointer value.

Let's put the alignment number right in the type as follows:

```
newtype Pointer (align :: Nat)      ⟵     Requires the KindSignatures
        = Pointer Integer                  extension to be enabled
```

The idea behind this representation is to store a value that should be multiplied by an alignment before being used as a pointer. For example, the `Pointer 2` value of the `Pointer 4` type corresponds to the pointer value 8. Thus we can be sure that every pointer value is properly aligned.

We can define the zero pointer with any alignment as follows:

```
zeroPtr :: Pointer n
zeroPtr = Pointer 0
```

Some functions over aligned pointers are simple. For example, to increment a pointer keeping its alignment, we should add 1, as shown next:

```
inc :: Pointer align -> Pointer align
inc (Pointer p) = Pointer (p + 1)
```

Despite being so simple, this definition guarantees that we don't change alignment. This is the type system at work.

The value of alignment is known at compile time, but sometimes we need to use it at run time. For example, to view a real pointer value, we have to multiply its value by the alignment. Thus, we need to bring a type-level value of alignment to the level of terms. This can be done by using the KnownNat type class provided by the GHC.TypeLits module as follows:

```
ptrValue :: forall align. KnownNat align => Pointer align -> Integer
ptrValue (Pointer p) = p * natVal (Proxy :: Proxy align)
```

Now we have only two lines of code. Nevertheless, this definition is tough. We should look closely at its components, shown next:

- The forall align part in the type signature makes the align type variable available in the right-hand side of the function's body. This ability is enabled by the ScopedTypeVariables GHC extension.
- The KnownNat type class defines the natVal method, which takes a type-level natural literal to its term-level integer counterpart.
- The natVal method takes Proxy (from Data.Proxy) as an argument. This means that we are interested not in a value but in a type, namely, the align type variable.

The ptrValue and inc work as expected, as shown here:

```
ghci> :set -XDataKinds
ghci> ptrValue (inc $ zeroPtr :: Pointer 4)
4
ghci> ptrValue (inc $ zeroPtr :: Pointer 8)
8
```

Note that we are obliged to specify the particular type in these examples. Otherwise, the type checker would be unable to find an instance of the KnownNat type class, hence its name—*known natural*—meaning known at compile time.

Creating a pointer requires more work: we need to make sure that a pointer is properly aligned first and then store the unaligned factor. The result is not guaranteed, so we should return Maybe (Pointer align). Again, here we need to consult a type-level alignment via natVal from KnownNat as follows:

```
maybePtr :: forall align. KnownNat align => Integer -> Maybe (Pointer align)
maybePtr p
  | remainder == 0 = Just (Pointer quotient)
```

```
| otherwise = Nothing
where
  (quotient, remainder) = divMod p (natVal (Proxy :: Proxy align))
```

This works, as shown here:

```
ghci> mbptr1 = maybePtr 24 :: Maybe (Pointer 8)
ghci> ptrValue <$> mbptr1
Just 24
ghci> mbptr2 = maybePtr 42 :: Maybe (Pointer 8)
ghci> ptrValue <$> mbptr2
Nothing
```

Now we have pointers that are guaranteed by the type system to be always properly aligned.

EXAMPLE: SUFFIXED STRINGS

For another example, suppose we want to implement ID management in our organization. The ID consists of the username and a department part, for example, "bravit@teachers" or "bravit@devs". We want to store only usernames and keep department information in a type. Thus we could type check operations over employees according to department-level policies.

EXAMPLE: KEEPING IDS SUFFIXED WITH TYPE LITERALS

📄 ch11/type-lits/SuffixedStrings.hs

⚡ *type-lits*

☞ We use Symbol to work with String literals at the level of types.

The suffixed String can be defined using the Symbol kind as follows:

```
data SuffixedString (suffix :: Symbol) = SS String
```

To create a value of this type, we can use the following function:

```
suffixed :: String -> SuffixedString suffix
suffixed s = SS s
```

Note that it is useful to have this function to avoid exporting the SS data constructor. Now we can allow creating suffixed strings but disallow pattern matching on them.

To view the full ID we should consult the type-level department info. We can do that with the symbolVal method from the KnownSymbol type class as follows:

```
asString :: forall suffix. KnownSymbol suffix =>
        SuffixedString suffix -> String
asString (SS str) = str ++ "@" ++ symbolVal (Proxy :: Proxy suffix)
```

Again, this brings a value from the level of types to the level of terms, as shown next:

```
ghci> :set -XDataKinds
ghci> id1 = suffixed "bravit" :: SuffixedString "teachers"
ghci> id2 = suffixed "bravit" :: SuffixedString "devs"
ghci> asString id1
"bravit@teachers"
ghci> asString id2
"bravit@devs"
```

We'll see more pragmatic applications of this technique later in this book.

11.3   *Computations over types with type families*

Sometimes we need to map types onto types. Type families allow expressing such computations: they map one or several types to a result, which is also a type. Haskell provides several flavors of type families. In this section, we'll discuss type synonym families (they don't create new types), data families (they allow defining new data types), and associated families (they are defined inside type classes). Another word that is often used to characterize type families is *indexed*. We use types as indices to type families to get resulting types.

We'll start with type synonym families. Their whole idea is to define a simple mapping over existing types.

11.3.1   *Open and closed type synonym families*

Type synonym families come in two flavors: *open* (when it is allowed to add new instances everywhere, even in other modules) and *closed* (when there is a closed list of instances). Let's discuss both with a simple example.

EXAMPLE: SIMPLE TYPES MANIPULATIONS WITH TYPE FAMILIES

📄   ch11/type-families/SimplifyWiden.hs

⚡   *type-families*

☞   We can map types to other types.

Suppose we want to simplify the types we use in a program. For example, we are porting an application to some other programming language with minimal types, say, Integer and String. The first step could be to transform all of our data. To do that, we need a type family that maps all types to one of the two allowed types as follows:

```
type family Simplify t        ⟵—— Declares the type family

type instance Simplify Integer = Integer
type instance Simplify Int = Integer
type instance Simplify Double = Integer          Defining equations
type instance Simplify String = String
type instance Simplify Char = String
type instance Simplify Bool = String
```

Let's explore this type family in the following GHCi session. First, what is its kind?

```
ghci> :set -XNoStarIsType
ghci> :kind Simplify
Simplify :: Type -> Type
```

We can also ask GHCi to do some type-level computations for us as follows:

```
ghci> :kind Simplify Bool
Simplify Bool :: Type
ghci> :kind! Simplify Bool
Simplify Bool :: Type
= String
```

Note the bang in :kind!—it forces GHC to reduce a type family application.

It is not enough to describe this transformation at the level of types. We have to process our data also. As usual, with functions that should be able to process data of different types, we have to define a type class as follows:

```
class Simplifier t where
  simplify :: t -> Simplify t
```
The type of result is computed from t by Simplify.

Now we provide instances to implement the transformation itself. Here I use the most trivial transformations imaginable, as shown next:

```
instance Simplifier Integer where
  simplify = id

instance Simplifier Int where
  simplify = fromIntegral

instance Simplifier Double where
  simplify = round

instance Simplifier String where
  simplify = id

instance Simplifier Bool where
  simplify = show

instance Simplifier Char where
  simplify = (:"")
```

The simplify function can now be used as `Double -> Integer`, `Bool -> String`, or `Char -> String`, as shown here:

```
ghci> simplify (3.14 :: Double)
3
ghci> simplify True
"True"
ghci> simplify 'x'
"x"
```

Again, a synonym type family describes how types are mapped onto other types. To implement a function that uses a type family in its type, we define a type class and instances or call another function that we've already defined in a type class.

Open type families are quite limited. For example, there is no way to say something like *simplify all other types to* String. The reason is straightforward: a user should have an ability to add more type family instances later. A catchall instance would conflict with them.

For another simple example of type families, let's look at closed type families. The difference is that with open type families, we are free to add type instances whenever we like, whereas closed ones allow only a fixed list of instances. The following type family defines a way to widen the type of a value. Note the where keyword in the first line:

```
type family Widen a where
  Widen Bool = Int
  Widen Int = Integer
  Widen Char = String
  Widen t = String          ⟵──── A catchall instance
```

Note that it's okay to have the last instance correspond to all the other types. This type family can't be extended later. Once we've defined this type, it's impossible to add a transformation for another type.

Again, we transform types from one to another and need a function to do an actual job, as follows:

```
class Widener a where
  widen :: a -> Widen a

instance Widener Bool where
  widen False = 0
  widen True = 1

instance Widener Int where
  widen a = fromIntegral a

instance Widener Char where
  widen c = [c]
```

The following examples demonstrate that everything works as expected:

```
ghci> widen False
0
ghci> :type widen False
widen False :: Int
ghci> widen 'x'
"x"
ghci> widen (1 :: Int)
1
ghci> :type widen (1 :: Int)
```

```
widen (1 :: Int) :: Integer
ghci> widen (widen True)
1
```

We can also add instances for other types. For example, `widen` should return `String` for them, as shown next:

```
instance Widener Double where
  widen = show
```

Closed type synonym families give more information to the compiler, so it is more flexible to work with them. Let's look at a more useful example of using closed type synonym families.

11.3.2 *Example: Avoid character escaping in GHCi*

An old inconvenience exists in GHCi for everyone using non-English alphabets. GHC `Show` instances escape all the characters except the first half of the ASCII table. Unfortunately, `Show` is used by default for printing values in GHCi. For example, this is how I see my name written with the Cyrillic alphabet in GHCi:

```
ghci> "Виталий"
"\1042\1080\1090\1072\1083\1080\1081"
```

Whenever we write some value in GHCi, it is automatically replaced by the `print` function with that value as an argument. The `print` function refers to the `Show` instance, and we have character codes printed as a result. Fortunately, GHCi provides the `-interactive-print` flag, which allows replacing the default `print` function with something else. The only requirement for such a function is that it should have the following form: `C t => t -> IO ()`, where `C` is absolutely any constraint. This flexibility comes from the fact that this function is inserted in the type checker when all checks have been done already.

Let's implement such a function. Our goal is to make its use transparent for a user. The user shouldn't do anything about types; it should work just as the traditional `print` function.

> **EXAMPLE: AVOID CHARACTER ESCAPING IN GHCI**
>
> 🗋 ch11/type-families/Unescape.hs
>
> ⚡ *type-families*
>
> ☞ We can transform types with type families and type classes transparently.

The root of the problem is the `Show` instance for `Char`. It does all the escaping. Suppose we have our own `Char` as follows:

```
newtype UnescapingChar = UnescapingChar {unescapingChar :: Char}
```

We can implement the Show instance for it without any escaping as follows:

```
instance  Show UnescapingChar  where
    showsPrec _ (UnescapingChar '\'') = showString "'\\''"
    showsPrec _ (UnescapingChar c)    =
      showChar '\'' . showLitChar' c . showChar '\''

    showList cs = showChar '"' . showLitString' (map unescapingChar cs)
                . showChar '"'

showLitChar' :: Char -> ShowS
showLitChar' c s | c > '\DEL' =  showChar c s
showLitChar' c s = showLitChar c s

showLitString' :: String -> ShowS
showLitString' []          s = s
showLitString' ('"' : cs) s = showString "\\\"" (showLitString' cs s)
showLitString' (c   : cs) s = showLitChar' c (showLitString' cs s)
```

Here I mostly reuse the implementation of the Show Char instance, except that there is no character escaping anymore. With the previous instance defined, many Haskell users outside North America should be happy:

```
ghci> 'ë'
'\235'
ghci> UnescapingChar 'ë'
'ë'
```

The problem is that no one uses this nice UnescapingChar and never will. Moreover, we can't teach GHCi to treat the '?' literal as a value of the UnescapingChar type. Here comes an idea: why not transform the type of a given value using type families? We could take any type with Char somewhere inside it and transform it to the same type with Char replaced by UnescapingChar. We'd like to have the following mapping over types:

- Char goes to UnescapingChar.
- Maybe Char becomes Maybe UnescapingChar.
- [Char] becomes [UnescapingChar].
- Either String String becomes Either [UnescapingChar] [UnescapingChar].
- All unapplied type constructors (such as Maybe or Either) and concrete types (such as Int or Double) remain unaffected.

This is the corresponding type family:

```
type family ToUnescapingTF (a :: k) :: k where          ◁─── We use PolyKinds.
  ToUnescapingTF Char = UnescapingChar          ◁───  Char becomes UnescapingChar.
  ToUnescapingTF (t b :: k) = (ToUnescapingTF t) (ToUnescapingTF b)   ◁─┐
  ToUnescapingTF a = a          ◁───                                     
                                                  The applied type constructor
          Everything else is unaffected.          requires recursive processing.
```

Concrete types are processed as follows:

```
ghci> :kind! ToUnescapingTF Char
ToUnescapingTF Char :: Type
= UnescapingChar
ghci> :kind! ToUnescapingTF Int
ToUnescapingTF Int :: Type
= Int
```

We handle all the hard cases with the second equation, which follows. It works for both fully applied type constructors and partially applied ones, thanks to kind polymorphism.

```
ghci> :kind! ToUnescapingTF (Maybe Char)
ToUnescapingTF (Maybe Char) :: Type
= Maybe UnescapingChar
ghci> :kind! ToUnescapingTF (Either String)
ToUnescapingTF (Either String) :: Type -> Type
= Either [UnescapingChar]
```

Now we need a function to process values. As usual, we define it in a type class as follows:

```
class ToUnescaping a where
    toUnescaping :: a -> ToUnescapingTF a
```

Our original goal was to show all the types with the Show instance modulo escaping characters. Note that due to using newtype for UnescapingChar, the type resulting from ToUnescapingTF t shares the same run-time representation as t. This allows us to use the following dirty hack to implement a ToUnescaping instance for every type with the Show instance:

```
instance Show a => ToUnescaping a where
    toUnescaping = unsafeCoerce
```

The unsafeCoerce function implements toUnescaping by doing nothing. Its only role is to persuade the type checker that everything is all right. To show any type t, we need the following two instances:

- ToUnescaping t to run the toUnescaping processing
- Show (ToUnescapingTF t) to show the result

We can combine these two constraints into one using the ConstraintKinds GHC extension as follows:

```
type UnescapingShow t = (ToUnescaping t, Show (ToUnescapingTF t))
```

Finally, we can write the following replacements for show and print:

```
ushow :: UnescapingShow t => t -> String
ushow = show . toUnescaping

uprint :: UnescapingShow t => t -> IO ()
uprint = putStrLn . ushow
```

Every type with the Show instance automatically satisfies the UnescapingShow constraint. The latter function fits an -interactive-print perfectly, as shown next:

```
ghci> :set -interactive-print=uprint
ghci> "Vogt Nyx: »Büß du ja zwölf Qirsch, Kämpe!«"
"Vogt Nyx: »Büß du ja zwölf Qirsch, Kämpe!«"
ghci> "Voix ambiguë d'un cœur qui au zéphyr préfère les jattes de kiwi"
"Voix ambiguë d'un cœur qui au zéphyr préfère les jattes de kiwi"
ghci> "Ζαφείρι δέξου πάγκαλο, βαθῶν ψυχῆς τὸ σῆμα"
"Ζαφείρι δέξου πάγκαλο, βαθῶν ψυχῆς τὸ σῆμα"
```

The problem is solved! And yes, my name is also printed correctly now:

```
ghci> "Виталий"
"Виталий"
```

> **NOTE** Unfortunately, this implementation of the uprint function gives us only a partial solution to the original problem. We use type families to replace Char with UnescapingChar in parameters of type constructors. Parameters to data constructors are invisible for type families. To provide a full solution, one needs to analyze values instead.

11.3.3 *Data families*

Besides type synonym families, GHC also gives us *data families*, indexed family-related counterparts to algebraic data types. With data families, we define new data types for every instance. Data families are always open. There is no closed variant.

For a simple example of a data family, let's define a memory-efficient listlike data structure as follows:

- To store a list of (), one could use an Integer number that counts a number of elements.
- To store a list of Bool, one could use an Integer as a collection of bits with another Integer to count the number of elements in a list.

EXAMPLE: IMPLEMENTING A LISTLIKE DATA STRUCTURE

📄 *ch11/type-families/XListable.hs*

⚡ *type-families*

☞ Data families provide a unified interface to different data representations.

The following definition of the XList data family implements this plan:

```
data family XList a
newtype instance XList () = XListUnit Integer
data instance XList Bool = XBits Integer Integer
```

XListUnit and XBits are data constructors that create values of XList () and XList Bool, respectively. Note that to provide an instance, we can use both data and newtype declarations with the regular limitations of the latter (only one data constructor with one field). Whenever we have an idea to represent a list of something in some special way, we are free to extend this definition by adding an instance.

To define functions able to work with these list representations, we have to declare a type class with instances corresponding to the types we want to store in a list. For example, let's define three such functions as follows:

```
class XListable a where
  xempty :: XList a
  xcons :: a -> XList a -> XList a
  xheadMay :: XList a -> Maybe a
```

We'd like to construct empty lists with xempty, add an element to the beginning of a list with xcons, and check the first element with xheadMay. An instance for an () looks like the following:

```
instance XListable () where
  xempty = XListUnit 0

  xcons () (XListUnit n) = XListUnit (n + 1)

  xheadMay (XListUnit 0) = Nothing
  xheadMay _ = Just ()
```

Storing Bool values is a little bit harder, as shown next:

```
instance XListable Bool where
  xempty = XBits 0 0

  xcons b (XBits bits n) = XBits (bits * 2 + if b then 1 else 0) (n + 1)

  xheadMay (XBits bits n)
    | n <= 0 = Nothing
    | otherwise = Just (bits `mod` 2 /= 0)
```

Now we can define functions that work with different list implementations without knowing which one is actually chosen. For example, the following function creates an empty list, adds the given element to the beginning, takes the first element back, and checks whether it is the same as what was given:

```
testXList :: (Eq a, XListable a) => a -> Bool
testXList a = xheadMay (xcons a xempty) == Just a
```

Running this function with differently typed arguments works as expected, as shown here:

```
ghci> testXList ()
True
ghci> testXList True
True
ghci> testXList False
True
```

Data families serve as regular data types while providing different run-time representations, depending on the type parameters. We can always come up with the new representation for our own brand-new data type and immediately receive every piece of functionality available for the data family.

Injectivity as a property of type families

Note the following property of data families: a resulting data constructor determines a type index in the left-hand side of the data family instance declaration in a unique way. Any two different data constructors correspond to different indices. In mathematics, this property is called *injectivity*. Also note, type synonym families in general do not have this property: several instances may easily share the same resulting type.

GHC provides the `TypeFamilyDependencies` extension, which allows adding injectivity annotations to type synonym families. It was partly motivated by the `vector` library, which provides the `Mutable` type family. The goal of this type family is to compute a mutable counterpart to immutable vectors, as shown next:

```
type family Mutable v = mv | mv -> v
```

The actual definition is a little bit harder because it uses kind signatures (vectors depend on a type of an element), but they are irrelevant here. The main point is that a resulting type determines an argument in a unique way. This dependency is specified by the `| mv -> v` component of the definition: once you know `mv`, you know an exact `v` also. This simplifies type inference and eliminates some uses of the `Proxy` data type, whose only goal is to deliver additional information about types.

11.3.4 *Associated families*

Historically, type families were first introduced into GHC/Haskell as type components of type class definitions. They were associated with type classes. The motivating example was separating a graph interface from an internal representation. Let's look at an example.

EXAMPLE: UNIFIED INTERFACE FOR GRAPHS WITH DIFFERENT REPRESENTATIONS

    🗋   ch11/type-families/Graphs.hs

    ⚡   *type-families*

    ☞   Associated families work well with type classes.

A graph is a mathematical object. It consists of vertices and the edges between them. Suppose edges are directed so that every edge has a source and a target, which are vertices. A vertex may have incoming and outgoing edges. There are many possible graph representations, for example, adjacency matrices, incidence matrices, or lists of edges. All these representations are expected to support a common interface.

Our first goal is to provide an interface for a graph without fixing any details about representation. That means that we should provide functions that don't use specific types, which is where type families shine. The following code demonstrates a fragment of such an interface:

g is a type variable for a graph representation.

Associated type family: the type of vertices depends on the type of the graph.

Associated data family: the data type for edges will get data constructors in instances.

```
class Graph g where
    type Vertex g
    data Edge g
    src, tgt :: Edge g -> Vertex g
    outEdges :: g -> Vertex g -> [Edge g]
    -- other methods
```

Source and target of the given edge: types depend on a graph representation.

List of outgoing edges

A real graph interface could have dozens of methods. Even now, in this limited form, we can define functions that are able to work with any representation. For example, the following function computes a list of neighboring vertices to the given one. It maps over outgoing edges and collects their targets.

```
neighbors :: Graph g => g -> Vertex g -> [Vertex g]
neighbors g v = map tgt (outEdges g v)
```

The `isLoop` function from the following code snippet checks whether the given edge is a loop (its source and target are the same vertices):

```
isLoop :: (Graph g, Eq (Vertex g)) => g -> Edge g -> Bool
isLoop g e = src e == tgt e
```

Note that we can easily add constraints, such as `Eq (Vertex g)`, although we have no information about an actual `g` graph representation. This function will work with all the representations given that their vertex type implements an `Eq` instance.

Implementing `Graph` instances is outside the scope of the book, so I limit myself to the type families' parts of them. In the first instance, shown next, a graph is a list of edges, every edge is a pair of vertices, and a vertex is an `Int` number:

```
newtype EdgesList = EdgesList [Edge EdgesList]
```
◁—— **Edge representation is not known yet.**

```
instance Graph EdgesList where
    type Vertex EdgesList = Int
    data Edge EdgesList = MkEdge1 (Vertex EdgesList) (Vertex EdgesList)
    src = undefined
    tgt = undefined
    outEdges = undefined
```

Vertices are represented with Int values.

Edge representation is a pair of vertices.

We can now create a graph using the following representation:

```
g1 :: EdgesList
g1 = EdgesList [MkEdge1 0 1, MkEdge1 1 0]
```

The second representation could be a map from a vertex to a list of vertices adjacent to it, as follows:

```
import Data.Map (Map)
import qualified Data.Map as Map (fromList)

newtype VertexMap = VertexMap (Map (Vertex VertexMap) [Vertex VertexMap])

instance Graph VertexMap where
  type Vertex VertexMap = String
  data Edge VertexMap = MkEdge2 Int (Vertex VertexMap) (Vertex VertexMap)
  src = undefined
  tgt = undefined
  outEdges = undefined

g2 :: VertexMap
g2 = VertexMap (Map.fromList [("A", ["B"]), ("B", ["A"])])
```

In this representation, vertices are given as String values. Every edge has a multiplicity count in addition to a pair of vertices. Both g1 and g2 graph values represent the same graph, demonstrated in figure 11.3.

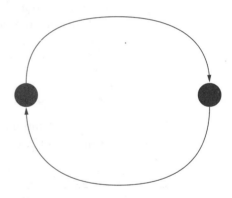

Associated type and data families are very good at the task of separating an interface from an internal representation. Remember, we almost always need to write type classes and instances when using any type families, associated or not. This is why it's a good idea to try associated families in the first place. Moreover, compiler error messages could be more infor-

Figure 11.3   Simple graph with two vertices and two edges between them

mative in the case of associated families because there is always additional information about a type class.

11.4   *Generalized algebraic data types*

Our next topic, generalized algebraic data types, is a Haskell feature that may be seen as a closed data family, although it originated in Haskell as an extension of regular algebraic data types. It subsumes several other type-level techniques that were used before it was introduced. Let's discuss one small example here to get a first glimpse.

We'll start with regular algebraic data types. The following Dyn algebraic data type allows storing string, char, or Boolean values as one variable:

```
data Dyn = S String | C Char | B Bool
```

We can easily put several such values in a list [Dyn] and print them all. Unfortunately, with this approach, we are losing control over those values at the type level. They are indistinguishable: we can't express a type of S components exclusively or write a function returning String, Char, or Bool, depending on the content.

The Haskell type system has a feature that allows this sort of type-level control, namely, generalized algebraic data types, or GADTs for short. It's crucial to understand what exactly is *generalized*. In Dyn, we can think of the S, C, B data constructors as functions as shown here:

```
S :: String -> Dyn
C :: Char -> Dyn
B :: Bool -> Dyn
```

The types here demonstrate that we lose type information. We have only Dyn afterward.

Now, what about parameterized data types? Don't they keep that information about the type? The convenient Maybe a algebraic data type has two data constructors, Just and Nothing, with the following types:

```
Just :: a -> Maybe a
Nothing :: Maybe a
```

Though we keep a in the type of a result, we are not allowed to restrict it. It's always Maybe a. Consequently, if we have a value of Maybe a without any constraints on a, there is not much we can do with it. Basically, we can just pass it around, and that's all. Generalized algebraic data types lift these limitations by allowing data constructors to return a data type parameterized by the specific types.

11.4.1 Example: Representing dynamically typed values with GADTs

Let's apply GADTs to the problem of representing dynamically typed values.

EXAMPLE: REPRESENTING DYNAMICALLY TYPED VALUES WITH GADTS

📄 ch11/dynvalues-gadt.hs

⚡ *dynvalues-gadt*

☞ GADTs allow keeping and using information about types after constructing a value.

For example, in the following code, we define a GADT for dynamic values, keeping track of their original types:

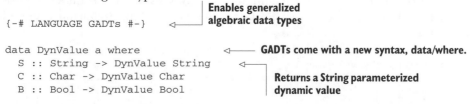

```
{-# LANGUAGE GADTs #-}          ◁──── Enables generalized
                                      algebraic data types

data DynValue a where           ◁───── GADTs come with a new syntax, data/where.
  S :: String -> DynValue String  ◁─
  C :: Char -> DynValue Char
  B :: Bool -> DynValue Bool            Returns a String parameterized
                                        dynamic value
```

With a GADT like this, we can easily and safely get back to a value of the original type as follows:

```
getValue :: DynValue a -> a
getValue (B b) = b
getValue (C c) = c
getValue (S s) = s
```

Note that different equations of the function definition return different types depending on the constructor, as shown next:

```
ghci> getValue (B True)
True
ghci> getValue (S "hello")
"hello"
```

It's also easy to print a dynamic value as follows:

```
printValue :: DynValue a -> IO ()          b has type Bool, and GHC knows how to print Bool.
printValue (B b) = print b     ←──────┐
printValue (C c) = print c        ←────┘   c is of type Char, which can be printed.
printValue (S s) = print s          ←────── s is a String, which can be printed also.
```

In functions like this one, GHC figures out what can be done with a value based on its type. It can find all the corresponding instances, which is the usual blessing of a type system.

We can print all the elements in a `[DynValue String]` list as follows:

```
ghci> mapM_ printValue [S "hello", S "bye"]
"hello"
"bye"
```

Now I feel you want to ask me about a list with differently typed dynamic values like `[S "hello", B True]`. The answer is no, we can't do that. What type is it expected to have? `[DynValue a]`? Well, we already know that it is a shortcut for `forall a. [DynValue a]`. Is there such an a type that would allow its value being either `String` or `Bool`? In Haskell, clearly, no.

Moreover, is it possible to write a function of the `a -> DynValue a` type? In fact, we cannot provide `DynValue a` *for all types*. We are limited to `DynValue String`, `DynValue Char`, and `DynValue Bool`. It's not a bug; it's a feature. We wanted exactly that: we wished to be limited by those types and have additional control over them as a result.

Fortunately, we have a technique that gives us a workaround, and it also uses GADTs. We can hide a type inside a value by using the following wrapping of the GADT:

```
data WrappedDynValue where
  Wrap :: DynValue a -> WrappedDynValue
```

Note that there is no parameter in the `WrappedDynValue` type. It has the `Type` kind. The value inside it has one. The a type variable used in the `Wrap` constructor is traditionally called *existential*: it exists somewhere inside a value. Haskell supports special syntax for existential types like this one, but it is now subsumed by GADTs.

Rewriting existential types with GADTs

You may remember from chapter 7 that we've already seen existential types in the definition of the following `SomeException` data type:

```
data SomeException = forall e . Exception e => SomeException e
```

We could easily rewrite it with a GADT as follows:

```
data SomeException where
  SomeException :: Exception e => e -> SomeException
```

The meaning is the same as before.

The `WrappedDynValue` GADT can now be used to create a dynamic value, say, from the given `String`, as shown next:

```
fromString :: String -> WrappedDynValue      We can't return Dynamic a for all a,
fromString str                                so we wrap it as an existential.
  | str `elem` ["y", "yes", "true"] = Wrap (B True)
  | str `elem` ["n", "no", "false"] = Wrap (B False)     Here we construct and
  | length str == 1 = Wrap (C $ head str)               wrap Dynamic Bool.
  | otherwise = Wrap (S str)
                                                Dynamic Char can be constructed
  The default result—a wrapped DynValue String   from a one-element String.
```

To do something with the wrapped value, we should unwrap it first. Let's, for example, print a wrapped dynamic value, as shown next:

```
printWDValue :: WrappedDynValue -> IO ()      Unwrapping gives us DynValue a,
printWDValue (Wrap dv) = printValue dv        which can then be printed.
```

In the following GHCi session, we create dynamic values from strings, wrap them, and print them:

```
ghci> printWDValue (fromString "y")
True
ghci> printWDValue (fromString "hello")
"hello"
```

Finally, let's process a list of `Strings`, turn every value to wrapped dynamic values, and then print them:

```
ghci> mapM_ (printWDValue . fromString) ["y", "no", "xxx", "c"]
True
False
"xxx"
'c'
```

This was a very basic example of GADTs, but it demonstrates the following main points regarding them:

- We get additional control by keeping specific types as parameters to a GADT type constructor.
- We can always get back to the original types and do whatever they support.
- We can use existential typing techniques to build GADTs from other types and pass those wrapped types around until we need the power of original types.

11.4.2 *Example: Representing arithmetic expressions with GADTs*

Any application operates over some domain: we introduce objects, subjects, processes, and analyses from the domain and represent them as code entities (data structures and functions). Domain entities usually have many restrictions, and we normally want to express them in the programming language. Depending on the power of the language, we can express some of them as types (and then get more control from the compiler) or invent our own ways to keep an eye on them (such as testing).

We'll get back to a domain we've already discussed earlier in this book, namely, arithmetic expressions, and see how to employ the Haskell type system to work with them.

EXAMPLE: REPRESENTING ARITHMETIC EXPRESSIONS WITH GADTS

🗋 expr/gadts/

⚡ *expr-gadt*

☞ GADTs add type control to arithmetic expressions.

We have the following data type representing arithmetic expressions with algebraic data types:

```
data Expr a = Lit a | Add (Expr a) (Expr a) | Mult (Expr a) (Expr a)
```

This representation supports an easy way to evaluate an expression to a number, as shown here:

```
myeval :: Num a => Expr a -> a
myeval (Lit e) = e
myeval (Add e1 e2) = myeval e1 + myeval e2
myeval (Mult e1 e2) = myeval e1 * myeval e2
```

How would we extend this `Expr` a type to Boolean expressions? They are not numbers, so we cannot simply use the a type variable for `Bool` because then we'd have to deal with additions and multiplications of Booleans. Moreover, we'd like to have conditional expressions once we have Booleans. What about some bridge between numbers and Booleans such as is-zero checks?

Remember that every data constructor for the `Expr` a algebraic data type returns `Expr` a. We can make this fact visible by enabling the `GADTSyntax` GHC extension as follows:

```
{-# LANGUAGE GADTSyntax #-}

data Expr a where
  Lit :: a -> Expr a
  Add :: Expr a -> Expr a -> Expr a
  Mult :: Expr a -> Expr a -> Expr a
```

Despite the syntax, this definition has absolutely the same meaning as the previous one. Enabling the `GADT` GHC extension gives us the ability to specify types on a per-constructor basis and add new constructors we need as follows:

```
{-# LANGUAGE GADTs #-}

data Expr a where
  NumLit :: Num a => a -> Expr a        <——|  Changed
  BoolLit :: Bool -> Expr Bool              <——— New
  Add :: Num a => Expr a -> Expr a -> Expr a
  Mult :: Num a => Expr a -> Expr a -> Expr a
  IsZero :: (Num a, Eq a) => Expr a -> Expr Bool   <——— New
  If :: Expr Bool -> Expr a -> Expr a -> Expr a   <——|
                                                      |  New
```

Evaluation is still an easy walk, as shown here:

```
myeval :: Expr a -> a
myeval (NumLit e) = e
myeval (BoolLit b) = b
myeval (Add e1 e2) = myeval e1 + myeval e2
myeval (Mult e1 e2) = myeval e1 * myeval e2
myeval (IsZero e) = myeval e == 0
myeval (If be e1 e2) = myeval (if myeval be then e1 else e2)
```

GADT constructors bring their own constraints to the corresponding lines. That's why we can do addition or comparison whenever needed. Let's look at an example:

```
expr1 = Add (NumLit 5) (NumLit (-5))
expr2 = If (IsZero expr1) (NumLit 0.5) (NumLit 1)
```

We can ask GHC to check the type of the second expression and evaluate it as follows:

```
ghci> :type expr2
expr2 :: Expr Double
ghci> myeval expr2
0.5
```

Any attempt to construct a wrong expression fails with a type error as follows:

```
ghci> :type IsZero (BoolLit True)

<interactive>:1:1: error:
    • No instance for (Num Bool) arising from a use of 'IsZero'
    • In the expression: IsZero (BoolLit True)
```

So we've got type checking for our domain for free. Well, not that free. Now it's much harder to construct these extended expressions programmatically (as we did in chapter 5 while implementing the shunting-yard algorithm). First, it's impossible to define a `String -> Expr a` function, because with this type, we should provide the result of any type (remember, we have an implicit `forall a` in the type). Despite that, depending on the given `String`, it can be either `Bool` or some numeric type. We already know how to deal with that. We define an existential wrapper, such as the following:

```
data SomeExpr where
  Some :: Expr a -> SomeExpr
```

Then we should think of defining a `String -> SomeExpr` function.

Second, the problem is hard, even with an existential wrapper. In that algorithm, we were building an expression from the smaller subexpressions. Suppose we have two `SomeExpr` values, which should become arguments to `Add`. Do you see the problem? How should we make sure that the types inside those subexpressions are the same? We need some sort of type equality to reason about that. We'll get back to the corresponding techniques later in this book.

11.5   *Arbitrary-rank polymorphism*

Searching over the internet for an arbitrary-rank polymorphism in Haskell or the `RankNTypes` GHC extension, we find thousands of explanations and plenty of theoretical examples we never encounter in industry. Yes, I did that, too. In this short section, I try to present this topic differently. First, I define the meaning of an arbitrary-rank polymorphism from the Haskell type system's point of view. Second, I describe the most popular use cases in Haskell libraries.

11.5.1 *The meaning*

Let's think about what it means for a function in Haskell to be polymorphic. Suppose we have a function like this one:

```
len :: [a] -> Int
```

There is an implicit `forall a` in the beginning, so the full type is `forall a.[a] -> Int`. Polymorphism here means that we are allowed to use the `len` function with any list, no matter the type of element. This sort of polymorphism is also called parametric polymorphism. There is another type of polymorphism, ad hoc polymorphism, which is expressed in Haskell with type classes as follows:

```
inc :: Num a => a -> a
```

The `inc` function can be used with any type that has an instance of the `Num` type class. To allow using `inc` with a type, we have to implement `Num` for it. This is why it is called *ad hoc*, which is literally translated as *to this* in English. We add support for this particular type when needed.

Suppose now we want to write a function that processes a list of `Int`: we want to apply a given function to every `Int`. We can implement it as follows:

```
processInts :: (Int -> Int) -> [Int] -> [Int]
processInts f xs = map f xs
```

Thanks to the Haskell type system, we are allowed to use it with `inc`—`processInts inc [1,2,3]` gives us the result we expect. In addition to all the functions of the `Num a => a -> a` type, we can also use `processInts` with the `Integral a => a -> a` functions and naturally with the `Int -> Int` functions. Is this a good thing? Well, not necessarily. As we know, a type system is a tool to express our ideas as well as to limit us. How do you say in Haskell, "I want to use the `processInts` function with every function of the `Num a => a -> a` type, no less, no more?"

One solution is to change the type as follows:

```
processInts :: Num a => (a -> a) -> [a] -> [a]
```

But that's not what we want—we do want to process lists of `Int`! We may wish to use some specific `Int` value inside, for example.

What about the following?

```
processInts :: Num a => (a -> a) -> [Int] -> [Int]
```

Unfortunately this gives a type error: we could use this function with any function of the `a -> a` type for any `Num a` type, for example, with a `Double -> Double` function. This naturally abuses the type system. So Haskell prevents this by disallowing such a behavior.

This situation is precisely where we need arbitrary rank polymorphism. It is enabled by the `RankNTypes` GHC extension and allows us to write the following type signature:

```
processInts :: (forall a. Num a => a -> a) -> [Int] -> [Int]
```

The only functional argument to `processInts` allowed now is any function that uses `Num a` exclusively. Technically, this function uses rank-2 polymorphism: we count polymorphic declarations in function arguments to the left of ->. If some function takes a rank-2 polymorphic function as an argument, then it's counted as rank-3 polymorphic, and so on.

Compare the following four types:

```
                                              Rank 0, nonpolymorphic function
(Int->Int) -> [Int] -> [Int]        <———┘
forall a. Num a => a -> a -> [Int] -> [Int]   <———┘  Rank 1
(forall a. Num a => a -> a) -> [Int] -> [Int]   <——— Rank 2
((forall a.Num a => a -> Int) -> Int) -> [Int] -> [Int]   <——— Rank 3
```

We don't have to use `forall` with type classes. It's okay to be parametrically polymorphic also, as shown next:

```
someFunc :: (forall a. a -> a) -> Int -> Int
```

It's hard to come up with meaningful arguments for such a function except for the identity function. In addition, we can play with `undefined` or exceptions.

Note that the `RankNTypes` GHC extension makes type inference impossible in general. So, when used, it requires top-level type signatures almost all the time. This is not a problem, because it is a good idea to write type signatures for all the top-level function definitions anyway.

11.5.2 Use cases

If we look at the packages on Hackage, we see three main use cases for arbitrary-rank polymorphism. First, it is used to abstract an interface in a controlled way, as we discussed in the previous subsection. Second, it is used to structure computation steps and embed steps from other computations. The `mask` function from the GHC runtime exceptions API is the most used example of this behavior. Third, it's used to create type-controlled separate computations as in the `ST` monad. Let's discuss these use cases one by one.

ABSTRACTING INTERFACES

It seems that abstracting function arguments is the most popular way to use the `RankNTypes` GHC extension in Haskell libraries.

> **EXAMPLE: ABSTRACTING INTERFACES FOR NUMERIC COMPUTATIONS**
>
> 🗋   ch11/nummod-rank-n/
>
> ⚡   *nummod-rank-n*
>
> ☞   We use `RankNTypes` to limit ways to implement an interface.

We may often see the library author giving us something like the following:

```
newtype NumModifier = NumModifier {
    run :: forall a. Num a => a -> a
  }
```

To write the following `NumModifier` declaration, you need the `RankNTypes` extension. The user doesn't need it.

```
processInts :: NumModifier -> [Int] -> [Int]
processInts nm xs = map (run nm) xs

ghci> processInts (NumModifier (+1)) [1,2,3]
[2,3,4]
```

Even without declaring a `newtype`, the following type pattern is used very often:

```
(forall a. SomeClass a => <function over a>) -> <other arguments and result>
```

It is often the case that the other arguments implement `SomeClass` a, thus allowing us to apply a rank-2 polymorphic argument to them. As a result, we are limited to functions that work for every `SomeClass` a value.

MASKING EXCEPTIONS

The second use case comes from the `Control.Exception` module, the following `mask` function:

```
mask :: ((forall a. IO a -> IO a) -> IO b) -> IO b
```

We'll discuss this function in great detail in chapter 16, so I'll limit myself here by explaining its type. We can see a couple of interesting features in it. First, it's a rank-3 polymorphic function, because its first argument `(forall a. IO a -> IO a) -> IO b` is rank-2 polymorphic. Second, no type-level connection exists between types a and b because there is no common type class. So, this differs from the previous use case.

Let's read the function type from the inside out as follows:

1 We have an `IO` computation, `forall a. IO a -> IO a`—let's call it an *inner computation.*

2 There is also an *outer computation*, `(forall a. IO a -> IO a) -> IO b`, which is able to run the inner computation inside it.

3 We have the `mask` function, which returns a result of an outer computation.

The type of the outer computation allows applying the inner computation to any particular type, just as we applied polymorphic functions to `Int` recently. So we have the following scenario of using the `mask` function:

1 We implement an outer computation, which does the following:
   – Creates (or acquires somehow) some value of any type it needs in the `IO` monad
   – Applies a given inner computation to that value (or any `IO` computation over it)
   – Produces some final result of type b

2 The `mask` function executes that outer computation by *providing* it some particular inner computation.

What could that inner computation supplied by mask do? Well, it could execute a given IO action in some specially crafted context, which differs from the context of the other parts in the outer computation.

Note that all this reasoning is done based on the type of the mask function exclusively. We don't refer to the exceptions API. In fact, the mask function is used to implement the so-called resource-acquisition-release pattern, which is an industry-standard resource-processing practice. This pattern describes the following three stages:

- Resource acquisition
- Resource processing
- Resource release

The mask function allows running these stages in a concurrent setting with different strategies, whether or not the exceptions from other threads (so-called asynchronous exceptions) could be raised during the current stage. Normally, resource acquisition and release run with the exception-raising threads blocked, whereas an inner computation with whatever is inside it (resource processing) may be interrupted due to an exception from some other thread.

By having the rank-3 polymorphic type, the mask function implements this logic without knowing any details of an outer computation. It is usually used as follows:

```
mask $ \ restore -> do      ◁——— The restore argument is supplied by the mask itself.
  x <- acquire
  restore (someComputation x) `onException` release
  release
```

This implementation guarantees that the resource will be released, no matter what. The restore function, provided by the mask implementation, switches the exception-raising strategy to the opposite of what was used before the mask function was called.

The exceptions package provides a monadically abstracted version of mask as a method of the MonadMask type class as follows:

```
mask :: MonadMask m => ((forall a. m a -> m a) -> m b) -> m b
```

This interface is basically the same except for using m instead of IO. We'll get back to the mask function in chapter 16.

STATEFUL COMPUTATIONS IN THE ST MONAD

And the last use case combines rank-2 polymorphism with phantom types. We've already discussed the ST monad in chapter 5. Let's get back to it and explain what was going on there in terms of the type system. The Control.Monad.ST module provides the following runST function to run a computation:

```
runST :: (forall s. ST s a) -> a
```

This is a perfect example of rank-2 polymorphism. The type of every computation in the ST monad mentions this s type variable without instantiating it (giving it some particular type value). Other ST-related types, such as STRef mutable references, have this s, too. If we have an ST computation, then we can run it with runST and get a result.

Suppose we've decided to return from an ST computation not a regular result but an ST reference instead as follows: runST (newSTRef 0).

Figure 11.4 illustrates the types of the corresponding computation and its components. We can see that returning a reference would result in violating the scope of the s type variable, so it's prohibited by the type system. Consequently, s cannot escape an ST computation. The different computations always stay strongly separate from each other.

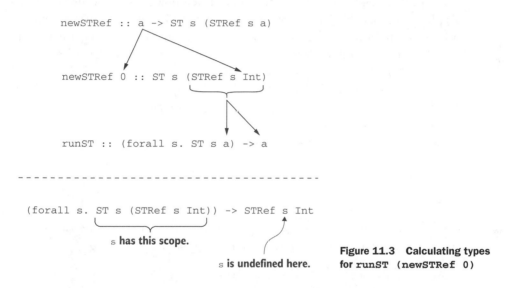

```
newSTRef :: a -> ST s (STRef s a)


newSTRef 0 :: ST s (STRef s Int)



runST :: (forall s. ST s a) -> a


- - - - - - - - - - - - - - - - - - - - - - - - - - - - - - - - - - -

(forall s. ST s (STRef s Int)) -> STRef s Int
```

s has this scope.

s is undefined here.

Figure 11.3 Calculating types for runST (newSTRef 0)

Why is this a feature? Well, this gives us a way to introduce stateful computations into a realm of pure functions in a controlled manner. We may want this to deal with performance issues without compromising purity. Escaping references from an ST computation could lead to mutating values between their uses in an unexpected way.

11.6 Advice on dealing with type errors

Programming with types is always fun, but it often involves a lot of pain. Unfortunately, the compiler is not always able to give us clear error messages if something goes wrong with types. In the last section of this chapter, we'll talk about several ways to make type-level programming in Haskell less painful.

11.6.1 Be explicit about types

The first piece of advice is to be explicit about types in our code. This should be a very strict rule for top-level declarations. We need this explicitness not only for documentation purposes but also to guide type inference. The compiler has to check whether the inferred type is the same as specified by the user. Although type inference algorithms in Haskell are powerful, sometimes it's not enough, particulary in the presence of type families.

GHC supports local type signatures, as shown next. Feel free to use both in GHCi and in code.

```
ghci> a = (read "37" :: Integer) + 5
ghci> :type a
a :: Integer
ghci> a
42
```

This could be helpful with numeric literals if we know precisely which type we need at this place. It is also helpful everywhere inside complex expressions. We may be wrong about something we have in a very long expression: adding a local type signature is like asking the compiler whether or not it agrees. These type signatures are free to us at run time. In fact, they can make our program even faster, if types inferred by the compiler are too general. If we need Int, it's okay to say that explicitly and help the compiler avoid introducing unnecessary polymorphism.

Local type signatures can't be written in all cases, however. Suppose, for example, that we are implementing a function similar to map as follows:

```
mymap :: (a -> b) -> [a] -> [b]
mymap _ [] = []
mymap f (x:xs) = f x : mymap f xs
```

Is it possible to add a local type signature to f x in the last line of the definition? Unfortunately, no. We want to write something like the following:

```
mymap f (x:xs) = (f x :: b) : mymap f xs
```

This code would lead to a strange type error saying that b is not the same as b1. This is because we refer to another b, not the b from the type signature. The ScopedType-Variables GHC extension allows referring to the b type variable from the main type signature, as shown in the following example:

```
{-# LANGUAGE ScopedTypeVariables #-}  ⊲——— Enables the extension

mymap :: forall a b. (a -> b) -> [a] -> [b]  ⊲——— Introduces the type variables explicitly
mymap _ [] = []
mymap f (x:xs) = (f x :: b)   ⊲┐
    : mymap f xs               │ Refers to a type variable introduced
                               │ in the top-level type signature
```

The ScopedTypeVariables GHC extension is mighty when we deal with type errors in our functions. When writing instances, the InstanceSigs GHC extension is another friend: it allows us to write a specific type signature for a type class method implementation. I've used it several times in this book. It helps us to understand what should be done in the code while we write it.

11.6.2 Ask the compiler

The compiler can give us a lot of additional information regarding types if we ask. For example, we've looked at explicit `forall`s in type signatures several times in this chapter, as shown next:

```
ghci> :set -XNoStarIsType
ghci> :set -fprint-explicit-foralls
ghci> :type map
map :: forall {a} {b}. (a -> b) -> [a] -> [b]
ghci> :type length
length :: forall {t :: Type -> Type} {a}. Foldable t => t a -> Int
```

The same flag can be given to the GHC compiler itself. As a result, GHC uses it to give more information in type error messages. In fact, GHC has many `-fprint-*` flags that print additional information hidden by default. They are listed in the section on compiler verbosity options in the GHC User's Guide.

Moreover, we can ask GHC to tell us the type of a variable if we are lost in types. Let's get back to our `map` implementation, shown here:

```
mymap :: (a -> b) -> [a] -> [b]
mymap _ [] = []
mymap f (x:xs) = _ : mymap f xs
```

The underscore in the last line is a typed hole. If GHC finds a hole in an expression, it reports its type as follows:

```
• Found hole: _ :: b
      Where: 'b' is a rigid type variable bound by
            the type signature for:
              mymap :: forall a b. (a -> b) -> [a] -> [b]
    ...
```

If we replace the underscore with `(f _)`, then the compiler says that we have a hole of type `a`. It's also possible to use named holes, that is, any name beginning with an underscore. GHC reports all the holes it finds and provides their names and types. It can also offer suggestions of what could potentially be valid hole fits. The section on typed holes in the GHC User's Guide provides all the details on this.

By using typed holes, we are moving toward type-driven development: we write types first and then see which values could be used to satisfy them. GHC could be of great help in this process.

Typed holes are used for expressions. To have somewhat close behavior in types, we can use the `PartialTypeSignatures` GHC extension. Holes in types are traditionally called wildcards. We denote them by underscores and can give them names (when the `NamedWildCards` GHC extension is enabled). One difference is that GHC can sometimes infer types for wildcards and compile the program anyway. This extension is often used together with `ScopedTypeVariables` to solve hard puzzles with types in our code.

11.6.3 *Saying more about errors*

One more thing: if we develop a type-level interface for our library, then we should strive to help users working with it. The `GHC.TypeLits` module provides a tool for defining custom compile-time type errors, which consists of the following two components:

- The `TypeError` type family, which can be used by a library developer to generate a type error
- The `ErrorMessage` data type, to construct a specific error message

You could use these custom compile-time errors in several contexts, for example:

- To prohibit some of the arguments to the type family by returning `TypeError`
- To react on an attempt to use some prohibited instance

The documentation for the `GHC.TypeLits` module mentions the corresponding examples.

Summary

- It is crucial to understand the main Haskell components of type-level programming: terms, types, and kinds.
- Data constructors can be promoted to types and type constructors to kinds by the `DataKinds` GHC extension.
- Use type families to describe generic interfaces to libraries and hide an implementation behind type class instances.
- Use generalized algebraic data types (GADTs) to control values of different types under one GADT umbrella.
- Learn the main ways to use higher-ranked polymorphism in industrial Haskell.
- Help the compiler by providing explicit type signatures.
- Ask the compiler for help with types.

Metaprogramming
in Haskell

This chapter covers

- Haskell features to support deriving type class instances automatically
- Exploiting a generic representation for any data type to write data-type-generic code
- Generating code at compile time with Template Haskell

When we write code in Haskell, we call it programming. When we write code that generates or processes other code on our behalf, we call it *metaprogramming*, or *generative programming*. With metaprogramming techniques, we usually automate repetitive boilerplate code, which is too dull to write manually. This leads to boosting developer productivity. Sometimes, there is a price to pay—such code can be quite hard to write and maintain.

In Haskell, we have the full spectrum of metaprogramming features, ranging from those that are almost free for developers to some quite demanding of their skills. In this chapter, we'll discuss three such features. We'll start with the mechanisms to derive instances automatically. No Haskell program today avoids instance derivation, and GHC does its best to generate appropriate implementations. We have several ways to derive instances, and we have to discuss all of them to know which one should be used in a particular situation. Then we'll turn to data-type-generic programming. This technique allows us to treat any data type and its value as a data structure of some other specific data type, called a *generic representation*. This lets us write code with respect to the generic representation, not the original data type itself. Thus, this generic code can be applied to many different data types that have nothing in common. Finally, we'll explore Template Haskell, the full-blown compile-time metaprogramming tool, which allows us to write code that is executed at compile time and generates other code that is then compiled as usual.

The two latter techniques are essential to implement certain complex and performant libraries, and we've already used some of them. For example, the `cassava` library uses data-type-generic programming to generate instances for reading user-defined data types from CSV files. We've used it for the `stockquotes` project. Whenever a library needs some supporting code on the client's side, it provides Template Haskell functions to generate it. We'll see several such examples in the rest of this book.

12.1 Deriving instances

We've already derived dozens of instances in this book. This feature has existed in Haskell since almost the very beginning. Shortly after introducing type classes in the 1990s, it became clear that implementing instances manually was extremely ineffective. Writing the same code again and again isn't very appealing (at least to Haskellers). Originally, we could derive instances for a small list of type classes supported by the compiler (such as `Eq`, `Ord`, and `Show`). The corresponding algorithms were built into the compiler, and there were no ways to extend them.

In this section, we'll explore modern GHC features that support instance derivation. We now have many more possibilities than ever before.

12.1.1 Basic deriving strategies

It's crucial to understand the following essential principles about instance derivation:

- Deriving an instance means generating an implementation for methods of type classes by the compiler.
- GHC supports several strategies to generate code. Since GHC 8.2, we can choose which strategy we want to use.
- Generated code is type-checked and compiled. Thus, it's undesirable to generate incorrect code, because users would face an error in code they didn't write and may not be aware of.

Remember that we use the `deriving` clause on `data` (or `newtype`) declarations to ask a compiler to derive instances. We can also use standalone deriving via the `Standalone-Deriving` GHC extension. The ideas we'll discuss next don't depend on the actual way you run deriving algorithms, so I assume that we always use the `deriving` clause.

EXPLORING DERIVED CODE

If something goes wrong, we can look at the code that was generated for us. GHC supports the `-ddump-deriv` flag to dump all the generated instances.

EXAMPLE: EXPLORING DERIVED CODE

   📄 ch12/deriv/basic-deriv.hs

   ⚡ *basic-deriv*

   ☞ We can explore the generated code.

Let's explore instances generated for the following trivial piece of code:

```
type Name = String
type Age = Int
data Student = Student Name Age
  deriving Eq
```

We ask GHC to generate the `Eq` instance. If we run it with the `-ddump-deriv` flag, we see the following `Eq` instance:

```
instance GHC.Classes.Eq Main.Student where
    (GHC.Classes.==)
      (Main.Student a1_a2j7 a2_a2j8)
      (Main.Student b1_a2j9 b2_a2ja)
    = (((a1_a2j7 GHC.Classes.== b1_a2j9))
          GHC.Classes.&& ((a2_a2j8 GHC.Classes.== b2_a2ja)))
```

GHC uses the full qualification and randomly generated names in this instance. If we strip off all these things, we have the following trivial implementation in disguise:

```
instance Eq Student where
    (==) (Student a1 a2) (Student b1 b2) = (a1 == b1) && (a2 == b2)
```

Two values of the `Student` type are equal if their first fields are equal and their second fields are equal.

Remember, the `Eq` type class provides another `/=` operator for inequality. Where is it? Well, it has a default implementation. GHC reports it also, though not as a derived instance but as a filling in of the method body, as shown next:

```
==================== Filling in method body ====================
GHC.Classes.Eq [Main.Student]
  GHC.Classes./= = GHC.Classes.$dm/= @(Main.Student)
```

The `/=` method body refers to a default `$dm/=` method implementation. Note the visible type application in the previous code: `@(Main.Student)`. GHC explicitly instantiates the default implementation of the `Student` type.

Once we have this instance defined, we can use it as if we implemented it manually. Exploring generated instances may be useful if we want to find sources of inefficiency. It may be the case that a compiler doesn't know the best way to implement an instance. In such cases, we avoid instance derivation and implement it manually.

DERIVING STRATEGIES

GHC supports the following strategies to derive instances:

- `stock` strategy refers to specific type classes with deriving algorithms built into GHC.
- `anyclass` strategy allows us to derive empty instances. No methods are generated for them. This makes more sense if we have default implementations in type class definitions.
- `newtype` strategy supports generating instances for `newtype` declarations. The code for those instances is the same as the code for the underlying types.
- `via` strategy allows us to give an example of how the code should be generated. GHC then follows an example and generates code correspondingly. This strategy is the most recent one; it has been available since GHC 8.6.

These strategies are guarded by the corresponding GHC extensions. Nevertheless, it's easy to come up with a situation where more than one strategy is enabled and can be applied. Suppose we have a `newtype` declaration and a type class with a default implementation. If both `newtype` and `anyclass` strategies are enabled, a compiler has to decide between them. Although GHC has an algorithm to choose a strategy to be used by default, it's safer to avoid it. After all, we always know what should be done in a particular instance. Since GHC 8.2, we have the `DerivingStrategies` extension to specify a strategy explicitly. Let's do that in a simple example.

EXAMPLE: DERIVING STRATEGIES

☐   ch12/deriv/strategies.hs

⚡   *strategies*

☞   We have to specify a strategy, even for trivial data types.

Suppose we have the following `newtype` for representing ages:

```
newtype Age = Age {age :: Int}
```

We want to do a lot of things with it, including the following:

- Use it as a number (e.g., to supply numeric literals as values or compute age differences).
- Print it.
- Encode it to JSON.

Thus, we need instances of the `Num`, `Show`, and `ToJSON` type classes.

> **NOTE** The latter `ToJSON` type class comes from the `aeson` package. We've already used it in the `suntimes` example in chapter 7.

The `Show` type class is the stocked one: GHC knows how to generate its instances. The `Num` type class isn't stocked. The only way to derive it is to reuse the underlying `Int` type and an implementation for it (this is a `newtype` strategy). The `ToJSON` type class has a default implementation (suitable for the `anyclass` strategy) for any data type, which also has an instance of the `Generic` type class from the `GHC.Generics` module. The latter type class happens to be also stocked. It becomes available after enabling the `DeriveGeneric` GHC extension. Figure 12.1 summarizes all these requirements.

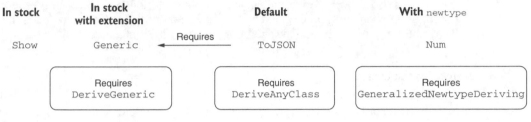

Figure 12.1 Required instances

Given all this, we are ready to derive them all. First, we need a whole bunch of GHC extensions:

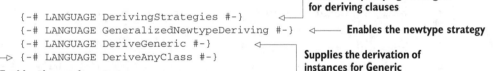

```
{-# LANGUAGE DerivingStrategies #-}          Allows for specifying strategies
{-# LANGUAGE GeneralizedNewtypeDeriving #-}  for deriving clauses
{-# LANGUAGE DeriveGeneric #-}               Enables the newtype strategy
{-# LANGUAGE DeriveAnyClass #-}
                                             Supplies the derivation of
Enables the anyclass strategy                instances for Generic
```

Second, we write several `deriving` clauses in the `newtype` declaration as follows:

```
newtype Age = Age {age :: Int}
  deriving stock (Show, Generic)
  deriving newtype (Num)
  deriving anyclass (ToJSON)
```

Running the following code demonstrates that everything works:

```
theAge :: Age          Uses Num for treating the 33
theAge = 33            numeric literal as an Age value

main :: IO ()
main = do              Uses Show for printing
  print theAge
  print $ encode theAge        Uses ToJSON for encoding
```

It also results in printing the following:

```
Age {age = 33}
"{\"age\":33}"
```

Problems with unspecified deriving strategies

Note that with all the extensions shown earlier enabled, the following code compiles, though with plenty of compiler warnings:

```
newtype Age = Age {age :: Int}
  deriving (Show, Generic, Num, ToJSON)
```

Moreover, it results in an exception at run time, as shown here:

```
Age {age = *** Exception: strategies.hs:10:28-30: No instance nor
    default method for class operation fromInteger
```

GHC has decided to go with the `anyclass` strategy for both `Num` and `ToJSON` instances, consequently arriving at a broken implementation of the `Num` methods. It's always better to use explicit deriving strategies and say what we actually need.

DERIVING STOCK CLASSES

GHC supports deriving the following seven type classes from scratch (all of them come from the Haskell 98 Report): `Eq`, `Ord`, `Enum`, `Ix`, `Bounded`, `Read`, and `Show`. The `Ix` type class defines a common interface for array indices. We've used the other classes many times in this book.

Besides them, current GHC versions derive the following instances with the corresponding extensions enabled:

- `Generic` and `Generic1` with `DeriveGeneric`. We'll get to these type classes in the next section.
- `Functor` with `DeriveFunctor`.
- `Foldable` and `Traversable` with `DeriveFoldable` and `DeriveTraversable`, respectively.
- `Typeable` and `Data` from the `Data.Typeable` and `Data.Data` modules with `DeriveDataTypeable`. These types provide one way to look at run-time representations of Haskell values and an additional approach to generic programming, different from what I present in this chapter. They are also used to introduce dynamic types to Haskell (see `Data.Dynamic` for details).
- `Lift` with `DeriveLift` to be used with the `template-haskell` package. More on that later in this chapter.

Algorithms that derive these instances are described in the GHC User's Guide. Let's now move to more advanced strategies: `newtype` and `via`. The `via` strategy may be seen as a generalization of the `newtype` strategy. Both of them allow us to derive non-trivial instances for classes unknown to a compiler. This creates a problem of type safety: how to guarantee type correctness for generated instances. Let's see how to solve it.

12.1.2 *The problem of type safety and generalized newtype deriving*

Introducing `newtype` declarations and deriving instances from the underlying representation is a traditional Haskell approach. In this section, we'll discuss why this is possible and which problems we could face when using this strategy to derive instances.

THE COERCIBLE CONSTRAINT AND THE COERCE FUNCTION

Let's get back to another version of the earlier `Age` and `Student` examples. We'll explore `newtype` declarations and discover more tools to work with them.

EXAMPLE: USING THE COERCE FUNCTION

📄 ch12/deriv/coerce.hs

⚡ *coerce*

☞ Writing code for newtypes can be often avoided.

Suppose we have the following `newtype` declaration and a function:

```
newtype Age = Age Int
  deriving (Show)

toAges :: [Int] -> [Age]
toAges = map Age
```

We want to turn a list of `Int` values into a list of ages. We know that due to the use of a `newtype` declaration, `Age` and `Int` share the same run-time representation. What about `[Age]` and `[Int]` or `Maybe Age` and `Maybe Int`? It'd be highly desirable for them to share the same representation also. This means that the `toAges` function should do literally nothing, and we should get the same list of `Int`s as a result. Is our compiler smart enough to optimize away the call to `map` in the implementation of `toAges`? Well, the power of the GHC optimizer has some limits. Fortunately, we can help the compiler and ourselves by avoiding writing `map` at all.

If we have types that share the same run-time representation, we can `coerce` between them. This functionality is provided by the `Data.Coerce` module from `base`. We've already met this function in chapter 9 when we discussed rewriting rules. Dealing with `newtype` declarations is another vital usage for it. Let's try to use the `coerce` function to reimplement `toAges` as follows:

```
import Data.Coerce

...

toAges' :: [Int] -> [Age]
toAges' = coerce
```

This code compiles successfully and works. No `map`, no explicit data constructors. Note that this code requires nothing besides importing the module and using `coerce`.

The coerce function has the following type:

```
coerce :: forall (k :: RuntimeRep) (a :: TYPE k) (b :: TYPE k).
          Coercible a b => a -> b
```

This is a highly polymorphic type; it works with all the run-time representations, boxed and unboxed, lifted and unlifted. Remember that Int and our Age both belong to the Type kind, which is defined as follows:

```
type Type = TYPE LiftedRep
```

The Coercible constraint is quite special. We are not allowed to define instances of Coercible manually. GHC infers them for us. When we write a newtype declaration, GHC infers the corresponding instance of Coercible. In our example, we have Coercible Age Int generated. Moreover, GHC lifts this instance to Coercible [Age] [Int] automatically. It is also able to use symmetry and get Coercible Int Age and Coercible [Int] [Age]. It's the latter instance that allows us to use coerce instead of implementing toAges with map.

All right, let's define the Student data type containing information about name and age and try to coerce on it as follows:

```
data Student ageType = Student String ageType

check :: Student Int -> Student Age
check = coerce
```

Note the ageType type variable in the data-type definition. We want to be flexible in storing ages. We have Coercible (Student Int) (Student Age) lifted from Coercible Int Age, so this compiles.

Let's make an age representation a little bit more complex. The age may be missing now, as shown next:

```
data Student1 ageType = Student1 String (Maybe ageType)

check1 :: Student1 Int -> Student1 Age
check1 = coerce
```

It still works with Coercible (Student1 Int) (Student1 Age). Is it possible to coerce everything to everything? Hopefully not. Let's continue our experiments on student representations as follows:

```
data Student2 m ageType = Student2 String (m ageType)

check2 :: Student2 Maybe Int -> Student2 Maybe Age
check2 = coerce
```

Now, this results in the following somewhat misleading error message:

```
• Couldn't match type 'Int' with 'Age'
      arising from a use of 'coerce'
```

So it was possible in all the examples before, but now GHC can't do that. What's the difference? It looks like GHC doesn't trust the m type variable. When it was Maybe in the type declaration, GHC was perfectly fine with it. Here is the point: what if m changes a representation somehow? Even though we have Maybe in the position of m in check2, GHC is still not happy about it.

Okay, let's replace this m with something more precise. How about the following identity type family?

```
type family Id t
type instance Id t = t
```

Types t and Id t are clearly identical, including their run-time representation. Let's use this type family in the following variation on the Student data type declaration:

```
data Student3 ageType = Student3 String (Id ageType)
```

Structurally, this declaration is the same as the one for Student1. Do we have Coercible (Student3 Int) (Student3 Age)? In other words, are we allowed to write the following function?

```
check3 :: Student3 Int -> Student3 Age
check3 = coerce
```

Well, GHC complains again:

```
• Couldn't match type 'Int' with 'Age'
      arising from a use of 'coerce'
```

So the answer is no. Even though the Id type family doesn't change the run-time representation, GHC still prohibits coerce.

Now the question is, how does GHC decide what is allowed and what is not? The answer is the roles system. Let's discuss it now.

ROLES FOR TYPE VARIABLES

The following are our variations on the Student data type declaration:

```
data Student  ageType = Student  String ageType
data Student1 ageType = Student1 String (Maybe ageType)
data Student2 m ageType = Student2 String (m ageType)
data Student3 ageType = Student3 String (Id ageType)
```

We try to use the `coerce` function to coerce between `Int` and `Age` as an `ageType` type variable. We can do that for `Student` and `Student1` but can't for `Student2` and `Student3`. What's the difference?

The difference is the *role* of the `ageType` type variable that is inferred by GHC. The three possible roles follow:

- The *phantom* role corresponds to phantom types that we've discussed in the previous chapter. Their values don't exist at run time, so they don't interfere with `coerce` at all.
- The *representational* role refers to type variables that are used to describe the run-time representation. We can coerce between types in positions with representational roles.
- The *nominal* role doesn't give us any information on the representation. These variables stand for their names, nothing else—that's why they are called nominal. For example, `key` in `Map key val` has a nominal role. We are not allowed to coerce between types in positions with nominal roles.

The `ageType` type variable has a representational role in the `Student` and `Student1` types. It has a nominal role in `Student2` and `Student3`. That's why we have the corresponding `Coercible` instances for the former examples and not for the latter. But how do we know the role of the type variable?

GHC infers these roles based on how a type variable is used. The `ageType` type variable is used to represent the second argument to the `Student` data constructor. Thus, its role is representational. The same rule applies to the `Maybe a` type: a here has a representational role—`ageType` in `Student1` stays representational because it is used in a representational position.

In `Student2`, we know nothing about `m`. It can potentially change the representation of `ageType` somehow; that's why `ageType` is considered nominal. Yet, `m` itself has a representational role.

Variables in type families and type classes are always considered with nominal roles. This explains why we can't coerce in `Student3`, even though the types have absolutely identical representations. This is just a limitation of the current role system—it can't handle this case.

We cannot persuade GHC to consider a type variable having a representational role if it infers a nominal role for it: this would break the type system. When the Haskell role system is too weak, but we are sure that it's okay to coerce, we can use the `unsafeCoerce` function from `Unsafe.Coerce` instead. The following code compiles successfully:

```
check3' :: Student3 Int -> Student3 Age
check3' = unsafeCoerce
```

Remember, we used this function in the previous chapter to define the `toUnescaping` function (ch11/type-families/Unescape.hs). The role system prohibits such cases with the combination of type families and type classes, although it works with `unsafeCoerce`.

Sometimes we want to restrict inferred roles and prevent generating unnecessary `Coercible` instances. We can do that with role annotations, available with the `Role-Annotations` GHC extension.

Writing the following prohibits coercions between `Student Age` and `Student Int`:

```
{-# LANGUAGE RoleAnnotations #-}

type role Student nominal
data Student ageType = Student String ageType
```

Note again, this works only to restrict a role: we can declare phantom roles as representational and representational roles as nominal, but not the other way around.

You can find more about roles and role inference in the GHC User's Guide. An interested reader is advised to read the "Safe Zero-Cost Coercions for Haskell" paper published in the *Journal of Functional Programming* in 2016 and available online as a preprint at https://www.microsoft.com/en-us/research/uploads/prod/2018/05/coercible-JFP.pdf to get even more details on this topic.

> **READING PAPERS ON HASKELL FEATURES** I can't stop recommending that everyone read papers that introduce or describe Haskell features. These papers almost always start with an accessible introduction and provide enough motivation and technical information for developers in the beginning sections. Then they usually go deeper into type system details, proofs, and other mandatory academic stuff that is definitely not easy reading unless you do research in programming languages. But remember: an abstract, an introduction, and a motivation section are for us, the Haskellers. Many papers can be found at https://wiki.haskell.org/Research_papers. Go read them and enjoy the beauty of Haskell.

DERIVING INSTANCES WITH GENERALIZEDNEWTYPEDERIVING

Now that we've discussed the `Coercible` constraint and the role system, it's easy to explain the `newtype` strategy for deriving instances. It turns out that implementing any method is as easy as writing `coerce`.

> **NOTE**
>
> 🗋 ch12/deriv/newtype.hs
>
> ⚡ *newtype*
>
> ☞ We can implement instances for `newtype` declarations manually or with an extension.

Suppose we have the following declaration:

```
{-# LANGUAGE DerivingStrategies #-}
{-# LANGUAGE GeneralizedNewtypeDeriving #-}

newtype Age = Age Int
  deriving newtype (Eq, Ord)
```

How does GHC generate the required instances? It coerces implementations for the underlying type (here, `Int`) of all the methods. For example, we have the following `Eq` instance:

```
instance Eq Age where
  (==) = coerce ((==) :: Int -> Int -> Bool)
```

The `(==)` operator for `Age` is the same as the one for `Int`. GHC uses the `Coercible Int Age` constraint to `coerce` those functions.

Deriving the `Ord` instance follows the same strategy. The only required `compare` method is implemented as follows:

```
instance Ord Age where
  compare = coerce (compare :: Int -> Int -> Ordering)
```

The same idea works with more sophisticated type classes. For example, we derived instances for monad stacks several times in this book as follows:

```
{-# LANGUAGE GeneralizedNewtypeDeriving #-}

newtype MyApp a = MyApp {
    runApp :: StateT Int IO a
  }
  deriving (Functor, Applicative, Monad, MonadIO)
```

GHC generates the following `Functor` instance:

```
instance Functor MyApp where
  fmap :: forall a b. (a -> b) -> MyApp a -> MyApp b
  fmap = coerce (fmap :: (a -> b) -> StateT Int IO a -> StateT Int IO b)
```

I've used the `InstanceSigs` and `ScopedTypeVariables` to define this instance. GHC may do this a little bit differently, but the idea is the same. We bring type variables into the scope and use `coerce` with the right types. For example, GHC 8.8 with the `-ddump-deriv` gives me the following (after cleaning the names):

```
fmap = coerce                                                          Coerces from
        @((a -> b) -> StateT Int IO a -> StateT Int IO b)    <──       this type
An fmap over    @((a -> b) -> MyApp a -> MyApp b)        <───
StateT Int IO   |─> (fmap @(StateT Int IO))                     Coerces to this type
is coerced.          :: forall (a :: TYPE LiftedRep)    <───
                          (b :: TYPE LiftedRep).          a :: Type
Resulting type of
fmap for MyApp  |─> (a -> b) -> MyApp a -> MyApp b
```

Remember that `coerce` has two implicit type arguments to coerce from and to. They are given here with the visible type applications (the `TypeApplications` GHC extension). Then we say that we'd like to coerce from `fmap` for `StateT Int IO` and finally give the resulting type of `fmap` we define. Remember that `TYPE LiftedRep` is aliased as the `Type` kind.

All the other instances are generated the same way.

READING GENERATED TYPES AND CODE Knowledge and experience come with extensive practice. Understanding Haskell types and code may be hard at first. I believe that reading types and code generated by GHC is yet another useful exercise when learning Haskell. An idea is not to give up in the very beginning when we see a long text with fully qualified or mangled names but to try to understand and interpret the structure behind it.

Note that the `GeneralizedNewtypeDeriving` GHC extension fails to generate instances if there are no appropriate `Coercible` instances around. The whole roles and `Coercible` ideas have arisen from a bug in older GHC versions. Suppose we have the following type family:

```
type family Inspect t
type instance Inspect Int = Bool
type instance Inspect Age = Int
```

We already know that the `t` type variable here has the nominal role, so there is no `Coercible (Inspect Age) (Inspect Int)` instance, though we still have `Coercible Age Int`. Suppose we also have the `inspect` function defined in a type class with an instance for `Int` as follows:

```
class Inspector a where
  inspect :: a -> Inspect a

instance Inspector Int where
  inspect n = n > 0
```

The result is of Inspect
Int type, which is Bool.

The question is, is it possible to derive the `Inspector` instance for `Age` using the newtype strategy? Remember that the newtype strategy here is replacing an implementation for `Age` with an implementation for `Int`. An ability to do that would mean that we have a result of type `Bool` (`Inspect Int`) interpreted as a value of type `Int` (`Inspect Age`). By doing so, we'd break the Haskell type system. Imagine this: it was possible in GHC for several years that we could see actual bits of `True` and `False` in memory as if we were C programmers! Let's check if it's possible now using the standalone deriving, as shown next:

```
deriving newtype instance Inspector Age
```

This results in the following type error:

```
• Couldn't match representation of type 'Bool' with that of 'Int'
      arising from a use of 'coerce'
    • In the expression:
        coerce
          @(Int -> Inspect Int) @(Age -> Inspect Age) (inspect @Int) ::
          Age -> Inspect Age
```

GHC generates an instance with `coerce`, and then the type checker figures out that this `coerce` invocation cannot be type-checked. We are on the safe side with the available and nonexistent `Coercible` instances!

12.1.3   *Deriving by an example with DerivingVia*

Our last strategy is the `via` strategy. Its overall idea is extremely simple. We give GHC an example of a type that already implements the instance we need and say, "Generate an implementation in the same way but replace types with ours, please." Note that this strategy generalizes the `newtype` strategy as follows: the given example of type is simply an underlying type in the `newtype` declaration. Let's look at several simple examples.

EXAMPLE: USING DERIVINGVIA

🗋   ch12/deriv/via.hs

⚡   *via*

☞ It's easy to derive instances automatically once we have an example.

GHC generates identical instances in the following code:

```
{-# LANGUAGE DerivingStrategies #-}
{-# LANGUAGE GeneralizedNewtypeDeriving #-}
{-# LANGUAGE DerivingVia #-}

newtype Age = Age Int          ⟵──┤ Int is an underlying type for Age.
   deriving newtype (Eq, Ord)  ⟵──── Instances for Int are reused.

newtype Age' = Age' Int              ┐ Int is given as an example
   deriving (Eq, Ord) via Int   ⟵───┘ to derive Eq and Ord.
```

In fact, we don't need the `GeneralizedNewtypeDeriving` GHC extension anymore: the `DerivingVia` extension was introduced in GHC 8.6.

> **TIP**   The `via` strategy was introduced by the "Deriving Via or, How to Turn Hand-Written Instances into an Anti-Pattern" paper (https://www.kosmikus .org/DerivingVia/deriving-via-paper.pdf), which is nicely written and easily accessible. I recommend reading it to understand the `via` strategy in full detail. This paper provides many practical examples of how to use this strategy and the ideas behind its implementation.

Why is generalized newtype deriving not enough? We know that some types may potentially have different instances capturing different ideas. In Haskell, we use `newtype` wrappers to distinguish between them. For example, the `Data.Monoid` provides several ways to implement instances for `Maybe  a`. There is a default instance that requires having the `Semigroup` instance for `a`. We can wrap the `Maybe  a` value with `Alt`, which prefers the first available not-`Nothing` value. We can also add the `Dual` wrapper to get the opposite behavior (preferring the last available not-`Nothing` value).

Let's look at an example. We have the following variation of the annoying `Age` type, now with a potentially missing value:

```
newtype MAge = MAge (Maybe Int)
```

Deriving `Semigroup` and `Monoid` instances with a `newtype` strategy requires having them for `Int` (that is the default for `Maybe a`). Unfortunately, there are none. One option is to add a layer or two of wrappers to the `MAge` type. This is not desirable because stacking wrappers makes using the type less convenient. With `DerivingVia`, we can instruct GHC to follow the `Alt Maybe Int` example when deriving the instance we want as follows:

```
newtype MAge = MAge (Maybe Int)
  deriving (Semigroup, Monoid) via (Alt Maybe Int)
```

We can also use the syntax with `StandaloneDeriving` as shown next:

```
deriving via (Alt Maybe Int) instance Semigroup MAge
deriving via (Alt Maybe Int) instance Monoid MAge
```

If we prefer to take the last available not-`Nothing` value, we go with `Dual` as follows:

```
newtype MAge = MAge (Maybe Int)
  deriving (Semigroup, Monoid) via (Dual (Alt Maybe Int))
```

Basically, we instruct the compiler with the desired way to implement instances. Both `Dual` and `Alt` are new types defined in the `base` library. They implement instances for both `Semigroup` and `Monoid` type classes. The `Semigroup` instance for `Alt` over `Maybe a` prefers the first-given not-`Nothing` alternative in the implementation of the (`<>`) operator from `Semigroup`. The instance for `Dual` swaps arguments to `<>`. For us, these provided instances are no more than patterns to define instances for our own `newtype` declaration. We say, "Make it just as in the instance of `Dual (Alt Maybe Int)`," meaning prefer the first, but swap arguments and make the results prefer the last alternative. Consequently, we have a simple declaration with the desired instances and no boilerplate with excessive wrappers or manual implementation.

12.2 *Data-type-generic programming*

Even though we've seen very flexible tools to derive instances, it turns out that in practice, these are not enough. Depending on the actual type structure, we often need to implement them differently. The problem is a necessity to have an instance for every type we have in our program. We'd like to write code generically, meaning that we want to deal not with a plethora of data types but with a single representation for all of them.

A NOTE ON SUM AND PRODUCT TYPES   Such a representation is built around a concept of *sum* and *product* types. Basically, the sum of several types is a type with every value belonging to one of those types. The product of several types is a type with every value consisting of values of all those types. The latter is well known in other programming languages. It corresponds to *tuples*, *structures*, or *records*. The former makes its way to mainstream programming languages in a relatively limited form of *enumerations*. In Haskell, we have both with the plain old `data` declaration via | and parameters to data constructors.

Data-type-generic programming in Haskell is supported by the `GHC.Generics` module, which provides such a representation. The most common usage for it is to write such instances that serve well for almost all the data types. Then we cook such generic instances and make them ready for the `anyclass` deriving strategy.

We've already seen `GHC.Generics`. We used it to generate instances to read values from CSV files or compose JSON requests. The `text-show` package provides a way to derive instances of the `TextShow` type class for our types using the `Generic` instances. The `deepseq` package uses them to evaluate values to normal forms. Now it's time to understand what data-type-generic programming is and how to use it in our own libraries.

First, we'll look at the representation of Haskell data types as defined by `GHC.Generics`. Second, we'll look at examples of how to process it.

12.2.1 *Generic data-type representation*

We'll start by exploring the idea of generic representation. Which information can we mine out of a value and its type?

EXAMPLE: VIEWING GENERIC REPRESENTATIONS

🗋   ch12/generics/view-generic.hs

⚡   *view-generic*

☞ We can explore a generic representation of data types.

Let's look at the following data type:

```
data Status = Ok | Err
```

Here I collect all the facts about this type:

- It's a data type, defined in the `Main` module of the `main` package (these names are used in GHC by default); it's not a `newtype`.
- Its name is `"Status"`.
- It has two data constructors. We can take either to construct a value.

- The left (first) data constructor is named `"Ok"`: it has no arguments, it is not a record selector, and it is supposed to be used in prefix form (as we usually do with data constructors).
- The right (second) data constructor is named `"Err"`: it has no arguments, it is not a record selector, and it is also supposed to be used in prefix form.

That's it. One may think that this is trivial and extremely boring information. Well, I agree. Nevertheless, having a representation means having all the information.

Now, suppose we have the `Ok` value. This is what we know about it:

- It was constructed with the left data constructor.
- Its data constructor has no arguments.

We can teach GHC to represent all this information as types and values as follows:

```
{-# LANGUAGE DeriveGeneric #-}

import GHC.Generics

data Status = Ok | Err
  deriving Generic
```

The `Generic` type class provides one associated type family and a couple of functions, as shown next:

```
class Generic a where
  type Rep a :: Type -> Type
  from :: a -> Rep a x
  to :: Rep a x -> a
```

For example, let's look at the type of the `from Ok` value, shown here:

```
ghci> :type from Ok
from Ok
  :: D1
       ('MetaData "Status" "Main" "main" 'False)
       (C1 ('MetaCons "Ok" 'PrefixI 'False) U1
        :+: C1 ('MetaCons "Err" 'PrefixI 'False) U1)
       x
```

It is extremely important to correlate this information to a collection of trivial facts about the `Status` type I showed earlier. We have a data type (`D1`) with some *metainformation* regarding names and the fact that this is not a `newtype` (see `'False` in the `'MetaData` type constructor). We have two data constructors combined with the (`:+:`) type operator. These constructors are also described with metainformation (name, fixity, being a record selector). Their arguments are given with `U1` (no arguments). Finally, we also have the `x` type variable, which is not used anyway, so we can safely ignore it.

Note that this type exploits several type-level features we discussed in the previous chapter, including data kinds (ticked names!) and the type-level `String`. When we process the values of such types, we can use `KnownSymbol` to bring names to a value level and process them accordingly.

The `from Ok` value itself is simpler, as shown next:

```
ghci> from Ok
M1 {unM1 = L1 (M1 {unM1 = U1})}
```

Here is the pattern: `M1` constructs a value, which is `L1` with an argument that is constructed with `M1` again and `U1` inside. `L1` corresponds to the left data constructor; `U1` corresponds to the absence of arguments to it. The left data constructor has no arguments, see? We also have `M1` as a building block of such a representation.

We can build such types and the corresponding values manually (given that we've enabled all the required extensions) as follows:

```
errVal :: D1
          ('MetaData "Status" "Main" "main" 'False)
          (C1 ('MetaCons "Ok" 'PrefixI 'False) U1
           :+: C1 ('MetaCons "Err" 'PrefixI 'False) U1)
          x
errVal = M1 {unM1 = R1 (M1 {unM1 = U1})}
```

Here, I construct the `Err` value. The only difference with `from Ok` is that I use `R1` instead of `L1` when building the value. The type is clearly the same. We can turn this value back to `Status` with the `to` function as follows:

```
ghci> to errVal :: Status
Err
```

What if we have fields in the constructors? The `GHC.Generics` module gives us the `(:*:)` operator. Suppose we have the following type for requests with `String` and `Int` fields:

```
data Request = Request String Int
  deriving Generic
```

The type of its generic representation follows (I'm using an associated type family directly with the GHCi `:kind!` command):

```
ghci> :kind! Rep Request
Rep Request :: * -> *              It's a data type.
  = D1
       ('MetaData "Request" "Main" "main" 'False)      Data-type metainformation
       (C1                                        Data
          ('MetaCons "Request" 'PrefixI 'False)   constructor    Constructor metainformation
          (S1
              ('MetaSel                  First field (selector)
```

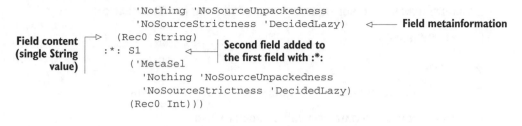

Field content (single String value) → (Rec0 String)

'Nothing 'NoSourceUnpackedness
'NoSourceStrictness 'DecidedLazy) ◄─── **Field metainformation**

:*: S1   ◄─── **Second field added to the first field with :*:**

('MetaSel
'Nothing 'NoSourceUnpackedness
'NoSourceStrictness 'DecidedLazy)
(Rec0 Int)))

The (`:+:`) and (`:*:`) operators can be used to represent any number of data constructors and constructor fields, respectively. A type with three data constructors could use the following somewhere inside it:

```
... :+: (... :+: ...)
```

Constructor field values at run time are represented with the `K1` data constructor as follows:

```
ghci> from (Request "req" 0)
M1 {unM1 = M1 {
    unM1 = M1 {unM1 = K1 {unK1 = "req"}}
            :*: M1 {unM1 = K1 {unK1 = 0}}
  }}
```

First value (arrow points to the M1 {unM1 = ... "req" line)
Second value ◄─── (the :*: M1 ... line)

Thus, the `Generic` type class allows us to go from a value to its generic representation and back. We also have the `Generic1` type class to represent type constructors of the `k -> Type` kinds. We can derive it with `DeriveGeneric`, too. Once we have those instances generated, we can go between values and their representations. I recommend looking through the documentation of the `GHC.Generics` module to see a thorough description of all the types used here.

12.2.2 Example: Generating SQL queries

Now let's do something useful with a generic representation. We want to generate `INSERT` SQL queries for our data types to store their values in a database. The idea is to take a data type, such as

```
data Student = Student {studentId :: Int, name :: Text, year :: Int}
```

and generate a SQL query like the following for a given value:

```
INSERT INTO students (studentId, name, year) VALUES (18265, "John Doe", 2)
```

Clearly, we don't want to limit ourselves to the `Student` type. We could also work with another data type, such as

```
data Course = Course {courseId :: Int, title :: Text, instructor :: Text}
```

Thus, we have to program generically.

EXAMPLE: GENERATING SQL QUERIES FROM A GENERIC REPRESENTATION

📄   ch12/genSQL/

⚡   *generic-sql*

☞   We can generate an INSERT query for any given data type.

EXPLOITING OUTCOMES IN DATA-TYPE-GENERIC PROGRAMMING

Suppose we have the following type class:

```
class ToSQL a where
  insertInto :: Text -> a -> Text
```

Its goal is to generate INSERT queries. We'd like to use it as follows:

```
{-# LANGUAGE OverloadedStrings #-}
{-# LANGUAGE DerivingStrategies #-}
{-# LANGUAGE DeriveGeneric #-}
{-# LANGUAGE DeriveAnyClass #-}

import GHC.Generics
import Data.Text (Text)
import qualified Data.Text.IO as TIO

import GenericSQL

data Student = Student {studentId :: Int, name :: Text, year :: Int}
  deriving stock Generic
  deriving anyclass ToSQL

data Course = Course {courseId :: Int, title :: Text, instructor :: Text}
  deriving stock Generic
  deriving anyclass ToSQL

main :: IO ()
main = do
  TIO.putStrLn $ insertInto "students" (Student 18265 "John Doe" 2)
  TIO.putStrLn $ insertInto "courses" (Course 1 "Math" "Jane Doe")
```

The result follows:

```
$ cabal -v0 run generic-sql
INSERT INTO students (studentId, name, year) VALUES (18265, "John Doe", 2)
INSERT INTO courses (courseId, title, instructor)
➥ VALUES (1, "Math", "Jane Doe")
```

This code is simple. For every data type that we need to insert into a database, we derive both Generic and ToSQL using different strategies. We already know that the anyclass strategy requires having a default implementation. So our insertInto should have one. Let's do that.

EXTRACTING INFORMATION FROM A GENERIC REPRESENTATION

First, we need to extract all the information from a generic representation provided by the `Generic` instance. Which information do we need? Well, it's a list of field names and a list of values. Note that this information goes partly from a type declaration (selector names, such as `"studentId"` or `"name"`) and partly from a value itself (`18265` or `"John Doe"`). Extracting it from a type requires writing a type class and instances as usual. We start with a type class as follows:

```
class ToColumnsValuesLists f where
  toColumnsValues :: f a -> ([Builder], [Builder])
```

The idea is to go over a run-time representation once and collect two lists: one with selector names and the other with the corresponding values. Note that I use `Builder` from the `TextShow` module for performance reasons when building the resulting `Text` value. The SQL queries may be quite large.

Let's implement instances, starting with the simplest one. If we have a data type represented with `U1`, then it has no fields at all, so the resulting lists should be empty, as shown here:

```
instance ToColumnsValuesLists U1 where
  toColumnsValues _ = ([], [])
```

If we have several fields, then the data type is represented by the (`:*:`) type operator. In this case, we should first extract information from both parts, left and right, and then combine it in the resulting lists as follows:

```
instance (ToColumnsValuesLists a, ToColumnsValuesLists b) =>
              ToColumnsValuesLists (a :*: b) where
  toColumnsValues (a :*: b) = (columns1 <> columns2, values1 <> values2)
    where
      (columns1, values1) = toColumnsValues a
      (columns2, values2) = toColumnsValues b
```

Note the context in the instance head: we require both sides of `:*:` to implement our type class. Note also that the (`:*:`) operator exists both at the type level (we have it in the instance head) and the value level (we pattern match over it). We traverse over both levels simultaneously. The implementation itself is trivial.

Now to the interesting part: extracting metainformation should be done from the `M1` type. The `M1` type has the following four type parameters:

```
newtype M1 (i :: Type) (c :: Meta) (f :: k -> Type) (p :: k)
```

The first one corresponds to a represented component (the data type itself, constructor, or selector). We have several type aliases for these components, as shown next:

```
type D1 = M1 D
type C1 = M1 C
type S1 = M1 S
```

The second parameter contains metainformation, which clearly depends on a component. The third parameter specifies a type whose representation we are constructing. The last parameter is the represented type itself.

We ignore most of the information, so let's define the following instance to traverse over:

```
instance (ToColumnsValuesLists a) =>
                ToColumnsValuesLists (M1 i c a) where
  toColumnsValues (M1 a) = toColumnsValues a
```

We are interested only in the selector's names, so we define an overlapping instance for this particular case as follows:

```
instance {-# OVERLAPPING #-} (ToColumnsValuesLists a, Selector c) =>
                ToColumnsValuesLists (M1 S c a) where
  toColumnsValues s@(M1 a) = (fromString (selName s) : columns, values)
    where
      (columns, values) = toColumnsValues a
```

The `selName` function comes from the `Selector` type class. It uses the `KnownSymbol` under the hood to give us information from the type level.

Finally, we should extract values, as shown next. They are represented with `K1`.

```
instance TextShow a => ToColumnsValuesLists (K1 i a) where
  toColumnsValues (K1 a) = ([], [showb a])
```

For simplicity reasons, I don't want to consider other cases, such as several data constructors in one data type, data types that don't use record syntax, or recursive data types. All of these can also be represented with `GHC.Generics`, and the documentation is quite good. The code we already have is going to work for the simplest case, and that's enough for our goals. Note that plenty of practical data types follow this trivial structure: one data constructor, a record syntax, and as many selector fields as necessary. At least, it works for our `Student` data type, as shown next:

```
$ cabal repl generic-sql
ghci> :set -XOverloadedStrings
ghci> toColumnsValues (from $ Student 18265 "John Doe" 2)
(["studentId","name","year"],["18265","\"John Doe\"","2"])
```

Our next step is to use all this extracted information to build a SQL query.

PREPARING A TYPE CLASS FOR DERIVING INSTANCES WITH A DEFAULT IMPLEMENTATION
Now we use the extracted information to provide a default implementation for the `insertInto` method of the `ToSQL` type class.

We'd like to have the following function:

```
insertIntoDefault
  :: (Generic a, ToColumnsValuesLists (Rep a)) => Text -> a -> Text
```

Note the constraints: we require an *a* type having a generic representation and an ability to extract columns and values from its representation. With these constraints available we can implement it as follows:

```
insertIntoDefault table val =
  toText $ "INSERT INTO " <> fromText table <> " "
           <> buildersToList columns
           <> " VALUES " <> buildersToList values
  where
    (columns, values) = toColumnsValues (from val)
```

The buildersToList constructs a parenthesized list of the given arguments, as shown next:

```
buildersToList :: [Builder] -> Builder
buildersToList [] = "()"
buildersToList (x:xs) = singleton '(' <> x <> go xs    -- "(..
  where
    go (y:ys) = showbCommaSpace <> y <> go ys           -- .., ..
    go []     = singleton ')'                           -- ..)"
```

We are now very close to the final step: we have to introduce this default implementation to the ToSQL type class. Remember that it is defined now as follows:

```
class ToSQL a where
  insertInto :: Text -> a -> Text
```

Our idea is to say that insertInto is the same as insertIntoDefault. One problem here is that these two functions have different types. Let's look at them once again in the next code sample:

```
insertInto :: ToSQL a => Text -> a -> Text
insertIntoDefault
  :: (Generic a, ToColumnsValuesLists (Rep a)) => Text -> a -> Text
```

The types are the same, although the constraints are different. For such situations, GHC provides the DefaultSignatures extension. With this extension enabled, we can provide a specific signature for a default implementation as follows:

```
class ToSQL a where
  insertInto :: Text -> a -> Text

  default insertInto ::
      (Generic a, ToColumnsValuesLists (Rep a)) => Text -> a -> Text
  insertInto = insertIntoDefault
```

This means these constraints will be in effect if an instance uses the default implementation. Otherwise, the user is free not to introduce them.

Getting back to the beginning, we see that all these constraints are met with our data types, for example:

```
data Student = Student {studentId :: Int, name :: Text, year :: Int}
  deriving stock Generic
  deriving anyclass ToSQL
```

First, we derive the `Generic` `Student` instance, and the first constraint is satisfied. Second, we ask GHC to derive a default implementation of `ToSQL` with the `anyclass` strategy. At this moment, GHC checks whether we satisfy the second constraint, namely, `ToColumnsValuesLists (Rep Student)`. That means that we should have the `ToColumnsValuesLists` instances for all the representational types used to represent a `Student`. Note we don't have to implement instances for all the representational types provided by `GHC.Generics`.

Let's try to derive the `ToSQL` instance for our `Status` type as follows:

```
data Status = Ok | Err
  deriving stock Generic
  deriving anyclass ToSQL
```

GHC complains, as shown here:

```
• No instance for (ToColumnsValuesLists
                   (C1 ('MetaCons "Ok" 'PrefixI 'False) U1
                   :+: C1 ('MetaCons "Err" 'PrefixI 'False) U1))
    arising from the 'deriving' clause of a data type declaration
```

Well, we've intentionally decided to ignore such data types, so it's fine.

Data-type-generic programming works perfectly well with data types, their run-time and type-level representations, default signatures for type class methods, and deriving default instances with the `anyclass` strategy. Nevertheless, that's not enough. GHC provides the ability to generate any code at compile time without such limitations as having a data type, type class, and so on. The corresponding instrument is called Template Haskell. Let's move to it now.

12.3 *Template Haskell and quasiquotes*

When GHC compiles our code, it starts with parsing. As a result of parsing, it creates an *abstract syntax tree* (AST). Template Haskell (TH) allows us to explore this tree and generate new nodes. The compiler then continues the compilation of the code, including what we've generated. In this section, we'll look at different TH features by implementing a series of simple examples in a tutorial style. Then we'll discuss quasiquotations, a mechanism that allows enriching code in Haskell with literally anything. We'll end up with a complex example of implementing classical mechanisms for distributed computations and remote procedure calls (or remote function calls in this case).

THE RISKS OF USING TEMPLATE HASKELL Template Haskell is intimately tied to the GHC internals. It was never standardized. There are always risks of breaking code under GHC updates. As a rule, it's better to avoid using Template Haskell in production code.

12.3.1 A tutorial on Template Haskell

One thing that should be understood from the very beginning is that Template Haskell runs at compile time. This puts many limitations on how we write programs with TH. We'll meet them shortly, but let's start with the simplest things. Our first problem is how to build an AST manually and insert it into the code.

QUOTES AND SPLICES

Let's fire up GHCi, enable the `TemplateHaskell` extension, and import the main TH module as follows:

```
ghci> :set -XTemplateHaskell
ghci> import Language.Haskell.TH
ghci> runQ [| 1 + 2 |]
InfixE (Just (LitE (IntegerL 1))) (VarE GHC.Num.+) (Just (LitE (IntegerL 2)))
```

We have many interesting things here. The `[| ... |]` brackets are called Oxford brackets. They are used to define a computation in the very special `Q` monad. In some sense, they create a *quote* with Haskell code. We can look at an AST that corresponds to this quote by running this `Q` computation with the `runQ` function.

The result of `[| 1 + 2 |]` is an infix expression built from two integer literals and the `+` operator. Note how this description corresponds to the AST in the previous GHCi session. Every Haskell code element has a corresponding data constructor in this AST. Because we have these constructors, we can build our own AST nodes as follows:

```
ghci> answer = LitE (IntegerL 42)
ghci> :type answer
answer :: Exp
```

The next step is to splice this node to the code itself. We do that with the `$(...)` instruction, whose argument should be a `Q` computation, as shown next:

```
ghci> $( pure answer )
42
```

Let's construct the 1+2 expression manually with AST data constructors and splice it in GHCi to see a result as follows:

```
ghci> expr = InfixE (Just (LitE (IntegerL 1))) (VarE (mkName "+")) (Just
➥  (LitE (IntegerL 2)))
```

Note the `mkName` function, which gives us a value of the `Name` type used to refer to a name in an AST. A spliced expression is immediately evaluated in GHCi as shown next:

```
ghci> $( pure expr )
3
```

We don't have to use GHCi. We can do the same thing in our program. One of the limitations I mentioned earlier is that we are not allowed to splice TH definitions created in the same module—they should always be defined elsewhere.

EXAMPLE: INTRODUCING TEMPLATE HASKELL

🗋   ch12/th/hello/Hello.hs

🗋   ch12/th/hello/Main.hs

⚡   *hello-th*

☞ We should create and splice TH definitions in separate modules.

The following is the simple TH definition in the separate module. It's an expression in the Q monad, which prints a `String`.

```
{-# LANGUAGE TemplateHaskell #-}
module Hello where
import Language.Haskell.TH

hello :: Q Exp
hello = [| putStrLn "Hello world" |]
```

Now we can splice it in `Main` as follows:

```
{-# LANGUAGE TemplateHaskell #-}
module Main where

import Hello

main :: IO ()
main = $hello
```

Note that we don't need parentheses if we splice a single name. This program works as expected, as shown next:

```
hid-examples $ cabal -v0 run hello-th
Hello world
```

Besides expressions (the `Exp` type), Haskell ASTs may contain declarations (`Dec`), types (`Type`), and patterns (`Pat`). We can construct and splice all of them.

GENERATING EXPRESSIONS

In Haskell, we have the following convenient functions:

```
fst :: (a, b) -> a
snd :: (a, b) -> b
```

Unfortunately, no such functions exist for tuples with three elements. Or seventeen. Wouldn't it be nice to have all of the following functions, too:

```
proj_17_0  (x0,_,_,_,_,_,_,_,_,_,_,_,_,_,_,_,_) = x0
proj_17_1  (_,x1,_,_,_,_,_,_,_,_,_,_,_,_,_,_,_) = x1
proj_17_2  (_,_,x2,_,_,_,_,_,_,_,_,_,_,_,_,_,_) = x2
proj_17_3  (_,_,_,x3,_,_,_,_,_,_,_,_,_,_,_,_,_) = x3
proj_17_4  (_,_,_,_,x4,_,_,_,_,_,_,_,_,_,_,_,_) = x4
proj_17_5  (_,_,_,_,_,x5,_,_,_,_,_,_,_,_,_,_,_) = x5
proj_17_6  (_,_,_,_,_,_,x6,_,_,_,_,_,_,_,_,_,_) = x6
proj_17_7  (_,_,_,_,_,_,_,x7,_,_,_,_,_,_,_,_,_) = x7
proj_17_8  (_,_,_,_,_,_,_,_,x8,_,_,_,_,_,_,_,_) = x8
proj_17_9  (_,_,_,_,_,_,_,_,_,x9,_,_,_,_,_,_,_) = x9
proj_17_10 (_,_,_,_,_,_,_,_,_,_,x10,_,_,_,_,_,_) = x10
proj_17_11 (_,_,_,_,_,_,_,_,_,_,_,x11, , , , , ) = x11
proj_17_12 (_,_,_,_,_,_,_,_,_,_,_,_,x12,_,_,_,_) = x12
proj_17_13 (_,_,_,_,_,_,_,_,_,_,_,_,_,x13,_,_,_) = x13
proj_17_14 (_,_,_,_,_,_,_,_,_,_,_,_,_,_,x14,_,_) = x14
proj_17_15 (_,_,_,_,_,_,_,_,_,_,_,_,_,_,_,x15,_) = x15
proj_17_16 (_,_,_,_,_,_,_,_,_,_,_,_,_,_,_,_,x16) = x16
```

Well, maybe not. Anyway, let's generate them as our next example.

EXAMPLE: GENERATING FUNCTIONS PROJECTORS FOR TUPLES

☐ ch12/th/projectors/

⚡ *projectors*

☞ We can construct expressions in several ways.

Our first goal is to implement the following function:

```
proj :: Int -> Int -> Q Exp
```

It takes a total number of elements and an element we are interested in and returns a corresponding projector (a whole function). We could use it as follows:

```
main = do
  putStrLn $ $(proj 3 1) (undefined,"Success!",undefined)
  putStrLn $ $(proj 4 2) (undefined,undefined,"Success!",undefined)
  putStrLn $ $(proj 5 4) (undefined,undefined,undefined,undefined,"Success!")
```

The easiest way to start writing TH definitions is to explore code with Oxford brackets. For example, what's the AST for the \(x, _, _) -> x lambda function?

```
ghci> runQ [| \(x, _, _) -> x |]
LamE [TupP [VarP x_0,WildP,WildP]] (VarE x_0)
```

Here we've got many keys. Now it's clear how to construct tuples (TupP with a list of arguments), how to refer to _ (WildP), and how to build a lambda (LamE). Thus, the plan is as follows:

1 We build a list of patterns of the given size to construct a tuple.
2 We build the body.
3 We build the lambda itself.

The name in this lambda should not interfere with anything else. TH gives us the newName function to generate a fresh variable name. The first implementation follows:

```
proj n k = do
    x <- newName "x"          ◁──────  Creates a new name for a variable
    let mkPat j                        Puts a variable into the requested position
          | j == k = VarP x    ◁────
          | otherwise = WildP  ◁────   Puts in an underscore otherwise
    pure $ LamE [TupP $ map mkPat [0..n-1]] (VarE x)  ◁─┐ Constructs the
                                                         resulting lambda
```

This function works as expected, for example:

```
ghci> $(proj 3 2) ("aaa", "bbb", "ccc")
"ccc"
```

Unfortunately, we've completely forgotten to check our arguments. If we use incompatible arguments, GHC complains, as shown here:

```
ghci> $(proj 3 4) ("aaa", "bbb", "ccc")

<interactive>:11:3: error:
    • The exact Name 'x_a92y' is not in scope
        Probable cause: you used a unique Template Haskell name (NameU),
        perhaps via newName, but did not bind it
        If that's it, then -ddump-splices might be useful
    • In the untyped splice: $(proj 3 4)
```

TIP GHC error messages usually try to be very helpful. The previous one, for example, suggests using the -ddump-slices GHC option to see the generated code. The problem in this particular example is clear. We refer to a variable that is not in a tuple. In general, it is an extremely good idea to look at the code that was generated by TH to find out what exactly went wrong.

Let's add parameter checks as follows:

```
proj n k
  | n > 1 && 0 <= k && k < n = do
    -- same as before
  | n <=1 = fail "Wrong number of tuple elements (must be > 1)"
  | otherwise = fail $ "Incorrect projection: "
                  <> show k <> " of " <> show n <> " elements"
```

The `fail` method causes GHC to print an error message at compile time. Let's try to use $ (proj 3 4) in Main.hs, for example:

```
putStrLn $ $(proj 3 4) ("aaa","bbb","ccc")
```

That results in the following error message at compile time:

```
ch12/th/projectors/Main.hs:8:16: error:
    • Incorrect projection: 4 of 3 elements
    • In the untyped splice: $(proj 3 4)
    |
8 |    putStrLn $ $(proj 3 4) ("aaa","bbb","ccc")
    |               ^^^^^^^^^^
```

This approach, when we construct an AST node with data constructors, quickly becomes too clumsy. In most cases, it's better to delegate some parts of construction to GHC itself with quotes and splices.

GENERATING EXPRESSIONS WITH A COMBINATION OF QUOTES AND SPLICES

Template Haskell allows nesting splices and quotes. In the following implementation of the `proj` function, we use quotes to construct a lambda:

```
proj n k
  | n > 1 && 0 <= k && k < n = do
      x <- newName "x"
      [| \ $(mkArg x) -> $(varE x) |]      ←——  Splices inside a quote
  | n <=1 = fail "Wrong number of tuple elements (must be > 1)"
  | otherwise = fail $ "Incorrect projection: "
                 <> show k <> " of " <> show n <> " elements"
  where
    mkPat x j
      | j == k = varP x
      | otherwise = wildP
    mkArg x = tupP $ map (mkPat x) [0..n-1]
```

There are more changes in this code. Note that now I'm using varE, varP, wildP, and tupP instead of VarE, VarP, WildP, and TupP. These functions return their results in the Q monad already, so they are composed better with the $(...) splice operator that expects Q a values inside it. Let's compare types of TupP and tupP as follows:

```
TupP :: [Pat] -> Pat      ←——  Data constructor for Pat
tupP :: [PatQ] -> PatQ    ←——  Works with Q values
type PatQ = Q Pat         ←——  Type alias for Q values
```

Many AST data constructors have their functional counterparts defined in the `Language.Haskell.TH.Lib` module.

GENERATING DECLARATIONS

The lambda functions we've generated are expressions. Now let's generate all the projectors for a given number of elements in a tuple. Thus, we need *declarations* with function names, bodies, and type signatures. In fact, type signatures are optional, as GHC infers them anyway.

We begin with the names as follows:

```
mkProjName :: Int -> Int -> Name
mkProjName n k = mkName $ "proj_" <> show n <> "_" <> show k
```

Generating a function declaration is also simple, as shown here:

```
mkProjDec :: Int -> Int -> Q [Dec]
mkProjDec n k = [d| $nm = $(proj n k) |]
  where
    nm = varP $ mkProjName n k
```

Note the [d| … |] Oxford brackets. They give us a list of declarations. We can look at the following result:

```
ghci> runQ $ mkProjDec 2 1
[ValD (VarP proj_2_1) (NormalB (LamE [TupP [WildP,VarP x_0]] (VarE x_0))) []]
```

The ValD declaration is used to declare values (without arguments). The NormalB constructor corresponds to a regular function body as opposed to pattern-guarded ones. These constructors were generated thanks to [d| … |].

Generating a type signature is surprisingly hard. Let's explore type signatures with quotes first, as shown next:

```
ghci> :set -XTemplateHaskell
ghci> runQ [t| (a, b) -> a |]
<interactive>:2:11: error:
    • Not in scope: type variable 'a'
    • In the Template Haskell quotation [t| (a, b) -> a |]
  ...
```

This simple type is wrong, according to Template Haskell. It looks like we should introduce a and b first with the forall keyword (the output is formatted by me for convenience) as follows:

```
ghci> runQ [t| forall a b.(a, b) -> a |]
ForallT [PlainTV a_0,PlainTV b_1] []
  (AppT
    (AppT
        ArrowT
        (AppT
            (AppT (TupleT 2) (VarT a_0))
            (VarT b_1)
        )
    )
    (VarT a_0)
  )
```

We should generate a list of type variables, send them to `forall`, and then construct a tuple with types and build a type for a function from a tuple to a resulting type (which is called `ArrowT` and represents an `->` arrow). The main operation for type construction is `AppT`—we should use it to provide tuple elements and arrow arguments.

This plan is implemented in the following example:

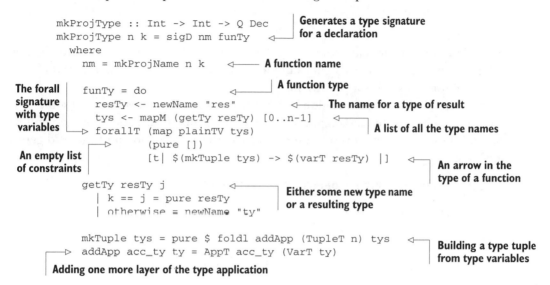

Note that I've used `[t| ... |]` Oxford brackets to build a resulting type declaration for a function. This saves a couple of explicit data constructors.

To reach the original goal, we should generate a whole bunch of projectors for the given sizes as follows:

```
mkProjectors :: [Int] -> Q [Dec]
mkProjectors = fmap concat . mapM projectors
  where
    projectors n = concat <$> mapM (mkProj n) [0..n-1]
    mkProj n k = (:) <$> mkProjType n k <*> mkProjDec n k
```

Here we combine type signatures with function declarations and concatenate all of them in the resulting list of `Dec` values ready to be spliced. The splicing itself should be done in `Main`, for example:

```
$(mkProjectors [2..10])
```

Template Haskell then generates something like the following:

```
proj_2_0 :: forall res_a8Cd ty_a8Ce. (res_a8Cd, ty_a8Ce) -> res_a8Cd
proj_2_0 = \ (x_a8Cf, _) -> x_a8Cf
proj_2_1 :: forall ty_a8Ch res_a8Cg. (ty_a8Ch, res_a8Cg) -> res_a8Cg
proj_2_1 = \ (_, x_a8Ci) -> x_a8Ci
...
```

This was not easy to develop. The main problem is that Template Haskell data types are very complex, with plenty of types and data constructors. We should always explore and experiment.

We haven't touched on one thing yet: we've generated code, but we've never consulted the compiler about the code that we wrote. This process is called *reification*. Let's talk about it now.

REIFICATION

Sometimes we need to learn something that we already have in our code before generating something new. In the next example, we'll look at existing data declarations and generate some code to support them.

In general, the term reification means turning something abstract into something concrete. In Template Haskell, we reify names into full information about the entities behind those names. As a result, we can inspect this information and use it to generate code.

EXAMPLE: GENERATING PREDICATES FOR DATA TYPES

📄   ch12/th/predicates/

⚡ *predicates*

☞ We can generate code based on the code we already have.

Suppose we have the following data type for representing geometric shapes:

```
data Shape = Circle Double
           | Square Double
           | Triangle Double Double Double
```

Sometimes we need to use the following predicates:

```
isCircle :: Shape -> Bool
isSquare :: Shape -> Bool
isTriangle :: Shape -> Bool
```

Though they can be easily implemented, it's quite boring to write them down. Well, let's generate them! After all, this is our main solution to every problem in this chapter. The plan follows:

1 Reify the given data-type name, and extract information about data constructors.
2 Write code to generate trivial predicate definitions with TH.
3 Use TH splices to actually generate code for predicates.

Let's write the function as follows:

```
mkPredicates :: Name -> Q [Dec]
```

It takes the name of the data type and gives back predicate declarations. The reification is done via the `reify` function as follows:

```
reify :: Name -> Q Info
```

This function gives back a lot of information, but we are interested in data constructors exclusively, as shown next:

```
extractConstructors :: Info -> [Con]
extractConstructors (TyConI (DataD _ _ _ _ cons _)) = cons
extractConstructors _ = []
```

There are several sorts of data constructors. We go with the simplest one, `NormalC`, and ignore the others as follows:

```
mkPredicate :: Con -> Q [Dec]
mkPredicate (NormalC name types) =
  [d|
     $predicate = \z -> case z of
                             $pat -> True
                             _ -> False
  |]
  where
    predicate = varP $ mkName $ "is" ++ nameBase name
    pat = conP name $ replicate (length types) wildP
mkPredicate _ = pure []
```

Here we build the predicate name using the `mkName` and `nameBase` functions. The latter function removes all the qualifications, if present. Then we build a pattern for the corresponding constructor. This requires providing the right number of wildcards in the pattern.

With this job done, it's easy to implement the required generator as follows:

```
mkPredicates :: Name -> Q [Dec]
mkPredicates name =
  reify name
  >>= fmap concat . mapM mkPredicate . extractConstructors
```

In the last step, we should refer to the name of the data constructor in the TH splice. We use the `''` prefix for that, as shown here:

```
$(mkPredicates ''Shape)
```

This instruction generates all the required predicates. We can use them as follows:

```
main = mapM_ print [isCircle s1, isSquare s2, isTriangle s3]
  where
    s1 = Circle 4
    s2 = Square 10
    s3 = Triangle 1 1 1
```

The `reify` function is extremely powerful: it opens the door to the compilation pipeline and reports almost every piece of information known to the compiler at the moment when TH is fired up.

QuasiQuotes

We've seen several examples of Template Haskell quotes in Oxford brackets. We can also define our own Oxford bracket processors, called *quasiquoters*. A quasiquoter is a value of the `QuasiQuoter` type defined in the `Language.Haskell.TH.Quote` module. This value should contain the following four functions as its fields for parsing quotes found in different contexts:

- As an expression
- As a pattern
- As a type
- As a top-level declaration

These functions should return the corresponding TH data types in the `Q` monad. Whenever GHC meets a quasiquotation, it calls the corresponding function and splices its result back to the code. Let's look at an example. Remember that Haskell doesn't contain any multiline `String` literals. It's easy to implement them with quasiquotes.

EXAMPLE: IMPLEMENTING MULTILINE STRING LITERALS

📄   ch12/th/mstr-lits/

⚡   *mstr-literals*

☞ We can introduce new language features with `QuasiQuotes`.

We implement the following trivial quasiquoter:

```
module Str where

import Language.Haskell.TH
import Language.Haskell.TH.Quote

str = QuasiQuoter {
        quoteExp = stringE
      , quotePat = undefined
      , quoteType = undefined
      , quoteDec = undefined
      }
```

The whole idea behind this quasiquoter is to take a `String` inside Oxford brackets and turn it into a `String` expression. The `stringE` function from Template Haskell does precisely that. We leave all other functions unimplemented because we don't expect multiline `String` literals in other contexts except for expressions.

To use this quasiquoter, we should enable the `QuasiQuotes` GHC extension, import the corresponding module, and write Oxford brackets as follows:

```
{-# LANGUAGE QuasiQuotes #-}
module Main where

import Str

verse :: String
verse = [str|What needs my Shakespeare for his honoured bones,
The labor of an age in pilèd stones,
Or that his hallowed relics should be hid
Under a star-ypointing pyramid?
Dear son of Memory, great heir of fame,
What need'st thou such weak witness of thy name?
Thou in our wonder and astonishment
Hast built thyself a live-long monument…|]

main :: IO ()
main = putStrLn verse
```

If we run this program, the `String` is printed as it was defined, as shown next:

```
$ cabal -v0 run mstr-literals
What needs my Shakespeare for his honoured bones,
...
```

In general, we have to implement parsing of quote content by ourselves. Let's now move to a much more sophisticated example where we exploit Template Haskell and quasiquotes.

12.3.2 *Example: Generating remote function calls*

The theory of distributed computing describes several approaches to distributed communications. The most popular nowadays is explicit message passing. With this approach, both communicated sides send and receive messages. In the 1980s and 1990s, another approach was widely used, namely, remote procedure calls or remote method invocation. In this model, it looks like we call a procedure or a method of some object as usual, but it's actually executed on the remote machine. We have a client that initiates communication and a server that serves a request. In the background, all arguments to the procedure called by a client are serialized into an envelope, sent over the network, received at the server side, deserialized, and processed. Results are then sent back in the same way. Clients in this model traditionally use blocking calls to wait for results.

In this section, we'll implement *remote function calls*, an approach to distributed computing with a functional programming flavor. I wouldn't recommend using this approach in industry nowadays. Nevertheless, it's a good exercise in Template Haskell. We'll develop a library and a sample application to demonstrate its usage.

SAMPLE APPLICATiON: SENDING PINGS AND ECHO REQUESTS OVER THE NETWORK

Let's start with a sample application. It consists of a client and a server with a few common definitions.

EXAMPLE: SENDING PINGS AND ECHO REQUESTS BETWEEN A CLIENT AND A SERVER

    📄   ch12/rpc/ping/

    ⚡ *ping-client*

    ⚡ *ping-server*

    ☞ We can call functions on a client that runs on a server.

Our application is only about 50 lines of Haskell code. Almost all the functionality is hidden in the library. Clients and servers share data types and an environment for executing code. The following are some common definitions.

EXAMPLE: SENDING PINGS AND ECHO REQUESTS BETWEEN A CLIENT AND A SERVER

    📄   ch12/rpc/ping/PingCommon.hs

    📄   ch12/rpc/ping/client.hs

    📄   ch12/rpc/ping/server.hs

    ⚡ *ping-server*

```haskell
{-# LANGUAGE DeriveGeneric #-}
{-# LANGUAGE DeriveAnyClass #-}
{-# LANGUAGE DerivingStrategies #-}
module PingCommon where

import GHC.Generics
import Data.Serialize      ⟵——— The module from the cereal package

import RpcCommon           ⟵——— The module from our rpc-lib internal library

instance RemoteState Integer where        ⟵——— State for one client-server session
    initState = 0

type RemotePing a = RSIO Integer a        ⟵——— Main application monad to work with

data PingAnswer = PingAnswer String Integer   ⟵┐  Data type used as a
    deriving stock (Show, Generic)               │  result of the ping call
    deriving anyclass Serialize
```

Every value sent over the network should be properly serialized. We use the cereal library, which uses GHC.Generics to implement default serialization methods. We'll come to the serialization later in this section.

    The client uses QuasiQuotes to generate remote function stubs and calls them in a simple communication session, as shown next:

```haskell
{-# LANGUAGE QuasiQuotes #-}
import Control.Monad
import Control.Monad.Trans
```

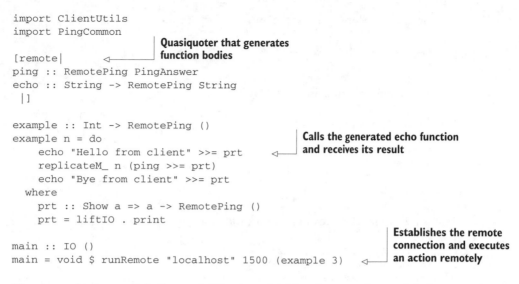

```
import ClientUtils
import PingCommon
```

Quasiquoter that generates function bodies

```
[remote|
ping :: RemotePing PingAnswer
echo :: String -> RemotePing String
 |]

example :: Int -> RemotePing ()
example n = do
    echo "Hello from client" >>= prt
    replicateM_ n (ping >>= prt)
    echo "Bye from client" >>= prt
  where
    prt :: Show a => a -> RemotePing ()
    prt = liftIO . print

main :: IO ()
main = void $ runRemote "localhost" 1500 (example 3)
```

Calls the generated echo function and receives its result

Establishes the remote connection and executes an action remotely

The server is also straightforward. We give trivial implementations of the remote functions and start serving requests as follows:

```
{-# LANGUAGE TemplateHaskell #-}
import Control.Monad.State
import ServerUtils
import PingCommon

ping :: RemotePing PingAnswer
ping = do
  modify (+1)
  n <- get
  liftIO $ putStrLn $ "Ping received/answered with " <> show n
  pure $ PingAnswer "OK" n

echo :: String -> RemotePing String
echo msg = do
  liftIO $ putStrLn $ "Echo message: " <> msg
  pure msg

genServer ['ping, 'echo]

main :: IO ()
main = server "localhost" 1500
```

Generates the server function to serve requests to the ping and echo functions

Note how we refer to the declared functions with 'ping and 'echo. The tick here is used to get the TH Name of the corresponding functions. Remember, we've used double ticks to refer to type names before. Note also that there is no explicit Template Haskell splice for genServer here. GHC allows calling TH functions as top-level declarations without the $(…) syntax.

If we run the server, it blocks and waits for requests, as shown next:

```
$ cabal -v0 run ping-server
...
```

Running a client results in the following output:

```
$ cabal -v0 run ping-client
"Hello from client"
PingAnswer "OK" 1
PingAnswer "OK" 2
PingAnswer "OK" 3
"Bye from client"
```

The server logs the following communication also:

```
LOG: 127.0.0.1:61767 New connection
Echo message: Hello from client
Ping received/answered with 1
Ping received/answered with 2
Ping received/answered with 3
Echo message: Bye from client
LOG: 127.0.0.1:61767 Connection closed
```

Now let's see how all this stuff is implemented.

COMMUNICATION MODEL: REMOTE FUNCTION CALLS

We want to implement the following communication model in our library:

1 The client calls a function, which is actually a *stub*.
2 This stub packs all the arguments with a function name and sends them over the network to the server.
3 The server receives a request, unpacks it, looks up the requested function, and calls it with the arguments provided with the request.
4 The function is evaluated on the server and gives back a result.
5 The server packs the result and sends it back to the client.
6 The client's stub receives the result, unpacks it, and gives it to a caller.

While packing and unpacking values, we have to follow a specific strategy. We use serialization and deserialization for Haskell values. We work with bytestrings to pack them into envelopes that we send over the network. These envelopes contain a size field and a payload of this size. Whenever we receive an envelope, we receive the payload size first and then wait for the payload of that size. This method is important to deserialize values properly.

Figure 12.2 presents the overall process of making a single function call, from initiating it down to getting a result, and provides some details on the internal processes. For example, I've decided to make a tuple from all the function arguments to make serialization and deserialization easier. Note that I'm striving for simplicity, not practicality here. In fact, nesting tuples introduces unnecessary overhead. We may have functions with any number of arguments in our remote interface, but the functions we actually execute over the network will have only one argument, which is a tuple. All these intermediate functions will be generated by Template Haskell, so the user doesn't have to bother about it.

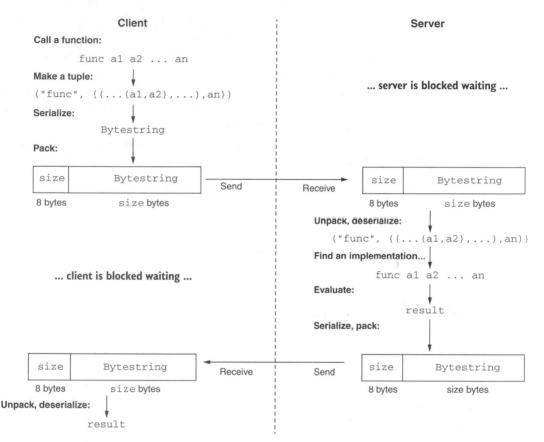

Figure 12.2 Communication model: a single function call

LIBRARY STRUCTURE
Now let's get closer to the library code.

EXAMPLE: LIBRARY THAT IMPLEMENTS RPC-STYLE CALLS

   🗋 ch12/rpc/lib/

   ⚡ *rpc-lib*

   ☞ We hide all the implementations details in the internal library.

We have the following modules:

- RpcCommon provides common definitions used by other modules and clients. These include mainly data types and the RSIO monad stack, which combines the Reader, State, and IO monads.
- ClientUtils and ServerUtils provide interfaces for clients and servers, respectively. They reexport many required definitions from other modules and implement client- and server-specific functionalities.
- RemoteIO implements value passing with serialization and provides wrappers over networking primitives.
- DeclsGenerator is a module for generating code for clients and servers with Template Haskell. Both the remote quasiquoter and genServer used in the previous sample application are defined in this module.
- RemoteParser provides a utility function to parse a remote interface as a list of type signatures we've used in the client definition.

We have about 220 lines of code in the library. Nevertheless, it's not going to be an easy walk, because the code is quite convoluted. Note that I won't talk about components we've already discussed many times earlier in this book, such as monad stacks and exception handling. Refer to the previous chapters if you need to refresh your memory.

VALUE PASSING AND NETWORKING

Passing values between clients and servers is a well-known problem. Our key ingredient for value passing is the Serialize type class, provided by the cereal library. We use it mostly through the following couple of functions:

```
encode :: Serialize a => a -> ByteString
decode :: Serialize a => ByteString -> Either String a
```

They are implemented through the low-level put and get methods of the Serialize type class. Encoding always runs smoothly, but decoding may occasionally fail. That's why the decode function gives us Either String a back. The left component contains an error message.

EXAMPLE: LIBRARY THAT IMPLEMENTS RPC-STYLE CALLS

🗋   ch12/rpc/lib/RemoteIO.hs

🗋   ch12/rpc/lib/ClientUtils.hs

🗋   ch12/rpc/lib/ServerUtils.hs

Because we do decoding several times, we have the following data type to distinguish between stages:

```
data DecodeStages = Stage0 | Stage1 | Stage2
  deriving Show
```

The stages are as follows:

1   At Stage0, we decode the first field of an envelope (the size of the payload).
2   At Stage1, we decode the second field of an envelope to a ByteString.
3   At Stage2, we decode the ByteString to a value we expect (either a tuple with all the parameters or a result of a function call, depending on the side we are on).

The same stages are used to encode parameters in the opposite order, though we don't have to report them because we expect no problems during encoding.

The following function deals with processing decoding results:

```
unEitherStaged :: DecodeStages -> Either String a -> RSIO st a
unEitherStaged stage eValue = either (throwRemote . errMsg) pure eValue
  where
    errMsg msg = "Decoding error (" <> show stage <> "): " <> msg
```

We either return a decoded value or report an error within the monad stack.

Both encode and decode functions are used in the following callRemote function, which implements our remote function call model on the client side:

**Sends the request with the required
function name and encoded arguments**

```
type Operation = String
type RemoteAction st a b = a -> RSIO st b

callRemote :: (Serialize a, Serialize b) => Operation ->  RemoteAction st a b
callRemote operation params = do
    sendRSIO (operation, encode params)
    answer <- receiveRSIO                        ← Receives a result
    unEitherStaged Stage2 (decode answer)        ← Decodes the result
```

We'll get to sendRSIO and receiveRSIO shortly.

The server side stores the table with all the registered functions as follows:

```
type RPCTable st = [(Operation, RemoteAction st ByteString ByteString)]
```

Note that these functions operate on the server side over the ByteString encoded parameters. We'll use the following wrapper to generate such functions from the functions over serializable parameters:

```
runSerialized :: (Serialize a, Serialize b) =>
                 RemoteAction st a b ->
                 RemoteAction st ByteString ByteString
runSerialized action params
  = unEitherStaged Stage2 (decode params) >>= fmap encode . action
```

Note that the params argument of runSerialized refers to parameters of the resulting RemoteAction over ByteString.

For every request, the server looks up the RPCTable and calls the corresponding wrapped function as follows:

```
serveRequest :: RPCTable st -> RSIO st ()
serveRequest rpcTable = receiveRSIO >>= call >>= sendRSIO
  where
    call (operation, params) =
      case lookup operation rpcTable of
        Nothing -> throwRemote
                     $ "Unsupported operation (" <> operation <> ")"
        Just func -> func params
```

The sendRSIO and receiveRSIO functions are responsible for encoding and decoding at stages 0 and 1. They also initiate networking operations. The sendRSIO is implemented as follows:

The connection is kept in the Reader environment.

```
sendRSIO :: Serialize a => a -> RSIO st ()                Builds an envelope and
sendRSIO msg = do                                        sends it over the network
▷ conn <- ask
   liftIO $ connectionPut conn $ buildMsgEnvelope $ encode msg  ◁
  where
    buildMsgEnvelope payload = runPut $ do               ◁        Constructs an envelope
      putWord64be (fromIntegral $ BS.length payload) ◁            using low-level Serialize
▷     putByteString payload                                       methods
                                             Creates the size field as
  Creates the rest of the envelope           a big-endian Word64
```

The receiveRSIO deals with receiving messages over the network, staged decoding, and potential errors as follows:

```
receiveRSIO :: Serialize a => RSIO st a
receiveRSIO = ask >>= \conn ->                Receives the          Decodes the
                recvExact conn msgSizeField   size field            size field as a big-
Receives the                                                        endian Word64
payload    |    >>= unEitherStaged Stage0 . runGet getWord64be  ◁
           ▷    >>= recvExact conn . fromIntegral
                >>= unEitherStaged Stage1 . decode   ◁——— Decodes the payload
    where
      recvExact conn sz =
        catch (liftIO $ connectionGetExact conn sz)
              (\e -> if isEOFError e then throwM ConnectionClosed
                     else throwRemote (displayException e))
```

Note the type signatures of these functions, shown next:

```
sendRSIO :: Serialize a => a -> RSIO st ()
receiveRSIO :: Serialize a => RSIO st a
```

We can use them for sending and receiving both arguments and results, given that they are serializable. This creates a source of fragility in our implementations. If we send something unexpected at a particular point, then decoding fails, and we can't continue. Binary protocols are known to be extremely fragile and rarely used at the application level nowadays.

Thus, neither a client nor a server has to deal with encoding. Everything is done by the library.

As for networking, we use the following three libraries:

- `network` for basic definitions (such as the port number)
- `connection` for establishing client-server connections and sending and receiving packets over the network
- `network-simple` for simple server implementation

The main entry point for a client is the `runRemote` function, as shown next:

```
runRemote :: RemoteState st => String -> PortNumber -> RSIO st a -> IO a
runRemote host port computation = do
    conn <- remoteConnectTo host port
    res <- runRemoteConn conn computation
    liftIO $ connectionClose conn
    pure res
```

It establishes a connection to the specified server, runs all the operations, and closes the connection afterward.

The main entry point for a server is the `serveRPC` function, shown here:

```
serveRPC :: RemoteState st =>
            HostName -> PortNumber -> RPCTable st -> IO ()
serveRPC host portNum rpcTable =
    serve (Host host) (show portNum) procRequests
  where
    connParams = ConnectionParams host portNum Nothing Nothing

    procRequests (connSock, sockAddr) = do
      logConnection "New connection" sockAddr
      initCtx <- initConnectionContext
      conn <- connectFromSocket initCtx connSock connParams
      catch (runRemoteConn conn $ forever $ serveRequest rpcTable)
            (\(e :: RemoteException) ->
                logConnection (displayException e) sockAddr)

    logConnection msg sockAddr =
      putStrLn $ "LOG: " <> show sockAddr <> " " <> msg
```

The `serve` function from the `Network.Simple.TCP` module creates a separate thread for every incoming connection. We run the `procRequests` function in that thread.

GENERATING CLIENT DEFINITIONS

Now let's get to the main point: using Template Haskell. Remember that the client uses the following quasiquote to describe the remote interface:

```
[remote|
ping :: RemotePing PingAnswer
echo :: String -> RemotePing String
 |]
```

We should parse these type signatures and generate the `ping` and `echo` function stubs, which are responsible for sending requests to a server and receiving their results, respectively.

EXAMPLE: LIBRARY THAT IMPLEMENTS RPC-STYLE CALLS

🗋   ch12/rpc/lib/DeclsGenerator.hs

🗋   ch12/rpc/lib/RemoteParser.hs

The quasiquoter is defined as follows:

```
remote :: QuasiQuoter
remote =  QuasiQuoter {
    quoteExp = undefined,
    quotePat = undefined,
    quoteType = undefined,
    quoteDec = quoteFuncInfoDec
  }
```

We want to replace the quote with the generated function declarations, as shown next:

```
quoteFuncInfoDec :: String -> Q [Dec]
quoteFuncInfoDec quote = parseRemoteInterface quote >>= genClientStubs
```

Let's look at parsing interfaces first. Note the problem: we have to parse Haskell type signatures here. Clearly, this is not a problem we want to solve manually. Instead, we apply the following packages:

- `haskell-src-exts` to parse type signatures
- `haskell-src-meta` to turn parsed types to Template Haskell type representations

WARNING   These two packages for parsing Haskell sources are becoming part of history. It's not a good idea to start new projects that rely on them. Nowadays, GHC provides the GHC API for doing the same things. This API is accessible via the `ghc-lib-parser` package. Unfortunately, solving our easy problems with this highly sophisticated package is not that easy. That's why I've decided to use good old `haskell-src-exts` and `haskell-src-meta` in this book.

For every type signature, we'd like to get the following record:

```
data FuncInfo = FuncInfo {
    name :: String
  , ty :: TH.Type
  }
```

The `parseRemoteInterface` and `funcInfo` functions do all the work, as shown next:

```
parseRemoteInterface :: String -> Q [FuncInfo]
parseRemoteInterface quote = concat <$> mapM (funcInfo . parseDecl) funcs
  where
```

```
    funcs = filter (not . null) $ map (dropWhile isSpace) $ lines quote

funcInfo :: ParseResult (Decl SrcSpanInfo) -> Q [FuncInfo]
funcInfo (ParseOk (TypeSig _ ids t)) =
    pure $ [FuncInfo {..} | Ident _ name <- ids,
                           let ty = toType t]
funcInfo err =
    fail $ "Error when parsing remote interface (type signature expected)\n"
            <> show err
```

Here we use the `parseDecl` function from `haskell-src-ext` to parse a Haskell declaration. It gives us the `Decl` type, which contains all the details about the type signature wrapped into the `ParseResult` type. If parsing is successful, we look into the result and extract identifiers and their type. Finally, we create a list of `FuncInfo` from those identifiers and types converted with the `toType` function from `haskell-src-meta` to be compatible with Template Haskell types.

Now we need to generate function stubs as follows:

```
genClientStubs :: [FuncInfo] -> Q [Dec]
genClientStubs fis = concat <$> mapM (genClientStub "callRemote") fis
```

Remember that remote functions are allowed to have any number of arguments. We've decided to put all of them into a tuple. We can do that by calling the `curry` function several times as follows:

```
curryAll :: Int -> Q Exp
curryAll 0 = [| \f -> f () |]
curryAll 1 = [| id |]
curryAll n
    | n > 1 = [| curry . $(curryAll (n-1)) |]
    | otherwise = fail "curryAll argument can't be negative"
```

This Template Haskell code generates a lambda function, which creates a function with many arguments from a function with one argument given as a tuple. For example, with `curryAll 3`, we get the following:

```
ghci> :type $(curryAll 3)
$(curryAll 3) :: (((a, b1), b2) -> c) -> a -> b1 -> b2 -> c
```

The `(((a, b1), b2) -> c)` single argument function runs over the network, but the user works with the `a -> b1 -> b2 -> c` part of the generated function.

The client stub itself uses this function to build the declaration we need, as shown here:

Builds a function declaration from a name and a body

```
genClientStub :: String -> FuncInfo -> Q [Dec]
genClientStub callee FuncInfo {..} = do
    funcImpl <- funD funName [clause [] (normalB stubBody) []]    <——
    pure [typeSig, funcImpl]
  where
```

```
    funName = mkName name
    typeSig = SigD funName ty        ◁──┐  Builds a type signature from a name and a type
┌─▷ stubBody = [| $(curryAll (arity ty)) $ $(dyn callee) name |]
│
```
Builds a function body with currying

Note that some of the components are built purely with constructors (e.g., SigD for type signatures) whereas others require using Q computations (e.g., function declaration with funD). Just as before, we combine quotes with splices.

The dyn function creates a reference to a function from the String representation of its name. We use it to refer to the callRemote function. For example, if we call the echo function, the $(dyn callee) name part of the body generates callRemote "echo" augmented with argument currying.

The arity function inspects a Template Haskell type representation and determines the number of function arguments as follows:

```
arity :: Type -> Int
arity (ForallT _ _ rest) = arity rest
arity (AppT (AppT ArrowT _) rest) = arity rest + 1
arity _ = 0
```

This is a simplified version of such a function, though it works for most type signatures. The Type type has more than two dozen constructors, and using some of them in a type may lead to the wrong results.

GHC with the -ddump-splices flag reports the following generated functions for our ping client:

```
ping :: RemotePing PingAnswer
ping = ((\ f_akLr -> f_akLr ()) $ callRemote "ping")
echo :: String -> RemotePing String
echo = (id $ callRemote "echo")
```

Let's add the two-argument function as follows:

```
echo2 :: String -> String -> RemotePing String
```

Now we have the following function generated:

```
echo2 :: String -> String -> RemotePing String
echo2 = ((curry . id) $ callRemote "echo2")
```

The client is ready to work. Let's move to the server.

GENERATING SERVER DEFINITIONS

The server needs the server function working over the RPCTable with remote functions.

EXAMPLE: LIBRARY THAT IMPLEMENTS RPC-STYLE CALLS

[ ] ch12/rpc/lib/DeclsGenerator.hs

We generate both as follows:

```
genServer :: [Name] -> Q [Dec]
genServer names =
  [d|
    server :: String -> PortNumber -> IO ()
    server host port = serveRPC host port $(genRemoteTable names)
  |]
```

This function takes the names of functions that are supposed to be called remotely. We hand them to `RPCTable` augmented with serialization and deserialization. To do that, we first get their types and then wrap with `runSerialized` we've already discussed as follows:

```
genRemoteTable :: [Name] -> Q Exp
genRemoteTable names =
  mapM reifyFunc names
  >>= listE . map (genServerStub "runSerialized")
```

The `reifyFunc` function consults the compiler with `reify` and gives back the `FuncInfo` record, as shown next:

```
reifyFunc :: Name -> Q FuncInfo
reifyFunc nm = do
  VarI _ t Nothing <- reify nm
  pure $ FuncInfo (nameBase nm) t
```

The `genServerStub` builds an `RPCTable` entry for one remote function as follows:

```
genServerStub :: String -> FuncInfo -> ExpQ
genServerStub callee FuncInfo {..} =
    [| (name, $(dyn callee) $ $(uncurryAll (arity ty)) $(dyn name) ) |]
```

The `uncurryAll` does the opposite to the `curryAll` function, as shown here:

```
uncurryAll :: Int -> Q Exp
uncurryAll 0 = [| (const :: a -> () -> a) |]
uncurryAll 1 = [| id |]
uncurryAll n
  | n >1 = [| uncurry . $(uncurryAll (n-1)) |]
  | otherwise = fail "uncurryAll argument can't be negative"
```

For example, in our `ping-server`, we have the following code generated:

```
server_akVF :: String -> PortNumber -> IO ()
server_akVF host_akVG port_akVH
  = ((serveRPC host_akVG) port_akVH)
      [("ping", (runSerialized $ (const :: a_akVI -> () -> a_akVI) ping)),
       ("echo", (runSerialized $ id echo))]
```

Although not too much code is generated here, such code is extremely boring to write, so using Template Haskell definitely pays off.

Summary

- GHC provides very sophisticated instance-deriving mechanisms. Chances are we don't have to derive them manually.
- Specifying strategies for deriving clauses explicitly is generally considered good practice.
- GHC.Generics allows us to write code with respect to data-type representation and not the data type itself.
- We use data-type-generic programming with GHC.Generics to provide type classes suitable to work with default implementations.
- We use Template Haskell to generate any code we need that is too dull to write manually.
- Template Haskell is powerful, though writing it can be very hard and error prone.

More about types

13

This chapter covers

- Using types to direct processing stages
- Using types to implement safe interfaces
- Programming with dependent types in Haskell

We've discussed a lot of powerful Haskell features in the previous chapters. To keep the presentation simple, I tried to talk about them in isolation. Their powers become much stronger, however, when we use them in combination. We can achieve a huge boost in the expressiveness of our types together with the provable safety of our programs if we apply types, type classes, type families, GADTs, and Template Haskell at once. In this chapter, I demonstrate how we can do that in two extended examples.

In the first section we'll explore the usage of type families and type classes to describe and implement RESTful web services. We'll do that in the vein of the Servant library, the most-used Haskell library for implementing web services.

In the second section, we'll implement a safe type-controlled interface for elevators. Software correctness becomes of primary importance when we work with hardware devices. We'll use GADTs as the main building blocks to do fully featured type-level programming in Haskell, although we need almost everything else, too.

Along the way we'll implement *singletons*, special values that can be operated on both the term level and the type level. Singletons will bring us to the idea of dependent-type programming, when types depend on values. GHC does not yet support fully dependent types at the time of writing, though we can already use many dependently typed techniques.

13.1   *Types for specifying a web API*

When we teach numbers to small children, we never tell them about integer, real, or complex numbers. They are just numbers like 1, 2, 3. Children get used to different types of numbers later. It's not unusual to follow the same path with programs: we start with almost no types at all, using `String` to express almost everything, and then continue to build more sophisticated abstractions and apply more high-level typing machinery.

In this section, we'll build a prototype web service implementation from scratch: starting with the most basic implementation, we'll get to something similar to `Servant`, one of the most popular (and hard to understand) Haskell libraries featuring type-level programming at its best.

13.1.1   *Implementing a web API from scratch*

Our web service provides information about books: given a book ID, it returns the corresponding book's title, year of publication, and rating. We support HTTP requests like `"/title/1234"` or `"/rating/4321"`. For simplicity, let's assume that request is already split into components, such as `["title", "1234"]` or `["rating", "4321"]`. We will not try to maintain a book database: every correct request will return info about "Haskell in Depth", published in 2021, and rated as "Great", no matter the book ID given.

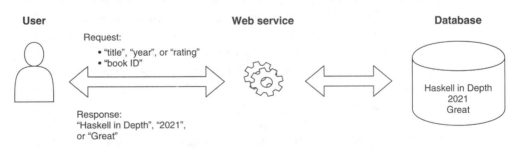

Figure 13.1   Prototype of a book information web service

Figure 13.1 illustrates what we are going to implement in this section.

STAGE 0: PROGRAMMING WITH STRINGS

At stage 0 of our implementation, we work with strings: both requests and results are strings. The only thing we should implement is how to determine results based on requests.

EXAMPLE: PROTOTYPE WEB SERVICE IMPLEMENTATION (STAGE 0)

☐   ch13/api/Api0.hs

⚡   *api-stage0*

The following example presents an original implementation:

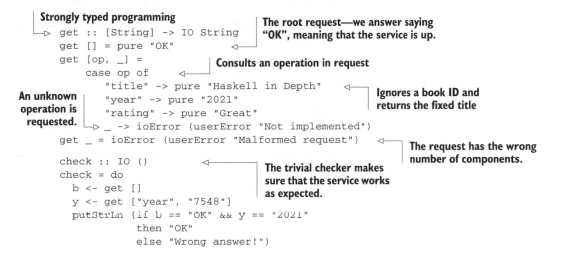

The get function is our main object in this project. It implements the whole service. Given a request, it generates the following response:

```
ghci> get []
"OK"
ghci> get ["title","1234"]
"Haskell in Depth"
```

The request is expressed with types as [String]. The response is also String. The service is [String] -> IO String, meaning that we work in the IO monad to do something real-worldish. Book IDs, year, and rating are all values of the String type.

Despite the simplicity, we still have basic error checking and tests.

STAGE 1: INTRODUCING TYPES

Our first goal is to introduce more types. Many components in our small program are begging for stronger typing, for example:

- Book rating and service status could be represented by a type enumerating possible values.
- One particular request handler deserves its own type.
- Request handlers could return specific types instead of plain String types.
- We could combine request handlers into one data structure, thus getting service as a value and the ability to write different implementations.
- We could also introduce *routing* as a separate stage with its own type. Routing is a procedure to find the particular handler for a request.

EXAMPLE: PROTOTYPE WEB SERVICE IMPLEMENTATION (STAGE 1)

☐   ch13/api/Api1.hs

⚡   *api-stage1*

☞   More types bring more structure to our data.

The easiest thing to do is to provide types for a book rating and a service status as follows:

```
data Rating = Bad | Good | Great
  deriving Show

data ServiceStatus = Ok | Down
  deriving Show
```

As for request handlers, one option is to define a type for one handler and a record for storing the service as a whole as follows:

```
type BookID = Int
type HandlerAction a = IO a
type ReqHandler a = BookID -> HandlerAction a

data BookInfoAPIImpl = BookInfoAPIImpl {
                        root :: HandlerAction ServiceStatus,
                        title :: ReqHandler String,
                        year :: ReqHandler Int,
                        rating :: ReqHandler Rating
                      }
```

We have a root request as an action without parameters returning `ServiceStatus`, whereas all other requests take `BookID` and return corresponding types. Thanks to this `BookInfoAPIImpl` record, we can provide a couple of different implementations, as shown next:

```
impl1 = BookInfoAPIImpl {
    root = pure Ok,
    title = \_ -> pure "Haskell in Depth",
    year = \_ -> pure 2021,
    rating = \_ -> pure Great
  }

impl2 = BookInfoAPIImpl {
    root = pure Down,
    title = \_ -> notImplemented,
    year = \_ -> notImplemented,
    rating = \_ -> notImplemented
  }
  where
    notImplemented = ioError (userError "not implemented")
```

This is a very important step: we've introduced the `BookInfoAPIImpl` type, and now we can separate service implementation from request processing. The `ReqHandler` a type synonym serves as a contract: all our request handlers have to agree to it. Once we have a notion of a handler, we can refine its type further and get more control over handlers. Here we are able to control a result type: it's impossible to return something that is not a `Rating` when handling the `rating` request.

Our types allow us to give a more precise meaning for routing, as shown here:

```
type Request = [String]
route :: BookInfoAPIImpl -> Request -> Maybe (IO String)
```

We take a service implementation with a list of request components and return an `IO String` action (`HandlerAction` a with a result encoded as a `String`), which can be `Nothing` if routing fails. Routing implementation is almost the same as before, though we have to take actions out of the given implementation and encode their results as follows:

```
encode :: Show a => HandlerAction a -> IO String
encode m = show <$> m

route :: BookInfoAPIImpl -> Request -> Maybe (IO String)
route impl [] = pure $ encode $ root impl
route impl [op, bid'] = do
  bid <- readMaybe bid'
  case op of
    "title" -> pure $ title impl bid
    "year" -> pure $ encode $ year impl bid
    "rating" -> pure $ encode $ rating impl bid
    _ -> Nothing
route _ _ = Nothing
```

We could also go with `Either` instead of `Maybe` to provide more information on mistakes (malformed requests or an unknown operation requested).

The `get` function is now a small wrapper for `route`, as shown next:

```
get :: BookInfoAPIImpl -> Request -> IO String
get impl xs =
  case route impl xs of
    Just m -> m
    Nothing -> pure "Malformed request"
```

The checker checks a particular implementation as follows:

```
check impl = do
  b <- get impl []
  answer <- get impl ["year", "7548"]
  putStrLn (if b == "Ok" && answer == "2021"
            then "OK"
            else "Wrong answer!")
```

The main result of this stage was introducing types to specify data and processing stages.

STAGE 2: SPECIFYING A WEB INTERFACE WITH TYPES

Let's move to the most interesting part: specifying a web API for our service. The idea is to put all the necessary information about the API, including the operations in requests, their parameters, and the results, directly into a type. We already know that we can use string literals in the types, so let's use that here, too.

   Once we have an interface described by a type, we need to write an implementation, that is, implement functions for every operation. Types of those functions should relate to a description in the interface. It turns out that we can use type families to compute types of functions in the service implementation.

EXAMPLE: PROTOTYPE WEB SERVICE IMPLEMENTATION (STAGE 2)

📄   ch13/api/Api2.hs

⚡   *api-stage2*

☞   Types can describe web interfaces.

The following list of GHC extensions and imported modules gives an idea of what we are going to use to achieve the goals stated earlier:

```
{-# LANGUAGE KindSignatures #-}
{-# LANGUAGE TypeOperators #-}
{-# LANGUAGE PolyKinds #-}
{-# LANGUAGE DataKinds #-}
{-# LANGUAGE TypeFamilies #-}

import Data.Kind
import GHC.TypeLits
```

We start with implementing a small type-level language for describing web interfaces. The following four data types set the basis for the interface and implementation types:

Describes the results:
what we are going to get

Captures a request parameter
of some given type

```
 data Get (a :: Type)

 data Capture (a :: Type)     ←

 data a :<|> b = a :<|> b     ←
 infixr 8 :<|>

 data (a :: k) :> (b :: Type)     ←
 infixr 9 :>
```

Lists the alternative
request operations

Adds a request
component

Note the precedence declarations: :> has higher precedence so that we can construct one operation and then use it in the list of other operations. Note also the polymorphic kind ::k in :>, which allows having whatever we like in the description of one operation, for example, Symbol. Only one of the data types, namely, :<|>, is not empty. We use it to build a list of implementations, whereas all others serve as types exclusively.

Technically, we could go with ordinary pairs, but it's more convenient to reflect the structure of the type itself.

With these data types, it's easy to describe an interface of our web service as follows:

```
type BookInfoAPI =
        Get ServiceStatus
  :<|> "title" :> Capture BookID :> Get String
  :<|> "year" :> Capture BookID :> Get Int
  :<|> "rating" :> Capture BookID :> Get Rating
```

Now look at the implementation we expect, shown next:

```
type HandlerAction a = IO a

type BookInfoAPIImpl =
        HandlerAction ServiceStatus
  :<|> (BookID -> HandlerAction String)
  :<|> (BookID -> HandlerAction Int)
  :<|> (BookID -> HandlerAction Rating)
```

Figure 13.2 describes the translation from an API type to an implementation type. Note the additional parentheses that reflect fixity and precedence of :<|> and :>.

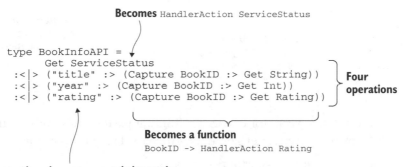

Figure 13.2 Translation from web API to implementation

Now it should be clear that the translation is automatic, and we have a tool to describe it—type families, as shown here:

```
type family Server layout :: Type
type instance Server (Get a) = HandlerAction a
type instance Server (a :<|> b) = Server a :<|> Server b
type instance Server ((s :: Symbol) :> r) = Server r
type instance Server (Capture a :> r) = a -> Server r
```

Layout is our API; Server layout is our implementation.

Get a translates to HandlerAction a.

Symbol is ignored.

A pair of requests becomes a pair of request implementations (handlers).

Capture a becomes a parameter to a request handler.

Implementations look different with this approach—they are not records anymore. They use the `:<|>` data constructor to reflect the API instead as follows:

```
impl1 :: Server BookInfoAPI
impl1 = pure Ok
        :<|> title
        :<|> year
        :<|> rating
   where
     title _ = pure "Haskell in Depth"
     year _ = pure 2021
     rating _ = pure Great
```

> The type of implementation is computed from BookInfoAPI.

Interestingly, if we replace `Server BookInfoAPI` in the type signature with `BookInfoAPIImpl`, shown earlier, we'll see no difference. These types are the same, according to GHC.

Because we've changed the representation of the service implementation, we should reflect these changes in routing as follows:

> The implementation is given as Server BookInfoAPI.

> Pattern matching on the implementation reflects the associativity of `:<|>` to the right.

```
route :: Server BookInfoAPI -> Request -> Maybe (IO String)
route (root :<|> _) [] = pure $ encode $ root
route (_ :<|> title :<|> year :<|> rating) [op, bid'] = do
   bid <- readMaybe bid'
   case op of
      "title" -> pure $ title bid
      "year" -> pure $ encode $ year bid
      "rating" -> pure $ encode $ rating bid
      _ -> Nothing
route _ _ = Nothing
```

> Pattern matches on the implementation to access all other handlers

We are almost done except for one thing. Routing itself can also be constructed automatically from an interface. Let's do that at the last stage of this example.

STAGE 3: IMPLEMENTING ROUTING WITH TYPE CLASSES

Let's look at our API once again:

```
type BookInfoAPI =
      Get ServiceStatus
  :<|> "title" :> Capture BookID :> Get String
  :<|> "year" :> Capture BookID :> Get Int
  :<|> "rating" :> Capture BookID :> Get Rating
```

How should we do routing based on it? Several guidelines follow:

- If our interface is simply `Get a`, we should return the corresponding encoded `HandlerAction a` with `Just`.
- If we have something like a `:<|>` b, we should try a first, and if it fails (we get `Nothing`), then try b. (This is a traditional `Alternative` instance behavior for `Maybe a`.)

- If we have "operation" :> a, we should consult the request we've got and check if it has the "operation" in it. Then we return either Nothing or do a (with the tail of the request as we've processed an operation already).
- If we have Capture a :> b, we should consult the current request component, turn it into an a (for simplicity) via the Read a machinery, and then proceed with b, supplying it with a discovered parameter.

This is clearly a type-directed procedure. We'd like to implement the route function based on the types of parameters. Isn't it plain old type classes and instances machinery? Well, it surely is.

EXAMPLE: PROTOTYPE WEB SERVICE IMPLEMENTATION (STAGE 3)

🗋 ch13/api/Api3.hs

⚡ *api-stage3*

☞ Implementation can be derived from a type.

To apply this idea, we need the following additional GHC extensions and a new module:

```
{-# LANGUAGE FlexibleInstances #-}
{-# LANGUAGE InstanceSigs #-}
{-# LANGUAGE ScopedTypeVariables #-}

import Control.Applicative ((<|>))   ◁─── For Maybe alternatives
```

The FlexibleInstances GHC extension is almost always needed when we define instances. Standard requirements for instances are very tight. For example, they allow only instances with the C (T a1 … an) head, where C is the class, T is a data type constructor, and the a1 … an are distinct type variables. FlexibleInstances allows arbitrary nested types instead. As for the two other extensions, we met them earlier in this book.

The route function is now the only method of the HasServer type class, as shown next:

```
class HasServer layout where
  route :: Proxy layout ->               We are interested in a
                                         type of API, hence Proxy.
         Server layout ->         ◁───── API implementation
         Request ->          ◁──┐
         Maybe (IO String)         List of request components
```

Resulting action ↦ (labels for `route ::` result line and `Maybe (IO String)`)

We have only one additional parameter to route: the type of the API. We'll use it extensively to exploit instance machinery.

Let's write the first instance for Get a, expecting an encoded HandlerAction a as a result as follows:

InstanceSigs helps to see the actual type signature.

We encode the handler and return it. There should be no request components at this stage.

```
instance Show a => HasServer (Get a) where
  route :: Proxy (Get a) -> HandlerAction a -> Request ->
    Maybe (IO String)
  route _ handler [] = Just (encode $ handler)   ◁──
  route _ _       _  = Nothing
```

Remember, we didn't do encoding when returning `String`. The following is an instance especially for `Get String`. It uses the `OVERLAPS` pragma to signal explicitly that it's a special case of `Get a`.

```
instance {-# OVERLAPS #-} HasServer (Get String) where
  route :: Proxy (Get String)
        -> IO String -> Request -> Maybe (IO String)
  route _ handler [] = Just handler
  route _ _          _ = Nothing
```

An instance for `:<|>` is straightforward. We choose either the first component or the second one, if the first one fails, as shown next:

```
instance (HasServer a, HasServer b) => HasServer (a :<|> b) where
  route :: Proxy (a :<|> b)
        -> (Server a :<|> Server b) -> Request -> Maybe (IO String)
  route _ (handlera :<|> handlerb) xs =
        route (Proxy :: Proxy a) handlera xs
    <|> route (Proxy :: Proxy b) handlerb xs
```

The most interesting case is processing `Symbol`, because we have to make sure that it matches the request component. We do that by the familiar `symbolVal` method of the `KnownSymbol` type class. If it doesn't match, the routing fails as follows:

```
instance (KnownSymbol s, HasServer r) => HasServer ((s :: Symbol) :> r) where
  route :: Proxy (s :> r)
        -> Server r -> Request -> Maybe (IO String)
  route _ handler (x : xs)
    | symbolVal (Proxy :: Proxy s) == x = route (Proxy :: Proxy r) handler xs
  route _ _         _                 = Nothing
```

And the final instance for `Capture a` is shown here:

```
instance (Read a, HasServer r) => HasServer (Capture a :> r) where
  route :: Proxy (Capture a :> r)
        -> (a -> Server r) -> [String] -> Maybe (IO String)
  route _ handler (x : xs) = do
    a <- readMaybe x                    ⟵——┐ Acquires a request parameter
    route (Proxy :: Proxy r) (handler a) xs  ⟵——┐
  route _ _        _       = Nothing          │ Sends the parameter to a handler
```

All these instances we just implemented do the actual routing job. Consequently, GHC decides what to do based on types. Types direct and lead an implementation.

The last thing to do is to replace `route` in the implementation of `get` and reflect this in `check` as follows:

```
get :: HasServer layout =>
      Proxy layout -> Server layout -> [String] -> IO String
get proxy handler request =
  case route proxy handler request of
```

```
        Nothing -> ioError (userError "404")
        Just m  -> m
check impl = do
  b <- get (Proxy :: Proxy BookInfoAPI) impl []
  answer <- get (Proxy :: Proxy BookInfoAPI) impl ["year", "7548"]
  putStrLn (if b == "Ok" && answer == "2021"
            then "OK"
            else "Wrong answer!")
```

We are done. Types are hard at work doing control, implementation constructing, and routing. Note that this technique doesn't depend on our example; it can be used for any web service. It is available to your projects via the `servant` library. Let's look at the same example implemented with `servant`.

13.1.2 Implementing a web service with servant

The `servant` library is much more complicated than what we've seen so far. Despite specifying a web interface with types and derived routing, it supports many ways to encode responses (plain text, JSON, etc.). Handlers in `Servant` are not simple `IO` actions. They use monad transformers instead. Nevertheless, the ideas we've got should help to explain `Servant`.

> **EXAMPLE: PROTOTYPE WEB SERVICE IMPLEMENTATION (SERVANT)**
>
> 🗋   ch13/api/ApiServant.hs
>
> ⚡   *api-servant*
>
> ☞ We use the `servant` library to implement web services.

Technically, `servant` is implemented as a bunch of packages. Normally, we use it together with other packages to get additional functionality. In this example, we need the following:

- `servant-server` as a starting point for servant-based web services
- `warp` as an HTTP server
- `blaze-html` and `servant-blaze` to generate and return HTML documents
- `aeson` to deal with JSON

The three main steps to implement the web service follow:

1 Describe the API.
2 Provide implementations for particular requests.
3 Derive server functionality and run it.

The first step with `servant` is almost the same as before, as shown here:

```
data Rating = Bad | Good | Great
  deriving (Show, Generic, ToJSON)

data ServiceStatus = Ok | Down
```

```
    deriving (Show, Generic, ToJSON)

type BookID = Int

type BookInfoAPI = Get '[JSON] ServiceStatus
                  :<|> "title"  :> Capture "id" BookID :> Get '[HTML] H.Html
                  :<|> "year"   :> Capture "id" BookID :> Get '[JSON] Int
                  :<|> "rating" :> Capture "id" BookID :> Get '[JSON] Rating
```

Note the following differences from our previous implementation:

- We need to derive `Generic` and `ToJSON` instances for `Rating` and `ServiceStatus` to make our types available for JSON encoding.
- We provide lists of particular available encodings in `Get` request components. Those are type-level lists. We write them with `'[…]` syntax. We've used trivial `String` encoding before.
- For the sake of demonstration, I return HTML for title requests and JSON for all other requests.
- The `Capture` request component requires `Symbol` to name an argument.

As the second step, we define an implementation as follows:

```
impl :: Server BookInfoAPI
impl = pure Ok
       :<|> title
       :<|> year
       :<|> rating
  where
    title _ = pure $ H.toHtml $ H.b "Haskell in Depth"
    year _ = pure 2021
    rating _ = pure Great
```

Just as before, all the types are under control. For example, the type checker makes sure that we do give HTML back in the second request handler.

Finally, we define a server application and run it. This includes deriving routing implementation and dealing with network communications. Thanks to the `servant-server` and `warp` packages, this takes only a couple of lines of code, as shown next:

```
app :: Application
app = serve (Proxy :: Proxy BookInfoAPI) impl

main :: IO ()
main = run 8081 app
```

The `serve` function takes a `Proxy` with type information about the API and derives all the actual routing implementation. It returns a `WAI` application, which is a standard interface for web applications in Haskell. The `run` function comes from the `warp` package. It implements an HTTP server able to serve any `WAI` application.

Let's run this program as follows:

```
$ cabal run api-servant
Up to date
...
```

The server blocks and waits for requests. Now we can either head to the browser and ask for `http://localhost:8081/` or use `curl` to retrieve the results as follows:

```
$ curl http://localhost:8081/
"Ok"
$ curl http://localhost:8081/title/1234
<b>Haskell in Depth</b>
$ curl http://localhost:8081/year/1234
2021
$ curl http://localhost:8081/rating/1234
"Great"
```

Note the rendered HTML returned as a result of the `title` request. Other results are JSON-encoded.

The `servant` library has very good documentation and a brilliant tutorial (https://docs.servant.dev/en/stable/tutorial/). I recommend going through it before using this library in practice.

13.2 Toward dependent types with singletons

The Haskell type system is quite weak in comparison with some other programming languages, such as Agda or Idris. Those languages support *dependent types*. This means that types may depend on values, and a type checker has access to those values. An ability to analyze values at compile time allows for fine-grained control over computations, their arguments, and results.

Although Haskell doesn't support dependent types yet, its type system is already powerful enough to express some of the techniques for programming with dependent types. Such tools as type classes and GADTs enable many of those techniques. In this section, we use them to provide a safe interface for elevators that move from floor to floor and manage their doors. This is a well-known state machine often used to present the corresponding ideas.

13.2.1 Safety in Haskell programs

Haskell developers often talk about the *safety* of their programs, but what does that actually mean? As usual, theory gives the right answer.

Unfortunately, in practice, types don't express every program property. Moreover, they are quite weak in describing values we get at run time from a user. Although we do try to parse external data into some internal types, we have some limits. For example, if a user provides a sequence of values at run time, we cannot reason about their number at compile time. We just don't know that number then.

> ### Theoretical notion of safety
>
> The usual definition of safety includes the following two parts:
>
> - *Progress* means that a well-typed program is either a value or can be evaluated further.
> - *Preservation* means that evaluation steps preserve types, so an initial program and a resulting value have the same type.
>
> Consequently, the program is considered safe if it features both progress and preservation. Theory suggests that once we've checked types, those types can be erased, and the computation goes smoothly without errors. These theoretical ideas are actually implemented in GHC. At the least, no types are left in a program at run time.

In general, we use types to check everything that can be checked at compile time. We write tests to check over program properties. Finally, we have to write run-time checks, report errors to a user using some sort of an exception-handling mechanism, or implement some workarounds like using default values or most appropriate values.

Consider, for example, the `head` function. If it's given an empty list, it throws an exception. This counts as unsafe behavior. We should check an argument before passing it to this function. Then we still have to look for workarounds if an argument is an empty list. Alternatively, we use functions that return `Maybe a`. Then the type system ensures that we've dealt with both potential results, `Just` or `Maybe` something. This is a step toward type safety. We could also use `NonEmpty` instead of ordinary lists.

Unfortunately, the safer an interface we have, the less convenient it usually is to use. With `Maybe` in a result, we have to implement two processing branches, even if we are absolutely sure that `Nothing` never arises. This is required by the types. In this section, we'll look at cases where we have to prove things to a compiler. These proofs can be quite hard to write—sometimes, it's even impossible.

I'd like to stress that *safe* and *unsafe* don't correspond to *good* and *bad* directly. It's safe to write unsafe programs in Haskell, given that we have tests and run-time checks. Nevertheless, for some sorts of software, the price of an error is too high. We'd like to apply whatever is available to reduce or completely eliminate the corresponding risks. Then we have to think hard, deal with sophisticated types, and write proofs.

An elevator-management system is definitely an example of such software. We don't want to have a door open when the elevator is not completely level with a floor. We don't want to allow it to move with open doors. We want to make it impossible to move higher than the top floor or go below the ground level. Surely, we can check that at run time, but we can also do the same at compile time using several quite clever techniques. This is our main focus in this section.

13.2.2 *Example: Unsafe interface for elevators*

Let's start with low-level operations over elevators. Hardware mostly comes with supporting C libraries and no type-level control at all. This is where we'll start.

EXAMPLE: LOW-LEVEL INTERFACE FOR ELEVATOR HARDWARE

🗋   ch13/elevator/Elevator/LowLevel.hs

We use the following interface for low-level operations:

```
up :: IO ()
up = putStrLn "Going up"

down :: IO ()
down = putStrLn "Going down"

open :: IO ()
open = putStrLn "Door is opening"

close :: IO ()
close = putStrLn "Door is closing"
```

Nothing is controlled in any way. This interface can be used in plenty of incorrect ways. It's clearly unsafe. Let's wrap it with something more usable.

EXAMPLE: UNSAFE INTERFACE FOR ELEVATORS

🗋   ch13/elevator/Elevator/Unsafe.hs

⚡   *unsafe-elevator*

☞   We implement unsafe interfaces with plenty of run-time checks.

We start by representing data. We have doors that can be either opened or closed, as shown here:

```
data DoorState = Opened | Closed
  deriving (Eq, Show)
```

We also have floors, as shown next:

```
newtype Floor = Floor Int
  deriving (Eq, Ord)
```

For simplicity, I limit the minimum and maximum floors with the Bounded instance as follows:

```
instance Bounded Floor where
  minBound = Floor 0
  maxBound = Floor 5
```

The elevator combines both door and floor, as shown next:

```
data Elevator = Elevator {
    current :: Floor,
    door :: DoorState
  }
  deriving Show
```

Now we can implement many trivial run-time checks as follows:

```
sameFloor :: Floor -> Elevator -> Bool
sameFloor fl el = fl == current el

isClosed :: Elevator -> Bool
isClosed el = door el == Closed

isOpened :: Elevator -> Bool
isOpened el = door el == Opened

belowTop :: Floor -> Bool
belowTop fl = fl < maxBound

aboveGround :: Floor -> Bool
aboveGround fl = fl > minBound
```

Whenever we want to go down, we want to make sure that there is something below. We should also check that the door is closed. We can implement this at run time and throw errors if something is wrong as follows:

```
down :: MonadIO m => Elevator -> m Elevator
down el@(Elevator fl@(Floor n) Closed)
  | aboveGround fl = do
      liftIO $ LL.down
      pure $ el {current = Floor (n - 1)}
  | otherwise = error "Elevator is on the ground floor"
down (Elevator _ Opened) = error "Door must be closed before move"
```

Note that I've switched to the `MonadIO m` context instead of working in the `IO` monad directly. This is often a good idea when wrapping low-level interfaces. We can now use our elevator in complex monad stacks based on `IO`.

When we write such code, we believe that all these exceptional situations never arise. After all, it's not the user who calls these functions—our other functions call them.

Opening doors requires the following checks:

```
open :: MonadIO m => Floor -> Elevator -> m Elevator
open fl el
  | sameFloor fl el =
      if isClosed el
      then do
        liftIO $ LL.open
        pure $ el {door = Opened}
      else error "Door is already opened"
  | otherwise = error "Can't operate the door with an elevator elsewhere"
```

Once again, this function shouldn't be called in the wrong environment. Unfortunately, we still have to check everything. And it's still possible that we made a mistake somewhere else and could call such a function in the wrong way.

The up and `close` functions are similar. Sometimes we should do something no matter the current situation. For example, we should ensure that a door is closed before the elevator moves, as shown next:

```
ensureClosed :: MonadIO m => Elevator -> m Elevator
ensureClosed el
  | isClosed el = pure el
  | otherwise = close (current el) el
```

Moving from one floor to another may require several up or down calls. We can implement this with recursion as follows:

```
moveTo :: MonadIO m => Floor -> Elevator -> m Elevator
moveTo fl el' = do
  el <- ensureClosed el'
  case compare fl (current el) of
    EQ -> pure el
    GT -> up el >>= moveTo fl
    LT -> down el >>= moveTo fl
```

Here we compare a required floor with a current one and make a decision on the direction to move.

Finally, we have the following function that gives all the instructions to elevator hardware when it is called from one of the floors:

```
call :: MonadIO m => Floor -> Elevator -> m Elevator
call fl el = do
  liftIO $ putStrLn $ "Call to: " <> show fl
  if sameFloor fl el
    then (if isOpened el then pure el else open fl el)
    else (moveTo fl el >>= open fl)
```

Let's use this simple interface in a small demo program.

EXAMPLE: USING AN UNSAFE INTERFACE FOR AN ELEVATOR

    ch13/elevator/UseUnsafe.hs

    unsafe-elevator

We have an elevator with a closed door on the ground floor as our starting point, as shown here:

```
gfElevator :: Elevator
gfElevator = Elevator (Floor 0) Closed
```

Then we interpret command-line arguments as a list of required floors and execute corresponding elevator commands as follows:

```
main = do
    floors <- map read <$> getArgs
    foldM_ traceTo gfElevator (map Floor floors)
```

```
where
  prt el = print el >> pure el
  traceTo el fl = call fl el >>= prt
```

One example of running our simulation follows:

```
$ cabal -v0 run unsafe-elevator -- 3 1 0
Call to: Floor 3 of 5
Going up
Going up
Going up
Door is opening
Elevator {current = Floor 3 of 5, door = Opened}
Call to: Floor 1 of 5
Door is closing
Going down
Going down
Door is opening
Elevator {current = Floor 1 of 5, door = Opened}
Call to: Floor 0 of 5
Door is closing
Going down
Door is opening
Elevator {current = Floor 0 of 5, door = Opened}
```

It seems we did everything right. It may be the case, but the interface we've used is error prone and unsafe. Let's look at how Haskell can make it safer.

13.2.3 *Dependent types and substituting them with singletons*

We consider an interface safe when more things are expressed and controlled with types. In the previous version, both the door and the floor were values. The type system knew almost nothing about them. To make an interface safer, we have to bring them to type level somehow. Then we could express something like the following:

- This function can be called only when the door is closed.
- We can go down because we are not on the ground floor.
- We are below the top floor, so we can go up.

Is it possible? We don't know the actual user requests in advance. It turns out, yes, this is possible. In fact, we can think differently. We assume that we have precise information at compile time. The compiler makes sure that all the preconditions are met and then compiles our code as usual. Later we'll see how to bridge our compile-time assumptions with actual user requests.

As I've mentioned several times, in languages with dependent types, it's possible to use values (such as door state or floor number) directly at the level of types. This is not possible in Haskell, at least at the time of writing. So, we need a workaround. The idea is simple: to bring values to type level, we introduce a whole bunch of types with only one value in each of them. Such types, just as sets with a single element, are called *singleton types* or simply *singletons*. If every such type has only one value, then we can easily go between term level and type level. If we have a value, then we know its type (as always in Haskell). With singletons, if we have a type, we can be 100% sure about the value also, because only one value exists.

We already know that part of the job is done by the `DataKinds` GHC extension, which promotes data constructors to type constructors and types to kinds. Let's look at another part.

EXAMPLE: TYPE-SAFE DOOR OPERATIONS

We use state machines in software to represent processes and protocols quite often. In this section, we'll apply singletons to control state machine behavior. Let's take the doors as the simplest possible example of a state machine.

> ### EXAMPLE: TYPE-SAFE DOOR OPERATIONS
>
> ☐   ch13/doors/SingManual.hs
>
> ⚡   *door*
>
> ☞ We can introduce singletons manually.

Doors can be either closed or opened. We can open them or close them. We should also be able to make them (or initialize them). Figure 13.3 illustrates doors as state machines with their states and operations over them.

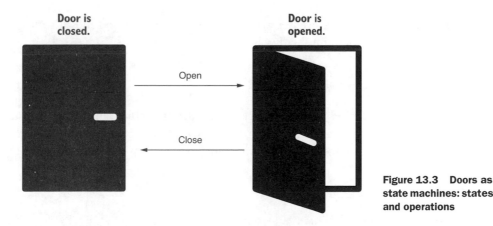

Figure 13.3   Doors as state machines: states and operations

Our goal now is to represent doors as a data type and prevent incorrect operations such as closing already closed doors or opening already opened doors.

We start with the following data type describing door states:

```
data DoorState = Opened | Closed
  deriving Show
```

With the `DataKinds` GHC extension, we get types `Opened` and `Closed` right away. Note that the promoted types have no values. Let's define two singletons for them as GADTs as follows:

```
data SDoorState (s :: DoorState) where
  SClosed :: SDoorState Closed
  SOpened :: SDoorState Opened
```

The `SDoorState Closed` type is a singleton. There exists only one value of this type, namely, `SClosed`. The `SDoorState Opened` is another singleton.

> ## GADTs and local assumptions
>
> The `SClosed` and `SOpened` values of the `SDoorState Closed` and `SDoorState Opened` types defined earlier are aliases to the following:
>
> ```
> SClosed :: s ~ Closed => SDoorState s
> SOpened :: s ~ Opened => SDoorState s
> ```
>
> The `s ~ Closed` and `s ~ Opened` are type equality constraints. Whenever we pattern match over the `SDoorState s` value and bring one of the `SClosed` or `SOpened` data constructors into scope, we bring equality assumptions as well. They are called local assumptions because they exist locally in the corresponding branch of pattern matching. Consequently, pattern matching over singletons gives us information at both the term and type levels.

The `SClosed` and `SOpened` values are explicit singletons. Sometimes it's more convenient to work with them implicitly via the following type class:

```
class SDoorStateI (s :: DoorState) where
  sDoorState :: SDoorState s
```

If we have the `SDoorStateI` type class among the constraints, we can use the `sDoorState` method to acquire an explicit singleton and then pattern match over it. This type class has the following two trivial instances:

```
instance SDoorStateI Opened where
  sDoorState = SOpened

instance SDoorStateI Closed where
  sDoorState = SClosed
```

Now we are ready to describe the door itself, as shown next:

```
data Door (s :: DoorState) where
  MkDoor :: SDoorStateI s => Door s
```

We build the door with the `MkDoor` data constructor. Note that it has no arguments. Instead, it introduces the `SDoorStateI` constraint. Depending on the door type we actually build, `Door Closed` or `Door Opened`, GHC adds the corresponding instance.

Suppose we have the `MkDoor` value. How do we get its state? Is it opened or closed? Here is how singletons come into play. We should consult the corresponding `SDoorStateI` instance, get a singleton, and pattern match over it, as shown here:

Introduces the s type variable explicitly to refer to it later

Introduces the SDoorState1 instance, which comes with MkDoor

```
doorState :: forall s. Door s -> DoorState
doorState MkDoor =
  case sDoorState :: SDoorState s of
    SOpened -> Opened
    SClosed -> Closed
```

Pattern matches over the singleton associated with the current door

If we replace the `MkDoor` pattern on the left-hand side with `_`, no corresponding `SDoorStateI` instance would be available. GHC would complain then. It's very important to understand that type-level information comes with values. We access it via pattern matching.

The `doorState` function goes one way, from a type to a value. We can use it to define the `Show` instance as follows:

```
instance Show (Door s) where
  show d = "Door " <> show (doorState d)
```

Sometimes, we don't need to refer to singletons. For example, in the following two functions, it's enough to control the types:

```
open :: Door Closed -> Door Opened
open _ = MkDoor

close :: Door Opened -> Door Closed
close _ = MkDoor
```

Behind the scenes, GHC works hard and adds the corresponding `SDoorStateI` instances to `MkDoor`. Of course, it disallows using `open` with the opened door and `close` with the closed one.

As we discussed in chapter 11, we can't write a function that returns `Door s` for some particular `s` depending on the user input. Instead, we hide this `s` inside an existential (see section 11.4.1 for a refresher):

```
data SomeDoor where
  SomeDoor :: Door s -> SomeDoor

deriving instance Show SomeDoor
```

Now it's easy to parse user input and build a door as follows:

```
parseDoor :: String -> Maybe SomeDoor
parseDoor "Opened" = Just $ SomeDoor (MkDoor :: Door Opened)
parseDoor "Closed" = Just $ SomeDoor (MkDoor :: Door Closed)
parseDoor _ = Nothing
```

By providing an explicit type signature to MkDoor, we ask GHC to add the corresponding SDoorStateI instance.

For the real problem, let's implement the following function that takes a door and switches its state. If it was closed, it opens it. If it was open, it closes it. We don't know the resulting type in advance, so we have to hide it inside SomeDoor.

```
switchState :: forall s. Door s -> SomeDoor
switchState door@MkDoor =
  case sDoorState :: SDoorState s of
    SOpened -> SomeDoor (close door)
    SClosed -> SomeDoor (open door)
```

The switchState function begins similar to doorState. We introduce the s type variable explicitly to be able to refer to it later. Then we pattern match over the MkDoor constructor to access the corresponding singleton. Finally, we pattern match over the singleton. Here's where the magic begins. Remember, the SOpened value comes with the s ~ Opened local assumption. GHC brings it into scope in the first case. This allows us to apply the close function safely. The door is clearly opened here both at term level and at type level. The second case works alike under the s ~ Closed assumption. We simply can't get this wrong. And yes, it's not magic—it's just precise information about types available to GHC thanks to our singletons.

THE SINGLETONS PACKAGE

The definitions that support singletons can be generated automatically. This functionality is implemented by the singletons library. Let's revisit the doors example with singletons.

EXAMPLE: TYPE-SAFE DOORS WITH SINGLETONS

  ☐   ch13/doors/SingGen.hs

  ⚡ *door-gen*

  ☞ We can generate definitions that support singletons.

Generating singletons requires enabling more GHC extensions than we need when writing them manually. The following is the list of them in this example:

```
{-# LANGUAGE DataKinds #-}
{-# LANGUAGE ScopedTypeVariables #-}
{-# LANGUAGE GADTs #-}
{-# LANGUAGE TypeOperators #-}
{-# LANGUAGE KindSignatures #-}
{-# LANGUAGE StandaloneDeriving #-}
```

```
{-# LANGUAGE TemplateHaskell #-}
{-# LANGUAGE TypeApplications #-}
{-# LANGUAGE TypeFamilies #-}
{-# LANGUAGE UndecidableInstances #-}
{-# LANGUAGE InstanceSigs #-}
```

We've already met all of them! We need only one module and a Template Haskell splice, as shown next:

```
import Data.Singletons.TH

$(singletons [d|
 data DoorState = Opened | Closed
  deriving Show
 |])
```

Here we declare that we want to turn `Opened` and `Closed` into singletons. This TH splice generates the following:

- `SDoorState s` type with values `SOpened` and `SClosed`. The type name is an alias to `Sing`.
- `SingI s` type class instances for `SOpened` and `SClosed`. This type class provides the `sing` method (analogous to the `sDoorState` method from the previous version).
- The `fromSing` method, which returns the original `DoorState` value when given the corresponding singleton.

We can reimplement the `Door` type and the `doorState` function using the generated functions as follows:

```
data Door (s :: DoorState) where
  MkDoor :: SingI s => Door s

doorState :: forall s. Door s -> DoorState
doorState MkDoor = fromSing (sing :: SDoorState s)
```

The `switchState` function now refers to `sing` when acquiring the singleton, as shown next:

```
switchState :: forall s. Door s -> SomeDoor
switchState door@MkDoor =
  case sing :: SDoorState s of
    SOpened -> SomeDoor (close door)
    SClosed -> SomeDoor (open door)
```

Everything else is the same as before. The `singletons` library saved us several lines of boilerplate defining types, type classes, and instances supporting singletons.

> **TIP** There is much more about singletons to learn and understand. I recommend reading an entertaining tutorial (https://blog.jle.im/entries/series/ +introduction-to-singletons.html) by Justin Le if you want to dive deeper.

13.2.4 *Example: Safe interface for elevators*

Let's get back and see how singletons can help us to provide a type-safe interface for elevators. Our plan is as follows:

1 We start with floors and ensure the safety of moving from one floor to another.
2 Then we define an elevator with respect to a current floor and a door either opened or closed on the current floor. We are going to provide basic operations over elevators first.
3 After that, we define a high-level interface for elevators.
4 With a type-safe interface ready, we need to bridge it with user input.
5 Finally, we run a simulation as in the previous attempt and see that nothing bad can ever happen.

EXAMPLE: A SAFE INTERFACE FOR ELEVATORS AND A SIMULATION

🗋   ch13/elevator/Elevator/Safe/

🗋   ch13/elevator/Elevator/Safe.hs

🗋   ch13/elevator/UseSafe.hs

⚡   *elevator*

☞ We can use many type-level features to ensure the safety of our interfaces.

Clearly, this road is longer than before. Safety costs a lot in both time and complexity of development.

FLOORS AND PROOFS

We don't have to use the `singletons` package all the time to work with singletons. As an alternative, we could write our own singleton definitions manually. We can also use singletons provided by third-party libraries. For example, to implement floors, we need type-level natural numbers. Although we have type-level natural numbers in `base`, they are quite limited in their features and don't support singletons. A handful of external packages also provide type-level natural numbers of differing quality. Some of them depend on the `singletons` package, whereas others don't.

I've decided to use the implementation of type-level natural numbers in the `fin` package by Oleg Grenrus. This library supports the singleton style without heavy dependencies. The features provided are absolutely appropriate for our goals.

The `Data.Type.Nat` module from the `fin` package provides the main `Nat` functionality. We have the following:

- The `Nat` type for natural numbers
- The corresponding `SNat` type for singletons (one singleton type for every natural value)
- The `SNatI` type class to acquire the corresponding singleton

The `Nat` type is defined as follows:

```
data Nat = Z | S Nat
```

We have a zero `Z` and the next number expressed as `S` to the given `Nat`. For example, one is `S Z`, two is `S (S Z)`, and so on. Singletons are built from these data constructors.

We also use the `Data.Type.Nat.LE` module with type-level comparisons.

EXAMPLE: A SAFE INTERFACE FOR ELEVATORS AND A SIMULATION

📄 ch13/elevator/Elevator/Safe/Floor.hs

What is the floor? It is described by two numbers: a maximum number of floors and a current floor that must be less than or equal to the maximum floor. Consequently, we need two numbers to describe not only a floor but also the relationship between them. Note that this relationship should exist at run time because otherwise, it would be impossible to reason about it. Let's describe this requirement as a type alias as follows:

```
type GoodFloor mx cur = (SNatI mx, SNatI cur, LE cur mx)
```

Note that `GoodFloor` is a constraint, as shown here:

```
ghci> :kind GoodFloor
GoodFloor :: Nat -> Nat -> Constraint
```

It consists of the following three constraints:

- `SNatI mx` means that we can always get a singleton that corresponds to the `mx` natural number.
- `SNatI cur` does the same for a current floor.
- `LE cur mx` means that `cur` is less than or equal to `mx`.

Every floor must follow these constraints, so we can specify them as requirements for the `MkFloor` data constructor as follows:

```
data Floor (mx :: Nat) (cur :: Nat) where
  MkFloor :: GoodFloor mx cur => Floor mx cur
```

Thus, whenever we've got the `MkFloor` data constructor, we also have the following:

- Instances of `SNatI mx` and `SNatI cur`, so we can get the corresponding singletons and numbers as types and values
- An instance of the `LE cur mx` type class that is a type-level proof that $cur \leq mx$

Note that we don't need to have the current floor as a value in the `MkFloor` data constructor because we can always get it through the singleton machinery. For example, let's define an instance of the `Show` type class as follows:

```
instance Show (Floor mx cur) where
  show MkFloor = "Floor " <> show (snatToNat (snat :: SNat cur))
                <> " of " <> show (snatToNat (snat :: SNat mx))
```

The `snat` method comes from the `SNatI` type class. It returns the singleton corresponding with the required type-level natural number. We specify this number via the local type signature as follows:

```
snat :: SNat cur
```

The `snatToNat` method gives us a value corresponding to the given singleton. It has the following type:

```
snatToNat :: forall n. SNat n -> Nat
```

We can print a floor in GHCi, as shown next:

```
ghci> MkFloor :: Floor Nat5 Nat0
Floor 0 of 5
```

Note the type-level `Nat5` and `Nat0` names provided by the `Data.Type.Nat` module.

How do we check if we are allowed to go to the next floor? We must be below the top, as shown here:

```
type BelowTop mx cur = LE (S cur) mx
```

So the next floor, `S cur`, must be less than or equal to the maximum floor. Once this constraint is satisfied, we can go to the next floor as follows:

```
next :: BelowTop mx cur => Floor mx cur -> Floor mx (S cur)
next MkFloor = MkFloor
```

This short definition is not simple. Let's discuss what is going on behind the scenes. First, from the `BelowTop` constraint, we have proof that cur+1 $\leq$ mx. Second, as a result of pattern matching over `MkFloor`, we have instances of `SNatI` mx, `SNatI` cur, and a proof that cur $\leq$ mx. GHC checks if it has enough to build a `MkFloor` of the resulting `Floor mx (S cur)` type by trying to satisfy the required `GoodFloor mx (S cur)` constraint. It turns out that everything is here, so the `next` function is type-checked with no complaints.

> **TIP** I believe that understanding the logic behind the compiler helps us write code faster because we don't try to guess what the compiler would need. Instead, we can act preemptively and provide everything in advance.

Going to the previous floor is harder. We want to implement a function with the following type signature:

```
prev :: forall mx cur. Floor mx (S cur) -> Floor mx cur
```

The S cur is clearly aboveground, so we can safely go down. By pattern matching over the Floor mx (S cur) argument, we could obtain GoodFloor mx (S cur), which provides SNatI mx, SNatI (S cur), LE (S cur) mx. To build the resulting Floor mx cur, GHC needs GoodFloor mx cur made up of SNatI mx, SNatI cur, and LE cur mx. Do we have enough? Well, not quite. SNatI mx is surely with us. Unfortunately, we don't have SNatI cur and LE cur max. We should *prove* that these requirements can be obtained from SNatI (S cur) and LE (S cur) max. Figure 13.4 illustrates what is given and what GHC needs to compile the prev function.

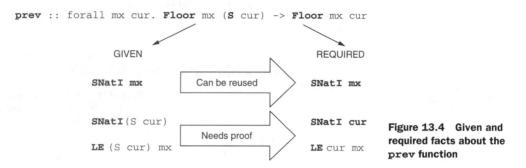

Figure 13.4 **Given and required facts about the prev function**

> **IMPORTANT** This is the first moment in this book where we need to prove something. When we bring values to the type level, we make type inference much harder. The algorithms behind type checking can't deal with that. This is a theoretical limitation. Consequently, the compiler needs our help. Doing proofs for the compiler becomes unavoidable when we write programs with dependent types.

The fin package provides the following handy functions to help GHC with proofs:

```
withSNat :: SNat n -> (SNatI n => r) -> r
withLEProof :: LEProof n m -> (LE n m => r) -> r
```

We can start writing a proof with the following scheme:

```
prev MkFloor =
  withSNat _ $
    withLEProof _
      MkFloor
```

Note a couple of holes in this code. To fill the first one, we need the SNat cur singleton. To fill the second one, we need the LEProof cur mx value. This would give us the required SNatI cur and LE cur mx to complete the proof and build MkFloor with the required type.

Writing proofs manually requires understanding the structure of the corresponding values. Let's dive into that. The SNat singleton of Nat is defined as follows:

```
data SNat (n :: Nat) where
    SZ :: SNat 'Z
    SS :: SNatI n => SNat ('S n)
```

We have SNat (S cur). It was clearly built with SS, not SZ. If we pattern match on this SS, we could get the required SNat cur instance from the SS constraint via the snat function from the SNatI cur instance. This proof needs access to the cur type variable, so we write it in the where block as follows:

```
prev :: forall mx cur. Floor mx (S cur) -> Floor mx cur
prev MkFloor =
  withSNat snatCur $
    withLEProof _
      MkFloor
  where                                                    Pattern matches over
    snatCur :: SNat cur      ◁──┐  Required singleton       the available singleton
    snatCur = case snat :: SNat (S cur) of ◁──┘
                  SS -> snat          ◁────        The only possible case brings the
    ...                                            SNatI cur instance into a scope, and
                                                   we are ready to go.
```

Note that it would be a mistake to write the SZ case. This branch is inaccessible. GHC knows that and gives us a warning.

Let's deal with LE. In mathematics, cur ≤ mx follows from cur+1 ≤ mx. To prove that, we take an evident inequality cur ≤ cur+1 and apply transitivity of ≤ to the two latter inequalities. The problem is to prove this to GHC. The LE type class defines only one method, as shown next:

```
class LE n m where
    leProof :: LEProof n m
```

The definition of the LEProof data type follows:

```
data LEProof n m where
    LEZero :: LEProof 'Z m
    LESucc :: LEProof n m -> LEProof ('S n) ('S m)
```

We can think of these two constructors as the definition of an LE relation. Zero is less than or equal to everything. If n ≤ m, then n+1 ≤ m+1. To make proofs easier, the Data.Type.Nat.LE provides several *lemmas*. In general, a lemma is a subproof—a proof whose main value is in its use as a building block in other proofs. It isn't of much interest in and of itself. In our case, lemmas are functions, as shown in the next example:

```
leZero :: LEProof Z n
leSucc :: LEProof n m -> LEProof (S n) (S m)
leRefl :: forall n. SNatI n => LEProof n n
leStep :: LEProof n m -> LEProof n (S m)
leTrans :: LEProof n m -> LEProof m p -> LEProof n p
leStepL :: LEProof (S n) m -> LEProof n m
lePred :: LEProof (S n) (S m) -> LEProof n m
```

Remember, we have LE (S cur) mx. This gives us the leProof value of the LEProof (S cur) mx data type. We need LEProof cur mx and immediately see that it's enough to apply the leStepL function to leProof. This gives us the final implementation of prev, as shown here:

```
prev :: forall mx cur. Floor mx (S cur) -> Floor mx cur
prev MkFloor =
  withSNat snatCur $
    withLEProof leCur
      MkFloor
 where
  snatCur :: SNat cur
  snatCur = case snat :: SNat (S cur) of
              SS -> snat
  leCur :: LEProof cur mx
  leCur = leStepL leProof
```

If we don't have an appropriate lemma, we can always pattern match over constructors of LEProof and prove individual cases.

The proof strategy

Writing proofs may be extremely hard unless we try to follow some strategies. I recommend doing proofs as follows:

1. Understand which constraints we already have, explicitly and implicitly.
2. Understand what we need to compile code successfully.
3. Make sure that something you want to prove makes sense in mathematics. Attempts to prove incorrect facts will take forever with no chance of success.
4. Look through constructors and helper functions available from the library.
5. Find something close to what you need and construct the proof.

Although the last point may sound like "do the job," I found this strategy quite effective.

We are not done with floors yet. Later we'll need to do the following things:

- Make sure that two given floors are the same.
- Create floors with the given parameters.

Let's do that now.

FLOORS, EQUALITY, AND DECIDABILITY

If we are given two floors, how do we make sure that they are equal? Remember that we have to work at the type level and analyze the equality of types. For example, we could have Floor mx from and Floor mx to. Are they equal? Another issue is how to convey the information about their equality to the type checker.

Let's use the functionality from the Data.Type.Equality module. We already know the type equality constraint, denoted as ~. If GHC sees the n ~ m constraint in the scope, it allows the use of n and m equally. The Data.Type.Equality introduces the :~: data type whose constructor Refl (short for reflexivity) brings the ~ type equality constraint by pattern matching.

We can implement the following function that establishes the equality of two floors:

```
sameFloor :: forall mx to from.
             Floor mx to -> Floor mx from -> Maybe (to :~: from)
```

If to is the same as from, we get Just Refl with the to ~ from constraint at the type level. Otherwise, we get Nothing. Comparing Nat values is ubiquitous, and the Data.Type.Nat from the fin package gives us the following eqNat function precisely for that:

```
eqNat :: forall n m. (SNatI n, SNatI m) => Maybe (n :~: m)
```

Now we should expose all the local assumptions that come with floors and apply eqNat, as shown next:

```
sameFloor MkFloor MkFloor = eqNat
```

This function works as expected, as shown here:

```
ghci> sameFloor (MkFloor :: Floor Nat5 Nat3) (MkFloor :: Floor Nat5 Nat3)
Just Refl
ghci> sameFloor (MkFloor :: Floor Nat5 Nat3) (MkFloor :: Floor Nat5 Nat0)
Nothing
```

Note that the Refl value is useless by itself, but it brings the type equality constraint into scope if we pattern match over it.

As for creating Floor mx cur values, we need to make sure that cur ≤ mx. The problem is that we should do that at the level of types to introduce the LE cur mx constraint into MkFloor. Thankfully, the LE relation is *decidable*.

A NOTION OF DECIDABILITY   Decidability is a theoretical idea. It relates to decision problems, that is, problems with yes or no answers. We say that such a problem is decidable if there exists an algorithm that answers with either yes or no within a finite amount of time.

The decidability of the LE relation comes in the form of the following function from the Data.Type.Nat module:

```
decideLE :: forall n m. (SNatI n, SNatI m) => Dec (LEProof n m)
```

The Dec data type comes from the following dec package by Oleg Grenrus:

```
data Dec a
    = Yes a
    | No (Neg a)

type Neg a = a -> Void
```

If we get `Yes`, then we have a proof of a. If we get `No`, then we have a negation of a, which is a function from a to `Void`. The latter type is defined in `Data.Void`; it has no values at all. Consequently, it is impossible to construct a value of the `Void` type. This is one of the traditional definitions of negation: the negation of a thing is an ability to build `Void` when given this thing.

Negation as a computation

The definition of negation provided earlier may be hard to understand. It's easy with `Bool` values when we say that negation of `True` is `False` and vice versa. When it comes to more general systems of logic, however, this simple idea no longer works. Instead, we use a computational definition. If we can compute something, then it is a truth. The `Void` type is a pure falsehood, because it has no values that could be computed by definition. The `No` data constructor gives us a function from a to `Void` that means the following two things:

- We can apply this function and compute a value of `Void` when given a value of a.
- There are no values of a in existence, so there is nothing to which we could apply the function.

The definition of `Void` rules out the first alternative, so the second one is true: there are no values of a. Consequently, we relate the a type to falsehood, and the negation of a is a truth.

I recommend reading about the Curry–Howard correspondence that relates types to propositions and explains a lot about the theoretical underpinnings of what we are doing here with proofs. This Wikipedia article (https://en.wikipedia.org/wiki/Curry–Howard_correspondence) could be a good start. The "Proposition as Types" paper by Philip Wadler (https://homepages.inf.ed.ac.uk/wadler/papers/propositions-as-types/propositions-as-types.pdf) is great and a very accessible source to learn about this.

The following function attempts to create a floor using the decidability of `LE`:

```
mkFloor :: forall mx cur. (SNatI mx, SNatI cur) => Maybe (Floor mx cur)
mkFloor =
  case decideLE :: Dec (LEProof cur mx) of
    Yes prf -> withLEProof prf $ Just MkFloor
    No _ -> Nothing
```

We execute the decidability of `LE`, and if there is a proof, we build a floor. Otherwise, we return `Nothing`. Note that we have everything we need at the `Yes` branch to build a value of `Floor mx cur`. Both `SNatI` instances are available from the type signature, `LE cur mx` appears as a result of decideLE. With these assumptions, the GoodFloor mx cur constraint is fully satisfied. GHC has no complaints and compiles this code successfully.

TYPE ELEVATOR AND SAFE PRIMITIVE OPERATIONS OVER IT

An elevator is a door that is either opened or closed and a floor. We should be able to move an elevator up and down, as well as open and close the door.

EXAMPLE: A SAFE INTERFACE FOR ELEVATORS AND A SIMULATION

🗋   ch13/elevator/Elevator/LowLevel.hs

🗋   ch13/elevator/Elevator/Safe/Operations.hs

As for doors, we explored them earlier in this chapter, so why not reuse them? Let's generate singletons with the singletons package as follows:

```
$(singletons [d|
 data Door = Opened | Closed
  deriving (Eq, Show)
  |])
```

We build an elevator from a floor and a door, as shown here:

```
data Elevator (mx :: Nat) (cur :: Nat) (door :: Door) where
  MkElevator :: SingI door => Floor mx cur -> Elevator mx cur door
```

The SingI type class comes with the singletons package. The Template Haskell splice shown earlier generated its instance for the Door type, among other things. Information about the floor exists as mx and cur type variables, but it is also available through the MkElevator argument. We can extract it as usual, as shown next:

```
currentFloor :: Elevator mx cur door -> Floor mx cur
currentFloor (MkElevator fl) = fl
```

To translate information from the door type variable to values, we use the singleton machinery as follows:

```
currentDoor :: forall mx cur door. Elevator mx cur door -> Door
currentDoor (MkElevator _) = fromSing (sing :: Sing door)
```

The sing method gives us the current door singleton (available from the MkElevator context), and fromSing translates it to Door.

We can apply the following two current* functions to show an elevator:

```
instance Show (Elevator mx cur door) where
  show el =
    "Elevator {current = " <> show (currentFloor el)
    <> ", door = " <> show (currentDoor el) <> "}"
```

Remember, we have the low-level elevator operations. We can call them now in the corresponding type-safe functions.

The up and down functions are almost trivial because the main job was done before in the next and prev functions for floors, as shown here:

```
import Elevator.Safe.Floor
import qualified Elevator.LowLevel as LL


...

up :: (BelowTop mx cur, MonadIO m) =>
      Elevator mx cur Closed -> m (Elevator mx (S cur) Closed)
up (MkElevator fl) = do
  liftIO $ LL.up
  pure (MkElevator $ next fl)

down :: MonadIO m => Elevator mx (S cur) Closed -> m (Elevator mx cur Closed)
down (MkElevator fl) = do
  liftIO $ LL.down
  pure $ MkElevator $ prev fl
```

Note that both functions require the door being closed at the level of types. This is type safety at work. It is impossible to apply these functions to an elevator with opened doors or to doors whose state is not established (proved) at the level of types.

Opening and closing doors is also trivial, as shown next:

```
open :: MonadIO m =>
        Floor mx cur -> Elevator mx cur Closed -> m (Elevator mx cur Opened)
open _ (MkElevator fl) = do
  liftIO $ LL.open
  pure (MkElevator fl)

close :: MonadIO m =>
        Floor mx cur -> Elevator mx cur Opened -> m (Elevator mx cur Closed)
close _ (MkElevator fl) = do
  liftIO $ LL.close
  pure (MkElevator fl)
```

Note that we require the current floor of an elevator and the floor of the request to be the same. It's simply impossible to open the door on some floor with an elevator on a different floor. There is no such functionality in our interface.

What if we have a door with an unknown type-level state? Well, we can always consult the corresponding singleton and use local assumptions that come with it as follows:

```
ensureClosed :: forall mx cur door m. MonadIO m =>
                Elevator mx cur door -> m (Elevator mx cur Closed)
ensureClosed el@(MkElevator fl) =
  case sing :: Sing door of          | door ~ Closed: no need to close it.
    SClosed -> pure el         <------┘
    SOpened -> close fl el      <------ door ~ Opened, so we are allowed to close it.
```

To open the door, we ensure that the floor is the same first as follows:

```
ensureOpenedAt :: forall mx cur door m. MonadIO m =>
  Floor mx cur -> Elevator mx cur door -> m (Elevator mx cur Opened)
ensureOpenedAt fl el@(MkElevator _) =
  case sing :: Sing door of          | door ~ Opened
    SOpened -> pure el        <───────┘
    SClosed -> open fl el      <────── door ~ Closed
```

Let's review our elevator interface so far. First, we control elevator moves and make sure that the door is always closed as follows:

```
up :: (BelowTop mx cur, MonadIO m) =>
      Elevator mx cur Closed -> m (Elevator mx (S cur) Closed)
down :: MonadIO m => Elevator mx (S cur) Closed -> m (Elevator mx cur Closed)
```

Second, we control doors and how they change their state, as shown next:

```
open :: MonadIO m =>
        Floor mx cur -> Elevator mx cur Closed -> m (Elevator mx cur Opened)

close :: MonadIO m =>
         Floor mx cur -> Elevator mx cur Opened -> m (Elevator mx cur Closed)
```

Third, we can operate over doors with an unknown state as follows:

```
ensureClosed :: forall mx cur door m. MonadIO m =>
                  Elevator mx cur door -> m (Elevator mx cur Closed)
ensureOpenedAt :: forall mx cur door m. MonadIO m => Floor mx cur ->
                  Elevator mx cur door -> m (Elevator mx cur Opened)
```

We are now close to the hardest part of the solution: deciding how to move if we get a request from a particular floor.

DECIDING ELEVATOR MOVES

Suppose we get a request at floor `to`, and an elevator is at floor `from`. Which elevator command should we issue to fulfill the request? The `up` and `down` functions have their own requirements. We have to make sure that they are satisfied at compile time.

EXAMPLE: A SAFE INTERFACE FOR ELEVATORS AND A SIMULATION

🗋   ch13/elevator/Elevator/Safe/Moves.hs

Let's define a type for moves with all the constraints hidden within the constructors as follows:

```
data Move mx to from where
  StandStill :: Move mx to to
  GoingUp :: BelowTop mx from => Move mx to from
  GoingDown :: from ~ S fl => Move mx to from
```

Note that these constraints are enough to go either up or down. Our main goal now is to define the following function:

```
decideMove :: forall mx to from.
  Floor mx to -> Floor mx from -> Move mx to from
```

Whenever we have `to` and `from`, we have the following three possible cases:

- Floors are the same, so an elevator shouldn't move at all.
- `to < from` and an elevator goes down.
- `to > from` and an elevator goes up.

Figure 13.5 presents the steps we have to follow to decide which case we are in.

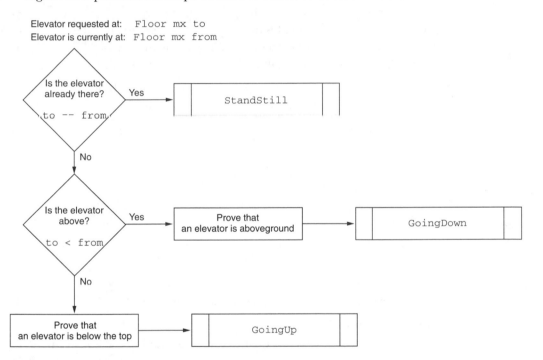

Figure 13.5   Deciding elevator moves

We need two decidability algorithms now: one for equality and another for LE. The `fin` package provides both, as shown next:

```
discreteNat :: forall n m. (SNatI n, SNatI m) => Dec (n :~: m)
decideLE :: forall n m. (SNatI n, SNatI m) => Dec (LEProof n m)
```

The proof structure follows:

```
case discreteNat :: Dec (to :~: from) of        to == from
    Yes _ -> _
    No _ ->              to /= from
```

```
                    case decideLE :: Dec (LEProof to from) of
to < from  └──▷  Yes _ -> _
                    No _ -> _      ◀────  to > from
```

Interpreting the results of Dec (to :~: from) is the easiest, as shown next:

```
case discreteNat :: Dec (to :~: from) of
    Yes Refl -> StandStill
    No to_neq_from ->
      ...
```

Pattern matching on Refl brings to ~ from into scope. This is enough to construct a StandStill. The No case gives us a value of Neg (to :~: from), that is, a function from to :~: from to Void. We'll see how to use it shortly.

The decideLE algorithm decides between to ≤ from and to > from. Note that the first alternative is not enough to go down. What we need is from ~ S f1 for some f1. Is it possible to prove this fact? Well, we have to use the following:

- to ≤ from (aka LEProof to from) from the Yes branch of decideLE
- Neg (to :~: from) from the No branch of discreteNat

From these two facts we should be able to infer that to < from so from is clearly aboveground, as shown next:

```
case decideLE :: Dec (LEProof to from) of
        Yes to_le_from ->
            withAboveGround to_le_from to_neq_from GoingDown
        No _ -> _
  where
      withAboveGround :: LEProof to from -> Neg (to :~: from) ->
                         (forall f1. from ~ S f1 => r) -> r
      ...
```

As usual with proofs, we have the following two main tools:

- Appropriate functions in the library
- Pattern matching over data constructors to get additional constraints

Remember, the LEProof data type has the following two constructors:

```
LEZero :: LEProof Z m
LESucc :: LEProof n m -> LEProof (S n) (S m)
```

The first one says that to ~ Z and the second one immediately reports that from ~ S _. We can use the second one to solve that branch as follows:

```
withAboveGround (LESucc _) _ r = r
```

As for the first one, to ~ Z, it's time to analyze a singleton for from, as shown here:

```
withAboveGround LEZero neq r =
    case snat :: SNat from of
      SZ -> _
      SS -> _
```

Is it possible for `from` to be equal to `Z`? The `from ~ Z` constraint is introduced with the `SZ` singleton. Remember, we already have `to ~ Z` and `Neg (to :~: from)`. Clearly, we have a contradiction, and we have to make it visible. The idea is to construct `Refl` of the `to :~: from` type from `to ~ Z` and `from ~ Z` and then pass it to the `neq` function of the `Neg (to :~: from)`. This gives us `Void` because negation is a function to `Void`. From `Void`, we can get anything with the `absurd` function. It's okay to call such a function because we know that this case is impossible, although the compiler can't see it by itself.

The `SS` case trivially gives us the required `S _` structure to `from`. Consequently, we arrive at the following definition of `withAboveGround`:

```
withAboveGround :: LEProof to from -> Neg (to :~: from) ->
                   (forall fl. from ~ S fl => r) -> r
  withAboveGround (LESucc _) _ r = r
  withAboveGround LEZero neq r =
    case snat :: SNat from of
      SZ -> absurd $ neq Refl
      SS -> r
```

In the last branch, we have to deal with `Neg (LEProof to from)` and arrange going up as follows:

```
case decideLE :: Dec (LEProof to from) of
        ...
        No to_gt_from ->
           withLEProof (belowTop to_gt_from) GoingUp
  where
    belowTop :: LE to mx => Neg (LEProof to from) -> LEProof (S from) mx
    ...
```

Here we have an easy exercise in proofs. Looking through available lemmas, we quickly find the following solution:

```
belowTop neg = leTrans (leSwap neg) leProof
```

The `leSwap` gives us `LEProof (S from) to`, which is clearly a negation of `LEProof to from`. `leProof` is of the `LEProof to mx` type, and we get the desired `LEProof (S from) mx` by transitivity.

Finally, we have the following implementation with all the proofs:

```
decideMove :: forall mx to from.
  Floor mx to -> Floor mx from -> Move mx to from
decideMove MkFloor MkFloor =
  case discreteNat :: Dec (to :~: from) of
```

```
        Yes Refl -> StandStill                  <---- to == from
        No to_neq_from ->
          case decideLE :: Dec (LEProof to from) of
            Yes to_le_from ->                    <---- to < from
              withAboveGround to_le_from to_neq_from GoingDown
            No to_gt_from ->                     <---- to > from
              withLEProof (belowTop to_gt_from) GoingUp
  where
    belowTop :: LE to mx => Neg (LEProof to from) -> LEProof (S from) mx
    belowTop neg = leTrans (leSwap neg) leProof

    withAboveGround :: LEProof to from -> Neg (to :~: from) ->
                       (forall fl. from ~ S fl => r) -> r
    withAboveGround (LESucc _) _ r = r
    withAboveGround LEZero neq r =
      case snat :: SNat from of
        SZ -> absurd $ neq Refl
        SS -> r
```

Once again, note the strategy: exploit decidability, analyze what we have and what we need, write type signatures, and fulfill them with either available lemmas or on a case-by-case basis through pattern matching. Unfortunately, it takes a lot of time. Programming with safety in mind is hard.

HIGH-LEVEL ELEVATOR INTERFACE

All the hard work is already done. We only need to define functions for a high-level elevator interface and bridge them with the user input.

EXAMPLE: A SAFE INTERFACE FOR ELEVATORS AND A SIMULATION

🗋   ch13/elevator/Elevator/Safe.hs

The decideMove function analyzes the current situation in full detail. We can use it as follows:

```
moveTo :: MonadIO m =>
          Floor mx to -> Elevator mx from Closed -> m (Elevator mx to Closed)
moveTo fl el =
  case decideMove fl (currentFloor el) of
    StandStill -> pure el
    GoingUp -> up el >>= moveTo fl
    GoingDown -> down el >>= moveTo fl
```

The DecideMove data constructors bring all the constraints into scope so that we can use up and down safely. Note the recursion in moveTo. Every invocation works with all the choices for the to and from types. As a result, we end up at the desired floor.

To call an elevator at the given floor, we define the following function:

```
call :: MonadIO m =>
        Floor mx to -> Elevator mx from door -> m (Elevator mx to Opened)
call fl el = do
```

```
liftIO $ putStrLn $ "Call to: " <> show fl
case sameFloor fl (currentFloor el) of
  Just Refl -> ensureOpenedAt fl el
  Nothing -> ensureClosed el >>= moveTo fl >>= open fl
```

Everything we've defined before is in use here. Thanks to the types, it's almost impossible to do something wrong in this function. I recommend experimenting with this code to see the type errors that arise from any attempt to break the protocol.

Unfortunately, functions like this can't be used by a user, because their arguments are fixed in types. There are no types at run time, so we need a bridge. As usual, we use existentials for that as follows:

```
data SomeFloor (mx :: Nat) where
  MkSomeFloor :: Floor mx cur -> SomeFloor mx

data SomeElevator (mx :: Nat) where
  MkSomeElevator :: Elevator mx cur door -> SomeElevator mx
```

I've left the maximum number of floors fixed in types, meaning that this characteristic is really fixed at run time. Now we need a way to create a floor from the user input. For example, we can use the `Natural` type from `base`. Our next goal is to write the following function:

```
mkSomeFloor :: forall mx. SNatI mx => Natural -> Maybe (SomeFloor mx)
```

To make it possible, we have to bring the given natural number to the level of types. We need the following two functions from the `fin` package:

```
fromNatural :: Natural -> Nat
reify :: forall r. Nat -> (forall n. SNatI n => Proxy n -> r) -> r
```

The first one gives us `Nat` from `Natural`. The second one introduces the singleton, which corresponds to the given `Nat`. The only problem is to specify the types we need. We can do that as follows:

```
mkSomeFloor :: forall mx. SNatI mx => Natural -> Maybe (SomeFloor mx)
mkSomeFloor cur = reify (fromNatural cur) (fmap MkSomeFloor . toMbFloor)
  where
    toMbFloor :: SNatI fl => Proxy fl -> Maybe (Floor mx fl)
    toMbFloor _ = mkFloor
```

The only role of the `toMbFloor` auxiliary definition is to set specific types. Then we use `mkFloor` defined earlier and put everything inside a `SomeFloor mx` wrapper.

It's instructive to look at the definition of `reify` from the `Data.Type.Nat` module. There is no magic in it—simply recursion over natural numbers and plenty of explicit types, as shown next:

```
reify :: forall r. Nat -> (forall n. SNatI n => Proxy n -> r) -> r
reify Z     f = f (Proxy :: Proxy 'Z)
reify (S n) f =  reify n (\(_p :: Proxy n) -> f (Proxy :: Proxy ('S n)))
```

Note how we use recursion to introduce all the `SNatI n` instances for all `n` less than `S n`. Once we have all of them, GHC can easily construct `SNatI` for the current `Nat` value in the request.

The input from a user comes in the form of `Some*` types. To execute actual elevator operations, we need to extract their content and then put the result back as follows:

```
callSome :: MonadIO m =>
            SomeFloor mx -> SomeElevator mx -> m (SomeElevator mx)
callSome (MkSomeFloor fl) (MkSomeElevator el) =
  MkSomeElevator <$> call fl el
```

With this function, we are ready to run a simulation.

RUNNING A SIMULATION

This is the final part of the example. We do the same thing as with the unsafe interface, but now we expect no run-time errors. We've eliminated them completely.

EXAMPLE: A SAFE INTERFACE FOR ELEVATORS AND A SIMULATION

□   ch13/elevator/UseSafe.hs

⚡   *elevator*

We have the following elevator installed:

```
type MX = Nat5

gfElevator :: Elevator MX Nat0 Closed
gfElevator = MkElevator (MkFloor :: Floor MX Nat0)
```

Suppose we are given a list of `SomeFloor MX` values as a sequence of user requests. We can serve all of them in order as follows:

```
simulate :: [SomeFloor MX] -> IO ()
simulate = foldM_ traceToSome (MkSomeElevator gfElevator)
  where
    prt el = print el >> pure el
    traceToSome el fl = callSome fl el >>= prt
```

The source of requests is irrelevant. For example, we can get them from the command-line arguments, as shown next:

```
main :: IO ()
main = do
    args <- getArgs
    let mbFloors = mapM (mkSomeFloor . read) args
```

```
case mbFloors of
  Nothing -> putStrLn "Incorrect floors"
  Just floors -> simulate floors
```

This elevator can't do anything wrong, thanks to the types.

I wouldn't argue that this type-safe version is better. It's safer, that's for sure. It may be more performant due to the absence of run-time checks, but it's much harder to write. It's harder to extend the functionality. As usual, we have to take many factors into account when developing software.

Summary

- We use types to define a language that describes some entities from the application domain. A web API is just one example.
- Type classes and their instances can be used to implement behavior, depending on the specific types.
- Haskell has limited support for dependent types in the form of singletons.
- When using dependent types, we have to prove facts to GHC.
- Type-safe interfaces allow eliminating run-time checks.

Part 5

Haskell toolkit

Haskellers use all the language features we've discussed so far to develop very nice libraries. In this part, we'll look at those libraries and apply them to solve real-world software developer problems. We'll process data files in streaming pipelines going from raw bytes to final results by efficient reading, parsing, and calculating. We'll access data in data structures and databases. We'll also learn essential topics in concurrency. This part could be 10 times longer because software problems are countless, but I believe that all the readers at this point are ready to learn the tools they need all by themselves. Good luck!

Data-processing pipelines

Many applications share a similar structure: they read a data source, transform data to a form suitable for processing, process data somehow, prepare results, and present those results to a user. We call this structure a *data-processing pipeline*. The `stockquotes` project from chapter 3 was a simple example of such an application. In real-world applications, we need to take special care to keep performance and memory usage under control.

Figure 14.1 presents a pipeline starting from a data source and ending up at a resulting output. The term *pipeline* suggests having different stages. We do different things at those stages. At every stage, we have data in some form in the beginning and produce data in some new form as a result.

In this chapter, we'll discuss Haskell tools that allow us to implement data-processing pipelines. Although particular stages can be very specific, we need to

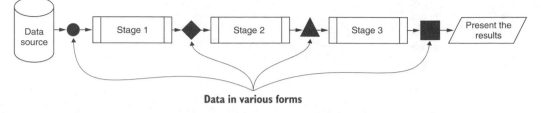

Figure 14.1   General data-processing pipeline

organize them at least. We'll start with discussing a problem and implementations of streaming as a solution for organizing pipelines and stages.

Then we'll continue with talk about things that can be useful at various stages of pragmatic data-processing pipelines. In the second section, we'll discuss efficient input/output, parsing data, and tools to manipulate complex data structures that often arise at latter stages. Finally, we'll discuss one practical example where we'll apply all these tools to a small data-processing application.

All the libraries we discuss in this chapter are usually considered quite sophisticated. They use higher-order abstractions and advanced type system features. Getting familiar with them is a good stress test for the things we've learned so far in this book.

14.1 *Streaming data*

Let's get back to figure 14.1. Every stage of a pipeline either transforms data or computes some additional information. We may want to do input/output, parse data, or analyze it. Data between those stages exists in various forms. We may start with a sequence of bytes and end up with quite sophisticated data structures.

Here we already have a problem. If we have a lot of data, keeping it in memory as a whole may not be efficient or even possible. The traditional Haskell approach of lazy input/output, unfortunately, has its drawbacks. It's difficult to predict the memory footprint or avoid leaks. We need another solution. The Haskell community has formulated the following desired properties:

- Code for stages should be clearly distinguished, giving us composability.
- We should be able to run various effects of choice (such as input/output) as we process data.
- Data should be processed in chunks of a predictable size to avoid memory leaks.

In Haskell, we have several libraries that provide us with such solutions. They implement a streaming data approach. Let's discuss this approach in general and then move to the particular implementations.

14.1.1 *General components and naive implementation*

Suppose we have a data source. It can be a file, a network socket, a database, or something else. The data source gives us data in some particular form, which is usually a sequence of something, for example, raw bytes, UTF-8 characters, or rows of a database table. We can interpret data sources as producers of data. Once we have a sequence of data items, we want to process them as follows:

- Individually, by transforming every piece of data into a new form
- In groups, by collecting individual pieces into chunks and transforming chunks into a new form

As a result of a single processing stage, we have a sequence of something again. At the end of the day, we want to consume a sequence into a result that can be either a big data structure that contains everything or some new information we've computed from a sequence.

Producing, processing, and consuming data are well-known stages of data processing. The crucial point is that we don't want to run them in a waterfall model by producing all the data first, then processing all of them, and finally consuming them. Instead, we stream data over these stages by running the corresponding code once we've got enough data. Consequently, there should be no clear division between stages at run time. With this streaming approach, all the stages fuse into one big loop, responsible for everything.

Unfortunately, these stages may be hard to distinguish in practice. We may want to compute some parts of a result while processing data or even while producing them.

Note, traditional list processing in Haskell follows the same ideas: we generate lists, map some functions over them, and fold them into something else. GHC works hard to avoid keeping whole lists in memory and fuses calls to functions, as we discussed in chapter 9. We may think of streams of data as a generalization over lists that allows running monadic effects at the time of processing.

The streaming approach belongs to a long tradition of writing interfaces to process data sequences in a resource-controlled manner. It started with an abstraction of *iteratee*, discovered by Oleg Kiselyov, and evolved into powerful, extremely efficient industrial-level libraries, including the following two most powerful:

- `conduit` by Michael Snoyman
- `pipes` by Gabriel Gonzalez

These packages underpin whole ecosystems of packages that give access to various data sources and ways to process and consume data. These ecosystems are described in many tutorials and are well established and widely applicable to implement data-processing pipelines. The documentation is also very good. Despite that, I've decided to talk about the third competitor, the `streaming` library. It's relatively new, adopts the recent innovations, and provides a cleaner and simpler interface. As a result, it's easier to teach. Arguably, it's also more efficient in many cases.

Let's start implementing a streaming library from scratch and then see the same approach used in a real Haskell package.

WHAT'S A STREAM?

In Haskell, we have the `[a]` type, which expresses an idea of storing a sequence of elements of type a. To express the idea of having a result of processing such a list, we can use a pair: `([a], r)`. To produce such a list using some user input or any other effectful computation, we can add a monad as follows:

```
Monad m => m ([a], r)
```

One issue with this type is that we have an action that gives us a whole list and a result back. We want to avoid this. Instead, we'd like to allow interspersing actions and elements freely, without fixing a particular order.

EXAMPLE: IMPLEMENTING STREAMS FROM SCRATCH

🗋   ch14/stream.hs

⚡   *stream*

Thus, we arrive at the following type that expresses all the ideas I've just mentioned:

The stream contains elements of type e.
```
data Stream e m r = Element e (Stream e m r)
                  | Action (m (Stream e m r))
                  | Result r
```
The stream is generated by monadic actions.

The stream has a result of type r.

We can have empty streams, as shown here:

```
empty :: Stream e m ()
empty = Result ()
```

Or we can have streams with all the constructors interweaved, as in the following one running in the IO monad:

```
stream :: Stream Int IO ()
stream = (Element 1
             (Action (putStrLn "some action" >>
                   pure (Element 2
                        (Action (putStrLn  "finish" >> pure empty))
                   )
             )
          )
       )
```

Processing such a stream requires a recursive function. Let's write one to reveal what's going on inside this stream as follows:

```
printStream :: (Show e, Show r) => Stream e IO r -> IO ()
printStream (Result r) = putStrLn $ "Result: " <> show r
printStream (Element e str) = do
  putStrLn $ "Element: " <> show e
  printStream str
printStream (Action mstr) = do
  putStr "Run action: "
  str <- mstr
  printStream str
```

Running this function on `stream` gives us the following:

```
ghci> printStream stream
Element: 1
Run action: some action
Element: 2
Run action: finish
Result: ()
```

We may want to consume the whole stream by computing the sum of all the elements in it, as shown here:

```
ssum :: (Num e, Monad m) => Stream e m r -> m (e, r)
```

Note the type of the result: we want to keep both the sum and the result of the stream processing. As usual, we want to keep types as general as possible, so we have `Num e` and `Monad m` constraints. An implementation is also recursive, as shown next:

```
ssum (Result r) = pure (0, r)
ssum (Action m) = m >>= ssum
ssum (Element e str) = (\(acc, r) -> (acc + e, r)) <$> ssum str
```

Runs an action to get a stream and processes further

Adds a current element to an accumulator

If we run the `ssum` function on the `stream` we defined earlier, we get the following output:

```
ghci> ssum stream
some action
finish
(3,())
```

Note that we can't avoid running actions that are encapsulated in the `stream`. Remember the `Action` data constructor? The rest of a stream is the result of such an action, so we have to execute it in order to continue processing a stream.

Converting any list to a stream is also easy, as shown next:

```
each :: [e] -> Stream e m ()
each [] = Result ()
each (x:xs) = Element x (each xs)
```

The stream constructed with each has no actions at all, so summing it up gives us a result right away, as shown here:

```
ghci> ssum $ each [1..10 :: Int]
(55,())
```

Thus, we have a stream as a succession of available elements or actions that produce the rest of a stream.

GENERALIZING ELEMENTS TO FUNCTORIAL STEPS

Our stream Element data constructor is a pair in disguise: we have an element and the rest of a stream. If we look at the corresponding clauses of the printStream and the ssum functions, we immediately see that they share the same pattern as follows:

- Do something specific with an element (print it or add it to an accumulator).
- Make a recursive call to consume the rest of a stream.

The latter step resembles the functorial behavior of a pair: fmap f (a, b) applies f to the second component. Every Haskeller in such a moment thinks something like the following: why not generalize this data constructor to a Functor and see how that works? Let's make this generalization in our Stream data type.

EXAMPLE: STREAM ELEMENTS AS FUNCTORS

☐   ch14/simple-streaming.hs

⚡   *simple-streaming*

In addition to replacing Element with a general functor that returns the rest of a stream, I change other names to match those used in a library we are going to use later as follows:

```
data Stream f m r = Step (f (Stream f m r))
                  | Effect (m (Stream f m r))
                  | Return r
```

Our empty stream follows:

```
empty :: Stream f m ()
empty = Return ()
```

Creating a stream with an effect can be implemented as follows:

```
effect :: Monad m => m r -> Stream f m r
effect eff = Effect $ Return <$> eff
```

To express the idea of a stream element, we use a tailor-made pair that can be easily turned into a Functor, as shown next:

```
data Of a b = a :> b
  deriving Show

instance Functor (Of a) where
  fmap f (a :> b) = a :> f b
```

Note that `Functor` operates on the second component, leaving the first one unmodified. We can now interpret streams with elements of type `a` as those having the `Stream (Of a) m r` type. This particular functor is one way to give the form of a step. We'll see others shortly.

The following function creates a stream with one element:

```
yield :: a -> Stream (Of a) m ()
yield a = Step (a :> empty)
```

We can also implement constructing `Of a` streams from lists as shown here:

```
each :: [e] -> Stream (Of e) m ()
each [] = Return ()
each (x:xs) = Step $ x :> each xs
```

Sometimes, we need to operate over the first element of the `Of` pair. To make this easier, let's implement the `Bifunctor` instance as follows:

```
instance Bifunctor Of where
  bimap f g (a :> b) = f a :> g b
```

This type class provides the `first` and `second` functions to operate over the first and second pair of components independently.

Computing the sum of stream elements is almost the same as before, as shown next:

```
ssum :: (Num e, Monad m) => Stream (Of e) m r -> m (Of e r)
ssum (Return r) = pure (0 :> r)
ssum (Effect m) = m >>= ssum
ssum (Step (e :> str)) = first (+e) <$> ssum str
```

Here I've used `Bifunctor` to simplify accumulating elements.

Final stream printing is also possible, almost without modifications, as follows:

```
printStream :: (Show e, Show r) => Stream (Of e) IO r -> IO ()
printStream (Return r) = putStrLn $ "Result: " <> show r
printStream (Effect m) = do
  putStrLn "Run action:"
  str <- m
  printStream str
printStream (Step (e :> str)) = do
  putStrLn $ "Element: " <> show e
  printStream str
```

Let's check whether these functions work:

```
ghci> printStream $ yield (1 :: Int)
Element: 1
Result: ()
ghci> printStream $ each [1..5 :: Int]
Element: 1
Element: 2
Element: 3
Element: 4
Element: 5
Result: ()
ghci> ssum $ each [1..5 :: Int]
15 :> ()
```

Generalization to functors is used in Haskell very often. Another traditional thing is to check whether our type is a monad. It turns out, `Stream f m` is a monad over the type of the streaming result.

STREAM AS A MONAD

Being a monad means being both a `Functor` and an `Applicative`. We start with the `Functor` instance. To apply a function to a streaming result, we have to get it first. Consequently, we loop over a stream to reach the final `Return` data constructor as follows:

```
instance (Functor f, Monad m) => Functor (Stream f m) where
  fmap :: forall a b. (a -> b) -> Stream f m a -> Stream f m b
  fmap fun = loop
    where
      loop :: Stream f m a -> Stream f m b
      loop (Return r) = Return (fun r)      ⟵──┐  Applies the given function
      loop (Effect m) = Effect (fmap loop m)  ⟵──── Loops over the monadic effect
      loop (Step f) = Step (fmap loop f)      ⟵──┐
                                                 └ Loops over the functorial step
```

I use the `ScopedTypeVariables` GHC extension to tie the `loop` internal function with the type of `fmap` and help the reader with information about types. Both `fmap loop m` and `fmap loop f` expressions are responsible for delivering the given function to the final destination. Note that here we use the generalization we made earlier.

It turns out that implementing the `Monad` instance is easier than doing so for `Applicative`. The idea is the same: loop over the effects and steps until we reach `Return` and then apply a function to the streaming result, as shown next:

```
instance (Functor f, Monad m) => Monad (Stream f m) where
  (>>=) :: forall r r1.
           Stream f m r -> (r -> Stream f m r1) -> Stream f m r1
  stream >>= fun = loop stream
    where
      loop :: Stream f m r -> Stream f m r1
      loop (Return r) = fun r
      loop (Effect m) = Effect (fmap loop m)
      loop (Step f) = Step (fmap loop f)
```

Note one difference, though: a `Functor` keeps a structure of a stream unchanged, but a `Monad` is more powerful. Compare the ways we process the `Return r` stream constructor. The second argument to `(>>=)` is a function that returns a new stream. As a result, we get the ability to concatenate streams.

Now we have to provide the `Applicative` instance. We can do that by exploiting the `Monad` we've just defined as follows:

```
instance (Functor f, Monad m) => Applicative (Stream f m) where
  pure r = Return r
  (<*>) = ap
```

The `ap` function uses the `Monad` constraint to implement the functionality of `(<*>)`. It's safe to implement `(<*>)` through it.

Once `Stream f m` is a monad, we can use `do` notation for it. For example, we can define a stream with three elements and a couple of actions as follows:

```
stream1 :: Stream (Of Int) IO ()
stream1 = do
  yield 1
  effect (putStrLn "action 1")
  yield 2
  effect (putStrLn "action 2")
  yield 3
```

Remember, both the `yield` and `effect` functions give us streams built with two constructors (`Step`/`Effect` and `Return`). Thanks to monadic machinery, they are concatenated into a stream with six constructors. Running `printStream` on this combined stream gives the following result:

```
ghci> printStream stream1
Element: 1
Run action:
action 1
Element: 2
Run action:
action 2
Element: 3
Result: ()
```

With functorial steps and a monad for a stream, we've got more. In fact, we've implemented a *free monad*.

STREAM AS A FREE MONAD

The `Stream f m r` data type implements the abstract concept of a free monad. Let's compare it with the corresponding data type in the `free` package as follows:

```
data Stream f m r = Step (f (Stream f m r))
                  | Effect (m (Stream f m r))
                  | Return r

data Free f a = Pure a | Free (f (Free f a))
```

The `Return` data constructor corresponds to `Pure`, and `Step` to `Free`.

The `Free` type expresses the idea of layering computations in an unrestricted way (hence *free*) and producing some combined final result. We have either a result (the `Pure` data constructor) or some computation (with `f` as a functor) that wraps another layer with the same result type (the `Free` data constructor). We have a general way to implement a `Monad` instance for any such type, hence the term *free monad*. We've already implemented it in the `Monad` instance for `Stream`.

Such data types are traditionally used to store and manipulate computations without executing them. We can add, remove, or replace layers until we are ready to interpret them. We run this interpretation by looping over the whole structure and doing something meaningful along the actual execution.

The same idea is used in the `Stream f m r` type: we build a stream as a succession of steps (functorial layers), but we don't attempt to execute those steps right away. Instead, we enrich them with new effects by changing monads or change their form by switching functors. We can do that via maps from a `Stream f m1 r` into a `Stream f m2 r` or from a `Stream f1 m r` into a `Stream f2 m r`. This allows us to go from a declaratively described processing pipeline to a big loop at run time that executes all the effects, interprets the steps at once, and lets us avoid storing all the data in memory.

Particular effects come from the stages of a pipeline we are implementing. We prefer to describe stages independently (in a declarative way) but want to execute each action once it has enough data. So we fuse effects from different stages into one combined effect.

Depending on what we have in a stream (a step, an effect, or a result), a stream interpreter chooses what to do at run time. By writing stream-processing functions, we construct such a stream with functorial layers and effects. Figure 14.2 illustrates the relationship between a declarative pipeline description and streaming at run time.

A note on library design

Haskell library authors are always willing to apply abstract concepts to their code. Then they have the following choices:

- Use an abstract concept, and expose it to the user.
- Use an abstract concept under the hood, but hide it from the user via module import/export mechanisms.
- Reimplement an abstract concept manually.

Exposing an abstract concept to users could make it harder for them to learn a library if they don't know this concept. On the other hand, if they do know it, it's easier for them. More abstraction provides more power, but only if we are able to control it. Magic can destroy a novice wizard, you know.

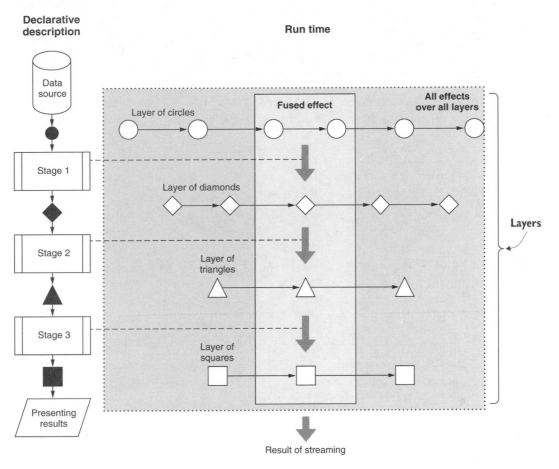

Figure 14.2 Stream in a nutshell

IMPLEMENTING FUNCTOR GENERAL FUNCTIONS

There is not much sense in generalizing, unless we can do something interesting. For example, let's implement the following quite general rank-2 function, which replaces a Functor in the given Stream with something else:

```
maps :: (Functor f, Monad m) =>
        (forall x. f x -> g x) -> Stream f m r -> Stream g m r
```

Note the first argument: this function replaces the functor but leaves the value inside it unchanged. Why? Because it's under forall, we can't do anything with it other than pass it around. Thus, we are guaranteed that the stream structure remains unchanged.

An implementation loops over the stream structure and exploits the monad (for Effect) and the functorial (for Step) fmap as follows:

```
maps fun = loop
  where
    loop (Return r) = Return r
    loop (Effect m) = Effect (fmap loop m)
    loop (Step f) = Step (fun (fmap loop f))
```

Consequently, `maps` doesn't touch effects but works on steps. We can use it to implement a function similar to `map` over lists, as shown next:

```
mapOf :: Monad m => (a -> b) -> Stream (Of a) m r -> Stream (Of b) m r
mapOf fun = maps (first fun)
```

A quick check in GHCi shows that it works:

```
ghci> ssum $ mapOf (*2) $ each [1..3 :: Int]
12 :> ()
```

For another example of `Functor` general functions, let's implement the `zipsWith` function as follows:

```
zipsWith :: Monad m
  => (forall x y p . (x -> y -> p) -> f x -> g y -> h p)
  -> Stream f m r -> Stream g m r -> Stream h m r
zipsWith fun = loop
  where
    loop (Return r) _ = Return r
    loop _ (Return r) = Return r
    loop (Effect m) t = Effect $ fmap (flip loop t) m
    loop s (Effect n) = Effect $ fmap (loop s) n
    loop (Step fs) (Step gs) = Step $ fun loop fs gs
```

This highly general function zips two streams together using a function over their functorial steps. We return if one of the given streams returns (just as traditional `zipWith` works on the shortest list). We leave effects untouched, continuing with their results (this is what `fmap` does). Finally, we apply the given function to the functorial steps once we have them exposed.

For streams `Of a`, we could put elements into a pair as follows:

```
zipPair :: Monad m =>
           Stream (Of a) m r -> Stream (Of b) m r -> Stream (Of (a, b)) m r
zipPair = zipsWith fun
  where
    fun p (e1 :> x) (e2 :> y) = (e1, e2) :> (p x y)
```

Functors can be easily composed. This idea is implemented by the `Compose` type in the `Data.Functor.Compose` module from `base`. This type is defined as follows:

```
newtype Compose f g a = Compose { getCompose :: f (g a) }
```

We can use this type and its `Functor` instance to compose any two given streams as follows:

```
zips :: (Monad m, Functor f, Functor g)
    => Stream f m r -> Stream g m r -> Stream (Compose f g) m r
zips = zipsWith fun
  where
    fun p fx gy = Compose (fmap (\x -> fmap (\y -> p x y) gy) fx)
```

Note, this function exploits a new form of a step, namely, `Compose f g`. One application for composed steps is to turn one of them into an effect, as shown here:

```
decompose :: (Monad m, Functor f) =>
              Stream (Compose m f) m r -> Stream f m r
decompose = loop
  where
    loop (Return r) = Return r
    loop (Effect m) = Effect (fmap loop m)
    loop (Step (Compose mstr)) = Effect $ do     <--  The outer Functor becomes
      str <- mstr                                      an enclosing Effect.
      pure (Step (fmap loop str))    <------  The inner Functor remains a Step.
```

Remember the `maps` function that switches functors? We can use it with `Compose` to insert a monadic effect into every layer of a stream as follows:

```
mapsM :: (Monad m, Functor f, Functor g) =>
         (forall x . f x -> m (g x)) -> Stream f m r -> Stream g m r
mapsM fun = decompose . maps (Compose . fun)
```

For example, we can add any monadic effect to a stream `Of` a without hurting the stream elements, as shown next:

```
withEffect :: Monad m =>
              (e -> m ()) -> Stream (Of e) m r -> Stream (Of e) m r
withEffect eff = mapsM go
  where
    go p@(e :> _) = eff e >> pure p
```

Compare the following three stream-processing pipelines:

```
ghci> ssum $ each [1..3 :: Int]
6 :> ()
ghci> ssum $ withEffect print $ each [1..3 :: Int]
1
2
3
6 :> ()
ghci> ssum $ withEffect print $ withEffect (\_ -> putStr "Element: ")
          $ each [1..3 :: Int]
Element: 1
Element: 2
Element: 3
6 :> ()
```

We've managed to add a couple of independent effects into a pipeline, and they work together for every functorial step as one combined effect.

STREAM AS A RESULT AND A FUNCTORIAL STEP

As a final example of what can be achieved with this simple implementation of streaming, let's implement splitting a stream into fragments of fixed size (chunks). Let's start with the splitsAt function, shown here:

```
splitsAt :: (Monad m, Functor f) =>
            Int -> Stream f m r -> Stream f m (Stream f m r)
splitsAt n str = ...
```

The goal is to process the first n elements of the given stream and return everything else as a result of streaming. Remember, we never put any limitations on the type of the streaming result, so why not have a stream as a result?

The implementation follows the same pattern: we loop over the stream structure and count steps. Once we have enough, we stop and send the rest of the stream to Return as follows:

```
splitsAt = loop
  where
    loop n stream
      | n > 0 =                          ◁────── Needs to loop over
         case stream of
            Return r -> Return (Return r)   ◁──── The stream has ended.
            Effect m -> Effect (fmap (loop n) m)   ◁────── Loops over an effect
            Step f  -> Step (fmap (loop (n-1)) f)  ◁──
      | otherwise = Return stream
```

Returns the rest of a stream as a streaming result

The stream has ended.

Loops over an effect

Loops over a step and decrements the steps counter

Now to the chunking implementation. If we need chunks of size n, the idea is to take the first step and then use splitsAt (n-1) to complete the chunk. The problem is how to express a chunk. Is it a good idea to represent it with lists having the Stream (Of [a]) m r stream as a chunking result? Well, no. We want to avoid lists with their hard predictable memory usage altogether. Why not use Stream f m itself as a functorial step? It's a Functor, and it expresses the idea of successive elements. Thus, we arrive at the following type and implementation of the chunksOf function:

```
chunksOf :: forall f m r. (Monad m, Functor f) =>
            Int -> Stream f m r -> Stream (Stream f m) m r
chunksOf n = loop
  where
    cutChunk :: Stream f m r -> Stream f m (Stream (Stream f m) m r)
    cutChunk str = fmap loop (splitsAt (n-1) str)

    loop :: Stream f m r -> Stream (Stream f m) m r
    loop (Return r) = Return r
    loop (Effect m) = Effect (fmap loop m)
    loop (Step fs) = Step (Step (fmap cutChunk fs))
```

The `cutChunk` function is responsible for cutting one chunk of a stream and continuing looping over the rest of it. The `loop` function constructs a stream of streams with two `Step` data constructors and runs `cutChunk` over the original step.

A quick test shows that we are good:

```
ghci> ssum $ withEffect print $ mapsM ssum $ chunksOf 2
         $ each [1,1,1,1,1 :: Int]
2
2
1
5 :> ()
```

We have a stream of streams as a result of `chunksOf`, so we can run functions over substreams with `mapsM`. This is where generalization really shines.

Note that we don't introduce a new data structure to describe chunks of stream elements. The free stream structure is already powerful enough to express them. This is one of the main features of the streaming approach we are working on.

All the implementations in this section follow closely the implementations in the actual `streaming` package. The `Stream f m r` type is absolutely identical there. Let's move to that package and see how to use it. The implementation details should be clear by now.

14.1.2 *The streaming package*

Let's look at the functionality that streaming libraries provide by comparing them with regular Haskell lists.

EXAMPLE: TABULATING NUMBERS WITH SUMS

Suppose we have many integer numbers, and we want to tabulate them, that is, print in several columns. We also want to compute the sum of all the numbers given as we process them.

EXAMPLE: SUMMING AND TABULATING NUMBERS WITH STREAMS

📄 ch14/sumtab.hs

⚡ *sumtab*

☞ Streaming libraries try to mimic list-processing operations.

☞ Streaming libraries focus on memory usage and performance.

In terms of lists, the solution is easy, as shown here:

```
import Data.Text (Text)
import Data.Text.IO as TIO
import TextShow
import qualified Data.List.Extra as LE

withTab :: Int -> Text
```

```
withTab num = showt num <> "\t"

tabulateL :: Int -> [Int] -> [Text]
tabulateL cols ns = map mconcat $ LE.chunksOf cols $ map withTab ns

sumAndTabL :: Int -> [Int] -> IO Int
sumAndTabL cols ns = do
  mapM_ TIO.putStrLn $ tabulateL cols ns
  pure $ sum ns
```

We turn every given number into `Text`, break lists into chunks of the required size, concatenate components of every chunk, print the results line by line, and also return the sum. For example, we could get the following result with the [1..9] list in three columns:

```
ghci> sumAndTabL 3 [1..9]
1    2    3
4    5    6
7    8    9
45
```

Unfortunately, this simple solution isn't a good one in terms of performance. The problem is that we should traverse the whole list of numbers twice. Note the `sumAnd-TabL` function: there are two references to `ns` in two consequent `IO` steps. As a result, we have to keep this list in memory. This is unsatisfactory if a list is sufficiently large. We could make a list larger and run the program with the `+RTS -s` flag to see the actual stats on memory usage.

Is it possible to rewrite this program and avoid keeping the whole list in memory? Absolutely. We could write the following much more efficient implementation:

```
sumAndTabL1 :: Int -> [Int] -> IO Int
sumAndTabL1 cols ns = foldM prtLineSum 0 $ LE.chunksOf cols ns
  where
    prtLineSum !acc xs = do
      TIO.putStrLn $ mconcat $ map withTab xs
      pure $ acc + sum xs
```

This function does the same thing as before, but it works in constant memory. No more storing the whole list in memory. Have we lost anything? Unfortunately, yes. We've lost compositionality. Remember, we had the `tabulateL` and `sum` functions before, and now their code is interleaved inside the implementation of the `sumAndTabL1` function. This would become a huge problem if we want to interleave the functionality of more than a couple of functions. So, what's the right solution? Here come the streaming libraries, specifically designed to deal with problems like this one.

INTRODUCING THE STREAMING PACKAGE

The streaming package functionality is split between the two following modules:

- The Streaming module defines the main Stream type and the most general functions over it.
- The Streaming.Prelude module gives access to many stream functions over the streams of elements of particular types.

Note the Prelude part in the name of the second module. It refers to the idea that this module provides functions similar to those found in the standard Haskell Prelude module.

Let's import these modules as follows:

```
import Streaming as S
import qualified Streaming.Prelude as S
```

The Streaming module gives us the Stream type. It represents a succession of steps, though we don't have access to the corresponding data constructors. Instead, we can use the following wrappers, available from the Streaming module:

```
wrap :: (Monad m, Functor f) => f (Stream f m r) -> Stream f m r
effect :: (Monad m, Functor f) => m (Stream f m r) -> Stream f m r
```

We also have the following instances available:

- Stream f m is a Functor, an Applicative, and a Monad treated as a computation, resulting in an r.
- Stream f m is also an Alternative that allows us to glue streams together stepwise.
- Given that m is a MonadIO, Stream f m is also a MonadIO.
- Stream f is a monad transformer that adds streaming abilities to the underlying monad.
- Given that r is a Monoid, Stream f m r is also a monoid.

Many other instances can be found in the documentation. Interestingly enough, there are no Foldable or Traversable instances. We can't simply go over every element in a stream, because that would break its internal structure. Traversing over streams is handled internally and exposed by some dedicated functions we'll discuss shortly.

The Of type is used in streaming to represent stream elements. The only difference from our earlier implementation is that the first component of a pair is strict. It turns out that this is crucial for performance. Just as before, we construct the Of pair with the (:>) data constructor. We can also get its components via the pattern matching or with the S.fst' and S.snd' functions.

LISTS/STREAMS ANALOGY IN TYPES

In our example, we have the following list-processing functions:

```
tabulateL :: Int -> [Int] -> [Text]
sumAndTabL :: Int -> [Int] -> IO Int
```

Their counterparts for streams look very similar, as shown here:

```
tabulateS :: Int -> Stream (Of Int) IO r -> Stream (Of Text) IO r
sumAndTabS :: Int -> Stream (Of Int) IO r -> IO Int
```

I've simply replaced `[Int]` with `Stream (Of Int) IO r`. Now we have a stream of `Int` numbers processed in the `IO` monad. (Remember, we need to print the numbers in columns.) Note that the `r` result type is left unspecified. In general, we replace any list `[a]` with `Stream (Of a) m r`. By doing that we promise to use the `m` monad effects while processing the stream elements and return the `r` value later when the stream processing is over.

There is a price to pay—types become more complex. The good news is that we have more power now. First, we have a monad; second, we've got an idea of a result right in the type of a stream.

SIMPLE STREAMING FUNCTIONS

Let's implement the streaming analog to the `tabulateL` function. Let's revisit it first here:

```
tabulateL :: Int -> [Int] -> [Text]
tabulateL cols ns = map mconcat $ LE.chunksOf cols $ map withTab ns
```

We've used several list functions here. We can rewrite them in terms of streams. Let's start with mconcat as follows:

```
mconcat :: Monoid a => [a] -> a
S.mconcat :: (Monad m, Monoid w) => Stream (Of w) m r -> m (Of w r)
```

In `S.mconcat`, we reduce a stream of `w` typed values to a single value. There is no stream anymore: the resulting action works in the `m` monad, and the resulting pair contains both an mconcat result and a stream-processing result. Consequently, we've kept the lists/streams analogy and provide additional abilities (monad and a stream-processing result).

The `S.mconcat` function belongs to a family of folding functions. The following two are the most general folds in `streaming`:

```
fold :: Monad m =>
        (x -> a -> x) -> x -> (x -> b) -> Stream (Of a) m r -> m (Of b r)
foldM :: Monad m =>
        (x -> a -> m x) -> m x -> (x -> m b) -> Stream (Of a) m r -> m (Of b r)
```

Just as regular folds, they take a function over an accumulator and individual stream element, an initial accumulator value, and a stream of values. They also take a third argument, which is a function converting an accumulator to another type. Note that these functions keep the stream-processing result.

We'll need the following streaming sum and length functions shortly. They belong to the folds family also.

```
S.sum :: (Monad m, Num a) => Stream (Of a) m r -> m (Of a r)
S.length :: Monad m => Stream (Of a) m r -> m (Of Int r)
```

Remember, folding consumes a stream giving the following two different results:

- The result of folding
- The result of streaming

There are also variations of folding functions giving back only one of those results.

In chunksOf, the lists/streams analogy becomes a little bit harder to see, as shown next:

```
LE.chunksOf :: Int -> [a] -> [[a]]
S.chunksOf
  :: (Monad m, Functor f) => Int -> Stream f m r -> Stream (Stream f m) m r
```

Note that the streaming chunksOf doesn't use Of; it uses a general Functor. It works with any form of a step. The most important thing here is how we express a list of lists. We use the Stream (Stream f m) m r type for that. Remember that Stream f m is a Functor, so we can use it as a form of a step.

One would expect something like the following to express a list of lists:

```
Stream (Of (Stream (Of a) m r)) m r
```

But this would require having the whole inner stream computed. We don't expect that with streaming. An implementation behind Stream (Stream f m) m r guarantees that there will be no unnecessary bookkeeping while grouping individual elements besides some almost ephemeral borders between groups.

As for the mapping over stream elements, the choice is extremely rich. We'll need only a couple of functions in our examples, but many others are available.

Instead of the one regular map, we'll use the following two:

```
map :: (a -> b) -> [a] -> [b]
S.map :: Monad m => (a -> b) -> Stream (Of a) m r -> Stream (Of b) m r
S.mapsM :: (Monad m, Functor f) =>
           (forall x. f x -> m (g x)) -> Stream f m r -> Stream g m r
```

The S.map function looks similar to map. The S.mapsM is more general. It allows replacing a functorial form of a step by doing something in a monadic computation given as the first argument. In our example, we'll need it to transform a chunked stream of the type `Stream (Stream (Of Text) IO) IO r` to `Stream (Of Text) IO r`.

With these functions in our hands, we arrive at the following implementation of `tabulateS`:

```
tabulateS :: Int -> Stream (Of Int) IO r -> Stream (Of Text) IO r
tabulateS cols str = S.mapsM S.mconcat $ S.chunksOf cols $ S.map withTab str
```

Let's write out the specific types in this particular function as follows:

```
S.map :: (Int -> Text) -> Stream (Of Int) IO r -> Stream (Of Text) IO r
S.chunksOf ::
          Int -> Stream (Of Text) IO r -> Stream (Stream (Of Text) IO) IO r
S.mconcat :: Stream (Of Text) IO r -> IO (Of Text r)
S.mapsM :: (Stream (Of Text) IO r -> IO (Of Text r)) ->
        Stream (Stream (Of Text) IO) IO r ->
        Stream (Of Text) IO r
```

These functions let us flow from the original `Stream (Of Int) IO r` to `Stream (Of Text) IO r`. Whenever we have a generic type, it's always a good idea to specify it in the particular circumstances. This helps us understand what is going on.

To test this implementation, we'll need more functions. First, we can use the `S.each` function to build a stream from a list. Second, we can print every `Text` element in a stream by mapping `TIO.putStrLn` over it with the `S.mapM_` function as follows:

```
S.mapM_ :: Monad m => (a -> m x) -> Stream (Of a) m r -> m r
```

This function keeps the stream-processing result but eliminates everything else, including the stream itself.

Let's try `tabulateS` in GHCi as follows:

```
ghci> S.mapM_ TIO.putStrLn $ tabulateS 3 $ S.each [1..9]
1    2    3
4    5    6
7    8    9
```

Remember that we haven't tried to compose tabulating with the computing of the sum yet. Right now, streaming may look like an inconvenient and verbose replacement for lists. Stay tuned.

TO COPY OR NOT TO COPY

Doing two different things with the same data can be problematic. It helps if we can copy it, but we'd prefer to avoid that. With streams, we can pretend that we are copying things while describing a pipeline, but under the hood, we manipulate the stream structure without duplicating data. Copying is an abstraction in `streaming` that allows us to compose different processing stages into one data-processing pipeline.

As we've already discussed, a stream represents a succession of steps. Copying a stream corresponds to making those steps more complex and adds more processing actions to them. Those additional actions come from different stages of a pipeline.

Let's look at how copying is expressed in types in the following example:

```
S.copy :: Monad m => Stream (Of a) m r -> Stream (Of a) (Stream (Of a) m) r
```

This function gives us a stream back. In this stream, we have steps in the same form `Of a` as before but in a different monad. The `Stream (Of a) m` is precisely a new step monad: it's an `m` monad transformed.

For the simple example of copying, let's compute the sum and the length of the given stream as follows:

```
ghci> S.length $ S.sum $ S.copy $ S.each [1..9 :: Int]
9 :> (45 :> ())
```

Both the `S.sum` and `S.length` functions participate in computing the results of streaming. Thanks to the `copy` function, we can get the combined result as a pair of `Int`s and a pair, as shown next:

```
ghci> :t it
it :: Of Int (Of Int ())
```

It may be useful to see how types are changed along the previous pipeline. Let's break it down as follows:

```
ghci> :set +t
ghci> s1 = S.each [1..9 :: Int]
s1 :: Monad m => Stream (Of Int) m ()
ghci> s2 = S.copy s1
s2 :: Monad m => Stream (Of Int) (Stream (Of Int) m) ()
ghci> s3 = S.sum s2
s3 :: Monad m => Stream (Of Int) m (Of Int ())
ghci> res = S.length s3
res :: Monad m => m (Of Int (Of Int ()))
```

Note that `S.sum` works over a stream with a transformed monad whereas `S.length` operates in the original one. This will be important later, when we have effects and want to understand which effects come first. We'll see that effects in the original monad are executed earlier.

The `copy` function is often used via the simple `S.store` wrapper defined as follows:

```
store :: Monad m =>
         (Stream (Of a) (Stream (Of a) m) r -> t) -> Stream (Of a) m r -> t
store f x = f (copy x)
```

This function copies the stream and runs a streaming function over the copy. Then we can continue the pipeline, assured that the first streaming result is properly stored until the end of streaming.

Now we are ready to implement the streaming function similar to the `sumAndTabL` defined earlier and reprinted here for convenience:

```
sumAndTabL :: Int -> [Int] -> IO Int
sumAndTabL cols ns = do
  mapM_ TIO.putStrLn $ tabulateL cols ns
  pure $ sum ns
```

The idea is to store the sum of numbers first and then continue with tabulating them as follows:

```
sumAndTabS :: Int -> Stream (Of Int) IO r -> IO Int
sumAndTabS cols =
  fmap S.fst' . S.mapM_ TIO.putStrLn . tabulateS cols . S.store S.sum
```

This looks like plain old list processing via function composition. But note that we've also got a perfectly composed processing of "a copy" of a stream. The final `fmap S.fst'` extracts the sum computed at the start of the pipeline from the streaming result.

Running the `sumAndTabS` function gives us the same results as the `sumAndTabL` function, as shown next:

```
ghci> sumAndTabS 3 (S.each [1..9])
1    2    3
4    5    6
7    8    9
45
```

Now we've got an implementation that runs in constant memory and is quite performant. What's even more important, it's quite simple.

The `copy` function behavior may be difficult to comprehend. Let me demonstrate it once again by the following extremely simple pipeline:

- We have a stream of characters.
- We print every character as it is.
- We also print its code.

The goal is to keep the printing of a character and its code separate.

EXAMPLE: DEMONSTRATING S.COPY BEHAVIOR

📄 ch14/chars.hs

⚡ *chars*

☞ S.copy enriches steps with more actions instead of copying data.

Suppose we have the following functions to print characters and their codes:

```
printChar :: Char -> IO ()
printChar c = putChar c >> putChar ' '

printCode :: Char -> IO ()
printCode = print . ord
```

Let's turn them into stream-processing stages as follows:

```
printChars :: MonadIO m => Stream (Of Char) m r -> m r
printChars = S.mapM_ (S.liftIO . printChar)

printCodes :: MonadIO m => Stream (Of Char) m r -> m r
printCodes = S.mapM_ (S.liftIO . printCode)
```

We try to be as general as possible. We don't fix the monad. We also keep the streaming result, though we don't produce one in these functions. Both functions can be used independently, as shown here:

```
ghci> printChars $ S.each "haskell"
h a s k e l l
ghci> printCodes $ S.each "haskell"
104
97
115
107
101
108
108
```

Now let's use `S.copy` and run them over the "copies" of the stream as follows:

```
ghci> printChars $ printCodes $ S.copy $ S.each "haskell"
h 104
a 97
s 115
k 107
e 101
l 108
l 108
```

We have cleanly separated stages, but we also see that the effects are interleaved. There is no need to store all the data in memory. As expected, we process characters one by one, in constant memory.

   Note the order: the `printCodes` function executes steps in a modified monad, the one provided by the `S.copy`. This transformed monad complements actions of the original one coming from the `main`, namely, the `IO` monad. The `m` monad in the type of `printCodes` refers here to the transformed `Stream (Of Char) IO` monad. Its action follows the actions of the underlying IO monad provided by printChars. That's why we have characters printed first and their codes next.

The streaming package contains many more streaming functions. Refer to the documentation for the details.

It should be clear that the streaming package is not about processing lists. In the next session, we'll link it to real-world problems and see what can be done during pipeline stages.

14.2 Approaching an implementation of pipeline stages

Many problems can be solved using the streaming data approach. Consequently, many packages may be required to implement particular stages. Those packages don't have to be closely related to the streaming package. Nevertheless, we may benefit from a close integration in many cases.

In this section, we'll look at the following packages that belong to the streaming package ecosystem:

- streaming-bytestring allows working with files and their content. This package is meant to be a replacement of the bytestring package. It uses the streaming approach under the hood.
- streaming-utils provides wrappers for several data sources and makes it easier to communicate with them.

We use the streaming-utils to bridge the parser combinators found in the attoparsec package and the streaming ecosystem. We'll also look at the lens library, which doesn't relate to streaming at all but can be used with deeply nested data structures, which are quite common in the latter stages of data-processing pipelines.

14.2.1 Reading and writing data efficiently

The first problem of every data-processing pipeline is how to read data from a data source. Surely, we don't want to get all the data in memory at once. That means that we should keep a connection (file descriptor, network socket, or a database connection) as long as we work through the pipeline. We should also be able to release all the acquired resources (close file descriptors, etc.) in due time. All that said, we do want a program to look like we read all the data at once.

Let's look at the solution to the problem of copying a file. We want to copy a given file and report the number of bytes copied.

EXAMPLE: COPY FILE WITH STREAMING

🗋 ch14/copy.hs

⚡ *copy*

The traditional bytestring package gives us the ByteString type for arrays of Word8 values. Here we use the Streaming.ByteString module from the streaming-bytestring package. It gives us the effectful ByteString m r type, which is the

`Stream (Of ByteString) m r` in disguise. Most of the operations in this module mimic those from the `Data.ByteString`. We can use them or switch to the `streaming` operations, if needed.

To copy a file, we need to read it and then write all the content into another file. We also need to store the length of the file. Reading and writing in `Streaming.ByteString` can be done with the following functions:

```
readFile :: MonadResource m => FilePath -> ByteString m ()
writeFile :: MonadResource m => FilePath -> ByteString m r -> m r
```

Note the `MonadResource m` constraint. It comes from the `resourcet` package, which allows safe resource allocation and guarantees that it will be released at the due time. This package does the hard work of exception handling and prevents resource leaks efficiently. To run the `MonadResource` computation, we need to use the `runResourceT` function. It works well with any `IO` computations (and any `MonadIO` monad stacks).

The following function copies a file using the streaming approach:

```
import Streaming
import Streaming.ByteString as BS
import Control.Monad.Trans.Resource

copyFile :: FilePath -> FilePath -> IO Int
copyFile fIn fOut = do
  (len :> ()) <- runResourceT
                $ BS.writeFile fOut
                $ BS.length
                $ BS.copy
                $ BS.readFile fIn
  pure len
```

Note that we use `BS.copy` to compute the number of bytes copied. `BS.length` adds the length to the final streaming result, and we extract it by pattern matching.

When using the streaming approach, writing functions in a left-to-right (or bottom-up) manner quickly becomes irritating. For such cases, we normally use the `(&)` operator from the `Data.Function` module. It reverses the order of application so that we can write `arg & fun`. With this operator, we can write pipeline stages in a more traditional manner as follows:

```
copyFile :: FilePath -> FilePath -> IO Int
copyFile fIn fOut = runResourceT $ do
  (len :> ()) <- BS.readFile fIn
                & BS.copy
                & BS.length
                & BS.writeFile fOut
  pure len
```

We start with reading the file, copy it, compute the length, and then write the original content to a new file. Finally, we run all the computation in a resource-aware environment.

All the streaming libraries give some form of efficient input/output guaranteed to work in the constant memory. We can easily check this with memory profiling via the +RTS flags.

14.2.2   *Parsing data with parser combinators*

Parsing is often used at early pipeline stages to get away from raw bytes and move toward more sophisticated data structures. Figure 14.3 presents parsing as a pipeline stage.

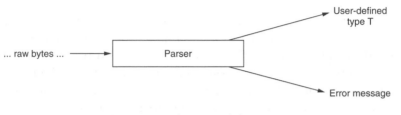

```
parse :: ByteString -> Either ErrorMsg T
```

Figure 14.3   Parsing a pipeline stage

Usually, we expect having the following function as an interface to any parsing library:

```
parse :: ByteString -> Either ErrorMsg T
```

In Haskell, there is a long tradition of implementing particular parsers using parser combinators because it's a nice example of using features of the Applicative and Monad type classes. Consequently, books about Haskell rarely avoid implementing parser combinators from scratch. Many libraries already implement this approach, including most notably the following:

- parsec is a de facto standard without too much development nowadays.
- megaparsec can be seen as a modern actively developed fork of parsec.
- attoparsec concentrates on performance and implements incremental parsing, when we have data partially supplied.
- trifecta features good diagnostics and follows the same line as other parser combinator libraries.

NOTE   All these libraries are described in many tutorials available online. For example, I can recommend a thorough tutorial (https://markkarpov.com/tutorial/megaparsec.html) on megaparsec written by Mark Karpov. That tutorial features a good range of problems that can be solved by parser combinator libraries.

Instead of implementing parsing combinators from scratch or describing a range of features of some parsing library, I'll focus on one practical example of parsing routine CSV files to give an idea of what a parsing library is like. In this section, we'll parse a

CSV file of the simplest format as a list of lists of `Text` and see how parsing can be embedded into pipelines. In the last section of this chapter, we'll introduce parsing CSV files into a pipeline of stages.

The two steps in using any parser combinator library follow:

- First, we describe our expected input and show how it corresponds to an output.
- Second, we implement the actual parsing.

Let's look at both stages in order.

DESCRIBING INPUT WITH PARSER COMBINATORS

We decided to parse CSV files. Let's ignore the possibility of having single-quoted or double-quoted fields for simplicity. The goal is to parse the following quotes.csv file from chapter 3:

```
day,close,volume,open,high,low
2019-05-01,210.520004,64827300,209.880005,215.309998,209.229996
...
```

We want to produce the `[[Text]]` data type as a result of parsing. To do that, we should write several parser combinators that correspond to the following elements of a CSV file:

- A field
- A record as a collection of comma-separated fields
- A file as a collection of end-of-line-separated fields

Hey, what's a combinator?

Chances are the word *combinator* used in a context of parsing makes no sense to you. In fact, it's yet another way to describe a computation. Traditionally, computations are described in mathematics with functions. Functions have arguments. To describe a computation, we show a way to go from the arguments to the result of a function. For example, the following function says how to increment a number by 1: `\x -> x + 1`.

Now, suppose we have primitive operations `inc`, `dec`, `repeat5`, `andThen`, and so on. We can use them to express computations like the following:

- `repeat5 inc` increments a value five times.
- `andThen inc dec` asks for incrementing followed by decrementing.

As a result, we have a computation described without an argument at all. This is precisely the idea of a combinator pattern used to define the interfaces of many Haskell libraries. At the end of the day, we apply a combined combinator to a value but can avoid this final application as long as needed.

Note that this meaning of a combinator doesn't correspond directly to the one used in theoretical computer science, so don't be confused. The following wiki page gives more details on these two meanings: https://wiki.haskell.org/Combinator.

EXAMPLE: PARSING A SIMPLE CSV FILE

ch14/csv-simple.hs

csv-simple

We are parsing byte strings into texts using the attoparsec library. Let's start with importing the corresponding modules as follows:

```
import Data.ByteString (ByteString)
import Data.Text (Text)
import qualified Data.Text.Encoding as T
import Data.Attoparsec.ByteString.Char8 as A
import Control.Applicative
```

What's a CSV field? Well, it's a sequence of any characters that are not either ',' or end-of-line characters. (I intentionally ignore the full CSV field syntax with quotes and escaping.) This description corresponds to the following parser combinator:

```
field :: Parser ByteString
field = A.takeWhile (\c -> c /= ',' && c /= '\r' && c /= '\n')
```

Note that we have no arguments to parse. They will be supplied later. Parser is a monad that keeps track of current input and parsing results. The takeWhile function has no ByteString as an argument; it's also a combinator. Nevertheless, it describes the underlying computational process very clearly. It instructs a parser to consume all the input until it encounters either a field separator or an end-of-line character.

The Parser ByteString type of the field combinator promises a ByteString as a result of parsing. We'd like to get a Text field instead. The Data.Text.Encoding module provides the decodeUtf8 function to make a decoding, as shown next:

```
textField´ :: Parser Text
textField = T.decodeUtf8 <$> field
```

Now, what's a CSV record? It's a sequence of text fields, separated by a field separator. We can specify a particular field separator using the char ',' combinator. The sepBy1 combinator expresses the idea of being separated by something as follows:

```
record :: Parser [Text]
record = textField `sepBy1` (char ',')
```

The 1 in sepBy1 means that there should be at least one field in a record. At this point, we could run the program in GHCi and try our combinators out as follows:

```
ghci> :set -XOverloadedStrings
ghci> parseOnly record "1,2,3"
Right ["1","2","3"]
```

We need this to treat a String literal as a ByteString.

The "1,2,3" literal is parsed successfully. The parseOnly function applies a combinator to a ByteString and gives back either an error message or a parsing result.

Finally, we are ready to describe what a CSV file is. Unfortunately, even with simple formats like this one, we can encounter various gotchas. For example, we don't know in advance whether there is an end-of-line character after the final line of the file. We should be ready for both sorts of input, with or without it.

Parsers express options in the input like that using the Alternative features. We can try the first combinator. If it fails, we go with the second one. Following is how we can use this to describe an end-of-file character:

```
endOfFile :: Parser ()
endOfFile = endOfInput <|> endOfLine *> endOfInput
```

The endOfInput and endOfLine combinators are provided by the attoparsec libraries as well as Applicative and Alternative instances for Parser a. Remember the next types:

```
(<|>) :: Alternative f => f a -> f a -> f a
(*>) :: Applicative f => f a -> f b -> f b
```

The Alternative instance for Parser a takes the first parser that succeeded. The (*>) operator ignores the result of its left argument.

Now, the CSV file is a record followed by a sequence of line ends and records until the end of a file as follows:

```
file :: Parser [[Text]]
file =
  (:) <$> record
      <*> manyTill (endOfLine *> record)
                   endOfFile
```

The manyTill combinator applies the first combinator repeatedly until the second one is successfully applied. The attoparsec library provides many other combinators to parse data; you may find them in the documentation on Hackage.

RUNNING A PARSER ON A STREAMED BYTESTRING

Once we have our combinator, we can apply it to the data. As I mentioned earlier, the attoparsec is capable of incremental parsing, so we can feed it with partial data as it goes. This is a particularly important feature in streaming. In this simple example, we don't need it. The parseOnly function is enough in our case. It has the following type:

```
parseOnly :: Parser a -> ByteString -> Either String a
```

To apply it, we can write the trivial main function shown next:

```
import qualified Data.ByteString as B

-- ...

main :: IO ()
main = B.readFile "data/quotes.csv" >>= print . parseOnly file
```

To apply attoparsec to the streamed data, we can use an adaptor defined in the Data.Attoparsec.ByteString.Streaming module provided by the streaming-utils package. The adaptor has the following type:

```
parsed
  :: Monad m                        Attoparsec parser
  => Parser a      <—               combinator for type a          Streams with
  -> ByteString m r           <—    Streams with raw bytes         parsed values
  -> Stream (Of a) m (Either (Message, ByteString m r) r) <—┘      of type a
```

Note the type for the result of streaming. We can get an error message with the rest of the streamed ByteString m r if there is any error in the input. We can use the following quite general function to throw this result away if we don't need it:

```
Data.Functor.void :: Functor f => f a -> f ()
```

Combining the reading of a file into a streamed ByteString with parsing, we arrive at another possible implementation of the main function, as shown next:

```
import qualified Streaming.Prelude as S
import qualified Streaming.ByteString as BS
import Control.Monad.Trans.Resource
import Data.Attoparsec.ByteString.Streaming
import Data.Function ((&))
import Data.Functor (void)

-- ...

main = runResourceT $
          BS.readFile "data/quotes.csv"
        & parsed file
        & void
        & S.print
```

Note that this program doesn't actually stream due to the implementation of the file parser combinator. It waits for the end of file explicitly, keeping all the data in memory, and then produces a final result. We'll write a properly streaming program later in this chapter.

Interestingly, the following list of dependencies looks quite impressive for such a small program:

```
text
attoparsec
bytestring
```

```
streaming-utils
streaming-bytestring
streaming
resourcet
```

Clearly, we need neither the streaming approach nor parsing with combinators to parse CSV files. It's better to go with a more high-level package instead. We've already used cassava for that. Nevertheless, this combination of techniques will be very useful later in this chapter because we'll need to parse CSV data while partially ignoring some parts of the relatively large input. This is where parsing data as a whole may be overkill in terms of performance.

14.2.3 *Accessing data with lenses*

When we work through data-processing pipelines, our data becomes more and more complex. The data may be deeply nested or contain potentially missing parts or many instances of those parts. Some of the parts may be containers of some sort, for example. Working with the data implies reading or modifying parts, changing forms, and transforming data as a whole. In Haskell, we have a general approach to manipulate data often called *optics*. We have our own glasses, telescopes, and microscopes (or optics, in a word) to work with data and their components.

Several libraries implement this approach. In this chapter, we'll use the lens library developed by Edward Kmett. He is known as one of the most *category-theory-*inclined Haskell developers. This fact affects his libraries a lot. Nevertheless, I'll try to persuade the reader that it is possible to use the lens library efficiently without understanding a thing about categories. Unfortunately, I'll have to restrain myself from talking about the implementation details of this library.

The number of explanations about lenses on the internet is overwhelming. It seems only monad tutorials are more popular. Fortunately, lenses are one of those things that often need two explanations before anyone knows what you are talking about, as Owl put it in one of the stories about Winnie the Pooh.

A GENERAL APPROACH TO WORKING WITH DATA

The lens package provides several so-called optical devices with more or less fancy names, including Lens, Prism, and Iso. Let's try to understand the problems they solve first and then give them a more precise meaning.

We already know that complex data structures in Haskell are built out of the following two simple "bricks":

- Product types (structures, records, etc.) allow building data from parts or components with a tuple as a typical example.
- Sum types (enumerations or alternatives) allow their values to take one of various alternative forms; Bool and Either a b are both examples of sum types.

We use the same two bricks in the definition of algebraic data types. With them, we can construct everything as complexly as we need. To work with data built this way, we write functions as clauses with pattern matching and corresponding bodies.

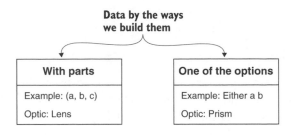

With parts

Example: (a, b, c)

Optic: Lens

One of the options

Example: Either a b

Optic: Prism

Figure 14.4 Optics reflecting the ways we build data structures

The optics approach provides a couple of devices that reflect these ways of building values, namely, `Lens` and `Prism`, illustrated in figure 14.4.

As a whole

Example: any type

Optic: Iso

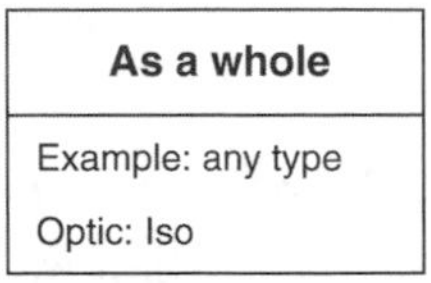

Figure 14.5 Optics for working with data as a whole

Sometimes we need to work with data as a whole without looking at the parts or inspecting actual forms. There is a device for that also, called `Iso`, presented in figure 14.5.

We use yet another way to build data, namely, putting it into a collection. This is not a primitive brick but a combination of sum and product types. Nevertheless, we work with containers too often to avoid having a dedicated device for them, called `Traversal` and presented in figure 14.6.

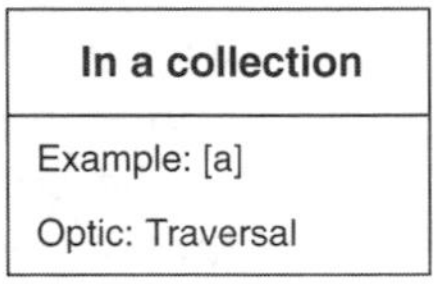

In a collection

Example: [a]

Optic: Traversal

Figure 14.6 Optics for processing data collections

Note that with collections, things can get complicated. For example, any data as a whole can be considered as a collection of one element. Whenever we are looking for a particular form of data of a sum type, we can either get it or not. Suppose we are looking for a value inside `Maybe a`. We can either get it in `Just`, or it can be missing because of a `Nothing`. So we have a collection of either 0 or 1 element. Any data, no matter how we've built it, is subject to processing as a whole via `Iso`. At the end of the day, we may consider elements of a collection as parts of data and work with them appropriately via `Lens`. It turns out that optical devices relate to each other, and we can use some of them instead of others.

Now let's look at the following operations we apply to data:

- We may want to get some part of the data; there is `Getter` for that.
- If we need to change some part or apply a function to it, we use a `Setter`.
- When working with collections, we may want to fold them into a single value; we have `Fold` for that.

Figure 14.7 illustrates the devices that reflect operations over data.

Even though we talk about operations over data, we still talk about data. We think about it as *gettable, settable,* or *foldable.* The distinction between these sorts of data is not trivial. For example, foldable can easily be gettable. It can't be settable, though, because we don't know which particular value of a foldable collection should be set.

You see that we can describe our data in terms of the ways we build it and in terms of the operations we apply to it. This idea fits a unified framework, presented in figure 14.8.

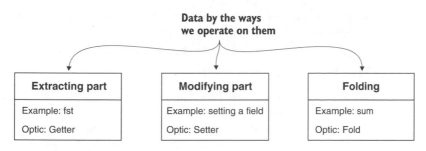

Figure 14.7 Optics for operating over data

Note the arrows. They denote a sort of subtyping. We can consider any Iso being a Lens, or Prism being a Traversal, but not the other way around.

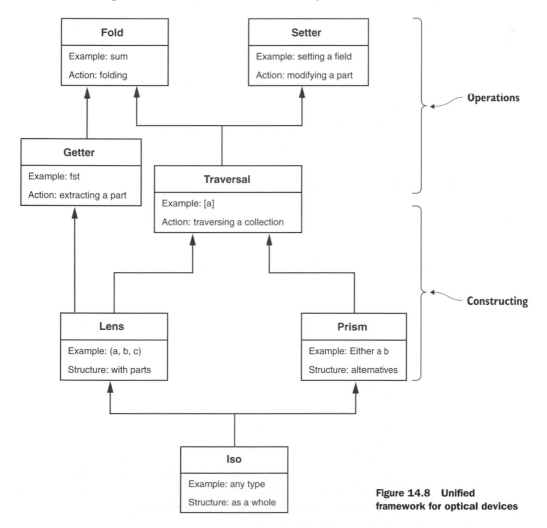

Figure 14.8 Unified framework for optical devices

All right, we have all those devices and have an idea what we need them for. The question is, what are they in terms of Haskell? Well, that's easy: they are just functions. We also call them functional references, because they refer to something about data (a part, an element inside a collection, an operation, etc.).

> **TIP** Unfortunately, the types of those functions may be quite hard to understand. They use a lot of polymorphism, monadic machinery, and plenty of category theory constructions. Mostly, it's okay to forget about all that. The `lens` library gives us type synonyms that hide those function types, though we can still spot them occasionally in error messages. I suggest closing your eyes at those moments.

Now, to work with data we need the following three ingredients:

- The data itself
- Functional references (lenses et al.)
- Functions (or operators) to apply functional references to data

Functional references are quite independent and can be composed without any data at all—they are functions, after all. So we use them as combinators. Once we've defined what we need, we apply the result to our data. Let's move on to examples.

BASIC USAGE OF THE LENS LIBRARY

We are not trying to do something meaningful in the following examples. Instead, we concentrate on the most basic usage.

EXAMPLE: USING BASIC LENSES

☐   ch14/lens-ex.hs

⚡   *lens-ex*

Let's import the main `lens` package module first as follows:

```
import Control.Lens
```

We are starting with the simplest data structure—a tuple with two elements—and we want to look inside, as shown here:

```
$ cabal repl lens-ex
ghci> pair = ("hello, world", '!')
ghci> view _1 pair
"hello, world"
ghci> view _2 pair
'!'
```

We have a `pair` data structure. The `_1` and `_2` are functional references for tuples to retrieve the first and the second tuple components, respectively. The `view` function allows getting a referenced value from data. Let's look at their types, as shown next:

```
_1 :: Lens' (a, b) a
_2 :: Lens' (a, b) b
view :: Lens' s t -> s -> t
```

We have two arguments to the `Lens'` type constructor. The first one denotes the data structure; the second one denotes the part we are referencing.

Note, these types are simplified. If we check them in GHCi, we may see something different. Also note, though, that these types are not wrong. The Haskell type system allows us to give different names to the same types. It also allows us to treat them with more or less generality, thanks to polymorphism. Would it be a lie to say that we have the `id` function of type `Int -> Int` in Haskell? Not really, even though the *actual* type is `forall a. a -> a`.

Getting back to the previous example: we have data, a functional reference pointing to one of the parts, and a function to apply the reference to the data. In addition to the latter function, the `lens` package provides the `(^.)` operator with its arguments flipped, as shown next:

```
ghci> pair ^. _1
"hello, world"
ghci> pair ^. _2
'!'
```

Many functions for applying functional references have corresponding operators. As a result, there are too many of them, so using them extensively may make reading the code much harder.

To set a pair component, we can use the `set` function or the corresponding `(.~)` operator as follows:

```
ghci> set _1 "bye" pair
("bye",'!')
ghci> _1 .~ "bye" $ pair
("bye",'!')
ghci> pair & _1 .~ "bye"
("bye",'!')
```

Note the use of `($)` and its flipped variant `(&)` in the latter examples. We need them to construct a functional reference before applying it to the data.

To apply a function over a data component, we use `over` or the `%~` operator as follows:

```
ghci> over _1 length pair
(12,'!')
ghci> _1 %~ length $ pair
(12,'!')
ghci> pair & _1 %~ length
(12,'!')
```

In what follows, I'll use the `(&)` operator with data to the left because I find it clearer.

If our data is nested, we use regular function composition via the (.) operator as shown next:

```
ghci> view (_2._1) (False, pair)
"hello, world"
ghci> (False, pair) ^. _2 . _1
"hello, world"
```

Thanks to precedence, we don't need parentheses for functional references when we use the (^.) operator.

Let's now take a data structure with a list inside it as follows:

```
ghci> points = ("points", [(1, 1), (0, 1), (1, 0)]) :: (String, [(Int, Int)])
```

We can ask for a list of pairs, as shown next:

```
ghci> view _2 points
[(1,1),(0,1),(1,0)]
```

To look deeper, we can't use view. Instead, we have the toListOf function shown here:

```
ghci> toListOf (_2 . folded . _1) points
[1,0,1]
```

Here we take the first components of the pairs in the list. The folded functional reference means that we should go over the list components. Here we apply the _1 reference to them.

The corresponding operator is called (^..), as shown next:

```
ghci> points ^.. _2 . folded. _1
[1,0,1]
```

To get an element by its index, we can use ix as follows:

```
ghci> toListOf (_2 . ix 1) points
[(0,1)]
ghci> points ^.. _2 . ix 1
[(0,1)]
```

We can also set those first components to something different, say, the 'x' character, though folded is not enough in that case (it's not about changing values after all!). We need traverse for that, as follows:

```
ghci> set (_2 . traverse . _1) 'x' points
("points",[('x',1),('x',1),('x',0)])
ghci> points & _2 . traverse . _1 .~ 'x'
("points",[('x',1),('x',1),('x',0)])
```

Note that we've changed the type. This is also possible with lenses. Whenever we can set values, we can also apply a function to them as follows:

```
ghci> over (_2 . traverse . _1) (*100) points
("points",[(100,1),(0,1),(100,0)])
ghci> points & _2 . traverse . _1 %~ (*100)
("points",[(100,1),(0,1),(100,0)])
```

Let's work with data containing `Either a b` inside, as shown next:

```
ghci> info = ("info", Right 5) :: (String, Either String Int)
```

`Either a b` gives us an example of a `Prism`. We can look at the second pair component as usual:

```
ghci> view _2 info
Right 5
```

To look down further and get five occurrences of `view` is not enough. There can be no `Right` constructor at all. Prisms give us the `preview` function or the (^?) operator to try looking inside. It returns `Maybe a`. We can mention the form of data we are interested in with the `_Right` and `_Left` prisms as follows:

```
ghci> preview (_2 . _Right) info
Just 5
ghci> preview (_2 . _Left) info
Nothing
ghci> info ^? (_2 . _Right)
Just 5
```

Setting and applying a function can be done as usual:

```
ghci> info & _2 . _Right .~ (0 :: Int)
("info",Right 0)
ghci> info & _2 . _Right %~ (+1)
("info",Right 6)
```

All the optics can be applied to user-defined types. Suppose we have the following types:

```
data Point = Point {_x :: Double, _y :: Double}
  deriving Show

data Segment = Segment {_beg :: Point, _end :: Point}
  deriving Show
```

Note the _ prefixed names. We can define lenses for them using the `TemplateHaskell` GHC extension and the following splices:

```
makeLenses ''Point
makeLenses ''Segment
```

Remember, top-level Template Haskell declarations don't require $(...) syntax.

We can construct the following list of segments:

```
segs :: [Segment]
segs = [Segment (Point 0 0) (Point 100 0),
        Segment (Point 100 0) (Point 0 100),
        Segment (Point 0 100) (Point 0 0)]
```

Let's run some queries on it. For example, we can ask for starting points of all the segments as follows:

```
ghci> toListOf (folded . beg) segs
[Point {_x = 0.0, _y = 0.0},Point {_x = 100.0, _y = 0.0},Point {_x = 0.0,
➥ _y = 100.0}]
ghci> segs ^.. folded . beg
[Point {_x = 0.0, _y = 0.0},Point {_x = 100.0, _y = 0.0},Point {_x = 0.0,
➥ _y = 100.0}]
```

We can also set every y of every segment's end to 0, as shown next:

```
ghci> segs & traverse . end . y .~ 0
[Segment {_beg = Point {_x = 0.0, _y = 0.0}, _end = Point {_x = 100.0, _y =
➥ 0.0}},...]
ghci> set (traverse . end . y) 0 segs
[Segment {_beg = Point {_x = 0.0, _y = 0.0}, _end = Point {_x = 100.0, _y =
➥ 0.0}},...]
```

To move every segment's beginning on 100 along the x-axis, we could write the following:

```
ghci> over (traverse . beg . x) (+100) segs
[Segment {_beg = Point {_x = 100.0, _y = 0.0},...]
ghci> segs & traverse . beg . x %~ (+100)
[Segment {_beg = Point {_x = 100.0, _y = 0.0},...]
```

As a last example, let's write a function to move every point of every segment on the (d, d) vector. We could do that by composing with the over function as follows:

```
move :: Double -> [Segment] -> [Segment]
move d = over (traverse . beg . x) (+d)
       . over (traverse . beg . y) (+d)
       . over (traverse . end . x) (+d)
       . over (traverse . end . y) (+d)
```

Lenses are first-class values, so we can put them into a list. Let's use this idea to write another version of the move function, shown here:

```
move' :: Double -> [Segment] -> [Segment]
move' d = compose [ over (traverse . point . coord) (+d)    ← Composes a list of functions over [Segment]
                  | point <- [beg, end],                    ← For all segment points
                    coord <- [x, y]]
  where
    compose = appEndo . foldMap Endo    ← A Monoid instance for Endo does the job.
```

For all coordinates

The `foldMap` function has the following type:

```
foldMap :: (Foldable t, Monoid m) => (a -> m) -> t a -> m
```

The `Endo a` newtype is a wrapper over `a->a` functions (they are called *endomorphisms*—sorry about that). We refer to the wrapped function via the `appEndo` function. The `Monoid` instance for `Endo` is implemented to build a composition of two such functions. After folding the list of `[Endo [Segment]]`, we get the desired move as a function from `[Segment]` to `[Segment]`.

Let's relate the following bunch of functions and operators to our general framework:

- `_1` and `_2` are lenses for tuples.
- `view` and `(^.)` work with getters.
- `set`, `(.~)`, `over`, and `(%~)` work with setters.
- `folded` is a `Fold`.
- `toListOf` works with any `Fold`.
- `traverse` is a `Traversal`.
- `ix` implements indexing in a traversal.
- `_Left` and `_Right` are prisms for `Either a b`.
- `preview` and `(^?)` work with prisms.

These are the most-used ingredients of lenses. Many more types, functions, and operators are out there. I suggest looking at the big picture in the first page of the documentation to the `lens` package on Hackage: https://hackage.haskell.org/package/lens. Figure 14.8 is in fact an extremely simplified view of that picture. The big `lens` picture is a key to finding the right tool within the `lens` package, though it may be scary to look at it the first thousand times. Believe me, it makes sense eventually.

We are now ready to apply everything we've discussed so far in this chapter to organize our own data-processing pipeline.

14.3 Example: Processing COVID-19 data

This chapter was written when the COVID-19 virus was spreading over the world. We already have a lot of data about it. Let's extract some of the data and do basic computations over it. My goal is to present a sample data-processing pipeline, not to get some remarkable insights.

14.3.1 The task

Let's take publicly available data about COVID-19 from the Our World in Data website: https://ourworldindata.org/coronavirus-source-data. They distribute data in various formats. We'll go with CSV. The data for August 14, 2020, is available in the `hid-examples` package. To save space, I've added the gzipped CSV file.

EXAMPLE: PROCESSING COVID-19 DATA

◻   data/owid-covid-data.csv.gz

This CSV file contains a lot of data. There are 36 fields and 36,775 records in total. Every record corresponds to one day's worth of information for a particular country. There are also additional records with accumulated data. As is always the case with real-world data, it is not perfect. Many fields are missing, and a lot of information is repeated in many lines.

Our task is to go over this file and extract the following information about every country:

- ISO code, name, continent, current total cases, and deaths
- Some general stats about the country (population, density of population)
- Per-day information about new cases and deaths

This information corresponds to the following CSV file fields:

```
iso_code,continent,location,date,total_cases,new_cases,total_deaths,new_deaths,
⇒ <14 FIELDS SKIPPED>,population,population_density,<OTHER FIELDS>
```

Then we are going to accumulate the population and cases and deaths for the continents and the world in general.

To process the file, we have to create a pipeline with the following stages:

1   Read the file.
2   Unzip it.
3   Split to lines.
4   Group the lines referring to one country.
5   Parse country data into a data structure.
6   Compute information about the continents and the world in general.
7   Print data about every country.
8   Print stats about the continents and the world.

Figure 14.9 presents the overall pipeline.

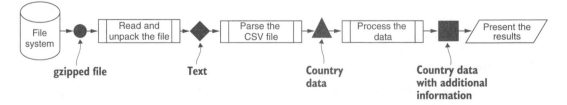

Figure 14.9   Pipeline structure for the COVID-19 data-processing application

The following is an output from the last stage we'd like to get (data for August 14, 2020):

```
Continent/population/cases/deaths
Africa/1339423921/1085589/24680
Asia/4607388081/5399479/115546
Europe/746573436/3087691/207384
North America/591242473/6239663/240036
Oceania/40958320/24606/394
South America/430461090/5052258/171093

World population/cases/deaths:
7756047321/20889286/759133
```

We'll apply a `streaming` ecosystem for reading, unzipping, and parsing the given file. We'll also use `attoparsec` to parse data about the countries. Once we have country data, we'll use a `lens` to do the computations.

Why couldn't we simply use `cassava` to deal with a `Vector` of records from CSV right away? Well, this would be impractical for three reasons. First, we are not interested in all the data; we need only a small part of it. There is no need to keep everything in memory after we've read a file. Second, for almost any field, we have missing data in some of the records. With `cassava`, we'd have to use `Maybe` a for every field. With manual parsing, we can silently skip lines if they miss that small portion of data we really need. Third, we'd have to deal with repeated data anyway, so why not ignore them while parsing?

Let's get to the code.

EXAMPLE: PROCESSING COVID-19 DATA

☐   ch14/covid/

⚡   *covid*

We have the following three modules in this project:

- `CovidData` describes our data structures and provides functions for them; it uses the `lens` package to access data.
- `CovidCSVParser` provides all the parser combinators and parsers to parse the data we are interested in and to skip everything else.
- `Main` defines and runs a data-processing pipeline.

We'll talk about everything we do during the various stages to process data first and then organize those stages into a pipeline.

14.3.2 *Processing data*

In this section, we'll describe the data, parse it from byte strings, and compute statistics. Note that the data-streaming approach allows independent development of particular stages. We'll decide what to do on every stage and then start thinking about combining them together.

DATA STRUCTURE

We want to avoid repetitiveness in our data, so we'll use hierarchical data structure.

EXAMPLE: PROCESSING COVID-19 DATA

    ch14/covid/CovidData.hs

The data about one country is described with the `CountryData` data type as follows:

```
data CountryData = CountryData {
    _iso_code :: ByteString,
    _continent :: Text,
    _name :: Text,
    _current_total_cases :: Int,
    _current_total_deaths :: Int,
    _days :: [(Day, DayInfo)],
    _stat :: CountryStat
  }
```

Only the first three fields are directly available in the data file. We have to provide the others by either computations or grouping.

The `DayInfo` contains information about daily cases and deaths, as shown next:

```
data DayInfo = DayInfo {
    _cases :: DayCases,
    _deaths :: DayDeaths
  }

data DayCases = DayCases {
    _total_cases :: Int,
    _new_cases :: Int
  }

data DayDeaths = DayDeaths {
    _total_deaths :: Int,
    _new_deaths :: Int
  }
```

Finally, we have the following general statistics about countries:

```
data CountryStat = CountryStat {
    _population :: Int,
    _population_density :: Maybe Double
  }
```

To use this hierarchical data structure with the `lens` package, we make lenses as follows:

```
makeLenses ''CountryData
makeLenses ''DayInfo
makeLenses ''DayCases
makeLenses ''DayDeaths
makeLenses ''CountryStat
```

With lenses, we have easy access to any level of this hierarchy. We'll look at examples shortly.

PARSING DATA

The CSV file we have contains a lot of repetitive and unnecessary data. We'd like to avoid parsing it, so our plan of parsing follows:

1   Parse the original file to a sequence of pairs with a country code and the rest of a line.
2   Group lines referring to one country together.
3   Parse the first line of a group.
4   Parse every other line by taking the interesting parts and skipping everything else.

Figure 14.10 presents these steps over the given CSV file.

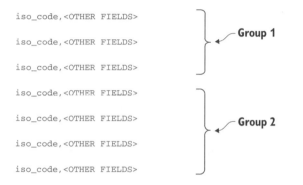

Figure 14.10   Parsing the CSV file with COVID-19 data

Here we discuss implementing steps 1, 3, and 4 with `attoparsec`, leaving step 2 for streaming.

EXAMPLE: PROCESSING COVID-19 DATA

🗋   ch14/covid/CovidCSVParser.hs

The `attoparsec` package allows parsing `ByteString` data. Because we are interested in parsing a text file, we import the corresponding module:

```
import Data.Attoparsec.ByteString.Char8 as A
```

At step 1, we are parsing the given `ByteString` into a sequence of values of the following type:

```
data CountryCodeWithRest = CountryCodeWithRest {
    code :: ByteString
  , rest :: ByteString
  }
```

We have to know where our lines end, as shown next:

```
notEOL :: Char -> Bool
notEOL c = c /= '\n' && c /= '\r'
```

This is the parser combinator for country codes. We take three characters and then expect a field separator as follows:

```
countryCode :: Parser ByteString
countryCode = A.take 3 <* char ','
```

Thanks to the `(<*)` operator, the result of `char ','` will be ignored. To parse the whole line, we parse country codes and the rest of the line as follows:

```
countryCodeWithRest :: Parser CountryCodeWithRest
countryCodeWithRest =
  CountryCodeWithRest <$> countryCode
                      <*> A.takeWhile notEOL
                      <* endOfLine
```

Some of the lines don't refer to a particular country. Let's skip them completely, as shown here:

```
skipLine :: Parser ()
skipLine = skipWhile notEOL <* endOfLine
```

Now we should combine the two earlier parsers and provide a result for every line. We can use `Maybe` for that as follows:

```
countryCodeWithRestOrSkip :: Parser (Maybe CountryCodeWithRest)
countryCodeWithRestOrSkip =
  Just <$> countryCodeWithRest <|> const Nothing <$> skipLine
```

The `Alternative` instance for `Parser a` prefers the first successful parser. Note that in this case, the second one can't fail, so we are guaranteed to get `Nothing` if the line doesn't have a country code.

We are done with step 1. Now let's parse the rest of the line. Our basic field parser combinators are as follows:

```
field :: Parser ByteString
field = takeTill (\c -> c == ',') <* char ','

textField :: Parser Text
textField = decodeUtf8 <$> field

skipField :: Parser ()
skipField = skipWhile (\c -> c /= ',') <* char ','

intField :: Parser Int
intField = (decimal <|> pure 0) <* skipField
```

We use various `attoparsec` combinators to get the parts we want. The `decodeUtf8` function comes from the `Data.Text.Encoding` module. Note the overly permissive `intField` parser: it allows us to parse values like `"1000.0"` or `""` as `Int` values. If we can parse a decimal number, we skip the rest of the field.

Now we are ready to parse a line with full information (the country code field was parsed earlier) as follows:

```
fullCountryData :: ByteString -> Parser CountryData
fullCountryData code =
  CountryData <$> pure code
              <*> textField -- continent
              <*> textField -- name
              <*> pure 0 -- current total cases
              <*> pure 0 -- current total deaths
              <*> dayInfo
              <* count 14 skipField
              <*> statInfo
```

The `count` combinator repeats its argument the given number of times, so we skip 14 fields we are not interested in. This code is extremely fragile. Let's hope the data format will never change! Alternatively, we could rely on column names in the first line of the CSV file, but that would bring a lot of complications to this simple example.

To parse information about the particular day, we use the following straightforward parser combinator:

```
dayInfo :: Parser [(Day, DayInfo)]
dayInfo = (\a b -> [(a,b)]) <$> dayParser <*> dayInfoParser
  where
    dayParser =
      fromGregorian <$> decimal <* char '-'
                    <*> decimal <* char '-'
                    <*> decimal <* char ','

    dayInfoParser = DayInfo <$> dayCasesParser <*> dayDeathsParser
    dayCasesParser = DayCases <$> intField <*> intField
    dayDeathsParser = DayDeaths <$> intField <*> intField
```

We also need to parse stats as follows:

```
statInfo :: Parser CountryStat
statInfo = CountryStat <$> intField -- population
                       <*> (option Nothing $ Just <$> double)    ⟵ Density
```

Here I use the `option` combinator that can give us `Nothing` if the parser for population density fails.

If we are interested in per-day information only (that's the case for all country lines after the first one), then we skip the continent and country name, as shown next:

```
dayInfoOnly :: Parser [(Day, DayInfo)]
dayInfoOnly = count 2 skipField *> dayInfo
```

We are done with parser combinators. Let's now define a couple of parsers for the first line in a country group and for the rest of the lines as follows:

```
parseFullCountryData :: CountryCodeWithRest -> Maybe CountryData
parseFullCountryData CountryCodeWithRest {..} =
  either (const Nothing) Just $ parseOnly (fullCountryData code) rest

parseDayInfo :: CountryCodeWithRest -> [(Day, DayInfo)]
parseDayInfo CountryCodeWithRest {..} =
  fromRight [] $ parseOnly dayInfoOnly rest
```

We'll call these functions from the pipeline stages.

ACCESSING COUNTRY DATA WITH LENSES

Let's get back to our data structures. We have a couple of problems. First, we need to populate country data created from the first line in a country group with a list of per-day information. Second, we have empty current total fields for cases and deaths. They should be computed from the list of per-day information.

EXAMPLE: PROCESSING COVID-19 DATA

⬚   ch14/covid/CovidData.hs

We solve both problems in the following function:

```
withDaysAndTotals :: CountryData -> [(Day, DayInfo)] -> CountryData
withDaysAndTotals countryData ds =
    withDays & current_total_deaths .~ ctDeaths
             & current_total_cases .~ ctCases
  where
    withDays = countryData & days %~ (++ ds)
    ctDeaths = maxOfDays (deaths . total_deaths) withDays
    ctCases = maxOfDays (cases . total_cases) withDays

    maxOfDays what = maximum1Of (days . folded . _2 . what)
```

The only new thing here is the maximum1Of function. It comes from Fold and can work with almost any sort of optics. We use it here to extract maximum values of the total_deaths and total_cases fields deeply nested in our data structure.

We can use lenses in any situations when we need access to data. For example, we can define the following TextShow instance with them:

```
instance TextShow CountryData where
  showb cd = fromText (cd ^. name)
             <> " "
             <> showb (cd ^. stat . population)
             <> " "
             <> showb (cd ^. current_total_cases)
             <> " "
             <> showb (cd ^. current_total_deaths)
```

This instance provides output like the following:

```
United States 331002647 5248242 167110
```

ACCUMULATING STATS

To accumulate statistics, we can use the following data type:

```
data AccumulatedStat = AccumulatedStat {
    _acc_population :: Int,
    _acc_total_cases :: Int,
    _acc_total_deaths :: Int
  }

makeLenses ''AccumulatedStat
```

Note that we don't have to use the lenses we have. It's perfectly okay to use pattern matching, as in the following TextShow instance:

```
instance TextShow AccumulatedStat where
  showb (AccumulatedStat pop tc td) =
    showb pop <> "/" <> showb tc <> "/" <> showb td
```

The accumulation itself can be implemented via Semigroup/Monoid machinery shown next:

```
instance Semigroup AccumulatedStat where
  (AccumulatedStat a b c) <> (AccumulatedStat a' b' c') =
      AccumulatedStat (a+a') (b+b') (c+c')

instance Monoid AccumulatedStat where
  mempty = AccumulatedStat 0 0 0
```

At some point, we'll need to go from country data to AccumulatedStat as follows:

```
fromCountryData :: CountryData -> AccumulatedStat
fromCountryData cd =
  AccumulatedStat (cd ^. stat . population)
                  (cd ^. current_total_cases)
                  (cd ^. current_total_deaths)
```

Lenses work well here. In some cases, ordinary functions are much better than lenses. Consider the problem: we'd like to compute stats per continent and want to use `Map Text AccumulatedStat` for that. As we go over the countries while streaming data, we consider them as parts of the corresponding continent and include them in the stats as follows:

```
import Data.Map (Map)
import qualified Data.Map as M

...

considerCountry :: Map Text AccumulatedStat
                   -> CountryData
                   -> Map Text AccumulatedStat
considerCountry stats cd =
     M.insertWith (<>) (cd ^. continent) (fromCountryData cd) stats
```

The `insertWith` function is able to insert new data or combine it with something already present in the `Map`. This function takes a function to combine new and old data, a key, data itself, and a `Map`.

We can express the same operation with lenses, but the result, shown next, is a little bit further from being readable unless you are a lenses guru:

```
considerCountry stats cd =
   stats &
      let new = fromCountryData cd
      in at (cd ^. continent) %~ Just . maybe new (<> new)
```

The stats we've accumulated should be presented to the user as follows:

```
instance TextShow (Map Text AccumulatedStat) where
  showb stats = M.foldlWithKey' withEntry "" stats
    where
      withEntry b nm st = b <> fromText nm <> "/" <> showb st <> "\n"
```

We also need to compute world data, as shown here:

```
worldStats :: Map Text AccumulatedStat -> AccumulatedStat
worldStats = M.foldl' (<>) mempty
```

All this information will be printed at the end of our pipeline.

14.3.3 Organizing the pipeline

We've reached the final point of this project. We are ready to organize the data-processing pipeline.

EXAMPLE: PROCESSING COVID-19 DATA

    📄 ch14/covid/Main.hs

Let's start with the modules we need. We've got quite a lot of them, as follows:

```
import Streaming
import Streaming.Zip (gunzip)
import qualified Streaming.Prelude as S
import Control.Monad.Trans.Resource
import qualified Streaming.ByteString.Char8 as C
import qualified Data.Attoparsec.ByteString.Streaming as ABS
import Data.Text (Text)
import qualified Data.Text.IO as T
import TextShow
import Data.Map (Map)
import qualified Data.Map as M
import Data.Function (on, (&))

import CovidData
import CovidCSVParser
```

The pipeline itself should be pretty clear by now, as shown next:

```
main :: IO ()
main = do
  r <- runResourceT $
        C.readFile "data/owid-covid-data.csv.gz"
      & gunzip
      & ABS.parsed countryCodeWithRestOrSkip
      & void
      & S.catMaybes
      & S.groupBy ((==) `on` code)
      & mapsM tryMkCountryData
      & S.catMaybes
      & S.store (S.fold considerCountry M.empty id)
      & printCountryData
  printStats $ S.fst' r
```

We read, unzip, parse, group on country lines, turn them into `CountryData`, compute stats, print country data, and print stats. We are using `catMaybes` a couple of times to get rid of any cases of `Nothing` that may appear in a stream during the preceding stages. We know that thanks to the `streaming` library, we should have no problems with memory usage and performance. The library will make sure that we have a big loop over the file content.

    To conclude this project, let's work out a couple of details. First, we should discuss building `CountryData`. Second, we should talk about printing.

The `tryMkCountryData` function is responsible for building `CountryData` from a substream of byte strings, grouped by the country code. We use it as follows with `mapsM`, hence its type:

```
tryMkCountryData :: Monad m =>
    Stream (Of CountryCodeWithRest) m r ->
    m (Of (Maybe CountryData) r)
```

The whole substream should be turned into a `Maybe CountryData` as shown next:

Augments data from the first line with days and totals

Inspects the first line in the substream

```
tryMkCountryData str =
    S.next str >>= either noCountryData withCountryData
  where
    withCountryData (line1, otherLines) =
      case parseFullCountryData line1 of
        Nothing -> S.effects otherLines >>= noCountryData
        Just cd -> first (Just . withDaysAndTotals cd)
                    <$> (S.mconcat $ S.map parseDayInfo otherLines)

noCountryData = pure . (Nothing :>)
```

The first line can't be parsed; skips other lines.

Extracts per-day information from the rest of the lines

Sends Nothing to the parent stream

Note the next function type shown here:

```
S.next
  :: Monad m =>
     Stream (Of a) m r -> m (Either r (a, Stream (Of a) m r))
```

We can get either a streaming result if the given stream is over (in `Left`) or the next element with the rest of the stream (in `Right`). We consume the result of `S.next` with the `either` function by providing functions responsible for either case.

The `noCountryData` function is not only responsible for sending `Nothing` to an original stream. It's also able to keep the streaming result if there was one. Its type follows:

```
noCountryData :: Monad m => r -> m (Of (Maybe a) r)
```

In its implementation, we use the `pure` function to get through `m` and the `:>` operator to construct the proper `Of` functor value with the given streaming result.

As for printing results, we print country data along the pipeline as we get to it as follows:

```
printCountryData :: (MonadIO m, TextShow a) => Stream (Of a) m r -> m r
printCountryData str = do
  liftIO $ T.putStrLn "Country population cases deaths"
  S.mapM_ (liftIO . printT) str
```

> **Partial type signatures**
>
> The easiest way to get the type of the inner function is to give it a *partial* type signature as follows:
>
> ```
> where
>     noCountryData :: _
>     noCountryData = pure . (Nothing :>)
> ```
>
> The compiler immediately reports the inferred type. This can be helpful to understand what is going wrong with the code.

To print the statistics we've accumulated, we just use the `TextShow` instances defined earlier, as shown next:

```
printStats :: Map Text AccumulatedStat -> IO ()
printStats stats = do
  T.putStrLn "\nContinent/population/cases/deaths"
  printT stats
  T.putStrLn $ "World population/cases/deaths: "
  printT $ worldStats stats
```

And we are done with the streaming.

Summary

- Streaming is a default approach when we need to process a lot of data.
- Several important families of streaming libraries exist, including `conduit`, `pipes`, and `streaming`.
- Streaming allows us to organize data-processing pipelines.
- We often need parsing as one of the stages. In Haskell, we do that with a parser combinator library.
- Complex, deeply nested data structures often arise at latter stages of pipelines; we use optics such as the `lens` package to deal with them.

15
Working with
relational databases

This chapter covers

- Relating Haskell data to database data
- Writing and executing SQL queries
- Structuring programs that need access to databases

Accessing a database is an important part of any backend program. In this chapter, we'll look at several approaches to access relational databases in Haskell. As usual, we'll focus on Haskell features that make programming with databases safe. This includes type checking for values we send or receive from a database. Although NoSQL databases are also popular within the Haskell community, I've decided not to mention them in this book. The main reason behind this decision is that the corresponding libraries suggest a rather straightforward approach to communicate with databases and don't rely on any of the sophisticated Haskell features.

Just as in other programming languages, Haskell database interfaces are extremely diverse. With some of them, we merely construct queries and run them against a database. With more sophisticated interfaces, we can avoid writing queries and do regular programming instead.

Although many database access packages are able to work with different databases, in this chapter, we'll use one particular database, namely PostgreSQL, which is widely used with Haskell software in industry.

The following is a list of questions we have to answer when we want to access any database with any package:

- How does data in a database relate to Haskell data types?
- How do we construct a query to a database?
- How do we run the query we've constructed and access the results?

Different packages give different answers. It's useful to do the same thing with several of them to see the spectrum of possibilities. In this chapter, we'll discuss the following packages:

- HDBC, a rather old package that can be used with many databases
- postgresql-simple, a midlevel package that provides many convenient wrappers for low-level functionality
- hasql, another midlevel package that features very good performance
- opaleye, a package that provides a sophisticated high-level interface to databases, exploiting many type system features

For every package, we'll write a program with the same functionality, which I describe shortly.

15.1 Setting up an example

In this chapter, we'll implement an application that works with a film database. We'll look at its content and manipulate it. I assume that the reader has some knowledge of SQL and some experience using databases. To run the examples, we need a working PostgreSQL database instance. The PostgreSQL website provides all the necessary instructions at https://www.postgresql.org/download/.

> **IMPORTANT** Examples that depend on PostgreSQL aren't built by default. To enable building them, once you have PostgreSQL installed, uncomment the flags: with-pg line in the cabal.project.local file in the root folder of the hid-examples project. Should you use stack to build this project, the corresponding flag can be set in stack.yaml.

15.1.1 Sample database

We'll use an abridged version of the Sakila sample database (https://dev.mysql.com/doc/sakila/en/), which is often used to illustrate database features. This database contains data about content and processes of a DVD-rental store's network. I've borrowed three tables about films and their categories from this sample database. Figure 15.1 presents the tables we are going to use.

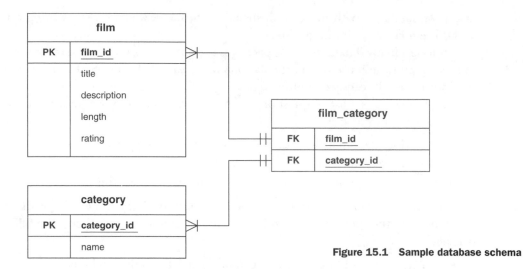

Figure 15.1   Sample database schema

EXAMPLE: FILMS SAMPLE DATABASE

📄   data/films/

The database schema is described by SQL CREATE commands in the films-schema.sql file. We have the following three tables:

- category contains the names of film categories with their corresponding numeric identifiers.
- film contains information about films, such as their titles, descriptions, lengths, and ratings.
- film_category defines a many-to-many relationship between films and categories, so that we can assign several categories to a film and any category to several films.

To make things more interesting on the Haskell side, we use nonstandard SQL types. For example, to represent the rating, we use the following ENUM:

```
CREATE TYPE mpaa_rating AS ENUM (
    'G',
    'PG',
    'PG-13',
    'R',
    'NC-17'
);
```

We also combine nullable and non-nullable fields. For example, in the film table, we have the following two nullable fields:

```
CREATE TABLE film (
    film_id integer DEFAULT nextval('film_film_id_seq'::regclass) NOT NULL,
    title text NOT NULL,
```

```
        description text,
        length smallint NOT NULL,
        rating mpaa_rating
);
```

Two other tables are simpler, as shown next:

```
CREATE TABLE category (
        category_id integer DEFAULT nextval('category_category_id_seq'::regclass)
            NOT NULL,
        name text UNIQUE NOT NULL
);
CREATE TABLE film_category (
        film_id integer NOT NULL,
        category_id integer NOT NULL
);
```

We have a lot of sample data, including 16 various categories and 1,000 fictional films. To recreate the sample database on a reader's machine, we can issue the following commands:

```
$ psql -c 'create database sakila_films'
$ psql -d sakila_films -a -f data/films/films-schema.sql
$ psql -d sakila_films -a -f data/films/films-insert.sql
```

The `psql` utility usually comes with the PostgreSQL database server distribution. Depending on the actual installation, it may be required to provide the username and the password via the -U and W options. If we connect to a server, then we should also provide the hostname and the port number via the -h and -p options.

15.1.2 Sample queries

Many things can be queried, even in such a small database. For example, we can ask for the films in it, as shown here:

```
$ psql -d sakila_films
sakila_films=# SELECT film_id, title, length, rating FROM film;
 film_id |             title             | length | rating
---------+-------------------------------+--------+--------
       1 | ACADEMY DINOSAUR              |     86 | PG
       2 | ACE GOLDFINGER                |     48 | G
      19 | AMADEUS HOLY                  |    113 | PG
      20 | AMELIE HELLFIGHTERS           |     79 | R
 ...
```

To count the total number of films in the database, we can issue the following query:

```
sakila_films=# SELECT count(*) FROM film;
 count
-------
  1000
(1 row)
```

We'll also be interested in films that satisfied some constraints, for example, those longer than the given number, as shown next:

```
sakila_films=# SELECT film_id, title, length, rating FROM film
sakila_films-# WHERE length >= 185;
 film_id |        title       | length | rating
---------+--------------------+--------+--------
     141 | CHICAGO NORTH      |    185 | PG-13
     182 | CONTROL ANTHEM     |    185 | G
     212 | DARN FORRESTER     |    185 | G
...
```

To look at the particular film categories, we should join several tables as follows:

```
sakila_films=# SELECT category.name FROM film
sakila_films-# JOIN film_category USING (film_id)
sakila_films-# JOIN category USING (category_id)
sakila_films-# WHERE title = 'MODERN DORADO';
    name
-------------
 Documentary
(1 row)
```

Besides SELECT queries, we also need to manipulate the data. For example, let's update a film's rating as follows:

```
sakila_films=# UPDATE film SET rating = 'G' WHERE title = 'MODERN DORADO';
UPDATE 1
```

To add a new category, we use the INSERT query, as shown next:

```
sakila_films=# INSERT INTO category (name) VALUES ('Art');
INSERT 0 1
```

In many cases, we also need to get the corresponding category_id that was generated while inserting the new record as follows:

```
sakila_films=# SELECT lastval();
 lastval
---------
      17
(1 row)
```

Alternatively, we could issue the next INSERT/RETURNING query:

```
sakila_films=# INSERT INTO category (name) VALUES ('Anime')
sakila_films-# RETURNING category_id;
 category_id
-------------
          18
(1 row)
```

The RETURNING part is specific to PostgreSQL and may not be available when using database-agnostic packages.

Finally, we'll need to unassign a film category, as shown here:

```
sakila_films=# DELETE FROM film_category
sakila_films-# USING film, category
sakila_films-# WHERE category.name = 'Documentary'
sakila_films-# AND film.title = 'MODERN DORADO'
sakila_films-# AND film_category.film_id=film.film_id
sakila_films-# AND film_category.category_id=category.category_id;
DELETE 1
```

To restore the database after experiments with it, we can run the recreate.sh script provided in data/films/.

In what follows, we'll see how to issue these and similar queries from a Haskell program using different database packages. But before we move to that, let's describe our data using Haskell data types. Their representation shouldn't depend on how we work with a database.

15.1.3 *Data representation in Haskell*

Although the data we have to describe in our Haskell program is derived from a database, we usually don't want to depend on database-specific ways to work with that data. Let's describe all the film information, disregarding a particular database access package first, and then see how to relate it to the actual database interface.

EXAMPLE: INFORMATION ABOUT FILMS IN HASKELL

🗋 ch15/FilmInfo/Data.hs

☞ Data can be represented, no matter the database package chosen.

Let's start with numeric identifiers. PostgreSQL uses 32-bit integers to represent them. This type corresponds to Int32 in Haskell. Instead of using Int32 right away, we could use the following newtype declaration:

```
newtype FilmId = FilmId Int32
```

In fact, we do it in two steps. First, we define a newtype without specifying an actual type as follows:

```
newtype FilmId' a = FilmId a
```

Then we fix it via a type synonym, as shown next:

```
type FilmId = FilmId' Int32
```

This will enable automatically generating more definitions that we'll need later. The category identifiers are represented in the same way, as shown here:

```
newtype CatId' a = CatId a
type CatId = CatId' Int32
```

We'll also need the following type for representing film lengths:

```
newtype FilmLength' a = FilmLength a
type FilmLength = FilmLength' Int32
```

> **ON USING NEWTYPES FOR DATABASE FIELDS** Note that I've decided to declare three newtypes for the same Int32 type. This allows us to control our types in Haskell and prevents many mistakes. In fact, I made one such mistake while writing examples for this chapter. I mixed up film ID and category ID, and GHC was silent about that because I used Int32 for both. With newtype definitions, this sort of error is ruled out.

To represent film ratings, we use the following Rating data type:

```
data Rating = G | PG | PG13 | R | NC17
  deriving Show
```

We'll need to convert between literals and ratings often, so let's implement auxiliary functions for that. To get a literal representation from a Rating value, we use the following function:

```
fromRating :: IsString p => Rating -> p
fromRating G = "G"
fromRating PG = "PG"
fromRating PG13 = "PG-13"
fromRating R = "R"
fromRating NC17 = "NC-17"
```

The reverse transformation requires Maybe because it is not guaranteed, as shown next:

```
toMaybeRating :: (Eq p, IsString p) => p -> Maybe Rating
toMaybeRating "G" = Just G
toMaybeRating "PG" = Just PG
toMaybeRating "PG-13" = Just PG13
toMaybeRating "R" = Just R
toMaybeRating "NC-17" = Just NC17
toMaybeRating _ = Nothing
```

Now we are ready to declare the FilmInfo data type. We use the same abstract data/type synonym technique for that as follows:

```
data FilmInfo' i t d l r = FilmInfo {
    filmId :: i
  , title :: t
```

```
    , description :: d
    , filmLength :: l
    , rating :: r
    }
type FilmInfo = FilmInfo' FilmId Text (Maybe Text) FilmLength (Maybe Rating)
```

Note that we use `Maybe` to represent nullable values (description and rating). This is the traditional technique used with all the database access packages.

Some of the data types have no direct relation to a database. For example, the following `FilmCategories` data type represents the full film information, including all the categories that are assigned to it:

```
data FilmCategories = FilmCategories FilmInfo [Text]
```

Apart from data declarations, the `FilmInfo.Data` module defines the `TextShow` instances and functions to print data in various formats.

We are now ready to connect to a real database and get data from it.

15.2 Haskell database connectivity

We start with the `HDBC` package, the oldest package to connect to databases in Haskell. It doesn't use sophisticated Haskell features. It is also database agnostic and can be used with many different databases via a general ODBC interface.

EXAMPLE: USING HDBC TO WORK WITH THE POSTGRESQL DATABASE INSTANCE

📄 ch15/hdbc.hs

⚡ *hdbc*

15.2.1 Connecting to a database

The `HDBC` package requires drivers to connect to specific databases. We can use the `HDBC-postgresql` package as a driver to a PostgreSQL database. This package provides the `Database.HDBC.PostgreSQL` module. We'll need only the one following function from it:

```
withPostgreSQL :: String -> (Connection -> IO a) -> IO a
```

This function takes a database connection string and a computation that runs over an established connection. We can use it as follows:

```
demo :: Connection -> IO ()
demo conn = do
  ...

main :: IO ()
main = withPostgreSQL connString (handleSqlError . demo)
 where
   connString = "host=localhost dbname=sakila_films"
```

The `handleSqlError` function from the `Database.HDBC` module wraps an `IO` computation, catches all the SQL-related errors, and reports them.

15.2.2 *Relating Haskell data types to database types*

Every database access package should provide a way to relate Haskell data to database data and back. This problem is handled in `HDBC` by the `Convertible` type class, the `SqlValue` type, and the following functions:

```
toSql :: Convertible a SqlValue => a -> SqlValue
fromSql :: Convertible SqlValue a => SqlValue -> a
```

The `SqlValue` is able to store numbers, texts, dates, and times in different forms. The `HDBC` package provides many instances of the `Convertible` type class for various Haskell types. When working with our own types, we can either use `toSql` and `fromSql` on internal data components whose types are known to `HDBC` or write our own instances. For example, we can write the following `Convertible` instances:

```
instance Convertible FilmId SqlValue where
  safeConvert (FilmId i) = safeConvert i

instance Convertible FilmLength SqlValue where
  safeConvert (FilmLength l) = safeConvert l

instance Convertible Rating SqlValue where
  safeConvert r = safeConvert (fromRating r :: Text)

instance Convertible CatId SqlValue where
  safeConvert (CatId i) = safeConvert i
```

As a result, we can use `toSql` on our own data types. It seems that using `fromSql` on an underlying representation is convenient enough and obviates the need for writing the corresponding instances. For example, let's convert a list of `SqlValues` to a value of the `FilmInfo` data type as follows:

```
fiFromList :: [SqlValue] -> FilmInfo
fiFromList [fid, ttl, desc, l, r] = FilmInfo {
    filmId = FilmId $ fromSql fid
  , title = fromSql ttl
  , description = fromSql desc
  , filmLength = FilmLength $ fromSql l
  , rating = (fromSql r :: Maybe Text) >>= toMaybeRating
  }
fiFromList _ = error "unexpected result (fiFromList)"
```

Note that we use the `Maybe Text` type to call `fromSql` on a description and a rating. This handles the problem of nullability of the corresponding fields for us.

Whenever we ask for data from a database, the HDBC package gives us a [[Sql-Value]] list. The outer list refers to a list of table rows. The inner list corresponds to a list of fields in a request. Let's write a couple of convenience functions to convert these results from a database. Sometimes we want to get one particular value, as shown next:

```
fetchSingle :: (Monad m, Convertible SqlValue a) =>
               String -> [[SqlValue]] -> m a
fetchSingle _ [[val]] = pure $ fromSql val
fetchSingle what _ = error $ "Unexpected result: " ++ what
```

fetchSingle uses its first argument for error reporting when we don't have a single result. We could expect either one or no results instead, as shown here:

```
fetchMaybe :: Monad m => ([SqlValue] -> a) -> [[SqlValue]] -> m (Maybe a)
fetchMaybe fromRow (row:_) = pure $ Just $ fromRow row
fetchMaybe  _ _ = pure Nothing
```

We'll use these functions, depending on what we expect from a request.

This approach doesn't attempt to check types at compile time. The only thing that is actually checked is whether the type has a Convertible instance. We can easily try to convert a film description to a film ID, and GHC wouldn't complain. Of course, there will be an exception at run time, but is that sufficient for us Haskellers nowadays? The other packages we discuss in this chapter are less permissive as we'll see shortly.

15.2.3 *Constructing and executing SELECT queries*

As the first example of a SELECT query, let's fetch all the films from the database as follows:

```
allFilms :: Connection -> IO [FilmInfo]
allFilms conn = map fiFromList <$> quickQuery conn select []
  where
    select = "SELECT film_id, title, description, length, rating FROM film"
```

We have a SQL query and the quickQuery function from the Database.HDBC module that does all the work. Its type is shown next:

```
quickQuery
  :: IConnection conn =>
     conn -> String -> [SqlValue] -> IO [[SqlValue]]
```

The quickQuery function takes a connection, a SQL query as a value of the String type, and a list of request parameters. There are no parameters in our query, so the list is empty. This function returns a list of rows with every row represented as a list of type SqlValue. Note that almost any change in the order of fields in the SELECT query would result in an exception due to conversions in fiFromList.

In the next example, we issue a SQL query about a number of films in our database:

```
totalFilmsNumber :: Connection -> IO Int64
totalFilmsNumber conn = do
  res <- quickQuery conn "SELECT count(*) FROM film" []
  fetchSingle "totalFilmsNumber" res
```

Just as before, we don't have any parameters.

The parameterized queries are used when we want to issue a SQL query that depends on some data external to the database itself. For example, we can ask for all the films that are longer than some given length as follows:

```
filmsLonger :: Connection -> FilmLength -> IO [FilmInfo]
filmsLonger conn len =
    map fiFromList <$> quickQuery conn select [toSql len]
  where
    select = "SELECT film_id, title, description, length, rating"
             <> " FROM film WHERE length >= ?"
```

The parameter is mentioned as `"?"` in the SQL query, and its actual value is provided when we run the query. Note that thanks to the `Convertible` instance defined earlier, we can use `toSql` on a value of the `FilmLength` type.

We can use parameters of any types. In the following function, we use the title of a film as a parameter to a SQL query:

```
findFilm :: Connection -> Text -> IO (Maybe FilmInfo)
findFilm conn filmTitle = do
    res <- quickQuery conn select [toSql filmTitle]
    fetchMaybe fiFromList res
  where
    select = "SELECT film_id, title, description, length, rating"
             <> " FROM film"
             <> " WHERE title=?"
```

Quite often, we have to issue several SQL queries to get the result we need. For example, the following function takes a list of film titles and gives us back a list of FilmCategories:

```
filmsCategories :: Connection -> [Text] -> IO [FilmCategories]
filmsCategories conn films = do
    stmt <- prepare conn selectCats          ◁──┐  Prepares the query
    catMaybes <$> mapM (runSingle stmt) films    │  for execution
  where
    selectCats = "SELECT category.name FROM film"
                 <> " JOIN film_category USING (film_id)"
                 <> " JOIN category USING (category_id)"
                 <> " WHERE title = ?"
    runSingle stmt filmTitle = do
      mfilm <- findFilm conn filmTitle
      case mfilm of
```

```
    Nothing -> pure Nothing
    Just film -> withCategories film stmt
withCategories film stmt = do
  _ <- execute stmt [toSql $ title film]
  cats <- fetchAllRows' stmt
  pure $ Just $ FilmCategories film $ map (fromSql . head) cats
```

|← **Executes the query
  with parameters**

In such situations we have to run the same query many times with different parameters. The HDBC package supports the prepare/execute approach. First, we prepare a statement. Second, we execute it against the particular parameter values.

> **NOTE** Depending on the database and the library, we could rewrite the film-Categories function using a single SQL query. In this book, we are concerned with Haskell programming, not writing SQL. That is why some of our examples may feature less-efficient SQL queries.

15.2.4 *Manipulating data in a database*

Besides selecting data, we also need to insert, update, or delete data. These queries don't return results from a database. Instead, they usually return the number of affected rows. For such queries we can use the run function as follows:

```
run :: IConnection conn => conn -> String -> [SqlValue] -> IO Integer
```

In the following function, we update the rating of a given film:

```
setRating :: Connection -> Rating -> Text -> IO Integer
setRating conn fRating filmTitle = do
  res <- run conn "UPDATE film SET rating = ? WHERE title = ?"
          [toSql fRating, toSql filmTitle]
  commit conn
  pure res
```

Note the commit IO action. The HDBC package runs every statement within a transaction. It doesn't guarantee the visibility of a database-changing query to other database users until we issue the COMMIT instruction. The actual behavior depends on the database, though.

When we insert data, for example, if we want to add a new category, we don't know the ID that it is going to get. One option is to run the specialized SELECT query right after the INSERT as follows:

```
newCategory :: Connection -> Text -> IO CatId
newCategory conn catName = fmap CatId $ do
  cnt <- run conn "INSERT INTO category (name) VALUES (?)" [toSql catName]
  if cnt /= 1
    then error "Inserting category failed"
    else quickQuery conn "SELECT lastval()" [] >>= fetchSingle "category_id"
```

Deleting can be also done with the run function. We can use the following function to unassign the given category from the given film:

```
unassignCategory :: Connection -> Text -> Text -> IO Integer
unassignCategory conn catName filmTitle =
    run conn delete [toSql catName, toSql filmTitle]
  where
    delete = "DELETE FROM film_category"
        <> " USING film, category"
        <> " WHERE category.name = ? AND film.title = ?"
        <> "       AND film_category.film_id=film.film_id"
        <> "       AND film_category.category_id=category.category_id"
```

Let me stress again: there is almost no safety checking on the list of parameters to the SQL query or the correctness of the query itself. All the checks are postponed until run time.

15.2.5 *Solving tasks by issuing many queries*

When working with databases, we almost always have the following choices:

- We can write one big SQL query that does everything.
- We can do the job by running several smaller queries independently.

Let's explore the second alternative. Suppose we want to assign an additional category to a film. This category can be already defined in the database, or it can be completely new. If it exists there, then it can be already assigned. The film must be present in the database; otherwise, we can't do anything.

Let's solve this task in several steps. We already have the newCategory function that inserts a category, but we don't check if the category exists. The following function tries to locate the category in the database:

```
catIdByName :: Connection -> Text -> IO (Maybe CatId)
catIdByName conn catName =
  quickQuery conn "SELECT category_id FROM category WHERE name = ?"
              [toSql catName]
  >>= fetchMaybe (CatId . fromSql . head)
```

We can now get a category ID or add a new one as follows:

```
findOrAddCategory :: Connection -> Text -> IO CatId
findOrAddCategory conn catName = do
  cats <- catIdByName conn catName
  case cats of
    Nothing -> newCategory conn catName
    Just cid -> pure cid
```

To assign a category to a film, we need the ID of the latter, as shown here:

```
filmIdByTitle :: Connection -> Text -> IO (Maybe FilmId)
filmIdByTitle conn filmTitle =
  quickQuery conn "SELECT film_id FROM film WHERE title=?" [toSql filmTitle]
  >>= fetchMaybe (FilmId . fromSql . head)
```

Once we have both IDs, we should check whether the category is already assigned as follows:

```
isAssigned :: Connection -> CatId -> FilmId -> IO Bool
isAssigned conn cid fid = do
  res <- quickQuery conn ("SELECT count(category_id) FROM film_category"
                      <> " WHERE category_id = ? AND film_id= ?")
                    [toSql cid, toSql fid]
  cnt <- fetchSingle "isAssigned" res
  pure $ cnt > (0 :: Int64)
```

We run the next check before assigning a category:

```
assignUnlessAssigned :: Connection -> CatId -> FilmId -> IO Integer
assignUnlessAssigned conn cid fid = do
  b <- isAssigned conn cid fid
  case b of
    True -> pure 0
    False -> run conn insert [toSql cid, toSql fid]
 where
   insert = "INSERT INTO film_category (category_id, film_id) VALUES (?, ?)"
```

Finally, we can combine the functions defined earlier to get the desired functionality, as shown next:

```
assignCategory :: Connection -> Text -> Text -> IO Integer
assignCategory conn catName filmTitle = do
  cid <- findOrAddCategory conn catName
  mFilmId <- filmIdByTitle conn filmTitle
  case mFilmId of
    Nothing -> pure 0
    Just fid -> assignUnlessAssigned conn cid fid
```

Note that we don't run any SQL queries in the latter function directly. We orchestrate them through the auxiliary functions.

Let me summarize the HDBC approach:

- The SqlValue type can hold any value received from a database.
- Conversions from and to SqlValue are implemented via the Convertible type class instances.
- We can write parameterized SQL queries and execute them against a database.
- The result from a database is given back to us as a list of rows or the number of rows affected, depending on the function we use.

The main drawback of HDBC is that we have almost no type checking over the values we send to the database or receive from it. We'll see how this approach evolved into much more sophisticated techniques implemented in other database access packages.

15.3   *The postgresql-simple library*

The second database access package we are going to discuss is the `postgresql-simple` package. It's definitely a step forward in terms of type safety.

EXAMPLE: USING THE POSTGRESQL-SIMPLE PACKAGE

◻   ch15/pg-simple.hs

◻   ch15/FilmInfo/

⚡   *pg-simple*

15.3.1   *Connecting to a database*

We have the `connectPostgreSQL` function to connect to a database and the `close` function to close the connection. The `main` function can be implemented as follows:

```
main :: IO ()
main = do
  conn <- connectPostgreSQL connString
  demo conn
  close conn
 where
   connString = "host=localhost dbname=sakila_films"
```

In fact, working with a connection in this way is captured precisely by the `bracket` function from the `Control.Exception` module. This function guarantees that the connection will be closed, even if we have an exception. We could rewrite the `main` function using this approach as follows:

```
main :: IO ()
main = bracket (connectPostgreSQL connString) close demo
 where
   connString = "host=localhost dbname=sakila_films"
```

Let's discuss some more interesting features of this package.

15.3.2   *Relating Haskell data types to database types*

The `postgresql-simple` package delegates relations between Haskell and database types to the `FromField` and `ToField` type classes. The idea is to describe these relations first and then work as if all the query-running functions can consume and produce values of our own types.

The most interesting case is the `Rating` data type. The following is the implementation of the `FromField` type class for it:

```
module FilmInfo.FromField where

import Database.PostgreSQL.Simple.FromField
import qualified Data.ByteString.Char8 as B
```

```
import FilmInfo.Data

instance FromField Rating where
  fromField f Nothing = returnError UnexpectedNull f ""
  fromField f (Just bs) =
    case toMaybeRating bs of
      Nothing -> returnError ConversionFailed f (B.unpack bs)
      Just r -> pure r
```

The types that we use in the previous code follow:

```
fromField :: FromField a => FieldParser a
type FieldParser a = Field -> Maybe ByteString -> Conversion a
```

`Conversion a` is an `IO` action resulting in an `a` or reporting an error.

Once we have such an instance, we can get `Rating` values from a database without explicit conversions. Instances for every other type can be derived as follows:

```
deriving instance Generic FilmId
deriving newtype instance FromField FilmId
deriving newtype instance ToField FilmId

deriving instance Generic FilmLength
deriving newtype instance FromField FilmLength

deriving instance Generic CatId
deriving newtype instance FromField CatId
deriving newtype instance ToField CatId

deriving instance Generic FilmInfo
deriving instance FromRow FilmInfo
```

We need `ToField` instances if we plan to write values to a database, either as fields or as parameters. The `FromRow` type class is responsible for interpreting the whole table row as a value of a single type. We also have the `ToRow` type class that is responsible for writing to a database.

These instances make executing queries easier because we don't need to write explicit conversion operations.

15.3.3 *Executing queries*

We have the following functions to execute queries:

```
query  :: (ToRow q, FromRow r) => Connection -> Query -> q -> IO [r]
query_ :: FromRow r => Connection -> Query -> IO [r]
execute :: ToRow q => Connection -> Query -> q -> IO Int64
```

The first two functions are mainly for SELECT queries. The last one is for returning a number of affected rows. The q parameter is for parameters, if we need them. The only constraint for q is `ToRow` q. In most cases, we use tuples. If we need only one parameter, the library gives us the `Only` wrapper and the `fromOnly` function. The `Only` wrapper is also useful for getting a single field in a row.

Let's look at several examples. We can select all films as follows:

```
allFilms :: Connection -> IO [FilmInfo]
allFilms conn = query_ conn select
  where
    select = "SELECT film_id, title, description, length, rating FROM film"
```

Thanks to `FromRow` instances, we have no explicit conversion at all.

Getting a single result is also trivial, as shown next:

```
totalFilmsNumber :: Connection -> IO Int64
totalFilmsNumber conn = do
  [Only cnt] <- query_ conn "SELECT count(*) FROM film"
  pure cnt
```

We use `query` and `Only` to specify a single parameter to a query as follows:

```
filmsLonger :: Connection -> FilmLength -> IO [FilmInfo]
filmsLonger conn (FilmLength len) = query conn select (Only len)
  where
    select = "SELECT film_id, title, description, length, rating"
             <> " FROM film"
             <> " WHERE length >= ?"
```

Sometimes, we expect `Maybe` as a result with one parameter and a single field in the result, as shown next:

```
catIdByName :: Connection -> Text -> IO (Maybe CatId)
catIdByName conn catName =
    listToMaybe . map fromOnly <$> query conn select (Only catName)
  where
    select = "SELECT category_id FROM category WHERE name=?"
```

It's crucial to understand the types in the `catIdByName` function. Let's write out the specific types in play there as follows:

```
fromOnly :: Only CatId -> CatId
map fromOnly :: [Only CatId] -> [CatId]
listToMaybe :: [CatId] -> Maybe CatId
listToMaybe . map fromOnly :: [Only CatId] -> Maybe CatId
query :: Connection -> Query -> Only Text -> IO [Only CatId]
listToMaybe . map fromOnly <$>
    query conn select (Only catName) :: IO (Maybe CatId)
```

GHC then finds the right instances of `FromRow` and `FromField`—we are on the safe side.

When inserting values into a database, we exploit the corresponding `ToField` instances and the `ToRow` instances for tuples as follows:

```
assignUnlessAssigned :: Connection -> CatId -> FilmId -> IO Int64
assignUnlessAssigned conn cid fid = do
    b <- isAssigned conn cid fid
    case b of
      True -> pure 0
      False -> execute conn insert (cid, fid)
  where
    insert = "INSERT INTO film_category (category_id, film_id) VALUES (?, ?)"
```

We didn't provide the `ToField` instance for `Rating`, but we can use it as a query parameter anyway, as shown here:

```
setRating :: Connection -> Rating -> Text -> IO Int64
setRating conn fRating filmTitle =
  execute conn "UPDATE film SET rating = ? WHERE title = ?"
          (fromRating fRating :: Text, filmTitle)
```

All the other functions are implemented similarly.

The `postgresql-simple` package provides a simple interface for constructing and executing queries. It also features a nice way to relate Haskell and database values through the `ToField` and `FromField` type classes. The level of type safety is a bit higher than with `HDBC`, though it is still not perfect. This package is usually considered a midlevel interface. It uses the low-level `postgresql-libpq` package underneath.

15.4 *The hasql ecosystem*

Let's get to the third database access package, `hasql`. In fact, it is the root of the whole ecosystem, which includes about a dozen packages responsible for various features. In this section, I talk about `hasql` and `hasql-th`. We use the latter for constructing type-safe SQL statements and the former for everything else.

> **EXAMPLE: USING THE HASQL ECOSYSTEM**
>
> ☐   ch15/hasql/
>
> ☐   ch15/FilmInfo/Data.hs
>
> ⚡ *hasql*

15.4.1 *Structuring programs with hasql*

Figure 15.2 describes the structure of any program that uses the `hasql` ecosystem to access databases.

We start working with data, either query parameters or query results. The relationship between data in Haskell and data in a database is described by encoders (for parameters) and decoders (for results). Both encoding and decoding are usually done in applicative style. Once data relations are ready, we construct the SQL statements that we need in a program. We execute SQL statements in sessions. A session abstracts a single domain-specific problem and may involve executing as many SQL

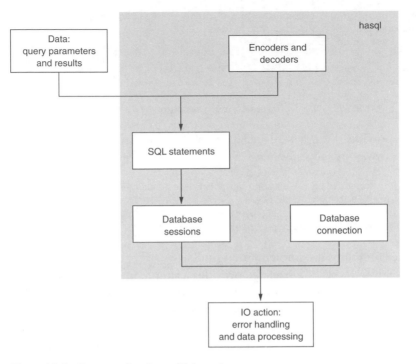

Figure 15.2   Program structure with `hasql`

statements as we need. From a technical point of view, any session is the `ReaderT Con-nection` transformer over the `IO` monad, so we have a connection inside every session. Once we've described every session, we establish a database connection and run our sessions in `IO` actions. At this last stage, we may encounter run-time database communication errors or receive the desired data.

Consequently, we have the following modules in our `hasql` model application:

- `FilmInfo.Data`
- `Statements`
- `Sessions`
- `DBActions`
- `Main`

Let's explore them in order, starting with `Statements`.

15.4.2 *Constructing type-safe SQL statements*

Every statement in `hasql` is a value of the two-parametric `Statement params results` type, where `params` and `results` refer to particular Haskell types. Parameters should be encoded into something suitable for a database. Results should be decoded to Haskell types.

Instead of using encoders and decoders directly, we'll apply the `hasql-th` package. Its goal is to parse SQL queries augmented with type annotations using Template Haskell and infer the required encoders and decoders.

EXAMPLE: USING THE HASQL ECOSYSTEM

🗋   ch15/hasql/Statements.hs

Let's look at the simplest example next:

```
import Hasql.Statement (Statement)
import Hasql.TH

countFilms :: Statement () Int64
countFilms =
  [singletonStatement|
    SELECT count(*) :: int8 FROM film        ◁──┐ SQL statement augmented
  |]                                             │ with a type annotation
```

We have a statement that counts films in a database. Its type is `Statement () Int64`, meaning that we have no parameters and precisely one result of the `Int64` type. The `hasql-th` package uses the `QuasiQuotes` GHC extension to parse SQL queries. The `singletonStatement` quasiquoter is responsible for processing queries that give exactly one row of a result.

We'll need the following quasiquoters in our application:

- `singletonStatement` for statements returning exactly one row of data
- `maybeStatement` for statements with either no or a single result
- `vectorStatement` for statements with many rows of results
- `rowsAffectedStatement` for statements that return the number of affected rows

Remember, we were inventing our own solutions to deal with these different forms of output. The `hasql-th` package has got us covered.

Note also the `int8` type annotation in the previous SQL query. It refers to a database type. The `hasql-th` package knows how to relate it to the `Int64` type in Haskell, so it can inject the corresponding decoder.

As our next example, let's select all the films from a database longer than a given length. The `hasql-th` package has no idea about our `FilmLength` or `FilmInfo`, but we do need a statement of the following type:

```
filmsLonger :: Statement FilmLength (Vector FilmInfo)
```

The SQL statement to select the corresponding films follows:

```
[vectorStatement|
    SELECT film_id :: int4, title :: text,
           description :: text?,
           length :: int4, rating :: text?
```

```
    FROM film
    WHERE length >= $1::int4
|]
```

We have two new features in this type-annotated SQL statement. First, note the use of text? to denote nullable fields. Second, we use $1 to denote a query parameter. Depending on the number of parameters, we use $2, $3, and so forth.

> **NOTE** In fact, both :: type annotations and $ enumerated query parameters are parts of the core PostgreSQL syntax. The hasql package extends it with ? nullability markers to denote Maybe values on the Haskell side.

The hasql-th package can't work with FilmLength directly. It expects the underlying Int32 type to fit the $1 parameter type. Let's extract that value as follows:

```
fromFilmLength :: FilmLength -> Int32
fromFilmLength (FilmLength len) = len
```

The hasql-th package can't produce FilmInfo either, but it can give us a tuple of the following type as a row, inferred from the type annotations inside the query:

```
(Int32, Text, Maybe Text, Int32, Maybe Text)
```

Let's implement the next function, which translates such a tuple to FilmInfo:

```
fiFromTuple :: (Int32, Text, Maybe Text, Int32, Maybe Text) -> FilmInfo
fiFromTuple (i, t, md, l, mr) = FilmInfo {
    filmId = FilmId i
  , title = t
  , description = md
  , filmLength = FilmLength l
  , rating = mr >>= toMaybeRating
  }
```

The only problem now is how to apply fromFilmLength and fiFromTuple to the statement parameters and results. Remember, every statement has the following type: Statement params results. Values of these type parameters are used in the opposite directions as follows:

- params are turned into values suitable for a database.
- results are created from database values.

Now, consider the situation: the hasql-th package is able to generate the following statement from the type-annotated SQL statement given earlier:

```
Statement Int32 (Vector (Int32, Text, Maybe Text, Int32, Maybe Text))
```

All these types are perfectly suitable to go to and from the database, but it'd be nicer to have `Statement FilmLength (Vector FilmInfo)` with our domain types instead. Therefore, we need to provide the following functions:

```
FilmLength -> Int32
Vector (Int32, Text, Maybe Text, Int32, Maybe Text) -> Vector FilmInfo
```

The first function returns a parameter suitable for a database from our domain value. The second one returns a result in our domain from a database value.

Note the asymmetry in these functions. To build `Statement p2 r2` from `Statement p1 r1` we need to provide the following:

- `p2 -> p1`
- `r1 -> r2`

It turns out that this asymmetry is perfectly encoded by the `Profunctor` type class from the `profunctors` package. This type class gives us the following methods:

```
lmap  :: Profunctor p => (a -> b) -> p b c -> p a c
rmap  :: Profunctor p => (b -> c) -> p a b -> p a c
dimap :: Profunctor p => (a -> b) -> (c -> d) -> p b c -> p a d
```

The good news is that the `Statement` type constructor has an instance of the `Profunctor` type class. Consequently, we can use the previous methods as follows:

```
lmap  :: (p2 -> p1) -> Statement p1 r1 -> Statement p2 r2
rmap  :: (r1 -> r2) -> Statement p1 r1 -> Statement p2 r2
dimap :: (p2 -> p1) -> (r1 -> r2) -> Statement p1 r1 -> Statement p2 r2
```

With these tools at hand, we can complete an implementation of the `filmsLonger` statement, as shown next:

```
filmsLonger :: Statement FilmLength (Vector FilmInfo)
filmsLonger = dimap fromFilmLength (fmap fiFromTuple)
  [vectorStatement|
     SELECT film_id :: int4, title :: text,
            description :: text?,
            length :: int4, rating :: text?
     FROM film
     WHERE length >= $1::int4
  |]
```

Sometimes we need to tweak only the results, as in the following statement:

```
filmIdByTitle :: Statement Text (Maybe FilmId)
filmIdByTitle = rmap (fmap FilmId)
  [maybeStatement|
     SELECT film_id::int4 FROM film WHERE title=$1::text
  |]
```

Or we may need to add a preprocessing step for parameters, as shown here:

```
setRating :: Statement (Rating, Text) Int64
setRating = lmap (first fromRating)
  [rowsAffectedStatement|
    UPDATE film SET rating = $1 :: text :: mpaa_rating
    WHERE title = $2 :: text
  |]
```

The previous example is particularly interesting. Besides `Profunctor`, we use the `first` function from `Bifunctor`. We already met them in the previous chapter. Note also the double type annotation for `$1`. The second one, `mpaa_rating`, is responsible for casting our text value for a rating to the corresponding enumeration type we've created in our database. This casting is done by PostgreSQL itself.

As a last example, let's check if a category is already assigned to a film as follows:

```
fromFilmId :: FilmId -> Int32
fromFilmId (FilmId a) = a

fromCatId :: CatId -> Int32
fromCatId (CatId a) = a

isAssigned :: Statement (CatId, FilmId) Bool
isAssigned = dimap (bimap fromCatId fromFilmId) isJust
  [maybeStatement|
    SELECT category_id::int4 FROM film_category
    WHERE category_id=$1::int4 AND film_id=$2::int4
  |]
```

We exploit the `maybeStatement` quasiquoter but ignore an actual result by using `isJust` to get the `Bool` value we are interested in. The parameters pair is transformed via the `bimap` method of the `Bifunctor` type class.

We'll get back to constructing statements in the end of the section devoted to `hasql`. For now, let's use the statements from the `Statements` module to define database sessions.

15.4.3 *Implementing database sessions*

The `Hasql.Session` module provides all the tools required to define sessions and run SQL statements inside them.

EXAMPLE: USING THE HASQL ECOSYSTEM

📄   ch15/hasql/Sessions.hs

A database session can be as simple as executing one SQL statement, as shown next:

```
import Hasql.Session (Session)
import qualified Hasql.Session as Session

import qualified Statements as Stmt

countFilms :: Session Int64
countFilms = Session.statement () Stmt.countFilms
```

It can also be more complex, executing many statements and sessions defined earlier as follows:

```
assignCategory :: Text -> Text -> Session Int64
assignCategory catName filmTitle = do
  cid <- findOrAddCategory catName
  mFilmId <- Session.statement filmTitle Stmt.filmIdByTitle
  case mFilmId of
    Nothing -> pure 0
    Just fid -> assignUnlessAssigned cid fid
```

Note that we do not communicate with a database while defining our sessions. There is no database connection in the code above. Consequently, we don't expect any database communication errors. `Session` is a monad that allows composing computations over databases. To get an actual result, we need to establish a connection and run a session.

15.4.4 *Running database sessions*

Running a session may reveal many sorts of errors. The database server may be down. The expected table might not be in the database. The queries we constructed may be wrong from a database point of view. Although the `hasql-th` package tries to check SQL statements as much as possible, the database always knows better.

> **EXAMPLE: USING THE HASQL ECOSYSTEM**
>
> 🗋   ch15/hasql/DBActions.hs
>
> 🗋   ch15/hasql/Main.hs

We ignore errors in our model database, so let's define the following wrapper to report any error and halt the program:

```
handleErrors :: IO (Either Session.QueryError a) -> IO a
handleErrors m = do
  r <- m
  case r of
    Right v -> pure v
    Left err -> error $ show err
```

Note the first argument. It's an `IO` action that resulted from any session we run using the following function:

```
run :: Session a -> Connection -> IO (Either QueryError a)
```

We already have our sessions. We get a connection in the `main` function as follows:

```
main :: IO ()
main = do
  Right conn <- Connection.acquire connectionSettings
```

```
    demo conn
  where
    connectionSettings =
      Connection.settings "localhost" 5432 "" "" "sakila_films"
```

Consequently, our database actions are simple wrappers over sessions. For example, we get the total number of films in the database as follows:

```
import qualified Sessions as Ses

totalFilmsNumber :: Connection -> IO Int64
totalFilmsNumber conn = handleErrors $ Session.run Ses.countFilms conn
```

Setting the rating and assigning a category are also trivial, as shown next:

```
setRating :: Connection -> Rating -> Text -> IO Int64
setRating conn newRating film =
  handleErrors $ Session.run (Ses.setRating newRating film) conn

assignCategory :: Connection -> Text -> Text -> IO Int64
assignCategory conn catName filmTitle =
  handleErrors $ Session.run (Ses.assignCategory catName filmTitle) conn
```

We construct the corresponding sessions using the parameters given and run them. Unfortunately, this simple scheme with constructing statements, defining sessions, and running them in IO becomes complicated if we want something that is not directly supported by the hasql ecosystem. Let's see what we need to do in such code by extending our model application with a new piece of functionality.

15.4.5 *The need for low-level operations and decoding data manually*

Suppose we need to save all the data about films into a text file. Suppose also that we have a huge table with films—millions of them. The only way we have, so far, to get all this data in hasql is selecting them to Vector FilmInfo, which means that we load all the data into memory. This is clearly not something scalable if the data is huge. One may argue that hasql makes it problematic by not providing us with lazy lists as all the other packages we've seen do. Unfortunately, that's not the root cause of the problem. Although other packages give us lazy lists in Haskell, more often than not, the underlying libraries will load all the data into memory anyway. The hasql package makes it clear by providing Vector instead of lists.

 To work with data without loading all of it into memory, we have to use database cursors. Let's do that with hasql low-level operations.

EXAMPLE: USING THE HASQL ECOSYSTEM

🗋   ch15/hasql/Statements.hs

🗋   ch15/hasql/Sessions.hs

🗋   ch15/hasql/DBActions.hs

Our goal is to implement the following database session:

```
processAllFilms :: (FilmInfo -> IO ()) -> Session ()
```

It can be used as follows:

```
printAllFilms :: Connection -> IO ()
printAllFilms conn =
  handleErrors $ Session.run (Ses.processAllFilms printFilm) conn
```

We need to create a database cursor and fetch elements from it by reasonable chunks until they are all fetched. This can be accomplished by issuing the following SQL queries:

```
BEGIN;
DECLARE films_cursor CURSOR FOR
  SELECT film_id, title, description, length, rating FROM film;
FETCH FORWARD 10 FROM films_cursor;
FETCH FORWARD 10 FROM films_cursor;
FETCH FORWARD 10 FROM films_cursor;
...
END;
```

For every chunk of `FilmInfo` values, we want to execute an action on every film.

Let's start with implementing the `FETCH` statement first. This is where we should decode data coming from the database into the `FilmInfo` values. All the decoders are defined in the `Hasql.Decoders` module. They should provide information about a type in a database, the nullability of a field, or other column- and row-decoding specifications. We can build our own types by declaring a decoder in applicative style.

In the following example, we define a statement manually by giving a SQL query and a decoder:

```
import qualified Hasql.Decoders as Dec
import qualified Hasql.Encoders as Enc

fetchFilmsChunk :: Statement () (Vector FilmInfo)
fetchFilmsChunk =
  Statement
    "FETCH FORWARD 10 FROM films_cursor"
    Enc.noParams                        ←——— We have no parameters.
    decoder
    True        ←——— The statement should be prepared.
    where
      decoder = Dec.rowVector $
        FilmInfo
          <$> (fmap FilmId . Dec.column . Dec.nonNullable) Dec.int4   ←—
          <*> (Dec.column . Dec.nonNullable) Dec.text
          <*> (Dec.column . Dec.nullable) Dec.text
          <*> (fmap FilmLength . Dec.column . Dec.nonNullable) Dec.int4
          <*> (fmap (>>= toMaybeRating) . Dec.column . Dec.nullable) Dec.text
```

Rows are decoded as Vector elements.

Wraps the nonnullable int4 column with FilmId

Constructs FilmInfo in an applicative style

Now we can use this statement to declare a whole session as follows:

```
processAllFilms :: (FilmInfo -> IO ()) -> Session ()
processAllFilms process = do
    Session.sql "BEGIN"
    Session.sql declareCursor
    fetchRowsLoop
    Session.sql "END"
  where
    declareCursor =
      "DECLARE films_cursor CURSOR FOR "
      <> "SELECT film_id, title, description, "
      <> "       length, rating FROM film"
    fetchRowsLoop = do
      rows <- Session.statement () Stmt.fetchFilmsChunk
      when (not $ V.null rows) $ do
        liftIO (V.mapM_ process rows)
        fetchRowsLoop
```

The main job is done in the fetchRowsLoop function. We execute the FETCH statement. If there is some data, we run the process function over it and go for the next iteration.

Note that it is possible to avoid using hasql-th for constructing a SQL statement and declare all the decoders and encoders manually as we did in this example, though it seems that the former approach is simpler.

15.5 *Generating SQL with opaleye*

In our final implementation of the model application, we don't write SQL at all. Instead, we generate all the SQL queries from Haskell code using the opaleye package. This package is based on the postgresql-simple package and reuses its functionality for connecting to a database. All other aspects of communicating with a database differ a lot.

EXAMPLE: USING THE OPALEYE PACKAGE

📄 ch15/opaleye/

📄 ch15/FilmInfo/

⚡ *opaleye*

15.5.1 *Structuring programs with opaleye*

Figure 15.3 illustrates the common program structure with opaleye and its zone of responsibility. First, we describe database fields and tables in terms of their relationships with Haskell types. Second, we construct SQL queries without actually writing them in SQL. Instead, we use the specialized monad syntax to say whatever we need. Third, we run those queries in IO actions against the previously established database connection.

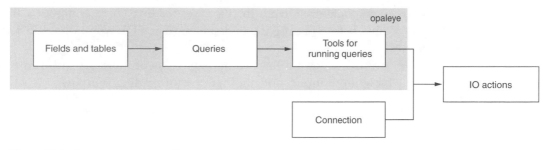

Figure 15.3   Program structure with `opaleye`

We have the following modules in our model application:

- `FilmInfo.Data` and `FilmInfo.FromField` are reused.
- `Tables` describes fields and tables in the database.
- `Queries` defines all the SQL queries we need.
- `DBActions` provides all the `IO` actions.
- `Main` runs the demo.

Let's discuss specific problems regarding the use of the `opaleye` package.

15.5.2 Describing database tables and their fields

Using `opaleye` starts with describing database tables. Table fields are considered something that can be written and read. We need descriptions for table fields at both the type level and the value level. The former is responsible for ensuring type safety. The latter is used in the actual processing at run time. The `opaleye` package uses profunctors to describe table fields and construct tables from them. Let's discuss this idea first and then move on to table descriptions.

EXPLOITING PROFUNCTORS AND PROFUNCTOR PRODUCTS

The `opaleye` package exploits a profunctor abstraction to describe fields. We already know that the `Profunctor` type class is defined by the following `dimap` method:

```
dimap :: Profunctor p => (a -> b) -> (c -> d) -> p b c -> p a d
```

Note the order of the arguments. It is often said that the first argument of `dimap` is applied *contravariantly* and the second one *covariantly*. This asymmetry corresponds to the asymmetry of writing and reading a field. When we want to write a field, we take a Haskell value and turn it into something suitable for a database. When we want to read a field, we take some value from a database and turn it into a Haskell value.

The writing and subsequent reading of a value may be interpreted as a computation from f to f'. Note that it's not necessary to have the same types here. For example, when we insert a record into a table, we don't specify id fields—they are computed by a database itself. For such cases, `opaleye` suggests using `Maybe f` as a type for writing and f itself for reading. The f and f' type variables may also refer to a user-defined type and a database type. In this case, reading corresponds to a final operation over a value before putting it to a database (e.g., SQL type casts). We'll see examples shortly.

Suppose we have the following field computations as profunctors with two type parameters, one for writing (input) and another one for reading (output):

```
f1 :: p wf1 rf1
f2 :: p wf2 rf2
f3 :: p wf3 rf3
```

To define a table with these fields, we need to combine types for writing and types for reading to get something like p (wf1, wf2, wf3) (rf1, rf2, rf3). This is where profunctor products become useful. If p has an instance of the ProductProfunctor type class, then we can apply the following function to it:

```
p3 :: ProductProfunctor p => (p wf1 rf1, p wf2 rf2, p wf3 rf3) ->
                             p (wf1, wf2, wf3) (rf1, rf2, rf3)
```

The p3 function then gives us a table with three fields described by a type for writing and a type for reading the whole record.

The product-profunctors package provides many functions like this one. Note that to use all of them, we need a computation in a profunctor. To get one, we can use Default instances and adaptors.

The Default type class defines the most meaningful def value of the p wf rf computation, depending on the wf and rf types.

Adaptors are functions that turn a user-defined type into field computations. For example, if we have the Foo a parameterized type, a profunctor-product adaptor would have the following type:

```
pFoo :: ProductProfunctor p => Foo (p wf rf) -> p (Foo wf) (Foo rf)
```

Remember that we defined all our types in FilmInfo.Data as parameterized types. Well, now we can finally use that. The product-profunctors package is able to generate both the Default instance and an adaptor function for such types with the following Template Haskell splice:

```
makeAdaptorAndInstanceInferrable :: String -> Name -> Q [Dec]
```

Now we are ready to define all of our fields and tables.

EXAMPLE: USING THE OPALEYE PACKAGE

🗋   ch15/FilmInfo/

🗋   ch15/opaleye/Tables.hs

RELATING HASKELL VALUES TO DATABASE VALUES

Let's start with film ratings. We already have the `Rating` type and the `FromField Rating` instance defined in `FilmInfo.FromField`. We define the following empty type to refer to a database value:

```
data PGRating
```

The `opaleye` package can reuse the `FromField` `Rating` instance defined for `postgresql-simple`, thanks to the provided `fromPGSFromField` function, as follows:

```
instance DefaultFromField PGRating Rating where
  defaultFromField = fromPGSFromField
```

The following is the profunctor we are interested in when defining the `Rating` computations for `opaleye`:

```
ToFields Rating (FieldNullable PGRating)
```

To define the `Default` instance for it, we need to consider the following:

- To write a `Rating` value to a database, we need to convert it to something appropriate first. A `Text` value should work. We have the `fromRating` function for that.
- To put a `Text` field into a database, we need to cast it to the `mpaa_rating` SQL type. The `opaleye` package provides the `unsafeCast` function for that.
- We can use the `Default ToFields Text (Field PGText)` instance provided by the package as a base for our own definition and then transform the `def` value from it via the `dimap` profunctor function.

All these ideas are implemented in the following instance:

```
{-# LANGUAGE MultiParamTypeClasses #-}
{-# LANGUAGE TypeFamilies #-}
{-# LANGUAGE FlexibleInstances #-}

instance pgf ~ FieldNullable PGRating => Default ToFields Rating pgf where
  def = dimap fromRating
              (unsafeCast "mpaa_rating")
              (def :: ToFields Text (Field PGText))
```

> **NOTE** Note that due to technical subtleties, we are not allowed to mention `ToFields Rating (FieldNullable PGRating)` in the instance head directly. `FieldNullable` is a type family. We are not allowed to invoke type families when defining an instance. The `...=>` part is used later during instance resolution, when it's perfectly safe to do computations over type families.

The good news is that `Rating` is the only type that requires these preparations. For all other fields, we can generate almost everything we need using Template Haskell as follows:

```
makeAdaptorAndInstanceInferrable "pFilmId" ''FilmId'
makeAdaptorAndInstanceInferrable "pFilmLength" ''FilmLength'
makeAdaptorAndInstanceInferrable "pFilmInfo" ''FilmInfo'
makeAdaptorAndInstanceInferrable "pCatId" ''CatId'
```

The adaptors and `Default` instances we've generated are not tied to `opaleye` exclusively. For example, the `pFilmId` adaptor function gets the following rather generic type:

```
pFilmId :: ProductProfunctor p =>
           FilmId' (p a1_0 a1_1) -> p (FilmId' a1_0) (FilmId' a1_1)
```

The generated instance of the `Default` type class for the `FilmId'` follows:

```
instance (ProductProfunctor p, Default p a a')
    => Default p (FilmId' a) (FilmId' a') where
  def = pFilmId (FilmId' def)
```

The `opaleye` package uses the generated adaptors and instances for user-defined types to derive instances for `ToFields` and other internal stuff.

DECLARING FIELDS AND TABLES

Now we are ready to declare fields and tables. The `film_id` field is defined as follows:

```
type FilmIdField = FilmId' (Field SqlInt4)
```

We relate `FilmId` to `SqlInt4`. We can use this field for reading. To write a `film_id`, we need a `Maybe`, as shown here:

```
type FilmIdFieldWrite = FilmId' (Maybe (Field SqlInt4))
```

We also need a type for reading and writing `FilmLength`, shown next:

```
type FilmLengthField = FilmLength' (Field SqlInt4)
```

We'd like to consider the whole `film` table record as a single `FilmInfo` field as follows:

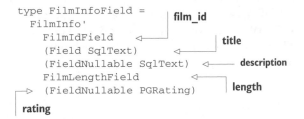

Note that we've specified both a type and nullability for every field. To write such a field, we need `FilmIdFieldWrite` for `film_id`, as shown next:

```
type FilmInfoFieldWrite =
  FilmInfo'
    FilmIdFieldWrite
    (Field SqlText)
    (FieldNullable SqlText)
    FilmLengthField
    (FieldNullable PGRating)
```

The `film` table is now described as follows:

```
filmTable :: Table FilmInfoFieldWrite FilmInfoField
filmTable =
  table "film"
        (pFilmInfo FilmInfo {
              filmId = pFilmId $ FilmId $ tableField "film_id"
            , title = tableField "title"
            , description = tableField "description"
            , filmLength = pFilmLength $ FilmLength $ tableField "length"
            , rating = tableField "rating"
            })
```

Note that the `Table` type constructor has two parameters: one for writing and another for reading. We construct its value via the product-profunctors machinery and extensive type inference for the `table` and `tableField` functions. As a result, we get a tool to read and write database fields of various types, either nullable or not.

Two other tables are simpler. We need to define `category_id` field for them as follows:

```
type CatIdField = CatId' (Field SqlInt4)
type CatIdFieldWrite = CatId' (Maybe (Field SqlInt4))
```

Both table definitions use p2 from `product-profunctors` to construct a table with two fields as a pair, as shown next:

```
categoryTable :: Table (CatIdFieldWrite, Field SqlText)
                       (CatIdField, Field SqlText)
categoryTable =
  table "category"
        (p2 ( pCatId $ CatId $ tableField "category_id"
            , tableField "name"))

filmCategoryTable :: Table (FilmIdField, CatIdField)
                           (FilmIdField, CatIdField)
filmCategoryTable =
  table "film_category"
        (p2 ( pFilmId $ FilmId $ tableField "film_id"
            , pCatId $ CatId $ tableField "category_id"))
```

The information about database tables we've provided is sufficient to generate SQL queries from Haskell code. Let's move to ways the opaleye package suggests to express our needs when communicating with a database.

15.5.3 *Writing queries*

We don't write SQL queries with opaleye. We write Haskell instead.

EXAMPLE: USING THE OPALEYE PACKAGE

□   ch15/opaleye/Queries.hs

SELECTING VALUES

Let's start with queries that select all the information from the tables we've defined. This is a pretty standard query, so the opaleye package provides the following selectTable function precisely for that:

```
filmSelect :: Select FilmInfoField
filmSelect = selectTable filmTable

categorySelect :: Select (CatIdField, Field SqlText)
categorySelect = selectTable categoryTable

filmCategorySelect :: Select (FilmIdField, CatIdField)
filmCategorySelect = selectTable filmCategoryTable
```

The opaleye package provides many functions that correspond to SQL aggregation operators. For example, we can easily compute all the films in the film table as follows:

```
countFilms :: Select (Field SqlInt8)
countFilms = aggregate countStar filmSelect
```

The opaleye package then turns definitions like this one into corresponding SQL queries.

We can also add conditions in the WHERE clauses, as shown next:

```
findFilm :: Text -> Select FilmInfoField
findFilm filmTitle = do
  film <- filmSelect
  viaLateral restrict (title film .== toFields filmTitle)
  pure film
```

Here we say that we expect only films with the specified title. The toFields function converts a Haskell value to a corresponding database value via all the machinery we discussed earlier. The .== operator compares database fields. The viaLateral and restrict functions refer to some internal opaleye machinery for defining subqueries. Although we didn't have to write subqueries with the previous database access packages, opaleye relies on them to provide genericity. It seems okay to use these functions to express our ideas without looking at their types and thinking about their precise meaning.

The functorial nature of the `Select` type constructor allows us to add postprocessing as follows:

```
filmIdByTitle :: Text -> Select FilmIdField
filmIdByTitle filmTitle = filmId <$> findFilm filmTitle
```

We can use other conditions besides equalities, too. For example, we can select films longer than a given length, like so:

```
filmsLonger :: FilmLength -> Select FilmInfoField
filmsLonger (FilmLength len) = do
    film <- filmSelect
    let FilmLength lenf = filmLength film
    viaLateral restrict (lenf .>= toFields len)
    pure film
```

Unfortunately, we have to unwrap the `FilmLength` newtype manually to apply the (`.>=`) operator.

In the following function, we select categories for the given film:

```
filmCategories :: Text -> Select (Field SqlText)
filmCategories filmTitle = do
  film <- filmSelect
  (ccatId, catName) <- categorySelect
  (fcfilmId, fccatId) <- filmCategorySelect
  viaLateral restrict $
        (title film .== toFields filmTitle)
    .&& (filmId film .=== fcfilmId)
    .&& (ccatId .=== fccatId)
  pure catName
```

This function generates a SQL query with several JOIN and WHERE clauses. Working with equalities over wrapped `id` fields is convenient thanks to the polymorphic (`.===`) operator provided by `opaleye`. Note that we've used the less polymorphic (`.==`) for the `title` field. Note also the (`.&&`) operator for adding AND to conditions in WHERE clauses.

MANIPULATING VALUES

The `opaleye` package provides `Insert`, `Update`, and `Delete` types to specify the corresponding SQL queries. They are usually used with various wrappers for most common tasks, such as `rCount` to get a number of rows affected or `rReturning` to apply a function to values in a query and give back its result.

For example, to insert a new category, we could write the following function:

```
newCategory :: Text -> Insert [CatId]
newCategory catName = Insert {
    iTable      = categoryTable
```

```
    , iRows        = [(CatId Nothing, toFields catName)]
    , iReturning  = rReturning (\(id', _) -> id')
    , iOnConflict = Nothing
    }
```

Note the `CatId Nothing` value for `category_id` in `iRows`. This means that we expect the corresponding `id` to be generated by a database. In `iReturning`, we specify a query result. We expected an identifier to be generated.

Updating a field looks similar, as shown next:

```
setRating :: Rating -> Text -> Update Int64
setRating fRating filmTitle =
  Update {
      uTable = filmTable
    , uUpdateWith = updateEasy (\film -> film {rating = toFields fRating})
    , uWhere      = \film -> title film .== toFields filmTitle
    , uReturning  = rCount
  }
```

The `updateEasy` wrapper specifies how to update the corresponding rows.

The deletion instruction follows the same pattern, as shown here:

```
unassignCategory :: CatId -> FilmId -> Delete Int64
unassignCategory catId' filmId' = Delete {
      dTable      = filmCategoryTable
    , dWhere =  \(fid, cid) -> (fid .=== toFields filmId')
                              .&& (cid .=== toFields catId')
    , dReturning  = rCount
    }
```

NOTE Interestingly, with the previous approaches, we were able to unassign a category given by a category title and a film title. I didn't manage to construct such a query (`DELETE` with joins) in `opaleye`. It seems that's a general problem with all the approaches that hide query construction from users. You can't express anything that was not foreseen and implemented by such a library author, although it's possible in SQL.

In all these functions, we specify a table, a condition for a `WHERE` clause, and an expected result. Special operations are also given as fields of the corresponding data type.

Once we have all our queries ready, we can run them.

15.5.4 *Running queries*

We'll use the following functions to run the queries we've defined:

- `runSelect`
- `runUpdate_`
- `runInsert_`
- `runDelete_`

All of them take a `Connection` and a query as arguments. Let's look at some examples.

EXAMPLE: USING THE OPALEYE PACKAGE

ch15/opaleye/DBActions.hs

To get a list of films, we execute the following `IO` action as follows:

```
import qualified Queries as Q

allFilms :: Connection -> IO [FilmInfo]
allFilms conn = runSelect conn Q.filmSelect
```

Expecting a single result can be implemented as follows:

```
totalFilmsNumber :: Connection -> IO Int64
totalFilmsNumber conn = do
  [cnt] <- runSelect conn Q.countFilms
  pure cnt
```

If we expect a result of either zero or one, we can play with a list returned by `runSelect`, as shown next:

```
findFilm :: Connection -> Text -> IO (Maybe FilmInfo)
findFilm conn = fmap listToMaybe . runSelect conn . Q.findFilm
```

Just as before, our `IO` actions may issue several requests, as shown here:

```
findOrAddCategory :: Connection -> Text -> IO [CatId]
findOrAddCategory conn catName = do
  cats <- runSelect conn (Q.catIdByName catName)
  case cats of
    [] -> runInsert_ conn (Q.newCategory catName)
    (cid:_) -> pure [cid]
```

The following additional type annotations may be necessary to help `opaleye` to infer types:

```
isAssigned :: Connection -> CatId -> FilmId -> IO Bool
isAssigned conn cid fid = do
  cats <- runSelect conn (Q.findAssigned cid fid) :: IO [CatId]
  pure (length cats > 0)
```

All the other `IO` actions follow the same patterns.

• The `opaleye` package turns writing SQL into Haskell programming. Unfortunately, this approach makes some things impossible to implement without resorting to `IO` actions. In addition, it makes Haskell coding harder, due to all those profunctors and type-level features.

Summary

- We have several approaches in Haskell to access relational databases, ranging from low-level to high-level.
- The HDBC package is the oldest and simplest package that allows working with almost any SQL database in existence.
- The postgresql-simple package provides a midlevel yet simple enough interface for PostgreSQL.
- The hasql package provides a type-safe performant interface for PostgreSQL with support for extensibility via additional packages.
- The opaleye package allows avoiding the writing of SQL queries altogether at the cost of sophisticated types and limited functionality.

Concurrency 16

Almost every server or desktop application nowadays runs concurrently over many CPU cores. Once the result of a limitation on increasing single-processor speed, this becomes an opportunity to organize our applications in new ways. An application becomes a collection of tasks that run in dedicated threads. For multithreading, we can use either operating system threads or library threads. The latter are lightweight, so we can run many of them. Threads work concurrently, so we need to synchronize them.

In this chapter, we'll discuss Haskell approaches to develop concurrent applications around threads. We'll start with a discussion of Haskell mechanisms to run computations concurrently. We are interested in both low-level mechanisms available to Haskell developers from the base package and more sophisticated high-level tools provided by other libraries. Once we can run threads, we need them to communicate with each other. We'll discuss how we do that in Haskell in the second section of the chapter.

567

Concurrent programming is generally considered a hard problem, no matter the language or the library we use. It's easy to make mistakes, though high-level approaches are usually better at keeping those mistakes under control. We'll discuss the best practices and see how to avoid common pitfalls.

16.1   *Running computations concurrently*

In this section, we'll discuss how to achieve concurrent execution within a Haskell program.

16.1.1   *An implementation of concurrency in GHC*

Most current operating systems support running several threads within a process. These OS-managed threads are quite heavy in terms of resources. Every process uses at least one OS thread but may ask the operating system to create more. To use threads at run time, a program must be linked with the version of the GHC runtime system that supports multithreading. This can be done by passing the -threaded flag to GHC. When using hpack or cabal, we can specify the following option in the executable section of the corresponding package description file:

```
ghc-options: -threaded
```

By default, the GHC runtime system uses only one OS thread that implements one virtual processor (also called a capability) for running any number of Haskell threads. To run the program over several OS threads (providing several capabilities), we should pass the -N <x> flag to the runtime system and give the specific number of OS threads we intend to use. Typically this number corresponds to the number of physical CPUs or CPU cores available on the computer system. Omitting the value means using all the physical processors.

Let's write the following trivial program and run it over several OS threads.

EXAMPLE: RUNNING A MULTITHREADED PROGRAM ON SEVERAL PROCESSORS

🗋   ch16/conc-hello.hs

⚡   *conc-hello*

```
import Control.Concurrent (getNumCapabilities)

main :: IO ()
main = do
  n <- getNumCapabilities
  putStrLn $ "This program runs over " ++ show n ++ " capabilities"
```

Running this program on my computer gives the following results:

```
hid-examples $ cabal -v0 run conc-hello -- +RTS -N2
This program runs over 2 capabilities
hid-examples $ cabal -v0 run conc-hello -- +RTS -N4
```

```
This program runs over 4 capabilities
hid-examples $ cabal -v0 run conc-hello -- +RTS -N
This program runs over 8 capabilities
```

As opposed to OS threads, the GHC runtime system implements library-managed lightweight threads. One OS thread may execute thousands of library threads by switching between them in short periods of time. We call this process preemptive multitasking. The GHC runtime system may send Haskell threads to any OS thread available at the moment, thus providing us more flexibility when structuring our applications.

Figure 16.1 shows the correspondence between OS threads and Haskell threads. It is expected that there are significantly more Haskell threads than OS threads at run time.

The multithreading runtime system in GHC was designed to allow running thousands of threads: they are rather cheap. Haskell threads are fully managed by the runtime system. It can migrate them between capabilities when

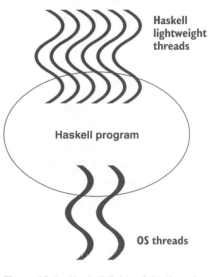

Figure 16.1   Haskell lightweight threads vs. OS threads in the GHC runtime system

needed, but we can fix a thread within the required specific capability, if needed. We can also create a bound thread that corresponds one-to-one to the OS thread. This is usually the case when dealing with non-Haskell libraries via foreign calls.

16.1.2 Low-level concurrency with threads

Now it's time to discuss how to run threads within a Haskell program.

MANAGING THREADS

For our first example of exploiting several threads, let's implement an application that prints a dot once a second while some other long-lasting action is in operation. This is often used like a progress bar to indicate that the process isn't stalled forever. Printing dots can be delegated to a separate thread while the main thread is responsible for performing the actual job.

> **EXAMPLE: PRINTING DOTS IN A SEPARATE THREAD**
>
> ☐ ch16/dots.hs
>
> ⚡ *dots*
>
> ☞ We can delegate nonessential operations to separate threads.

To solve this problem, we need to do the following:

- Run a thread that prints dots.
- Delay the thread for a second.
- Kill the thread once the job is done.

To this end, the `Control.Concurrent` module provides the following functions:

```
forkIO :: IO () -> IO ThreadId
threadDelay :: Int -> IO ()
killThread :: ThreadId -> IO ()
```

Note the `ThreadId` type. It refers to one Haskell thread. We run a new thread via the `forkIO` function and get the corresponding `ThreadId`. To delay the current thread for a given number of microseconds, we use the `threadDelay` function. To kill a thread from another thread, we use the `killThread` function.

Suppose we have the following extremely useful computation running for about five seconds:

```
oneSec :: Int
oneSec = 1000000 -- milliseconds

doSomethingUseful :: IO ()
doSomethingUseful = do
  threadDelay $ 5 * oneSec
  putStrLn "All done"
```

We also have the following dot-printing action that runs forever:

```
printDots :: Int -> IO ()
printDots msec = forever $ do
  putStrLn "."
  threadDelay msec
```

Note the simplicity of such an action. We don't have to think about the overall running time at all—the corresponding thread will be killed right on time.

Now we can run a dot-printing thread in the `main` function as follows:

```
main :: IO ()
main = do
  hSetBuffering stdout NoBuffering          <── Avoids buffering to
  putStrLn "Doing something useful"              see dots right away
  dotsPrinter <- forkIO (printDots oneSec)  <── Runs a thread
  doSomethingUseful
  killThread dotsPrinter      <── Kills the thread
  putStrLn "Exiting..."
```

Running this program gives the following output:

```
$ cabal -v0 run dots
Doing something useful
```

```
    .
    .
    .
    .
    .
All done
Exiting...
```

Note that we've got the expected behavior even with one capability (without the -N flag). Note also that we had to explicitly disable buffering for standard output. Otherwise, we could observe the delayed output.

In fact, dealing with standard output requires a lot of attention. A better practice could be to delegate all the output to one particular thread. Otherwise, we could observe a lot of interleaved output. Although GHC usually tries to avoid interleaving for single calls to putStr and other IO functions, consecutive calls may be interleaved.

In the following program, we run five threads that print the same line forever.

EXAMPLE: INTERLEAVING OUTPUT

ch16/interleaving.hs

⚡ *interleaving*

```
printHello :: IO ()
printHello = forever $ do
  putStr "Hello "
  putStrLn "world"

main :: IO ()
main = do
  _ <- replicateM 5 (forkIO printHello)
  threadDelay oneSec
```

We may observe the following lines in the standard output when running this program:

```
$ cabal -v0 run interleaving | sort | uniq
Hello
Hello Hello Hello Hello Hello world
Hello Hello Hello world
Hello Hello world
Hello world
world
```

The output from different threads was interleaved. As a result, we observe many combinations of the words "Hello" and "world" with the line break. Note that we don't have to kill threads—they will be killed automatically once the main function is over.

ASYNCHRONOUS EXCEPTIONS

We discussed *synchronous exceptions* in chapter 7. Concurrent execution makes way for *asynchronous exceptions*, those that are raised by another thread. In contrast to synchronous exceptions, we have absolutely no way to predict asynchronous exceptions inside the thread because they are not caused by actions we do in this thread.

Asynchronous exceptions are raised by the following function:

```
throwTo :: Exception e => ThreadId -> e -> IO ()
```

To use it, we should provide an ID for a target thread and a value of an exception. Note that this function doesn't require a specific type for an asynchronous exception. We can throw any exception using `throwTo`, thus making it asynchronous. It's impossible to check whether an exception we got was thrown synchronously or asynchronously.

Asynchronous exceptions are often used to kill a thread. The `killThread` we used previously is a small wrapper over `throwTo` that raises the `ThreadKilled` exception of the `AsyncException` type. The runtime system reports `StackOverflow` and `HeapOverflow` of the same type as asynchronous exceptions. We also have the `UserInterrupt` exception raised by pressing Ctrl-C.

In most cases, we react to an asynchronous exception by releasing all the resources we've previously acquired and terminating gracefully. The main problem with asynchronous exceptions is that they are not always desirable. There can be moments in a thread when we'd like to avoid them. For example, we wish to complete some critical process without interruptions, such as when we have acquire/release actions to work with external resources. We'd like to guarantee the completion of both `acquire` and `release`. Figure 16.2 illustrates such a situation.

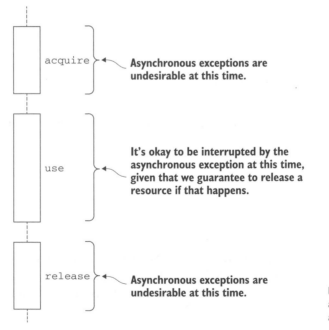

Figure 16.2 Acquire/release actions in the presence of asynchronous exceptions

Let's model an experiment to understand some of the problems around asynchronous exceptions. Note that this is not a real program: we'll use debug printing instead of doing the actual job.

EXAMPLE: EXPERIMENTS WITH ASYNCHRONOUS EXCEPTIONS

ch16/async-exc.hs

async-exc

Suppose we have the following functions that work with some resource:

```
acquire :: IO ()
acquire = do
  putStrLn "Start resource acquisition"
  threadDelay oneSec
  putStrLn "Resource is acquired"

release :: IO ()
release = do
  putStrLn "Start releasing the resource"
  threadDelay oneSec
  putStrLn "Resource is released"

use :: IO ()
use = do
  putStrLn "Begin using the resource"
  threadDelay (2 * oneSec)
  putStrLn "End using the resource"
```

It takes about a second to acquire and release a resource. We use this resource for two seconds. Let's forget about asynchronous exceptions for a moment and implement the following resource-processing action:

```
workWithResource :: IO ()
workWithResource = do
  acquire
  use `onException` release
  release
```

The `onException` function guarantees that if we have an exception during the `use` function, then the `release` function will be called. Suppose `acquire` and `release` functions can't throw an exception, so it seems we are on the safe side here. Note that `onException` doesn't stop the propagating of an exception. If we've got an exception during the `use` stage, the whole `workWithResource` action is aborted, so we never execute `release` twice.

In our experiment, we run `workWithResource` in a separate thread. This should take four seconds to complete. The idea is to see what is going on if we kill this thread sooner, as shown here:

```
experiment :: Int -> IO () -> IO ()
experiment timeout action = do
  thr <- forkIO action
  threadDelay timeout
  killThread thr
  threadDelay (2 * oneSec)
```

We run a thread, wait for a specified time-out, and then kill the thread. The last line is needed to make sure that we are done with this thread.

In the main function, we attempt to kill a thread during the following three different stages of execution:

```
main :: IO ()
main = do
  putStrLn "Asynchronous exception during `acquire`"
  experiment (oneSec `div` 2) threadUnsafe

  putStrLn "\nAsynchronous exception during `use`"
  experiment (oneSec + oneSec `div` 2) threadUnsafe

  putStrLn "\nAsynchronous exception during `release`"
  experiment (3 * oneSec + oneSec `div` 2) threadUnsafe
```

Running this program gives us the following output:

```
Asynchronous exception during `acquire`
Start resource acquisition

Asynchronous exception during `use`
Start resource acquisition
Resource is acquired
Begin using the resource
Start releasing the resource
Resource is released

Asynchronous exception during `release`
Start resource acquisition
Resource is acquired
Begin using the resource
End using the resource
Start releasing the resource
```

In the first experiment, the call to acquire was not completed. In the second experiment, we got an exception during use. It was not completed, but the resource was released, thanks to onException. In the third experiment, we have a problem once again. The resource was not released properly.

> ### Unexpected interruptions: Good or bad?
> You may wonder whether it is a good thing to have unexpected interruptions all over the program. I've already mentioned the good parts: it's often convenient to terminate a computation due to time-outs or the fact that we don't need its results anymore. There are also bad parts: some operations shouldn't ever be interrupted. Which ones? For example, it's always fine to interrupt pure computations; we have absolutely no problems with that. Remember, in Haskell, most of the program runs as a pure computation. If we've started reading a file, it's no problem to stop at any point, provided that we've closed it properly.

> We also want to have an ability to interrupt any blocking operations. We just don't want to be blocked forever! It may be the case that interruption is dangerous when we are doing foreign calls. Other programming languages don't tolerate unexpected interruptions. It seems that asynchronous exceptions are very useful in Haskell, but we need a special tool for those rare cases when we want to avoid them.

To hide some parts of code from the asynchronous exceptions, we use *masking*. The following three levels of masking are encoded as values of the `MaskingState` data type:

- `Unmasked`, when asynchronous exceptions are allowed; this is the normal state.
- `MaskedInterruptible`, when asynchronous exceptions are masked but may still be raised if we call interruptible operations (most blocking operations are interruptible).
- `MaskedUninterruptible`, when asynchronous exceptions are totally masked.

When we say that exceptions are *masked*, we mean that they may be thrown anyway but with the following caveats:

- The target thread doesn't notice them, so its execution is unaffected.
- The call to `throwTo` is blocked.

Once the target thread unmasks asynchronous exceptions or calls an interruptible operation in the `MaskedInterruptible` state, it receives the exception right away and the call to `throwTo` unblocks.

Thus masking affects the execution of both threads significantly, so it should be used with great care. For example, it's too easy to block everything (and become totally unresponsive) forever if we are too optimistic working in the `MaskedUninterruptible` state for a long time. To avoid such errors, the `Control.Exception` module provides a specially crafted interface, as shown next:

```
mask :: ((forall a. IO a -> IO a) -> IO b) -> IO b
uninterruptibleMask :: ((forall a. IO a -> IO a) -> IO b) -> IO b
```

We've already discussed the type of these functions in chapter 11. This type uses rank-3 polymorphism to express the following idea: an `IO` action in the argument (the one resulting in `IO b`) runs in a masked state but takes another action (the one resulting in `IO a`) as an argument and runs it in a state of the outer context. We'll see how to use these functions shortly.

> **IMPORTANT** Note that inner computation in both `mask` and `uninterruptible-Mask` doesn't run in an unmasked state. Instead, these functions restore the state of the outer context that may be either unmasked or masked. This prevents unexpected unmasking inside a computation with masked exceptions.

Let's get back to our experiments with asynchronous exceptions. Both `putStr` and `threadDelay` functions are blocking, so they are interruptible. Consequently, using them inside `mask` has no effect; they can still be interrupted. Let's use `uninterruptible-Mask` to demonstrate that asynchronous exceptions are really masked as follows:

```
workWithResourceSafe :: IO ()
workWithResourceSafe = uninterruptibleMask $ \restore -> do
    acquire
    restore use `onException` release
    release
```

We run both `acquire` and `release` with fully masked asynchronous exceptions and use `restore` of type `forall a. IO a -> IO a` to run `use`.

Running the same experiments as before with the `workWithResourceSafe` thread body gives us the following output:

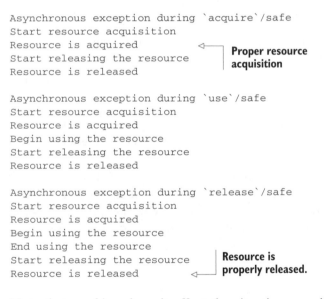

```
Asynchronous exception during `acquire`/safe
Start resource acquisition
Resource is acquired
Start releasing the resource
Resource is released
```
Proper resource acquisition

```
Asynchronous exception during `use`/safe
Start resource acquisition
Resource is acquired
Begin using the resource
Start releasing the resource
Resource is released
```

```
Asynchronous exception during `release`/safe
Start resource acquisition
Resource is acquired
Begin using the resource
End using the resource
Start releasing the resource
Resource is released
```
Resource is properly released.

Note that masking doesn't affect the situation running `use`. It runs with unmasked exceptions, just as before.

Chances that we actually need `uninterruptibleMask` in our programs are very small. It's safer to forget about it right away. Remember, it could easily lead to heavy deadlocks. Never repeat this experiment at home. The `Control.Exception` module provides other functions to control asynchronous exceptions, though they are also rarely used. Even the `mask` function is best not used directly but through the `bracket` function we already mentioned in chapter 7 and shown next:

```
bracket :: IO a -> (a -> IO b) -> (a -> IO c) -> IO c
```

We can now easily understand its implementation in base, as shown here:

```
bracket before after thing =
  mask $ \restore -> do
    a <- before
    r <- restore (thing a) `onException` after a
    _ <- after a
    pure r
```

It's useful to understand both the motivation and the pragmatics behind asynchronous exceptions, though using them directly is generally not recommended. In what follows, we'll discuss the higher-level interface for running threads that allows avoiding many complications of asynchronous exception handling.

16.1.3 *High-level concurrency with the async package*

The async package was written by Simon Marlow to provide a convenient layer for concurrent execution above the Control.Concurrent module. The Control.Concurrent .Async gives us the following:

- A concept and a type for asynchronous computation with a result. (Compare with threads: we never talked about their results.)
- An interface to spawn an asynchronous computation, wait for its result, or cancel it.
- A set of convenient utilities to spawn many concurrent computations at once using traditional Haskell data types and type classes (ranging from pairs and lists to generic Traversable).

ASYNCHRONOUS COMPUTATIONS

The idea of an asynchronous computation with a result is captured by the following Async a type provided by the Control.Concurrent.Async module:

```
data Async a
```

For example, Async Int is a type for asynchronous computation resulting in a value of type Int. The Async a type implements several type classes, including Functor, Eq, Ord, and Hashable. Consequently, we can easily do postprocessing or store an asynchronous computation in any container.

Every Async a is executed in a separate thread. We call such computations asynchronous because threads don't get blocked after starting them. We spawn a computation and then do our business, letting the computation proceed on its own. We can query Async a at any moment later to check whether the computation is over by using sort of a polling operation. We can also block on it while waiting for a result if we have nothing else to do. We can cancel it if we are not interested in the result anymore.

The `async` package allows us to work with many asynchronous computations simultaneously. In fact, we can use it to design the whole application as a collection of asynchronous computations spawned and completed in due time.

Let's look at various operations over asynchronous computations available in the `Control.Concurrent.Async` module.

SPAWNING AND QUERYING ASYNCS

We have the following two main ways to spawn an asynchronous computation:

```
async :: IO a -> IO (Async a)
withAsync :: IO a -> (Async a -> IO b) -> IO b
```

The first one, the `async` function, spawns an `IO a` computation given as an argument in a separate thread, giving us the `Async a` value as a result. At this point, we can do whatever we like with `Async a`.

The second one, the `withAsync` function, takes both an `IO a` computation and a function that processes its result. It wraps the `async` function and provides an additional value. The `withAsync` function guarantees that the supplied computation will be terminated once the processing function is completed. When using the `async` function, it's our responsibility not to forget about the computation we've spawned.

Let's revisit the "printing dots while doing something useful" example and reimplement it using `withAsync`.

EXAMPLE: PRINTING DOTS WITH ASYNC

⬚   ch16/dots-async.hs

⚡   *dots-async*

The `main` function is now simpler, as shown here:

```
main :: IO ()
main = do
  hSetBuffering stdout NoBuffering
  putStrLn "Start doing something useful"
  withAsync (printDots oneSec) $ \_ -> doSomethingUseful
  putStrLn "Exiting..."
```

We don't have to bother with thread IDs. In this particular example, we even ignore the computation itself. We know that it's guaranteed to terminate once we've completed `doSomethingUseful`.

Once we have a value of `Async a`, we can start querying it. First, we can wait until we have a result, as follows:

```
wait :: Async a -> IO a
```

Second, we can poll to see whether it's done, as shown next:

```
poll :: Async a -> IO (Maybe (Either SomeException a))
```

Getting `Just (Right result)` from the `poll` function means the computation has been completed and we have a result. Getting `Nothing` means that the computation is still in progress.

> **ASYNCHRONOUS COMPUTATIONS AND EXCEPTIONS** Both `wait` and `poll` functions make sure that we are aware of every unhandled exception raised inside the asynchronous computation. The `wait` function rethrows the same exception in the parent thread. The `poll` function gives it back in the `Left` branch of the `Either` data type. Thus, no exception inside a thread would go unnoticed.

The following function provides somewhat mixed behavior:

```
waitCatch :: Async a -> IO (Either SomeException a)
```

The `waitCatch` function blocks until the result is ready or a computation is terminated due to an unhandled exception. In the latter case, the exception is returned in the `Left` branch of `Either`.

Finally, we can cancel an asynchronous computation as follows:

```
cancel :: Async a -> IO ()
```

Let's use these functions in another incarnation of the printing-dots example.

EXAMPLE: PRINT DOTS AND CANCEL RANDOMLY

⬚ ch16/dots-async-cancel.hs

⚡ *dots-async-cancel*

In this version, we turn `doSomethingUseful` into an asynchronous computation. After two seconds of running it, we get a random `Bool` value and decide whether to continue the computation or cancel it. Here is the code:

```
main :: IO ()
main = do
  hSetBuffering stdout NoBuffering
  putStrLn "Start doing something useful"
  withAsync (printDots oneSec) $ \_ ->
    withAsync doSomethingUseful $ \useful -> do
      threadDelay $ 2 * oneSec
      interrupt <- getStdRandom uniform
      case interrupt of
        True -> cancel useful
        False -> wait useful >> pure ()
  putStrLn "Exiting..."
```

When we run this program, it may complete or terminate prematurely, depending on the random `Bool` value, for example:

```
$ cabal -v0 run dots-async-cancel
Start doing something useful
.
.
.
Exiting...
```

At this time we got `True` and stopped.

Suppose that we want to let the user decide whether to continue or terminate a computation. This is a little bit more difficult, because we need the following four computations:

- Printing dots
- Doing something useful
- Waiting for user input
- Implementing the cancelling logic

Waiting for user input may take forever, so we have to put it into a separate computation. We can implement the canceling logic in `main`, but what exactly should we wait for? Is it a user input or completion of the job? Well, we need to wait for the one that comes earlier. One option could be using `poll` for both computations in a loop, but this is not very convenient. Fortunately, we have a better option. The `Control.Concurrent.Async` module allows us to wait for several asynchronous computations simultaneously.

WAITING FOR MULTIPLE ASYNCS

Depending on our waiting scenario, the `Control.Concurrent.Async` module provides a plethora of waiting functions, including the following:

```
waitAny :: [Async a] -> IO (Async a, a)
waitEither :: Async a -> Async b -> IO (Either a b)
waitEither_ :: Async a -> Async b -> IO ()
waitBoth :: Async a -> Async b -> IO (a, b)
```

These functions wait for one or all of the given asynchronous computations. They either give us results or rethrow an exception raised during the computation. In addition, the `waitAny` function returns the first completed asynchronous computation. Catch-flavored functions return `Either SomeException a` instead of rethrowing an exception, and cancel-flavored ones cancel all the other given computations after completing the first one.

Let's reimplement the printing-dots example and give the user the chance to terminate the computation by pressing Enter.

EXAMPLE: PRINTING DOTS DEPENDING ON USER INPUT

ch16/dots-async-interrupted.hs

dots-async-interrupted

First, we add the following computation that waits for a user to press Enter:

```
waitEnter :: IO ()
waitEnter = getLine >> pure ()
```

In the `main` function, we start all the computations asynchronously and wait for the first one to complete, as shown here:

```
main :: IO ()
main = do
  hSetBuffering stdout NoBuffering
  putStrLn "Start doing something useful"
  withAsync (printDots oneSec) $ \_ ->
    withAsync waitEnter $ \enter ->
      withAsync doSomethingUseful $ \useful ->
        waitEither_ enter useful
  putStrLn "Exiting..."
```

Once any of the computations have completed, we leave the `withAsync` section, and every computation in progress is cancelled for us.

CONCURRENT DATA PROCESSING

Some patterns of concurrent execution arise so often that it makes sense to have a wrapper for them and avoid explicit concurrency functions altogether. For example, in the previous example, we spawned three computations and waited for the first one that completed, as shown next:

```
withAsync (printDots oneSec) $ \_ ->
    withAsync waitEnter $ \enter ->
      withAsync doSomethingUseful $ \useful ->
        waitEither_ enter useful
```

Instead of writing these three lines, we could use the following `race_` function:

```
race_ :: IO a -> IO b -> IO ()
```

Because we have three computations, we need to call the `race_` function twice as follows:

```
race_ (printDots oneSec) $
    race_ waitEnter doSomethingUseful
```

The behavior is the same as before. Note that we've eliminated explicit thread spawning completely.

If we are interested in results, we could use the following `race` function:

```
race :: IO a -> IO b -> IO (Either a b)
```

We also have functions to wait for all the results instead of the first one, including the following:

```
concurrently :: IO a -> IO b -> IO (a, b)
mapConcurrently :: Traversable t => (a -> IO b) -> t a -> IO (t b)
replicateConcurrently :: Int -> IO a -> IO [a]
```

These functions share the same strategy for exceptions: if one of the spawned computations throws an exception, then this exception is rethrown, and all the other computations are cancelled. These functions make it easy to organize the concurrent processing of all the values in a data structure or spawn many computations at once.

LINKING ASYNCS TOGETHER

In some cases, we still need to work with asyncs explicitly. For example, sometimes we need to arrange parent/child relationships. If the parent thread dies for some reason, then all its children should be killed. If we use `withAsync`, then we get such behavior automatically. Remember the following type:

```
withAsync :: IO a -> (Async a -> IO b) -> IO b
```

Once the function in the second argument returns, an asynchronous computation spawned for the first argument is cancelled. Sometimes we need this behavior, and sometimes we don't. Let's work through an example where we create a tree of threads.

EXAMPLE: SPAWNING A TREE OF THREADS

📄   ch16/tree-async.hs

⚡   *tree-async*

Suppose we have a type for a binary tree and a tree of such a type as follows:

```
data BinTree = Node Int BinTree BinTree
             | EmptyTree

tree :: BinTree
tree = Node 2
         (Node 3 EmptyTree EmptyTree)
         (Node 1 EmptyTree EmptyTree)
```

Functions for processing such a tree are usually recursive—for example, we can compute the maximum as follows:

```
treeMax :: BinTree -> Int
treeMax EmptyTree = 0
treeMax (Node n left right) =
  max n $ max (treeMax left) (treeMax right)
```

Alternatively, we could implement a bunch of type classes up to `Traversable` to get this and many other functions for free.

Now we want to process every node of the tree using the following function:

```
work :: Int -> IO ()
work sec = do
  threadDelay $ sec * oneSec
  putStrLn $ "Work is completed for " ++ show sec ++ " sec"
```

Processing a node with the value n takes precisely n seconds. How could we process the whole tree? We have two strategies. With the first strategy, we spawn processes, and they run independently of each other, as shown next:

```
spawnTree :: BinTree -> IO ()
spawnTree EmptyTree = pure ()
spawnTree (Node sec left right) = do
  _ <- async (spawnTree left)
  _ <- async (spawnTree right)
  work sec
```

Completing the call to `spawnTree` (processing one node of the tree) doesn't mean that we want to cancel the child threads.

Alternatively, we could arrange parent/child dependency and kill children whenever the parent thread completes as follows:

```
spawnTreeCancel :: BinTree -> IO ()
spawnTreeCancel EmptyTree = pure ()
spawnTreeCancel (Node sec left right) =
  withAsync (spawnTree left) $ \ _ ->
    withAsync (spawnTree right) $ \ _ ->
      work sec
```

The `withAsync` function does the job.

Finally, let's run both functions and compare the resulting output as follows:

```
main :: IO ()
main = do
  hSetBuffering stdout NoBuffering
  putStrLn $ "No children cancellation"
  spawnTree tree
  threadDelay $ (1 + treeMax tree) * oneSec
  putStrLn $ "\nWith children cancellation"
  spawnTreeCancel tree
  threadDelay $ (1 + treeMax tree) * oneSec
  putStrLn "Exiting..."
```

Note that after each call to `spawnTree`, we wait for sufficient time to allow all the threads to complete.

Running this program results in the following:

```
No children cancellation
Work is completed for 1 sec
Work is completed for 2 sec
Work is completed for 3 sec

With children cancellation
Work is completed for 1 sec
Work is completed for 2 sec
Exiting...
```

There are no traces of the three-second job in the second run because it was cancelled by withAsync, so the required dependency between asynchronous computations was established.

It's also possible to arrange dependencies between asyncs after they were spawned. The Control.Concurrent.Async module provides the following functions:

```
link :: Async a -> IO ()
linkOnly :: (SomeException -> Bool) -> Async a -> IO ()
```

These two functions link the given async to a current thread. The linking means that the exception raised in the Async will be rethrown in the current thread (wrapped in an ExceptionInLinkedThread). Unless handling this exception, the current thread will be killed. The linkOnly function allows providing a predicate that chooses an exception to propagate between threads.

We can also link two asynchronous computations together, as shown next:

```
link2 :: Async a -> Async b -> IO ()
link2Only :: (SomeException -> Bool) -> Async a -> Async b -> IO ()
```

All these function allow establishing any sort of a dependency between threads.

In fact, exception passing between threads is a simple form of interthread communication. In the next section, we'll discuss other tools designed to organize communication between threads.

16.2 *Synchronization and communication*

Synchronization is an extremely hard problem. The reader may have heard about semaphores, mutexes, critical sections, and things like that. Fortunately, they are not normally used in Haskell. We have better and more high-level tools to organize synchronization and communication between threads. In this section, we'll look at two such tools: synchronized mutable variables and software transactional memory. The latter is more novel and much easier to use in a safe manner. The former is simpler to understand at first. Both tools are used to implement sophisticated data structures for concurrent programs.

16.2.1 *Synchronized mutable variables and channels*

Let's start with the basic building block of concurrent communication in Haskell: a synchronized mutable variable, or `MVar`—a special sort of mutable reference that allows additional control in the concurrent settings.

MVARS AND OPERATIONS OVER THEM

A synchronized mutable variable is either empty or filled with some value. Whenever it is empty, we are allowed to put a value in it to make it full. Whenever it is full, we are allowed to take a value out of it and make it empty. Putting a value into an already full variable or taking a value out of an empty one leads to blocking a thread that executes such operations. This blocking behavior allows using such variables for synchronizing concurrent threads. A value of a mutable variable can be regarded as a message going from one thread to another. Consequently, we've got a communication mechanism as well.

Synchronized mutable variables are defined using the following data type:

```
data MVar a
```

We can create either an empty or a full mutable variable as follows:

```
newEmptyMVar :: IO (MVar a)
newMVar :: a -> IO (MVar a)
```

Once we have a variable, we can take or put values, as shown here:

```
takeMVar :: MVar a -> IO a
putMVar :: MVar a -> a -> IO ()
```

Figure 16.3 demonstrates the blocking behavior of these two functions over empty and full variables.

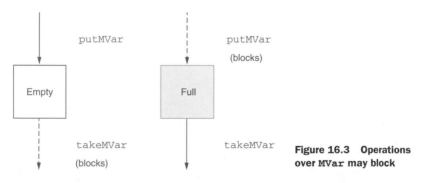

Figure 16.3 Operations over MVar may block

All the previous operations are executed atomically, meaning that no threads can execute them concurrently over the same variable. When some operation is blocked, other operations over the same variable are allowed. They can change the state of the variable, leading to unblocking blocked operations. There can be many threads blocked on the same variable. The GHC runtime system keeps track of them and checks whether they can proceed after any change of the variable.

For the first example of using an MVar, let's implement waiting for the completion of a thread spawned via a low-level forking mechanism. Remember, there is no such a functionality in Control.Concurrent.

EXAMPLE: WAITING FOR A THREAD COMPLETION

☐   ch16/wait-completion.hs

⚡   *wait-completion*

Suppose we have the following action taking some random time to complete:

```
randomDelay :: IO ()
randomDelay = do
  secs <- getStdRandom (uniformR (1, 5))
  putStrLn $ "Waiting for " ++ show secs ++ "sec"
  threadDelay $ secs * oneSec
```

We know that the following main function won't work as required:

```
main :: IO ()
main = do
  _ <- forkIO randomDelay
  pure ()
```

Once the main thread is completed, all other threads are automatically killed. Consequently, we have to wait for the completion of randomDelay. The easiest solution is to create an empty MVar in main and then wait until it's full. The thread then should put something into it when it's done. One problem is to guarantee that no matter what's going on inside the thread, we put something into the variable eventually. Putting a value as the final operation of the thread isn't an appropriate solution because we could get an exception during a thread execution and never reach that point. The Control.Concurrent module suggests using the following forkFinally function in such a situation:

```
forkFinally :: IO a -> (Either SomeException a -> IO ()) -> IO ThreadId
```

This function spawns a thread with an IO action in the first argument augmented with the try block followed by its second argument, as shown next:

```
forkFinally action and_then =
  mask $ restore ->
      forkIO $ try (restore action) >>= and_then
```

The try and and_then parts are executed with asynchronous exceptions masked, so all the guarantees hold.

Now we are ready to implement the correct version of the `main` function as follows:

```
main = do
  fin <- newEmptyMVar
  _ <- forkFinally randomDelay (\_ -> putMVar fin ())
  takeMVar fin
  putStrLn "Exiting..."
```

We are not interested in a particular value, so `MVar ()` for the `fin` variable works. The `main` function is now guaranteed to be blocked until the `randomDelay` thread is completed. It's easy to extend this example to wait for several threads by creating several such variables and waiting for all of them one by one.

We can use the same idea to organize the delayed start of the thread. To do that, we create another empty variable and insert a wait for it at the beginning. Once we put something in it, the thread continues as follows:

```
main :: IO ()
main = do
  start <- newEmptyMVar
  fin <- newEmptyMVar
  _ <- forkFinally (takeMVar start >> randomDelay)
                   (\_ -> putMVar fin ())
  threadDelay oneSec
  putMVar start ()        <——— Thread starts.
  takeMVar fin            <—
  putStrLn "Exiting..."     | Thread stops.
```

The `Control.Concurrent.MVar` module provides many other operations over `MVar`. Some of them block, whereas others allow testing a variable without blocking on it as follows:

```
readMVar :: MVar a -> IO a -- blocks if empty, doesn't change a value
swapMVar :: MVar a -> a -> IO a -- blocks if empty
tryTakeMVar :: MVar a -> IO (Maybe a) -- non-blocking
tryPutMVar :: MVar a -> a -> IO Bool -- non-blocking
withMVar :: MVar a -> (a -> IO b) -> IO b -- blocks if empty
...
```

It's crucial to understand the technical details behind these and other operations over `MVar`. Thus, careful reading of the `Control.Concurrent.MVar` module is highly recommended. Even then, programming with `MVar` is quite dangerous—it's to easy to introduce errors and end up with unresponsive programs or get unexpected exceptions.

CHANNELS

Synchronized mutable variables can be used to create more sophisticated data structures. One of the most useful examples of such a structure is a *channel*, that is, an unbounded FIFO queue. We can write to a channel and read from it. Reading from a channel may block if the channel is empty.

An interface of channels is very simple, as shown next:

```
data Chan a
newChan :: IO (Chan a)
writeChan :: Chan a -> a -> IO ()
readChan :: Chan a -> IO a
```

Figure 16.4 illustrates reading and writing operations over a FIFO channel.

writeChan   readChan

Figure 16.4   Reading from and writing to a channel

Let's use this interface to implement a traditional pattern of concurrent communication, namely, *producer/consumer*. Our problem is trivial: we have a list of numbers and want to compute their sum. To do that, we use a channel and two threads: one thread for sending numbers to a channel, and another one for reading and summing them up.

EXAMPLE: SUMMING NUMBERS WITH A PRODUCER/CONSUMER PATTERN

    ☐   ch16/sum-numbers.hs

    ⚡   *sum-numbers*

Our idea is to use the `Chan (Maybe Int)` type to represent a channel with numbers. We'll write `Nothing` into this channel when the numbers are over. Let's implement a producer thread first as follows:

```
sendNumbers :: [Int] -> Chan (Maybe Int) -> IO ()
sendNumbers xs ch = do
  forM_ xs $ \x -> do
    writeChan ch (Just x)
    threadDelay $ oneSec `div` 2
  writeChan ch Nothing
```

To make things more interesting, I've introduced a delay between writes to a channel. All numbers from the `xs` list are written to a channel wrapped with a `Just`.

The consumer thread should read from a channel (and block when there are no numbers). When it gets a number, it adds it to an accumulator. When it gets `Nothing`, it stops. The implementation is straightforward, as shown next:

```
sumNumbers :: Chan (Maybe Int) -> IO Int
sumNumbers ch = loop 0
  where
    loop !acc = do
      next <- readChan ch
      case next of
```

```
    Just n -> do
      putStrLn $ "We've got a number: " ++ show n
      loop (acc + n)
    Nothing -> do
      putStrLn "There are no more numbers"
      pure acc
```

Note that this action returns an accumulator. We'll use this to run an asynchronous computation. Note also that the channel is given as an argument to both thread actions. It is created in the `main` thread as follows:

```
main :: IO ()
main = do
  ch <- newChan
  summator <- async (sumNumbers ch)
  _ <- async (sendNumbers [1..5] ch)
  res <- wait summator
  putStrLn $ "Sum is " ++ show res
```

In the `main` function, we create a channel, spawn both threads as asynchronous computations, and then wait for the result of summing all the numbers. Running this program gives us the following output:

```
$ cabal -v0 run sum-numbers
We've got a number: 1
We've got a number: 2
We've got a number: 3
We've got a number: 4
We've got a number: 5
There are no more numbers
Sum is 15
```

If you run it, you'll see a delay when receiving numbers.

The `Chan` a channels are unbounded, meaning that an aggressive producer may quickly exhaust the memory available. Another problem is that our idea of sending `Nothing` to a channel to express the end of a channel stops working when we have several consumers. We'll discuss other channels later in this chapter.

POTENTIAL DEADLOCKS WITH MVARS

To support my claim about the potential danger when using `MVar` variables, let's look at an example. In this example, we'll create a couple of mutable variables, then take their values, compute the sum, and put it back to both variables.

EXAMPLE: LOOKING FOR DEADLOCKS

🗋   ch16/mvar-deadlocks.hs

⚡   *mvar-deadlocks*

☞   Programming with `MVar` is dangerous

The following `IO` action manipulates two `MVar`s:

```
action :: MVar Int -> MVar Int -> IO ()
action mv1 mv2 = do
  a <- takeMVar mv1
  b <- takeMVar mv2
  let s = a + b
  putMVar mv1 s
  putMVar mv2 s
```

Suppose, we've created the following two variables we want to manipulate:

```
var1 <- newMVar 1
var2 <- newMVar 2
```

Let's run the `action` function twice in separate threads as follows:

```
async1 <- async (action var1 var2)
async2 <- async (action var2 var1)
```

Oops, I've messed up the names of the variables. Is that a problem? Well, it depends on the actual execution order at run time. For example, everything could go smoothly, as shown here:

```
async1: takeMVar var1 -- SUCCESS, var1 is emptied
async1: takeMVar var2 -- SUCCESS, var2 is emptied
async2: takeMVar var2 -- BLOCKED, because var2 is empty
async1: putMVar var1 -- SUCCESS, var1 is full
async1: putMVar var2 -- SUCCESS, var2 is full, async2 is unblocked
async2: takeMVar var2 -- SUCCESS, var2 is emptied
async2: takeMVar var1 -- SUCCESS, var1 is emptied
async2: putMVar var2 -- SUCCESS, var1 is full
async2: putMVar var1 -- SUCCESS, var2 is full
```

Figure 16.5 illustrates the corresponding execution trace.

Unfortunately, we can have a problem with one particular execution order, as shown here:

```
async1: takeMVar var1 -- SUCCESS, var1 is emptied
async2: takeMVar var2 -- SUCCESS, var2 is emptied
async1: takeMVar var2 -- BLOCKED, because var2 is empty
async2: takeMVar var1 -- BLOCKED, because var1 is empty
-- DEADLOCK, both threads are waiting for each other
```

Thus, we have a potential deadlock. Let's run an experiment and count how often we have a deadlock in this code. The GHC runtime system can detect deadlocks and report them by throwing an exception. Let's count these exceptions while repeating the scenario described earlier many times.

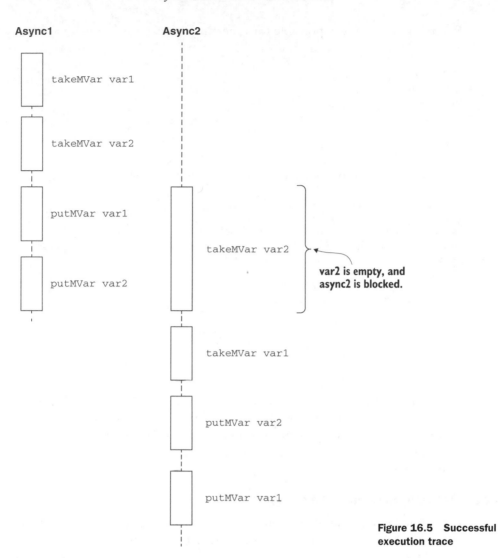

Figure 16.5 Successful execution trace

The following function creates variables and runs both actions once:

```
experiment :: IORef Int -> IO ()
experiment dlcnt = do
  var1 <- newMVar 1
  var2 <- newMVar 2
  async1 <- async (action var1 var2)
  async2 <- async (action var2 var1)        The order of variables
                                            is swapped.
  res <- try (waitBoth async1 async2)
  case res of
    Left BlockedIndefinitelyOnSTM           An exception raised by async
      -> modifyIORef' dlcnt (+1)            Increment counter
    _ -> pure ()
```

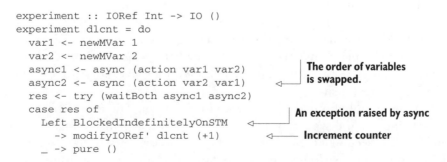

The main function is responsible for repeating this experiment many times, as shown here:

```
main :: IO ()
main = do
  dlcnt <- newIORef 0
  replicateM_ 10000 (experiment dlcnt)
  putStr "Number of deadlocks encountered: "
  readIORef dlcnt >>= print
```

I've executed this program several times; my results follow:

```
$ cabal -v0 run mvar-deadlocks -- +RTS -N
Number of deadlocks encountered: 1
 $ cabal -v0 run mvar-deadlocks -- +RTS -N
Number of deadlocks encountered: 2
 $ cabal -v0 run mvar-deadlocks -- +RTS -N
Number of deadlocks encountered: 2
 $ cabal -v0 run mvar-deadlocks -- +RTS -N
Number of deadlocks encountered: 5
$ cabal -v0 run mvar-deadlocks -- +RTS -N
Number of deadlocks encountered: 0
 $ cabal -v0 run mvar-deadlocks -- +RTS -N
Number of deadlocks encountered: 7
```

We see that the deadlock here is quite a rare event. We got it only a handful of times during thousands of runs. Anyway, we have to be extremely careful when working with synchronized mutable variables, because bad things can happen. In fact, it's better to avoid them altogether. In the next section, we'll discuss a more robust mechanism for implementing synchronization and communication in Haskell, namely, software transactional memory.

16.2.2 *Software transactional memory (STM)*

Let's think about a variable in memory in a concurrent program. We'd like to have access to this variable from many threads. Access means either reading or writing. We'd like to have writing as an atomic operation, meaning no two threads are allowed to write to a variable at the same time. In general, concurrent reading may be allowed. Unfortunately, even if we have an atomic write operation, this is not enough. For example, we'd like to increment a variable. We read it and then write an incremented value back. What if someone wrote a new value right at the moment between our reading and writing operations? Well, this intermediate change is lost. The problem is much more serious if we are talking about money, for one example. We don't want to lose money, that's for sure.

We have several approaches to tackle this problem. Traditionally, in concurrent programming, we use synchronization primitives and organize critical sections with them. A critical section is a piece of code that can access any shared resource such as a variable exclusively. No other thread is allowed to do the same while we are in a critical section. Programming with critical sections and other synchronization primitives is hard.

Another approach is traditionally used in databases. It is called transactions. We start a sequence of operations that are expected to run atomically all together. Once we complete a transaction, we either commit or abort it, depending on other transactions in a database. We abort our transaction in the presence of unintended changes initiated by other processes. If there are no such changes, we are allowed to commit. This approach has proved itself very appropriate for Haskell. Let's explore it with several simple examples.

STM TRANSACTIONAL VARIABLES AND STM TRANSACTIONS

STM controls access to transactional variables of the following type:

```
data TVar a
```

The most basic operations over them include the following:

```
newTVar :: a -> STM (TVar a)
readTVar :: TVar a -> STM a
writeTVar :: TVar a -> a -> STM ()
```

Note that all the operations work in the STM monad. To run any STM computation as an atomic action, we use the following function:

```
atomically :: STM a -> IO a
```

We call every STM computation a transaction. The atomically function executes this transaction. What can we do inside a transaction? Well, we can read and write transactional variables. When used concurrently from different threads, these operations can lead to a conflict. It's a conflict for different threads to attempt writing to the same variable at the same time. It's also a conflict to write to a variable that is read in the yet unfinished transaction. On the other hand, concurrent read operations don't lead to a conflict. If the GHC runtime system determines there is a conflict, it aborts all the concurrent transactions in the conflict and restarts them. When aborting a transaction, all the changes done during it should be reverted. That's easy if everything we are doing inside a transaction is limited to memory reads and writes. This is where monadic computations shine in Haskell. We are allowed to do only a small set of operations inside the STM monad. The Haskell type system ensures that we are doing nothing dangerous. Unfortunately, repeated conflicts and restarting transactions may still lead to degrading performance, but this is the price we pay for the convenience of STM.

Besides conflicts, we also have a need for manual abortion of a transaction. Suppose we've read some variables and realize that their values don't allow us to proceed at this moment. What should we do? As usual in concurrent programs, we should block until variables change their values. This block-until behavior is also implemented in STM transactions. We have the following functions to support it:

```
retry :: STM a
check :: Bool -> STM () -- retry if 'Bool' is false
```

Whenever we call `retry` or `check` inside a transaction, it is aborted, and the thread is blocked until one of the variables we've read inside a transaction changes its value. When that happens, our transaction is automatically restarted.

Let's look at an example. Suppose we have several threads. We want them to print `"Hello"` based on user choice. While the user is thinking, all the threads should be silent (i.e., blocked).

EXAMPLE: CONTROLLING THREADS WITH A TRANSACTIONAL VARIABLE

📄   ch16/ordered-threads.hs

⚡   *ordered-threads*

Suppose, we have the following five threads:

```
maxThread = 5
```

The idea is to use a transactional variable that is either 0 or the number of a thread. Whenever we set a variable to a number from 1 to 5, the corresponding thread should react by printing `"Hello"`. After reacting, the variable is set back to 0.

We can implement waiting for a specific number in an STM action as follows:

```
waitUnless :: TVar Int -> Int -> STM ()
waitUnless tv n = do
  n' <- readTVar tv          ⭤————————————┐  Reads the variable
  check $ n == n'      ⭤———— Blocks unless n == n'
```

Hello threads now can be implemented as follows:

```
hello :: TVar Int -> Int -> IO ()
hello tv n = forever $ do
  atomically $ waitUnless tv n        ⭤———— Runs an STM transaction
  putStrLn $ "Hello from thread " ++ show n
  atomically $ writeTVar tv 0         ⭤———— Sets the variable back to 0
```

Successful completion of a transaction guarantees that we've observed the number of the current thread, so we print `"Hello"` after `atomically` runs.

Communication with a user is a loop where we wait for an input and react to it by setting a transactional variable, as shown in the next code sample. Iterating this loop is allowed whenever a transactional variable is 0, so that no other thread should respond.

```
userLoop :: TVar Int -> IO ()
userLoop tv = do
  atomically $ waitUnless tv 0
  putStrLn $ "Enter thread number (1.." ++ show maxThread ++ "):"
  n' <- readMaybe <$> getLine
```

```
case n' of
  Nothing -> pure ()
  Just n -> when (1 <= n && n <= maxThread) $ do
    atomically $ writeTVar tv n
    userLoop tv
```

We ask for a thread number and then either stop or set a transactional variable and go for another iteration.

The `main` program is now trivial. We create a transactional variable, spawn all the threads, and proceed with `userLoop` as follows:

```
main :: IO ()
main = do
  tv <- atomically $ newTVar 0
  forM_ [1..maxThread] $ async . hello tv
  userLoop tv
```

Running this program gives the desired behavior, as shown next:

```
$ cabal -v0 run ordered-threads
Enter thread number (1..5):
3
Hello from thread 3
Enter thread number (1..5):
1
Hello from thread 1
Enter thread number (1..5):
5
Hello from thread 5
Enter thread number (1..5):
0
```

`Control.Concurrent.STM.TVar` provides several other convenient utilitics to work with transactional variables, including the following:

```
modifyTVar :: TVar a -> (a -> a) -> STM ()
swapTVar :: TVar a -> a -> STM a
registerDelay :: Int -> IO (TVar Bool)
```

The last function returns a transactional variable that is set to `True` after the given number of microseconds. This function can be used instead of `threadDelay`. Let's look at an example.

EXAMPLE: PRINTING DOTS FOR THE GIVEN TIME WITH STM

🗋 ch16/dots-stm.hs

⚡ *dots-stm*

To delay a thread, we first use `registerDelay` and then check the value of the resulting `TVar` as follows:

```
printDots :: IO ()
printDots = forever $ do
  putStrLn "."
  tv <- registerDelay oneSec
  atomically $ readTVar tv >>= check
```

In the `main` function, we run an asynchronous computation to print dots and then delay on a new transactional variable, as shown next:

```
main :: IO ()
main = do
  [sec] <- getArgs
  withAsync printDots $ \_ -> do
    tv <- registerDelay $ oneSec * read sec
    atomically $ readTVar tv >>= check
  putStrLn "Alarm!"
```

Let's run this program as follows:

```
$ cabal -v0 run dots-stm -- 3
.
.
.
Alarm!
```

The `async` and `stm` packages work nicely together. For example, we can wait for or poll an asynchronous computation inside an `STM` action as follows:

```
waitSTM :: Async a -> STM a
pollSTM :: Async a -> STM (Maybe (Either SomeException a))
```

In fact, the `async` package is implemented over `stm`. The `wait` function for `Async a` is a small wrapper over `atomically . waitSTM`.

STM QUEUES AND CHANNELS

Transactional variables are so much easier to work with than synchronized mutable variables; therefore, they were used to implement plenty of concurrent data structures. For example, many variations of queues and channels with different properties exist. Let's discuss their variety.

Both queues and channels implement first-in-first-out (FIFO) access to the elements. Queues are simpler and more performant. Channels are queues that support broadcasting, so there can be multiple readers receiving the same elements. Among other properties of queues and channels, we have the following:

- *Boundedness*—A bounded data structure has a capacity. Writing to such a structure blocks if there is no more space until some element is removed.
- *Closability*—Allows expressing the concept of a closed data structure. It is similar to keeping `Maybe a` in a structure with a guarantee to get `Nothing` forever once a structure is closed.

The plethora of queues and channels with these properties is available from two packages, `stm` and `stm-chans`, as shown next:

```
data TQueue a -- unbounded queue
data TBQueue a -- bounded queue
data TMQueue a -- closable queue
data TBMQueue a -- bounded closable queue
data TChan a -- unbounded channel
data TBChan a -- bounded channel
data TMChan a -- closable channel
data TBMChan a -- bounded closable channel
```

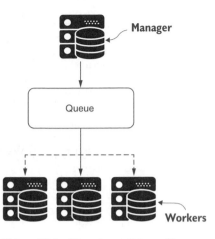

Figure 16.6   **Manager-workers pattern**

Let's revisit the summing-numbers example and use a closable bounded queue with many workers. Here we implement the traditional concurrent manager-workers pattern illustrated in figure 16.6. We have one thread for managing tasks and several others that work on those tasks. A queue used to store tasks guarantees that every task is received by exactly one thread.

EXAMPLE: SUMMING NUMBERS WITH A MANAGER-WORKERS PATTERN

    📄   ch16/sum-numbers-many-workers.hs

    ⚡   *sum-numbers-many-workers*

In this example, we use `TBMQueue Integer`. Boundedness guarantees fixed memory usage. Closability helps to inform workers that there is no more job to do. We don't need any broadcasting here, so a queue suffices.

Sending numbers to a queue is similar to what we've done before, as shown here:

```
sendNumbers :: [Integer] -> TBMQueue Integer -> IO ()
sendNumbers xs q = do
  forM_ xs $ \x -> do
    atomically $ writeTBMQueue q x
  atomically $ closeTBMQueue q
```

Both writing and closing are executed atomically as STM transactions. Note that due to boundedness, the call to `writeTBMQueue` may block.

Summing numbers is also similar to what we've done before, as shown next:

```
sumNumbers :: TBMQueue Integer -> IO Integer
sumNumbers q = loop 0
  where
    loop !acc = do                                        Reading gives
      next <- atomically $ readTBMQueue q    ◁┘           Maybe Integer.
      case next of
 Queue is    Just n -> loop (acc + n)        ◁──── Goes to the next iteration
 closed. └▷  Nothing -> pure acc
```

In the `main` function, we create a queue, spawn all the threads, and wait for results as follows:

```
main :: IO ()
main = do
    q <- newTBMQueueIO 10000          ← New bounded queue with
                                         10,000 elements max
    summators <- replicateM 5 (async (sumNumbers q))    ← Spawns workers-
                                                          summators
    _ <- async (sendNumbers [1..10000000] q)   ← Spawns the manager
    res <- mapM wait summators         ←
    putStrLn $ "Partial sums are:"         Waits for all the summators
    mapM_ print res
    putStrLn $ "Total sums is " ++ show (sum res)
```

Prints the partial sums from summators

Running this program reveals that individual workers are quite busy doing their jobs, as shown here:

```
$ cabal -v0 run sum-numbers-many-workers -- +RTS -N
Partial sums are:
10243402366553
9841958071164
10083187676303
9590442201639
10241014684341
Total sums is 50000005000000
```

If we run the same program several times, we see that partial sums always differ. The workers receive and sum different numbers depending on the order of execution.

Nothing could stop us from using several concurrent data structures in the same program. In the following example, we implement a publisher-subscriber pattern with a broadcasting channel and a destination queue. Figure 16.7 illustrates what we are going to achieve. The user inputs a number. This number is then sent to a broadcasting channel. Several threads (subscribers) receive this number and send a message about it to a queue. We also need a printer responsible for printing all the messages from a queue.

Figure 16.7   Publisher-subscriber pattern and a destination queue

EXAMPLE: IMPLEMENTING A PUBLISHER-SUBSCRIBER PATTERN WITH A CHANNEL AND A QUEUE

ch16/pub-sub.hs

pub-sub

Our publisher here is a user that inputs numbers and sends them to a closable channel as follows:

```haskell
publisher :: TMChan Int -> IO ()
publisher ch = do
  putStrLn "Enter next number: "
  x' <- readMaybe <$> getLine
  case x' of
    Just x -> do
      atomically $ writeTMChan ch x      <───── Sends a number
      publisher ch
    Nothing -> atomically $ closeTMChan ch   <───── Closes the channel
```

Goes to the next iteration

Printing messages from a destination queue is trivial, as shown next:

```haskell
printer :: TQueue (Int, Int) -> IO ()
printer q = forever $ do
  (n, x) <- atomically $ readTQueue q
  putStrLn $ "Subscriber " ++ show n ++
             " received number " ++ show x
```

Note that we don't use a closing queue here. No single subscriber knows when this queue should be closed. We'll have to kill the printer thread when there are no more subscribers left.

The subscriber reads from a channel and writes to a destination queue as follows:

```haskell
subscriber :: Int -> TMChan Int -> TQueue (Int, Int) -> IO ()
subscriber n inch outq = loop
  where
    loop = do
      next <- atomically $ readTMChan inch      <───── Reads a number
      case next of
        Just x -> do
          atomically $ writeTQueue outq (n, x)    <───── Writes to a queue
          loop
        Nothing -> pure ()   <───── The job is done because the channel is closed.
```

Goes to the next iteration

We'll need several subscribers, so let's spawn all of them as follows:

```haskell
spawnSubscribers
  :: Int -> TMChan Int -> TQueue (Int, Int) -> IO [Async ()]
spawnSubscribers total ch outq =
  forM [1..total] $ \n -> do
    inch <- atomically $ dupTMChan ch      <───── Duplicates a channel
    async $ subscriber n inch outq
```

Note that we have to duplicate a channel before giving it to a subscriber. Otherwise, we'd have no broadcasting.

Finally, we create all data structures and run the threads in the main function as follows:

```
main :: IO ()
main = do
  outq <- newTQueueIO
  withAsync (printer outq) $ \_ -> do
    ch <- newBroadcastTMChanIO
    subs <- spawnSubscribers 3 ch outq
    publisher ch
    mapM_ wait subs
  putStrLn "Exiting..."
```

Note that the broadcasting channel is created with the newBroadcastTMChanIO function. Once we have it, we can spawn all the subscribers and then start the publisher. When the publisher is done, we wait for all the subscribers to make sure that they've completed their job and then exit.

Experiments show that we are fine, as shown next:

```
$ cabal -v0 run pub-sub -- +RTS -N
Enter next number:
1
Enter next number:
Subscriber 1 received number 1
Subscriber 3 received number 1
Subscriber 2 received number 1
3
Enter next number:
Subscriber 3 received number 3
Subscriber 2 received number 3
Subscriber 1 received number 3
q
Exiting...
```

> **NOTE** In this chapter, we've discussed many small examples of using various tools for concurrent execution. I recommend reading *Parallel and Concurrent Programming in Haskell* by Simon Marlow (https://simonmar.github .io/pages/pcph.html) to dive deeper into the field of concurrent programming. The "Beautiful Concurrency" tutorial chapter (https://www.microsoft .com/en-us/research/publication/beautiful-concurrency/) by Simon Peyton Jones introduces STM with some very nice examples. The original paper on STM (https://www.microsoft.com/en-us/research/publication/composable-memory-transactions/) is also quite readable. Once you've mastered the details, I recommend watching the "Using STM for Modular Concurrency" talk (https://vimeo.com/452222780) by Duncan Coutts, devoted to designing large-scale concurrent programs.

Summary

- Most concurrent programs in Haskell should be implemented with the `async` and `stm` libraries.
- Low-level thread-running mechanisms and synchronized mutable variables are best avoided.
- STM queues and channels are used to implement traditional patterns of concurrent communication, such as manager-workers or publisher-subscriber.

appendix
Further reading

Books

- Simon Marlow is responsible for the current implementation of concurrency in Haskell. He wrote *Parallel and Concurrent Programming in Haskell* (https:// simonmar.github.io/pages/pcph.html).
- Simon Marlow and Simon Peyton Jones authored the great introduction to the internals of the Glasgow Haskell Compiler as a chapter for *The Architecture of Open Source Applications, Volume II*, available at https://www.aosabook .org/en/ghc.html.
- Simon Peyton Jones wrote the "Beautiful Concurrency" tutorial on Software Transactional Memory as a chapter of *Beautiful Code*. This chapter is available at https://www.microsoft.com/en-us/research/publication/beautiful-concurrency/.
- Alexander Granin, in *Functional Design and Architecture* (https://graninas .com/functional-design-and-architecture-book/), describes how to design functional programs at the industry level.
- Edwin Brady created the Idris programming language, which features dependent types. Reading his *Type-Driven Development with Idris* (https://www .manning.com/books/type-driven-development-with-idris) is a great way to see why we need dependent types in Haskell and what can be done with them.

Research papers

The number of research papers on Haskell that are published every year is overwhelming. I recommend following the Haskell Symposium (https://www.haskell .org/haskell-symposium/) as the main event for these kinds of papers. Other venues where one can find papers on Haskell are listed at https://wiki.haskell.org/ Conferences. Once you have the title of the paper you are interested in, it's usually easy to find the preprint in PDF. Remember, the introduction and motivation sections are usually quite accessible for a general reader.

index

X

Y

Z

RELATED MANNING TITLES

Get Programming with Haskell
by Will Kurt

ISBN 9781617293764
616 pages, $44.99
March 2018

Type-Driven Development with Idris
by Edwin Brady

ISBN 9781617293023
480 pages, $49.99
March 2017

Functional Programming in Scala
by Paul Chiusano and Rúnar Bjarnason
Foreword by Martin Odersky

ISBN 9781617290657
320 pages, $44.99
September 2014

For ordering information go to www.manning.com